POST-COMMUNIST PA[RTY SYSTEMS]

Competition, Representation, and Inter-[...]

Post-Communist Party Systems examines democratic party competition in four post-communist polities in the mid-1990s: Bulgaria, the Czech Republic, Hungary, and Poland. Legacies of pre-communist rule turn out to play as much a role in accounting for differences as the institutional diversity incorporated in the new democratic rules of the game. The book demonstrates various developments within the four countries with regard to different voter appeal of parties, patterns of voter representation, and dispositions to join other parties in legislative or executive alliances. The authors also present interesting avenues of comparison for broader sets of countries.

Herbert Kitschelt is a Professor of Political Science at Duke University. The European party system, social movements, and technology policy have been the focus of Professor Kitschelt's numerous publications. Kitschelt received the 1996 Woodrow Wilson Award for his book, *The Radical Right in Western Europe* (University of Michigan Press, 1995). His other recent books include *The Transformation of European Social Democracy* (Cambridge University Press, 1994) and his co-edited volume *Continuity and Change in Contemporary Capitalism* (Cambridge University Press, 1999).

Zdenka Mansfeldova is Senior Research Fellow for the Institute of Sociology at the Czech Academy of Sciences. Mansfeldova's primary interests are political parties, interest groups, and institutionalization of interest representation. She is author of a number of articles and book chapters about the Czech party system, civil society, and neo-corporatist forms of interest representation in Czech, German, and English.

Radoslaw Markowski is Head of the Electoral Studies Division for the Institute of Political Studies at the Polish Academy of Sciences. Since 1997 Markowski has also been Principal Investigator and Director of the Polish National Election Survey. Markowski publishes regularly in *Studia Polityczne,* discussing the topics pertaining to political behavior, party systems, and East Central European comparative politics. His recent publications include his co-edited book, *Predictions and Elections: Polish Democracy '95,* and his article "Political Parties and Ideological Spaces in East Central Europe," in *Communist and Post-Communist Studies* (September 1997).

Gábor Tóka is Assistant Professor of Political Science at the Central European University, Budapest. Professor Toka has published numerous articles on electoral behavior, political parties, and democratic consolidation in Eastern Europe. He is the editor of *The 1994 Elections to the Hungarian National Assembly* (Berlin: Sigma, 1995).

CAMBRIDGE STUDIES IN
COMPARATIVE POLITICS

General Editor
PETER LANGE   Duke University

Associate Editors
ROBERT H. BATES   Harvard University
ELLEN COMISSO   University of California, San Diego
PETER HALL   Harvard University
JOEL MIGDAL   University of Washington
HELEN MILNER   Columbia University
RONALD ROGOWSKI   University of California, Los Angeles
SIDNEY TARROW   Cornell University

OTHER BOOKS IN THE SERIES

The series list continues after the Index.

"POST-COMMUNIST PARTY SYSTEMS"

Competition, Representation, and Inter-Party Cooperation

HERBERT KITSCHELT

ZDENKA MANSFELDOVA

RADOSLAW MARKOWSKI

GÁBOR TÓKA

CAMBRIDGE
UNIVERSITY PRESS

PUBLISHED BY THE PRESS SYNDICATE OF THE UNIVERSITY OF CAMBRIDGE
The Pitt Building, Trumpington Street, Cambridge, United Kingdom

CAMBRIDGE UNIVERSITY PRESS
The Edinburgh Building, Cambridge CB2 2RU, UK   www.cup.cam.ac.uk
40 West 20th Street, New York, NY 10011-4211, USA   www.cup.org
10 Stamford Road, Oakleigh, Melbourne 3166, Australia
Ruiz de Alarcón 13, 28014 Madrid, Spain

First published 1999

Printed in the United States of America

Typeface Garamond no. 3, 10½/12 pt.   *System* MagnaType™ [AG]

A catalog record for this book is available from the British Library.

Library of Congress Cataloging in Publication data
Post-communist party system : competition, representation, and inter-
party cooperation / Herbert Kitschelt . . . [et al.].
p.   cm. – (Cambridge studies in comparative politics)
Includes bibliographical references.
ISBN 0-521-65288-X (hc.). – ISBN 0-521-65890-X (pbk.)
1. Political parties – Europe, Eastern. 2. Post-communism – Europe,
Eastern. 3. Europe, Eastern – Politics and government – 1989–
I. Kitschelt, Herbert. II. Series.
JN96.A979P67   1999
324.247 – DC21   98-46760
                                              CIP

ISBN 0 521 65288 X hardback
ISBN 0 521 65890 X paperback

CONTENTS

FIGURES AND TABLES

FIGURES

TABLES

ACKNOWLEDGMENTS

Our project would not have been possible without the financial support of a number of institutions. In 1993, a German Marshall Fund fellowship and a leave from Duke University permitted Herbert Kitschelt to devise a questionnaire and conduct an initial round of more than one hundred pilot interviews with politicians in the four East Central European countries. The International Research and Exchange Board (IREX) generously funded the main survey among more than five hundred politicians in the four countries that we conducted in 1994, and helped with travel expenses associated with our collaborative research and writing. Thanks are also due to Duke University and Humboldt University Berlin for providing travel funds to bring the co-authors of this study together repeatedly and to disseminate our findings at workshops with colleagues and graduate students.

Our project relies on the admirable cooperation of hundreds of members of parliament, party secretaries, and municipal councilors in the many Bulgarian, Czech, Hungarian, and Polish parties we cover in our study. In addition to filling out and commenting on our questionnaires, some of them set aside long hours to meet with Herbert Kitschelt both in 1993 and 1994 in order to discuss changes in their countries' domestic politics. For a foreigner whose lack of local language skills limited access to firsthand observation of the political process, these conversations were indispensable to gain a better understanding of the emerging democratic polities.

We also would like to thank our colleagues and graduate students in Bulgaria, the Czech Republic, Hungary, and Poland, who were involved in the collection, coding, and statistical analysis of our data. We owe special gratitude to Dobrinka Kostova, who is a research associate at the Institute of Sociology of the Bulgarian Academy of Science. Dr. Kostova managed our Bulgarian survey, but was unable to participate in the comparative analysis of our data. On the Czech

side, we are grateful to Lubomir Brokl for a continuous stream of critical sugges-
tions over the entire duration of our project and to Milan Tucek for directing the
coding of the Czech data and helping with the data analysis. In Hungary, we are
indebted to Péter Guba, who served as Herbert Kitschelt's research assistant in the
first round of interviews in 1993 and later conducted a number of interviews in
the main survey, as well as to Gabriella Tarjányi (TARKI, Budapest) who trans-
ferred the data to electronic files. Zoltán Kárpáti and members of the Institute for
Social Conflict Research of the Hungarian Academy of Science supervised the
interviewers in the main survey in 1994. In Poland, we owe thanks to the
Institute of Political Studies of the Polish Academy of Sciences for logistic support
and use of facilities. Above all, our gratitude is due to Pawel Grzelak who
provided indispensable and tireless help in preparing our data set and participating in the statistical data analysis. The survey data on the Bulgarian public were
generously made available to us by Geoffrey Evans and Stephen Whitefield, and
the Czech, Hungarian, and Polish mass surveys were collected and shared with us
by the Department of Political Science at the Central European University,
Budapest.

Over the years, a large number of colleagues read papers that eventually fed
into chapters of this study and listened to presentations on initial findings at
various annual meetings of the American Political Science Association and more
specialized conferences on post-communist politics in the Czech Republic, En-
gland, Germany, Hungary, Poland, and the United States. We particularly acknowledge the support of colleagues at our home institutions, the Central European University in Budapest, the Institute of Political Studies at the Polish
Academy of Sciences, the Institute of Sociology at the Czech Academy of Sciences,
Duke University, and Humboldt University Berlin. Among our colleagues who
work on overlapping research issues, we would especially like to highlight the
critical support we received from our friends at Oxford University, Geoffrey Evans
at Nuffield College and Stephen Whitefield at Pembroke College. Both share our
enthusiasm for the comparative analysis of post-communist democracies and
encouraged the progress of this project, although they disagree with some of its
propositions. In addition to their always insightful comments, we greatly appreciate their willingness to share their own survey of the Bulgarian population with
us. Finally, three friends and colleagues deserve special mention and thanks because they read and extensively commented on the entire penultimate draft of this
study: Peter Lange, Scott Mainwaring, and Denise Powers. Their critical remarks
made the printed version of the book leaner and (we hope) sharper – but thus also
more vulnerable to objections. We certainly were unable to remedy all the flaws
they discovered in our work, but we hope to have addressed at least some of their
concerns.

As always with complex research projects, the months and years we dedicated
to this study took their toll on our families and friends. At the same time, our
cooperation on this project has created new friendships that have enriched our
lives.

INTRODUCTION: DEMOCRACY AND PARTY COMPETITION

The collapse of communism across Eastern Europe was one of the final manifestations of a worldwide spread of democratization over a twenty-year period that began with Southern Europe in 1974, then continued in Latin America in the 1980s and subsequently moved on to Eastern Asia in the late 1980s and 1990s. Political scientists devoted much effort to account for the timing and modalities of political-regime change and the structural conditions and dynamic processes that made possible this "Third Wave" of democratization (Huntington 1991). But as we approach the turn of the century, we have only the most sketchy understanding of the *practice of democratic competition, representation, and policy making* in these new democracies. Political scientists have delivered few theoretically incisive comparative analyses of the way the new democracies actually work.

Much of the political science discourse is still mesmerized by an almost exclusive concern with the "survival" or "consolidation" of basic democratic regime parameters in Third Wave democracies, such as civil liberties, free elections, and legal-bureaucratic predictability. Contributors to this debate seek to specify the minimal conditions that make democratic rules of the game persist over time (cf. Linz and Stepan 1996: 7–37). But there may be no one set of baseline features that keeps democracy alive. Moreover, the focus on holistic questions of democratic consolidation has diverted attention from the specific mechanisms of electoral competition and legislative representation as well as the modes of interest intermediation in the policy-making process, all of which contribute to breathing life into the democratic framework. The literature is full of general talk about civil society, political society, and the rule of law, but mostly devoid of concrete comparative analyses of democratic processes. In the final analysis, whether democracy becomes the "only game in town" depends on the *quality of democratic interactions and policy processes* the consequences of which affect the legitimacy of democracy in the eyes of citizens and political elites alike. Thus it may be

1

impossible to say much about the holistic problem of "consolidation" without a close analysis of the conduct of political actors – parties, interest groups, and social movements – inside and outside the institutionalized arenas of democratic decision making.[1]

The debate on the role of presidentialism or parliamentarism for the survival of democracy vividly illustrates the consequences of a holistic approach to the problem of regime consolidation that disregards a close study of democratic processes.[2] Contributors typically speculate about the implications of institutional design for democratic survival in a highly generalized fashion without delving into the practice of democratic competition and legislative decision making in which the impact of alternative institutional arrangements on policy outputs, such as economic reform, and ultimately on the public perception of the legitimacy of the democratic order would surface. The debate may establish correlations between executive-legislative institutional designs and the durability of democracy, but it yields little insight into the mechanisms of how and why democracies reproduce themselves.

One central and indispensable aspect of democratic practice is electoral competition for legislative office and the associated formation of political parties. Given the holistic predisposition of much research on new democracies, the comparative analysis of parties and party systems in Third Wave polities is underdeveloped. There are case studies of individual parties and descriptions of party systems, but we cannot think of many theoretically sophisticated and empirically comparative studies that would explain alternative modes of party competition in the electoral arena and party strategy in legislative and executive settings within any sub-set of the new democracies. This generalization applies not only to the post-communist and East Asian democracies emerging late in the Third Wave of democratization, but even to Latin American polities where democratic process features, including the study of political parties, have been the object of surprisingly little comparative research.[3] To our knowledge, no one has attempted in a systematic, comparative, and empirically grounded fashion to analyze the linkage mechanisms between citizens and party elites in these countries or the alignments, if any, that divide parties and their constituencies. In the

---

[1]This, we take it, is an interpretation of O'Donnell's (1996) basic complaint about the "consolidation" literature. O'Donnell is interested in the quality of democratic procedures, what he calls the difference between "universalistic" and "particularistic" democratic practices, not just the tenacity of democracies to persist.

[2]We are particularly thinking of the contributions edited by Lijphart (1992) and Linz and Valenzuela (1994). Shugart and Carey (1992) and Mainwaring and Shugart (1997) constitute steps forward in analytical sophistication.

[3]Mainwaring and Scully's (1995) edited volume comes closest to our concerns because it makes a concerted effort to map levels of party system institutionalization. But this is only a beginning because no effort is made to explain the patterns of variance identified in this volume, or to link them to other properties of party competition.

present book, we make a start in this direction for a small number of Third Wave democracies. Our empirical reference cases are four post-communist East Central European democracies, but our agenda is to contribute to research on the practices of party competition, representation, and policy making in new post-communist polities and other democracies more generally. With this objective in mind, we develop theoretical arguments, explore empirical research procedures, and pursue modes of data analysis we hope to be useful to students of democratic polities not only in the post-communist region, but also in Latin America, East Asia, or even advanced industrial democracies.

Research on advanced industrial democracies, of course, has analyzed practices of interest articulation, aggregation, and collective decision making for decades. On the one hand, such research can inspire comparativists who turn to new democracies at the end of the twentieth century. On the other, comparativists of advanced industrial democracies have at times built on unquestioned theoretical assumptions that betray the historical idiosyncrasies of the countries they study. In this regard, research on the procedural quality of democracy in new polities may enable us to ask new questions and explore novel research strategies that may even feed back on the study of advanced industrial democracies.

Three tasks appear to us particularly important to characterize the quality of democratic procedures in order to promote a useful dialogue between students of "old" and "new" democracies. First, students of democracy must identify critical dimensions and variations in the modes of interest articulation and aggregation through parties, associations, and movements within and across democratic polities. This task is essentially descriptive, but is fruitful only if its empirical categories are already guided by theoretical interests that drive the second and the third task to explain democratic process features and to employ such features to account for the outputs and outcomes of the democratic decision-making process. Turning backward, diversity in modes of interest intermediation and collective decision making may be accounted for in terms of (1) the formal rules of the democratic games, as enshrined in constitutions and statutory law, and (2) the resource endowments and interest alignments of collective actors in light of historical pathways that have produced such constellations.

Our book attempts to shed light on a particular slice of political reality related to the first and second tasks, accounting for the formation and describing the dynamics of party systems in post-communist East Central Europe. In this introduction, we wish to argue that the study of party systems is critically important in the comparative analysis of democratic polities. We then sketch two explanatory strategies to account for the emergence of democratic process features and argue that they are actually complementary rather than competing, as is quite commonly believed in the literature on democratization. This introduction outlines themes and strategies of research only. We develop the concepts that characterize different democratic procedures and the specific theoretical propositions that inform our investigation of post-communist party system formation in the first two chapters of this study.

THE QUALITY OF THE DEMOCRATIC PROCESS

Normative democratic theory has always emphasized that the "rule of the people" lends itself to different interpretations and practices. Thus, theorists have distinguished classical and realist democracy (Schumpeter 1946), liberal and populist democracy (Riker 1982), representative, participatory, and deliberative democracy (Fishkin 1991), pluralist and corporatist democracy (Schmitter 1974), and a host of other "democracies with adjectives" (Collier and Levitsky 1997; Held 1987). It is much harder, however, to relate such abstract normative models to the empirical realities of democratic practice, as it results from the interaction of individual politicians and collective actors (movements, interest groups, parties) inside and outside a variety of institutional arenas (electoral contests, legislatures, cabinets, administrative agencies, courts).

At the most general level, democratic political processes vary with the *scope* of societal interests they permit to mobilize and gain access to representation and participation within procedures of collective political decision making, the *effectiveness* of such processes to yield results that affect people's life chances through binding policies or other techniques of allocating costs and benefits among societal constituencies, and the *volatility* of such processes and outcomes over time. In the past thirty years, perhaps the most ambitious effort to develop an empirically grounded typology of democratic polities based on distinct democratic process types is Lijphart's (1984) work on majoritarian and consensual democracies. We introduce his ideas here not to give them wholesale endorsement, but to highlight the critical significance Lijphart attributes to parties and party systems, our main subject of study in East Central Europe, in his analysis of democratic processes.

In fact, a distinction between democracies based on the number of parties and the number of dimensions of political alignment on which parties place themselves constitutes the core of Lijphart's uni-dimensional typology of democratic polities. These features, in turn, are partially correlated with institutional arrangements, such as electoral rules. The larger the number of parties and alignments in a polity, the broader tends to be the scope of representation and fewer interests may be excluded from access to the political arena. With an increasing number of actors and policy dimensions, however, efforts to build viable majorities and to agree on durable, binding policy decisions become more complicated. As a result, the effectiveness of policy making may decline, provided the players do not agree on techniques of consensus building that reduce transaction costs and give durability to policy compacts, such as oversized winning coalitions and dense networks of legislative bargaining facilitated by weak executive dominance. While consensual democracies excel in terms of inclusiveness, at the opposite end of the spectrum majoritarian democracies shine in terms of effectiveness. Majoritarian democracies include few parties and issue dimensions that divide them. They reduce the scope of political representation, but therefore are more likely to provide effective governance based on single-party majorities and an assertive executive that employs its legislative following to ratify executive policy choices. Whereas majoritarian democracies thus put a premium on effectiveness, they give less weight to inclusiveness and possibly to the stability of policy making.

Lijphart's typology squeezes many attributes of the democratic process into the single consensus-majoritarian dimension. The mobilization and conduct of interest groups is closely tied to the more consensual or competitive character of the polity (Lijphart and Crepaz 1991). Furthermore, legislative-executive designs, as indicated by the status and prerogatives of presidents in the government executive, relate to the consensual-majoritarian process dimension (Lijphart 1994b). Although Lijphart may go too far in claiming strong empirical associations of various democratic process attributes on a single dimension, we agree with the *central role he attributes to political parties and party systems for the quality of democratic procedures in different polities.* The anchor of the democratic polity is its representative format, constituted by parties as agents of interest intermediation that play in a variety of institutional arenas. In this spirit, our study of the nature of democratic processes in East Central Europe focuses on the emerging post-communist party systems to explore the citizen-party linkages they articulate and the alignments that transpire in the policy process.

An emphasis on political parties is not uncontroversial in the study of contemporary democracies. Theorists of interest group corporatism or of direct democratic plebiscitarianism have envisioned democratic procedures *without or with only a marginal involvement of political parties* in the process of interest intermediation. But neither corporatist nor plebiscitarian democratic ideas have yielded normatively coherent institutional design blueprints that are consistent with the essential baseline attribute of democracy, the equality of all competent citizens in the democratic process at least with regard to one aspect, the vote for legislative representatives in free and fair elections. Parties as associations of ambitious politicians who band together in the pursuit of elected office, by contrast, take as their starting point the electoral competition in territorially defined constituencies where each citizen enjoys the same weight in the choice among candidates. A more important deficiency of corporatist and plebiscitarian theories is their inability to identify empirical examples in complex societies, where corporatist or plebiscitarian techniques have displaced political parties. It may be ironic that corporatist interest intermediation has been most prominent in those polities, where organizationally powerful and ideologically coherent parties have a strong presence and delegate certain policy subjects to carefully constrained bargaining arenas among organized interests. Parties and legislatures here still determine the framework under the shadow of which corporatist bargaining takes place. In a similar vein, plebiscitarian decision procedures typically involve a legislative framework and an oversight process that determines when plebiscitarian procedures override other decision modes. Empirically, claims that parties and interest groups are involved in a zero-sum game to dominate the democratic policy process are ill-conceived. The presence of powerful political parties in the electoral arena may yield a positive-sum game in which parties, interest groups, and sometimes even social movements alike jointly reach higher levels of mobilization and influence in the policy process.

Because open fair elections are central for the functioning of democratic interest intermediation, our study of post-communist polities concentrates on the role of parties and their linkages to citizens. More specifically, we examine the extent to which programmatic appeals shape the bond between citizens and voters, the nature of alignments among parties in the competitive party system, the patterns of representation that characterize each party system, and the executive governance structures that result from them. In the comparative literature on advanced industrial democracies, some of these features have received a great deal of attention, but others relatively little. Conversely, an important aspect of party democracy in that literature plays only a very subordinate role in our own study, the number of parties in the democratic system and the resulting competitive strategies. Let us comment on each of these democratic process features, as they relate to the study of recently founded democracies.

First, much of the comparative literature on advanced industrial democracies takes the presence of parties and their linkages to citizens so much for granted that it does not systematically examine the *full scope of basic techniques parties may employ to appeal to voters and to build durable linkages to electoral constituencies.* In stylized fashion, the two most common ways political scientists have described solutions to the problem of citizen-party linkage in Western democracies may be labeled the behavioral "Michigan" model and the rational choice "Rochester" model. According to the Michigan model, electoral preferences rest primarily on citizens' affective identification with a party and unthinking habitual support for that party, whereas the Rochester model emphasizes rational deliberation by voters who compare their own ideal policy preferences with those of parties' policy records and advertised agendas. In the Rochester model, party identification reflects the sunk costs of past deliberations about the proximity of voters' and parties' programmatic positions.

In new democracies, affective and habitual party identification often is not an option due to the recent emergence of the party alternatives. Moreover, rational voting may be impaired where parties do not present voters identifiable program alternatives. It is therefore our first task to analyze the extent to which programmatic appeals and constituency linkages characterize new party systems and to explore alternative linkage techniques to which political entrepreneurs may resort. These may involve the deployment of charismatic leadership or of direct clientelist exchanges in which parties buy votes and financial backing for material advantages politicians disburse to their supporters after the election.

Consistent with much of the Western party system research, Lijphart (1984) *assumes* that parties situate themselves on programmatic issue dimensions or alignments, a belief shared by comparative-historical students of party divides (Lipset and Rokkan 1967) as much as formal theorists in the rational choice framework (e.g., Downs 1957). But in new Third Wave democracies, the quality of democratic processes may vary precisely because parties and entire party systems may violate the presumption of programmatic competition. To our knowledge, the literature on alternative linkage strategies and on the relevance of cohesive programmatic appeals for partisan politics is quite fragmentary and has yielded little systematic cross-national research. Given the practices of party competition in the United States, political scientists focusing on American democracy have devoted more attention to the variable programmatic coherence of parties than comparativists working on other advanced industrial democracies. Although the party systems of countries such as Austria, Belgium, Italy, and Japan suggest that parties employ clientelist linkages to instill voter loyalty in addition to or as partial substitute for programmatically cohesive appeals, the incidence of such practices has rarely found attention in systematic comparative treatments.[4] Particularly with regard to new Third Wave democracies, there is virtually no comparative research that would empirically determine party politicians' deployment of programmatic, clientelist, or charismatic linkage strategies, let alone systematic efforts to account for differences in linkage strategies across parties and countries.

Second, we analyze the nature of the programmatic divisions that emerge where programmatic appeals play an important role. Research pre-occupied with Western democracies, including that of Lijphart, has put considerable emphasis on the *content of political divides and competitive dimensions, conceived in terms of the interests and preferences of electoral constituencies* along which parties distinguish their positions, once they have decided to make partisan appeals primarily on programmatic grounds. What counts for the quality of democratic procedures is the nature of the stakes in political divides, the number of such divides, the relationship among such divides (crosscutting or reinforcing?) and the position of parties relative to each other on these divides (spread over the entire range of policy options or clustering around "centrist" appeals?). In our study, we analyze the emerging alignments both from the perspective of political elites who situate their own parties and their competitors in a system of alignments, as well as that of voters who perceive party alternatives through the lens of their personal preferences.

By comparing the social construction of party alignments from the perspectives of both voters and politicians, we already move to our third task, the study of *relations of representation* between partisan electorates and their legislators in the new democratic polities. While students of established Western party democracies have devoted some energies to the analysis of relations of representation in programmatically oriented party systems (e.g., Converse and Pierce 1986), surprisingly few comparative empirical studies have addressed the variability of relations of representation and accountability in democratic polities. This is all the more puzzling in light of the prominence questions of representation have for

---

[4]A partial exception is Katz (1980) who emphasizes the role of the electoral system in sustaining such practices.

normative democratic theory as well as for the empirical study of the legitimation of democratic political regimes.

Students of Western democracy often hypothesize a growing decoupling of politicians' and voters' preferences but rarely study this relationship empirically. Even more so, comparativists who examine Third Wave democracies often complain that parties do not represent their electoral constituencies, but this assertion is hardly ever empirically substantiated. The whole notion of "delegative democracy" (O'Donnell 1993) turns on the claim that political leaders can essentially dissociate themselves from their constituencies once in elected office and pursue private agendas without being held back by mechanisms instilling responsiveness and accountability to the democratic sovereign. Because of the importance of relations of representation for new democracies, we devote an entire chapter to this subject. In an effort to go beyond the existing literature, we distinguish specific modes of representation and theorize about their occurrence in the presence of different configurations of party competition.

The fourth and final democratic process feature we analyze in our study of post-communist East Central European polities moves the attention from "parties in the electorate" and parties as strategic actors in the electoral arena to the realm of legislative and executive politics. With regard to advanced industrial democracies, studies of the process of crafting majorities in legislatures and executives have proliferated, as evidenced by a large literature on coalition politics, but a detailed comparative exploration of coalition politics and majority formation in new Third Wave democracies is still lacking. In addition to the problem that students of non-Western democracies still have few data points to analyze coalition politics, such investigations may in some instances be hampered by the assumption of much Western coalition theory that parties are policy-seeking collective actors who appeal to voters based on rather unambiguous programmatic stances in the electoral arena and then employ these positions in the legislative arena to craft coalitions among competitors with overlapping, compatible preference schedules. Even in post-authoritarian democracies where programmatic appeals constitute a basic linkage strategy of parties to voters, the experience and recollection of suffering under the preceding non-democratic regime may invalidate the common hypothesis that parties with similar policy programs can enter coalition arrangements, if there is a deep regime divide between parties that overrules their policy commitments. The final substantive chapter of our study therefore explores the extent to which policy considerations shape the cooperation among parties in post-communist democracies as compared with the memories of the authoritarian experience and the sentiments that surround them.

As indicated earlier, we do not analyze the party system formats of new post-communist democracies, although in existing Western party system research *party system fragmentation* has played an important role. It appears both as an independent variable to predict parties' programmatic appeals in the electoral arena (Do such appeals converge on a "centrist" range or diverge sharply into polar opposites?) and the ease of coalition building in the legislative and executive arena as well as a dependent variable accounted for in terms of electoral laws and societal cleavage dimensions. Our decision not to focus on party system fragmentation results from the difficulty of determining the number of parties in many new democracies in a theoretically meaningful fashion. Where parties are "weak" (Sartori 1986) in terms of building cohesive programmatic commitments and internal organizational structures, they may not be the effective locus of bargaining in the legislative arena or of campaigning in the election arena. Instead, the meaningful unit of analysis may be situated *below the party level* in the various currents and factions subsumed under a single partisan label. Conversely, where several parties have similar programmatic appeals and thus are located in the same sector of a political alignment system, the relevant unit of analysis may be "blocs" of parties *above the individual party level* in the same political sector. Whether or not the party system format thus measures a significant attribute of a polity varies within democratic process features. If party systems employ other linkage techniques than programmatic appeals, such as clientelist or charismatic appeals, knowing the party system format may be even less informative for a study of democratic decision-making techniques and policy outputs.

By focusing on four important process features of party democracy, our book is meant to contribute more than merely a close analysis of party system formation in four East Central European countries less than half a decade away from their founding elections. Instead, we hope to provide an exemplary model for the study of party systems in Third Wave democracies both with regard to the theoretical propositions we explore as well as our empirical techniques of data collection and analysis that may serve as a positive or negative reference for future research on democratic party systems not only in post-communist polities but also in other regions of the world.

The four countries we have chosen for our empirical comparison quickly developed "consolidated" democratic regimes in the early 1990s in the minimalist sense that just about all relevant political actors and most citizens began to treat the rules of multi-party competition, together with the basic civil and political rights, as the "only game in town." Non-democratic alternatives have managed to excite only political fringe groups. Nevertheless, these four post-communist democracies permit us to explore the procedural qualities of democracy because they exhibit striking contrasts in the ways parties appeal to voters, represent electoral constituencies, and compete or collaborate with their rivals. Even in a comparison among post-communist democracies, the over-riding impression often is *divergence* more than *convergence* of democratic processes.

ACCOUNTING FOR DIVERGING DEMOCRATIC PRACTICES

Democratic procedures vary across countries and give rise to at least two questions of interest to students of comparative politics: first, how different democratic processes have come into existence and, second, how democratic procedures shape public policies and more generally affect the allocation and distribution of life chances among electoral constituencies. Ultimately, the second, forward-looking causal analysis of the nexus between democratic process and policy outputs and outcomes, particularly as they involve the political economies of the new democracies, may pose the most exciting challenges for comparativists. But this nexus is hard to trace in Third Wave democracies that have often existed for little more than a decade. Here it is methodologically difficult to attribute policy performance to the current procedures of democratic decision making without taking into account the complex interactions between remnants of the old authoritarian system that affect the resources of players and their power configuration and the evolving new political forces in the democratic polity. Policy outputs and outcomes may be as much a consequence of the old as well as the new polities. Democratic political institutions and power relations often are, to a considerable extent, still *endogenous* to the power constellations that existed when the demise of the old regimes occurred and the new democracies came into being. Short of fundamental social revolutions, these power relations usually evolve gradually in the new democracies. Because past and present are often so closely intertwined, statistical efforts to isolate the independent effect of current regime type on economic performance have encountered formidable estimation problems and yield contradictory results.[5]

Because of the linkages between non-democratic regimes and new democracies, a backward-looking causal mode of analysis that examines the conditions under which particular process features of democratic competition, interest representation, and policy making "lock in" is therefore a more tractable and indispensable analytical step that must precede studies of policy outputs and outcomes. Even though forward-looking causal analysis of the linkage between democratic processes and policy outputs and outcomes in the spirit of comparative political economy may be an ultimate objective of comparative analysis, one must not put the cart before the horse. A firm grasp of players and processes in new democracies is an essential pre-condition for the subsequent analysis of democratic performance. A backward-looking causal analysis of democratic processes may eventually help students of political economic performance in new democracies to distinguish between the "legacies" of pre-democratic power relations and the consequences of the new democratic rules of the game and the emerging power relations among strategic actors that can no longer be traced back to predemocratic origins.

Comparativists whose objective is to explain democratic process features such

---

[5]In addition to the extremely crude characterization of alternative regime types and the lack of a specification of interaction effects between old and new regimes, results of such studies suffer from problems of statistical model specification, variable sampling strategies, and the selection and operationalization of key theoretical and control variables (cf. Przeworski and Limongi 1993; Feng 1997; Leblang 1997).

as the programmatic structuring of parties, party alignments, and patterns of representation in established Western democracies usually first turn to the *formal democratic institutions,* defined by constitutions and electoral laws, as the relevant causal variables. We submit, however, that this theoretical approach seriously underspecifies the empirical research problem and may be particularly inappropriate for the study of newly emerging democracies.

In all democracies, societal relations of power and preference shape the demands that are channeled into the political process. Thus, although democratic institutions filter what makes it into decision-making arenas, they do not determine the substance, scope, and intensity of demands that seek access to the polity. For example, students of electoral systems know that electoral laws may constrain how many conflict alignments will be represented by parties in the legislature and what constituencies will make their voices heard in that arena. But such institutions do not determine the content and complexity of socio-economic and cultural alignments that seek political representation (cf. Cox 1997: chap. 11). In a similar vein, while electoral laws and the constitutionally prescribed interplay between legislatures and presidential executive may affect the extent to which parties are programmatically cohesive, within these constraints a range of non-institutional factors shapes the actual linkage strategies between citizens and politicians.

Two further conditions limit the explanatory power of formal institutions for democratic process features in new democratic polities. First, there is the problem of endogeneity. Political actors choose institutions in light of subjective expectations to maximize their own political leverage under the new rules of the game. Their demand for institutional arrangements thus is likely to be subjectively rational and can be explained in terms of their resource endowments and cognitive frameworks that may owe a great deal to their role inside and their experiences with old regime politics. Whatever institutions result from the inter-play of power-oriented and more or less resourceful political actors, they are initially an effect, but not a cause, of power relations. Institutions become exogenous to power relations and thus an independent force impinging on democratic process features in two cases. First, actors may choose bargaining strategies over institutions that are *objectively* undercutting their interests, but actors *subjectively believe otherwise* because they have cognitive maps and an understanding of institutional effects that is simply wrong. In that case, institutions, once chosen, limit the permissible strategies of actors to accumulate power in the new polity and force them to adapt to the new rules. Even where institutional choices initially coincide with the interests of the dominant actors, however, over time such actor constellations change. While new powerful actors may wish to change institutional arrangements, institutions often stay in place because no set of players is capable of paying the transaction costs to modify the institutional status quo. Also in this case, institutions become exogenous to power configurations and independently shape democratic processes.

In emerging democracies, the exogenous causal impact of new democratic institutions, however, is limited by a second condition that also has to do with the actors' cognitive capabilities and experience with the game under the new democratic institutions. Institutions may have equilibrium effects that emerge once actors have repeatedly interacted under democratic rules and have acquired a firm knowledge of the payoffs they and their competitors derive from the mutual choice of strategies in the existing power configuration. Before the political actors have gained such experience in repeated rounds of the game, however, democratic institutions may generate *transitional effects* that are quite different from their equilibrium effects. Actors may initially face too much uncertainty to choose what amounts to the best strategies under equilibrium conditions. If all actors face similar uncertainty about the payoffs of their own and their competitors' strategies, almost anything can happen. Thus, plurality electoral systems that make the emergence of two-party competition likely under equilibrium conditions may actually yield a proliferation of competing parties under disequilibrium conditions where voters do not recognize the two contenders for whom it might be worth voting strategically and where politicians do not know when to abandon a small party and join the bandwagon of the prospective winners (cf. Moser 1995; 1996).

For the explanation of democratic process features, we draw the conclusion that new democratic institutions cannot be the primary or exclusive forces that shape the practice of such polities. Instead, we need a "layered" explanatory strategy that gives primacy to the power configurations among actors that emerge from the old regime and shape the institutions and democratic procedures in the formative phase of the new democracies. Institutions lose their endogeneity and become external conditions impinging on the democratic process, if the institutions do not directly reflect power relations (because actors employed the wrong cognitive maps) or power configurations change sufficiently beyond the initial relations that prevailed during institutional bargaining. In this case, actors need sufficient chances to play the game repeatedly before their conduct may be accounted for by equilibrium models. Thus, explanations of democratic process features employ democratic institutions as a secondary cause that gains increasing efficacy as they age and involve more experienced political actors.

As a consequence, the dichotomy of explanations for democratic process features between "legacies" of the old regimes and "institutions" of the new democracies is false (Crawford and Lijphart 1995). Instead of constituting either-or alternatives, we need a *sequential model* that explains how over time institutions become relatively more important as exogenous determinants of democratic process features, while they are initially endogenous to the political process. The dichotomy between "legacies" and "institutional" explanations of processes in new democratic polities is even more misleading, if it is associated with the claim that historical "legacy" explanations identify culture as the causal agent, whereas institutional explanations favor actors' material political self-interests. Nothing could be further from the truth.

Legacy explanations claim that resource endowments and institutions that precede the choice of democratic institutions have a distinct impact on the observable political process under the new democratic regime. Moreover, such explanations claim that the democratic institutions themselves depend on legacies, because they are endogenously chosen by political actors emerging from the old pre-democratic systems. Power configurations under the old system and in the transitions process, mediated by the actors' well-understood self-interests and subjective cognitive maps, thus shape institutions to a considerable extent. Legacy explanations acknowledge that equilibrium-based institutional explanations of democratic processes are insufficient in new democracies, where actors face great uncertainty about the consequences of their actions and therefore cannot easily converge on equilibrium outcomes. The relative independent importance of institutions to account for policy processes and outcomes is thus initially modest, but significant in the long term.

Many students of democracy have recognized the sequential causal efficacy of political and economic legacies, first, and institutional rules, second, for democratic process features. Thus Lipset and Rokkan (1967) develop a two-stage model of political cleavage formation that begins with a historical account of the societal identities and alignments that came about under pre-democratic political regimes. In the second stage, these authors then determine how strategic moves of political actors at the time of democratization and the endogenous choice of institutions made it more likely that some societal alignments made it into the arena of party competition than others (cf. Rokkan 1977). Only in a third phase, democratic institutions themselves become constraints on the representation of political cleavage dimensions. In a similar vein, Katzenstein (1985) engages not only in a causally forward-looking study of how democratic process features translate into political-economic outcomes in small European democracies, but also traces these features back to democratic institutional choices (e.g., that of electoral systems) and the pre-existing power configurations that informed such choices.

Both of these exemplary studies combine legacies and institutions in their explanatory accounts in ways that emphasize two features relevant for the explanatory strategy pursued in our present book. First, the authors of these studies are eager to specify causal mechanisms that link various steps in the development of democratic procedures to each other. They do not rely on "long-distance" causality that associates political configurations hundreds of years ago with observed democratic procedures in the twentieth century. Second, in both instances, the democratic institutions constitute a second stage of the explanatory models that filter societal economic interest alignments. In both respects, these studies differ from Putnam's (1993) celebrated account of the causes and consequences of democratic process features in Italy. As numerous critics have pointed out, Putnam's study relies too much on "long-distance" causality from the thirteenth to the twentieth century that lacks intermediation by actor strategies and alignments in the intervening time period. Moreover, Putnam's account probes too little into the institutional frames that support political decision-making procedures in different time periods.

Our account of the divergence of democratic process features in post-communist East European democracies is in the spirit of linking legacy-based and institutional explanations. We show how the economic and political legacies of pre-communist and communist regimes affect the pathways of contemporary post-communist polities. Such legacies impinge on the rational, calculated, and deliberate actions of the emerging political players in the new regimes. Material endowments and cognitive orientations that civic actors had acquired and handed down to subsequent generations through political practices that go at least as far back as the inter-war period shape the political mobilization and rational bargaining during the transition to democracy and the construction of new democratic collective decision-making procedures. In part, the emerging formal institutions of democracy, codified in constitutions and electoral laws, are endogenous to the bargaining process in which historical legacies assert themselves. In part, they reflect contingent choices influenced by idiosyncrasies of the decision-making situation in an environment with considerable uncertainty about the identity of collective political actors, their interests, and their strategic options. These qualifications are not meant to deny the impact of new democratic institutions on political procedures. But even where formal institutions, such as electoral laws or constitutional relations between executives and legislatures, are identical in two post-communist polities, the political practices of party competition and representation may still differ, if these polities emerge from different political legacies, crystallized around diverging configurations of actors – around resource endowments and cognitive orientations that derive from pre-communist and communist rule.

CONCLUSION

By 1996 twenty-six independent countries had emerged from communist rule in East Central Europe and the former Soviet Union (FSU), but only nine had established reasonably democratic procedures of political representation and decision making. They included Bulgaria, the Czech Republic, Hungary, Poland, Slovakia, Slovenia, and the three Baltic countries of Estonia, Latvia, and Lithuania. A further ten countries straddled the border between democratic and authoritarian rule. They were Albania, Armenia, Croatia, Georgia, Kyrgyzstan, Macedonia, Moldova, Romania, Russia, and Ukraine. The remaining new polities, Azerbaijan, Belarus, Kazakhstan, Serbia, Tajikistan, Turkmenistan, and Uzbekistan, have adopted unambiguously authoritarian regimes.[6] A twenty-seventh entity, Bosnia, is difficult to count as a functioning polity. Among the

---

[6] Our judgment is informed by the 1996 Freedom House Survey Team report which scores all countries in terms of political rights (1 = democratic; 7 = undemocratic) and civil rights (1 = democratic; 7 = undemocratic). Unambiguous democracies have an average score of no worse than 3.0. Ambiguous democracies score between 3.5 and 4.5, authoritarian regimes between 5.0 and 7.0.

borderline cases, from 1996 to 1997 Macedonia, Moldova, Romania, and Russia appeared to be joining the definitely democratic countries, whereas Albania, Armenia, Kyrgyzstan, and possibly even Croatia and Slovakia were veering toward authoritarianism. This state of affairs is quite sobering in light of widespread exuberance in 1989 about the "end of history" and the decisive victory of Western economic liberalism and political democracy over rival ideologies with alternative conceptions of socio-political order.

The impressive divergence of the political and economic trajectory of post-communist polities in Eastern Europe and the former Soviet Union raises questions not only about the basic regime choice between democracy and authoritarianism but also the nature of the democratic processes that emerge in the new polities. The main theme of our study is to document and explain the similarities and differences in crucial features that characterize the democratic procedures of four post-communist democracies: Bulgaria, the Czech Republic, Hungary, and Poland. Because these democracies had existed for only four to five years when we conducted our field research and because politicians were still learning to cope with exceedingly complex policy agendas, we considered it prudent to leave the second analytical question of how democratic governance structures deliver policies and affect citizens' subjective and objective life chances for future research. Our investigation focuses on one key component of the democratic process, the electoral arena of party competition and voter representation. To a lesser extent, we also examine the propensities of parties to form legislative or executive (coalition) majorities that are able to deliver effective political governance. Electoral politics and party competition are critical ingredients of any democratic polity, although they do not exhaust the range of actors and institutions involved in democratic interest intermediation. The way parties operate and create linkages of accountability and responsiveness to citizens is likely to have major consequences for the viability of democracy and the quality of its outputs.

Our study addresses only one component of a more comprehensive agenda for the comparative analysis of newly emerging democracies that is likely to preoccupy political scientists for some time to come. We ignore the inter-play of electoral and party politics with other collective actors in the democratic polity, such as social movements and interest groups, and we do not study the connection between democratic process features and policy outputs and outcomes. Given that our study is limited to four polities only, it can provide only modest empirical support for general theoretical propositions. Future research should cover a more comprehensive set of post-communist polities to probe more systematically into the origins and consequences of democratic procedures of competition and representation. Our study thus has more an exploratory rather than a confirmatory character. It spells out and illustrates a range of hypotheses about a multitude of democratic process features that vary among post-communist democracies. Moreover, it brings some novel empirical research tools and analytical perspectives to bear on the study of democratic procedures. While many of the hypotheses we advance in our study might eventually be proved wrong, our work will have served its purpose if its conceptual innovations, theoretical propositions, and empirical research strategies inspire new and better comparative investigations.

Let us finally address one issue of terminology in this introduction. We refer to East European countries as post-communist democracies and to the old ruling parties as communist parties and their successors as post-communist parties, even where they technically had adopted other labels after their merger with socialist or social democratic parties in the 1940s. Thus, we label not only the Communist Party of Bohemia and Moravia as a communist party, but also the Hungarian Socialist Workers' Party and the Polish United Workers' Party. Our usage of a generic terminology for the old ruling parties is at variance with everyday practice. At least since the 1970s, Hungarian and Polish citizens and observers would have hardly employed the attribute "communist" or invoked communist ideology to characterize the actions and motivations of the ruling parties in their countries. We treat the notion "post-communist" as a generic concept applicable to all countries emerging from former communist regimes. With regard to individual parties, however, we apply the attribute "post-communist" only to the main successors of the old communist ruling parties since 1989, but not to other parties that populate the new East European party systems, even when their precursors participated in the party bloc alliances communists created at the time of their takeover between 1945 and 1949.

PART I

THEORY: PARTY SYSTEMS AND THE PROCEDURAL QUALITY OF POST-COMMUNIST DEMOCRACY

HISTORICAL LEGACIES AND STRATEGIES OF DEMOCRATIZATION: PATHWAYS TOWARD POST-COMMUNIST POLITIES

The breakdown of political and economic regimes always offers new political actors opportunities to deal creatively with a highly contingent and open range of possibilities in order to craft new institutions and power relations. Nevertheless, the creativity of actors is also constrained by the experiences of the past and the patterns of economic and political resource distribution under the old regimes. Whereas historians are typically fascinated by the openness of choice in situations of regime breakdown and the idiosyncrasies of the actors who take advantage of them, sociologists and political scientists tend to focus more on the regularities and continuities that exercise a persistent influence on the pathways of social and political transformation in crisis situations, mediated by actors' rational pursuit of power, wealth, or ultimate cultural values. In this vein, the profound diversity of post-communist polities may not predominantly result from random variation of actors' choices when faced with the collapse of the existing communist political and economic regimes. Although regime breakdown may make some actors imagine an almost infinite range of choices among alternative new social and political orders, the former institutions and resource distributions, together with entrenched mutual expectations about likely or appropriate behavior generated under the old regime, still affect actors' aspirations and practical moves when building a new order and thus circumscribe the feasible set of outcomes.

Both historical legacies and actors' strategic choices matter in the path-dependent process of creating new polities and economies. Legacies at least initially shape the resources and expectations that help actors to define their interests and to select the ways and means to acquire political power. In order to account for the varying development of parties and party systems in post-communist democracies, in this chapter we detail a simple analytical model that characterizes structural components of the diversity among the old communist regimes and associated pathways toward institutional change in the critical window of regime breakdown. In chapter 2, we then propose hypotheses explaining how diverse experiences and strategic configurations among actors before and during communist rule as well as in the transition to a new order affect the patterns of party competition and political representation that create qualitatively different processes of interest aggregation and collective decision making across the new democracies.

Accounts of political change that invoke path dependence often appear to command a compelling persuasiveness only because they seem to presuppose nothing more than a good narrative constructed around a linear chronology in which later events and institutional arrangements somehow follow from earlier ones. With the benefit of hindsight, a skilled storyteller may always identify attributes and episodes associated with the old regimes that foreshadow subsequent developments. In order to avoid such opportunistic theorizing and the related penchant toward idiosyncratic accounts geared to individual cases, arguments from path dependency must meet at least two standards to achieve explanatory bite. First, its advocates must formulate them at a level of sufficiently high conceptual generality to be testable against the experience of a variety of unexplored cases. This requires that we abstract from numerous historical particularities of each case and focus on attributes that vary systematically across classes of cases. Second, accounts based on path dependency must lay out a parsimonious logic detailing how and why actors with a capacity to process information, to define preferences, and to deliberate about alternative pathways choose particular strategies resulting in observable collective outcomes.

In this chapter, we propose such a logic for the subject of communist regime breakdown in three steps. First, we distinguish three variants of communist rule and discuss how these variants are themselves steeped in social and political-institutional antecedents, although we refrain from pursuing the causal chain further into the past, let alone explore the cultural correlates they are associated with. Next, we explore how these three configurations of communist rule opened up alternative strategic pathways of regime transition in the late 1980s. Finally, we sketch how the distinctive patterns of regime transition influenced the choice of new democratic rules of the game. After outlining the logic that connects resources, institutions, and political choices to alternative pathways of post-communist transformation, we discuss how our theoretical model applies to empirical cases in the communist hemisphere and justify the design of our empirical research in that light.

It is a matter of course that a logic of institutions and calculated strategic choices constructs an idealization not fully reflecting any particular historical case. Observers of political and economic regime change are therefore quite right to insist on the contingency of regime transitions in which actors must make choices under conditions of great uncertainty because unique constellations of institutions and actors, faced with a far-reaching breakdown of economic activity and political order, make it difficult for participants to define their preferences and collective identities or to select strategies that advance their objectives in light of their opponents' choices. Nevertheless, theory involves the construction of logically connected generalizations about the causal linkages between actions, events, and macro-institutions. If we endorse this epistemology of social science, then theory aims at highlighting the non-contingent, least probabilistic connections among elements within political processes at the expense of purely contingent choices that can be reconstructed only by a historical narrative.[1]

THREE MODES OF COMMUNIST RULE AND THEIR HISTORICAL ANTECEDENTS

While communist polities vary in many respects, two properties characterize alternative communist regime types that appear consequential for the transition to democracy and ultimately the quality of the democratic process in post-communist polities. The first dimension concerns the extent to which communist regimes rely on a formal-rational bureaucratic state apparatus that rules out corruption and clientelism, as opposed to a patrimonial administration based on personal networks of loyalty and mutual exchange, combined with patronage, corruption, and nepotism. The existence of formal bureaucracy may have lasting consequences for the construction of citizen-party linkages at the time of suffrage extension and on opportunities for rent seeking by members of the incumbent elite in the process of reassigning property rights. A good measure of formal-bureaucratic rule is the extent to which the state administration relied on corruption under communist rule. While a few scholars have attempted to determine practices of corruption under communism in comparative terms (Willerton 1992; Goetz 1995; Mildner 1995), we lack a broad and reliable data base in this regard. Nevertheless, comprehensive assessments of corruption in post-communist countries conducted by investment risk analysis firms may provide us with clues about administrative practices under the old regimes, as long as we accept the premise that such administrative practices are unlikely to have fallen simply out of the blue sky at the time of regime change in the late 1980s.[2]

The extent of communist systems' reliance on formal-bureaucratic rule depends on older patterns of state formation, economic development, and political mobilization. Where capitalist market economies had begun to take off before the advent of communism, they were intertwined with the development of more secure property rights hastened by and contributing to the development of a

---

[1]For this reason, authors such as Levine (1988), Remmer (1991, 1997), and Kitschelt (1992a, 1992b) have pointed out that the correct intuition of analysts who emphasize contingency – such as O'Donnell and Schmitter (1986) or DiPalma (1990) – unfortunately does not help us to make theoretical advances.

[2]For expert assessments of corruption in twenty-six post-communist countries, see *Central European Economic Review,* December 1995–January 1996, p. 9.

predictable formal-bureaucratic state apparatus. Moreover, in the more industrial economies powerful socialist and communist parties formed outside the state apparatus. Particularly the radical, communist working-class organizations had no access to state patronage and developed practices of citizen-elite linkage without clientelist material rewards to constituencies (cf. Shefter 1994). Consistent with the Leninist vanguard party model, these practices favored formal-hierarchical and rational-bureaucratic governance structures later on when strong communist parties assumed political rule. Conversely, where market economies and radical socialist parties were feeble before the advent of communist rule and where the state apparatus relied on patrimonial governance, later governing communist parties could resort to patrimonial techniques in their own governance structures.

The second dimension of variability among communist regimes concerns the mechanisms communist parties employed to instill compliance in the population or the extent to which communist rulers after Stalin's death and during the "post-totalitarian" transformation tolerated a modicum of economic or political pluralism under communist tutelage.[3] The two main compliance mechanisms are repression (the stick) and co-optation (the carrot), negative or positive incentives to promote cooperative conduct. While all communist regimes relied on a mix of both, the emphasis on each varied contingent upon the *parties' bargaining power vis-à-vis actual or virtual opponents.* This bargaining power, in turn, is linked to the skills and experiences of different political forces in the pre-communist period that constituted a virtual threat potential to the new incumbents of state power, once communist rule had been installed. Political and economic conditions preceding communist rule thus began to shape the feasible strategies of communist politicians after Stalin's death.

Different propensities for communist rulers to rely on repression, co-optation, and toleration of dissent come in at least three configurations characterized by different balances in the distribution of organizational resources. First, where socialist and communist parties as well as their bourgeois opponents were well organized in mass parties before the advent of communist rule, later communist governments primarily relied on repression and tolerated little dissidence. Second, where the socialist-communist left was weak in numbers and organization, but bourgeois and agrarian opponents strong, communist governments from the 1950s onward relied on direct bargaining or indirect tacit trades with a virtual and sometimes real opposition to find a modus vivendi. Third, where both the socialist-communist left as well as bourgeois political organizations were weak and only agrarians were able to mobilize a mass following around civic associations in the

---

[3]In contrast to the pluralism debates in the sovietology of the 1970s and 1980s where the key question was whether organized economic special interests (firms, sectors, regions) articulate conflicting demands and shape the policy process (cf. Hough 1977; Skilling 1983), we are returning here to the classic notion of pluralism concerned with free and voluntary political mobilization and contestation of elite positions (cf. Dahl 1971, 1989).

pre-communist era, communist rulers employed both strict repression and induce-ments of co-optation but did not tolerate dissent. Based on our two dimensions – formal bureaucratic rule and the balance of power between communists and their adversaries in pre-communist political regimes – we can now characterize three different modes of communist rule and their historical origins.

The first type of communist rule is *patrimonial communism*. It relies on vertical chains of personal dependence between leaders in the state and party apparatus and their entourage, buttressed by extensive patronage and clientelist networks.[4] At the apex of patrimonial regimes, political power is concentrated around a small clique or an individual ruler worshiped by a personality cult. The level of rational-bureaucratic institutionalization in state and party remains low because the ruling clique penetrates the apparatus through nepotistic appointments. In extreme cases, such regimes give rise to the "sultanistic" rule of an individual and his family (cf. Linz and Stepan 1996: 51–54). In patrimonial systems, rulers firmly repress any stirring of opposition demanding rights to participation or they co-opt potentially resourceful challengers through selective incentives (office, material privilege).

Patrimonial communism was likely to emerge in historical settings where a traditional authoritarian regime,[5] assisted by compliant religious leaders, ruled over societies of poor peasants (whether they were freemen or serfs), weak cities, a thin layer of ethnic pariah immigrant entrepreneurs and merchants, a small and geographically concentrated industrial working class, and a corrupt coterie of administrators dependent on the personal whims of the ruler. In such settings, communist insurrectionists were political entrepreneurs without a proletarian mass following who built political power on the mobilization of dissatisfied elements of the intelligentsia whom they were able to recruit from the offspring of the political and economic elite. Moreover, they sought support from the poor peasantry by promising to break up large estates and to give property rights to the peasantry, or, where peasants were a class of poor smallholders, to redistribute resources to the countryside from the ruler's fiscal apparatus in the capital city.

Once having assumed power with or without foreign help, communist parties easily crushed weak urban middle-class organizations. Patrimonial communists then constructed an industrial society at an initially dizzying pace by squeezing the peasantry and subsidizing the emerging heavy industries.[6] Patrimonial com-

---

[4]On the significance of clientelism and patronage in communist bureaucracy, see Goetz (1995) and Mildner (1995). To gauge the extent of patronage and clientelist administration in communist times, the best guide may be to rely on current estimates of corruption in post-communist bureaucracies. Such corruption scores highly correlate with our three types of communist rule. See note 2.

[5]Such regimes often did not impose constitutional restraints on the ruler. In addition to regimes without constitution, this also applies to polities where constitutions de facto cannot limit the exercise of political power.

[6]This pattern of industrialization represents an extreme form of import substituting industrialization (ISI) which far exceeded the milder Latin American cases, where the peasantry and the rural landlords were weakened but not wiped out.

munism presided over a prolonged era during which the peasantry's offspring enjoyed upward mobility into industrial jobs and the technical-administrative strata. Rapid economic growth due to the substitution of low-productivity agricultural jobs by employment in higher-productivity industrial manufacturing generated the resources to co-opt these new societal groups into the communist power structure and reinforce clientelist networks, an administrative practice assimilated from previous regimes.

An important cognitive legacy of the political-economic modernization under patrimonial communism is the lack of a popular memory of an urban middle class or of a proletariat that would have played a decisive role in the advancement of economic welfare before the advent of a modern industrial order created by communist party rule. Thus, patrimonial communism never had to confront an alternative vision and practice of modernization whose carriers had been crushed by the communist takeover. Once firmly entrenched in power, the patrimonial communist parties' mixture of repression and clientelist co-optation kept the emerging new urban industrial and white-collar middle strata compliant and preempted the rise of opposition forces that could have cultivated a new vision of modernity and challenged the party's exclusive claim to represent the only viable path to progress. On the eve of the communist collapse, patrimonial regimes therefore faced no significant internal opposition movements, except dispersed, isolated dissident intellectuals, unable to produce a sustained discourse or organize a professional cadre advancing a new vision of political-economic modernity. As a consequence, communist parties enjoyed not only the support of the country-side and of the industrial working class, but also of many new urban industrial and administrative strata that looked back on a lifetime of upward social mobility and improving living standards, at least until the end of the 1970s.

The second type of communist rule, *national-accommodative communism*, produced regimes with more developed formal-rational bureaucratic governance structures that partially separated party rule and technical state administration. Moreover, such regimes evidenced a greater propensity to permit modest levels of civil rights and elite contestation at least episodically, while relying more on co-optation than repression as ways to instill citizens' compliance. When Soviet support for Stalin's direct representatives in the leadership of communist parties throughout Eastern Europe waned by the mid-1950s, a number of East European regimes discovered they could govern only by broadening their societal support base. As a consequence, after sometimes bloody internal confrontations and even Soviet military interventions, indigenous communist rulers attempted to craft a tacit political and economic accommodation with their domestic challengers. They conceded modest steps toward economic or political liberalization in the hope of eliciting a modicum of popular acceptance of single party rule. To make such arrangements more palatable, they intimated that tacit mutual accommodation between ruling party and potential civic challengers was the only way to preserve an element of national autonomy from the Soviet hegemon. This modus vivendi of somewhat relaxed party control entailed a good deal of patronage politics and a sectorization of the state apparatus into competing interests vying for resources.

National-accommodative communism prevailed in countries or Soviet republics that emerged from semi-democratic and semi-authoritarian inter-war polities with rather vibrant political mobilization around parties and interest groups. Such countries had already undertaken significant steps toward industrialization but were saddled with inefficient state bureaucracies over-staffed by the offspring of a state-centered educated middle stratum unable to find work in private business. In these settings, urban-rural conflicts were particularly salient and congealed around intense party divisions, while industrial class conflict played a comparatively minor role in the crystallization of political divides.[7] In the inter-war period communist parties were marginal operations led by urban intellectuals, whereas middle-class nationalist and pseudo-liberal parties, together with powerful peasant parties, vied for political power. These contests often took place under the tutelage of semi-authoritarian leaders who maintained power through rigged elections that sustained the dominance of the urban centers with its administrative middle class over the countryside. After the installation of communism, the new rulers lacked a strong working-class movement as a natural power base. At the same time, they faced potentially mutinous urban and peasant constituencies. The existence of Catholic or Protestant churches, which had always insisted on their internal autonomy from political meddling and had on occasion actively shaped inter-war politics, gave communist regimes another reason to seek mutual societal accommodation.

The cognitive legacy of national-accommodative communism is the experience of multiple conflicting visions of modernity, one represented by the anti-communist urban and rural elites of the inter-war period, another by the communists themselves. The communist ruling parties thus could never claim the exclusive capacity to promote modernity. They therefore never ascended to the same ideological hegemony as in the patrimonial communist countries. Instead, national-accommodative communist regimes tolerated low-level dissident activities and sometimes even networks of dissident communication that congealed around liberal, rural-populist, or Christian conceptions. Under national-accommodative regimes, the Marxist-Leninist ideology began to wither earlier than in other communist regimes.

In the third type of communist rule, *bureaucratic-authoritarian communism*, opposition forces encountered a much harsher and more hostile climate than in national-accommodative communism, but for different reasons than in patrimonial communism. Bureaucratic-authoritarian communism came closest to the

---

[7]Rogowski (1989: 84) is somewhat ambiguous in his characterization of the cleavage structures in inter-war Eastern Europe. He wishes to claim that the dominant division is a class cleavage between capitalists and landowners, on the one side, and workers, on the other. Yet the "workers" are mostly poor peasants who mobilize against urban elites that are often difficult to characterize as capitalist entrepreneurs.

totalitarian model of a party state with an all-powerful, rule-guided bureaucratic machine governed by a planning technocracy and a disciplined, hierarchically stratified communist party. It relied on a tier of sophisticated economic and administrative professionals who governed a planned economy that produced comparatively advanced industrial goods and services. Bureaucratic professionalism and strict party discipline, however, were inimical to political bargaining with and mutual interest accommodation to potential outside challengers. Bureaucratic authoritarian communism resorted more to the repression and exclusion of sometimes vocal opposition movements than national accommodative communism. Given these characteristics, we have consciously chosen the Latin Americanists' concept of bureaucratic-authoritarianism to characterize this variant of communist rule. In fact, bureaucratic authoritarianism may be a more adequate description of certain communist regimes than of most Latin American authoritarian polities.[8] It is a form of political rule that coincides with a relatively advanced stage of capital intensive industrialization and relies on a technocratic governance structure that tolerates no political diversity.

Bureaucratic-authoritarian communism occurred in countries with considerable liberal-democratic experience in the inter-war period, an early and comparatively advanced industrialization, and a simultaneous mobilization of bourgeois and proletarian political forces around class-based parties beginning in the late nineteenth century. In the inter-war and immediate post–World War II democracies, strong disciplined communist parties either directly organized the working class or eventually took over such organizations from rival social democratic parties when the latter ceased to lead an independent life with the subordination of the East European satellite countries under Stalin's Soviet Union. The discipline of a revolutionary party created outside of and against existing political institutions and the rise of a modern professional state machinery under precommunist rule made the new communist regimes more resistant than other modes of communist rule to patronage and clientelist politics.[9]

Under bureaucratic-authoritarian communism, the ruling party's internal organizational strength and firm entrenchment in a broad industrial working class decreased its tolerance for political deviations. The balance of forces thus tilted in favor of repressive communist rule even in countries where pluralist civic and political mobilization in the inter-war period posed the potential challenge of an anti-communist insurrection later on. Whereas in patrimonial communism weak pre-communist pluralism, and above all the absence of urban political mobilization, accounts for the feebleness of the anti-communist opposition in the 1980s,

---

[8]We are building on O'Donnell's (1973) formulation and Collier's (1979) reconstruction of the concept, while recognizing that at least in Latin America many of its attributes never appear to have applied (Kaufman 1979) and therefore require revision of the theory (O'Donnell 1979).

[9]Our account is consistent with Shefter's (1994) finding that patronage and clientelist bureaucracies are less likely where political regimes rely on mass parties that were founded long before its supporters had access to the levers of the state.

in bureaucratic-authoritarian communism it is rather the organizational discipline and encapsulation of the working class that allowed ruling communist parties to prevail over a potentially strong challenge by opposition forces and to resist the temptation of seeking societal peace through accommodation with potential opposition forces.

In cognitive terms, the legacies of bureaucratic-authoritarian communism incorporate not a shortage but an abundance of competing models of socio-political modernization advanced by conflicting political actors in the inter-war period. Where declining growth rates showed the communist model of modernization to run into trouble, technocratic experimentation with economic reform, for example in the Prague Spring of 1968, were short-lived because they triggered an almost instant reawakening of a massive political opposition to communism. Unlike technocratic reformers under national-accommodative communism, the economic reformers under bureaucratic-authoritarian communism faced a party elite unwilling to make concessions for the sake of greater popular inclusiveness and economic efficiency. Communist parties in bureaucratic-authoritarian regimes remained more wedded to proletarian rhetoric and ideological orthodoxy than in national accommodative communism and, in some ways, even in patrimonial communism. Under the hegemony of orthodox Marxist-Leninist doctrines, bureaucratic authoritarian communist countries developed like pressure cookers with a muted and clandestine but potentially powerful opposition, building up steam that could blow the lid off the communist regime whenever the party's containment of opposition through repression showed signs of weakness.

Each of the three different communist regime types chose unique policy strategies to cope with the economic slowdown in the 1980s. These strategies had important consequences for economic liberalization and stabilization policies after 1989. Elites in national-accommodative communism had the strongest incentives to placate the population and maintain a modicum of political stability by increasing the supply of consumer goods. In these countries, foreign debt owed to Western banks and governments ballooned more than in other communist regimes in the 1970s and 1980s (cf. Comisso and Marer 1986; Poznanski 1986). In patrimonial or in bureaucratic-authoritarian communism, by contrast, the incumbent elites could afford to avoid major concessions to their citizens and therefore took fewer Western loans, kept tighter control of their external debt, and engaged in harsher economic retrenchment in the 1980s.[10]

At a superficial inspection, our argument concerning the origins and types of communist rule appears to invoke a model of political development very much akin to modernization theory, emphasizing the influence of economic affluence and growth as a determinant of political regime patterns. Indeed, we believe that modernization should not be considered merely a bad word, as long as theorists

---

[10]See for this comparison Tyson (1986: 258–80). Tyson refers to both bureaucratic-authoritarian and patrimonial systems (in our language) as "patrimonial" as opposed to the "collegial" systems of Hungary and Poland.

properly spell out the linkages between economic resource mobilization and institutional change. In the inter-war period, political regime forms and the development of civic political associations in Eastern Europe closely correlate with the relative size of the peasantry and the industrial sector. Differential industrial growth, however, may itself be grounded in institutional and cultural variations unexplored by modernization theory. Were we to pursue the origins of inter-war regional economic inequality in Eastern Europe backward before 1850 when most of the region was about equal in terms of poverty and dominated by agriculture, good candidates to explain subsequent differential growth rates would be the geographic incorporation into the divergent governance structures of the Prussian, Russian, Habsburg, or Ottoman empires, agrarian property rights, proximity to major trade routes, and even religious beliefs, together with associated practices of church-state relations (cf. Janos 1989; 1994; Schöpflin 1993; Offe 1994; Berglund and Aarebrot 1997).

More importantly for us, *there is no longer a close relationship between economic modernization and the type of communist rule by the 1970s or 1980s.* Patrimonial communist countries that began with a more "backward" economy in the 1940s often had pretty much caught up with their initially more advanced neighbors in national-accommodative or bureaucratic-authoritarian communist polities.[11] For this reason, the political institutions of communist rule, not levels of economic development, are the key determinants of political transformation strategies in the late 1980s and early 1990s. The resulting institutional differences in the post-communist polities may, however, influence subsequent differential pathways of economic reform and successful market liberalization in turn, thus translating institutional diversity again into varying levels of economic "modernity" (cf. Hellman 1996; Stark and Bruszt 1997).[12]

REGIME CHANGE BEYOND COMMUNIST RULE

A leading structural cause for the collapse of communism was the Eastern bloc's declining economic and technological performance throughout the 1970s and 1980s and its inability to stay abreast of an arms race with the United States paced by technological innovations difficult to nurture in a planned economy. Moreover, the Soviet Union's military defeat in a low-technology guerrilla war in Afghanistan weakened the governing elite. Once the dominant group of the Soviet elite began to opt for economic and institutional reform, its decision to abandon the Brezhnev doctrine of intervention in the domestic affairs of subsidiary communist countries and its willingness to grant more political autonomy to individual

---

[11] For a discussion of modernization theory and political change in Eastern Europe, see also Lewis (1997: 9–15).

[12] Our argument here is akin to Putnam's (1993: 152–62) in that we reverse the role of economic modernization and see it as a dependent variable affected by institutional and cultural arrangements.

Soviet republics profoundly altered the opportunities for regime change in the satellite countries and Soviet republics. Nevertheless, these changing external constraints on domestic power relations cannot explain the diverging pathways individual countries and former republics of the Soviet Union then chose to build new post-communist political orders. These pathways depend on the domestic distribution of political resources, mobilization capabilities, and cognitive orientations that grew out of their experiences with different modes of communist rule.

In the broader literature about "democratic transitions" it is quite controversial whether features of the old authoritarian regimes systematically relate to the pathways of political regime change. While some authors have postulated an association between modes of transition and the quality of the democratic outcomes,[13] few scholars have elaborated the connection between authoritarian regime form and the mode of transition itself.[14] Our own attempt to specify such a logic claims no more than to throw light on post-communist pathways of transition. We do not spell out a more general theory applicable to the strategic interaction between authoritarian regime incumbents and potential challengers in a wider range of authoritarian regimes.[15] Conceptually, our distinction among modes of transition from communist rule builds on existing typologies that characterize the alternative pathways by the varying resources and orientations of the competing actors shaping opponents' ability to challenge the incumbents and incumbents' propensity to make concessions to their challengers.[16]

First, where the incumbent communist elite continues to control most significant resources and public support while the democratic opposition remains weak, the elites maintain the political status quo *unless* an elite faction launches the transition by a *preemptive strike* because it expects to protect its long-term interests better by quick reform on its own terms than by passive resistance to weak opponents who are destined to grow stronger in a favorable international setting and eventually may sweep aside the entire ruling apparatus. The transitions literature refers to the preemptive strategies of incumbent elites also as imposition (Karl 1990), transformation (Huntington 1991: 124–42), transaction (Share and Mainwaring 1986), or agreed reform within the ruling bloc (Colomer 1991).

[13]See, for example, O'Donnell and Schmitter (1986), Przeworski (1986), Karl (1990), and Shain and Linz (1995).

[14]But see Huntington (1991: 110–13) who adopts a rather ad hoc classification of authoritarian regimes and a similarly questionable coding of regime transitions and hence finds few linkages. A more careful coding of African cases by Bratton and Van de Walle (1994), however, reveals interesting patterns.

[15]If dictatorships are relatively short-lived interruptions of democratic or semi-democratic regimes amounting to less than ten or twenty years, the relationship between type of rule and process of transition may be quite random because the regime types themselves are not well established and may permit a variety of transition modes. For comparative Latin American politics, it may therefore be less promising to search for a linkage between regime form and mode of transition than for sets of countries with long-term entrenched authoritarian regimes.

[16]This general argument is made by numerous authors, such as Etzioni-Halevy (1993), Friedheim (1992), Mangott (1992: 94), and Wasilewski (1992: 116–17).

In the 1980s, lopsided power balances favoring the incumbent communist party over weak, dispersed opposition groups typically occurred in *patrimonial communist regimes.* Once changes in the international situation made it uncertain whether communist rule could survive anywhere, factions of the incumbent elites had strong incentives to seize the initiative, displace the discredited top communist leadership, and engineer regime change via preemptive reform with only minimal input from the emerging democratic opposition forces. Indeed, most of the time the reformist currents within communist parties did manage to protect vital organizational and material resources of the former ruling parties during and in the initial aftermath of transitions by preemptive strike. In other cases, patrimonial communist rulers were so well entrenched that they only changed the label, the public ideology, and the symbols associated with their regime, but maintained the status quo apparatus of power.

In a second configuration of regime change, communist elites show signs of an increasing rift between hard-liners and reformers and have to reckon with an embryonic opposition with considerable capacity to network and appropriate resources for an eventual democratic mobilization. This situation prepares a regime transition based on *negotiation* between incumbents and opposition representatives. The ruling elites are too weak and divided to impose reform on their own initiative, but still sufficiently powerful to demand concessions from the challengers in exchange for a democratic opening. Eventually, the interaction of reformers in the regime camp and moderates within the opposition camp brings about a democratic transition by elite compacts rather than mass mobilization (Przeworski 1991: chap. 1). The literature refers to negotiated transitions also as democratization through pacts (Karl 1990), transplacement (Huntington 1991: 151–63), extrication (Share and Mainwaring 1986), or controlled opening to the opposition (Colomer 1991).

This second configuration of forces prevailed most clearly in the *national-accommodative communist regimes.* The regime incumbents were already weakened on the eve of the transition and in part predisposed to bargaining with an opposition that had comparatively strong resources, organizational skills, and public support. In the ensuing negotiated transitions, the counter-elites acquired the right to compete for positions of government power, but the previous communist incumbents did not lose all political and economic assets. Indeed, their willingness to embrace the new democratic order made them acceptable as fully recognized players in the new democratic order. Their rapidly changing reputation and popular appeal, together with their residual organizational strength, quickly enabled them to become serious democratic alternatives to the former dissidents' parties and to make another bid to win executive office by democratic means.

In the third configuration of regime transition, intransigent communist elites cling to power and apply repressive strategies until the bitter end. Opposition forces remain mostly submerged, but they network and control cognitive and cultural capacities that enable them to stage a short and sharp jolt of mass mobilization when the international situation becomes sufficiently favorable to wipe out the incumbent regime almost instantly (Kuran 1991; Lohmann 1994). In this case, regime change occurs by *implosion of the old order,* a process scholars have also called replacement (Huntington 1991: 142–51), breakdown (Share and Mainwaring 1986), or sudden collapse of the authoritarian regime (Colomer 1991). Where implosions take place, the former elites have the least bargaining power in the transition and are shunted aside by opposition forces that quickly gain organizational and ideological predominance. The former communist incumbents enjoy little opportunity to change their political appeal or to regain popular confidence under the new rules of democracy. It is unlikely that they become recognized as the leading opposition force to the new democratic polity.

Regime change by implosion characterizes *bureaucratic-authoritarian communism,* where the elites, based on the monolithic coherence of the communist party machines and long-standing support from the working class, intransigently refused to bargain for change, thus delaying any reform that would have enabled them to rescue some of their resources into a post-communist order. When the international domino effect in Eastern Europe triggered the generalized crisis of communism all around them in neighboring countries, the ruling parties swiftly succumbed to a sudden acceleration of mass protest in which the now liberated civic counter-elites, in conjunction with segments of the technical-administrative personnel in the bureaucratic-authoritarian state, took power. The new governments stripped the assets and dismantled the organizational apparatus of the former communist elite much faster and more thoroughly than their counter-parts in countries that had gone through preemptive or negotiated transitions.

None of the former communist countries experienced a fourth mode of democratic transition conventional terminology would associate with the classic case of regime change through *revolution.* Revolutions involve a sustained, accelerating political organization and mobilization of regime opponents from below who challenge a weakening, intransigent status quo elite. Revolutions bring about an open contest for power with a dual power structure ("revolutionary situation") and eventually displace the incumbents by the challengers' violent takeover of the executive and the coercive state machinery. The absence of revolutions in the demise of communist regimes may be due to the high concentration and coherence of the means of coercion in the communist state apparatus. The continued integrity of the military and the police made a direct violent challenge of the incumbent elites futile and compelled challengers to resort to softer and more incremental techniques of undermining the status quo.

THE CHOICE OF DEMOCRATIC INSTITUTIONS IN POST-COMMUNIST POLITICAL REGIMES

As a first approximation, we assume that rational actors prefer to choose political institutions that lock in permanent gains and impose lasting losses on their adversaries (Knight 1992; Przeworski 1991). Institutions cement power relations because they create high transaction costs for potential challengers intent to change. Dominant forces in the transition try to lock in their initial advantages through institutions that improve their expected chance to pursue important objectives, such as winning and maintaining political office. Placed in the context of path-dependent political change after communism, this distributive political rationale has a systematic and a random term. The choice of rules should be systematically associated with the varying resource endowments of the actors emerging from different types of communist regimes and transition processes. But at the same time, a host of idiosyncrasies ensures that institutional choice is not entirely endogenous to the logic of path dependency. Some of this non-endogeneity is consistent with rational institutional choice, some of it is not.

The expected popular strength of former communist incumbents is greatest after patrimonial communist regimes, followed by national-accommodative and bureaucratic-authoritarian polities. In polities emerging from patrimonial communism, the former ruling parties are generally likely to demand and often have sufficient leverage to obtain new democratic political rules that emphasize major-itarian principles, rewarding the strongest and most unified political actor with a disproportionate share of political power. To that end, communist successor parties may advocate single-member district plurality voting laws and a strong presidency with wide decree powers, a presidential veto difficult to override by the legislature, and presidential discretion in nominating, appointing, or dismissing members of the political executive. Communist successor parties may opt for the personaliza-tion of political office promoted by majoritarian electoral rules and personalized presidential power also because it enables them to gloss over their discredited ideology and instead direct voters' attention to the popularity, trustworthiness, and reliability of their candidates in electoral campaigns. Finally, they might hope that the power of their party apparatus has the greatest payoff in plurality elections. After patrimonial communism, however, even liberal-democratic forces may favor a constitutional arrangement with personalist representation and executive con-trol. In these settings, liberal democrats are typically weak, with volatile, thinly organized and faction-ridden parties configured around individual personalities. Such parties may embrace a constitutional design with a strong executive presi-dency, if they believe one of their politicians has a chance to win it.

In formerly bureaucratic-authoritarian polities, the incumbent communists command little support and are rapidly sidelined by a host of electorally popular new liberal-democratic contenders who are likely to advocate and obtain de-personalizing institutional rules that incorporate the proportional representation of electoral lists in legislatures and a parliamentary system that makes the chief executive dependent on parliamentary coalitions. A rational logic underlies the institutional choice. The new liberal-democratic contenders typically run under competing party labels and often lack well-known politicians. They therefore expect to gain more power by instituting rules of proportional representation and a depersonalizing choice of the executive.

In former national-accommodative communist countries, where communist successor parties have maintained some bargaining power and popularity based on their willingness to embrace reform, constitutional arrangements are likely to combine elements of proportional and plurality electoral systems or of parliamentary and presidential power. Here reform communists often hope to be electorally successful, based on their conciliatory approach to regime transition, and therefore advocate strong majoritarian democratic institutions. But the emerging field of dissident groups and parties mobilizes sufficient bargaining power to force the political incumbents to negotiate more proportional political rules and limits on presidential powers. Once defeated in founding elections and converted into quasi-social democratic parties, the communist successor parties then themselves embrace a parliamentary form of governance with proportional representation in the legislature.

Closer empirical inspection indeed reveals a moderate but robust association between communist regime type and critical institutional design choices. Yet new political institutions are not entirely endogenous to former communist power configurations and modes of political transition. Although this association illuminates the underlying "deep structure" of political resource distribution and power relations, it does not take into account the openness and vagaries of the transition and bargaining process that makes the idiosyncrasies of the political actors, their frequent miscalculations in single-shot bargaining games based on no prior experience, and matters of timing and sequence so important for the outcomes. Finally, the ideological bent of the actors may lead them to interpret their strategic prospects inaccurately and support institutional rules that may be at cross-purposes with their short- and long-term power strategies.

This is not the place to engage the subtleties of institutional choice in post-communist polities, a task that has yet to be attempted in a comprehensive comparative fashion.[17] Let us therefore simply indicate some of the reasons why the adoption of democratic institutions may diverge from the simple logic of communist regime–driven path dependency just sketched. First, all actors may act on myopic self-interest to obtain political power as quickly as possible, but conjunctural events in the transition process put power into different hands than the simple path-dependent model anticipates. Thus, in formerly patrimonial communist systems, where communist incumbents have no convincing personality to fill the presidential office but face a popular contender advanced by the regime dissidents, they may withdraw from constitutional proposals for a strong presidency. Conversely, politicians belonging to the anti-communist opposition may realize that they command only limited support in legislative elections, but nevertheless they favor a strong presidency if their man has the greatest opportunities to win the contest.

Second, the assumption of a myopic rationality of short-term office seeking itself may be inadequate to reconstruct the propensities of some actors involved in

---

[17]For elements of such an analysis, see Frye (1997), Elster (1993–94), Kitschelt (1994b), Lijphart (1992), Przeworski (1991), and Shugart (1993, 1996).

the bargaining game and to account for the eventual institutional choices that follow from it. On the one hand, actors may simply make errors in assessing their prospective strength in an open democratic contest. Thus, time and again, communist successor parties have overestimated their vote-getting capabilities and consequently advocated the adoption of the "wrong" electoral system (e.g., Hungary, Poland). On the other, parties may take long-term detrimental consequences of institutional choice into account even if such institutions look advantageous in the short run. Dominant parties in ethnically plural societies may refrain from imposing majoritarian institutions because of their long-term consequences on the support of disempowered minorities for the polity.

More generally, where parties have considerable organizational and programmatic coherence or command a crushing lead over competitors at least at the initial founding of democracy, they may develop a longer time horizon of office maximization that makes them prefer institutions even though they look quite irrational by criteria of short-term office seeking. For example, an initially dominant communist successor party may not wish to adopt a majoritarian electoral system because that would give the opposition very little legislative representation and could trigger a backlash in subsequent elections. In a similar vein, neither liberal-democratic nor socialist parties may see it in their interest to adopt personalizing electoral institutions – such as strong presidencies, plurality voting systems, or other electoral rules making the candidate rather than the party the focus of competition – because they tend to undermine the organizational coherence of the parties.

Parties representing sectional socio-cultural appeals, running under religious, peasant, nationalist, or ethno-cultural (minority or majority) labels, tend to prefer personalistic electoral systems, but usually with proportional representation, multi-member districts if they represent minorities. Nationalists may opt even for a strong presidency regardless of their initial chances to control it. Socio-cultural and sectional parties tend to *lack a theoretical conceptualization of the imperatives of economic reform that is highly salient on the post-communist legislative agenda* (see chapter 2). They shun firm commitments on economic policy making for fear of dividing their socio-cultural constituencies. Because they cannot build comprehensive socio-economic programs, they prefer personalistic electoral contests.

Third, a major problem in the negotiation of institutional rules is that the actors who participate in the design of the democratic polity often know they will change their "identity" through splits and mergers once the new rules come into effect. Moreover, there are often conflicts *within* collective bargaining units over the locus of interests that are to be satisfied. For example, are representatives of post-communist parties in constitutional negotiations acting in the office-maximizing interests of their parties or just their own presidential ambitions? Given these ambiguities about the identity of bargaining units, it is difficult to specify the articulation of interests and the resulting bargaining game a priori. And ex posteriori, it is always easy to read some kind of self-interested rationality back into the bargaining process, because observers reconstruct the identities of the relevant bargaining units from the ultimate outcomes of institutional choice. Where ambiguities about actors' identities and payoffs are great, psychological explanations based on focal points, past precedent, and the dissemination of foreign models ("learning") are often more plausible than rational self-interest reconstructions of bargaining situations.

The upshot of our brief discussion of institutional design in post-communist polities is to advance an argument based on structural path dependency *and* rationality, but to remain sensitive to the explanatory limits of this parsimonious approach. Contingent opportunities modify the circumstances under which actors formulate their myopically rational bargaining strategies. Some actors and circumstances promote hyperopic rationality of office seeking. And cognitive ambiguities about the expected payoffs of alternative institutional designs as well as the identity of the actors themselves make it sometimes difficult to apply a straightforward logic of rational self-interest at all. While institutional choice is partially path dependent, the new democratic institutions have sufficient autonomy to become determinants of party system features in their own right, a point we discuss in chapter 2.

THE VARIABILITY OF COMMUNIST RULE AND ITS LEGACIES

Table 1.1 summarizes the logic of the argument we have developed in the previous sections and advances a few amendments and specifications. The political-economic developmentalism that underlies the historically first "stage" of the model is captured by the antecedents of communism, the role of agriculture, and the nature of inter-war polities that shape the bargaining power of different actual or virtual actors over the communist regime form in the aftermath of the Stalinist "freeze" (1948–53). The diverse power balances within communist polities of the 1960s through 1980s, in turn, shape the trajectory of regime change in the late 1980s and early 1990s.

Our reconstruction of differences among communist regimes is entirely driven by *domestic politics,* but can be extended by incorporating the role of *the international political hegemony of the Soviet Union.* In that perspective, bureaucratic-authoritarian regimes emerge at the "front line" of the Iron Curtain where the Soviet empire constructed a hard shield against the capitalist world (GDR, Czech Republic). National-accommodative communism becomes possible only in the region of "logistic supply" (Poland, Hungary), and patrimonial communism prevails in the heartland of the Soviet Union (Berglund and Aarebrot 1997: 102). The internationalist argument is mostly collinear with the domestic politics argument and suggests one plausible additional causal chain that contributes to regime diversity in the communist bloc. Nevertheless, upon close inspection, the domestic explanation of diverse power structures has more explanatory bite, where one can disentangle geopolitical location from path-dependent institu-

Table 1.1. *Antecedents and consequences of three types of communist rule*

	Bureaucratic-authoritarian communism	National-accommodative communism	Patrimonial communism
Antecedents of communist rule			
Pre-communist political economy	Industrial capitalism, agriculture < 40% of employment	Partially industrialized market economy, agriculture > 40% and < 60% of employment	Agricultural pre-capitalist economy, agriculture > 60% of employment
Pre-communist political regime	Competitive representative democracy	Semi-authoritarian rule with "managed" party competition	Traditional authoritarian or absolutist rule
Mobilization of political forces	Highly mobilized urban middle strata, highly mobilized working class, agrarian pressure groups	Highly mobilized urban middle strata, unmobilized working class, strong agrarian mobilization	Demobilized urban middle strata, unmobilized working class, strong agrarian mobilization
Modes of communist rule			
Formal bureaucratization of the state apparatus	High levels of formal professional bureaucratization, low corruption	Intermediate levels of formal professional bureaucratization, low-medium corruption	Low levels of formal professional bureaucratization, high corruption
Methods to induce popular compliance with party authority	Repression: intense, co-optation: secondary	Repression: secondary, co-optation: intense	Repression: intense, co-optation: intense

Modes of transition from communism			
Incumbents	United, intransigent	Predominantly ready to offer concessions	Divided, personalist cliques
Challengers	Strong liberal democrats, weak nationalist groups	Strong liberal democrats and nationalists	Weak liberal democrats, strong nationalists
Transition process	Implosion of regime, short but sharp protest wave	Protracted negotiations between challenger and incumbent elites	Preemptive reform by incumbent elite faction
Consequences for democratic institutions			
Electoral laws	Proportional representation (PR), closed list	Mixed PR/plurality systems, open-list features	Plurality/majoritarian rules, open-list features in PR systems
Executive-legislative design	Parliamentary system with weak presidential powers	Cabinet with parliamentary responsibility, medium presidential powers	Strong presidential powers, weak parliaments

tional choice and power alignments. With its borders on capitalist Austria and "renegade" Yugoslavia, Hungary was not unambiguously situated in the region of logistic supply behind the front lines of the communist camp. Conversely, Bulgaria, as a Southeast European front-line state, develops a communist regime very different from that of the Czech Republic or the German Democratic Republic. In a similar vein, Romania is situated in the logistic supply region and has produced a national-patrimonial, yet not an accommodative form of communism. Finally, there is too much diversity among the successor states of the Soviet Union to make the international argument entirely convincing.

Different types of communist rule also correspond to the differential strength and orientation of anti-communist dissident forces in the transition, an observation that leads us to the subject of party system formation addressed in the next chapter. The organization, support, and ideological clarity of these forces and of their communist counter-parts, in turn, affects the institutional choices that configure the new polities. Liberal-democratic forces are stronger in formerly bureaucratic-authoritarian and national-accommodative communisms that had been preceded by episodes of democratic or semi-democratic rule. By contrast, in the patrimonial communist regimes, nationalist and ethno-cultural demands often appear divorced from liberal democratic aspirations. The contrasting features of regime legacies may tempt us to hazard a guess about the persistence and resilience of post-communist democracies. These opportunities appear greater in formerly bureaucratic-authoritarian and national-accommodative communist regimes than after patrimonialism. We do not directly discuss the stability of post-communist regimes in our study. But in subsequent chapters our characterization of the quality of the democratic process that emerges in most patrimonial communist countries would allow us to flesh out an argument that pathways from communist patrimonialism involve greater regime volatility.

To conclude this chapter, it is now time to associate concrete historical polities with the three logics of path-dependent transition and justify our selection of cases for the empirical analysis of this book. The four-volume set of country reports on the transition from communism covering the entire post-communist region, edited by Karen Dawisha and Bruce Parrott (1997), provides a useful introduction to pass judgment on the classification of cases in light of our typology. Given that our own expertise varies from country to country and that the case studies in Dawisha and Parrott's book series were not written with our analytical scheme in mind, table 1.2 should be read more as a set of descriptive hypotheses about the fit of countries rather than as a conclusive assessment of countries' communist regime forms and transition processes. Its heuristic value is to indicate how the theoretical argument about party system formation we develop in chapter 2 can be tested against cases not included in the present study.

Table 1.2 distinguishes among communist regime types, measured by repression, co-optation, and levels of corruption and among modes of transition from communist rule. Not surprisingly, we claim a strong association between regime type and mode of transition. Because we found it difficult to score a number of

Table 1.2. *Communist rule, mode of transition, and post-communist regime form*

	Bureaucratic-authoritarian communism	Mix of both	National-accommodative communism	Mix of both	Patrimonial communism
Transition by implosion	Czech Republic[a] German Democratic Republic[a]			Slovakia[a]	
Transition by negotiation		Poland[a]	Hungary[a] Slovenia[a] Croatia (1971)[b]	Estonia[a] Latvia[a] Lithuania[a]	Moldova[a] Armenia[b] Georgia[b] Macedonia[a] Bulgaria[a] Romania[a] Russia[a] Ukraine[a] Albania[b]
Transition by preemptive reform					
Regime continuity under new label and new personnel				Serbia[c]	Azerbaijan[c] Belarus[c] Kazakhstan[c] Kyrgyzstan[c] Tajikistan[c] Turkmenistan[c] Uzbekistan[c]

[a]Democratic.
[b]Semi-authoritarian.
[c]Authoritarian.

countries unambiguously, a problem encountered by almost any abstract classification scheme, let us explain a few entries in the table.

The single purest case of bureaucratic-authoritarian communism is the Czech Republic with a vibrant democratic pluralism in the inter-war period and a long history of working-class mobilization spearheaded by popular socialist and communist parties. In many ways, also the German Democratic Republic fits into this category, although the national question affected its internal dynamic of repression and resistance to change and finally in 1989–90 precipitated the quick demise of the entity's political independence. In those two countries, the "implosions" of fall 1989 clearly follow from regimes characterized by high repression, little co-optation, and low corruption. Civil society could rarely ever rise against communist rule. In the GDR, such efforts were confined to the uprising of 1953. In the Czech Republic, the Prague Spring of 1968 had quite a different character than the contestations of communist rule in national-accommodative communisms such as in Hungary, Poland, or even the Baltic republics of the Soviet Union. Whereas in the latter contestation came from below and outside the communist apparatus, the Czech reform was orchestrated from above by a technocratic reform current in the ruling party itself.

In the national-accommodative category we primarily find Hungary and Slovenia, which relied on co-optation more than repression and corruption as inducements to popular compliance with the communist regime. Also Poland fits this category, but it employed more repression against open dissident movements, though of an intermittent nature, than the other two countries.

A number of countries fit rather unambiguously into the patrimonial communist category of high repression, but also rampant corruption and co-optation. In at least four of them, above all Russia/Soviet Union, and later Bulgaria, Romania, and finally Albania, a preemptive strike of elements within the political elites engineered the political regime change of the late 1980s and early 1990s. In the others, the critical moment was the disintegration of the Soviet Union when the Russian political leadership headed by Yeltsin began to challenge the Soviet communist party and precipitated the coup attempt of August 1991. In those republics where the communist party leaders encountered only weak or moderate anti-communist nationalist challenges, they could either suppress these groups or co-opt them into what remained essentially unreformed power structures. The critical difference to the old regime is the new nationalist legitimation of political authority that displaces the communist rhetoric. It is no accident that none of the patrimonial communist countries where the old political apparatus could essentially maintain its control can be unambiguously classified as democratic by the late 1990s. The Ukraine is the only case where the mix of national and democratic challenges to communist rule has opened up the possibility of democratic consolidation. Also one former Yugoslav republic with a moderately strong nationalist challenge, Macedonia, offers similar prospects.

Within our scheme, it is hardest to classify those newly independent states formerly subjected to Soviet, Serbian, or Czech authority with very strong nationalist movements that succeeded in taking over state power at the inception of national sovereignty. Let us divide them into three sub-catgories. First, there are the three Baltic republics that were democratic and semi-authoritarian independent states with highly mobilized political associations in the inter-war period and a record of armed and unarmed opposition against Soviet authority from the 1940s to the 1980s. Here, the Soviet communist party's leadership at the republic level oscillated between heavy-handed repression and subtle efforts to craft inter-ethnic accommodation (cf. Misiunas and Taagpera 1993). In all three countries, important communist party leaders embraced the struggle for national independence in the late 1980s and engineered an essentially negotiated transition that allowed former communists to compete credibly within the new democratic frameworks.

The second set of newly independent countries includes Croatia and Slovakia. Here republic-level communist party leaderships fought with greater or lesser success for autonomy within a federalist framework and attempted to obtain backing for their strategies by national-accommodationist arrangements within their republics. At the same time, however, neither case has a civil society and a stock of pre-communist political experiences that could have propelled forward the elite's accommodation process from below. In both republics, therefore, the communist polities and their displacement display attributes that characterize patrimonial communism and its regime change through preemptive reform from above. As a consequence, the process features of new political regimes in the 1990s therefore are likely to share more with those emerging from patrimonial communism than others developing against the backdrop of bureaucratic-authoritarian or national-accommodative communism.

This argument applies with even greater force to a third set of new post-Soviet countries that had clearly patrimonial governance structures under the old regimes and no historical background of mobilization in civic political associations within what had been essentially agrarian societies. Here in the early 1990s non-communist nationalists initially prevailed over the ruling communist parties, whose leaders did too little, too late to seek accommodation with the new challengers. But the failure of Moldovan, Armenian, and Georgian nationalists to organize the new polities while finding a solution to the internal and external challenges of ethnic pluralism enabled politicians of the old party apparatuses to try their hand once more at organizing inter-ethnic accommodation within the realities of the new configuration of sovereign states.

CONCLUSION: EMPIRICAL RESEARCH STRATEGY

In order to explore the consequences of communist regime legacies and transition processes for the quality of democratic governance in the new post-communist polities, it is obviously critical to choose cases that exemplify a variety of pathways and constellations. In 1991–92 when we began to design our study, only a small minority of the emerging post-communist countries had already experienced a free founding election with open party competition, let alone a second election. This constrained our choices. With regard to bureaucratic-authoritarian communism, the Czech Republic was the logical reference case. Although the disappearance of the German Democratic Republic has rendered the Czech Republic the singular historical case that exemplifies this type of communist rule, its uniqueness does not discredit our theoretical framework. Following Sidney Verba (1967: 114–15), also unique historical events must be considered as conceptual classes for the purposes of comparative analysis, even if they occur only once in reality. In light of recent work on the comparative method (Ragin 1987; Fearon 1991), one could go even further. Logical rigor requires the construction of a complete set of types, *even if no empirically observable referents can be found to study some of the types thus constructed* ("counter-factuals"). All comparative and statistical reasoning involves counter-factuals in this sense. It is thus not so surprising that there may be "types" for which only one empirical referent can be detected.

The class of national-accommodative communist regimes in 1991 offered Poland and Hungary as the cases in which processes of party system formation could already be studied. Both are included in the empirical analysis of this book. Were we to replicate this study in the future, we would also want to include the three Baltic countries, Slovenia, and the two complex "mixed" cases of Croatia and Slovakia.

With regard to patrimonial communist systems, our choices in 1991–92 were seriously constrained. By then, only Bulgaria had gone through two essentially free elections, and we incorporated that country in our comparison. Romania constituted a borderline case with a founding election in 1990 that gave the anti-communist opposition little chance to mobilize effectively and a semi-authoritarian presidential regime headed by a former communist who only gradually inched toward the acceptance of the rules of democratic competition. Elections in Albania could be characterized in a similar fashion. All other patrimonial communist countries had not even attempted free multi-party elections by the time we began our study. Again, a replication of our analysis should include those countries that subsequently established democratic or semi-democratic rule, such as Albania, Macedonia, Moldova, Romania, Russia, and the Ukraine, but this was not a feasible research strategy from the vantage point of 1992.

Due to the historical realities of democratization in the early 1990s, our study cannot analyze the independent effect of ethnic pluralism and new state formation on the quality of democratic processes and party competition in post-communist regimes. Both ethnic pluralism and new state building may disorganize and crosscut divisions of competition emerging in more homogeneous countries. But because we could not study these alignments empirically in our current work, we sketch only a couple of related hypotheses in the next chapter, but leave an analysis of these problems to a future, more comprehensive comparative project with twelve to fourteen rather than only four post-communist democracies. In our sample, Bulgaria is the only country in which ethnic pluralism plays out in a limited fashion within the context of patrimonial communist legacies.

2

THE QUALITY OF POST-COMMUNIST DEMOCRACY: PATTERNS OF PARTY COMPETITION, REPRESENTATION, AND INTER-PARTY COLLABORATION

Democracy requires that all competent members of society enjoy essential civil and political rights to free, equal participation in the election of legislative representatives who control the government executive. The laws and constitutional stipulations about the election and the inter-play of legislative and executive branches shape relations of *representation* between citizens and political elites. From the bottom up, citizens are able to hold elected representatives *accountable* for their actions by endorsing or rejecting their reelection. From the top down, periodic elections make decision makers anticipate public accountability and encourage them to become *responsive* to citizens' demands. While even non-democratic regimes de facto involve some modicum of accountability and responsiveness between subjects and rulers, only democratic governance structures stipulate institutions with the explicit purpose to nurture relations of representation.

Civic and political rights determine a minimum floor for the operation of democratic representation. The *quality of democratic accountability and responsiveness,* however, hinges on the resources, skills, and dispositions of citizens and politicians as well as the specific design of constitutional and electoral rules that govern the inter-play between electoral constituencies and their representatives. Institutions shape the conversion of social preferences into political bargaining positions and binding allocations of valuable resources ("policies"). Neither societal re-

43

source distributions and corresponding political divisions alone nor political institutions, by themselves, determine the quality of the democratic process; rather their inter-play does. In all but very small communities, this inter-play is organized by *intermediary political and civic associations,* such as parties, interest groups, and social movements. The quality of democracy varies with the techniques political entrepreneurs employ to build such intermediaries, to rally a mass following, and to craft policies in competition and cooperation with other political associations, given the institutions of the polity.

Among intermediary associations, *political parties* play an exceptional role because most of the time rules of democratic competition enable them to field electoral candidates and coordinate the political actions of legislative representatives as well as government executives. While non-electoral interest associations undoubtedly affect the quality and vigor of a democratic polity, they have a fundamentally different status than parties. Only the latter organize the critical citizen-elite bonds through the electoral process. The election of legislative representatives from territorial constituencies is the only avenue of citizens' participation democratic constitutions can codify in sufficiently precise and enforceable terms to meet a baseline criterion of democratic legitimacy: the equal weight of all citizens in a fair process of political participation. All other conceivable models of functional collective political representation through interest groups have failed to meet the baseline conditions of free, equal and fair citizens' participation, including efforts to enshrine functional interest group democracy in corporate bodies of representation.[1] For this reason, the "hard core" of formal democratic institutions revolves around the mechanisms of citizens' territorial representation through general elections and legislatures. A comparison of the quality of emerging democratic polities therefore is well advised to focus on the relations of representation and executive governance that congeal around electoral competition in general and political parties in particular. Political analysts from Huntington's (1968) magisterial *Political Order in Changing Societies* to recent analyses of Third Wave democracies emerging since the 1980s have therefore emphasized the critical role of party systems in the new polities (cf. Bermeo 1990: 369; Lipset 1994: 14; Nelson 1993: 456–57). Relations of interest group intermediation and social movement mobilization are embedded into party systems that constitute relations of territorial representation.[2]

---

[1]For an early, but still valid critique of corporatist functional interest group democracy, see Weber ([1968] 1978: 297–99). Theories of corporate democracy cannot provide principles according to which interest groups would be included or excluded, how their votes would be weighted to satisfy the equality of citizens' criteria, and how the internal democratic organization of each group, and thus the liberty of each citizen, could be assured.

[2]The corporatism literature has often overlooked the close link between consensual or consociational party systems, to employ Lijphart's (1984) language, and corporatist interest intermediation (but see Lehmbruch 1977; Lijphart and Crepaz 1991). In a similar vein, the literature on political opportunity structure and social movements emphasizes the critical role of party systems (cf. Kitschelt 1986; Tarrow 1990; McAdam, McCarthy, and Zald 1996).

Four aspects of the quality of democracy, as it relates to the party systems of emerging post-communist polities, are at the heart of this study and constitute the dependent variables of our analysis. First, we analyze how politicians build linkages to electoral constituencies. Do they emphasize the charisma of their leaders, selective material benefits to clients, programmatic representation of voter preferences, or some combination thereof? Second, to the extent politicians build parties that engage in programmatic appeals, what sorts of substantive policy preferences do they incorporate in their messages and what kinds of competitive spaces do such programmatic commitments create in the electoral and legislative process? Third, what is the extent to which politicians' programmatic appeals correspond to their voters' preferences and constitute relations of representation? Finally, what is the effectiveness of the democratic polity to translate interest representation into public policy?

The intent of our investigation into the quality of post-communist democracy is entirely positive, not normative. We examine the conditions under which party systems develop specific attributes on the four dimensions we have just elaborated. Historical legacies and democratic institutions, in the terms specified in chapter 1, serve as the main predictors of patterns of post-communist democratic quality. In our study, we avoid addressing the positive reformulation of a normative assessment of democratic quality, namely accounting for the *durability* of democratic polities in light of the observed processes of political competition and decision making. Exploring the durability and resilience of polities characterized by varying attributes of their democratic processes would require us to overcome several obstacles we find insurmountable at this time. Above all, we would have to presume that the patterns of democracy we observe in East Central Europe in 1993–94 already constitute *steady equilibrium states* that may be more or less resilient to various challenges. Instead, what we observe in Eastern Europe is a *non-equilibrium process of learning in which political actors employ resources, legacies, and new institutional rules to explore particular patterns of democratic political interaction.* In no way do we assume that these explorations have reached a steady state. Our comparison of four countries analyzes different modes of democratic learning against the backdrop of legacies and institutions at a single point in time, about four years after the democratic opening in East Central European communist polities. Future research must add a longitudinal comparative dimension and account for the trajectory of learning and the retention of democratic processes over time, a project that would ultimately shed light on the durability of alternative democratic governance structures. Within the confines of our current project, we claim only that cross-nationally varying pathways of experimenting with democracy may anticipate different democratic procedural equilibria in each country at some future point in time. For now, we can try to account for *alternative modes of democratic learning,* but we have to shelve the positive study of questions concerning the durability of political regimes with alternative democratic procedures, let alone the normative evaluation of such alternatives. In a speculative fashion, we return to such questions briefly at the end of this book.

VARIETIES OF CITIZEN-PARTY LINKAGE

Parties are lasting coalitions of politicians who field candidates for legislative or executive office. Parties may play a wide range of roles in the political process, but political scientists typically single out as their core tasks the articulation and aggregation of political demands into bundles of policy preferences. More recent rational choice perspectives on political parties express the same task structure in a different language. Parties help citizens and politicians to overcome collective action problems in mobilizing demands and resolving problems of social choice in coordinating a myriad of diverse policy preference schedules.[3]

Voters cannot express demands on their own but rely on political entrepreneurs who act on their behalf. Parties enable such entrepreneurs to provide cheap ways for voters to choose among political agents likely to pursue their objectives. Parties solve the collective action problem by pooling resources and running under a joint label in electoral campaigns, which permit politicians to appeal to electorates more efficiently than by running individually. These gains from cooperation derive from technical economies of scale. The way to address collective action problems in a democratic polity, therefore, is for politicians to make *investments in the joint administrative infrastructure of a political party* that allows each politician to reach out to voters more efficiently and to channel resources toward potential supporters.

If voters' and politicians' preference schedules are highly diverse, chances are that the political process yields problems of social choice. In this instance, there is no conceivable democratic voting procedure that would identify a unique, socially preferred package of policies always winning the strongest popular support. Instead, depending on the voting rules and the decision-making agenda, different policies win and may even yield cycling policy choices. As a result, political decisions may be volatile, contingent upon agenda control and voting rules, even if underlying preference distributions are stable. Parties address the problem of social choice by bundling policy preferences. Over the critical range of policy issues they organize them based on a few simple underlying normative principles or pragmatic interests supported by a permanent coalition of politicians. Politicians thus minimize their transaction costs in legislative voting procedures by participating in parties that support permanent "package deals."[4] Parties overcome social choice problems by investments in *institutionalized procedures of conflict resolution and consensus building among politicians that result in packages of policies ("programs") supported by the entire party over an extended period of time.*

---

[3]The language of interest articulation and aggregation, of course, appears in the older literature, such as Almond and Coleman (1960) and Almond and Powell's (1978) textbook. Aldrich (1995) discusses the parallel rational choice formulation of parties' contributions to the democratic process most concisely.

[4]Logrolling, as alternative to party formation, results in short-term negotiated policy bundles involving high transaction costs in the negotiation and the enforcement of package deals.

Whether politicians create parties by making investments in administrative infrastructure and procedures of programmatic conflict resolution, however, is an empirical question. Ideal-typically we can distinguish four outcomes of party formation. We examine two of them more closely because they represent likely alternatives of post-communist party formation.

First, if politicians make investments in *neither* administrative infrastructure *nor* consensus building, they shun party formation and run as individual candidates with their own profile of political preferences or efforts to rally a following based on the authority of their unique personal qualities ("charisma"). Charismatic leaders consciously disarticulate policy commitments in order to avoid constituency divisions. Followers are inspired by solidary incentives to be physically and transfiguratively close to a leader with exceptional capabilities and personality traits. The leader-follower relationship is marked by asymmetry, directness, and, for the followers, great passion (Madsen and Snow 1991: 5). Charismatic citizen-elite linkages create a "delegative" democracy in which leaders claim a political mandate but shun accountability and responsiveness to their voters' policy preferences and material claims (O'Donnell 1993). Although some institutional settings of democracy may support charismatic representation, charismatic politicians and their electoral organizations are always likely to suffer the fate of routinization (Weber 1978). Followers demand material payoffs, a process that forces politicians to make investments in an organizational infrastructure, and/or in a convincing policy program, the crafting of which requires procedures of conflict resolution in the electoral organization.

A second form of citizen-politician linkage involves investments in procedures of consensus building, but not in technical-administrative organization. This arrangement represents the *legislative faction or proto-party* before the advent of electoral mass politics.[5] Politicians form coalitions around a variety of policies in the legislative arena. Without organizational infrastructure, however, such policy agreements, and hence the longevity of these coalitions, remain tenuous. Legislative alliances have little capacity for resource pooling and voter mobilization and therefore become obsolete with the advent of universal suffrage and mass politics that raise the stakes with regard to investments in the administrative infrastructure of parties. This leaves us with a third and fourth type of political party each of which in fact has been prominent in many democracies around the world.

In the third mode of party formation, politicians heavily invest in administrative-technical infrastructure, but shun those in procedures of consensus building around policy packages. They induce electoral constituencies to support their parties by offering direct selective material and symbolic advantages to those individuals who demonstrably support the party's candidates. Such *clientelist and patronage rewards* typically take the form of monetary transfers, gifts in kind, jobs in the public sector, preferential treatment in the allocation of social benefits (e.g.,

---

[5] Aldrich's (1995: chap. 3) description of efforts to overcome social choice problems in the first American Congress reflects this type of undertaking.

housing, welfare payments), regulatory favors, government contracts, and honor-ary memberships and titles. Depending on the setting, clientelism may be com-munal, rooted in durable, hierarchical personal ties of trust between locally based patrons and clients, or purely instrumental, based on contingent exchanges with a political machine.[6]

Clientelism is typically based on personalized exchange between politicians and clients, but in a routinized institutional mode with mutually calculable transactions rather than an extraordinary charismatic relationship. Politicians "buy" the acquiescence of constituencies through direct compensation for elec-toral support. In exchange, voters give up control over the politicians' pursuit of public policies and content themselves with the immediate tangible benefits derived from surrendering their vote. To become viable, clientelist exchange relations thus pre-suppose a heavy flow of material resources and extensive per-sonal networks. These result from politicians' investments in the organizational capabilities of a party to extract resources from clients and to redistribute them.

The fourth type of organizing party-centered, politician-constituency link-ages is through *programmatic parties* that compensate contributors *indirectly* by the policy packages politicians promise to pursue if elected to legislative and execu-tive office. Such parties also must make considerable administrative-infra-structural investments in mass democracies, but to a lesser extent than clientelist parties, because they do not rely on a direct and contingent exchange of votes for material advantages.[7] Programmatic parties, however, have to make substantial investments in *procedures of consensus building* that craft the policy "packages" around which politicians attract electoral constituencies. Program deliberations are time-consuming, but they are essential to make parties' future conduct calcu-lable for voters. This is not to say that programmatic parties serve the "common good," whereas clientelist parties serve "special interests." *What differs between the two types of parties is the procedural mode of compensating supporters (voters, members, activists) through direct or indirect exchanges.*

The four ideal types of party-based voter-politician linkages certainly do not exhaust the complexity of political reality. In practice, parties rely on a mix of charismatic, clientelist, and programmatic techniques. West European mass par-ties, for example, whether of social democratic, Christian democratic, or conserva-tive stripes usually appeal to policy programs, but they have also incorporated elements of charismatic leadership and clientelist exchange. Conversely, parties primarily based on clientelist machine politics may not be entirely devoid of programmatic signals. What varies, however, is the *mix of techniques,* because there are *trade-offs* between the different linkage mechanisms. The more a party moves

---

[6]A distinction among modes of clientelism can be found in Scott (1969) and Lemarchand (1988). Clientelism, of course, also appears in non-democratic regimes where it is centered around the executive state apparatus (cf. Chazan et al. 1992: chap. 6).

[7]In this technical sense, also "special interest parties," such as agrarian parties, are "pro-grammatic parties" as long as they benefit their constituencies *indirectly* through public policy provisions.

the personality of its leader into the foreground, the harder it is to elaborate programmatic packages or deliver benefits to clients, because the capriciousness of the leader tends to undercut such commitments. Both clientelist and programmatic linkages rely on durable mutual expectations and thus involve institutionalized relations of accountability and responsiveness among political actors that set them apart from the exercise of purely charismatic, extraordinary authority. At the same time, clientelist linkage building with its particularist networks of beneficiaries is often at odds with a party's universalist programmatic message. Parties then must choose between alternative mixes of linkage building.

The existence of diverse strategies to organize citizen-politician linkages inside democratic party systems raises the question of what are the causes and consequences of alternative arrangements. Why do some parties and party systems build linkages configured more around programmatic or clientelist appeals and incentives? Do parties and party systems based on different linkage strategies deliver diverging political-economic outcomes, such as economic growth, collective goods, and income distribution?

In our study, we focus on the procedural quality of democracy in emerging post-communist regimes and therefore address the causal question about origins only. More specifically, we now develop theoretical propositions about the conditions under which it is likely that parties develop *more or less programmatic cohesiveness*. For parties with weak programmatic cohesiveness to survive, they must sooner rather than later develop alternative charismatic or clientelist linkages. This does not imply, of course, that every party with low programmatic cohesiveness has already automatically built strong clientelist or charismatic bonds, particularly when we examine recently founded parties that may simply have not yet crafted *any* strong linkage mechanisms. We derive our propositions about the pathways of citizen-politician linkage building from a generalization of the legacies and institutions framework we have developed in chapter 1 and then apply them to post-communist East Central Europe.

LEGACIES

Socio-Economic Development

An important strand of the literature on elite-citizen linkages allows us to construct a simple three-stage model of modernization (cf. Eisenstadt and Roniger 1984: 163–64; Lemarchand 1988; Martz 1997). Clientelist relations are typically mechanisms of class control. In *agrarian societies* with feudal or patrimonial property rights, patrons and clients enter in localized dyadic long-term inter-personal relations, laced with an ideology of mutual trust and obligation that hides the coercive nature of the generalized exchange between patron and client.[8] The

---

[8]Of course, these clientelist relations do not necessarily involve political parties. Some ruling classes may abandon electoral competition and legislative representation, but nevertheless organize clientelist networks. Cf. Wiarda and Kline (1990: 71).

patron extracts material resources and loyalty and, in return, offers a variety of hedges against uncertainties caused by the marketplace, nature (crop failures, catastrophes), and predatory politicians.[9] In *societies with greater state and market incorporation and industrialization,* patron-client networks develop greater complexity and reach up into regional and national bureaucracies, while becoming more short-term, specific, and interest-based. This sort of clientelism typically revolves around the organization of "political machines" that lack the quality of personal trust. They prevail where local community orientation and deference patterns have weakened (Scott 1969).

Clientelism and patronage politics breaks down in the third stage with the appearance of a broad urban middle class, combining advanced education and higher income expectations. On the demand side, the middle class undercuts clientelism because machine bosses cannot offer the high-skill jobs and long-term career tracks typically sought by this stratum (Eisenstadt and Roniger 1984: 193). For middle-class voters, the opportunity costs of supporting clientelism simply become too high. Viewed from the supply side, politicians find it exponentially more costly to maintain clientelist exchanges. As they struggle to extract more resources for clientelist networks, they increasingly burden the business class with deadweight that impedes its competitiveness, particularly in the internationally exposed sectors.

Clientelist practices then prompt resistance not only for reasons of narrow myopic economic self-interest in urban middle strata. The cognitive sophistication of middle-class voters makes them aware of the reduction of economic efficiency and the sparse provision of collective goods through public policy that often coincide with clientelism. Hence "progressivist" middle-class movements with a broader and longer-term conception of the costs and benefits of clientelist voter-politician linkages begin to challenge party machines.

Two propositions follow from this theoretical argument about clientelism. First, at the level of party systems, economic development coincides with intensified challenges to clientelist arrangements and a transition to programmatic party competition. Second, at the level of individual parties, it is primarily the parties of the urban middle strata that challenge clientelist arrangements, which are more likely to endure in the countryside and in sectors of industrial manufacturing. Applied to post-communist democracies, clientelism should become distinctly more common in the economically more backward regions of Eurasia or certain poor Balkan countries (Macedonia, Bosnia, Serbia, Albania) and Moldova. Beyond that, however, the developmentalist argument has relatively little power

---

[9]For a good analytical summary of the elements involved in generalized clientelist exchange, see Eisenstadt and Roniger (1984: 48–49) and Roniger (1981). Lemarchand (1981: 15) provides a brief definition of clientelism that also emphasizes asymmetry, diffuseness, and reciprocity of the relationship. Our description of the clientelist generalized exchange is sufficiently abstract to avoid taking sides in the dispute between scholars who put more emphasis on the normative and moral orientation of participants in the exchange (Scott 1976) or their material self-interest (Popkin 1979).

to discriminate between bureaucratic-authoritarian, national-accommodative, and patrimonial communism, as most countries with diverse communist regimes are in the same general wealth bracket of between $4,000 and $6,000 per capita income at purchasing power parity in the mid-1990s. Given citizens' comparatively high education and economic expectations, clientelism may find little favor in the bulk of post-communist polities.

The divergence of citizen-elite linkages in advanced industrial democracies, however, teaches us that developmentalist accounts, by themselves, are insufficient to explain levels of programmatic party competition. The theory certainly cannot tell us why Italy, Japan, Austria, or Belgium has experienced strong challenges to its clientelist networks only in the past twenty years whereas many other countries never developed such ties or abandoned them long ago.[10]

The Timing of Professional Bureaucracy and Suffrage

Based on a comparison of programmatic party competition and clientelism in Britain, Germany, and France, Shefter (1994) has proposed a state- and politics-centered explanation. The timing of universal suffrage and bureaucratic professionalization is critical. Where the latter precedes the former, such as in absolutist states, politicians have no chance to avail themselves of the state apparatus as a trough of material incentives they can consume to build direct linkages to electoral constituencies.[11] That option is open to politicians only where democratization precedes bureaucratization. Moreover, it applies only to those parties that originate *inside* the pre-democratic regime elite. By contrast, the mass mobilization of lower-class challengers, such as workers' parties, never had access to state material resources prior to democratization. Where they develop before the advent of universal suffrage, they build contributions-based mass organizations to mobilize resources outside the state. Once democracy is achieved, such parties do not embrace patronage politics, but build a reputation of "clean government" parties (Shefter 1994: 30–32).

Thus, personalist, non-professional state machineries invite patronage and clientelism, whereas professionalized bureaucracies direct politicians toward programmatic competition. Shefter's propositions directly tie into our analysis of communist legacies. Bureaucratic-authoritarian communism is built on strong working-class mass parties and a pre-existing professional bureaucracy, thus inhibiting clientelist practices under communist rule. After communism, moreover, the old *insiders* of the regime, assembled around the post-communist party, are weak and cannot avail themselves of the state apparatus with rent-seeking strat-

---

[10]For assessment of elite-voter linkages across a broad set of countries, compare Eisenstadt and Roniger (1984: chaps. 4, 5) and De Winter, della Porta, and Deschouwer (1996).

[11]To be fair to Eisenstadt and Roniger's previously discussed work, even they do not exclusively rely on a developmentalist account, but also recognize the importance of weak state capacities for the strength of patronage networks (Eisenstadt and Roniger 1981: 284; 1984: 207, 264).

egies. The new rulers tend to be *outsiders* recruited from the regime opposition with few ties into the apparatus. It is hard for them to build clientelist linkages.

At the other extreme, patrimonial communism derived from pre-communist authoritarian regimes without professional state administration and yielded a proliferation of personalist, patronage-oriented practices inside communist rule. Because patrimonial communism was penetrated by personalist relations of clientelist linkage and the communist successor parties remain strongly entrenched with the advent of democracy, it is likely that post-communist politicians attempt to thrive on remodeling their networks toward different ends. Thus, new democracies with a strong presence of *old-regime insiders,* whether in post-communist parties or other new democratic parties, tend to offer a more fertile ground for clientelist party politics, advancing rent-seeking coalitions that repay the favors they receive in the privatization and liberalization process by clientelist linkages to party politicians.

One complication that goes beyond our legacies framework has to do with the formation of newly independent countries (cf. Evans and Whitefield 1993: 539–45). Regardless of pre-existing state traditions and communist regime practices, the founders of new states may succumb to powerful temptations to pack the emerging new state apparatus with personal followers and thus nurture clientelist party networks. In some of the Balkan and post-Soviet new states, low levels of socio-economic development and new state formation mutually reinforce clientelist, non-programmatic party formation. In others, such as Croatia or Slovakia, the patronage opportunities of new state formation may depress programmatic party formation, even where communist regime legacies alone are not particularly favorable to them.

The four countries we examine empirically in this book are, of course, all established states and Shefter's statist account of the clientelism–programmatic competition alternative provides a clear-cut prediction consistent with our legacies argument. Following Czech bureaucratic-authoritarian communism, we expect strong programmatic party formation in that country. By contrast, in Bulgaria, emerging from patrimonial communism, the parties' programmatic articulation will be much weaker. Finally, in formerly national-accommodative communist polities in Hungary and Poland, we anticipate intermediate conditions for programmatic party formation.

A familiar problem of path-dependency-based macro-historical explanations to suggest too much determinism surfaces also in Shefter's account. There is no appreciation of the independent role of *institutions of democratic competition* that may modify parties' linkage strategies, regardless of historical pathway and predisposition toward patronage politics. In a similar vein, *new political-economic resource distributions,* such as the growth of mixed economies, may put political-economic resources at the disposal of politicians, which may entice them to abandon programmatic competition in favor of patronage strategies, even where legacy arguments would expect different commitments. For example, Shefter's historical determinism cannot explain why some working-class mass parties, such as the Austrian socialists, developed strong patronage systems in the democratic polity.[12] In a similar vein, we must be sensitive to the institutional and political-economic cues in post-communist democracy that may make parties and party systems more inclined to follow programmatic or clientelist strategies as they evolve and entrench themselves. This dynamic may only partially be endogenous to historical legacies, as the choice of democratic institutions in Bulgaria may demonstrate.

INSTITUTIONS

Clientelist party-constituency linkages thrive on chains of personal relations between electoral constituencies and a hierarchy of representatives, reaching from the local to the national level in which each lower-level agent always serves as client to the next higher-level patron. Such linkages permit participants to monitor and to enforce the exchange of material and symbolic favors for votes and financial support throughout the polity. Conversely, depersonalized, anonymous relations between remote national "teams" of politicians and their electoral constituencies foster programmatic party-constituency linkages. Two institutional elements of democracy contribute a great deal to the extent to which relations of representation are (de)personalized: electoral laws and executive-legislative relations.

Electoral Laws

Electoral provisions that force politicians to run as teams in depersonalized electoral contests are large district magnitude combined with a closed-list ballot format and party control over the nomination and ordering of list members. In this arrangement, voters support party teams, not individual candidates. They cannot pick and choose individual candidates but must endorse entire packages of politicians running in very large electoral districts. Under these circumstances, candidates have incentives to craft their voter appeals around abstract policy principles rather than concrete commitments to provide favors to specific target constituencies.

At least three stipulations shaping the ballot format open the door to personalized electoral contests, particularly if they appear in combination (Carey and Shugart 1995). First, voters can choose individual candidates from multi-member lists ("open" lists). Second, votes accrue to individual list candidates only, but do not assist other members of the list (absence of "vote pooling"). Third, party members and leaders may have no control over the composition of the list, if voters and candidates choose the list composition themselves – for example, through primaries or special provisions such that sitting legislators can choose the

---

[12]As Geddes (1994: chap. 2) argues for Latin America, parties make the decision to professionalize the civil service, often a key resource of patronage politics, an object of competitive strategies.

list on which they run. Cary and Shugart show that the effect of district size is contingent upon ballot format and nomination powers. Single-member districts are by definition "closed" lists and, at least where the party controls the candidate nominations process, it limits the personalization of voter-candidate ties.[13] By contrast, in multi-member districts with open lists and no vote pooling, the personalization of electoral contests is intense, with or without party control over list nominations. Such systems produce virtually powerless parties without means to sanction legislators who somehow defect from a "party line."[14]

Two amendments are necessary to specify the relationship between electoral rules and citizen-party linkage strategies. First, closed-list multi-member districts only promote programmatic parties, if national electoral thresholds of representation eliminate minuscule parties from legislative representation.[15] Such micro-parties often organize around individual personalities and special interests, thus providing the equivalent to the personal vote. Second, the equilibrium effect of electoral systems emerges only over time, as political actors play multiple rounds of democratic competition. In an emerging democracy where no existing parties have the reputation and track record to be likely winners, single-member districts may encourage the proliferation of parties and candidates, each hoping to become the lucky winner (Moser 1995).[16]

Applied to our four countries, closed-list multi-member district electoral systems in Bulgaria and the Czech Republic produce the greatest support for cohesive programmatic parties over time. In Poland, where 391 of 460 members of the Sejm are elected in small to medium-sized (three to seventeen member) districts with personal preference votes but pooling of votes for each party that receives at least 5 percent of the national vote share, locally entrenched candidates may have a limited capacity to build clientelist power bases. As a counterweight, national closed party lists divide up 69 seats among only those parties winning more than 7 percent of the vote. Also Hungary offers a variety of incentives for programmatic cohesion. Regional closed-list multi-member districts and national compensation lists for parties receiving a disproportionally small share of seats in single-member constituencies foster parties' programmatic cohesiveness. By contrast, individual candidates have more leverage in the single-member districts with majoritarian run-off. In all four countries, however, parties control candidate

---

[13]Thus, it is inaccurate to focus on district size alone in determining the potential for direct voter-representative exchanges, as proposed by Rogowski (1987) or Kitschelt (1995a).

[14]Examples of high personalization of electoral contests include Brazil (Mainwaring 1991; Ames 1995a, 1995b), Colombia, and, to a lesser extent, Japan under the single non-transferable vote system (Cox and Rosenbluth 1995; Katz 1980).

[15]For the almost boundless literature on the relationship between electoral rules and party system fragmentation, see Grofman and Lijphart 1986, Taagepera and Shugart 1989, and Lijphart 1994a.

[16]Presidentialism may have a similar counter-intuitive effect to multiply electoral candidates rather than to reduce them due to plural or majoritarian electoral formula. Cf. Filippov and Shvetsova 1996.

nomination and thus undercut personalized candidate-constituency exchanges in favor of programmatic competition.

Executive-Legislative Design

Constitutions with powerful presidencies offer more opportunities for clientelist linkage, parliamentary dominance more chances to build programmatic parties. Presidential power depends less on the terms that govern the choice and the tenure of incumbents (direct popular election and fixed term in office) than on the specific executive and legislative powers vested in the office. Does the president appoint the cabinet, control foreign policy, command the military, and exercise significant legislative powers, such as the exclusive right to initiate legislation in certain policy domains, the right to veto legislative bills in their entirety or in specific provisions, and the right to govern by decree under specified circumstances and for limited periods of time?[17] Given that the powers of the presidency may vary widely, the "presidentialism" of a democratic polity is more a matter of degree than a matter of regime type.

Electoral arrangements are likely to affect programmatic or clientelist linkage building more so than do presidential powers (Linz 1994: 62). Nevertheless, at least four mechanisms suggest that a stronger presidential office tends to undercut programmatic party competition in favor of clientelist or even charismatic party-constituency linkages. First, where the powers of the presidency elevate the office far above any other electoral position, ambitious politicians tend to create personalized machines in order to promote their presidential aspirations. They build factions or currents inside larger parties or found their own candidate-centered parties. Because such electoral machines build on personalist loyalties and seek funding for a particular politician more than a program, they promote charismatic or clientelist linkages.

Second, the electoral system for the presidency – a nationwide single-member district with plurality or majority electoral formula – highlights more personality than program, especially where the parties have little control over the choice of candidate. The strongest candidates often have incentives to project the image of being politicians "above the parties" in order to assemble the widest possible electoral coalition. Candidates may converge to the middle of a programmatic policy space *or* "disarticulate" programmatic agendas altogether and build coalitions around clientelist exchanges extended to local notables delivering electoral support (Ames 1994).

Once in office, third and fourth mechanisms advance the clientelist inclinations of sitting presidents. Via powers of executive appointment, decree powers, and budgetary allocation to particularist constituencies, presidents may induce legislators, regardless of party affiliation, to support the personal presidential agenda. For this reason, strong presidential power clashes with a disciplined,

[17]For a detailed analysis of presidential powers, see especially Shugart and Carey (1992: chaps. 7 and 8) and Shugart and Mainwaring (1997).

"responsible" party system (Linz 1994: 35). In order to limit their bargaining costs, presidents aim at intermediately fragmented legislatures where they can craft alliances among a limited number of caucuses and groups on a case-by-case basis (Shugart and Mainwaring 1997). As a mirror image of presidential dispositions to employ patronage, legislators expect the chief executive to solicit their support by way of uniquely tailored material inducements rather than by appeal to the programmatic unity of a party.

Students of American politics have sometimes claimed a happy division of labor between constituency-serving, clientelist legislators and programmatically oriented presidents. While in strong presidential systems the president may pay relatively *more* attention to programmatic concerns than the legislators because his constituency ultimately is the national majority of the voting electorate, the clientelist temptations of such institutional arrangements are sufficiently strong to make presidents *less* inclined to pursue programmatically cohesive legislative coalitions than cabinets in a parliamentary system where executive power derives from the continuous support of the government by a majority party (coalition).

Applied to our new East Central European democracies, parliamentary governments with weak presidential powers prevail in the Czech Republic, Hungary, and Bulgaria, thus promoting programmatic party cohesiveness in the longer run. Only in Poland does the presidency have a limited range of important legislative powers that can undercut legislative party government, such as the three-fifths majority required in parliament to override a presidential veto. Strong presidential rule, however, tends to constrain programmatic party formation much more decisively in Russia or the Ukraine than in any of the East Central European democracies (Kubicek 1994; Filippov and Shvetsova 1995; Ordeshook 1995).

Combining electoral systems and legislative-executive design, institutional conditions that induce parties to gravitate toward programmatic party competition are strongest in the Czech Republic and Bulgaria. They are somewhat weaker in Hungary because of its mixed electoral system and in Poland with a mixed electoral system and some significant presidential powers. In a broader comparison of democratic institutional arrangements, also in these two countries incentives for programmatic party formation are much stronger than in many other East European, Latin American, or East Asian countries with institutions generating greater conduciveness to clientelist exchange relations and party patronage.

POLITICAL-ECONOMIC RESOURCES AND TIES

The legacies of pre-communist and communist polities and social organization shape both institutions and post-communist political-economic resource distributions. But the often profound post-communist economic changes also have the potential to diminish and to overcome the impact of legacies and affect the workings of institutions, if not institutional choice itself. Political-economic arrangements of post-communism are therefore not simply endogenous to institutions and legacies. They become productive forces themselves that shape citizen-party linkages in at least two conceivable ways.

First, where democratic political governance extends to a large share of the political economy – whether through public ownership, subsidies, or regulatory oversight – parties gain access to resources that permit them to organize direct clientelist material exchanges between partisan supporters and politicians. Examples are the clientelist politicization of corporate governance in countries such as Austria, Belgium, Italy, and, to a lesser extent, France after World War II (cf. Müller 1993), but also the delegation of public services such as health care, housing, or unemployment insurance to subsidiary party organizations. In all these instances, public funds come under the discretion of elected politicians who may disburse them contingent upon citizens' partisan loyalties.

When state-dominated corporate governance structures run into severe economic performance problems, they weaken and undermine clientelist partisan networks.[18] Moreover, citizens may become dissatisfied with the goods and services such arrangements deliver, a reaction that is often prompted by the *absence of choice among alternative providers* typical where state-regulated or administered services with partisan governance prevail. Particularly middle-class citizens with a taste for superior goods and services are likely to challenge such rigidities.

Second, a number of authors have linked increasing trade-exposure to the decline of clientelist partisan networks and rent-seeking coalitions in a variety of ways (Rogowski 1987; Frieden 1991; Frieden and Rogowski 1996). High exposure of an economy to the international marketplace makes distributive domestic coalitions with clientelist politics that shelter rent-seeking coalitions behind tariff walls and other protective devices unfeasible. Such democracies therefore set up political institutions (closed-list proportional representation electoral laws, parliamentarism) that inhibit clientelist party-citizen linkages and favor programmatic competition.

The argument is unconvincing for several reasons. In empirical terms, with appropriate statistical controls for the cultural heterogeneity of countries, there is no evidence that trade exposure yields democratic institutions inhibiting clientelist politics (cf. Boix 1997). Moreover, some highly trade-exposed economies developed strong distributive coalitions around clientelist partisan networks in the past (e.g., Austria, Belgium, Italy) or experience the breakdown of clientelist arrangements in a time of declining trade exposure (Japan, 1980–98).[19] In

---

[18]Such decline may be induced not primarily by international competition, but by technological and structural change of domestic economies.

[19]Contrary to Cox and Rosenbluth's (1995) argument about the link between increasing openness and the erosion of party-based clientelism, Japan's trade exposure, measured as the sum of exports and imports, declined from 28 percent in 1980 to 17 percent in 1995 (World Bank 1997: 219).

theoretical terms, institutions and collective action problems intermediate between trade exposure and domestic political power relations (Alt et al. 1996; Garrett and Lange 1996).

Post-communist democracies are obviously saddled with large state-controlled economic sectors with formidable performance problems. At the same time, the trajectory of such arrangements is in part endogenous to political-economic legacies, in part to conjunctural circumstances. The critical challenge of post-communism is to cut off socialist nomenklatura managers from the rent-seeking strategies they often pursue in collusion with the old party apparatus (cf. Aslund, Boone, and Johnson 1996). This apparatus has a tendency to turn into a political machine that promotes clientelism.

In general, the vigor of anti-communist forces under bureaucratic-authoritarian and national-accommodative communism advances economic reform more than in formerly patrimonial communism. Regardless of such legacies, however, where circumstances allowed liberal reformers to control the levers of power early in the democratic experience, they may promote market reforms that generate their own constituency (cf. Fish 1998; Jackson, Klich, and Poznanska 1996). Both historical legacies and the partisan stripes of the first several post-communist governments would lead us to expect rather more programmatic party formation in the Czech Republic, Hungary, and Poland where reform governments emerged earlier than in Bulgaria where, with the exception of an eleven-month interlude, the post-communist party never quite gave up control of the political economy until 1997.

FROM PARTY SYSTEM TO INDIVIDUAL PARTY: THE ROLE OF POLITICAL IDEOLOGY AND CONSTITUENCY IDENTIFICATION

So far, our analysis has attempted to account for differences in party-constituency linkages and partisan competitive strategies within a framework of systemic conditions that affect essentially *all* political parties operating in a polity. But the propensity of individual parties to seek out clientelist or programmatic linkage strategies may vary within political systems as well. Constituency characteristics and corresponding party ideologies are likely to be responsible for this variance.

By way of returning to the developmentalist argument discussed earlier, parties relying on educated middle-class constituencies are likely to abandon particularist appeals and linkage practices earlier than their competitors. The educational sophistication of such electorates, but also their material self-interests, derived from their insertion into the market economy, account for this orientation. More generally, however, all those parties that invoke *universalist ideologies, such as liberalism or socialism,* in order to reach out to encompassing electoral groups emphasize programmatic over clientelist linkage strategies with practices of particularist, personalized, and arbitrary, discretionary exchanges between politicians and specific citizen constituencies.

By contrast, parties that invoke cultural particularism and create friend-foe identities and divides based on nationality, ethnicity, race, language, or religion involve at least two mechanisms disposing politicians more toward clientelist linkage strategies. First, in order to maintain a broad following around a cultural identity, politicians may find it impossible to address crosscutting economic divides cast in a universalistic language of rights, obligations, and deserts. Politicians may venture to keep every group member happy through direct material side payments. Second, membership in socio-cultural categories is a matter of type rather than degree and much less subject to social mobility than adherence to occupational groups, economic sectors or classes, and social strata.[20] The ascriptive and categorical nature of group membership facilitates clientelist politics, because it reduces the transaction costs of organizing, monitoring, and enforcing direct selective exchanges between politicians and followers, particularly where patterns of residence facilitate in-group interaction and social control. As the boundaries between groups become sharply defined, politicians compete only for supporters within groups rather than across groups (Horowitz 1985: 334, 342). This tendency undercuts broad programmatic concerns and leads to a focus on specific group benefits and direct exchange relations. Furthermore, patterns of contiguous residence in a socio-cultural group, strong intra-group norms of conduct, and common membership in associations that appeal exclusively to the socio-cultural group (such as a party) enhance the chances that ethno-cultural politics yields clientelist networks. Network and associational ties help politicians to monitor and to enforce the exchange of votes for favors between patrons and clients. Structural background conditions, such as widespread poverty in the constituency group and the absence of a professional state apparatus, particularly in newly independent countries, further enhance the probabilities of clientelist network politics.

By organizing socio-cultural divisions through material rewards, clientelist networks may actually *pacify* them. At times, such arrangements yield consociational mechanisms of conflict resolution (Lijphart 1977). Conversely, clientelist networks can also compete with each other and generate a centrifugal process of socio-cultural polarization with outbidding by the most extreme forces within each camp.

As we discuss in the next section, the propensity of parties to align around universalistic or particularistic divides varies across post-communist polities. For our purposes, none of the four countries we examine has a strong nationalist mobilization or salient ethno-cultural divides, with the partial exception of Bulgaria. We therefore do not expect ethnic pluralism to constitute a major obstacle

---

[20]Where objectively "mixed" groups exist (e.g., the offspring of inter-racial or inter-ethnic unions), their members are often forced to choose between one or the other "pure" category.

to programmatic party formation and an inducement to clientelism in any of the four countries.

THE INTERACTION OF LEGACIES, INSTITUTIONS, AND POLITICAL-ECONOMIC CONDITIONS IN THE PROGRAMMATIC STRUCTURING OF PARTY COMPETITION

Theories of linkage formation based on legacies, institutions, political economy, and party alignments do not postulate mechanisms that are entirely independent from each other. For example, legacies influence institutions, political-economic arrangements, and even party alignments. Conversely, political-economic change may override legacies and institutions and affect political alignments. It would take a very large number of countries and parties to spell out the independent effect and the interaction of such conditions on the formation of citizen-party linkages. For the more limited tasks of our empirical analysis of four post-communist democracies, table 2.1 summarizes our expectations about the relative strength of programmatic citizen-party linkage building in the Czech Republic, Hungary, Poland, and Bulgaria. Were we to include other post-communist countries such as Croatia, Russia, Slovakia, or the Ukraine, the range of variance in the expected outcomes would increase considerably.

In general, conditions for programmatic party competition look most favorable in the Czech Republic and least auspicious in Bulgaria. Hungary and Poland constitute intermediate cases within the frame of reference set by our four countries, although the addition of further contrasting cases, such as Russia or Ukraine, would show that here also politicians face comparatively strong incentives to form programmatic parties. What the table glosses over is the *effect of learning over time and the associated changing efficacy of different forces impinging on the process of parties' linkage building.* Thus, it is reasonable to expect that at the beginning of post-communist democratization legacies are the strongest factor affecting programmatic or clientelist party formation, because institutions, political-economic reform strategies, and political alignments tend to be endogenous to legacies at that time or because actors have not yet learned to take advantage of the new arrangements. As time elapses, however, the independent causal efficacy of institutions and new political-economic relations is likely to assert itself. In this vein, the existing rules of democratic competition in Bulgaria in the long run may offer a slightly greater potential for programmatic citizen-party linkages than those of Hungary and Poland, although Bulgaria might trail these countries in the early decades of party formation. As a countervailing force, however, slow change in Bulgaria's state-dominated political economy may undercut programmatic linkages in its party system. Citizen-party linkages in emerging democracies are an important quality trait of democratic governance structures, but it is unlikely that we can account for them in terms of a simple, parsimonious theory.

Table 2.1. *Conduciveness of post-communist political settings to programmatic competition*

	Czech Republic	Poland	Hungary	Bulgaria
Legacies				
Economic development	High	High	High	High
Nature of communist rule	High	Medium	Medium	Low
	Bureaucratic-authoritarian	National-accommodative	National-accommodative	Patrimonial
Transition	Implosion/rupture	Negotiation with implosion	Negotiation	Preemptive reform
Institutions				
Depersonalization of the electoral contest	Strong	Medium strong	Medium strong	Strong
Parliamentary government/weak presidency	Strong	Medium	Strong	
Political economy				
Economic reforms undercutting rent-seeking coalitions	Medium	Medium	Medium	Weak
Political alignments				
Ethno-cultural homogeneity	Strong	Strong	Strong	Medium

DIMENSIONS OF PROGRAMMATIC COMPETITION

Legacies of inter-war and communist regimes affect not only the extent to which party systems in the new East European democracies build programmatic linkages to electoral constituencies, but also the nature of the parties' policy appeals and the configuration among parties with different appeals that emerge as powerful electoral contenders. Beyond legacies, current political-economic developments affect these divides as well. By contrast, the institutional arrangements of the democratic polities, primarily their electoral laws and executive-legislative inter-action, have little capacity to shape the substance of the programmatic divides parties articulate in the electoral arena. What they affect, however, is the channeling of the substantive alternatives into a greater or lesser number of parties.[21]

Analyzing party system divides requires a three-stage analysis. First, we must examine the social and economic divisions that may lend themselves to political representation. We are talking here about fundamental group distinctions in terms of citizens' traits, such as socio-demographic roles, cultural and political opinions, and associational affiliations outside the arena of party competition (cf. Rae and Taylor 1970). But not all sociological divisions also surface in party politics. As already Lipset and Rokkan (1967) argued, the resource distribution among strategic politicians and their skills in crafting electoral constituency alliances over long periods of time critically shape the *conversion of social into political divides.*[22] The second task, then, is to analyze how citizens' traits, opinions, and acts translate into party affiliations and identifications. Operationally, we wish to know when and why sociological divides enable us to predict voters' partisan preferences.

Beyond such affiliations, however, we are more specifically interested in those divisions that become critical for electoral competition. Here a third analytic task presents itself. As Sani and Sartori (1983) framed it, when do *divisions of voter identification* convert into *competitive dimensions?* In the offensive struggle to increase their following, politicians focus on those political divides where they expect to increase their electoral support by altering their policy positions or increasing the salience of their appeal. Defensive politicians, by contrast, invoke divides with firmly set partisan identifications where, as a consequence, the electorate displays little elasticity of party support contingent upon politicians'

---

[21]As Cox (1997: 203–21) argues, even party system fragmentation is not entirely an institutional effect, but depends on social and political divides. Moreover, the power of institutions to shape party systems involves a process of learning by politicians. Hence, short-term institutional effects are quite different from long-term equilibria of party system formats (cf. Filippov and Shvetsova 1995, 1996; Moser 1995, 1996).

[22]See also Rokkan (1977) for a more detailed discussion of the contingencies affecting this conversion.

efforts to modify their appeals. The third task, then, is to explore how political divides convert into *competitive dimensions* in party systems.

Several reasons are likely to limit the competitive space to a single dimension or at most two or three of them, such that politicians "map" individual issues onto the underlying dimension (Hinich and Munger 1990, 1992). First, most voters have limited information-processing capacities and therefore politicians must simplify their alternatives into packages guided by some underlying ideological principle (cf. Downs 1957: chap. 7). Second, politicians tend to map issue positions onto broader ideological dimensions as a coordinating device in legislatures. In exchange for sacrificing the specificity of representing voters' ideal positions in a multi-dimensional space, voters gain predictability over the legislative or executive actions promoted by their chosen party. When new salient issues appear, politicians may initially attempt to map them onto the existing dimension(s) of party competition. If that fails and a new crosscutting dimension of party competition emerges, the party system is likely to enter a period of instability in which new parties appear and old parties lose support. Where democratic institutions exist that enhance programmatic voter-party linkages, this process may induce politicians to reconfigure their political issue positions around a single new dominant competitive dimension.

So far, we have talked about social, political, and competitive divides and dimensions, yet not cleavages.[23] Divides and dimensions are cleavages only if they are *durable rather than transient*.[24] In democratic party systems as recently constituted as those of Eastern Europe, it is difficult to test which divisions qualify as cleavages, a reason why we avoid the language of cleavages in this book. Nevertheless, we conjecture that divides are more likely to turn into cleavages, if socio-demographic group traits and inter-group differences coincide with issue opinions and associative practices that divide the same groups. *The cumulative nature of divides based on group traits, affiliations, and opinions hardens into social or political cleavages* (Bartolini and Mair 1990: 215). Thus, where we observe that political alignments among parties are rooted in socio-demographic group traits, political opinions, and voluntary associations, it is quite plausible to expect that political divides and competitive dimensions are in the process of creating cleavages.[25] Our analysis now proceeds in two stages. First, we will discuss sociological moorings of divides in post-communist societies. We then turn to the political-institutional legacies and political-economic developments that involve strategic politicians to account for political divides and competitive dimensions in different post-communist systems.

[23]As Meisel (1974: 6) points out, Lipset and Rokkan do not make a systematic terminological distinction between cleavage, contrast, conflict, opposition, or strain.

[24]For this qualification, see already Berelson, Lazarsfeld, and McPhee (1954: 75).

[25]For this logic, see Knutsen and Scarbrough (1995).

POLITICAL PREFERENCES AND PARTY DIVIDES: A SOCIOLOGICAL VIEW

In their analysis of Western party systems, Lipset and Rokkan (1967) distinguish two social divides associated with the rise of nation-states – center-periphery ethnically based conflicts and religious divides about the control of culture and morality – and two further divides resulting from the industrial revolution – urban-rural and worker-capital class conflicts. This proposal requires updating for the analysis of post-communist democracies. Also here we wish to distinguish four divides partially corresponding to Lipset and Rokkan's typology. We collapse their two economic divides into a single more general divide between "social protectionist" forces advocating the political allocation of scarce resources and "liberal" currents calling for spontaneous, voluntary market allocation of such resources. We generalize their religious divide to a conflict over the modes of socio-cultural control, norms, and decision-making mechanisms, distinguishing a more "libertarian" view advocating autonomous individual choice of life-styles and norms where possible and participatory democratic collective choices where necessary from a more "authoritarian" view supporting collectively binding social norms and deference to hierarchically stratified decision-making powers. We adopt Lipset and Rokkan's center-periphery divide but disaggregate it into two conflict structures that do not necessarily coincide: first, a struggle between national closure and cosmopolitan opening and, second, a struggle between ethnic groups in socio-culturally divided societies. Finally, we add a divide that actually appears first in post-communist democracies: the tension between supporters and opponents of the old communist regime.

We argue that at the sociological level alone, we can generate only limited predictions about the likely political divides, the alignment among divides, and the competitive dimensions appearing in post-communist society. In order to sharpen our analysis, we must pay close attention to regime legacies and political-economic transformations in the early years of democratization. We turn to this task in the subsequent step of our analysis.

Political Regime Divide

Support and opposition to the old communist regime derives from citizens' location in the socio-political networks of party and mass organizations and from their economic status within the old system, but also from the experience of repression and injustice under communism. The more the old systems employed repression and the less they relied on co-optation, the more salient and durable the regime divide may remain for citizens' voting decisions. As we will see in the next section, however, strategic politicians play a role in complicating this simple rule of thumb.

At the individual level, workers whom the communist regime represented as the vanguard, but who actually had little control over their lives, initially might vent the most resentment against the old regime that lied about their true conditions.[26] This may explain why workers often abandon communist successor parties overproportionally in the first democratic elections. Also age, the extent to which one's identity is tied up in the communist regime, and the memory of economic improvement under communism in the 1950s and 1960s may influence the regime divide. Younger people who only experienced communism in decay and whose identity is less caught up in the old system are more likely to come down on the anti-communist side.[27]

Economic-Distributive Divide

Post-communist voters face uncertainty about their economic fortunes after the demise of the planned economy, but they know their personal resource endowments and current employment situation well enough to anticipate how successfully they might cope with a market economy. Moreover, given the intensely economic pre-occupation of Marxist ideology under the old regimes, even in the new democratic order voters are likely to employ interpretive frames that attribute high salience to distributive struggles. Lipset and Rokkan (1967: 34) may be correct that class divides in Western capitalism are weak, where universal suffrage precedes class organization, an argument also applied to Eastern Europe in the inter-war period and to Latin America (cf. Dix 1989; Luebbert 1991). In contemporary Eastern European democracies, however, experience with communism deeply entrenched beliefs and practices revolving around economic distribution.

In the most general terms, those who expect to become losers in the market economy tend to oppose economic reform and opt for a social-protectionist, administratively intermediated economy, whereas the likely winners of market liberalization support it. It may be too simple to characterize citizens' economic fortunes by Marxist class relations of ownership and control over the means of production, but class in the broader Weberian sense of "market position" clearly affects voters' economic preferences.[28] Being young, highly educated, and male and enjoying social ties to the managerial-professional stratum of the discarded economic planning apparatus all help to make individuals more sympathetic to market reforms. After all, young males tend to be weighed down less by family obligations than any other group and have a long career horizon. They are therefore less risk-averse than other citizens. High education and social ties in the economic elite quite clearly enhance individuals' capacity for flexible adjustment

[26]Thus in some countries, such as the German Democratic Republic, the relative size of the working class in a region may be positively associated with electoral support for market-liberal parties (cf. Cusak and Eberwein 1993).

[27]Magaloni (1997) developed the general idea that memories about old-regime performance, periodically updated by more recent events, affect people's orientation toward the pre-democratic incumbents in a formal and empirical fashion for the Mexican case.

[28]In modern empirical stratification analysis, the Weberian notion of class is probably best captured by Goldthorpe's (1987) division of socio-economic categories. For an application to Eastern Europe, see Evans (1995).

to new economic opportunities. At the other extreme, pensioners and particularly older women have the least to expect from economic reform and almost no capabilities to overcome economic hardship.

Also sectoral affiliations may make a difference for citizens' economic orientations, even if we grant some inter-sectoral labor mobility. Those working in most manufacturing industries, agriculture, or the political security apparatus fear most for their employment under a market-liberal order. For this reason blue-collar workers who may have initially supported liberal parties soon return to more social-protectionist parties (Tóka 1993; Hough 1994; Evans 1995). Employees in commercial, administrative, and social services have generally better prospects, even though they may suffer sharp temporary wage declines with economic reform.

There is quite robust evidence that highly educated, young, male voters tend to support market liberalization.[29] Because these variables are moderately to strongly collinear and also correlate with occupation, sector, and firm affiliation, the net effect of each variable on market-liberal attitudes or support of market liberal parties varies with the controls employed in multiple regression estimates. Moreover, much of the impact of socio-demographic traits and sectoral experiences of voters on market-liberal preferences is mediated through expectations about the performance of the economy as a whole or one's individual economic fortunes in the future.

Also the unfolding of economic reform cycles is unlikely to affect these relations between personal resource endowment, sectoral affiliation, and party preference. At the aggregate level, of course, parties that engage in macroeconomic reform may lose elections if they take place before the recovery has yielded results visible to a broad audience (O'Donnell and Schmitter 1986: 62; Przeworski 1991: chap. 4; Evans and Whitefield 1995b; Aslund et al. 1996). Beyond a brief window of "exceptional politics" (Balcerowicz 1995) most citizens may not interpret the fact that the economy is getting worse with rising unemployment as a prelude to things getting better.[30] At that point, it is particularly the economically most vulnerable groups that abandon market-liberal parties.

---

[29]On the role of education see Evans (1994), Wessels and Klingemann (1994), and Whitefield and Evans (1994) in multi-country comparisons. See also Duch (1993: 503), Miller, Hesli and Reisinger (1994, 1996), and White, Wyman, and Kryshtanovskaya (1995) on Russia; Millard (1994a, 1994b) on Poland; and Kitschelt, Dimitrov, and Kanov (1995) on Bulgaria. But see Finifter and Mickiewicz (1994) and Finifter (1996) for a dissenting opinion. On age, compare Wessels and Klingemann (1994) and Rose and Carnaghan (1994); on gender, the more mixed evidence reported in Evans (1994).

[30]Przeworski (1996) found a counter-intuitive positive relation between economic decline and liberal party support only with regard to inflation, not unemployment. But support for liberal parties is high in a high inflationary environment only as long as this situation coincides with low unemployment. Because efforts to drive down inflation usually produce more unemployment, short-term retrospective economic voting prevails.

Socio-Cultural Divide

As in Western democracy, socio-cultural libertarianism is greater among younger individuals and the more educated citizens who have more capabilities and ambition to govern their own lives in a complex, information-rich society. But sociologically these dispositions are aligned with different economic preferences than in the West, particularly in comprehensive welfare states, where many of the young and educated support a leftist, redistributive economic agenda at least through the 1980s and early 1990s (Kitschelt 1994a; McGann and Kitschelt 1995). In post-communism, socio-cultural libertarians also tend to be winners of the economic transformation and therefore support right-libertarian agendas (Kitschelt 1992).[31] They are opposed by left-authoritarians who invoke both social hierarchy and economic protection. It is questionable, however, to what extent this simple association helps us to predict party system alignments without considering the systemic context and the legacies in which parties situate themselves.

National-Cosmopolitan Divide

The logic behind this divide is identical to that driving the socio-cultural divide. Youth and education promote cosmopolitanism in a world where economic success depends on human capital and occupational flexibility. Both cognitive skills as well as economic self-interest thus orient some individuals toward economic openness and others toward closure. A linkage between cosmopolitan and social-libertarian orientations, on the one hand, and nationalism and authoritarian attitudes, on the other, is plausible as well. Nationalism opposes the penetration of Western individualism in favor of communitarian conceptions of identity. This communitarian orientation makes possible an affinity between nationalism and socio-cultural authoritarianism.

As with the previously discussed societal divisions, the trouble is that sociological arguments do not let us conclusively predict how political players in the post-communist regimes integrate nationalist or cosmopolitan appeals into their broader message. A purely sociological model would suggest that market-liberal parties support social libertarianism and cosmopolitanism. As we will see, however, this is a contingent alignment typical only for one of three regime legacies.

Ethnic Divides

No one is compelled to embrace the one proposition that ethnic self- and group-identity grows out of an unequal ethnic division of labor in order to accept the

---

[31]Based on surveys in ten post-communist countries, Whitefield and Evans (1994) found correlations between indices of economic and social liberalism of .33. For empirical evidence backing some of these affinities in Eastern Europe, see Evans (1994: table 11) with data on a wide range of countries. For select countries, see also Duch (1993) and Gibson and Duch (1993). In the communist world outside Eastern Europe, Nathan and Shi (1995) have explored the political correlates of education in contemporary mainland China.

other proposition that *group-related inequalities and inter-group comparisons are a critical ingredient of ethno-political mobilization and conflict.*[32] While group formation may not follow strict material self-interest, the latter plays a critical role in conflicts of interests and political mobilization. The greatest incentives for collective mobilization are experienced by those whose individual material payoffs are particularly contingent upon group membership in a positive or negative direction, when compared with the payoffs of individuals with equivalent personal resource endowments in another ethnic group. Thus the educated middle class of a subordinate group may engage in collective action, if the gap to its peers in the dominant group is particularly large. Conversely, the least-skilled individuals in a dominant group may push toward ethnic mobilization if their advantages are particularly large compared with individuals with equivalent market skills in the subordinate group.

Likely losers of the economic liberalization in all ethnic groups, however, are particularly prone to making their claims heard in ethnic-particularist terms. In the economic sphere, displacing markets by political allocation rules is a form of closure against competition. Economic allocation based on ethnic group membership rather than personal achievements is one rationale in a closed economy. Ethnic particularism and socio-economic protectionism thus tend to reinforce each other.

Things are more complicated when we turn to members of ethnic sub-groups with high human capital and skills to thrive in a market economy. If that stratum belongs to an initially underprivileged minority that cannot hope to redistribute resources through a majoritarian democratic political process, their high level of education and capacity to perform in a market environment may predispose them toward universalist policies of formal equalization that overcome ethnic divisions of labor. If that group, however, controls a majority of the vote, it may well opt for a particularistic program of inter-ethnic redistribution that deprives the elite of the old dominant minority group of its assets, unless the latter co-opts the former into a system of shared spoils. In post-communist countries, the temptation to do so is particularly high where Russian minorities were economically dominant but are now outnumbered by titular majorities whose elites wish to redress the balance of power in their own favor.

Well-endowed members of an initially overprivileged group face a reverse distribution of alternatives. If they are in the minority, they cannot resort to a democratic majoritarian political process to maintain it. Instead, they must seek compromises with the elites belonging to the subordinate challenging majority or

---

[32]Hardin's (1995) effort to reconstruct ethnic identification in terms of economic self-interest falters when he relies on the "comforts of home" as the ultimate benefit supplied by group membership. Theories of group formation based on communication (Deutsch 1953; Gellner 1983) and state formation (Horowitz 1985) are more plausible. Nevertheless, group inequalities (Ragin 1987: 135–36) or the changing balance of such arrangements (Olszak 1992; Nagel 1995) are critical for political mobilization.

support a universalistic system of non-ethnic political competition. Thus, the best options for the elites of Russian minorities in the "near abroad" may be to advance an accommodation with the elites of the titular majority. In all these cases, however, the salience of ethnic divides and the linkage into the system of competitive alignments depends on the regime trajectories to which we turn next.

REGIME LEGACIES, POLITICAL-ECONOMIC CHANGES, AND STRATEGIC POLITICIANS: INFUSING POLITICS INTO THE FORMATION OF REGIME DIVIDES

Predictions of political alignments and competitive dimensions based on economic and sociological conditions of cleavage formation alone provide a heuristic template against which to compare the actual complexity of post-communist party competition. The basic defect of purely sociological analysis is that it ignores the role of political elites in crafting party systems. The strategic configurations among elite players, in turn, evolve in diverse directions contingent upon the former communist regime type. In our second theoretical step, therefore, we specify expectations about the nature of party alignments and programmatic competition in the new democracies that emerge from the variety of bargains that communist rulers struck under the old regimes from the 1960s through 1980s and that shaped the modes of transition in the late 1980s.

For each post-communist pathway toward democratization, we discuss likely party alignments and competitive dimensions around the regime conflict, socio-economic distribution, socio-cultural arrangements, national autonomy, and ethnic differences. In conclusion, we speculate about the likely shape of a potential hegemonic political-economic bloc that entrenches itself by combining winners and losers in each polity. For developing societies, Huntington (1968: 434) has argued that such a bloc is successful only if it overcomes the tension between city and countryside.[33] But also hegemonic parties in advanced industrial societies after World War II, such as the Liberal Democrats in Japan or Christian Democrats in Italy and West Germany, crafted broad social coalitions between city, countryside, and segments of the working class around "social market" compromises that buffered the less adaptable groups from the vagaries of open competition with policies of social compensation (cf. Pempel 1990). The shape of equivalent coalitions may vary substantially across post-communist democracies.

---

[33]Huntington (1968: 434) writes: "The source of political modernity is the city; the source of political stability is the countryside. The task of the party is to combine the two. One major test of the institutionalization of a party and the adaptability of its leadership is the willingness of the latter to make the concessions necessary to win the support of the countryside. The strong parties and the stable party systems are those which meet this test. In a modernizing society, the successful party is born in the city, but matures in the countryside."

Bureaucratic-Authoritarian Communism

Three critical facts shape the impact of bureaucratic-authoritarian communism on the structuring of democratic party alignments in the late 1980s. They are (1) the presence of a recalcitrant, orthodox ruling party, steeped in a strong working-class movement with pre-communist origins, (2) a comparatively professionalized bureaucracy, and (3) a repressed but potentially strong civil society with skills and political interpretations that in part derive from a functioning inter-war democracy and the memory of capitalist industrialization. Overall, this arrangement places economic-distributive conflicts at the center of political competition.

First of all, a stubbornly orthodox communist party with a history of heavy-handed repression directed at actual and potential challengers incites a deep *regime divide*. But at the same time, this divide is mitigated by the electoral weakness of the post-communists. Marxist orthodoxy leads to self-isolation. Particularly when placed in an environment of relatively high economic development and a popular memory of successful capitalist development before the advent of communism, economic liberalism, or social democratic "mixed economy" programmatic visions have much magnetism to capture the spirit of the electorate. Finally, the regime divide between communists, a moderate social-protectionist camp, and unfettered market liberalists is perfectly collinear with the economic policy divide and is subsumed under the latter.

Second, because bureaucratic-authoritarian communism evolves from already rather highly industrialized economies with a salient economic-distributive divide that is translated into repressive class politics under communist rule and a continued "class position" of the communist successor party, political entrepreneurs in the post-communist democracies primarily lock onto economic themes to highlight their party programs and to diversify their competitive positions. Thus, two developments converge to highlight the economic divide as the dominant feature of party competition. From society, bureaucratic-authoritarian communism with a comparatively advanced industrial structure, based on high-skill labor and professionals, generates a relatively strong *demand* for market-liberal reform policies. From the emerging competitive arena, the existence of an orthodox-Marxist pole allows new political entrepreneurs to engage in strategies of "programmatic product differentiation" by offering moderate or liberal economic appeals. As a consequence, citizens and politicians identify the formal notions of "left" and "right" in the competitive space primarily with economic policy alternatives.

Third, other divides in democracies following bureaucratic-authoritarianism have only secondary importance and tend to constitute dimensions of party identification rather than party competition. The socio-cultural divide, for example, with religious issues and broader civic libertarian-authoritarian policy alternatives (law and order, public morality) generates only a weak crystallization of party alternatives. The same applies to the national-cosmopolitan divide. Political polarization between economic-distributive liberalism and intransigent social protectionism sufficiently "stretches" the economic dimension of competition to permit parties to diversify their appeals. At the same time, societal demand for a second dimension of party competition is limited. Early industrialization and secularization have removed the salience of many moral and gender-related issues from controversy. For that reason, the Catholic Church could never emerge as a formidable political actor fighting against bureaucratic-authoritarian communism and is now in a weak position with demands for new socio-cultural policies. Looking into the future, post-industrial conflicts over ecology, gender roles, and citizens' participation in policy making do not make an appearance as long as basic questions of economic production and distribution are at the top of the agenda.

Given that less educated citizens in precarious economic circumstances are most accessible to authoritarian appeals against individualism and universalistic competition, including international openness, political entrepreneurs seizing on authoritarian and nationalist visions tend to endorse also social-protectionist, anti-market positions. Such "left-authoritarian" appeals can survive as relatively small niche parties. Thus, the orthodox communist successor parties link authoritarianism, national isolation, and social protection. Other parties may offer variations on similar themes, all the way to the more "centrist" Christian democratic parties that subscribe to moderately social protectionist and traditionalist authoritarian positions.

Finally, if democracies after bureaucratic-authoritarian communism are ethnically divided, the precise nature of the group mobilization, as everywhere else, depends on the distribution of economic resources across majority and minority groups. Overall, however, because of the overriding salience of the economic conflict line, politicians tend to deemphasize particularistic ethnic divisions and convert them into problems of economic distribution.

The dominance of economic-distributive party competition after bureaucratic-authoritarian communism also implies that parties' electoral fortunes are quite responsive to economic developments. Where economic reform delivers growth and employment, it advances market-liberal parties in electoral contests, while economic performance problems boost moderately social protectionist alternatives. The success of economic reform feeds on itself, as does its failure.

Because of the salience of the economic-distributive divide and the strength of the market-liberal constituency after bureaucratic-authoritarian communism, market-liberal parties have a plausible chance to become hegemonic actors, as long as they are able to co-opt some of the sectoral losers in heavy industry and/or general state administration into the coalition. Alternatively, moderate social democrats could craft a similar coalition. But in such polities, neither communists nor national authoritarians can make a successful bid for electoral hegemony.

National-Accommodative Communism
The critical facts about democracy after national-accommodative communism are (1) a flexible, reformist communist successor party that embraces the foundations of a liberal democracy, and a capitalist economy, though with social correctives, (2)

a moderately professionalized bureaucracy, and (3) a rapidly growing civic and political society of parties and associations many of which began to organize before the advent of democracy. While the political regime divide is by and large subdued in this configuration, economic and socio-cultural alignments among parties are more complex than in democracies inheriting the bureaucratic-authoritarian legacy.

National-accommodative communist rulers had a propensity to manage democratic transitions through negotiations with personalities representing a vibrant emerging scene of opposition movements and challenging parties. The more techniques to increase compliance under the old system relied on co-optation rather than repression and the more the old system tolerated subdued forms of oppositional activity, the less political entrepreneurs can expect to politicize the regime divide in the new democracies.

After national-accommodative communism, questions of economic reform are, of course, highly salient, but political entrepreneurs encounter much greater obstacles to harness them for programmatic party competition than their counterparts after bureaucratic-authoritarian or patrimonial communism, because the communist successor parties accept essentials of liberal market reform and convert themselves into "center-left" new social democratic parties (cf. Deschouwer and Coppieters 1994; Lindstrom 1991: 273). At least initially, economic liberalization becomes a valence issue in which all parties try to surpass each other in proclaiming their own sincerity and competence to engineer economic reforms. Later on, it is not automatically the post-communist successor party that makes the most social-protectionist appeals because it also caters to a stratum of technocrats in the management of public and private firms who emphasize economic reform.

As a consequence, it is rather difficult for party politicians to differentiate party appeals on a reliable and permanent basis according to economic-distributive positions. National-accommodative communism imposes much stricter limits on employing economics as the most salient dimension of party competition or even voter identification than do other regime legacies. Vote-seeking politicians who rely on programmatic appeals therefore have incentives to invoke dimensions of competition that are other than economic. Societal conditions in post-communist democracies with national-accommodative regime legacies offer such opportunities with regard to *socio-cultural, national, or ethnic divides.* In other words, both societal conditions as well as politicians' incentives, taken together, create salient dimensions of competition with clearly differentiated party appeals that crosscut an economic competitive dimension to the extent non-economic issues can reach salience after national-accommodative communism. In contrast to bureaucratic-authoritarian legacies of democracy, it is anti-communist forces with diverse economic positions that have the greatest potential to embrace socio-culturally authoritarian, nationalist, or ethnically particularist positions and to advertise them in order to attract a following.

Several developments explain this outcome. The Catholic Church often served as a catalyst to organize the regime's accommodation with the opposition and non-communist parties build on the church's prestige with a more authoritarian socio-cultural appeal. At the opposite end of the spectrum are culturally more libertarian forces configured around both the reformist post-communists as well as liberal parties both of which endorse universalist standards of civic individualism. The quest for a non-economic competitive divide may also relate to the issue of *national autonomy or international integration*. While both the former communist ruling party as well as opposition groups implicitly invoked the preservation of national autonomy from the Soviet hegemon in their implicit bargains under the old regime, non-communist politicians can present themselves more credibly as protectors of national independence after the arrival of democracy and also build on a long tradition of political conflict about national autonomy during the interwar period under democratic and semi-authoritarian regimes.

The importance of socio-cultural and national appeals for competition among parties also yields a distinct semantic construction of the left-right language in the political discourse of formerly national-accommodative communist polities. Left and right relate primarily to socio-cultural issues, with rightist positions signifying policies of closure against autonomy of the individual, universalistic norms of conduct, multi-cultural tolerance, and participatory decision making, while leftist positions endorse such visions of political order.

The socio-cultural and national lines of conflict thus foster a *tripolar political divide between a secular, libertarian, and market-liberal camp, an equally secular and libertarian post-communist camp, and a national-authoritarian camp endorsing rather mixed economic positions*. In this latter camp, Christian-conservative parties have sufficiently removed themselves from the communist regime to present themselves as credible heirs of the national tradition and as critics of boundless market liberalism and individualism. In formerly national-accommodative communist arrangements where ethnic divides have become critical, a Christian-national camp may also invoke particularist ethnic positions, if it represents the ethnic majority. Because socio-culturally authoritarian, nationalist, and ethnically particularist parties appeal to less educated voters and often the losers of the economic liberalization process, they cannot afford to embrace uncompromising market-liberal politics.

As a result of the importance of a salient libertarian-authoritarian competitive axis and of limited diversification among the parties' economic positions, retrospective or prospective economic voting may play a somewhat more subdued role in government incumbents' and opposition forces' electoral fortunes than in other post-communist polities. True, successful government incumbent parties thrive on a country's superior economic performance, but voters' choices often derive more from non-economic rationales relating to parties' socio-cultural appeals.

In democratic polities emerging from national-accommodative communism, therefore, at least two alternative hegemonic coalitions contend for control of the executive. On one side, there are the secular-cosmopolitan-libertarian forces that may congeal around an alliance between liberal democratic and social democratic parties. On the other, a more religious-national-authoritarian camp may assert itself, again in possible alliance with market liberals. Distinctive parties endorsing market liberalism are comparatively weak after national-accommodative communism, but they may serve as power brokers between the post-communist, social democratic, and the non-communist, socially conservative Christian-national party sectors. Whereas bureaucratic-authoritarian communism gives rise to uni-dimensional competitive spaces configured around economics quite like the Anglo-Saxon and, in modified fashion, the Scandinavian party systems, party configurations in democracies after national-accommodative communism tend to resemble *tripolar systems of party divides situated in two dimensions* quite similar to those of Austria, Belgium, Germany, Italy, the Netherlands, or Switzerland until well into the 1960s. Tripolar configurations are a prospect not only for Hungary and Poland, but also for Slovenia, Croatia, and some of the Baltic countries (cf. Klingemann, Lass, and Mattusch 1994).

Patrimonial Communism

The traits of patrimonial communism that have momentous consequences for the democratic successor regime are (1) a rather intransigent ruling party that attempts to manage the regime transition through preemptive reform rather than negotiation, (2) a deeply corrupt, unprofessional state apparatus penetrated by personal clientelist networks, and (3) a weak, disorganized anti-communist opposition without practical political experience, ideological refinement, or the memory of a non-socialist project of societal development to look back upon. In this setting, market liberalism remains weak, but economic policy disagreements constitute one of several mutually reinforcing divides that contribute to a single overarching competitive dimension that creates a polarized system of alternatives.

The *regime divide* is probably deeper in past patrimonial communist regimes than elsewhere, because the former ruling parties governed through heavy-handed repression as well as material co-optation and now continue to command wide-spread electoral support after the demise of communism. Both the existence of extensive clientelist networks organized through the communist party as well as the absence of experience with a non-communist model of industrial political-economic development strengthens the appeal of the communist successor parties. Many citizens fear that an openness to liberal market institutions, to Western competitors and to cultural individualism undermines the economic and cultural viability of their life-styles supported by the post-communist party. At the same time, the opposition to communist rule lacks skills, organization, and an intellec-tual tradition that is steeped in pre-communist political mobilization. In such circumstances, a weak and divided opposition often has nothing to build on but anti-communist rhetoric, invoking the repressiveness of the old regime and the self-enrichment of its leaders, when it begins to develop a programmatic strategy. As this anti-communist strategy evolves, economic, socio-cultural, national, and sometimes even ethnic divides feed into a single super-dimension of competition with mutually reinforcing components. Parties that wish to block reform or even reestablish the old regime constitute one pole on this competitive dimension, a weaker and more diffuse market-liberal and socio-culturally libertarian and cosmopolitan camp the other.

In terms of the *economic distributive dimension,* post-communist forces clearly favor social-protectionist policies. Such policies command much more support than market-liberal reforms because patrimonial communist institutions have to undergo more profound reforms than those of other communist systems before they can support a capitalist market economy. The uncertainties of fundamental change generate aversions to the reform process. For example, the absence of even a modicum of professionalism in the state apparatus and the pervasiveness of patronage and clientelism in the old party machine is inimical to the orderly functioning of capitalist markets building on the rule of law (cf. World Bank 1997). Given these fundamental deficiencies of political governance, market-liberal reformers, at the end of the political spectrum opposite to that where post-communist standpatters situate themselves, find it difficult to craft effective programs for market liberalization, let alone to implement them. Indecisive partial reforms, in turn, may lead to a deterioration of the existing economic order without putting something more viable in its place and only enable economic elites or political cronies to appropriate state assets and collect public rents (cf. Aslund et al. 1996; Hellman 1998).

Because communist regimes implemented a nationally oriented, centrally directed economic development policy of import substitution and industrial autarky, it is easy to see how the supporters of the old order can seize on authoritarian-collectivist and nationalist appeals to reinforce their message. Such views transpose the idea of *closure against economic competition and universalistic norms of individualism* into the sphere of socio-cultural conduct and collective identities. Such messages resonate well with the core constituencies of social protectionist parties, namely less educated older citizens who often work in particularly inefficient sectors endangered by foreign competition (heavy industry, agriculture, security apparatus) or are pensioners and who therefore have a propensity to defend "closed" political modes of resource allocation. Both a cohort of "red" communist successor parties as well as a new cohort of "brown" nationalist and anti-liberal parties seize on the opportunity to combine economic protectionist with socio-culturally authoritarian and nationalist appeals. Given the weakness and internal division of liberalism after patrimonial communist rule and the mutually reinforcing economic, socio-cultural, and national divides, nationalist parties may obtain a powerful pivotal bargaining position between the post-communist social-protectionist and the liberal pole in the emerging party systems.

It is easy to see how in such polities *ethnic divides* provide grist for the mill of party competition and can easily be integrated into the super-dimension of left-authoritarian versus right-libertarian politics. Ethnic group claims, after all, often, though not always, embody the quest for particularistic advantages, consistent with a social and economic protectionism that allocates scarce resources based on the identity and status of the beneficiary rather than the play of market forces. In this sense, ethno-particularist appeals go over well with the likely economic losers of market liberalization within *each* ethnic segment of a polity. Whether in an ethnic minority or majority position, this electorate is already pre-disposed to support anti-liberal parties for economic reasons. Particularly in an environment with hesitant institutional economic reform combined with persistent and progressive decline in the standard of living, the popular call for particularistic principles of resource allocation according to ethnic group membership is likely to intensify. Thus, politicians opposed to market liberalization, socio-cultural libertarianism, and cosmopolitan openness tend to seize on ethnic animosities, whereas those with market-liberal orientations favor a depoliticization of ethnic group memberships.

After the breakdown of patrimonial communism, the formation of newly independent states governed by former ethnic minorities who now become titular majorities may complicate such alignments. Because the old communist party served the imperial hegemon and may therefore lack nationalist credentials, it may be displaced by nationalist forces who sometimes press for market reforms to undercut the old establishment. Confronted with weak liberal but strong nationalist parties, younger communists may seize the former ruling parties and embrace socio-economic reform and a conciliatory approach to nation building accommodating both the new titular majority group and the old hegemonic minority. While this outlook is not unlike that of reform-oriented communist parties in former national-accommodative communism, post-communists here face strong nationalist party contenders and weak liberal parties rather than both liberal and Christian-national parties, as in democracies evolving from national-accommodative communism.[34]

In general, after patrimonial communism the usually divided liberal democratic forces can rarely establish hegemony in the party system or even aspire to a gatekeeper role, tipping the balance between alternative coalitions. Post-communist and nationalist-protectionist forces lead the stronger constituencies so that liberal democrats can only govern as long as these stronger tendencies block each other.

Party Alignments and Competitive Dimensions: A Summary
Table 2.2 highlights the most important propositions about party alignments and competition that follow from each communist regime type for the formation of party alignments and dimensions of competition. Political and economic legacies of communist rule affect the demand and supply of parties. On the demand side,

---

[34]An extreme case for this dynamic would be Macedonia where the former ruling party now occupies the political sector endorsing economic liberalism and national accommodation with the Albanian minority. Also in Moldova and Slovakia reformist communist parties set themselves apart from nationalist parties with sometimes strong anti-communist rhetoric. A partial outlier is the Ukraine, where, as of 1997, the post-communists stand for national reconciliation, but not for economic reform.

they shape the extent to which citizens are averse to market liberalization or treat democratic politics as an opportunity to take revenge on their former communist rulers. On the supply side, legacies contribute to the competitive configuration among parties that affects politicians' choice to highlight or deemphasize non-economic divides and frame them in terms of conflict alignments that crosscut or reinforce the economic divide between social protectionism and market liberalism.

Both bureaucratic-authoritarian as well as patrimonial communism promote a *single salient competitive dimension with mutually reinforcing regime and economic divides and considerable polarization between the most extreme parties.* By contrast, national-accommodative communism gives rise to *crosscutting dimensions of competition* that yield three or four party camps, divided over economic and socio-cultural issues. The formal convergence of democracies with bureaucratic-authoritarian and patrimonial legacies, however, conceals profound differences between the two types. In the former, economic divides become salient to the detriment of regime-based, socio-cultural, national, and ethnic struggles, whereas in the latter divisions between parties on issues relating to the political regime divide, economic distribution, cultural libertarianism, national autonomy, and ethno-cultural particularism reinforce each other.[35] Moreover, whereas democracies after bureaucratic-authoritarian communism develop strong market-liberal parties against the backdrop of pre-communist democracy and industrialization, formerly patrimonial communist countries that never experienced economic and political mobilization before the advent of communist rule produce weak and divided market-liberal parties unable to stage a bid for hegemony in the new democratic polity.

POLITICAL REPRESENTATION AND EFFECTIVE GOVERNANCE

Citizens are ultimately interested in the extent to which politicians represent their demands and provide effective governance, not primarily the extent to which party systems are programmatically structured and develop specific competitive party alignments. Democratic elections create feedback loops of accountability and responsiveness that foster a certain convergence between the preferences of constituencies, as democratic principals, and their representatives, as legislative agents, and reward or punish the latter for their contribution to the governance of the polity. The extent to which this convergence occurs and the nature of governance, however, depends on numerous contingencies, such as institutional arrangements and power alignments among politicians. Political scientists have

[35]In this regard, see also Remington and Smith's (1995) analysis of the Russian party system based on a roll call analysis of legislative voting as well as Kitschelt and Smyth (1997) on political divisions in the Russian party system.

Table 2.2. *Regime legacies and political alignments in new post-communist democracies*

Legacies	Czech Republic	Poland	Hungary	Bulgaria
	Bureaucratic-authoritarian	National-accommodative	National-accommodative	Patrimonial
Transition	Implosion	Negotiation/implosion	Negotiation	Preemptive reform
Regime divide				
Identification divide	Strong	Medium-strong	Medium	Strong
Competitive divide	Weak	Medium-weak	Weak	Strong
Economic-distributive divide				
Identification divide	Strong	Medium-strong	Medium-weak	Strong
Competitive divide	Strong	Medium-strong	Medium-weak	Strong
Support of the market-liberal camp	Strong	Medium	Medium	Weak
Socio-cultural divide				
Identification divide	Strong	Strong	Strong	Medium
Competitive divide	Weak	Medium	Strong	Medium

National divide				
Identification divide	Weak	Medium	Medium	Strong
Competitive divide	Weak	Medium	Medium	Medium-strong
Ethnic divide				
Identification divide	Weak	Weak	Medium	Medium-strong
Competitive divide	Weak	Weak	Weak	Weak-medium
Alignment political divide	Economic divide dominant	Crosscutting economic and political-cultural divides	Crosscutting economic and political-cultural divides	Reinforcing economic and political-cultural divides
Potential dominant party coalitions	Market-liberal or social-protectionist	Post-communist or Christian-national; market liberals as intermediating force	Post-communist or Christian-national; market liberals as intermediating force	Post-communist or nationalist; weak liberal-democratic forces

often claimed that the institutional-political constellations that further representation may inhibit effective governance and vice versa. We will not directly probe here into the contingencies that are said to affect the trade-off between representation and effective governance. Instead, we wish to highlight how the diversity of communist legacies directly or mediated through institutional choice helps us to account for the varying quality of democratic procedures both in terms of representation and effectiveness of governance. Chapters 9 and 10 then show empirically that at least in the four countries we discuss one would be hard pressed to postulate a simple trade-off between representation and effective governance.

POLITICAL REPRESENTATION

Skeptics about post-communist democracy expect that the emerging East European polities are incapable of delivering representation because voters either have no clear policy preferences or do not support parties close to their own preferences. Politicians, in turn, lack knowledge of their potential constituencies' preferences. Our research proves these skeptics wrong. What is more important, however, is to account for the diversity of modes and issue areas of representation in such new democracies. Yet again, we argue that regime legacies shape the quality of the process of democratic interest aggregation and intermediation.

We focus on *substantive policy representation* of electoral constituencies by parties and bracket *social and statistical representation*. The latter concerns the sociodemographic attributes of voters and their legislative agents – for example, class, gender, race, religion, or ethnicity. Communist legislatures were models of social-statistical representation, but provided little substantive policy representation. In democracies, parties may use statistical representation (e.g., of women or cultural minorities) in order to highlight their substantive representation of constituency demands through specific programmatic policy commitments (to feminist ideas, the welfare of minorities, etc.) or even their clientelist affiliations. But also in these cases questions of substantive policy representation are much more important than the derivative social-statistical representation.

From time immemorial political theorists have debated the virtues and vices of two alternatives within the sphere of substantive representation: *mandate relationships,* in which electoral constituencies instruct legislative representatives to act on specific popular preferences; and *trustee relationships,* which leave it to elected representatives to pursue constituency preferences so to speak "better than voters understand these themselves," with the litmus test being the willingness of constituencies to reelect the trustee.[36] But the notions of mandate and trusteeship representation are too loose for the purposes of comparative empirical analysis. We would like to know, for example, in which way legislators diverge from their voters' preferences in trusteeship relations. Up to what point can we talk about

[36]Converse and Pierce (1986: chap. 16) discuss the related theoretical literature within the context of comparative politics.

trusteeship relations and when do we identify a breakdown of representative relations? For this reason, we first supply some crisper conceptions of political representation and then relate these to the diversity of post-communist democracy.

Mandate relationships minimize the distance between the policy preferences of a politician's (or a party's) own policy preferences and those of his or her mean voter on a salient issue k. If a party enacts this position through government policy, this practice is called *responsible party government*. In trustee relations, there may be a more significant gap between the preferences of politicians and their voters, but that disparity must conform to particular regularities to count still as representation. In figure 2.1, consider the first model, which maps the mean position of each party's voters (lower line) and politicians (upper line) on an arbitrary 100-point policy scale. The vertical lines indicate the correspondence between parties' constituencies and their representatives (electoral candidates or legislators). If we employ the voters' positions as predictors of the parties' positions, in model I the correlation is perfect ($r = 1.0$). But this information is insufficient to describe the representative relation in statistical terms. We also need to know the sum of differences in policy positions of each party's voters and representatives, the slope coefficients, and the intercepts of the regression.[37] In model I, the representative relation is perfect only because also the slope coefficient equals 1.0 and the intercept is 0. As a consequence, the sum of differences between the positions of each party's mean voter and her representative is 0.

Now consider model II in figure 2.1. Here the correlation between parties' mean voter and politicians' positions is 0, the slope coefficient is 0, the intercept is 50, and the average difference between voters' and politicians' mean positions is 24. Model II provides an extreme case of non-representation. As always, empirically interesting phenomena relevant for comparative analysis are situated somewhere between the conceptual ideal types captured by models I and II. Model III in figure 2.1 illustrates a situation where voter constituencies support systematically different positions than those their party representatives endorse. "Absolute" representation is comparatively weak, given the very substantial average deviation between each party's voter position and that of the same party's politicians (deviation D equals 20.0 units) and the large intercept of 20.0 points in the regression. Nevertheless, knowing an electoral constituency's position enables us to predict the position of the corresponding party perfectly (slope coefficient = 1.0; correlation = 1.0). In this case, parties are *responsive* to their voters, and they *relate* their positions to their electorates, although they do not *reflect* the constituencies' preferences. While parties fail in terms of *absolute representation*, indicated by the difference in average positions D and the intercept, they still manage to deliver perfect *relative representation*, measured by the slope coefficient and the correlation.

[37] We follow here and in subsequent paragraphs Achen's (1977, 1978) lucid discussion of the statistical analysis of representative relations.

Model I: Mandate Representation

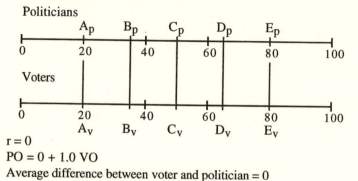

$r = 0$

PO = 0 + 1.0 VO

Average difference between voter and politician = 0

Model II: Absence of Representation

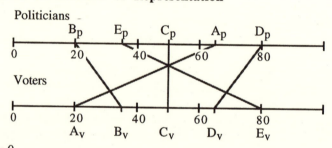

$r = 0$

PO = 50 + 0.0 VO

Average difference between voter and politician = 24

Model III: Trusteeship I - Relative, but no Absolute Representation

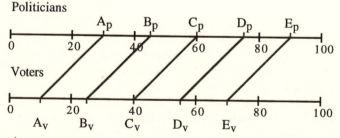

$r = 1$

PO = 20 + 1.0 VO

Average difference between voter and politician = 20

Figure 2.1. Models of representation

Model IV: Trusteeship II - Overstatement of Electoral Preference Divergence

Politicians

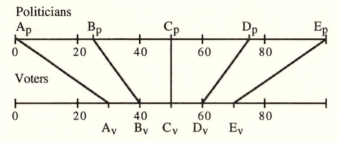

r = 1.0
PO = -75 + 2.5 VO
Average difference between voter and politician = 18

Model V: Trusteeship III - Relative Representation, but Downsian Centripetal Competition

Politicians

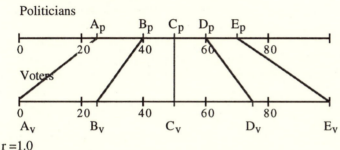

r = 1.0
PO = 30 + 0.4 VO
Average difference between voter and politician = 20

Figure 2.1. (cont.)

Model IV depicts an idealization of a voter-party alignment that will turn out to be empirically highly relevant. Partisan representatives overstate differences among voter constituencies. Also here, relative representation is high, with a perfect correlation of 1.0, yet a slope coefficient considerably greater than 1.0 and a negative intercept. The more negative the value of the intercept and the greater the slope coefficient, the more politicians *overstate* preference differentials among the various parties' electoral constituencies.

Three conditions may contribute to large slope coefficients and negative intercepts. First, these results indicate politicians' "issue leadership" and propensity toward centrifugal competition with an eagerness to signal "product differentiation" to the electorate. According to this *strategic interpretation,* politicians consciously overstate differences in the electorate – for example, in order to draw attention to their party.[38] Second, politicians' more radical positional scores may indicate only that they are *cognitively more certain* of their issue positions than are many voters. Because voters may feel less competent in assessing the issues, they may choose more centrist placements. Third, it is likely that mass surveys among partisan electorates generate more measurement error than surveys among political elites. The random noise of mass surveys makes partisan constituencies' average position regress to the mean position of the scale. This provides for a purely *technical-statistical interpretation* of voter-party differentials in issue positions.

Empirically, it would be fiendishly difficult to parcel out the relative effect of strategic, cognitive, and statistical influences on the slope coefficients, but their relative size may provide a crude yardstick. Coefficients still in the neighborhood of perfect responsiveness, somewhere between 1.0 and 2.0, may be caused by purely statistical and cognitive mechanisms. In these cases, party elites are unlikely to support substantively more extreme policies than their constituencies. If coefficients get numerically larger, however, the plausibility increases that the strategic interpretation of constituency-party differentials applies, and politicians indeed engage in centrifugal competition with radical issue leadership pursued at least by the outlying parties on each side of the issue dimension.

We therefore qualify as *polarizing trusteeship relation* between voters and politicians (trusteeship mark I) only those configurations where politicians' overstatement of voters' preference positions are sufficiently high to generate slope coefficients of at least 2.0, large differences of means (given our 100-point scales certainly greater than 10), and also large negative intercepts (of -50 or greater). As long as slope coefficients are between 1.0 and 2.0, differences of voters' and politicians' mean positions are small, and correlation coefficients comparatively high, we interpret the observed configuration findings as a *mandate relationship*. If slope coefficients are smaller than 1.0, differences of means are substantial and hence intercepts positive, then the party system articulates relations of *moderating trusteeship relation* (trusteeship mark II). Here politicians in different partisan camps *defy* voters' radicalism and consciously converge on a narrow common policy space (model V in figure 2.1). Also here, politicians are *absolutely* unrepresentative of their constituencies, indicated by a substantial D value and a large intercept, but *relatively* representative, signaled by slope and correlation coefficients. In both polarizing and moderating trusteeship relations, the correlation between voters' and parties' positions remains high.

Against the backdrop of these terminological and operational specifications, let us now ask the critical question when parties and party systems are likely to subscribe to different modes of political representation and how post-communist democracies might generate varying relations of political representation. We

---

[38]This interpretation does conform to Rabinowitz and McDonald's (1989) directional theory of voting, but it would also be consistent with a spatial theory of competition that allows for some issue leadership.

assume here that parties are vote-seeking or office-seeking or both. Purely policy-seeking parties with a long time horizon may always hope to persuade voters to a radical position in the long run, even if there is no evidence in elections that this may be happening. Such parties may therefore always engage in polarizing trusteeship, whereas vote- and/or office-seeking parties take into account contingencies of the party system in framing their policy positions.

Two systemic conditions of party competition are vital and interact with each other in shaping modes of political representation, the party system format and the electoral cycle. Two-party systems with vote- and office-seeking parties make competitors converge on the median voter and opt for moderating trusteeship (model V). In multi-party systems with four or more serious competitors, individual parties have incentives to spread out over the electoral space, thus producing mandate relations or polarizing trusteeship (model IV).[39] The electoral cycle and parties' opposition or government status, however, may modify these party strategies. Immediately after elections opposition and governing parties have the political-economic and electoral opportunity to show their partisan colors most sharply and engage in polarizing trusteeship relations (Alesina and Rosenthal 1995). Thereafter, the business of law making and reputation building ahead of a prospective election may force at least government parties to moderate their appeals. If partisan-based government policies deliver unpopular outcomes, government parties may have an incentive to move to the center, whereas opposition parties highlight their difference by more radical appeals. Model III (figure 2.1) describes the configuration that could result when the government is supplied by a more leftist coalition made up of parties A, B, and C against opposition D and E. Just before elections, however, governing parties may feel a need to reestablish their policy credentials and try to rebuild mandate relations, moving back to something in between model I and model IV (with slope coefficients between 1.0 and 2.0).

When we apply models of representation to post-communist democracies, general systemic conditions would predict mandate and polarizing trusteeship representation just about everywhere before and after elections because we are dealing with multi-party systems. Depending on the performance of government policy, sometimes a model III blend of polarizing trusteeship on the part of opposition parties and moderating trusteeship on the part of governing parties may occur. The critical difference between these democracies, however, appears when we consider the *issue arenas* or *competitive dimensions* on which politicians find it may pay to highlight polarizing or moderating trusteeship. Our hypotheses, summarized in table 2.3, follow directly from our theory of political divisions and competitive dimensions in the preceding section.

Because in the aftermath of bureaucratic-authoritarian communism only economic issues have high salience, we predict that relations of polarizing trustee-

---

[39]We assume here limits to strategic voting that may give parties incentives to gravitate toward the median voter even when the party system has four or more parties.

Table 2.3. *Regime legacies and modes of representation in new post-communist democracies*

	Czech Republic	Poland	Hungary	Bulgaria
Legacies	Bureaucratic-authoritarian	National-accommodative	National-accommodative	Patrimonial
Transition	Implosion	Negotiation/implosion	Negotiation	Preemptive reform
Alignment political divides	Economic divide dominant	Crosscutting economic and political-cultural divides	Crosscutting economic and political-cultural divides	Reinforcing economic and political-cultural divides
Economic-distributive issues	Polarizing trusteeship	Mandate relations or moderating trusteeship	Moderating trusteeship	Polarizing trusteeship
Absolute representation	Weak	Medium	Strong	Weak
Relative representation	Strong	Medium	Weak	Strong
Socio-cultural issues	Underdetermined	Polarizing trusteeship	Polarizing trusteeship	Polarizing trusteeship
Absolute representation	Uncertain	Weak	Weak	Weak
Relative representation	Uncertain	Strong	Strong	Strong
National and ethnic issues	Underdetermined	Polarizing trusteeship	Polarizing trusteeship	Polarizing trusteeship
Absolute representation	Uncertain	Weak	Weak	Weak
Relative representation	Uncertain	Strong	Strong	Strong

ship tend to be most likely here. On other issues in these systems, we have no definitive predictions about the likely configuration of political representation, but polarizing trusteeship is much less likely. By contrast, after national-accommodative communism, party competition highlights both economic and socio-cultural divides. Moreover, with regard to economic issues, reformist post-communist parties have pre-committed themselves to the acceptance of liberal reform and therefore cannot engage in strategies of polarization by embracing a strong anti-market social protectionism. Whereas polities emerging from national-accommodative communism may generate polarizing trusteeship relations on socio-cultural and national issues that in subterranean ways also reflect disappearing regime divides, such polities are much more likely to generate mandate relations or even moderate trusteeship on economic issues. In extreme cases, given that parties compete in a narrow space of economic policy alternatives, they may have trouble establishing relations of representation at all. In polities inheriting the legacies of patrimonial communism, finally, reinforcing competitive divides across economic, socio-cultural, and national issue dimensions are also likely to foster polarizing trusteeship relations in all these respects. Relations of representation thus assume distinct shapes across post-communist democracies.

THE EFFECTIVENESS OF DEMOCRATIC GOVERNANCE

A polity is governable if it is able to convert political preferences into binding policies that last. Parties further democratic governability if they create at least stable legislative but usually also stable executive majorities based on a single party or a coalition of parties that enact and implement binding policies. All else equal, durable and calculable legislative and executive majorities enhance the performance of public policy, particularly in a market economy that relies on private investors who shun uncertainty and demand political predictability. Legacies and institutions affect the probabilities that such lasting coalitions emerge in post-communist democracies. Both the extent of programmatic structuring of party systems as well as the nature of the competitive political divides are intervening variables through which the legacies of communist rule influence governance effectiveness. As we argued in the first chapter, institutions are partially endogenous to political legacies. Nevertheless, executive-legislative arrangements also exert an influence on effective democratic governance that deserves highlighting.

Party-citizen linkages constitute one factor that affects democratic governance. Where programmatic cohesiveness of parties is high, it is easier to produce effective governance than in systems where programmatic cohesiveness is low and/ or clientelist or charismatic linkages of politicians to the electorate prevail. Because democratic polities without programmatic competition do not solve the problem of social choice, legislators face high transaction costs in negotiating majority alliances that determine public policies, and such alliances quickly break apart. As a consequence, a lack of programmatic party competition yields a low and volatile legislative output in public policies. This does not necessarily imply unstable executives or democratic regime instability, as long as parties and governments can pay off their supporters through direct selective material exchanges. Conversely, programmatically structured party systems may not deliver stable governance if they are *highly polarized* on critical dimensions of competition (Huntington 1968; Sartori 1966).

On balance, however, post-communist systems that develop programmatic parties faster may have an edge in terms of policy production and particularly with regard to economic reform legislation. Hence, democracies in the footsteps of bureaucratic-authoritarian or national-accommodative communism may have an easier time to craft legislative and executive coalitions around consistent policy strategies. After patrimonial communism, legislative coalitions tend to be more factitious and brittle. Governments may still last, if they can appease their programmatically diffuse supporters by refraining from offensive legislation and offering side payments in terms of clientelist exchanges. In democratic polities after patrimonial communism, an additional challenge to effective governance stems from the nature of the substantive political alignments that may occur whenever parties do engage in programmatic competition. Due to mutually reinforcing issue divides on the competitive dimension, such systems may produce an intensity of polarization among parties that makes effective governing quite difficult.

The *alignment of partisan divides* plays a critical role for the quality of post-communist democratic governance in another way unfamiliar to students of conventional coalition theory. Such theories typically assume that parties in the legislative arena are policy-seeking entities.[40] They decide on coalition strategies based on the compatibility of their mutual policy programs and the leverage over policy making they gain from participating in legislative or executive coalitions (cf. Laver and Schofield 1990; Strom 1990; Schofield 1993). In this sense, a sharp polarization of parties on the most salient policy issues bodes ill for the formation of coalition governments (Dodd 1976). Still, there may be parties between the extreme poles of the competitive space that can muster sufficient support to constitute viable coalitions based on the proximity of their most salient policy positions.

The problem of this conventional spatial explication of legislative and executive coalitions, when applied to post-authoritarian democracies, however, is that it assumes parties are concerned in their strategic calculations about forward-looking policy issues, the resolution of which affects the distributive payoffs of electoral constituencies in the current round of decision making. But the theory has no *temporal depth* that would endow actors with memories of past episodes of

---

[40]We ignore here the very early theories of minimal winning coalitions that relied on politicians' quest for office alone.

interaction between rival political camps and distributive outcomes of such power relations. Regardless of future gains to be made by new coalitions, actors may have acquired *reputations* that make them unavailable for or unwanted in coalitions, no matter how much such liaisons would work to the mutual benefit of the potential partners. Particularly in post-communist democracies, such reputational barriers to coalition formation tend to build on deep *affective dislikes* between political parties that grow out of experiences with the communist regime. Thus, in the post-authoritarian situation, a *regime divide based on memories of past suffering and injustice* may make parties indisposed to mutual collaboration, regardless of how close they are in the policy space. Social-protectionist parties emerging from the opposition to communist rule, for example, may not wish to join a coalition with the successors of the former communist parties, even though their mutual policy concerns on salient political-economic and socio-cultural issues may be quite similar. Conversely, liberal democrats may not coalesce with communist successor parties that have embraced social democracy, because moral and symbolic considerations keep the former oppressed from teaming up with the party of their former oppressors. Policy distances between parties and the depth of the regime divide that separates them interact in shaping probabilities of coalition politics. The deeper the regime divide, the more likely even small policy differences among parties undermine their capacity to collaborate in legislative and executive coalitions.

In Eastern Europe, regime divides are most shallow after national-accommodative communism where the former ruling parties softened their authoritarianism decades before the demise of communism and negotiated the regime transition. In formerly bureaucratic-authoritarian systems, the regime divide is deep, but the communist successor party tends to be sufficiently isolated to contain resulting problems of governance. Because of the regime divide, governments tend to be skewed toward market-liberal coalitions. Any purely "leftist" social-protectionist coalition would have to include the former communists and non-communist social democrats, but the regime divide makes such alliances infeasible. The regime divide is probably the greatest obstacle to effective governance in formerly patrimonial communism. Here, market liberals can rarely cobble together viable legislative coalitions because popular preferences and legislative representatives tend to favor social protectionism. At the same time, social protectionist parties originating in the old communist system and those with an independent, usually nationalist or agrarian bent cannot collaborate with one another because of the deep regime divide.

Aside from political legacies, mediated by the programmatic structuring and the substantive alignment of party competition, also the new democratic institutions, on their own account, orient politicians' strategic actions and may nurture or undercut lasting legislative and executive majorities. In particular, this applies to the *legislative and executive powers of the presidency.* Where multi-partism in the legislature calls for collaborative party relations to pass legislation, a powerful presidency with legislative veto powers that are difficult to override, decree powers, or powers to appoint and remove cabinet members may hobble parties' capacity for effective governance. Presidents with ambitions to dominate the policy process may employ "divide and rule" tactics with the objective to prevent broad-based and durable legislative party coalitions that would reduce presidential influence over policy making. Presidential powers of patronage and executive appointment provide the institutional techniques to disorganize inter-party collaboration in the legislature. Multi-partism and powerful presidencies thus tend to undermine effective governance (Mainwaring 1993; Linz 1994; Ordeshook 1995; Przeworski 1996; Mainwaring and Shugart 1997).

In table 2.4, we have summarized how the four contingencies affecting democratic governance relate to our four empirical cases. In the Czech Republic, after bureaucratic-authoritarian communism, the patterns of programmatic party competition and the design of democratic institutions are likely to favor effective governance. Only the depth of the regime divide is an obstacle, but this remains surmountable as long as the post-communists remain isolated and attract only a small fraction of the electorate. Good prospects for governance also apply to Hungary, as one of our national-accommodative cases. Here the regime divide is likely to be shallow, policy divides tend to be narrow, and democratic institutions facilitate governance. Poland, as the other national-accommodative country in our sample, looks somewhat different. Conditions for programmatic competition are quite favorable, but the regime divide is somewhat deeper than in Hungary. Although the transition to democracy proceeded through negotiations, the bruising confrontation between the communist state and the Solidarność movement in the first half of the 1980s under martial law exacerbated the regime divide and has significantly complicated inter-party relations in the 1990s. What may have been more important, particularly before the passage of the new 1997 constitution, is that substantial presidential legislative and executive powers created institutional capabilities in the presidential office to undercut collaborative party relations and paralyze legislative majorities.

Overall, Bulgaria exhibits the least favorable conditions for effective governance among our four countries, although it does not reproduce the ideal-typical conditions our theory attributes to polities emerging from patrimonial communism. Its potential for programmatic competition is only moderately unfavorable, because in the longer run the closed-list system of proportional representation creates incentives for programmatic party competition and thus counter-acts the early influence of communist regime legacies that undercut governance by creating a deep regime divide and volatile, comparatively unstructured parties in programmatic terms. In the longer run, however, mutually reinforcing economic, socio-cultural, and collective identity-based divisions may create a polarized polity in which inter-party collaboration will be quite difficult to engineer. Bulgaria's regime divide is unfavorable for effective governance, but the absence of strong presidential powers may serve as an institutional counter-weight that facilitates coalition building. Other polities following patrimonial communism are more likely to develop personalist electoral systems and strong presidential powers,

Table 2.4. *Conditions favoring effective governance*

	Czech Republic	Poland	Hungary	Bulgaria
Legacies	Bureaucratic-authoritarian	National-accommodative	National-accommodative	Patrimonial
Transition	Implosion	Negotiation/implosion	Negotiation	Preemptive reform
Programmatic structuring	Favorable	Favorable	Medium favorable	Unfavorable
Limited polarization/no reinforcing divides	Medium favorable	Favorable	Favorable	Medium unfavorable
Weak regime divide	Medium favorable	Medium favorable	Favorable	Unfavorable
Parliamentary democracy/ weak presidential powers	Medium favorable	Medium unfavorable	Favorable	Favorable

such as Russia or the Ukraine – all conditions that erode effective legislative governance. Nevertheless, in relation to the comparison cases in our sample, Bulgarian democracy is likely to be less effective than its three Central European counterparts.

CONCLUSION

In this chapter we have outlined how legacies of communist rule affect the quality of democratic procedures in the fledgling post-communist democracies in at least four respects. At the same time, we have emphasized the idea that, over time, legacies may fade into the background and institutional incentives, together with political-economic arrangements, will play an increasingly critical role in shaping key attributes of the various polities' democratic political process. This applies in particular to citizen-party linkages and the problem of programmatic crystalliza-tion we discussed in the first section. It also applies to the effectiveness of governance, where the institutional design of executive-legislative relations is a decisive influence. With regard to the substantive policy divisions and competi-tive dimensions examined in the second section as well as the modes of political representation scrutinized in the third section, institutional arrangements are likely to gain only secondary importance. Here the old and the newly emerging political-economic and socio-cultural power relations within post-communist polities, in interaction with the format of party systems that influences the strategic alternatives vote- or office-seeking parties may pursue, are the critical forces that leave their imprint on the democratic process.

Let us conclude our theoretical exposition with another warning against interpreting our analysis of variations in the quality of democratic procedures across Eastern Europe in a normative fashion. Our analysis does not imply a normative democratic theory that would endorse a particularly "good" mode of voter-party linkage configuration of competitive alignments, mode of representa-tion, or effective governance. Our study does not venture into examining the consequences of alternative arrangements in terms of the longevity of democratic institutions, the political-economic performance of the democracies, or the popu-lar enthusiasm with the policy outcomes in different settings.[41] More specifically, it would be incorrect to read our study as the endorsement of a particular form of responsible party government that appears to be empirically most likely after bureaucratic-authoritarian communism. How the actual performance of democra-tic polities may be related to the quality of democratic procedures will have to be established in future studies independent from our current investigation.

[41]As we illustrate in chapter 3 (126–31), however, there is a striking correlation between patrimonial communist legacies, party system development, and an erratic economic reform process after 1990 in our four countries.

PART II

SETTING AND RESEARCH STRATEGY

FROM COMMUNIST RULE TO COMPETITIVE DEMOCRACY: FOUR CENTRAL AND EAST EUROPEAN COUNTRIES

Although Bulgaria, the Czech Republic, Hungary, and Poland shared the experience of communist rule in the shadow of Soviet hegemony since the 1940s, the arrival of democracy in each of these countries has been embedded in the diverging economic and institutional configurations of bureaucratic-authoritarian, national-accommodative, or patrimonial communism. In this chapter we sketch the trajectory of these four countries to illustrate the power of regime legacies, but also in order to show our awareness that beyond systematic path dependence the regime changes involve historical contingencies we can only narrate, but not incorporate into a parsimonious theoretical framework. Faced with an uncertain, open situation, new political actors with little experience are destined to experiment with innovative strategies and learn from feedback. The degrees of freedom the actors take advantage of, however, are limited by the distribution of resources and by mutual expectations about the relevant participants' strategic moves, both of which are influenced by historical legacies. Furthermore, the domestic actors cannot choose the international setting in which they are placed.

Strategic interaction in the initial phase of a new democracy is a non-equilibrium process. Because actors have limited experience, construct new institutions, and define their interests and strategies, it is unlikely that democratic arrangements as stable as those of Western democracies emerge quickly. The conduct of parties and the dynamic of party systems are a case in point. On the occasion of "founding elections" in the new democracies, crowds of political entrepreneurs enter the electoral arena with their own party labels in the hope of beating the odds, gaining popular notoriety and attracting a substantial electorate that permits them to stay in the public limelight and triggers a self-reinforcing process in which support for lesser contenders fades and then accrues to the early political frontrunners. The passage of time thus affects the process of party formation and citizen-elite linkage building. Party elites and voters go through a sequence of reciprocal signaling in which they reveal each other's "type," such as their willingness to demand or supply particular economic policies or special patronage incentives. Eventually they coordinate around particular patterns of linkage that are compatible with the institutional rules of democratic competition. The process in which parties clarify their voter appeal coincides with the disintegration of early anti-communist umbrella alliances ("forum" and "front" organizations or "citizens' lists") that combine politicians with rather disparate visions and ambitions to run together on a single ticket against the successors of the old ruling party in founding elections.

This chapter provides a narrative but analytically disciplined and highly condensed reconstruction of the liberalization process and its initial results in our four Eastern and Central European countries in the first half of the 1990s. We describe the actors and the settings in which our research takes place. Most importantly, we flesh out the independent variables that explain some, but not all, of the cross-national variations between the four countries with regard to their pathways of learning modes of democratic competition: their historical legacies, the resource distributions among critical actors in the transition beyond communism, the new rules of the democratic process, and the socio-economic trajectories since the beginning of the reform process. We cover the pre–World War II period and the crisis era of Stalinism and destalinization only in the briefest of terms in order to focus on the actual transition process and its results.[1] Our description always begins with Poland, the country that led the rest of Eastern Europe in dismantling communist rule. The communist elites in other countries monitored the Polish events and tried to learn from them. For this reason, timing and sequence of reform modify a purely internal path-dependent logic of political-institutional change.

REGIME LEGACIES, POLITICAL LIBERALIZATION, AND FOUNDING ELECTIONS

In Poland and Hungary, decades of tacit accommodation, mixed with occasional open conflict, between the communist elite and potential counter-elites preceded the final steps of liberalization and democratization in 1989–90. In the Czech Republic, the brief jolt of regime liberalization in the so-called Prague Spring of

[1]The historical literature on individual countries in Central and Eastern Europe is, of course, rich. Accounts that make an effort to compare their experiences are less common. Good comparative historical analyses can be found in Chirot (1986), Jelavich (1977), Rothschild (1974, 1989), Schöpflin (1993), Walters (1988), and, for a more limited time period, Janos (1989). An interesting attempt to combine comparative-historical with political science analysis is Ekiert (1996). Introductions to the monographic literature on individual countries are provided by Brown (1988), Crampton (1994), and Held (1992).

1968, when technocratically minded communist economic reformers unintentionally triggered a reform movement from below, was followed by two decades of communist elite intransigence that eventually yielded to the regime's sudden collapse in November 1989. Communist Bulgaria, finally, never experienced internal elite divides, reform from above, or protest movements from below from the late 1940s until the first half of 1989. Here, elements of the communist political elite themselves took the initiative in late 1989 to preempt popular pressure from below by reform from above.

POLAND

After gaining independence in wars pitting Poland against most of its neighbors between 1918 and 1921, the Polish inter-war republic organized democracy around parliamentary rule with a weak cabinet and presidential executive, modeled on France's Third Republic.[2] In 1926, the founder of the country, Jozef Piłsudski, took power in an army coup that emasculated the fragmented party system. Thereafter, Piłsudski ruled behind a veneer of continued quasi-parliamentary government with "managed" elections from 1926 until his death in 1935. Before Germany's attack and quick military victory in 1939, he was succeeded by a regime of colonels who unsuccessfully attempted to borrow techniques of mass mobilization from fascist Europe.

Under parliamentary democracy and then semi-authoritarian rule in the inter-war years, the main actors in the arena of party competition were an initially dominant socialist party that had a national cross-class appeal, as well as national democratic, peasant, and ethno-cultural parties, each relying on clearly distinct regional strongholds.[3] The radical socialist and later on communist party subscribed to explicit class politics but had a minute following, primarily among intellectuals and socially or ethnically marginal groups. It was unable to reach out to the small Polish working class and ignored the demands of the poor peasants. The political regime drove the party into illegality in 1919. Later on in 1930, an alliance with the Polish socialist party failed. Stalin further weakened communism in Poland by ordering the Comintern to dissolve the party in 1938 and by removing the resistance national communist leadership, headed by Władysław Gomułka, after 1947 (de Weyenthal 1978).

The communists' weak penetration of society before their takeover and the experience of non-communist civic and political associations, including the powerful Catholic Church, compelled the communist regime to cope with the crisis of Stalinism in the 1950s by accommodative strategies. In successive waves of protest in 1956, 1968, 1970, and 1976, intellectuals, students, peasants, and

[2]For a detailed description, see Davies (1984: chap. 3), Roos (1986: chap. 3), and Rothschild (1974: 27–72).

[3]Poland's electoral geography in the inter-war period and even after 1989 reveals the influence of the Polish divisions and the different styles of government under Habsburg Austria in Galicia, Prussia-Germany, and Russia. See Tworzecki (1996).

workers, often tacitly or openly supported by the church, voiced their demands in disruptive protest events, but failed to pool resources, build organizational vehicles, and engage in a deliberate strategy that might have divided the communist party leadership into hard-liners and reformers. Nevertheless, the opposition achieved a rollback of land reform, considerable autonomy for the Catholic Church, and a circumscribed area of civil liberties, though no collective representation.

A qualitative leap in the relations between government and citizenry occurred with the strike wave of August 1980 and the formation of the labor union Solidarność. It rallied workers, intellectuals, and eventually peasants under the umbrella of a single organization, achieved the endorsement of the Catholic Church, which began to serve as an intermediary between government and opposition, and engaged in a strategy of self-limiting protest that divided the incumbent communist party elite sufficiently to hold off repression of the movement for fifteen months until December 1981.[4] The imposition of martial law terminated Solidarność's legal activities and showed the continued resistance of the communist apparatus to profound reform, backed by the Soviet Union's increasing pressure on Poland to stay within the bounds of communist rule. But at the same time, internal tensions within Solidarność and its inability to coordinate its members around a reform program to address Poland's economic crisis contributed to the demise of the first sustained effort to challenge the Polish communist regime. The rulers' victory, however, proved Pyrrhic. They managed to drive Solidarność into the underground temporarily but failed to craft a societal coalition that could enact profound political-economic reform capable of addressing the grievances Solidarność had articulated on behalf of the vast majority of Polish citizens.

In the mid-1980s, the party leadership began to realize that it would be impossible to overcome the societal stalemate without inclusion of the opposition. It lifted martial law, acquiesced to a de facto toleration of oppositional news media and associations, and initiated a broad debate on economic reform that pushed market liberalization into the center of political attention. By 1987–88, when Gorbachev's reforms in the Soviet Union had created an international climate conducive to domestic changes, the Polish communist party made one last effort to push through an economic reform program without securing support of the opposition forces. To test the popularity of this initiative, the party scheduled a national referendum, which revealed the feebleness of its public support. As a consequence, the government switched to a strategy of dialogue and cooperation with the formally still illegal opposition movement and the church. Negotiations with Solidarność leaders began in 1988 and led to an agreement on free, but semi-

---

[4]Our account is particularly influenced by the interpretations of the Solidarity movement in Touraine et al. (1982), Staniszkis (1984), Ost (1990), and Ekiert (1996: chaps. 8–10). We find Goodwin's (1991) claim that Solidarność constitutes an autonomous working-class struggle with little contribution of the intellectuals implausible.

competitive, constrained elections in which a minority of seats in the legislature was to be openly contested in spring 1989.[5] In these negotiations, Solidarność representatives concentrated their demands on a democratic political opening, whereas government technocrats called for bolder economic reforms than the Solidarity representatives were willing to underwrite, because they had not yet fully designed their own economic liberalization policy.

Because of the constrained nature and the early scheduling of the June 1989 parliamentary elections, no differentiated spectrum of parties contested the seats to the legislature. Although some opposition groups outside the framework of Solidarity, such as the Confederation for an Independent Poland (KPN), presented their own candidates the bulk of electoral support in all openly contested seats to the lower house of the parliament, the Sejm, as well as 99 out of 100 seats in the newly created upper house, the Senate, went to Solidarity's Citizens' Committee with Lech Walesa, an electoral alliance without party character whose candidates had been personally nominated by Solidarność's unquestioned leader, Lech Walesa. Nevertheless, within Solidarność and beyond, considerable ideological and programmatic diversity lurked just under the surface of the electoral umbrella organization. Solidarność leftists in the opposition to communist rule, for example, disagreed with a strategy of economic market liberalization they deemed "reform through ruin" (Gortat 1994: 144). These divisions set the stage for the disintegration of Solidarność in subsequent phases of the transition process.

HUNGARY

Like Poland, Hungary had a semi-authoritarian inter-war political regime that permitted party competition and universal suffrage but "managed" elections and conferred executive power on an unaccountable chief executive. In the 1930s and 1940s, Hungarian governments more or less unsuccessfully attempted to adopt techniques of political mobilization gleaned from the fascist model, including a brief interlude with a fascist puppet regime under Nazi tutelage late in World War II.[6] Socialist and communist forces in inter-war Hungary were weak because of government repression, but also the weak socio-economic anchoring of its support base and the policies of the party leaders. The industrial working class was mostly limited to Budapest. Yet the party failed to win the poor peasantry with its program of socialist agricultural collectivization. As a consequence, the Budapest Soviet Republic of 1919 was easily swept from power by the counter-revolutionary army when it failed to rally the poor peasantry to its cause.[7] Much later the communists' urban isolation and lack of societal entrenchment made

---

[5]Detailed accounts of the Polish liberalization can be found in Friszke (1990), Grzybowski (1994), Ost (1990), Walicki (1991), Wesolowski (1990), and Zubek (1991).

[6]For inter-war Hungary, see especially Janos (1982: chaps. 5, 6), Hajdú and Nagy (1990), Ormos (1990), and Tilkovszky (1990).

[7]Among many others, on the Hungarian revolution of 1919, see Kovrig (1979: chap. 2) and Janos (1982: chap. 4).

itself felt in the free elections of 1945 and the semi-free elections of 1947 when peasant and urban middle-class parties resoundingly beat the communist party, although the latter benefited from support by the Soviet High Command and already controlled the domestic police apparatus.[8]

As in Poland, Hungarian resistance to Stalinism in 1953–56 occurred against the backdrop of widespread popular experience with non-communist political mobilization. But because the critical showdown between Stalinist party and civic opposition in 1956 shook the communist regime much more profoundly than in Poland, the Hungarian "critical juncture" precipitated a different pathway toward tacit national accommodation (cf. Ekiert 1996: chap. 4). After a six-year period of intense repression in which Moscow-backed forces around János Kádár recreated the communist party apparatus essentially from scratch, in the early 1960s the rulers adopted a strategy of social consensus building by emphasizing economic liberalization and the satisfaction of consumer demands more than by tolerating spaces for political dissent. Political liberalization made headway only in the final period of accommodation in the 1980s when Hungary's increasing economic difficulties and foreign indebtedness undermined regime popularity and compelled the ruling elite to seek out new avenues to maintain the tacit accommodation between potential challengers in the opposition and the incumbent regime.

Similar to Poland, lengthy negotiations between government and incipient opposition forces preceded the decisive democratic opening. But here three differences to Poland facilitated the early formation of competing parties within the opposition movements. First, Hungary lacked the Solidarność experience of open, polarized confrontation with the communist leadership in the early 1980s that rallied opposition forces under a single umbrella and later delayed the formation of parties with coherent political appeals. Second, reformist politicians in the Hungarian party leadership around Imre Pozsgay nurtured and cultivated populist-national opposition forces from the mid-1980s onward and did everything to set them apart from liberal-democratic dissidents.[9] Finally, the timing of the Hungarian democratization in summer 1989 after the Polish communists' unambiguous defeat in the June 1989 semi-competitive Sejm elections convinced the Hungarian reform-minded communists to opt for completely open and democratic elections. This opportunity encouraged numerous cliques of political entrepreneurs to field their own parties rather than to support a single anti-communist alliance.

Already in September 1987, a humanistically educated intelligentsia primarily from small and medium-sized towns founded the Hungarian Democratic Forum (MDF) in the presence of Imre Pozsgay, the head of the communist party's

---

[8]The weakness of the domestic communist cadre organization when it emerged from clandestine activities after World War II certainly facilitated the takeover by the Muscovite party functionaries (cf. Kovrig 1979: 165–69).

[9]For an excellent account of the Hungarian opposition outside the communist party, see Tőkés (1996: 181–200).

Patriotic People's Front. Budapest intellectuals' circles instead gravitated toward the Alliance of Free Democrats (SzDSz), founded in November 1988 and a semi-legal critical student movement created the Alliance of Young Democrats (Fidesz). Moreover, various historical parties, such as the agrarian Independent Smallholders' Party (FKGP), the Christian Democratic People's Party (KDNP), the social democrats, and the Hungarian People's Party appeared in late 1988 and contested the first free elections of March 1990.

CZECHOSLOVAKIA

In contrast to Poland and Hungary, Czechoslovakia was a functioning liberal democracy in the inter-war period with a programmatically crystallized party system, configured around class, religious, and ethno-regional divisions with tightly organized, if not polarized, mass parties.[10] Whereas much of East Central Europe was an industrial backwater before 1945, Bohemia was in the heartland of early European industrialization from the nineteenth century onward. Moreover, the absence of an indigenous aristocracy since Habsburg's takeover in the seventeenth century facilitated democratization and land reform in 1919. In Hungarian-governed, predominantly rural Slovakia, by contrast, a different, less institutionalized party system developed after the founding of the Czechoslovak Republic.[11]

Most important for the comparison and contrast with other Central European countries is the continuous legality and electoral strength of socialist and communist parties in the Czechoslovak first republic until 1939. The social democrats attracted strong labor unions with a Marxist appeal (Mamatey 1973: 106), while the communists mobilized marginal rural labor and ethnic minorities, such as the Slovak Hungarians, making it the second strongest national party in 1925 (Suda 1980: 83–84). The party resisted Stalinization for a considerable period of time and then lost support when it finally succumbed to it in 1930. Later in the 1930s, it managed to bounce back and extend its influence into the urban working class when it adopted a patriotic, anti-fascist alliance strategy consistent with Comintern guidelines (Suda 1980: 151). Building on this track record, it emerged as the overall strongest party with 37.9 percent of the vote in the free and fair legislative election of 1946, garnering a greater vote share in the highly industrialized Czech lands than in predominantly rural Slovakia.[12]

[10]On inter-war democracy in Czechoslovakia, see Bankowicz and Dellenbrant (1988: 89–92), Krejci (1990: chaps. 6–7), and Rothschild (1974: 73–135).
[11]Slovakia's political divisions revolved around religion and national autonomy. In contrast to Czech democracy, Slovakia also produced a popular quasi-fascist movement, institutionalized in a German puppet state on the eve of World War II.
[12]The regional discrepancy is due not only to differences in social structure. Many new residents in areas of Bohemia from which ethnic Germans had been expelled in 1945 supported the communists as the guarantor that the Germans would not be permitted to return.

When the communist coup abolished liberal democracy in February 1948 and forced the socialist rump party into fusion with its dominant communist partner, the ruling elite could rely on a powerful, disciplined, and thoroughly indoctrinated working-class organization. Its organizational resources permitted the party to resist destalinization and suppress all stirrings of anti-communist opposition. Only when weak economic performance in the 1960s led economic technocrats to search for more efficient governance structures, an effort ultimately spearheaded by a new party leadership in early 1968, could a principled political opposition take advantage of the opening and precipitate the Czechoslovak "spring without summer." After the Soviet occupation of August 1968 suppressed these forces, communist traditionalists inimical to any association with dissidents reasserted themselves. A range of liberal-democratic opposition groups, most notably Charta 77, mushroomed underneath the surface of a tight, repressive communist regime, but they had to wait until international circumstances were sufficiently favorable to hasten the sudden collapse of the existing power structure in November 1989. While the bureaucratic-authoritarian communist regime produced an economic planning technocracy that was definitely not involved in overt opposition activities, this technocracy rapidly defected when the end of communist rule was in sight. Its cadres facilitated Czechoslovakia's quick cross-over to a liberal democracy.[13]

Triggered by the sudden collapse of the communist regime in the German Democratic Republic and the opening of the Berlin Wall on November 9, 1989, student demonstrations in Prague on November 17 initiated a short wave of intensifying public protests. A general strike then brought the Czechoslovak ruling party to its knees. Within a month, the leading literary figure within the Czech human rights movement, Václav Havel, was elected president and the old party elites had departed from power. When the all but unprepared opposition leadership took over the helm of government, it retained second-tier communist administrator-technocrats, such as the new prime minister, Marian Calfa, who resigned from the ruling party in early November 1989. Calfa formed a caretaker government until the election of June 1990 and then was reconfirmed by the new democratic federal parliament until the election of June 1992.

With no pre-existing proto-parties on the scene after the sudden collapse of the communist regime, political support initially congealed around broad anti-communist electoral alliances that emphasized civil rights and democratic reforms in the Czech and Slovak republics, the Civic Forum in the Czech Republic and Public against Violence in Slovakia. In this situation, the anti-communist um-

---

[13]Our analysis agrees with Linz and Stepan's (1996: 322–23) characterization of the Czechoslovak transition as collapse. Like them, we believe that the conception of regime collapse needs further analytical work. But rather than focusing on the defection of the coercive apparatus from the communist regime in its final days (p. 322), we emphasize the bureaucratic-authoritarian technocracy. Not by accident, many leading members of the post-1992 governing parties, including the Czech prime minister, come from the relatively non-political, if not anti-political, technocratic stratum of the old regime.

brellas emphasized the personal qualities of their leaders and indulged in anti-party slogans ("Parties are for party men, Civic Forum is for everyone"). Neverthe-less, already in 1990 surveys reveal that a larger majority of Czechs and Slovaks believed that parties are essential for the democratic process than did respondents in Hungary or Poland (Brokl and Mansfeldova 1992: 185–86). Opting for an anti-communist anti-party organization was only a stopgap measure due to the circumstances of the transition.

BULGARIA

Before World War II, Bulgaria was an agrarian society with an urban intel-ligentsia and middle class small even by Central European standards. The country experienced only one short episode of democracy from 1918 to 1923, which ended in a bloody coup of right-wing military forces, endorsed by the tsar, that termi-nated the elected government of the radical peasant party, which itself had become increasingly authoritarian.[14] Since liberation from Turkish rule in 1876–78, Bulgaria had been a monarchy with a liberal constitutional veneer, but the de facto rule of strongmen or urban cliques configured around volatile, personalist parties that treated the weak, non-professional bureaucracy as their patronage turf (Crampton 1987: 40). In 1923, after the radical agrarian interlude, Bulgaria reverted first to a semi-constitutional authoritarianism without entrenched par-ties and then, until Soviet occupation in 1944–45, to one-man rule by the Bulgarian tsar after an army coup in 1934.

After World War I, the Bulgarian communist party emerged from a sectarian fringe organization as the second largest party behind the peasant party. For want of an industrial working class and of rural support, the communists relied on the urban public sector, primarily the postal and railroad employees. After a commu-nist insurrection in late 1923, the party had been confined to clandestine activities except during a brief interlude in the early 1930s. Between 1941 and 1944, the party staged an armed resistance against the Bulgarian government, then allied to Nazi Germany. Because the party's resistance fighters were all but wiped out, the victorious Russian troops could install a communist party leadership of Moscow émigrés headed by Georgi Dimitrov. The communist party quickly suffocated contending parties and liquidated their most important leaders. It then went on to conduct internal purges that peaked in 1949.[15]

In the 1950s, the Bulgarian communists were a thoroughly stalinized party without episodes of regime liberalization (Bankowicz 1994b). This changed little with the stepwise displacement of Bulgaria's "little Stalin," Vulko Chervenkov, by Todor Zhivkov between 1956 and 1962. The stability of Bulgarian communist

---

[14]On the peasant government, see Bell (1977) and Oren (1973: 5–42). On Bulgarian history since liberation from the Ottoman overlordship in general, compare Crampton (1987), Jelavich and Jelavich (1977: 128–40, 158–69, 192–96), and MacDermott (1962).

[15]On the history of Bulgaria's communists, see especially Bell (1986) and Oren (1973).

rule is symbolized by Zhivkov's long incumbency at the party's helm from 1956 until November 1989. In that time period, the communist party oversaw the transformation of Bulgaria from a peasant to an industrial society, a process accompanied by impressive economic growth and improvements in the national living standard. Because Bulgaria lacked significant indigenous "bourgeois" experiences of democratic political participation before 1945 and created a broader intelligentsia only under communist rule, the regime faced little opposition and could easily repress or co-opt emerging challengers. The only reform effort was led by Zhivkov's daughter Ludmilla whom he groomed as his successor in the late 1970s. With her premature death, however, her reformist entourage faded from the inner political circle.

Because of Russia's involvement in the Bulgarians' liberation from the Turks in the nineteenth century and the Nazi dictatorship in the twentieth century, Bulgarians in general and communists in particular looked toward Russia for leadership. Gorbachev's policies therefore left a faint echo even within the closed Bulgarian political elite, yet prompted only timid reforms. A liberalization of the Bulgarian election law in 1988 led to a small proportion of constituencies with multi-candidate elections (Ashley 1990: 312). In early 1989, some lonely reformists in the communist party began to organize a "Club for Glasnost and Perestroika." In the same year, others made modest efforts to found a Bulgarian human rights committee, to mobilize ecologists against nuclear power and pollution, and to protect the Turkish minority against the ethnic-nationalist propaganda of the Bulgarian Communist Party (BCP). Dissidents also founded an independent labor union, Podkrepa ("support"), reminiscent of Poland's Solidarity. But the regime subjected the various dissident organizers to arrests and repressive harassment that made participation exceedingly costly. The key characteristic of the Bulgarian liberalization process is therefore the absence of a sophisticated dissident elite and of protest traditions that would have given challengers the necessary experience to confront the communist party effectively in 1989–90 (Karasimeonov 1992; 1994).

Given this international and domestic setting, decisive political change could come only from within the party elite in the late 1980s. Internal dissatisfaction of BCP leaders with Zhivkov's efforts to impose his own son as his successor led sitting foreign minister Petur Mladenov to stage a well-prepared coup with consent of the Bulgarian military leadership, ousting Zhivkov from office on the day after the Berlin Wall came down. Although Mladenov initially sought to limit the liberalization of the communist regime, mass demonstrations of largely unorganized protestors in December 1989 forced the new rulers to accept round table discussions, but under rather different terms than in Hungary or Poland. In Bulgaria, it was clear that the newly renamed Bulgarian Socialist Party (BSP) was the dominant force at the table. The first round of discussions in January and February 1990 ended without agreement and the opposition resorted to public disruptive protests to make its voice heard. Negotiations were resumed in March and yielded an agreement on early elections in June 1990.

The political liberalization of winter 1989–90 triggered a proliferation of new parties and political clubs, but with initially little capacity to bundle electoral constituencies under the roof of any single association. Historical parties that existed intermittently during the pre–World War II regimes began to organize again, such as the social democrats, the democrats, the radical democrats, and various peasant parties. In addition, human rights groups, ecologists, and associations defending the Turkish minority appeared on the political scene. Recognizing political fragmentation as a weakness when dealing with the BSP behemoth, most opposition groups agreed to join an umbrella organization, the Union of Democratic Forces (SDS), yet without relinquishing their organizational autonomy. In contrast to Central European countries, in Bulgaria the communist successor party won the founding election based on strong support in the countryside, an inexperienced and divisive opposition alliance, and at least minor electoral fraud. It then formed a new government with cabinet members entirely drawn from its own ranks.

PARTY FORMATION AND CONSTITUTIONAL BARGAINING

We discussed in chapter 1 that the design of democratic institutions is to a considerable extent endogenous to the type of communist rule and the bargaining situation among self-interested political actors in the transitions process. With regard to electoral laws and executive-legislative designs, bureaucratic-authoritarian communism followed by an implosion of the old regime thus is likely to produce proportional representation within a parliamentary democracy, national-accommodative communism with negotiated transitions is more likely to yield "mixed" electoral laws with plurality and personality representation and a significant presidential authority in the democratic process, and finally patrimonial communism with preemptive reform is likely to result in candidate-centered electoral laws and strong executive and legislative presidential authority. In our brief sketch of constitutional design in the four East Central European countries, we will focus on developments that *diverge* from this simple logic and can be accounted for only in narrative terms due to timing and sequence and the contingent fortunes of critical actors.

POLAND

Poland's negotiated transition embarked on democratization at a time when it was not yet clear that the Soviet Union would relinquish its grip on the former satellite countries. Here the Solidarność opposition accepted the dominant role of the communist party for a limited number of years in order to protect the country from Soviet intervention and to bring about a gradual transition. Hence, the ruling party could put its stamp on the temporary electoral law and the executive parliamentary relations hammered out in the spring 1989 round table discussions. The participants agreed to create a strong, but indirectly parliament-elected presidency with powers to dissolve the legislature, to veto legislation with a two-thirds override requirement for both houses of parliament, and executive jurisdiction over defense and foreign policy cabinet appointments. Parliamentary elections in June 1989 allocated only a third of the lower-house seats by open competition in single-member constituencies. Ballots indicated only candidates' names, not party affiliations. Thus the ruling party successfully insisted on a personalization of the democratic process – presidentialism plus personalized legislative elections – and made only the concession to create an upper house of parliament, the Senate, that would be freely elected with a double-member district system, again featuring candidates more than parties. In accordance with these rules, the incumbent communist party ran a campaign around personalities rather than programmatic issues.[16] The Polish rulers, however, just as their Hungarian counter-parts later on, completely miscalculated their own party's performance and, as a consequence, lost just about all the seats that were openly contested.[17]

With the decomposition of both the ruling party and of Solidarność's legislative caucus between 1989 and 1993, Poland went through two further rounds of negotiation about the electoral system. In the fragmented party system of 1990 and 1991 where no individual actor could hope to benefit from plurality voting rules, most legislators favored and adopted a system of list proportional representation with minor advantages to large parties (Holzer 1992: 14; Rapaczynski 1991: 606). When these rules produced an extremely fragmented legislature that was unable to bring about government stability, in 1993 most legislators supported an electoral reform establishing among other stipulations a national 5 percent threshold of legislative representation and an allocation of seats according to multi-member districts with personal preference votes.[18] Ironically, in the 1993 parliamentary election, this law eliminated several post-Solidarność parties from legislative representation that had strongly supported it.

The erosion of communist party rule prompted the resignation of the sitting communist president, General Wojciech Jaruzelski, in 1990. Lacking viable party organizations and programmatic cohesiveness, not only Solidarność's

[16]Barany and Vinton (1990: 197) write: "The political establishment designed its election campaign to blur the distinction between official candidates and those of Solidarity. The official campaign was perversely apolitical, with the communist party choosing candidates familiar to the public, but for reasons other than political involvement, and emphasizing their personalities rather than their convictions or political experience."

[17]Wesołowski (1990: 440–41) concludes: "This [electoral system] set up was intended to enable the Communist Party to hold power and the opposition to express criticism. But the negotiated balance of power was destroyed by the electors who decided not to ratify the pact."

[18]Further safeguards against fragmentation were that only parties larger than 7 percent of the national vote would be entitled to participate in the distribution of a national tier of legislative seats. Furthermore, coalitions of two independent parties would have to top 8 percent of the national vote to qualify for any seats.

charismatic leader but also his then rival, the sitting prime minister Tadeusz Mazowiecki, endorsed a further strengthening of the presidential office through direct elections. But after Walesa's election in December 1990 and with the gradual crystallization of party alternatives, constitutional bargaining over the so-called Little Constitution 1992 and the final constitution in 1997 inched the outcome closer to what the simple bargaining theory expects after national-accommodative communism. The dominant parties in the legislature managed to whittle away presidential powers gradually, benefiting the prime minister and cabinet members, who are accountable to parliament. In 1992, the president lost the right to appoint or dismiss the prime minister and to dissolve parliament, except in narrowly defined circumstances. In 1997, the presidency also lost the prerogative to appoint the "power ministries" (foreign affairs, defense, interior) and saw its veto powers in the legislative process diluted from a two-thirds to a still respectable three-fifths legislative override in both houses of parliament.

While President Walesa before 1992 and even under the Little Constitution had considerable capacity to affect the legislative decision-making process and to undermine the stability of cabinet government, with the consequence of weakening the formation of cohesive parties, his successor Alexander Kwasniewski had fewer options at his disposal after the passage of the 1997 constitution. Although the consolidation of the party system tended to sideline the sitting president, the 1989 status quo of relatively strong presidential powers made it impossible for the parties to move to a fully parliamentary system. Thus, timing and sequence, in inter-action with a regime-based path dependency, made Poland end up with a by and large parliamentary democracy that still incorporates distinctive presidential power in the legislative process.

HUNGARY

In the round table negotiations between ruling party and a cartel of opposition groups in summer of 1989 and the ensuing seven months until the first parliamentary election of March–April 1990, the relations among the various parties changed considerably.[19] In summer of 1989, after the defeat of the Polish ruling party in a semi-open election, the ruling Hungarian Socialist Workers' Party opted for full democratic competition to boost its election chances. Moreover, it advocated a personalist electoral contest featuring a choice of 75 percent of all legislators through first-past-the-post (FPTP) single-member plurality elections and the remainder based on proportional representation. As opinion polls and by-elections lowered the communist negotiators' electoral expectations, the party eventually agreed with the opposition to an exceedingly complicated mixed

---

[19]For a detailed account of the pre-history and the process of the negotiated opening in Hungary, see Bozóki (1988; 1990; 1993), Bruszt (1990), Bruszt and Stark (1991), Jenkins (1992), Márkus (1994), Rácz (1991), Schöpflin (1991), and, most recently, the detailed study by Tökés (1996: 305–98).

system in which a little less than half of 386 parliamentary seats are allocated by a majoritarian runoff system among three top contenders in the first round of voting and the remainder by regional and national party lists initially subject to a 4 percent minimum threshold of national party support that was elevated to 5 percent in 1994.[20] With hindsight, the socialists as well as most of their competitors, except the Hungarian Democratic Forum (MDF), would have received more legislative representation and greater bargaining power over government, had they agreed to a straight closed-list proportional representation system. But the timing of the negotiations in 1989 and the false image of electoral momentum communist negotiators attributed to their own party, even as the party's popular support in opinion polls fell below the 30 percent mark, shaped the bargaining outcome. None of the parties foresaw that the law would deliver legislative hegemony to the MDF in the first legislative period and to the social democratically restyled former communists in the subsequent term.

In 1989, the incumbent socialists also preferred a strong executive presidency, which they expected to fill with Imre Pozsgay, the popular reformer from their own ranks. While some opposition parties accepted early presidential elections, the socialists underestimated the strength and mobilizing capacity of the liberal-democratic opposition forces who preferred early parliamentary elections and a weak presidency. The Alliance of Free Democrats (SzDSz) and the Alliance of Young Democrats (Fidesz) successfully mobilized for a referendum in December 1989 that rejected the compromise formula, postponed presidential elections, and established a parliamentary democracy in Hungary. After the parliamentary elections of spring 1990, the MDF and the SzDSz agreed on a presidential office with preciously little formal political power. The incoming president, the writer Arpad Göncz whom the SzDSz had nominated, has been mostly confined to ceremonial tasks, but did intervene in several bitter controversies to test the constitutional bounds of presidential authority.[21]

By combining a mixed personalist-proportional electoral system and a weak presidency, the outcome of the Hungarian bargaining process over critical rules of the democratic game are thus consistent with expectations based on a path-dependency model predicting rules as endogenous to the national-accommodative communist regime. Only presidential power may have turned out somewhat weaker than the endogeneity model would have suggested.

CZECH REPUBLIC

Consistent with the bargaining powers of the critical actors emerging from bureaucratic-authoritarian communism, the Czech Republic adopted a uniformly depersonalizing system of democratic rules with closed list proportional represen-

---

[20]Detailed analyses of the choice of the Hungarian electoral law can be found in Hibbing and Patterson (1992), Kukorelli (1991), and Racz (1991).

[21]As Baylis (1996: 320) points out, in Hungary and elsewhere presidents have tried to stand up to "reckless populism" and efforts to undermine democratic fairness.

tation and a weak presidency. The intransigent communist party had no bargaining power and was in any case too unpopular to hope for gains through a strong presidency or majoritarian electoral laws. Given the great uncertainty about the identity and strength of political parties, it was easy for the broad spectrum of non-communist liberal-democratic, Christian, or regionalist politicians to settle on an electoral system with list proportional representation but a rather tough threshold of parliamentary representation (5 percent in the Czech or Slovak republics), together with an indirectly elected, ceremonial presidency.[22]

The major challenge to the new rules came from newly elected president Václav Havel. Lacking a powerful party organization behind him and deeply inspired by an anti-party conception of democracy, Havel repeatedly brought his considerable prestige to bear on proposals for constitutional changes that would have strengthened presidential authority and personalized electoral contests for the legislature.[23] The legislative parties, however, all but unanimously rejected his bid for more presidential powers. His call for a majoritarian electoral system was seconded by the largest party in government, Václav Klaus's Civic Democratic Forum (ODS), but did not resonate well with the other coalition partners. Also the breakup of Czechoslovakia in the aftermath of the 1992 election left the basic institutional principles of the new democracy untouched.

BULGARIA

Although the successor to the Bulgarian communist party, the BSP, was the dominant actor during the transition and emerged as the winner of the first free elections, Bulgaria did not, like other formerly patrimonial communist polities, adopt a personalist electoral law and a powerful directly elected presidency.[24] The BSP's initial bargaining stance called for such arrangements, but contingent events forced the party to abandon its initial preferences and settle for a democratic design that contradicts the path-dependency prediction.

With regard to the electoral law, two considerations led the BSP to accept a mixed system of multi-member district proportional representation with a 4 percent threshold and single-member district majoritarian representation to elect the grand constitutional assembly in June 1990. First, public demonstrations and riots of opposition supporters in the capital made BSP negotiators willing to

[22]This electoral law was passed, although many experts involved in the negotiation process had preferred either a mixed electoral system or straight FPTP to preempt the extreme multi-partyism that had characterized the first Czechoslovak republic.

[23]Havel wanted stronger powers to dismiss parliament, a direct popular election of the president, and greater emergency decree powers (cf. Cutler and Schwartz 1991: 544–52).

[24]Many other polities emerging from patrimonial communism in fact confirm this expectation. Among those which have a relatively high level of civic and political rights and thus approach democratic rule are Moldava, Romania, Russia, and the Ukraine. We do not count the Eurasian republics, all of which have strong presidencies, because here democratic competition is nothing but a thin veneer disguising authoritarian rule.

compromise with the still weakly organized opposition. Second, these conflicts also made BSP politicians aware of the fact that it would completely delegitimize elections, if a majoritarian electoral law led to an overwhelming majority of former communists in the parliament. Later on, as BSP support began to erode after the first election, pure short-term self-interest motivated BSP negotiators to agree to a straightforward system of closed-list, multi-member district proportional representation with a 4 percent cutoff of representation that would advantage a multiple of larger parties but deprive small splinter parties of representation. This rule was agreeable to the main opposition force, SDS, because it would keep the constant stream of small groups of defectors from the alliance powerless and outside parliament.

In a similar vein, historical events also forced the BSP to abandon its initial stance on executive-legislative powers. When it became known that its hitherto popular communist leader, Petur Mladenov, whom parliament had elected president in early 1990, had called for sending out tanks against anti-communist demonstrators in December 1989, Mladenov had to resign and the BSP agreed to elect a renowned literary and democratic opposition personality, Zhelu Zhelev, to the presidency. In return, the BSP now pushed for weak presidential powers. The presidency was made a popularly elected office but essentially confined to ceremonial tasks.[25] Thus, by 1992 Bulgaria ended up with rules of the democratic game one would rather expect in formerly bureaucratic-authoritarian or national-accommodative communist polities, were it not for short-term conjunctural factors that made rational politicians seek different arrangements. Within the group of formerly patrimonial communist countries, Bulgaria is the most glaring case in which a structuralist-plus-rational choice logic of path dependency alone cannot account for key elements of the constitutional compact.

THE ITERATION OF THE ELECTORAL GAME AND THE SHAKEOUT PARTIES

With the iteration of the democratic electoral game, many early parties at the time of regime change disappeared from the political scene. On the one hand, selective attention to politicians in the media, primarily to those participating in legislatures and executives, let many contenders that failed to win parliamentary seats fade into the background. Politicians with similar appeals and linkage strategies to electoral constituencies then teamed up under the umbrella of the same party label. On the other, many political entrepreneurs discovered that they are not cut out for the tough world of democratic competitive politics Max Weber likened to the "tenacious boring of hard boards." Intellectuals particularly are often given to abstract, discursive, and complex reasoning that yields propositions

---

[25]On the Bulgarian design of democratic competition, see Ashley (1990), Höpken (1990), and Hoppe (1991).

its authors consider indubitable truths. Because such reasoning is hard to com-municate to large audiences and undercuts a favorable disposition toward political bargaining and compromise, intellectuals often turned away from the routines of legislative politics, the challenges of party building, and the myriad of mundane distributive struggles over economic reform, such as the budget process, that a new post-communist competitive democracy involves. Professional politicians with organizational tenacity and willingness to compromise in the pursuit of political office displace intellectuals on the political center stage (Agh 1994). Because our detailed empirical analysis probes the extent to which political legacies and new democratic rules shape the configuration of competing parties, in the current chapter we now introduce our four countries' democratic politics by providing only a simple chronological sketch of the relevant parties and their electoral careers during the first six to eight years of democratic competition. Our surveys among politicians and voters took place in 1993–94. Our brief overview thus permits us to situate the moment of data collection within the longer stretch of party system development in each country.

POLAND

Poland democratized first, still under the shadow of the Brezhnev Doctrine, but trailed Hungary and the Czech Republic in terms of party system formation because with Solidarność the country had an encompassing anti-communist um-brella organization that only gradually began to unravel and spawn individual parties. This process accelerated in the course of the year 1990. Many participants in the Solidarność movement rejected the formation of parties (Lewis 1994: 785–90), but the iterative game of party competition compelled movement entrepre-neurs to focus on the electoral and legislative arena.

The progressive dissolution of Solidarność began within twelve months after the free but restricted parliamentary election of June 1989, after which the Solidarity electoral list formed a majority coalition headed by prime minister Tadeusz Mazowiecki, supported by the former minor agrarian and middle-class bloc parties subordinated to the ruling Polish Socialist Workers' Party. By November 1990, Solidarity's Civic Parliamentary Caucus (OKP) had divided into no fewer than nine components, many of which revolved around individual political entrepreneurs who attempted to found their own personal parties (Gebethner 1991: 244–45). And two former Solidarność colleagues became bitter rivals in the struggle for the presidency that sitting communist president Wo-jciech Jaruzelski offered to vacate – Mazowiecki and Lech Walesa, the charismatic leader of the Solidarność movement and ultimate winner of the presidency.

As a consequence of Solidarność's disintegration and of the new proportional representation election law, the first fully free legislative election of 1991 yielded a highly fragmented party spectrum and legislature (see table 3.1). Nevertheless, the subsequent mutation of the Polish party system reveals three "blocs" or "sectors" of political forces around which politicians orbit. The first sector consists

Table 3.1. *Elections in Poland*

	November 1990 presidential election: Votes, first round	October 1991 legislative election		September 1993 legislative election		September 1997 legislative election	
		Votes %	Seats	Votes %	Seats	Votes %	Seats
Post-communist and other left parties							
Alliance of the Democratic Left (SLD)/ Social Democracy of the Polish Republic (SdRP)	Wlodzimierz Cimosczewicz, 9.2%	11.98	60	20.41	171	27.13	164
Polish Peasant Party (PSL)	Roman Bartoszcze, 7.2%	8.67	48	15.40	132	7.31	27
Union of Labor (UP)		2.05	4	7.28	41	4.74	0
Liberal democrats							
Democratic Union (UD)	Tadeusz Mazowiecki, 18.1%	12.31	62	10.59	74		
Liberal Democratic Congress (KLD)		7.48	37	3.99	0		
Beer Lovers' Party (PPPP)		3.27	13	—	—		
Freedom Union (UW)		—		—	—	13.37	60

Christian nationals and conservatives							
Christian National Union/Fatherland (ZChN)	Lech Walesa, 40.0%	9.84	53	6.38	0		
Center Alliance (PC)		8.71	44	4.42	0		
Solidarity (NZSS "S")		5.05	27	4.90	0		
Non-Party Bloc to Support Reforms (BBWR)		—	—	5.41	16		
Coalition for the Republic (KdR)		—	—	2.70	0		
Peasant Alliance (PL)		5.50	28	2.30	0		
Solidarity Election Action (AWS)		—	—	—	—	33.83	201
Movement for the Reconstruction of Poland (ROP)		—	—	—	—	5.56	6
Nationalists and others							
Confederation of Independent Poland (KPN)	Leszek Moczulski, 2.5%	8.58	46	5.77	22		
Party X	Stanislaw Tyminski, 23.1%	0.47	0	2.74	0		
Union of Real Politics (UPR)		2.25	3	3.18	0		
League of Self-Defense (Samoobroma)		—	—	2.78	0		
Pensioners' Parties		—	—	1.75	0		
Other	2.18, 1.63	13.84	35	9.81	0	4.30	2
Effective number of parties		14.69	10.93	9.81	3.87	4.60	2.95

of successor organizations of the old regime, the post-communist Social Democracy of the Polish Republic (SdRP) with its support organizations in the Alliance of the Democratic Left (SLD) and the Polish Peasant Party (PSL), but also one splinter of the Solidarność movement, the Union of Labor (UP). Overall, this sector grew from 21 percent of the vote in 1991 to 43 percent in 1993 and slightly declined to 39 percent in the 1997 election. Within this sector, however, votes increasingly concentrate on the SLD/SdRP electoral list, particularly after its candidate Aleksander Kwasniewski won the presidential office in 1995. Internally the SLD alliance is divided, however, between the All-Polish Trade Union Alliance (OPZZ), the former official communist union that now insists on strict social protectionist policies, and the SdRP leadership with a predominantly more technocratic and liberal approach.[26] SLD and PSL furnished the cabinet supported by majority legislative coalitions from 1993 to 1997 under several prime ministers. These governments became possible because the PSL had made a big comeback in 1993, but its patronage-oriented policies alienated many voters most of whom defected to the SLD in the 1997 legislative election.

The second party sector includes the two post-Solidarność parties, Democratic Union (UD) and Liberal Democratic Congress (KLD), that merged into a single organization shortly after our 1994 survey, since then called Freedom Union (UW). Also the Beer Lovers' Party (PPPP) of 1991 was in the orbit of this constellation before it disappeared from the scene. UW and its predecessors have maintained rather loose party organizations with distinct market-liberal, social-liberal, and Christian Democratic wings. The fortunes of this sector have declined from roughly 23 percent in 1991 to 13.5 percent in 1997, but the concentration of votes on a single party, led by the finance minister of the 1989–90 Mazowiecki government, Leszek Balcerowicz, have increased this bloc's bargaining power.

The third sector, whose members roughly subscribe to Christian-national symbols, is the most complex and changing sector of Polish politics. Here we encounter most of Solidarność's fission products that divided and recombined in different ways in the 1991, 1993, and 1997 parliamentary elections and the 1995 presidential race. Overall, the electoral size of this sector varies between 27 percent (1993) and 34 percent (1997). The electoral defeat of the constituent parties within this sector both in the 1993 legislative election and then again in the 1995 presidential election, when in addition to Walesa at least three other presidential candidates originated from the Christian-national political segment later in 1996–97, enabled the leader of the Solidarność union, Marian Krzaklewski, to craft a broad alliance named Solidarity Election Action (AWS). After the alliance's victory, Krzaklewski began to convert it into a single centralized party. Later chapters identify and discuss the obstacles the new leader must overcome on the path to reaching this objective. At the time of our survey in 1993–94, the most important constituents of the Christian-national sector were the Christian National Union (ZChN), the Center Alliance (PC), the electoral list

[26]For divisions in the SLD, see Zubek (1995).

Solidarity (NZSS 'S'), and the Non-Party Bloc to Support Reforms (BBWR). Essentially most of the politicians belonging to these parties, and some of the nationalists from the Confederation of Independent Poland (KPN), joined the AWS in 1997.

After coalitions led by liberal democrats Mazowiecki (UD) and Jan Kristof Bielecki (KLD), the Christian national bloc furnished two prime ministers of weak coalition governments in 1992 and 1993, Jan Olszewski and Hanna Suchocka. The internal divisions in this party sector, as well as the perpetual conflicts between the cabinet and the sitting president, Lech Walesa, contributed to the demise of these parties in 1993. After his stint as prime minister, Olszewski moved increasingly into the nationalist bloc and founded the Movement for the Reconstruction of Poland (ROP). In 1997, ROP may have benefited from the disappearance of the major anchor party of nationalist politics, the KPN.

In addition to these major parties, in 1990 a vaguely populist-nationalist maverick candidate, Stanislaw Tyminski, received more than one-fifth of the popular vote in the first round of the presidential elections, but the Party X he subsequently founded remained marginal. Another marginal populist-nationalist appeal, particularly in the countryside, developed around the League of Self-Defense (Samoobrona) under Andrzej Lepper who received only 1.3 percent in the 1995 presidential elections. Support for Party X and the league may indicate citizens' alienation from mainstream politics more than a distinctive political demand pattern.

Overall, in the evolution of Polish parties we observe a consolidation of alternatives around a handful of electorally attractive parties. A commonly used index measuring the "effective" number of parties at the electoral level and in the legislature captures this movement quantitatively. This value represents the inverse of the summed squares of the fraction of votes (seats) each party receives in an election (in parliament).[27] At the electoral level, party system fragmentation in Poland fell from an effective party index of 14.69 in 1992, extraordinarily high by international standards, to no more than 4.60 by 1997 (table 3.1). Legislative fragmentation also dropped steeply from 10.93 in 1991 to no more than 2.95 in 1997, a rather modest value by international comparison standards.

HUNGARY

Due to its negotiated political opening and the absence of a strong anti-communist umbrella organization, Hungarian parties began to form early before the first free election in April 1990. Moreover, in contrast to Poland, only those Hungarian parties gained legislative representation in subsequent democratic

[27]To take a simple example, if two parties receive 50 percent of the vote, the index value is calculated as

$$\frac{1}{.50^2 + .50^2} = \frac{1}{.50} = 2.0.$$

election of 1994 and 1998 that had already won seats in 1990. In terms of political sectors, however, the various streams of party development in the Hungarian system are quite similar to what we have already observed in Poland.

First, there is a post-communist political sector, which, by contrast to Poland, does not include a strong peasant party, but from 1990 on has been dominated by the reformist successor to the ruling Socialist Workers' Party, the Hungarian Socialist Party (MSzP). After an initial defeat in the 1990 election, it made a strong comeback in 1994 that was sustained in 1998 (see table 3.2). The MSzP is outflanked by a more orthodox communist splinter group that has run under the label of Workers' Party (MP) since 1994 but has remained marginal in the electoral arena.

Second, like Poland, Hungary has a liberal-democratic stream of political parties, initially consisting of the SzDSz and the Fidesz. As a result of Fidesz's electoral defeat in 1994 and of the SzDSz's decision to join a coalition government with the MSzP, Fidesz moved away from the liberal sector and increasingly began to attract the former voters of the Christian-national-populist party sector. This strategic change is reflected in the new name of the party, Fidesz-Hungarian Civic Party. Taking these changes into account, electoral support for the liberal sector fell from over 30 percent in 1990 and 27 percent in 1994 to a much smaller share for the SzDSz in 1998. The decline of the liberal party sector primarily benefited the post-communist MSzP, but also some of the other parties.

Third, the Christian-national party sector has undergone more turmoil and internal divisions and fusions than other sectors in Hungary, just as in Poland. While the MDF emerged as the bloc's strongest party in 1990, promising a policy of incremental reform, it remained only slightly ahead of its intra-bloc competitors in the 1994 election and then disintegrated in the subsequent electoral term, together with the KDNP. Many of MDF's and KDNP's politicians and electoral supporters joined Fidesz, which experienced a strong upswing of electoral support. Others benefited the political fortunes of the Independent Smallholders' Party (FKGP) with a more nationalist and social protectionist rhetoric. In the hands of its autocratic leader, Jozsef Torgyán, this party survived a severe crisis when most of its sitting legislators challenged the leadership in the 1990–94 term and eventually fielded a new party unsuccessfully. The continued electoral success of the FKGP is likely to have held a surge of other nationalist parties at bay, such as the Party of Hungarian Justice and Life (MIEP), a militant nationalist offshoot of the MDF that nevertheless attracted a critical mass of supporters after the demise of the MDF in 1998. Both Fidesz and FKGP also benefited from the dissolution of another party in the Christian national sector, the small Christian democrats (KDNP), who lost their place between the grindstones of its two competitors within the same sector.

Divisions between moderates and national-populist politicians inside the Christian national parties, particularly the MDF, in the years prior to the 1994 legislative election made the socialist party the major beneficiary at the polls. Under these circumstances, a low-key campaign with muted rhetoric was suffi-

Table 3.2. *Elections in Hungary*

	March–April 1990		May 1994		May 1998	
	Votes %	Seats	Votes %	Seats	Votes %	Seats
Hungarian Socialist Party (MSzP)	10.89	33	32.96	209	32.3	135
Hungarian Socialist Workers' Party/Workers' Party (MP)	3.68	0	3.18	0	4.1	0
Agrarian Alliance	3.13	0	2.10	1		
Alliance of Free Democrats (SzDSz)	21.39	93	19.76	70	7.9	24
Alliance of Young Democrats (Fidesz) (1998: Fidesz-Hungarian Civic Party)	8.95	22	7.00	20	28.2	148
Hungarian Democratic Forum (MDF)	24.73	165	11.73	37	3.4	17
Christian Democratic People's Party (KDNP)	6.46	21	7.06	22	2.1	0
Independent Smallholders' Party (FKGP)	11.73	44	8.85	26	13.8	48
Party of Hungarian Justice and Life (MIEP)	—	—	1.58	0	5.6	14
Other parties	9.03	0	5.78	0	2.6	0
Effective number of parties	6.76	3.74	5.54	2.89	4.63	3.42

cient to win the election. The relatively united appearance the MSzP was able to create before the May 1994 election should not let us overlook the deep divisions between labor-union wing and party technocracy that initially marred the MSzP's rule after 1994 until the economy began to recover remarkably in 1997–98 as a consequence of economic austerity policies adopted in 1995. In this regard, the MSzP's coalition with the SzDSz after the former's 1994 election victory served the purpose to bind the party leadership's hand and blame the early negative effects of economic austerity policies on the liberal coalition partner, when opposition from the social-protectionist wing arose within the MSzP. Beyond that, the coalition broadened the government's popular support base in two critical respects. The MSzP had won a parliamentary majority of 52 percent of the seats based on only 33 percent of the vote. In order to preempt extra-institutional protest, an oversized, inclusive coalition government therefore became imperative to establish the legitimacy of the executive. A coalition with the SzDSz as an organization of former anti-communist dissidents was also likely to strengthen the MSzP's image as a reliable democratic force.

Hungary, like Poland, combines volatility and stability in its emerging party system. The post-communist left has made a dramatic recovery since 1990, while the market-liberal and culturally libertarian forces have declined electorally and legislatively; the Christian-national sector underwent sharp decline in 1994 and equally sharp resurgence in 1998. Nevertheless, our index of effective parties shows that also in Hungary these changes have been accompanied by an overall drop in the electoral and legislative fragmentation of the party system.

CZECH REPUBLIC

The Czech party system develops in rather different fashion than in Hungary or Poland. First of all, the main communist successor party, the Communist Party of Bohemia and Moravia (KSCM) was electorally defeated in 1992, but never made a comeback thereafter. Various efforts by reformist leaders to take over the apparatus failed and the resulting splinter parties quickly vanished. At the same time, the KSCM held on to a large organizational base amounting to at least 350,000 members as late as 1992, whereas the corresponding communist successor parties in Hungary and Poland shrank to a few tens of thousands of members in the same time period (Kopecky 1993). Because the KSCM lacked an innovative leadership that could have overcome the conservatism of its mass apparatus and adapt to the democratic polity, the main beneficiary of growing disenchantment with economic reform in the mid-1990s was the Czech Social Democratic Party (CSSD). It emerged as the most popular opposition party before the 1996 election due to its endorsement of liberal democracy with social protection (Vermeersch 1994). Already in 1996, after the party had overcome divisive internal leadership battles, the election showed the party neck and neck with the leading government party ODS (table 3.3). The demise of another party alliance of the left, the Liberal Social Union (LSU), which captured almost as many votes in 1992 as the CSSD,

Table 3.3. *Elections in the Czech Republic*

	June 1990		June 1992		June 1996	
	Votes %	Seats	Votes %	Seats	Votes %	Seats
Civic Forum	53.15	66				
Civic Movement (OH)/Free Democrats (SD), SD-LSNS			4.60	0	2.05	0
Civic Democratic Party (ODS)			29.73	76	29.62	68
Civic Democratic Alliance (ODA)			5.93	14	6.36	13
Left Bloc/Communists (LB/KSCM)	13.48 (KSCM)	14	14.05 (LB)	35	10.33 (KSM) 1.40 (LB)	22 0
Czech Social Democrats (CSSD)			6.53	16	26.44	61
Liberal Social Union (LSU)			6.52	16		
Christian Democratic Union/People's Party (KDU-CSL)	8.69	7	6.28	15	8.08	18
Republican Party (SPR-RSC)			5.98	14	8.01	18
Movement for Local Democracy – Society for Moravia and Silesia (HSD-SMS)	7.89	9	5.87	14	1.14[a]	
Pensioners for Life Securities (DZJ)					3.09	0
Democratic Union					2.80	0
Other parties	3.18		14.51	0	0.70	0
Effective number of parties		1.89	7.69	4.80	5.33	4.14

[a]Three successor lists.

also helped the rise of the social democrats. The LSU failed to build a coherent party out of a loose alliance of proto-parties and thus drove voters into the arms of the CSSD.

In contrast to Poland and Hungary, where the liberal-democratic party sectors gradually eroded after the founding elections, in the Czech Republic such parties appeared to establish a lasting political hegemony after 1990. Václav Klaus, the finance minister of the transitional governments in 1990 through 1992, quickly took advantage of the disintegration of the Civic Forum, the anticommunist umbrella organization that won the 1990 parliamentary election in the Czech Republic, by setting up a parliamentary club with a strongly promarket and Western orientation inside OF already in October 1990. This club then rapidly evolved into a centralized proto-party that constituted itself as the Civic Democratic Party (ODS) in February 1991 (Juberias 1992: 153–57). The other successful spin-off from OF, the Civic Democratic Alliance (ODA), had already formed in early 1990 but fielded candidates under the OF umbrella in June 1990. The party attracted intellectuals and spoke to socio-cultural political concerns, but it nevertheless agreed with the technocrat Klaus on questions of economic liberalism and democratic principles from the beginning. The probably most prominent failure of OF successor organizations is the Liberal Club (OH) that eventually renamed itself Free Democrats (SD). It attracted many OF intellectuals and leaders of the anti-communist opposition but could not develop a programmatic profile quickly enough. ODA and ODS politicians often accused the OH/SD of representing nostalgia going back to the illusions of a third way between capitalism and socialism nurtured by participants in the 1968 Czech dissident movement. The party could never effectively fight this image.

ODS and ODA as governing parties since 1992 propagated the rhetoric of liberal market reform, but in their economic policies never forced the major industrial and financial enterprises to abide by hard budget constraints, rationalize production, and thereby create unemployment that would hurt the electoral support of the governing parties. These policies resulted in low productivity growth, an increasing trade deficit, bank failures, and eventually a decline in economic growth. As the consequence of an ensuing economic crisis in 1997 and 1998, both ODS and ODA suffered in the opinion polls but still commanded support far above the levels obtained by economically liberal parties in Hungary or Poland. In late 1997, the Klaus government had to resign. Within months, influential politicians began to abandon the ODS and set up their own marketliberal party alternative that is intended to be free from public association with the failed Klaus policies. When our data collection took place in 1993–94, Klaus's ODS was probably near the height of its popularity. Nevertheless, also in 1997–98 the market-liberal, conservative party spectrum attracted upward of one-third of the electorate in opinion polls.

Parties with Christian-national or national-populist outlook play a relatively limited role in the Czech Republic. The most important party is the Christian

Democratic Union – Czech People's Party (KDU-CSL). The party appeals to practicing Catholics, but also takes a strong stance on socio-economic issues, carefully trying to balance market-liberal and social-protectionist considerations. While in government alliance with the ODS and ODA, it was always seen as a potential coalition partner for a CSSD with moderate policy appeal, and it certainly contributed to Klaus's downfall in 1997. Another small Christian democratic party, the KDS, ran on the ODS ticket in 1992 and decided to merge with ODS in 1996.[28]

In addition to the small, but rather stable Christian democrats, the Czech Republic also has a more intensely nationalist-populist party called Republicans (SPR-RSC) who receive substantial electoral support especially in the industrial region of northern Bohemia, where a xenophobic rejection of immigrants and of the Roma minority living in the Czech Republic reaches receptive ears among the unemployed industrial work force. The Republicans carved out a unique electoral market niche in the 1992 and 1996 elections. The same cannot be said about a regionalist-particularist appeal launched by Moravian and Silesian politicians, initially running under the label of Movement for Local Democracy – Society for Moravia and Silesia (HSD-SMS). The party could not find a lasting mechanism to attract voters and broke into splinter groups when its support base collapsed in 1993–94.

Comparing the 1992 and 1996 legislative elections in the Czech Republic (table 3.3), the failure of Václav Klaus's coalition government to hold on to its parliamentary majority was due not to a demise of support for the governing parties, but the realignment of the social-protectionist camp around the social democrats. The Czech elections of 1996 show relatively little volatility between the more social-protectionist and the more market-liberal blocs. Although the economic crisis of 1996–97, the ensuing fall of the Klaus government, and the installation of a caretaker government until new elections in June 1998 dramatically affected the fortunes of individual parties and politicians, these developments had relatively less influence on the underlying strength and relations between party blocs where all evidence points toward only moderate volatility.

BULGARIA

In the aftermath of patrimonial communism, the Bulgarian post-communists never experienced the sharp drop in electoral support sustained by their counterparts in Central Europe. In fact, they won almost an absolute majority of the electorate and a clear majority of the legislature in the June 1990 founding elections (see table 3.4). Nevertheless, faced with the exigencies of economic

---

[28]Some of its sitting members of parliament, however, defected to the KDU. And its leader, who served as finance minister in the final Klaus government in 1997, belonged to the group of ODS politicians who founded a new conservative party.

Table 3.4. *Elections in Bulgaria*

	June 1990		October 1991		December 1994		April 1997	
	Votes %	Seats	Votes %	Seats	Votes %	Seats	Votes %	Seats
Bulgarian Socialist Party (BSP)	47.15	211	33.14	106	43.50	125	22.0	58
Democratic Alliance for the Republic (DAR) (includes BSDP 1994)	—	—	—	—	3.48	0		
Coalition Euro-Left	—	—	—	—	—	—	5.6	14
Bulgarian Agrarian National Union (BZNS)/ People's Union (1994 only)	8.03	16	3.86	0	6.51	18		
BZNS/Nikola Petkov	—	—	3.44	0	—	—		
United Democratic Forces (1997) (SDS + BZNS + Democratic Party + BSDP + small parties)								
Union of Democratic Forces (SDS)	36.20	144	34.36	110	24.23	69	52.2	137
Union of Dem. Forces - Center (includes BSDP 1991)	—	—	3.20	0	—	—	—	—
Union of Dem. Forces - Liberals	—	—	2.81	0	—	—	—	—
Movement for Rights and Freedoms (DPS) (1997: Union for National Salvation)	6.03	23	7.55	24	5.44	13	7.60	19
Bulgarian Business Bloc (BBB)	—	—	1.32	0	4.72	13	4.90	12
Other	2.59	—	10.82	0	12.12	0	6.70	—
Effective number of parties	2.75	2.14	4.19	2.41	3.87	2.73	3.09	2.52

reform in 1990, soon strong tensions appeared within the party between a social democratic reform wing and various conservative standpatters and nationalists (cf. Ishiyama 1995: 161–62). After a wave of demonstrations instigated by the opposition parties, the post-communist cabinet gave way to an all-party government in which opposition politicians were put in charge of the economy. Even in its first electoral defeat of October 1991, however, the BSP still collected more support than any Central European post-communist party at the time of its rebound in the second democratic election. In fact, after failed attempts by the anti-communist Union of Democratic Forces (SDS) to build majority support around economic reform and civil liberties, the BSP made a comeback and again won a majority of parliamentary seats in 1994. The following three years saw a repetition of deep internal strains in the BSP over economic reform policies, presided over by a weak cabinet under Zhan Videnov. Its anti-reform governance of the economy first led to a grain shortage, triggered by the export of grain licensed to shady trading organizations run by individuals close to the government. Later, the spiraling corruption and crony capitalism instigated by the former nomenklatura stratum running the government led to a breakdown of the banking system, due to cheap loans pumped into bankrupt state enterprises, and eventually hyper-inflation accompanied by a collapse of the currency and escalating unemployment. Even in this situation, the April 1997 election still left the BSP with 22 percent electoral support, plus an additional 6 percent for a small reformist wing that finally made itself independent of the communist successor party.

Compared with Central Europe, anti-communist market-liberal and democratic politicians had a much harder time in Bulgaria to stage a bid for power, given their lack of experience and the absence of a history of dissident movements. The umbrella organization of initially most anti-communist groups, the Union of Democratic Forces (SDS), offered a picture of progressive internal division and external fragmentation from 1990 until 1996. The alliance was governed by an executive committee in which radical anti-communist splinter groups from the Sofia region were overrepresented and marginalized or drove out more moderate organizations with larger membership, such as the social democrats, a peasant party list, later the Alternative Social Liberals and finally the Democratic Party.[29] Even Alexander Yordanov, the speaker of parliament and SDS legislator, was forced to resign in 1993 when he disagreed with the SDS's strategy to boycott the parliament and engage in street politics. As a result of these developments, by early 1994, the SDS parliamentary caucus had lost 36 of its originally 110 members in 1992, far exceeding the still substantial loss rates of the BSP (7 of 106) and of the DPS (6 of 24).

[29]In retrospect, Stojan Ganev, the Dimitrov government's foreign minister, writes about the operation of the SDS executive: "In the SDS a totalitarian structure prevailed which saw its first task in surveillance of the SDS's political leadership and thus the key personalities on whose support the SDS government depended" (*Südosteuropa,* Vol. 44, Nos. 3–4 [1995]: 221).

After the October 1991 election, the BSP fully relinquished executive power for only about fifteen months, during which the SDS led a minority government, tolerated by the Turkish minority's party, the Movement for Rights and Freedom (DPS), until the SDS proved incapable of holding together the parliamentary majority. A non-partisan government with support of part of the post-communist parliamentary caucus then persevered until new elections in late 1994 in which the BSP won an absolute majority of the legislative seats. The internal divisiveness of the anti-communist SDS government and its inability to craft a viable coalition alienated voters and revived the BSP's fortunes (Karasimeonov 1995: 580). On the one hand, the SDS government had engaged in harsh macro-economic austerity policies that alienated its partner, the DPS. On the other, the SDS was internally incapable of agreeing on and implementing structural economic reforms. In their anti-communist zeal, SDS radicals in the government were more concerned with excluding members of the old elite from private business opportunities than with the sober task of creating a functioning market economy (cf. Bell 1997: 379). More pragmatic politicians were forced out under the SDS prime minister Filip Dimitrov, who saw every opposition to his policies as inspired by communist machinations.[30] When former SDS leader and sitting president of the republic Zhelu Zhelev criticized the SDS cabinet and party executive because of the alliance's restrictive policies toward the unions, the free press, and the Orthodox Church, Dimitrov accused him of playing into communist hands. This division prompted further departures from the SDS (Bankowicz 1994b: 234). And after the fall of Dimitrov's SDS cabinet radical SDS legislators even instigated a hunger strike to force the resignation of democratically elected president Zhelev whom they suspected to be a communist "agent," because he did not try to force the non-partisan but communist-supported government by Ljuben Berov out of office. SDS core activists and leaders thus did not overcome their anti-institutional orientation conceived in their struggle against an overpowering BSP in 1990, even once democratic rules of competition were in place.

Numerous "centrist" parties and electoral lists that politicians founded when they dropped out of the SDS tried to counteract the polarization of Bulgarian politics, but could not combine forces and overcome the 4 percent electoral threshold of parliamentary participation in 1991, 1994, and 1997. Probably the only thing BSP and SDS agreed on in the 1990s was the almost exclusive allocation of television campaign time to the three main parliamentary parties, BSP, SDS, and DPS (Crampton 1995: 238). Thus, both the inexperience and divisiveness of Bulgarian politics as well as the rules of the game kept new contenders outside parliament. An example of this tendency is also one of the historical

---

[30]Dimitrov's anti-communist reflexes were so strong that he even accused private business leaders and the union Podkrepa, the product of the anti-communist opposition movement in 1989, to be "natural allies" of the post-communist socialist party, when they objected to some of his policies (cf. Engelbrekt 1992).

parties, the Bulgarian Agrarian Union (BZNS). It reverted in 1991 to a pattern of internecine struggle and ran under different labels, none of which won sufficient support to enter parliament. In 1994, one of its factions teamed up with a former SDS constituent party to form the People's Union, which barely overcame the threshold of representation.

Only two further parties have made it into the Bulgarian parliament in 1994 and 1997. First, the Turkish minority party DPS coheres around demands for the protection and subsidization of its clients but lacks a broad economic program and coalition strategy (Ganev 1995). Second, a populist protest party called Bulgarian Business Bloc and led by a Bulgarian media entrepreneur with American passport, George Ganchev, won seats in 1994 and 1997 with social protectionist slogans. Both in the 1991 and the 1996 presidential elections, Ganchev finished third with 17 (1991) and 22 percent (1996) of the vote. His appeal as a political outsider was similar to Tyminski's maverick campaign in Poland in 1990. As a politician thriving on protest against the establishment but weak in building a constructive alternative, Ganchev proved incapable of holding together his party's parliamentary group in the 1994–97 term. Nevertheless, unlike Poland, in Bulgaria a charismatic outsider did not fade from the political scene but could in fact increase his support throughout the 1990s.

The economic mismanagement and social disintegration under the last BSP government until 1997 created a crisis sufficiently deep to bring various factions and former constituents of the SDS back together and renew the alliance under the label of United Democratic Forces in 1997. Unlike other post-communist countries in Central Europe, Bulgaria thus ends up before its fourth post-communist election where other countries started out in 1990, with an anti-communist umbrella coalition that defeats the communist successor organization. Nevertheless, the parliamentary institutions of Bulgarian politics and the country's election law may facilitate the formation of programmatically sharper parties over time. Under the impact of the deep crisis and the lessons of the past failed SDS government, it appears that the new leaders around Prime Minister Kostov may be more skilled in crafting a viable party out of the political alliance patchwork that presented itself as main counter-force to the communists in the 1997 election.

Because party labels may mean less in Bulgaria than in the other three countries, we may understate the true fragmentation of electoral and legislative politics, if we calculate the effective number of Bulgaria's parties based on the electoral alliances that presented themselves in each election (table 3.4). Following conventional calculations, Bulgaria has much less party system fragmentation than Central European countries. Given the alliance status of one or both of the main players, however, these figures do not reflect the true level of fragmentation in Bulgarian politics. In many ways, the main antagonists in Bulgarian politics between 1990 and 1997, the BSP and the SDS, constitute little more than mirror images of each other. Exposed to rules of democratic competition, neither of them could build viable parties that would not hemorrhage dissenters continuously.

CONSEQUENCES OF PARTY GOVERNMENT: PATHWAYS TOWARD ECONOMIC REFORM

Where vigorous anti-communist parties displaced the ruling elites in the immediate aftermath of the transition and where social democratized post-communist parties followed suit, the process of economic reform has gone much further than where post-communist parties clung to power and reluctantly made way for weak anti-communist forces (cf. Aslund et al., 1996; Fish 1998; Hellman 1998). Moreover, early reformers have suffered less economic dislocation and pulled faster out of the restructuring crisis than countries on the slow track. Of course, these causal linkages have to be placed within a broader political-economic setting. Opposition forces tend to be much stronger in countries emerging from bureaucratic-authoritarian or national accommodative communism than in formerly patrimonial communist countries where the elites staged preemptive reform. Further, it is formerly bureaucratic-authoritarian and national-accommodative communism where the new rules of democratic governance depersonalize political authority and thus limit presidential powers. The extent of economic reform strongly correlates with limited presidential power (Hellman 1996: 51–55). To underscore these points, we briefly review some general economic performance indicators in our four East Central European polities through the mid 1990s.

Based on background conditions, we would expect that the Central European countries have made considerably more *effort* to introduce liberal market regimes and show substantially better *economic performance* than Bulgaria. Table 3.5 provides several indicators of governments' policy effort since 1989. The World Bank's index of economic liberalization measures the extent to which domestic economic transactions, external transactions, and the entry of new firms have been liberalized. It weighs a number of components and checks results against related measures developed by the European Bank of Reconstruction and Development. Although there is an element of arbitrariness involved in the scoring and weighting of essentially qualitative institutional reforms, the differences between the Central European countries, on the one hand, and Bulgaria, on the other, suggest that party government indeed does matter. Bulgaria had a substantially lower liberalization score throughout the 1990–95 period and in that period's final year than the other three countries. Moreover, the change from the average to the final year (line 1.3) is particularly small in Bulgaria, suggesting an only intermittent, halting reform process. In a similar vein, Bulgaria's private sector, as measured by the GDP share of all companies with private majority ownership, has grown slower and remained much smaller than in the other economies (lines 2.1 through 2.3). It is therefore not surprising that Bulgaria has attracted the smallest amount of foreign direct investment, when measured relative to the size of its GDP (line 3).

Figures in table 3.6 indicate whether reform efforts have been blessed with economic success. All four post-communist countries went through a deep valley

Table 3.5. *Institutional and structural change in East Central Europe*

	Bulgaria	Czech Republic	Hungary	Poland
1. Institutional liberalization				
1.1. Index of economic liberalization: average value 1989–95	5.0	6.6	7.2	7.2
1.2. Index of economic liberalization: 1995 value	6.1	9.3	9.0	8.9
1.3. 1995 improvement over the average	+1.1	+2.7	+1.8	+1.7
2. Private sector share of GDP				
2.1. Share in 1990 (%)	10	6	19	27
2.2. Share in 1995 (%)	36	70	60	58
2.3. Increase 1990–95	+26	+64	+41	+31
3. Cumulative foreign direct investment as % of the 1994 GDP	4	13	31	7
4. Percent of age cohorts in secondary education (% female/ male) in 1993	70/66[a]	88/85	82/79	87/82

[a]In 1980, 84/85.
Sources: World Bank 1996: lines 1.1–1.3 (p. 14), lines 2.1.–2.3 (p. 15), line 3 (p. 64), line 4 (pp. 200–1).

of economic decline during the restructuring crises of the early 1990s, but the three East Central European countries with more consistent and vigorous reform programs show more progress than Bulgaria. Among them, Poland has the best record and it is the country with the most radical approach after 1989. Hungary's macro-economic change was in part delayed until 1995. But it started catching up in 1996 and 1997 after the socialist government imposed budgetary austerity. In the Czech Republic, inefficient economic governance structures not revealed by the overall reform index slowed down the economic recovery after 1995. The big divide, however, is between the three Central European countries, on one side, and Bulgaria, on the other.

Is the recovery in Poland only due to the fact that its economy fell much more than that of other countries in the 1980s? Averaging rates of growth or contraction between 1984 and 1994 does not confirm this picture. Poland with the most radical economic austerity package in 1989–90 still has the best performance, followed by Hungary and the Czech Republic. As before, Bulgarian economic performance trails the Central European countries (line 1.10).

Table 3.6. *Performance of East Central European economies*

	Bulgaria	Czech Republic	Hungary	Poland
1. Economic growth (% GDP)				
1.1.　1990	−9.1	−1.2	−2.5	−11.6
1.2.　1991	−11.7	−14.2	−7.7	−7.0
1.3.　1992	−6.0	−6.4	−4.3	+2.6
1.4.　1993	−4.2	−0.5	−2.3	+3.8
1.5.　1994	+/−0.0	+2.6	+2.5	+5.5
1.6.　1995	+2.4	+5.0	+2.0	+7.0
1.7.　1996 (est)	−10.9	+4.1	+1.0	+6.0
1.8.　1997 (est)	−7.0	+1.0	+3.0	+5.5
1.9.　1997 GDP as % of 1989 GDP (= 100)	61.33	89.43	91.51	110.52
1.10.　Average economic growth 1985–94 (% GDP)	−2.7	−2.1	−1.2	+0.8
2. Cumulative inflation (1989–96) (1989 = 100)	16,372	304.8	493.0	4,628
3. Unemployment 1996 (% of labor force)	12.5	3.5	10.5	13.6
4. Per capita income GDP in 1995 (in $)				
4.1.　Current exchange rates	1,538	4,814	3,840	2,410
4.2.　Purchasing power parity	4,190	9,770	6,410	5,400

5. Income inequality				
5.1. Gini coefficient in 1992–93	30.8	26.6	27.0	27.2
5.2. Ratio of income between top and bottom quintile	4.73	3.56	3.85	3.94
6. Foreign debt 1994				
6.1. As percent of GDP, current dollars	104.8	29.7	70.1	46.2
6.2. As percent of GDP, purchasing power parity	29.9	10.7	44.3	20.3
6.3. As percent of export earnings	193.1	56.8	260.9	195.0
7. Export performance				
7.1. Total exports 1994 (million $)	3,900	14,000	7,600	17,000
7.2. Total exports 1996 (million $)	4,900	21,700	14,200	24,400
7.3. Change in exports 1994–96 (%)	+26.0	+55.0	+86.8	+43.5
8. *Cumulative flow of foreign direct investment per capita, 1989–96 ($ CAP)*	51	692	1,300	140

Sources: European Bank of Reconstruction and Development 1997: lines 1.1–1.9, 3, 4.1, and 4.2, 7.1–7.3, and 8 (pp. 219, 221, 225 and 231). World Bank 1996: line 1.10 (p. 173), line 2 (p. 174), line 5 (pp. 196–7), line 6 (pp. 220–1). World Bank 1996: lines 1.1–1.6. and 1.9 (p. 173), all except 1996 data contributing to the calculation of line 2 (p. 174), line 3 (p. 174), line 4 (pp. 188–9), line 5 (pp. 196–7), line 6 (pp. 220–1), and line 7.1 (pp. 216–17). *Business Central Europe*, December 1996/January 1997: all estimates for 1996, based on information provided by the European Bank for Reconstruction and Development.

Economic growth is a rather abstract concept that citizens experience only through its correlates, such as inflation, unemployment, and income. Different reform trajectories in the four countries have produced contrasting patterns of inflation over the past seven years. In 1996, Bulgarian inflation reached an estimated 320 percent annual rate, whereas inflation in the East Central European countries had come down into the 10–30 percent annual inflation range. Cumulated from 1989 (=100) to 1996, Bulgaria's price index climbed four times as much as Poland's, and between 33 and 54 times as much as Hungary's and the Czech Republic's (line 2). Curiously, Bulgaria's easy money policy throughout much of the past seven years did not pay off in short-term employment. In spite of its expanding money supply, the Bulgarian unemployment rate is in the same range as Hungary's and Poland's (line 3). The Czech unemployment rate appears to be substantially lower, but this is in part due to accounting procedures that determine the total pool of employment seekers, in part due to the survival of financially non-viable enterprises.[31] Bulgaria trails the other three countries' per capita GDP (line 4), but only because of its dismal economic performance since 1990 (line 1.9), not because of a developmental handicap. Still in 1990, its purchasing-power-parity-corrected per capita income was equal to or greater than that of Poland.

One might presume that communist countries with less market liberalizing reform efforts preserve more equality among their citizens, but data for 1992 and 1993 do not bear out this expectation (lines 5.1. and 5.2). It is the Czech Republic that has the greatest income equality, but the differences to Hungary and Poland are so small that measuring errors make them virtually indistinguishable. Again, Bulgaria, the least reformed country, trails the pack by a substantial margin. In just about every respect, economic reform efforts highly correlate with performance. Of course, it would take a much more sophisticated econometric model with appropriate controls to claim a causal relation between these variables, but the figures are suggestive and the pattern holds up in broader comparative analysis (Aslund et al. 1996). As Hellman (1998) has argued, partial reform allows rent-seeking "winners" of the early reform measures to lock in their gains and redistribute national income in their favor.

A common argument against the comparison we have just drawn is that Bulgaria and to some extent Hungary have fared so much worse because they carry a much heavier load of hard-currency external debt than do the Czech Republic and Poland. A cursory look at the debt-GDP ratio in current dollars seems to prove the point (line 6.1). Bulgaria's current external debt is greater than a whole

---

[31]Comparing employment as a percentage of the total population between the ages of fifteen and sixty-four, the Czech labor market has shrunk almost as much as in Poland and Hungary. Moreover, the Czech Republic's lower unemployment is partially due to the liberal government's reluctance to enforce bankruptcy laws and to instruct commercial banks, which are still dominated by state ownership, to liquidate insolvent companies.

year's GDP, Hungary's and Poland's somewhat better, and the Czech Republic's is best. But this comparison suffers from a serious endogeneity problem. If a country's domestic economy is inefficient, it will not generate the exports that make debt service tolerable and reduce indebtedness in the longer run. For example, Czech exports increased by half between 1994 and 1996, Poland's by almost as much, Hungary's by a quarter, but Bulgaria's by a paltry 8 percent, although the embargo on trade with its neighbors in former Yugoslavia was lifted in that time period (lines 7.1 through 7.3). If a country's exports are weak, trade and current-account balances may turn negative unless the domestic currency declines, typically below its purchasing power parity rate. We can thus partially bracket the endogeneity problem by calculating each country's external debt to GDP ratio at purchasing power parity GDP rates (line 6.2). By this measure, Hungary's debt is substantially greater than Bulgaria's, which now looks more similar to Poland. Also a calculation of debt/export ratios shows that Hungary is worse off than the other countries and Bulgaria is burdened not significantly more than Poland (line 6.3).

Our comparative data suggest that external constraints, by themselves, do not explain the dramatic differences in economic performance between these four countries. There is at least strong circumstantial evidence that efforts to achieve domestic market liberalization affect the economic performance of post-communist economies quite substantially. Domestic effort, in turn, hinges on party government – the willingness and capacity of democratically elected executives to redress the problems of the inherited socialist planned economy. This does not, of course, imply that market liberalization has been advanced as vigorously and as successfully as one could theoretically imagine in the three East Central European countries. Thus, the Czech Republic has suffered from an underregulated financial sector and poor governance structures of privatized companies that translated into low investment and productivity growth rates since 1995 and eventually triggered a large trade deficit, accelerating inflation, and an increase in unemployment when the government finally began to fight these problems in 1997. Poland's social democratic-peasant government dragged its feet on the privatization of state companies and protected the agricultural sector from international competition. And the Hungarian governments, at least until 1995, were unable or unwilling to accelerate the speed of market liberalization. Nevertheless, compared with other countries in the post-communist cohort, and particular to the offsprings of patrimonial communism, they have gone furthest toward market capitalism.

CONCLUSION

The main purpose of this chapter has been to provide a stylized narrative that introduces the settings for our empirical research and describes political-economic legacies and new democratic institutions that we expect to influence the dynamics of post-communist party competition. Although all four countries experienced communist rule for roughly the same time periods, these systems evolved in rather different contexts and with hitherto quite different results in the new democracies. It is now time to take a closer look at the patterns of party competition we encounter in the four countries drawing on our own empirical analysis.

4

EMPIRICAL RESEARCH STRATEGY

Our principal research tool is a survey among politicians of just about all electorally relevant parties in Bulgaria, the Czech Republic, Hungary, and Poland. We conducted the pilot study with politicians at the national level (legislators, party executives, and secretaries) throughout 1993. Our main study in winter–spring 1994 targeted middle-level politicians and party functionaries in four regions of each country. The time points of pilot and main study are sufficiently close to each other to let them serve as mutual validity checks for each other. Future research should multiply the time points of observation and increase the intervals between each measurement in order to capture dynamic change in the party systems. We supplement our elite study by population survey data to explore the correspondence of elite and voter positions and perceptions of the political landscape. In this chapter we explain the design of our empirical instrument and introduce technicalities of the elite survey analysis.

SURVEYING EXPERTS OR POLITICAL ELITES

Studies of party elites are rather uncommon in the empirical literature on party competition and they have proceeded along two different avenues. On the one hand, researchers have surveyed party politicians, such as convention delegates, candidates for legislative office, or legislators, and compared their policy positions with those of their voters.[1] On the other, political scientists have asked panels of academic experts on individual countries or entire regions to rate party positions on a left-right scale (e.g., Castles and Mair 1984). In a similar vein, Laver and

[1] An example is the European Political Parties Middle Level Elite survey on which Dalton (1985) and Iversen (1994) draw.

133

Hunt (1992) asked national panels of political scientists to rate the parties of their own country in terms of the positions they take on a variety of policy issues and the salience they attribute to these issues.[2] Respondents scored parties on fine-grained 20-point scales so as to enable the experts to accommodate subtle distinctions among parties in the more fragmented party systems, such as Denmark or Finland. From these expert judgments, the authors then produced a road map of each country's political space of competition via factor analyses and other statistical techniques that estimate the dimensionality of the issue space and the position of individual parties in that space.

In the Laver-Hunt expert technique, panelists provide a comprehensive view of the party system, because they compare all parties' positions and judge each position in view of the competitors' positions. Moreover, expert panels have an air of objectivity that does not accrue to politicians' judgments in surveys because politicians may have strategic incentives to misrepresent their positions. Politicians' surveys also typically lack a comparative dimension. They ask respondents to report their own policy preferences, not those of their party, as a whole, or those of its competitors. Conversely, politicians' surveys have the advantage of furnishing a more direct source of parties' stances on political issues than expert judgments. Most important, they permit researchers to examine the internal cohesion or diffuseness of parties rather than to assign parties a single value on policy issues, as do existing expert surveys. Our study blends elements of the Laver-Hunt expert technique with a politicians' survey. We ask politicians themselves to rate their own parties' and their competitors' political appeals. Like Laver and Hunt, we do not explore their private opinions, but central tendencies of their parties. Moreover, as in all expert surveys, these politicians assess all relevant national parties' positions on the issues, not just those of their own.

By asking politicians to rate *all* parties on *each* issue, we can also explore their tendencies toward strategic (mis)representation of their own and other parties. By comparing whether politicians from party A rate their own party's position on issue k different from the ratings party A receives on k from politicians belonging to parties B, C, or D, we can detect systematic asymmetries that indicate strategically different representations of a party's position by insiders and outsiders. If there is no systematic difference in the scoring of party i on issue k by respondents from *all* parties, the "subjective" judgmental scores gain "inter-subjective" validity and are as good as "objective" evaluations by some group of omniscient outside observers, unless, of course, we assume that the very fact of being a politician produces a strategic distortion in the perception of party politics. If a party's own politicians assign it a different position on an issue than politicians belonging to

[2]Laver and Hunt also asked experts to rate parties' internal power structure and propensities to trade policy for office concerns. In the pilot study of our project, it turned out that East European parties have too little experience with intra-party decision making and cross-party strategic interaction to permit politicians to address these questions in a reliable fashion. Such topics may be included in future studies of post-communist party systems.

its competitors, we encounter a *systematic asymmetry of judgments,* which requires detailed exploration. In the pilot study phase of our project, we also compared judgments of party positions by national expert panels with those of politicians themselves and could not find any substantial differences between these two types of respondents. The critical topic we can address better by politicians' than experts' surveys concerns the internal homogeneity or heterogeneity of parties' programmatic appeals, as reflected by the variance of politicians' judgments, an issue we address more formally in the last part of this chapter.

In addition to experts' and politicians' surveys, there are at least two other techniques to explore party positions. One technique is that of legislative roll call analysis, but this is applicable only in the few legislatures where such roll calls are frequently taken. Moreover, in parliamentary systems where the government depends on the confidence of the legislative majority, roll calls measure more party *discipline* than *ideological cohesiveness* and electoral appeal. Another method is the content analysis of party programs that helps us to identify a party's position within the competitive space of a party system, but also does not allow us to explore the programmatic cohesiveness of parties. A major cross-national study of European party systems has employed that method (Budge, Robertson, and Hearl 1987; Budge and Laver 1992). Content analysis of party programs, however, raises difficult questions of validity and reliability, particularly in the context of East European party systems. In such democracies, the declarative status of party manifestos is not yet constrained by a lengthy history and public reputation of parties. As a consequence, the gap between parties' words and deeds may be particularly glaring. In our politicians' surveys, we instructed interviewers to tell respondents to base their party policy assessments not just on manifestos, but also the media appearances of party leaders, the parties' speeches in parliament and other public fora, and the parties' activities in the legislative process. In addition to validity problems with the content analysis of party manifestos, there are also difficult problems of measurement and reliability. Even when applied to West European party systems, such content analyses at times generate rather implausible party scores.[3]

SELECTION OF POLICY ISSUES

Our questionnaire asks politicians of all significant parties in the four countries to rate their own parties and their competitors on a variety of political issues and to assess the salience of each issue for the party of the respondent. We framed the questions in light of a theory of political semantics that postulates three levels of political reasoning and rhetoric. At the most abstract level, politicians invoke general principles and concepts that are closely related to debates in political philosophy and to broad ideological battle lines: liberalism, egalitarianism, com-

[3]For a critique of Budge, Robertson, and Hearl (1987), see Kitschelt (1994a: 202).

munitarianism, tradition and modernity, religious values or secularism, and "left" versus "right" placements. At the second and less abstract level, politicians voice general preferences within specific policy areas that circumscribe the jurisdiction of agencies, offices, and arenas of decision making. These preferences typically concern rules to allocate scarce resources among competing claims and institutional designs that govern the allocation process. At the third and most concrete level, participants in political debates voice opinions about legislative bills or concrete political decisions. In a language reminiscent of Talcott Parsons's general theory of action, the first semantic level of political debate concerns *principles and values,* the second level focuses on *norms and institutions,* and the third level deals with *operational objectives, facilities, and instruments.*

Citizens usually lack the time and cognitive sophistication to process information about the myriad of concrete, operational policy decisions processed through the political system at any given time. To get a sense of how politicians handle concrete decisions, information misers will look for simple cues from politicians formulated at a high level of abstraction (principles and values, left-right placements). Based on such signals, citizens may infer politicians' preferences over institutional design and rules of collective resource allocation.[4] Although politicians pitch their public electoral appeals primarily in terms of highly abstract ideological concepts, in the case of salient issues they may be pushed to move down to the level of institutional choice and rules of decision making at which they are compelled to reveal how they intend to deal with complicated trade-offs among policy options and resource allocation.

This intermediate level of abstraction at which politicians talk about norms and institutions that drive their policy preferences, therefore, is particularly important for electoral campaigns where not only the mass media but also political interest groups force politicians to reveal their ways to cope with resource scarcities. While politicians may wish to avoid a level of concreteness at which internal party divisions gain a sharp relief for obvious strategic reasons, the publicness of political debates in democratic polities may give them no choice but to take a stance on salient issues that speaks to questions of institutional design and norms of resource allocation. As parties become more concrete in their policy programs, they also run the risk of appearing less united, as representatives begin to argue over policy trade-offs that can be glossed over at the level of pure political principles. The more a party presents itself as divided, the less confidence voters may have in its policy-making ability and the sincerity of its central policy commitments. It is precisely this competence and coherence of parties in dealing with hard policy choices that the mass media and politicians in rival parties may wish to probe into in order to discredit a party in the eyes of at least moderately

[4]We are following McCubbins and Lupia (1998) that a significant part of the electorate employs abstract principles to derive concrete policy positions. For a more skeptical position that citizens "make up" their opinions about principles of resource allocation as they respond to a questionnaire, see Zaller (1993).

sophisticated voters. At least in democracies where legacies and institutions nudge parties toward programmatic competition, their ability to indicate norms of resource allocation and institutional designs they wish to employ in order to address salient policy issues may therefore be important for their competitive success.

If our claim is correct that the intermediate level of abstraction in political discourse is vital for inter-party competition and the construction of citizen-party linkages, where conditions for programmatic competition are favorable we should find a rather tight linkage between abstract ideological cues (values and principles) and middle-level programmatic policy commitments (norms and institutions) in the belief systems of policy makers. To a comparatively lesser extent, voters may evidence a similar ability to see the inter-relations among parties' policy positions. The tightness of such "ideological constraint" (Converse 1964), of course, varies with contextual attributes of the party system, such as the complexity of the lines of political divisions in the competitive arena and the opportunities for clientelist linkage building.

Because we attribute critical importance to the intermediate level of semantic abstraction in policy debates among politicians and in the information processing of the politically more sophisticated voters who monitor parties' moves in the arena of competition in a general way, we pitch most of the policy scales on which we ask politicians to rate their own parties and their competitors to that level. Party scores at this level allow us best to detect the internal programmatic cohesiveness or division of parties over policy and their position vis-à-vis competitors in the electoral game.

Policy issues included in our questionnaire had to meet two further criteria. First, they had to be sufficiently salient to matter for a party's appeal. A number of questions included in our pilot study did not meet that test. For example, questions on gay rights simply do not register with post-communist mass publics and politicians and therefore yield "noisy," manufactured responses or simply non-response. Second, policy issues had to be at least moderately controversial among politicians. We therefore tried to frame policy choices as much as possible in terms of *positional alternatives* rather than *valence issues* on which all parties declare to pursue the same objective but dispute each other's competence in achieving the desired policy. With appropriate framing, most valence issues reveal a core of spatial-positional disagreements among politicians and parties. For example, everyone claims to fight pollution, inflation, and unemployment, but only some would do so if such policies involve trade-offs, such that environmental protection reduces growth, inflation dampens investments, and fighting unemployment creates large budget deficits. Policies concerning inflation and unemployment are thus not really disjointed valence issues but involve trade-offs on a common underlying economic policy dimension ranging from state-led expansionary and redistributive fiscal and monetary policies, at one extreme, to market-liberal visions at the other extreme where governments do little else than guarantee the stability of the currency.

Nevertheless, we do not suggest that all policy conflicts rely on spatial rather than valence competition. The empirical analysis of our survey responses in fact allows us to probe into the extent to which issues mobilize valence or spatial competition. *Systematic asymmetries* where party insiders ascribe different positions to their party than outsiders are a good gauge for the presence of valence issues. Politicians here fight not over which policy is correct, but which party comes closer to the generally recognized correct policy position.

Table 4.1 lists the issue scales as well as the more abstract ideological scales that survived our pilot study and were included in the main survey in the four countries in 1994. The issue wording in the English master questionnaire, as applied to Poland, is provided in appendix II. This version served as the reference text for translations into the national languages and was compared with reverse translations into English. In a number of instances, we made small semantic adjustments to fit a question to the national context.[5] Context-free semantic identity of translated texts may, in different settings, present rather different pragmatic stimuli to respondents. In each setting, survey respondents build on unique political experiences and perceptions of acute political controversies. For this reason, exact semantic equivalence in the translation of questionnaires into different languages may often create only the illusion of direct comparability, but constitute a misleading methodological criterion to enhance the validity of comparison across national borders. We have therefore taken the liberty to adjust the framing of policy issues to the particular context of each country.

We can roughly divide the issues that made it into the 1994 questionnaire into three bundles. The first group of issues concerns economic and social policies that directly affect the distribution of scarce material and financial goods. Five rather concrete policy choices each of which involves trade-offs and one abstract scale tap the socio-economic policy area in the survey. Social policy is represented by the question of whether health care should emphasize security by making all citizens contribute to a comprehensive public coverage scheme, or individuality by relying on private insurance schemes (VAR 30). Two questions concern macro-economic changes in the governance structures of firms and the fiscal and monetary policy. One of them probes into the size of the desirable private or public sector, taking short-term consequences for unemployment into account (VAR 31). The other scores parties on the priority of fighting inflation or unemployment in governments' fiscal and monetary policies (VAR 33). Two further questions throw light on different aspects of the distribution of income and property rights from a more micro-economic perspective. First, we asked politicians to rate parties' positions on the trade-off between an accelerated timetable of privatization and considerations of distributive justice in the implementation of privatization programs (VAR 32). Next, politicians scored parties' positions on the desirability of

---

[5]This applies especially to the authority-autonomy in education item (VAR 41), the issue of immigration (VAR 36), the role of churches (VAR 39), and the urban-rural difference (VAR 40).

Table 4.1. *Issues and ideological scales in the politicians' survey*

Variables	Point 1	Point 20
Political issue scales		
VAR 30: Social security	Citizens pay	Compulsory insurance
VAR 31: Market–state	Privatize all	Substantial public sector
VAR 32: Speed vs. justice of privatization	Justice	Speed and efficiency
VAR 33: Inflation vs. unemployment	Fight inflation	Fight unemployment
VAR 34: Foreign investment	Welcome	Dependence
VAR 35: Income taxation	More progressive	More equal
VAR 36: Immigration[a]	Restrictive	Permissive
VAR 37: Women at work	Subsidize kindergartens	Women stay home
VAR 38: Abortion[a]	Extreme pro-life	Extreme pro-choice
VAR 39: Churches and schools	Should influence	Should not
VAR 40: Urban–rural	Neutral or pro-urban	Agrarian
VAR 41: Authority-autonomy in education	Authority	Autonomy
VAR 42: Environment protection	Industry first	Environment
VAR 43: Censorship	Permit	Prohibit
VAR 44: Former communists	Discriminate	Equal rights
VAR 45: National issue I		
Bulgaria	Pro-Turkish	Anti-Turkish
Hungary	Anti-irredenta	Irredenta
VAR 52: National issue II		
Bulgaria	Pro-Turkish	Anti-Turkish
Abstract ideological concept scales		
VAR 46: State intervention–free market	State	Free market
VAR 47: Individual–tradition	Freedom	Tradition
VAR 48: National–pan-European	Nation	Europe
VAR 49: Clerical–secular	Clerical	Secular
VAR 50: Left–right	Left	Right

[a]Not asked in Bulgaria.

more progressive or more proportional income taxes (VAR 35). Finally, at the most abstract level, politicians placed parties on a scale ranging from endorsement of free markets to support of state interventionism in the economic process (VAR 46).

A second group of issues is likely to involve both economic-distributive and non-economic, socio-cultural connotations. Here we first presented the issue of foreign investment in and international economic integration of the new capitalist domestic economies: do such developments help or do they hurt economic fortunes? On the one hand, this question may tap distributive anxieties or hopes associated with an internationalization of the economy, but on the other it may involve national pride and foreign-policy concerns irreducible to distributive considerations (VAR 34). In a similar vein, the issue of social policies to encourage women's employment in formal labor markets (VAR 37) entails both a cultural frame (gender roles) as well as an issue of distributive economics (equality between the sexes, resources for public child care facilities). Also assistance to agricultural interests (VAR 40) may tap economic distribution as well as potential cultural conflicts between city and countryside. Even the environmental protection question (VAR 42) has an economic-distributive side rather than merely a health and cultural life-style side, because we asked respondents to assess how parties would decide a conflict between jobs and environmental protection. Finally, the pure left-right scaling of the parties (VAR 50) may involve a variety of cultural and economic meanings contingent upon the competitive environment of a party system.

The final group of questions concerns primarily cultural issues that cannot be directly projected onto economics. Among them, we include the issues of coping with immigrants from different cultures (VAR 36), women's choice of abortion (VAR 38), the influence of the churches over public school curricula (VAR 39), the role deference to authority and tradition or individual autonomy should play in public education (VAR 41), tolerance for freedom of the press or compliance with a dominant moral standard in the mass media (VAR 43), and the question of how former communists should be treated in the new democratic polities (VAR 44) – should they be permitted to participate or should they be excluded and punished for past deeds? At the more abstract-ideological level, we asked politicians to scale parties in their countries on preferences over more collectivist and traditional versus more individualist and modern orientations (VAR 47), a more national or a more pan-European vision (VAR 48), and a greater or lesser separation of religion and politics (VAR 49).

In Bulgaria, we were unable to ask two of the cultural issues in a meaningful way and had to change a third in a rather fundamental fashion. The question that needed substantial reformulation concerns the control of the churches over education, a non-issue in a country with a predominantly Orthodox clergy that always subordinated itself to the state. In its stead, we substituted a question that explores how willing parties are to protect the Bulgarian Orthodox state church from the rise of proselytizing fundamentalist Protestant sects. The first of two issues we entirely dropped in Bulgaria is that of coping with cultural diversity due to immigration (VAR 36). Given the country's economic feebleness at the time of our survey and its geographic location, emigration rather than immigration was the problem. Second, abortion is available upon demand, and this practice is a non-issue in the political arena. In place of these two questions, we inserted two other questions that are salient in Bulgaria and have to do with its ethno-cultural pluralism. Should ethnic Turkish children receive school instruction in Bulgarian or in Turkish (VAR 36)? Should Bulgaria consider Turkey a partner or an adversary in the region (VAR 45)? In a similar vein, for Hungary we added a scale about parties' willingness to fight for the rights of Hungarian ethnic minorities in surrounding countries.

Not only the decision to include an issue in our questionnaire but also the decision to exclude an issue require justification. First of all, foreign affairs is somewhat underrepresented, particularly relations with the former Soviet Union and Russia, but also the integration into the Western NATO defense alliance system. In our survey, only the policy scale dealing with foreign investment and economic interdependence (VAR 34) and the more abstract ideological scale on national versus pan-European development (VAR 48) address the foreign-policy complex. In 1993–94 NATO and EU membership were nowhere particularly salient topics of political debate and, with the partial exception of Bulgaria, they have very much the character of valence issues, with most politicians in East Central Europe preferring NATO and EU membership.

Also certain areas of domestic policy have found little resonance among politicians in our pilot study and therefore disappeared from the main survey. The probably most glaring omission concerns questions of fighting crime and creating law and order. In the pilot study in 1993, we discovered that such issues were gradually becoming more important, but that parties had not yet started to define the issue in terms of positional nor valence competition. A replication of our study in the late 1990s would probably yield a rather different picture. In the intervening years, this issue complex has become salient and divisive on the political agenda of post-communist countries.

THE PARTY SAMPLE

In each country, we sought to interview an almost equal number of politicians from all "relevant" parties in four sub-national districts. As our formal criterion of party relevance, we included all those parties that had received a minimum of 4 percent of the vote in the most recent election preceding our survey. We then added parties that attracted close to 4 percent electoral support in opinion polls taken shortly before our politicians' survey. Table 4.2 lists all the parties we covered in our survey, together with their abbreviations, as they are employed in each country's national language. Appendix I provides all abbreviations, full national language labels, and English translations of party names. We have provi-

Table 4.2. *Relevant parties in the four countries*

Type of party	Bulgaria	Czech Republic	Hungary	Poland
Post-communist parties	Bulgarian Socialist Party (BSP)	Left Bloc (LB) (Communist Party of Bohemia and Moravia, KCSM)	Hungarian Socialist Party (MSzP)	Alliance of the Democratic Left (SLD)/Social Democracy of the Polish Republic (SdRP)
Peasant Parties	Bulgarian Agrarian National Union (BZNS)	Liberal Social Union (LSU)	Independent Smallholders' Party (FKGP)	Polish Peasant Party (PSL)
Social democrats	Bulgarian Social Democratic Party (BSDP)	Czech Social Democrats (CSSD)	—	Union of Labor (UP)
Other labor	—			Solidarity (NZSS "S")
Christian parties	—	Christian Democratic Union (KDU)	Christian Democratic People's Party (KDNP)	Christian National Union (ZChN)
Populist-national parties	—	Republican Party (SPR-RSC)	Party of Hungarian Justice and Life (MIEP)	Confederation of Independent Poland (KPN)
Bourgeois conservatives	Union of Democratic Forces (SDS)	Czech Civic Democratic Party (ODS) Christian Democratic Party (KDS)	Hungarian Democratic Forum (MDF)	Non-Party Bloc to Support Reforms (BBWR) Center Party (PC)
Free-market liberals	—	Civic Democratic Alliance (ODA)	Alliance of Young Democrats (Fidesz)	Liberal Democratic Congress (KLD)
Social liberals	—	Civic Movement (OH)/Free Democrats (SD)	Alliance of Free Democratic Union (SzDSz)	Democratic Union (DU)
Ethnic parties	Movement of Rights and Freedoms (DPS)	Moravian and Silesian Association (HSD-SMS)	—	—

sionally listed the parties by general programmatic "families" to simplify a comparison of the party systems. At this point, not much weight should be placed on the assignment of parties to families. It is simply an ordering and classifying device. As we know already from our brief historical sketch, parties belonging to the same "family" but located in different countries may have rather different careers and strategic propensities. Moreover, a few of the parties whose politicians we surveyed in 1994 no longer exist in the late 1990s, having merged with parties in their general ideological vicinity.

Almost all the parties whose politicians we intended to interview cooperated with our project. With the benefit of hindsight, we did not approach one party, George Ganchev's Bulgarian Business Bloc (BBB), that turned out to be significant in a later election. In 1993–94, in our pilot study politicians from other Bulgarian parties could not attribute any specific policy positions to a proto-party that was then still mostly a one-man show, thus generating non-responses in the scoring practices of most politicians. By ignoring the BBB, however, we do underestimate the programmatic "noisiness" and diffuseness of the Bulgarian party system, an issue to which we return in the next chapter.

In the Czech Republic and in Hungary, the most nationalist-populist parties, the Czech Republican Party (SPR-RSC) and Istvan Csurka's Party of Hungarian Justice and Life (MIEP), refused to cooperate with our project. The refusal of committed nationalists is, of course, in the logic of their political objectives. Why should they support a "cosmopolitan" research project building on methods and theories of "Western" social science? Fortunately, we encountered no such problems of access among the more nationally oriented Polish parties, such as the Confederation of Independent Poland (KPN). Our data reveal that Polish politicians belonging to other parties view the KPN as much less extremist than Czech and Hungarian politicians score the SPR-RSC and the MIEP. This moderation is also reflected in the KPN's approach to our project. In Poland, the true equivalent to the Czech Republicans and the Hungarian MIEP would have been Samoobrona, the League of Self-Defense, which primarily mobilizes small segments of the rural underclass, and Stanislav Tyminski's Party X. Both of these parties fell short of attracting sufficient electoral support to merit inclusion in our study. On SPR and MIEP policy positions, we have gathered the perceptions of evaluators belonging to other parties, but we have no internal assessments of policy positions.

The most serious limitation of our elite survey is due to the partial noncooperation of the major Czech government party of the day, the Civic Democratic Party (ODS). The ODS party secretaries held the opinion that, given the electoral size of the party, our project should be obliged to interview a greater number of its politicians than those of other parties. We were unsuccessful in our efforts to explain to the responsible officials that our research question would not call for a proportional mapping of the individual parties and that considerations of relative size, if relevant, could be incorporated through appropriate weighting techniques. In spite of the recalcitrance of national party officers, we gained a modicum of interviews with ODS politicians through local and regional access (55 percent of the target number). Moreover, we also covered politicians from the small Christian Democratic Party (KDS) that merged with ODS in 1994–95. Its respondents are close to the ODS in almost all ideological positions, save the ODS's secular appeal. Taking ODS and KDS respondents together, we interviewed almost as many politicians as in all the other major Czech parties.

Several parties we did cover in the 1994 politicians' survey lost their electoral significance by the late 1990s or participated in new party configuration. In the Czech Republic, this applies to the Liberal Social Union (LSU), which was already in a process of decomposition at the time of our interviews in 1993 and 1994, the regionalist Moravian-Silesian party (HSD-SMS, before several name changes and splits), and the Free Democrats (originally OH, later SD). In Hungary, the MIEP received only a tiny fraction of the vote in the 1994 parliamentary election but then made a comeback in the 1998 election when it benefited from the near extinction of the Hungarian Democratic Forum (MDF), from which its leaders had originally defected. Most important, in Hungary between 1994 and 1998 the Alliance of Young Democrats (Fidesz) managed to reposition itself in the competitive space and absorb the MDF's and the Christian national KDNP's voters. In a similar vein, in Poland by the late 1990s none of the parties in the Christian national political sector whose politicians we interviewed in 1994 still existed. As we explained in the preceding chapter, these parties joined hands under two umbrella coalitions for the 1997 legislative elections.

Whereas in our pilot study we primarily interviewed national party politicians, such as sitting members of parliament or party secretaries in the national party headquarters, in our main politicians' survey in 1994 we chose to sample middle-level party politicians in four different regions of each country. The idea was to explore whether the unique regional conditions of party competition affect the politicians' cognitive maps of the party system or whether politicians perceive a nationally uniform system of party competition. Our choice of middle-level regional politicians for the main survey also resulted from a desire to prevent a "capital city" or "politician-intellectual" bias in our results. Our choice of respondents is meant to assure that we would capture images of party competition in the minds of politicians more representative than a thin top layer of prominent national leaders. We intend to learn something about party competition as a broad cross section of active politicians in the new democracies perceives it. After all, the task of citizen-elite linkage building and crafting parties' programmatic appeals extends beyond a few top personalities to a broader political cadre even in an age of television. It includes large numbers of politicians who participate in the governance of their polity on behalf of their parties at the local, regional, or national levels.

In order to test for regional disparities in the perception of party competition, we selected districts with highly diverse characteristics. In each country, one region is always the national capital in which the service sector (including the core state administration) and professionals are overrepresented while agriculture is underrepresented in comparison with the national average. Parties growing out of the dissident movements against communism tend to perform particularly well in the capital and other large cities. We therefore chose as our second and third research sites regions with a high share of industrial employment or agriculture. In both types of regions, the strength of the social protectionist or of nationalist parties tends to be greater than the national average. Finally, in each country we selected a fourth "wild card" region with unique characteristics that cannot be generalized across our set of four countries. In Bulgaria and the Czech Republic the obvious choice was to include areas with strong support for regional or ethno-cultural parties, such as Moravia and southeastern or Danube Bulgaria where a significant Turkish-speaking Islamic minority resides. The criterion of choice for the fourth district is somewhat more arbitrary in Hungary and Poland, but also captures territorial variance. In Poland we decided to incorporate the East/West Poland A/Poland B distinction. In Hungary, we selected a district in the more affluent western region of the country close to the Austrian border.

In Bulgaria, the survey included the regions of Sofia (capital), Plovdiv (industrial center), Dobrich (agrarian area), and Haskovo (an area with a strong Turkish-speaking minority population). In the Czech Republic, interviews covered the regions of Prague (capital), Most (industrial center), Blansko (Moravian and agricultural), and Kladno (no unique social-structural characteristics, but comparatively strong electoral performance of the opposition parties). In Hungary, we surveyed politicians in Budapest (capital), Miskolc (industrial center), Hodmeszö-varsahely/Csongrad (agricultural), and Szombathely in western Hungary (an area with a strong religious cultural background). In Poland, we chose Warsaw (capital), Katowice (industrial center), Bialystock (agriculture, Eastern), and Zielona Gora (a comparatively well-off city in Western Poland).

When we began our data analysis, we quickly discovered that regional variations in the perception of party stances and competitive configurations are negligible. In all four countries, it is appropriate to talk about "nationalized" systems of party competition, even though the relative electoral strength of the parties varies across localities.[6] In none of the four countries, however, is the variance of party strength across regions great by international comparative standards. In postcommunist polities, extreme regional variations may be a feature of ethnically more divided societies, not of the four countries we incorporate in our study. Because regional variations are modest, we disregard them in our data analysis and focus on parties' issue positions and their overall ideological appeal, together with the features of national party systems, as the relevant units of analysis. Moreover, a comparison between the results of the 1993 pilot study among parliamentarians and national party executives with the 1994 main survey among middle-level party representatives reveals no significant disparities. Without fail, the results of the main survey confirm the preliminary findings of the pilot study reported in

[6]For a good analysis of regional variation of party strength in Poland, compare Tworzecki (1996: chap. 3).

Kitschelt (1995c). In this book, we therefore confine our data analysis to the main 1994 surveys and need not engage in a detailed comparison of pilot and main study.

Depending on the number of parties we covered in each country, we interviewed between three and five politicians of each party in each of the four regions. The totals amount to between 25 and 35 politicians per region. In Bulgaria, where our study includes five parties, we completed 100 interviews. In the Czech Republic, with interviewees from nine parties, we collected 135 interviews. In Hungary, with politicians from six parties, we completed 126 interviews and in Poland, with ten parties, 120 interviews. The number of interviews per party is lowest in Poland with 12 respondents from ten parties, in Bulgaria and in Hungary it is highest with 20–23 respondents from five to six parties. In the Czech Republic, the average is 15 interviews per party (see table 4.3).

After selecting the research sites in each country, we contacted the local parties and requested interviews. Given the nature of our research, a random sampling process among local politicians would have been superfluous or infeasible. In quite a few parties, it proved not easy to identify the four or five key politicians we wished to interview in each locality because parties have small cores of activists and elected representatives. In each country, political science graduate students conducted most of the interviews after having been trained for the specific purposes of this study. The training and supervision of interviewers was the responsibility of the national investigators of our project.[7]

THE COMPARISON OF ELITE AND MASS DATA

Originally we intended to confine our study to an analysis of party politicians' perception of the competitive electoral arena. As we progressed in our research, we became keenly aware that information about the relation between elite appeals and citizens' political preferences in electoral politics is vital for our exploration of the procedural quality of post-communist democracies. We began to think about ways to tie our project into the broad stream of empirical studies on democratic representation. Do voters endorse parties that have similar positions as those they subscribe to themselves? Or are there discrepancies and disjunctures between elite and mass that reflect the precarious status of the new democracies?

In our effort to explore democratic party representation, we were handicapped by the absence of a population survey component from our original research design. Ideally, our study would have asked population samples in all four countries to rate each party on exactly the same issues we submitted to politicians. Moreover, respondents would have indicated the salience of the issues for each

---

[7]The national project directors are three of the four co-authors of this study (Zdenka Mansfeldova, Radek Markowski, and Gábor Tóka) plus Dobrinka Kostova in Bulgaria who was unable to participate in the data analysis.

Table 4.3. *The sample of politicians in the four countries*

Bulgaria	
Bulgarian Socialist Party	20
Bulgarian Agrarian National Union	20
Bulgarian Social Democratic Party	20
Movements for Rights and Freedoms	20
Union of Democratic Forces	20
Total	100
Czech Republic	
Left Bloc/Communist Party of Bohemia and Moravia	21
Liberal Social Union	18
Czech Social Democratic Party	20
Christian Democratic Union/People's Party	20
Civic Democratic Alliance	19
Free Democrats	14
Moravian and Silesian Association	6
Civic Democratic Party	11
Christian Democratic Party (KDS, joined ODS)	6
Total	135
Hungary	
Hungarian Socialist Party	23
Independent Smallholders Party	20
Christian Democratic People's Party	22
Alliance of Free Democrats	21
Alliance of Young Democrats	23
Hungarian Democratic Forum	17
Total	126
Poland	
Alliance of the Democratic Left/Social Democratic Party of Poland	12
Polish Peasant Party	12
Union of Labor	12
Solidarity (electoral list)	12
Christian National Union	12
Democratic Union	12
Liberal-Democratic Congress	12
Confederation for an Independent Poland	12
Non-Partisan Bloc for Political Reform	12
Center Alliance	12
Total	120
Total interviews, four countries	481

party and then revealed their own positions and party preference. Reality fell considerably short of this research design. For three of the four countries – the Czech Republic, Hungary, and Poland – the Central European University population surveys, conducted every six months in 1993 and 1994, invited respondents to indicate their own position on a number of policy issues presented in formulations quite similar to those included in the elite survey. Moreover, the population surveys feature a wealth of additional policy items that are worded in ways rather dissimilar from those in the elite questionnaire but are likely to tap similar issue dimensions as items included in the elite survey. With regard to all policy issues, respondents in the population surveys indicate their own personal policy preference, while in the elite survey we obtained respondents' perceptions of the parties' preferences on policy issues. While one can make a case that elite respondents' perceptions of their own parties' positions are likely to be close to their personal policy preferences, perceptions still measure a somewhat different aspect of political reality than preferences.

We were unable to identify a Bulgarian population survey completed sufficiently close to the date of our elite survey with the appropriate array of questions to match the political elite study. Our colleagues Geoffrey Evans and Stephen Whitefield, however, permitted us to analyze their Bulgarian population survey data from 1993. Although the items included in that questionnaire have a less close match to our elite study than the CEU surveys, they nevertheless enable us to engage in a modicum of comparison between elite and population preferences in the political arena. In chapter 8, we explain in greater detail how we relate the CEU surveys and the Bulgarian survey to our elite study. We wish to underline again that our methods and procedures are imperfect, but that the results strike us as rather robust and consistent with a clear interpretation of party-citizen linkages.

MEASURING PARTIES' POLICY POSITIONS AND PROGRAMMATIC COHESION

Before we turn to the substantive analysis of our data, we would like to give readers a feel for the kinds of data and measures we generate with our elite survey. This section is particularly relevant for the statistical analysis presented in the subsequent chapters on the programmatic structuring of party competition (chapters 5 and 6). In our survey, politicians place parties' policy positions and ideological tendencies on scales. Some of the variance among the scores respondents attribute to party j on an issue k are due to measurement error, particularly because we employ Laver and Hunt's fine-grained 20-point scale. In retrospect, the objections of respondents and colleagues that this scale requires too sophisticated judgments from politicians and should be replaced by a shorter ten-point scale strikes us as sound and we would recommend using a shorter scale in future research.[8] Another component of the variance between judges' scores of the same parties' issue position, however, is not measurement error, but permits a substantive interpretation. It reflects true uncertainty or intra-party conflict over a party's issue position. Thus, if we assume that the measurement error in respondents' judgment constitutes a random background noise that does not systematically vary across parties or countries, differential levels of variance in judges' assessment of parties' issue positions provide a measure of parties' internal cohesiveness.

The most straightforward measure of parties' internal programmatic cohesiveness we employ in subsequent chapters of this book is the standard deviation of the policy positions politicians i ascribe to party j on issue k. This measure allows us to determine a party's internal coherence "behind the back" of each respondent to our survey questions. Interviewers were also instructed to give politicians a direct chance to indicate parties' policy heterogeneity. If respondents thought a party covered a whole range of positions or expressed internal divisions on an issue, they could circle regions or disjointed positions on the 20-point scales to indicate a party's stances (e.g., positions 4–9, or 3–5 and 11–12). Because few respondents systematically employed that scoring option, we do not consider it in our analysis. Where respondents did circle regions rather than individual scores on the scale, we calculated the mean value to reflect their party scores (e.g., a range of 4–9 translates into a score of 6.5).

In order to appreciate how respondents' issue scores for each party can be analyzed, table 4.4 presents a simple fictitious example of a party system with four parties A_R, B_R, C_R, and D_R, and five evaluators A_1 (belonging to party A_R) through D_1 (belonging to party D_R). In the upper panel, in the first four columns, informants rank the parties' positions on issue k on 20-point scales. The first five rows provide the raw scoring of the parties by each of the evaluators and each evaluator's mean score for *all* parties taken together. This mean represents their "anchor point" for assessing the parties on the scale (1.1 through 1.5). Line 1.6 indicates the mean score for each party rated by all judges. Line 1.7 gives the standard deviation of the five judges' assessments of each party. Let us examine how the evaluators contribute to different standard deviations of the parties' positions on issue k. Evaluators A_1 and B_1 assign different values to the same parties, but the policy "distances" between the parties are exactly identical in the judgment of both evaluators. In other words, the two evaluators have different "anchor points" in the interpretation of the end points of the scale, but they agree on the relative distances of the parties from each other. Consider the issue whether parties endorse privatization of public enterprises, even if this policy creates unemployment, at one end of the scale (score = 1) versus the maintenance of a large sector of state enterprises to prevent unemployment, at the other end of the

---

[8]Expert and politicians' surveys modeled on our research instrument and conducted in Slovakia, the Baltic countries, and Russia in 1997 have adopted a ten-point scale to remedy this problem.

Table 4.4. *Demonstration of the judging process with fictitious data*

	Parties rated				Mean value "anchor point"
	A_R	B_R	C_R	D_R	
Absolute rating of the parties A_R through D_R on one issue					
Party identity of the judges					
1.1. A_1	4	8	12	16	10
1.2. B_1	2	6	10	14	8
1.3. C_1	9	6	13	17	11.25
1.4. C_2	8	10	11	12	10.25
1.5. D_1	15	12	6	4	9.25
1.6. Judges' party means	7.6	8.4	10.4	12.6	
1.7. Judges' party standard deviations	5.02	2.61	2.70	5.18	
1.8. Judges' party standard deviations excluding D_1	3.30	1.91	1.29	2.22	
Rating of the parties A_R through D_R on one issue relative to each other[a]					
2.1. A_1	−6	−2	+2	+6	0
2.2. B_1	−6	−2	+2	+6	0
2.3. C_1	−2.25	−5.25	+1.75	+5.75	0
2.4. C_2	−2.25	−0.25	+0.75	+1.75	0
2.5. D_1	+5.75	+2.25	−3.25	−5.25	0
2.6. Judges' party means	−2.15	−1.45	+0.65	+3.45	
2.7. Judges' party standard deviation	4.80	2.75	2.24	4.88	
2.8. Judges' party standard deviations excluding D_1	2.16	2.09	.60	2.09	

[a]Removal of the "anchor point."

scale (score = 20). Then both evaluators A_1 and B_1 see party A_R as the most market-liberal party, but interpret its position as somewhat different relative to their personal conception of what an extreme market-liberal policy might look like. A_1 and B_1 also see parties C_R and D_R closer to the social protectionist-statist extreme of the scale. While they assign different absolute scores to each of the parties, both evaluators see the same distances between them and party A_R.

The party j-issue k judgments of evaluators C_1 and C_2 are quite different from those of A_1 and B_1. C_1 essentially ranks parties B_R through D_R in a rather similar way as the previous judges, but clearly diverges on party A_R, which she considers to be much less market-liberal than judges A_1 or B_1 claim. Evaluator C_2 agrees with A_1 and B_1 on the ranking of the parties, but she places all parties much closer to each other than is warranted in the opinion of A_1 and B_1. C_2 is much more skeptical vis-à-vis claims of big programmatic differences in the three parties' positions than A_1 and B_1. In spite of these elements of heterogeneity, the judgments of A_1 through C_2 are roughly consistent, reflected in the rather modest standard deviations that each of the four evaluators' judgments generates for each party's position (line 1.8).

This general picture changes once we add evaluator D_1. This respondent fundamentally disagrees with her colleagues not only on the precise scores assigned to each party, but also on the rankings of the four parties relative to each other. For her, party A_R is most social-protectionist and party D_R most market-liberal. Given the very small number of respondents, D_1's judgments constitute influential outliers relative to the other four respondents' judgments that dramatically increase the standard deviations of the jk party scores, as reflected in line 1.7. Fortunately, in the larger samples with 100+ judges for each party's issue position we have obtained in each of our countries a few outliers, which affect the general picture much less dramatically.[9]

Now imagine that all evaluators A_1 through D_1 belong to the same party A_R. The high variance of their judgments of party A_R on issue k (S.D. = 5.02) would then entail that the party is intensely divided on the issue of market liberalization, provided the respondents deem the issue to be salient for party competition. Imagine, instead, that evaluator D_1 belongs to party D_R, while all other respondents belong to party A_R, B_R, and C_R. Imagine further that fellow party members who are not depicted in table 4.4 share the judgments their representatives A_1 through D_1 have announced. We then encounter a situation of systematic "asymmetric judgment," where the party affiliation of the judges, rather than the

---

[9]Nevertheless, outliers may be annoying. In the pilot study, we found that respondents sometimes confused the end points of the scales in the questionnaire and thus placed parties exactly in the opposite order they had intended. Interviewers were trained to catch such mistakes while respondents were completing the questionnaire, but in a few instances in each country the response pattern shows that we were unable to eliminate the problem entirely. Fortunately, these mistakes do not appear in such a fashion that they would systematically bias results. But they make the heterogeneity of party placements appear greater than it actually is.

identity of the rated party, determines how respondents score parties A_R, B_R, . . . on issue k. If you belong to D, you rate A as a social-protectionist party, but if you belong to A, you see it as a market liberal party. In most instances of salient policy problems, systematic asymmetry is a sure sign that respondents identify a valence issue of party competition. In contrast to positional or "spatial" issues where parties may announce diverging policy preferences, because voters disagree on the best policy, in the case of valence issues, politicians know that most voters have a clear and overwhelming preference for a single position. Under those circumstances, parties do not compete so much by advertising different issue positions, but by claiming to approximate the dominant popular position more closely and more competently than their competitors. As a consequence, evaluators from different parties dispute each other's ability to represent the dominant position.

Whether an issue is a valence or a spatial issue of competition is a matter of degree, determined by how lopsided the known or expected voter distribution of preferences over issue k actually is. In our example, the respondents believe that support for market liberalism approximates a valence issue, because all judges consider their own party to be closest to a market-liberal position. Even partisans of D_R insist on being market liberals, although judges belonging to the other parties depict D_R as a social-protectionist party. The respondents' scores show, however, that market liberalism is not a complete valence issue, because supporters of parties B and C are quite willing to indicate that their parties do not take extreme pro-market positions. There may be a range of "acceptable" alternative positions to that of complete market-liberal privatization.

Going back to lines 1.7 and 1.8 in table 4.4, note that the judges assess the relative homogeneity of each party's appeal on issue k quite differently. They see that parties A_R and D_R are programmatically quite incoherent, whereas they attribute rather coherent views to parties B_R and C_R. Moreover, if we remove the outlier judge D_1, then party D_R's cohesiveness is almost as high as that of parties B_R and C_R, while party A_R still displays a much greater standard deviation than its competitors. To some extent, the size of standard deviations in each party's position may be inflated by the judges' varying anchor points. By expressing a party's position relative to the mean of a judge's assessment of *all* parties rather than the absolute values of the scale, we remove the effect of that anchor point.[10] In table 4.4, this operation clarifies that judge A_1's and B_1's scores of the four parties are identical (lines 2.1 and 2.2). Moreover, the use of relative scores in some

[10]Alternatively, we could have standardized each respondent's party scores and thus corrected not only for the mean value, but also the variance in respondents' raw scores. This mathematical operation, however, makes the tacit assumption that the absolute distances between parties' scores and the greater or lesser polarization judges see between parties on an issue are meaningless because they say more about the respondent's psychological disposition to assign extreme scores than the actual greater or lesser polarization of parties' issue positions. Psychological dispositions may play a role at the individual level, but if we assume a random distribution of dispositions across parties, they should wash out when we compare parties' mean positions based on substantial samples of politicians judging parties in their country.

cases substantially reduces the standard deviations of a party j's rating by judges i on issue k (lines 2.7 and 2.8 compared with lines 1.7 and 1.8).

In our data set, the simple removal of personal anchor points of political judgments reduces standard deviations of party j's position on issue k on average by about 20 to 30 percent. Given our 20-point scale, standard deviations of parties' relative scores in the range of 3.0 or less indicate a rather strong convergence in the evaluators' placement of a party on an issue, standard deviations between 3.0 and 3.5 signal intermediate agreement on a party's position, and standard deviations greater than 3.5, and certainly those beyond 4.0, indicate rather high diffuseness or disagreement about a party's position.

UNITS OF MEASUREMENT AND UNITS OF ANALYSIS

In light of these considerations, we can define the units of measurement, the units of analysis, and the nature of comparison we propose in our empirical analysis with greater precision. Our *unit of measurement* is politician i's score of party j on issue k. The unit of measurement is *not* each rated party A_R, B_R, C_R . . . as a whole, or the individual respondent i, but the i.j.k scores of a particular party on an issue by a particular respondent. Thus, the number of observations of parties' positions on issue k is the number of respondents, multiplied by the number of parties they score.

Our unit of measurement, however, is not our unit of analysis. We do not attempt to explain why this or that respondent i scores parties j on issues k in a particular fashion. It would be a study in cognitive or political psychology to explain why party judgments vary across individual respondents. Our study includes no individual-level variables *other than the respondent's party affiliation* that would allow us to predict the peculiar scoring habits of individual politicians. Our study aims at the comparison of *attributes that characterize the scored collectivities,* such as the individual parties A_R, B_R, C_R . . . or the attributes of entire party systems. At the lowest level of aggregation, we compare traits of parties, perceived by all politicians in a country or only those politicians who belong to the party. Such traits are their perceived average issue positions, the cohesiveness of such positions, and the salience the party attributes to these positions. This information allows us to compare parties' attributes within the same party system. At the next level of aggregation, we are interested in the way parties bundle issue positions – that is, their composite political stances in the issue space ("programmatic appeal"). Here we explore how their own or all parties' issue stances "hang together" and produce low-dimensionality political divides and competitive dimensions.

At the highest level of aggregation, we compare the configuration of parties' political appeals *within* party systems *across* our four countries. For example, we wish to determine whether the average programmatic structuring of their competitive stances varies across countries. At this level, we explore the contribution of systemic properties, such as legacies of communism and institutional design features of the democratic rules, to the patterns of party competition.

Because our analysis is concerned with aggregate differences across issues, parties, and party systems, we do not worry much about the *size of our politicians' samples*. In each country, our main survey solicited interviews with between 100 and 135 respondents. On each issue, this generated between 500 and 1,200 judgments of party positions (number of respondents times parties judged). Respondents passed between 2,000 and 2,400 judgments on each party (number of respondents times issues judged). By standards of survey research, our samples are small, but given the design of our study and our respondents' level of cognitive refinement and political involvement, our approach offers rather robust opportunities to draw descriptive inferences.

Cross-issue and cross-national comparison of parties' issue positions with quantitative scales involves obvious risks. Can we say that a difference of 14 points on a 20-point issue scale between the most extreme parties in country X means the same thing as a similar distance of the extreme parties' positions on that same issue in country Y? If, for example, the Bulgarian and the Hungarian post-communist successor parties receive the same relative j.k score of +6 (once respondents' individual anchor points have been removed) on the issue scale for market liberalism versus social protectionism, are we entitled to infer that the two parties advocate *the same substantive policy positions* on economic policy? Can we even say that they are equally social protectionist relative to the other parties in their own system? In fact, it is well possible that a +6 score in Hungary signals a more market-liberal position than in Bulgaria, because the entire spectrum of Hungarian parties may be much more favorably disposed toward capitalist market economics. Moreover, the true distance between Hungarian socialists and their competitors may be smaller than in Bulgaria, because most parties are involved in a centripetal competition. The problem is that judges assess parties only within a single national system and do not base their judgments on comparisons of domestic and foreign parties' positions on the same issues. This yields the methodological problem for comparative research that respondents' anchor points may vary cross-nationally, but we have no technique of removing this effect. As a consequence, when we employ quantitative evidence in cross-national comparisons, we must be sensitive to context conditions that surround the national party systems.

PART III

THE STRUCTURING OF PARTY COMPETITION

5

PROGRAMMATIC CITIZEN-ELITE LINKAGE STRATEGIES ACROSS POST-COMMUNIST POLITIES

In the early phase of post-communist democratic party competition, legacies of the old regime constitute more powerful constraints or facilitators of programmatic competition than the new democratic institutions by themselves. According to this logic, among our four cases, we expect the strongest programmatic crystallization in the Czech Republic, a formerly bureaucratic-authoritarian regime. Programmatic crystallization may be weaker in Hungary where a negotiated regime transition against the backdrop of a national-accommodative communist regime makes it difficult for parties to develop clear programmatic profiles on salient socio-economic issues. Poland may be situated somewhere in between these two countries, combining an essentially national-accommodative communist regime whose ruling party toward the end embraced market and democratic liberalization with a transition process characterized by both negotiation and confrontation between an old ruling party and new challengers. Overall the least programmatic structuring we expect in Bulgaria where a weak and divided liberal-democratic political sector and a comparatively popular, but programmatically disorganized post-communist party emerge from the ruins of patrimonial communism.

In this chapter, we explore the empirical plausibility of these claims, but also confront an argument that runs counter to our explanation of cross-national diversity in the programmatic crystallization of party systems. Is it not simply the fragmentation of party systems that covaries with greater or lesser programmatic crystallization? Let us first, however, introduce four measures that bear on our assessment of programmatic crystallization in post-communist democracies.

ATTRIBUTES OF PROGRAMMATIC CRYSTALLIZATION

Parties that compete on programmatic appeals concentrate their messages on a few salient policy issues that serve voters as signals conveying the party's broader programmatic principles. Hence a cross-national comparison of programmatic structuring must focus on parties' salient issues. Although the salience of issues varies among parties, the exigencies of the competitive struggle, with no party capable of controlling the political agenda alone, typically force all parties to address a common set of issues. Even Christian parties cannot run just on moral issues or peasant parties only on agricultural subsidies; they also have to position themselves in the broader competitive arena.[1] We first explore, therefore, which issues enjoy sufficiently high political salience to matter for party competition.

Next, we construct a simple measure of parties' and party systems' *programmatic crystallization* around each issue. This measure is the standard deviation of a party j's position on issue k, as scored by all respondents i. Programmatic structuring is high, when the standard deviation of judges' scores is low. This presupposes that *both* the respondents who belong to party j *as well as* those who belong to other parties assign about the same score on the 20-point scale to party j on issue k. Thus, a party's programmatic structuring on an issue is high only if there is a *symmetry of perceptions among politicians of all parties* – that is, a general agreement on where that party stands on the particular issue. When *all* politicians from *all* parties agree where *each* party stands on issue k, political elites, but also voters, experience a minimum of confusion about the alternatives among which they have to decide.

We engage in a variety of tests to explore whether our raw measure of programmatic crystallization or its inversion, programmatic diffuseness, really represents the phenomenon of programmatic party cohesion we are interested in. In this chapter, we investigate whether our measure of programmatic diffuseness is nothing but an artefact of two other phenomena, *political polarization* or *asymmetric judgments* among politicians belonging to different parties. We measure programmatic polarization as the standard deviation of the mean issue positions all respondents assign to each party j on each issue k. Thus, if the four parties A, B, C, and D receive mean positions of A = 4, B = 8, C = 12, and D = 16 on our 20-point scale, then the inter-party issue polarization (S.D. = 5.16) is greater than were they to receive average scores of 7, 9, 11, and 13 (S.D. = 2.58). If parties are polarized, politicians and voters find it cognitively less challenging to identify their positions. In this sense, polarization covaries with programmatic crystallization. Probably for this reason, Huntington (1968: 416) argues that the perception of some programmatic polarization helps to tie voters to parties and thus to

---

[1] Issues that parties "own" in the sense of an issue theory of party competition (Budge and Farlie 1983) are therefore more points in a broad competitive space than independent dimensions of competition.

entrench broad-based competitive party systems, although in the long run *less* polarization may be more conductive to democratic stability. Programmatic polarization allows politicians and the electorate to see the programmatic stakes in the competitive game and realize that political participation matters.

In part, the covariation of polarization and programmatic crystallization may occur for purely technical reasons. Where programmatic diffuseness is high, because politicians perceive party j to take very different positions on issue k, the mean value of their policy scores for party j regresses toward the median on the 20-point scale. If programmatic diffuseness is a common phenomenon for most relevant parties in a system, all the parties' mean policy positions k will be close to the median of the scale and this configuration yields a low polarization score. We need to explore, therefore, in our empirical research whether purely technical effects of programmatic diffuseness account for low polarization. Of course, extreme parties may display considerable programmatic diffuseness (high standard deviations of politicians' scoring of their issue positions), while moderate parties are programmatically crystallized (low standard deviations). Low polarization in a party system therefore does not necessarily imply the absence of programmatic party competition. Comparing entire party systems, if the correlation between programmatic diffuseness and systemic polarization varies across polities, only substantive differences between party systems, not technical effects of a regression of party average position to the mean, can account for this pattern.

A party system may appear to be programmatically diffuse not because the politicians of a party j send diffuse messages about its position on issue k, but because politicians belonging to other parties systematically challenge party j's self-perception on issue k. They try to persuade voters that party j really takes a different position than its own politicians advertise. Here the seeming programmatic diffuseness of party j on issue k derives not from a random process of noisy evaluation of jk positions by all judges but from the *systematic asymmetry* of judges' assessments, resulting from the interaction effect of evaluator i's own party affiliation with the identity of the party j scored on issue k. We can empirically measure the presence of systematic asymmetries by estimating how much variance the i*j interaction effect of judges explains in predicting party j's position on k, net of the direct effects of i and j on k. As discussed in the previous chapter, such systematic asymmetries may substantively tap strategic configurations of inter-party *valence competition.*

In sum, we employ three different, but complementary measures of programmatic crystallization. Our master variable is a gross measure of parties' programmatic diffuseness, based on the standard deviations of all respondents' scores assigned to a party. At the level of party system, we measure the average diffuseness of all parties j on issue k. We can then further probe into the nature of programmatic diffuseness by analyzing party system polarization and asymmetric judgments. Programmatic crystallization, polarization, and systematic asymmetries matter most, of course, where issues are highly salient. For this reason, our comparative analysis begins with issue salience.

ISSUE SALIENCE

Table 5.1 depicts the mean salience that all respondents, regardless of party affiliation, assign to each issue in their own country. Unlike the 20-point issue position scales, the salience scale ranges from a low of score 1 to a high score of 5. Politicians rank none of the issues that made it into the final questionnaire as unimportant with mean scores of less than 3.0, an intended effect of the construction of our questionnaire. Nevertheless, there remain interesting patterns of variation between medium and highly salient issues across our four countries.[2] This divergence of issue salience comes to the fore even when we aggregate sets of issues according to the three broad categories introduced in chapter 4, economic, "mixed," and political-cultural issues. While these summary averages mask some interesting variance on individual issues, they nevertheless highlight the more general patterns.

Where an issue's mean salience score approaches the maximum value 5.0, there is preciously little variance among the judges, whether within or across parties. Where the score is at or below 4.0, politicians belonging to some parties may attribute distinctly less salience to the issues than those of others. Such inter-party variance is predictable on the issue of church influence in schools, which is more salient primarily for judges belonging to Christian parties. Urban-rural issues tend to be more salient for judges from agrarian parties than for those of the other parties, but usually not by much. The most interesting differences on salience ratings are indeed revealed by the cross-national and cross-issue variance presented in table 5.1.

Focusing on the cross-national comparison, Bulgarian respondents, at one extreme, find more issues highly salient for their parties' electoral appeals than Czech or Polish respondents, at the other extreme. Hungarian respondents are somewhere in the middle, but closer to the Bulgarian ratings.[3] One possible interpretation is that Bulgarian politics in 1994 was more highly charged with policy controversies, for example, because the country found itself without a stable government majority and faced a deep political crisis that raised a wide variety of pressing issues. What makes this argument plausible, of course, is the legacy of patrimonial communism that enabled the old ruling party to maintain a high level of societal entrenchment and resist a political adaptation to a capitalist liberal democracy.

[2]Details of the questionnaire construct are discussed in chapter 4. Please also note the difference in the formulation of the church-state question (VAR 39) in Bulgaria as opposed to the three East Central European countries and the addition of national issue items in Bulgaria and Hungary (VAR 45 and 52).

[3]Note that this interpretation does not hinge upon a direct comparison of issue salience scores across countries. Cross-nationally we compare only the salience differentials that respondents within each country see across issues. The standard deviation of the mean salience ratings across issues is only .32 in Bulgaria, .35 in Hungary, .38 in the Czech Republic, and .48 in Poland.

There is, however, a rather different interpretation for the same cross-national pattern. Whether politicians belong to the old Bulgarian ruling party or its opponents, they have *little capacity to distinguish between more important and less important issues*. The ability to discriminate among issues in the electoral competition characterizes politicians' programmatic linkage building to electoral constituencies. By establishing clear salience differentials among policy issues and highlighting a few critical issues as most salient, politicians help voters to create a map of the arena of party competition without overloading their capacity to process information. In contrast, where politicians declare everything to be important, maybe nothing is important for them at all, because they do not know how to prioritize their attention.

If this interpretation is correct, the inability of Bulgarian politicians to discriminate among more or less salient issues should coincide with a high programmatic diffuseness of the parties, a topic we explore next, and with a rather loose linkage between parties' positions across a set of policy issues, a topic we address in chapter 7. Where politicians are confused about their own parties' and their competitors' issue positions, they also have difficulties in discriminating among more or less salient policy questions.

Our data in table 5.1 also reveal interesting patterns across issue areas. It is obvious that economic issues have the highest salience in all countries (grand average: 4.49). All politicians clearly perceive economic problems as the critical issues driving the agenda of post-communist polities. They are followed by the "mixed" issues with economic and socio-cultural cues (grand average: 4.15) and, at some distance, by the purely political-cultural issues everywhere deemed much less important (grand average: 3.83). Hungarian respondents, however, judge political-cultural issues as substantially more salient for political competition than their counter-parts in the Czech Republic or Poland. We will revisit this observation in chapter 7 where we demonstrate that in Hungary socio-cultural issues have the relatively greatest capacity to structure party competition.

Beyond these general comparative cross-national and cross-issue relations, table 5.1 reveals a number of more idiosyncratic, but nevertheless intriguing patterns significant for the broader study of post-communist polities. First of all, in the mixed economic-cultural category, child care policy and women's labor market participation (VAR 37) receives below-average ratings in all four countries, *although* women everywhere were probably the greatest losers of the political-economic transition. This pattern highlights that post-communist politicians pay generally little attention to the special burdens imposed on women by the transition process. By contrast, in the same package of issues, environmental protection (VAR 42) receives generally high salience ratings. We show below, however, that this issue does not enter the arena of spatial party competition.

Among political-cultural issues, at first sight a somewhat obscure issue, the priority for authority or individual autonomy as an educational value (VAR 41) strikes a relatively strong chord with politicians who rate it as the generally most important issue in that class. We chose this issue as a tracer of parties' more

Table 5.1. *Salience of the political issues (averages for all parties/country)*

	Bulgaria	Czech Republic	Hungary	Poland	Mean/all countries
Economic issues					
VAR 30 Health/social security	4.8	4.3	4.5	4.4	4.5
VAR 31 Privatization, scope	4.8	3.9	4.8	4.5	4.5
VAR 32 Speed/justice of privatization	4.8	4.2	4.6	4.6	4.55
VAR 33 Fighting inflation or unemployment	4.8	4.2	4.7	4.6	4.58
VAR 35 Progressive or flat income taxation	4.7	4.0	4.1	4.4	4.30
VAR 46 Markets or planned economy[a]					
Mean	4.78	4.12	4.54	4.50	4.49
"Mixed" economic and cultural issues					
VAR 34 Foreign direct investment	4.3	3.9	4.3	3.9	4.10
VAR 37 Public child care and women's employment	3.9	3.7	4.2	3.7	3.88
VAR 40 Urban versus rural concerns	4.5	4.3	4.6	3.8	4.30
VAR 42 Environmental protection versus economic growth	4.5	4.4	4.3	4.1	4.33
VAR 50 Left-right placement of the parties[a]					
Mean	4.3	4.08	4.35	3.88	4.15

Political and cultural issues

VAR 36 Acceptance of immigrants	N.A.	3.5	3.7	3.0	3.40
VAR 38 Women's choice of abortion	N.A.	3.3	4.1	3.7	3.70
VAR 39 Church influence on school [Bulgaria: Orthodox Church]	4.3	3.1	4.1	3.7	3.80
VAR 41 Authority or individual autonomy in education	4.6	3.8	4.1	4.0	4.13
VAR 43 Moral censorship in mass media	4.4	3.9	4.0	3.5	3.95
VAR 44 Former communists in political life	4.4	3.8	3.5	3.4	3.78
VAR 45 National issue I	3.8	N.A.	4.3	N.A.	4.05
VAR 47 Individualism versus traditionalism[a]					
VAR 48 Patriotism versus cosmopolitanism[a]					
VAR 49 Clerical-secular[a]					
VAR 52 National issue II	4.2	N.A.	N.A.	N.A.	N.A.
Mean	4.28	3.57	3.97	3.55	3.83
Grand mean, all issues	4.45	3.89	4.24	3.95	4.12

[a]No salience ratings of the abstract ideological scales.

general propensities toward political-cultural authoritarian or libertarian policies (permissiveness toward individual social non-conformity, political tolerance, maybe even strategies of coping with crime). A further notable issue concerns the treatment of former communist officials in public life (VAR 44). Salience ratings on this issue directly reflect political legacies. The salience of the decommunization issue relative to other political-cultural issues is high in Bulgaria and the Czech Republic, but extremely low in Hungary and Poland. In Bulgaria, where democracy emerged by preemptive reform from patrimonial communism, or in the Czech Republic, where it resulted from the implosion of bureaucratic-authoritarian communism, the recalcitrance of the old ruling parties to accept the new liberal-democratic environment endows the issue of decommunization with considerable salience. By contrast, after negotiated transitions in Hungary and in Poland, there is comparatively less controversy over the treatment of former communists. In Hungary, the salience of this issue trails the average salience of all issues by a greater margin than anywhere else.

PROGRAMMATIC CRYSTALLIZATION OR DIFFUSENESS?

If political parties build programmatic appeals to electoral constituencies on salient issues, they must express unambiguous policy positions that are widely agreed on by their own politicians and recognized by their competitors. As a first rough approximation at the level of the party *system,* we measure the standard deviations all respondents i attribute to each party j on issue k and then calculate the average of these values for each country by issues k and issue areas in table 5.2. In this simple calculation, we do not weight the contribution each party's score makes to the mean overall programmatic diffuseness of the system by the electoral size of that party. Nor do we distinguish between the contribution of a party's own politicians and of politicians belonging to competitors to the overall diffuseness of a party's programmatic position. Of course, we begin with this simple aggregate analysis because closer scrutiny later on corroborates the basic inferences we draw from our first rough cross-national and cross-issue comparison.[4]

The small number of cases does not permit us to run significance tests on cross-national differences among the standard deviations. But differences in average programmatic diffuseness of .4 to .8 across polities and issue areas are rather substantial. Moreover, the *consistency of the patterns of diversity across countries and across issue areas* makes us confident that our results reflect not merely a random pattern but systematic variance. The observed pattern of differences in program-

---

[4]Results reported in table 5.2 are weighted for missing responses such that respondents from each party have the same weight on the final determination of a party's issue diffuseness. Because non-responses are rarely a problem, the results obtained after weighting politicians' responses in this fashion diverge little from an analysis of the unweighted raw data.

matic structuring also closely conforms to those already established in the pilot study of 1993 (Kitschelt 1995c).

The country-by-country comparison of programmatic diffuseness in table 5.2 reveals that, on almost every issue, the Bulgarian party system has the least programmatic crystallization.[5] On the highly salient economic issues, Bulgarian parties appear particularly confused, with standard deviations of party positions about .74 greater than the average values for the other three countries. The equivalent differential on mixed issues is .49 and on political-cultural issues .65. The contrasts between Bulgaria and Central Europe are particularly sharp, when we compare programmatic crystallization on economic issues in Bulgaria, on the one hand, to that of party systems in the Czech Republic and Poland, on the other. Similar contrasts between Bulgaria and Hungary/Poland appear on political-cultural issues. There can be little doubt that Bulgarian politicians send a cacophony of mixed signals to the voters. In-depth open-ended interviews conducted in the winter 1993 pilot study confirmed this picture. Politicians belonging to all relevant Bulgarian parties appeared to be ill-prepared to discuss their own parties' and their competitors' issue positions, once they were asked to go beyond general rhetoric about the deep political divide between the post-communist and the anti-communist "liberal" camp and address parties' issue positions.

Among the three Central European countries, the Czech Republic shows the greatest programmatic crystallization on the most salient economic and mixed issues, closely followed by Poland, which also has a moderately clear programmatic crystallization on economic issues. Here, bureaucratic authoritarianism with the collapse of an intransigent ruling party in the Czech Republic or a mixed negotiated-confrontational transition in Poland/Hungary, by contrast, is programmatically somewhat more diffuse on economic policy issues, but therefore more sharply contoured around the mixed and the political-cultural issues than are the Czech Republic and, to a lesser extent, Poland. Our theoretical argument can easily account for these cross-national differences. In Hungary, national-accommodative communism and negotiated transition undercut a deep programmatic division on economic issues among the viable parties. Given parties' broad agreement on market reforms, politicians face great difficulties in identifying or articulating each party's distinctive programmatic stance. As we will explore later, maybe in Hungary economic reform has more the status of a valence issue than elsewhere in Central Europe.

The greater programmatic crystallization on political-cultural issues in Hungary and Poland than in the Czech Republic is intelligible in light of social and political legacies. The Czech Republic's industrialization, secularization, and early class cleavage shaped not only the nature of its communist regime but also the emerging configuration of competition in its aftermath, such that economic issues

[5]Only with regard to environmental protection (VAR 42) and authority in education (VAR 41) Bulgaria comes in second place behind the Czech Republic.

Table 5.2. *Programmatic diffuseness of the political issues (averages for all parties/country)*

	Bulgaria	Czech Republic	Hungary	Poland	Mean/all countries
Economic issues					
VAR 30 Health/social security	3.68	3.16	2.90	3.08	3.24
VAR 31 Privatization, scope	4.12	3.03	3.69	3.33	3.54
VAR 32 Speed/justice of privatization	4.68	3.30	4.09	3.53	3.90
VAR 33 Fighting inflation or unemployment	3.84	2.84	3.63	3.35	3.42
VAR 35 Progressive or flat income taxation	4.42	3.31	3.71	3.49	3.73
VAR 46 Markets or planned economy	3.66	2.99	3.04	3.25	3.24
Mean	4.06	3.10	3.51	3.34	3.50
"Mixed" economic and cultural issues					
VAR 34 Foreign direct investment	3.96	3.00	3.73	3.41	3.53
VAR 37 Public child care and women's employment	4.16	3.35	3.30	3.76	3.64
VAR 40 Urban versus rural concerns	3.38	3.12	3.26	3.09	3.21
VAR 42 Environmental protection versus economic growth	3.14	3.29	3.07	2.89	3.10
VAR 50 Left-right placement of the parties	3.58	2.80	2.09	3.08	2.89
Mean	3.64	3.11	3.09	3.25	3.27

Political and cultural issues

VAR 36	Acceptance of immigrants	N.A.	N.A.	3.29	3.24	3.41	3.31
VAR 38	Women's choice of abortion	N.A.	N.A.	2.96	3.10	3.04	3.03
VAR 39	Church influence on school [Bulgaria: Orthodox Church]	3.42	2.83	2.69	2.73	2.91
VAR 41	Authority or individual autonomy in education	3.84	3.96	2.80	3.30	3.48
VAR 43	Moral censorship in mass media	4.06	3.72	3.43	3.32	3.63
VAR 44	Former communists in political life	3.86	3.66	3.24	2.73	3.37
VAR 45	National issue I	3.66	N.A.	3.47	N.A.	[3.57]
VAR 47	Individualism versus traditionalism	4.24	3.75	3.01	3.15	3.54
VAR 48	Patriotism versus cosmopolitanism	3.74	3.46	3.01	2.96	3.29
VAR 49	Clerical-secular	4.04	3.05	2.59	2.96	3.16
VAR 52	National issue II	3.62	N.A.	N.A.	N.A.	N.A.
	Mean	3.83	3.41	3.06	3.07	3.34
Grand mean, all issues		3.83	3.24	3.20	3.20	3.37

express relatively sharper party alternatives. In Poland and Hungary, by contrast, before communism politics revolved much more around religious-cultural and political divides; opposition figures and incipient politicians inspired by these divides then promoted the civic mobilization that compelled communist rulers to seek an accommodation with the subterranean opposition forces, for example, by invoking national autonomy, and they resurface in the process of democratization as divisions among the non-communist parties and the post-communist successor parties.

Also with regard to programmatic crystallization, a few comments on cross-national patterns of the programmatic diffuseness characteristic of individual issues are instructive, although a comparison of results by entire sets of economic or political-cultural policies is probably more robust. First, consider the highly abstract ideological symbolic principles (VAR 46 through 50) in comparison to the more concrete operational policy issues (VAR 30 through 45 and 52). Almost without fail, politicians provide marginally or considerably sharper, more co-herent judgments of the parties' programmatic locations with regard to the general principles when compared with their party scores on the more concrete issues. There is a symbolic element in the broad ideological descriptions of parties that allows politicians to situate them more easily on those than on operational economic and cultural policy problems. Politicians' judgments of parties' posi-tions on the more concrete operational policy questions are more diffuse because of limitations to politicians' knowledge about operational party positions and disagreements about how policy positions derive from the better-understood general ideological principles. Among economic issues, the lack of detailed knowledge and coherent operational positions might reduce programmatic crys-tallization on the rather "technical" policy issues most significantly. Particularly income taxation (VAR 35), mode of privatization (VAR 32), and handling short-term inflation-unemployment trade-offs in fiscal policy making (VAR 33), while being recognized as very important (average salience values of 4.3, 4.58, and 4.55 in table 5.1), may strain some respondents' cognitive faculties.

The extent to which programmatic clarity on symbolic ideological cues exceeds that on operational questions of policy is much greater in Hungary and somewhat greater in Poland than in the Czech Republic and Bulgaria. In the latter two countries, the averages of programmatic crystallization attributed to operational and ideological issue conceptualizations barely differ. But in Hungary, average programmatic diffuseness is 3.33 for operational policy issues and a low 2.75 for symbolic programmatic positions. In Poland, that same comparison yields averages of 3.23 and 3.08. In countries where democratic transitions pro-ceeded through negotiation and where democratic competition, particularly around salient economic issues, has a more centripetal character, politicians find it easier to pinpoint symbolic-ideological differences between the parties than clear-cut differences between parties' operational policy positions.

Overall, the ranking of the four countries on our raw index of programmatic crystallization agrees with our ranking of the countries based on their issue salience profiles. Politicians in the Czech Republic signal the greatest capacity to engage in programmatic competition. They discriminate in the sharpest fashion among more or less salient issues and their judgments of party positions on the most salient economic issues indicate considerable programmatic crispness. The Polish politicians follow next both in terms of the programmatic crystallization of party positions as well as their ability to discriminate among more important and less important policy issues. Third, Hungarian politicians rate the salience of mixed and political-cultural issues relatively higher than their colleagues in the Czech Republic and Poland. At the same time, Hungarians are also able to express a sharper programmatic crystallization of the party systems around these issues than respondents from other countries. By contrast, the programmatic crystallization of the Hungarian party system around the most salient economic issues trails that of the Czech Republic and Poland. Bulgaria, finally, indicates the lowest degree of programmatic crystallization on our two measures.

POLARIZATION OR "SPREAD" AMONG PARTIES

As argued earlier, technical and substantive reasons make it likely that programmatic crystallization is related to politicians' perceptions of programmatic polarization within the party system. Politicians tend to spread the perceived mean positions of parties j on issue k more widely across our 20-point scale for one of two reasons. Either they find the positions of the parties *clear*, even though they may be *close to each other*, but employ the entire space offered by the scale to represent each party's specific position; or they believe the parties' positions are *both clear and distant* from each other and therefore deserve scores near the opposite extreme poles of the scale. Empirical studies of competitive polarization in cross-national perspective typically fail to distinguish these two interpretations of survey response patterns.[6] Because in both interpretations, a higher value on the polarization measure implies greater programmatic crystallization, for the purposes of our study we need not worry about the extent to which high polarization values really indicate deeply incompatible party programs. In order to signal our inability to tell whether our measure taps a party system's actual polarization or the politicians' varying cognitive certainty about party positions, we usually refer to the "spread" of party positions across the issue scale rather than to political polarization. Spread is measured as the standard deviation of the mean scores politicians assign to each party on the 20-point issue scales. Table 5.3 reports results by issue and country.

---

[6]An example is the influential study by Sani and Sartori (1983). They interpret greater distances between parties on the left-right scale as an indicator of greater political polarization. While this interpretation may be correct in some comparisons, in others the more "polarized" countries simply may have more programmatically crystallized party competition.

Table 5.3. *Spread/polarization on the political issues (averages for all parties/country)*

	Bulgaria	Czech Republic	Hungary	Poland	Mean/all countries
Economic issues					
VAR 30 Health/social security	2.3	4.3	1.9	3.5	3.00
VAR 31 Privatization, scope	4.0	4.8	2.6	3.9	3.83
VAR 32 Speed/justice of privatization	1.5	4.5	3.3	3.8	3.28
VAR 33 Fighting inflation or unemployment	3.0	4.8	2.2	4.1	3.53
VAR 35 Progressive or flat income taxation	1.1	4.3	1.7	3.7	2.70
VAR 46 Markets or planned economy	3.6	4.5	3.1	4.2	3.85
Mean	2.58	4.53	2.47	3.87	3.36
"Mixed" economic and cultural issues					
VAR 34 Foreign direct investment	3.5	5.1	4.0	4.4	4.25
VAR 37 Public child care and women's employment	1.1	3.6	3.6	3.0	2.83
VAR 40 Urban versus rural concerns	3.6	4.6	3.0	4.1	3.83
VAR 42 Environmental protection versus economic growth	2.0	1.4	0.9	1.1	1.35
VAR 50 Left-right placement of the parties	4.5	5.0	5.0	4.4	4.73
Mean	2.94	3.94	3.30	3.40	3.40

Political and cultural issues

VAR 36 Acceptance of immigrants	N.A.	2.1	3.2	2.9	2.73
VAR 38 Women's choice of abortion	N.A.	4.8	5.8	5.5	4.02
VAR 39 Church influence on school [Bulgaria: Orthodox Church]	2.3	5.2	6.3	5.5	4.83
VAR 41 Authority or individual autonomy in education	2.5	2.0	5.3	4.0	3.45
VAR 43 Moral censorship in mass media	1.6	2.4	4.7	4.0	3.07
VAR 44 Former communists in political life	5.0	4.3	5.4	6.1	5.20
VAR 45 National issue I	4.6	N.A.	5.4	N.A.	5.00
VAR 47 Individualism versus traditionalism	2.6	2.8	5.6	4.4	3.85
VAR 48 Patriotism versus cosmopolitanism	1.9	3.4	4.6	4.6	3.63
VAR 49 Clerical-secular	2.7	5.2	6.1	5.3	4.83
VAR 52 National issue II	4.4	N.A.	N.A.	N.A.	N.A.
Mean	3.01	3.58	5.24	4.70	4.06
Grand mean, all issues	2.86	3.96	4.19	4.13	3.71

Overall, an argument from communist legacies leads us to expect the highest spread on the most salient economic issues in the Czech Republic. In countries with reformist former ruling parties and negotiated transitions, polarization on economic issues should be less pronounced. Particularly in Hungary with a long tradition of economic reform, chances of polarizing party competition on economic issues are pretty remote, a result confirmed by table 5.3. Instead, polities emerging from national-accommodative communism display considerable party polarization on socio-cultural issues.

In Bulgaria, finally, the programmatic diffuseness of the parties dampens polarization and spread among the parties' mean policy positions, particularly on the salient economic issues. Moreover, the weakness of liberal-democratic political forces after patrimonial communism and the entrenched clientelist character of the communist party machine, offering networks of party-constituency linkage not mediated by programmatic appeals, contribute to the observed pattern.

Comparing the interaction effect between national political setting and policy area, we find a similar pattern as in the case of programmatic crystallization before. In the Czech Republic, the highly salient economic issues are most crystallized and they also generate more spread among parties than "mixed" or political-cultural issues. Conversely, in Hungary the highly salient economic issues are not only associated with rather diffuse programmatic party images, but they also generate little spread among the parties. In fact, here the spread of parties is lower than in Bulgaria where for technical reasons we would expect the least spread, given the parties' highly diffuse programmatic positions. But Hungarian political and cultural issues generate not only sharp programmatic party images, but also divide parties into clear-cut camps.

Poland is situated somewhere between the Czech and the Hungarian configuration. The spread of its parties on economics is almost as high as in the Czech Republic, while its spread on political and cultural issues almost rivals that of Hungary. Poland is thus the country in our comparison that shows programmatic articulation of party positions over the widest range of programmatic issues. Because spread on political-cultural issues is so pronounced in Hungary and Poland, their average spread over the entire universe of policy issues and ideological orientations surpasses that of the Czech Republic.

Irrespective of country, politicians everywhere see more spread on the most abstract scales of economic and ideological party positions (VAR 46 and VAR 50) than on the concrete issue dimensions. Greater cognitive competence to assess parties' general ideological appeals than operational policy positions as well as the symbolic character of the abstract principles may account for this difference. Politicians may appeal to broad socio-economic programmatic alternatives, but when they are compelled to get down to the level of concrete policy programs, these differences become more blurry.

Although we are most interested in variations of programmatic clarity, table 5.3 still makes it tempting to diverge from our main theme and interpret our empirical observations as valid indicators of substantive political polarization. If we make that leap of faith, it is quite telling that economic issues generate moderate but not extreme programmatic spread in most countries with index scores not exceeding 5.0. What has vanished from politicians' intellectual horizon is a radical programmatic alternative to market liberalism, and this absence of fundamental competition among rival conceptions of the economic order shows up in politicians' perceptions of inter-party distances. Instead, the issues with the greatest spread, with polarization scores between 5.0 and 6.3, revolve around religious-cultural questions (VAR 38, 39, 49) and, to a somewhat lesser extent, around left-right party placements (VAR 50) and the question of national economic autonomy (VAR 34).

All of these issues are outflanked, however, by the high degree of polarization the question of decommunization and of relations to the old regime generates across the entire set of countries (VAR 44: four-country polarization average of 5.20). In the three party systems with elaborate programmatic structuring, however, the salience of the decommunization issue is either very low (Hungary and Poland) or below average (Czech Republic). Here, democratic competition is unlikely to be affected by a deep regime divide. Only in the least crystallized system, Bulgaria, is the "systemic" question of decommunization not only highly polarizing, but also rather salient in absolute and even in relative terms (compare table 5.1). This polarization derives from the relationship between the old communist elite and its antipodes in the aftermath of the Bulgarian transition by preemptive elite reform, a process that slows down the crystallization of programmatic competition around all other economic and cultural issues, but increases polarization around the historical regime divide.

SYSTEMATIC ASYMMETRIES IN PARTY COMPETITION

Our data interpretation has so far assumed that the measures of programmatic diffuseness and inter-party spread reflect the actual state of programmatic crystallization in parties, not some kind of systematic asymmetry between parties in which judges from one party dispute the other party's position on an issue. Instead, one might hypothesize that high diffuseness is a consequence of asymmetries between politicians' judgments of party positions. Diffuseness thus may not reflect lack of programmatic crystallization but parties' appeal to valence issues as the main operating mode of electoral competition and legislative debate.

If this alternative interpretation is true, issues on which countries display the highest level of programmatic diffuseness (i.e., the highest standard deviations of judges' evaluations of party positions) should also exhibit the greatest systematic asymmetry. Overall, countries with the highest average diffuseness should also evidence the highest level of asymmetry. Hence, based on our previous results,

Bulgarian parties would be expected to be most vigorously engaged in valence competition, followed by Hungarian and Polish parties on economic issues and the Czech parties on political-cultural issues.

In order to estimate systematic asymmetries, we regress the position assigned to each party j on issue k on (1) the party label of the evaluated party, (2) the party membership of the respondent i, and (3) the *interaction term* between the evaluated party label j and the evaluator i's party affiliation (i*j). Since our independent variables are nominally scaled, we employ an ANOVA routine designed for nominally scaled variables. *The percentage of variance explained by the interaction term, compared to an equation that does not contain the interaction term, indicates the level of systematic asymmetry and thus valence competition.*

Before turning to systematic asymmetries in the evaluation of parties' policy positions, as a comparative standard, consider the ultimate case of systematic asymmetry, sympathy toward one's own and toward other parties. In our questionnaire, we asked respondents to indicate sympathies for their own and for all the other competing parties on a 20-point scale.[7] Quite obviously, all politicians choose their own party to be most sympathetic and place all the others far behind. How a respondent evaluates the sympathetic nature of another party depends *on her own party membership compared with the evaluated party (i*j),* not the identity of the evaluated party itself. Statistical analysis of this perfect valence issue yields between 50 and 72 percent variance explained by systematic asymmetry in each country.[8]

Now by comparison, consider the systematic asymmetries in politicians' evaluations of the parties' issue positions. Table 5.4 reports the explained variance the interaction term i*j accounts for in respondents' evaluation of the parties' positions for each issue. First of all, systematic asymmetries explain only between 3 and 24 percent of the variance of respondents' evaluations of parties' issue positions. Furthermore, the cross-national and cross-issue variance in programmatic diffuseness we reported earlier (table 5.2) covaries little with levels of systematic asymmetry. As a consequence, in most instances, programmatic diffuseness genuinely appears to derive from uncertainties about parties' true positions, not from systematic asymmetries in respondents' evaluations of the parties.

Bulgarian politicians who have the greatest trouble in identifying the programmatic appeal of their parties do not express an overproportional share of systematically asymmetric judgment, as is evidenced particularly by the rather modest variance that systematic asymmetry explains on economic and "mixed" issues. Thus, high levels of programmatic diffuseness in Bulgaria are *not* due to systematic asymmetry, but to actual diffuseness of politicians' ratings, regardless of whether they belong or do not belong to the party they rate. Hungary, by

---

[7]We analyze patterns of party sympathies as a measure of dispositions to collaborate with other parties extensively in chapter 10.

[8]The numbers are 50 percent in the Czech Republic, 55 percent in Bulgaria, 65 percent in Poland, and 72 percent in Hungary.

contrast, displays greater issue asymmetry on economic and mixed issues than the other countries. Hungarian parties, of course, reveal greater programmatic diffuseness and less spread on precisely these issues (cf. tables 5.2 and 5.3). In Hungary, our empirical findings, particularly those on social security (VAR 30), the general abstract-ideological question of market economy (VAR 46), and international openness of market transactions (VAR 34), suggest a strong dosage of valence competition that creates the appearance of greater programmatic diffuseness than there actually is. Different parties dispute each other's position on salient issues: post-communists claim that Christian nationals or liberals are much more anti-welfare state, and thus distanced from the electorate's valence position, than the latter admit. Liberals and Christian nationals, in turn, ascribe much more desire to keep elements of socialist planning and control of direct foreign investment to their socialist competitors than the socialists would affirm themselves. After negotiated transition to democracy both the successor parties of the old communist regime as well as their liberal, Christian, or nationalist challengers agree on the fundamentals of a social market economy and now often fight over who can attain this objective best.

If we compare issues across countries, one issue generates above average systematic asymmetry in all four countries, environmental protection (VAR 42). Given the high pollution in communist industrial societies, the issue is rather salient (table 5.1), associated with moderate diffuseness (table 5.2) and next to no spread or polarization among the parties (table 5.3). It is, to a considerable extent, a valence issue, even though the policy issue is framed as a trade-off between environmental protection and economic growth. Because most people value environmental protection, most parties try to present themselves as pro-environmentalist. The issue generates considerable systematic asymmetry, because parties present themselves as more environmentalist than their competitors admit.

Returning to the broader comparative analysis, however, patterns of valence competition, as measured by systematic asymmetries, cannot explain the diversity of programmatic structuring across countries or issue areas. Hungary with moderate rather than low levels of systematic asymmetry on salient economic issues, is the partial exception. Nevertheless, the data reported in table 5.4 certainly do not bear out any revision in our assessment that the Czech Republic has the programmatically most crystallized, structured system of party competition, followed by Poland, Hungary, and Bulgaria.

PATTERNS OF PARTY COMPETITION: A SYNTHESIS

In figure 5.1 we have visualized the countries' averages for levels of diffuseness, salience, polarization, and asymmetry for each of the three broad issue areas we

Table 5.4. *Asymmetry of the parties' issue positions (averages for all parties/country)*

	Bulgaria	Czech Republic	Hungary	Poland	Mean/all countries
Economic issues					
VAR 30 Health/social security	11	4	15	5	8.75
VAR 31 Privatization, scope	6	4	7	7	6.00
VAR 32 Speed/justice of privatization	4	3	8	5	5.00
VAR 33 Fighting inflation or unemployment	3	4	7	4	4.50
VAR 35 Progressive or flat income taxation	10	5	5	8	7.00
VAR 46 Markets or planned economy	3	6	22	5	6.50
Mean	6.17	4.33	10.7	5.67	6.29
"Mixed" economic and cultural issues					
VAR 34 Foreign direct investment	6	3	13	6	7.00
VAR 37 Public child care and women's employment	12	7	5	7	7.75
VAR 40 Urban versus rural concerns	5	5	9	4	5.75
VAR 42 Environmental protection versus economic growth	9	17	24	15	16.25
VAR 50 Left-right placement of the parties	3	3	2	6	3.50
Mean	7.00	7.00	10.6	7.60	8.05

Political and cultural issues

VAR 36	Acceptance of immigrants	N.A.	11	5	8	8.00
VAR 38	Women's choice of abortion	N.A.	5	5	3	4.33
VAR 39	Church influence on school [Bulgaria: Orthodox Church]	19	3	3	3	7.00
VAR 41	Authority or individual autonomy in education	6	12	4	7	7.75
VAR 43	Moral censorship in mass media	13	10	4	6	8.25
VAR 44	Former communists in political life	8	9	4	3	6.00
VAR 45	National issue I	2	N.A.	4	N.A.	3.00
VAR 47	Individualism versus traditionalism	11	11	2	5	7.25
VAR 48	Patriotism versus cosmopolitanism	10	7	7	4	7.00
VAR 49	Clerical-secular	8	4	3	3	4.50
VAR 52	National issue II	2	N.A.	N.A.	N.A.	
	Mean	8.78	8.00	4.1	4.67	6.31
	Grand mean, all issues	7.55	6.65	7.53	5.70	6.72

Issue Salience

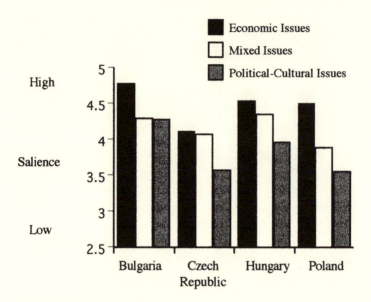

Programmatic Diffuseness

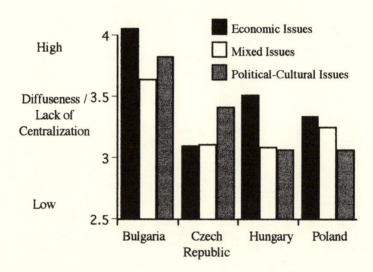

Figure 5.1. Configurations of party competition: Countries and issue areas

Spread / Polarization

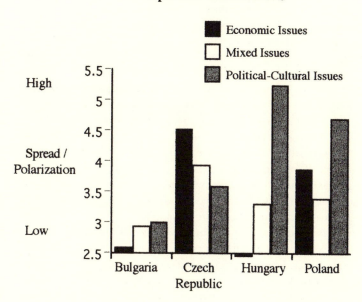

Systematic Asymmetries

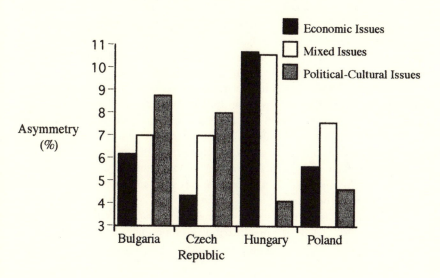

Figure 5.1. (cont.)

have created. This display highlights the important cross-national variances. In the Czech Republic, the parties' programmatic diffuseness is lowest, particularly on the most salient economic issues, where also issue positional spread among the parties is high, yet political asymmetries are low. The Czech Republic thus projects the image of a party system that is divided on economics between programmatically crystallized parties.

At the other extreme is Bulgaria with high diffuseness, particularly on the important economic issues, little capacity to discriminate between more or less important issues and low positional spread among the parties. The Bulgarian pattern clearly derives from its trajectory of democratization. The post-communists are either internally divided between hard-liners and reformists in the major urban areas or still well-entrenched in the countryside and can afford not to compete on distinctive political messages, whereas the anti-communist opposition is fluid, if not chaotic, internally deeply divided, and incompetent to sustain a programmatic discourse on any field of policy making.

Between these two extremes we encounter democracies evolving through negotiated transitions promoted by a former ruling party that essentially agrees to the democratic and capitalist institutions of the successor regime. Particularly in Hungary, polarization on the salient economic issues is low and diffuseness is high, but not because of a simple lack of programmatic structuring. Here systematic asymmetries – that is, valence competition – contribute to the appearance of programmatic diffuseness. Most relevant parties perceive that capitalism, with the "human" face of comprehensive social security, is a popular valence position and they dispute each other's competence to deliver policies that realize this overwhelming popular preference. Poland, finally, is somewhere located between the Hungarian and the Czech configuration. As in Hungary, its level of programmatic crystallization and polarization is particularly high on the less salient political-cultural issues. As in the Czech Republic, however, its politics tends to be also relatively polarized and crystallized on economics.

Let us now consider the inter-relations between the various properties of programmatic structuring we have examined in this section (table 5.5). The unit of analysis is the national score on each issue for the four variables that characterize the structuring of party competition. The number of cases on which correlations are based ranges from 15 (for those involving the measure of salience) to 21 (for correlations without the salience measure) in each country and from 60 (for correlations with salience) to 81 (for correlations without salience) in the pooled sample of the four countries.[9]

Policy salience is pretty much an independent variable that does not, by itself, covary with the other three attributes of programmatic structuring in significant ways. When we pool all four countries, salience appears to be associ-

---

[9]As will be recalled from table 5.1, there are no salience measures for the abstract-ideological dimensions, including left-right self-placement.

Table 5.5. *Relations between salience, diffuseness, polarization, and systematic asymmetries*

	Bulgaria	Czech Republic	Hungary	Poland	All
Salience – diffuseness	+.22	+.10	−.15	+.22	+.42**
Salience – polarization	−.17	−.25	−.47	−.19	−.37**
Salience – asymmetry	−.14	+.24	+.34	+.09	+.18
Diffuseness – polarization	−.38	−.72*	−.44	−.42	−.58**
Diffuseness – asymmetry	+.02	+.68*	+.12	+.22	+.22**
Polarization – asymmetry	−.54	−.78**	−.65*	−.89**	−.68**

*p = .01 (1-tailed significance); **p = .001 (1-tailed significance).

ated with programmatic diffuseness in a statistically significant manner, but this correlation masks the country effect created by Bulgarian politicians who attribute higher salience to all issues, while simultaneously exhibiting the highest programmatic diffuseness in their assessments. With respect to the relationship between salience and polarization and salience and asymmetries, the only results worth highlighting are the specific correlations for Hungary. In Hungary, the most important issues – that is, the questions of economic distribution and governance structures – generate less polarization among the competing parties and more systematic asymmetries. This captures the interpretation we have given on previous pages. Because of the convergence of post-communist and anti-communist parties on market economics, economic issues tend to have the character of valence issues more in this country than in the Czech Republic or Poland. There is, however, a slight general tendency across all four countries to reduce party polarization/spread, if issue salience is high. This may reflect the constraint that no party can seriously reject market reform out of hand after the collapse of the planned socialist economy.

For technical and substantive reasons, our theoretical argument and our statistical operationalization suggest systematic linkages between diffuseness, polarization, and asymmetries. While technical reasons may explain a baseline tendency across all four countries to generate covariance among these variables,[10] substantive reasons account for the varying strength of these associations within each country and the pooled cross-national set. Technically, diffuseness reduces polarization because high standard deviations of party scores nudge parties' mean

[10] If asymmetries are high, then our measure of spread cannot assume a high value because parties' mean positions gravitate toward the mean of the 20-point scale. At the same time, systematic asymmetries represent a special case of the more general concept of programmatic diffuseness.

values toward the center of the scale and thus diminish the standard deviation of all parties' mean values. The tendency that polarized issues yield more programmatic crystallization therefore prevails in all countries, but for *substantive reasons* it is most pronounced in the Czech Republic. Here, in the aftermath of bureaucratic-authoritarian communism and a sudden democratic transition by implosion of the old regime, parties tend to crystallize around economic and mixed issues more than after negotiated transitions or preemptive elite reform by elements of the communist elite.

Systematic asymmetries technically boost our measure of programmatic diffuseness, but table 5.5 shows that the correlation is quite modest and varies from country to country, a tendency technical considerations cannot account for. Only in the Czech Republic, there is a rather strong positive correlation between diffuseness and asymmetry across the entire set of issues. This, again, underlines the comparatively high programmatic crystallization of the Czech party system. As the example of environmental protection in the Czech Republic shows, even where issues *appear* to be programmatically quite diffuse, closer inspection shows that systematic asymmetries, not some random diffuseness of parties' issue positions, drive this result.

Everywhere spread/polarization and systematic asymmetries are negatively correlated, because the latter produce high standard deviations of parties' policy positions and lead to a regression of their average issue positions toward the mean. But given that the strength of such correlations again varies cross-nationally, technical reasons cannot be the only explanation for the observed association. The correlation between spread and systematic asymmetries is most pronounced in the two countries with the highest programmatic crystallization, the Czech Republic and Poland. The underlying political logic for this substantive relationship is straightforward. Where respondents signal a great deal of spread between parties, parties' positions are sharply defined. Politicians find it hard to engage in valence competition, measured by systematic asymmetries, if parties have sharply defined positions. Not by chance, therefore, the negative correlation between spread/polarization and asymmetries is weakest in Bulgaria, which has the least programmatic crystallization.

To conclude this analysis, let us distinguish more comprehensively between patterns of competition in our four countries. We first choose a "deductive" route that highlights the alternatives clearly but loses a great deal of information in the empirical display of results. We therefore also pursue a more "inductive" route that yields empirically more sophisticated, but theoretically more blurry results. For our argument, it is critical that both methods support the same results.

If we dichotomize the three parameters of party system structuring that characterize alternative patterns of competition most clearly – issue salience, programmatic diffuseness, and spread/polarization – into "high" and "low" values around the grand mean value for all four countries, we obtain eight competitive configurations within which we can further distinguish between high and low levels of systematic asymmetry (table 5.6).[11] Empirically, this procedure allows us to examine issue clusters around modes of party competition and compare the distribution of such modes within and across countries. In the four countries, taken together, we have eighty-one policy issues and general ideological principles on which we can score modes of party competition. With regard to the general ideological principles, we lack salience scores. For the purpose of complete classification, we presume here that the salience of these principles is equal to the average of the class of issues (economic, mixed, or political-cultural) to which they belong.

In the electoral game, salient issues are most central for parties' efforts to build programmatic linkages (section A of table 5.6). Among the highly salient issues, low diffuseness of parties' positions is the mark of crystallized programmatic competition. Within that group of issues, we can further distinguish between high inter-party spread of positions (configuration 1) and low spread (configuration 2). Empirically, only two of the four high-crystallization types are common: *spatial competition* with high spread ("centrifugal, polarized, competition")[12] *and* low asymmetry (1.1 configuration 1: 16 issues out of 81 in the four countries) and *valence competition* with low spread ("centripetal competition") *and* comparatively high asymmetry (1.2 configuration 2: 8 issues). Centripetal spatial competition is, of course, feasible, but rarely occurs in our sample.[13] Crystallized programmatic competition with high polarization and systematic asymmetries, however, may be logically and mathematically difficult to conceive. In our sample, highly polarized programmatic competition applies particularly to economic issues in the Czech Republic and political-cultural issues in Hungary. Poland associates a few economic issues with this configuration, whereas Bulgaria does not have a single high crystallization and high polarization case (line 1.1.1 in table 5.6). Highly crystallized issues with significant asymmetries occur primarily on economics in Hungary (line 1.1.2).

High salience issues may also yield *diffuse competition* with low programmatic crystallization. In this class of cases, issues may display the capacity for high or low polarization (configurations 3 and 4 under 2.1 and 2.2). Where spread/polarization is high and asymmetry low, parties appear not to have made up their mind on a policy issue (2.1.1: 4 issues). If asymmetries are high as well (2.1.2: 3 issues), parties are not only extremely polarized, but also dispute each other's

---

[11]We have corrected this dichotomization slightly for the cutoff point of the salience variable. Rather than 4.2, we have chosen 4.1 as the lower bound value for the "high-salience" category in order to correct slightly for the overrepresentation of Bulgaria among the most salient issues. This correction is justified in light of the indiscriminate fashion in which Bulgarian respondents award high salience ratings.

[12]We are aware that our choice of terminology here buys into the strong interpretation of our measure of spread as indicating actual polarization rather than merely cognitive clarity about party positions.

[13]This result is in agreement with the positive theory literature arguing that multi-party spatial competition promotes a spreading out of the parties over the entire policy space.

Table 5.6. *The structuring of party competition: Issue configurations in four post-communist democracies*

	Bulgaria	Czech Republic	Hungary	Poland
Part A: High-salience issues				
Configuration 1				
1. Crystallization high				
1.1. Polarization high				
1.1.1. Low asymmetry	No case	VAR 30 (economic) VAR 32 (economic) VAR 33 (economic) VAR 40 (mixed) VAR 46 (economic)[a] VAR 50 (mixed)[a]	VAR 38 (cultural) VAR 39 (cultural) VAR 41 (cultural) VAR 47 (cultural)[a] VAR 48 (cultural)[a] VAR 50 (mixed)	VAR 31 (economic) VAR 33 (economic) VAR 46 (economic)[a]
1.1.2. High asymmetry	No case	No case	No case	No case
Configuration 2				
1. Crystallization high				
1.2. Polarization low				
1.2.1. Low asymmetry	No case	No case	VAR 37 (mixed) VAR 42 (mixed) VAR 30 (economic)	No case
1.2.2. High asymmetry	VAR 42 (mixed)	VAR 42 (mixed) VAR 30 (economic) VAR 40 (mixed) VAR 46 (mixed)[a]		VAR 42 (mixed)
Configuration 3				
2. Crystallization low				
2.1. Polarization high				
2.1.1. Low asymmetry	VAR 31 (economic) VAR 50 (mixed) VAR 52 (cultural)	No case	No case	VAR 32 (economic)
2.1.2. High asymmetry	VAR 44 (cultural)	No case	VAR 34 (mixed) VAR 45 (cultural)	No case

Configuration 4
2. Crystallization low
2.2. Polarization low

2.2.1. Low asymmetry	VAR 32 (economic) VAR 33 (economic) VAR 34 (mixed) VAR 40 (mixed) VAR 41 (cultural) VAR 46 (mixed)[a]	No case	VAR 31 (economic) VAR 33 (economic) VAR 35 (economic)	VAR 35 (economic)
2.2.2. High asymmetry	VAR 30 (economic) VAR 35 (economic) VAR 39 (cultural) VAR 43 (cultural) VAR 47 (cultural) VAR 48 (cultural) VAR 49 (cultural)	No case	VAR 32 (economic)	No case

Part B: Low-salience issues

Configuration 5
3. Crystallization high
3.1. Polarization high

3.1.1. Low asymmetry	No case	VAR 31 (economic) VAR 34 (mixed) VAR 35 (economic) VAR 38 (cultural) VAR 39 (cultural)	VAR 44 (cultural)	VAR 38 (cultural) VAR 39 (cultural) VAR 40 (mixed) VAR 41 (cultural) VAR 43 (cultural) VAR 44 (cultural) VAR 47 (cultural)[a] VAR 48 (cultural)[a] VAR 49 (cultural)[a]
3.1.2. High asymmetry	No case		No case	No case

Table 5.6. (*cont.*)

	Bulgaria	Czech Republic	Hungary	Poland
Configuration 6 3. Crystallization high 3.2. Polarization low				
3.2.1. Low asymmetry	No case	VAR 37 (cultural)	VAR 36 (cultural)	No case
3.2.2. High asymmetry	No case	VAR 36 (mixed)	No case	No case
Configuration 7 4. Crystallization low 4.1. Polarization high				
4.1.1. Low asymmetry	VAR 45 (cultural)	VAR 49 (cultural)[a]	VAR 43 (cultural)	VAR 34 (mixed)
4.1.2. High asymmetry	No case	VAR 44 (cultural)	No case	No case
Configuration 8 4. Crystallization low 4.2. Polarization low				
4.2.1. Low asymmetry	No case	VAR 48 (cultural)[a] VAR 41 (cultural) VAR 43 (cultural) VAR 47 (cultural)[a]	No case	VAR 37 (mixed)
2.2.2. High asymmetry	VAR 37 (mixed)		No case	VAR 36 (cultural)

[a] Issue lacks salience rating (broad ideological conceptualizations) and is entered into the same salience bracket as more concrete policy issues in the same class (economic, mixed, cultural) in the same country.

positions. This may not be a case of valence competition, but of policy extremism where each party tries to outbid its competitor in radicalism. Consider the issue of how former communists should be treated in Bulgaria (VAR 44). Here the antipodes – the post-communist BSP and the anti-communist SDS – internally disagree on how to treat former communists, although they tend toward opposite poles of the scale. Moreover, those belonging to these parties attribute to their own parties more radical policies than perceived by respondents belonging to other parties.

Where spread/polarization is low (configuration 4), the low asymmetry cases display exceptional intra-party diffuseness about issues (2.2.1 in table 5.6: 10 issues), whereas in the high asymmetry cases valence competition adds to the confusion (2.2.2 in table 5.6: 8 issues). Hungarian economic policy competition displays these configurations because, after a national-accommodative communism with economic reform and a negotiated transition, parties cannot easily differentiate their economic policy appeals from one another. For different reasons, economic and a number of non-economic policy issues generate similar structural attributes of party competition (diffuseness, low polarization, high salience) in Bulgaria. Here parties have few skills and cognitive resources that would facilitate their programmatic crystallization. As a consequence, they show high diffuseness on just about all of the most salient policy issues, economic or otherwise.

The four low-salience configurations in part B of table 5.6 are not entirely irrelevant for party-citizen linkages. Parties may crystallize around programmatically clear but low-salience issues and thus bind considerable electoral constituencies to their own organizations. Such "identification issues" are particularly powerful, if they are associated with high spread/polarization (configuration 5, line 3.1: 15 cases). Identification issues do not involve high asymmetries (line 3.1.2). Politicians from different parties know where the major players stand and do not dispute such claims. Table 5.6 reveals that particularly cultural issues in the Czech Republic and Poland tend to be identification issues in this sense. Where policy salience is low, programmatic crystallization is high, but where spread/polarization is low, issues tend to gravitate toward a consensus among the parties. This configuration is not interesting for party competition and occurs only three times in our analysis (configuration 6, line 3.2.).

Finally, there are issues that have low salience and low crystallization, a sure sign that parties see these issues as irrelevant for the current electoral marketplace and their voter-party linkages. Where spread/polarization is high, the issue has either recently faded or is about to take off (configuration 7 in line 4.1: 5 cases). Where also spread/polarization is low, the issues are clearly not on the agenda of the relevant parties (configuration 8 in line 4.2: 7 cases).

Table 5.6 highlights the cross-national differences in profiles of party competition, primarily on the high-salience issues. Here the Czech Republic promotes high crystallization and polarization on economics, but pushes political-cultural issues down to the status of identification issues. By contrast, Hungary organizes spatial competition primarily around political-cultural issues and relegates economics into the realm of more diffuse programmatic crystallization and/or high asymmetries. Poland, again, is located somewhere between these two profiles. Its political-cultural issues give rise to party identification, while programmatic competition takes place primarily around select economic issues. Bulgaria, finally, fails to organize sharply contoured patterns of programmatic competition in 1994 and relies on parties with diffuse appeals, sometimes involving valence competition, sometimes a centrifugal dynamic of mutual outbidding.

Issues subsumed under configurations 1, 2, and 5 indicate an institutionalization around programmatic party competition, whereas issues in configurations 3 and 4 are tracers of a highly unstable, fluid, maybe even programmatically unintelligible competitive situation. Counting the ratio of issues in each country in these two broad categories, the odds are most clearly in favor of democratic procedures around programmatic competition in the Czech Republic (the ratio is 12:0), followed by Poland (14:2) and Hungary (13:6). Bulgaria again is out of the other countries' league (1:17). Of course, this does not rule out that in Bulgaria democracy stabilizes around other political linkage strategies, such as clientelism, a topic we return to in the next chapter.

The dichotomization of our four properties of party competitiveness around mean values and the rigid deductive combinatorics of eight competitive configurations involves some arbitrariness and a considerable loss of empirical information. To test the robustness of our conclusions, we perform a hierarchical cluster analysis with squared Euclidean distances and complete linkage estimation in order to generate types of issue-based party competition inductively and compare their occurrence across countries. This method groups cases (policy issues) together in "clusters" based on the relative similarity of their members in terms of our four attributes that characterize patterns of political competition. As the number of clusters decreases, their internal heterogeneity increases. The cutoff point for the reduction of clusters is the stage beyond which a major jump in the internal heterogeneity of the clusters occurs. Table 5.7 lists the eight clusters we obtained, the median values of each cluster on the four structural properties of competition we have distinguished, and the number of issues in each country, divided between political-cultural and economic/mixed issues, that fall into a particular cluster.[14]

[14]Two technical features of the cluster analysis should be clarified. First, we lack salience values for VAR 46 through 50 (the general ideological principles) in the four countries so that these issues could not be included in the original cluster analysis. We were able to estimate the likely cluster membership of these cases, however, by a discriminate analysis with the cluster membership of the other 61 cases as the dependent variables, and spread, noise, and asymmetry, the variables on which we have values for VAR 46 through 50, as the independent variables. Second, in the cluster analysis we have employed a different measure of diffuseness we term "noise." It represents the residual unexplained variance when a party j's position on issue k in a country is estimated with the identity of the judge's i party affiliation, the identity of the party j, and the interaction term between both as the predictor variables. The "noise" measure, however, highly correlates with the previously employed measure of programmatic diffuseness ($r = .73$).

Table 5.7. *Cluster analysis of issue competition: Results of a solution with eight clusters*

	Clusters							
	A	B	C	D	E	F	G	H
Properties of the cluster members (mean values)								
Salience	3.8	4.0	4.2	4.2	4.4	4.4	4.3	4.2
Diffuseness/noise[a]	21.4	31.8	41.0	53.6	65.0	83.5	57.3	71.8
Spread/polarization	5.5	4.7	3.9	3.2	2.3	1.4	2.1	1.4
Asymmetry	3.4	4.7	6.4	6.5	8.7	7.8	19.7	16.2
Issues belonging to each cluster								
Bulgaria								
Economic + mixed	—	—	2	4	2	3	1	1
Political-cultural	—	2	1	—	4	—	—	—
Czech Republic								
Economic + mixed	3	6	1	—	—	—	—	1
Political-cultural	2	1	2	—	3	—	2	1
Hungary								
Economic + mixed	1	—	2	2	2	1	2	1
Political-cultural	5	4	—	1	—	—	—	—
Poland								
Economic + mixed	—	4	5	1	—	—	—	1
Political-cultural	3	3	2	1	—	—	—	—

Note: Hierarchical cluster analysis with squared Euclidean distances and complete linkage agglomeration method with pooled cross-national data ($N = 61$). After 53 stages, the analysis produces 8 clusters with an absolute heterogeneity = 171. Further steps dramatically increase the heterogeneity of the clusters ($54 = 329$; $56 = 489$; $58 = 852$; $60 = 5,066$).
[a]For the calculation of this modified measure of diffuseness, see footnote 14.

In a rough approximation, as we move from clusters A to H, cluster members' mean values of issue salience increase, diffuseness and systematic asymmetry, increase, whereas spread/polarization decreases. The extreme cluster A has high spread/polarization, but moderate salience, diffuseness, and asymmetry. The other extreme H combines issues with high diffuseness, asymmetry and salience, but low spread/polarization. A definite break occurs between clusters A through C, on one side, and clusters D through H, on the other. The former three clusters have considerably lower diffuseness and higher polarization than the latter five, but also include some highly salient issues in clusters B and C. Clusters A through C thus approximate spatial competition, whereas the D through H set involves valence competition (particularly in sets G and H) or low structuring of programmatic competition.

The profile of issues in each of the four countries generates a cross-national distribution of issues that supports an interpretation quite similar to that suggested by table 5.7. In the Czech Republic programmatic spatial competition (clusters A–C) is strong on economic and mixed issues (10 out of 11 issues), but weaker on political-cultural affairs (5 out of 10 issues). In Poland, both types of issues involve programmatic party appeals with high issue salience (spatial competition) or less salient identification issues (together 9 out of 11 economic issues, 8 out of 9 political-cultural issues). In Hungary, spatial crystallized competition is primarily a preserve of political-cultural issues (9 out of 10), whereas economic and mixed issues tend to be diffuse or valence issues (8 out of 11). In Bulgaria, very few issues are programmatically crystallized around spatial divisions (5 out of 20 in A–C) or valence competition (2 out of 20 in G or H), whereas most are situated among the highly diffuse configurations of competition (13 in D–F).

SPATIAL COMPETITION AND PROGRAMMATIC STRUCTURING

Our core argument is that diversity in the institutionalization of "real existing" socialism beginning in the 1950s and 1960s and eventually the character of each country's transition to democracy in the 1980s have a critical impact on the shape of early post-communist democratic politics. Programmatic party structuring around the most salient economic issues is most pronounced in countries where bureaucratic socialism imploded and the old elites had little bargaining power, it is second highest in countries where national-accommodative communism was put to rest by negotiations between declining old and rising new elites, and it is weakest in countries where segments of the incumbent elite within the context of patrimonial communism engineered the transition to democracy through a preemptive strike.

In this explanatory framework, the *number of relevant parties* in each competitive democracy is at most an epiphenomenal correlate of the regime transition and of the newly forming lines of conflict that are increasingly constrained by the new institutional rules of party competition. But it has little independent power to structure party competition and determine the extent of programmatic crystallization. There is, however, a counter-argument to our explanation that is inspired by a modified Downsian view of party competition. It holds that the number of parties in a system determines the programmatic crystallization of each party. According to Downs (1957), in a two-party system characterized by no threat of new competitors entering the electoral arena, a single dimension of competition, rational voters who support the party closest to their own political ideal point, and no voter abstention, office-seeking parties advertise policy positions close to those of the median voter. But Downs's theorem is sensitive to uncertainty about voters' knowledge of parties' positions and politicians' uncertainties about voters' distribution of preferences. As a variant on his original theme that attributes more weight to such uncertainties, we might expect parties competing for the median voter to be programmatically diffuse undertakings advertising all things to all (wo)men. Instead of making a precise appeal to the preference schedule of the median voter, parties may "disarticulate" their programmatic positions under conditions of uncertainty about voters' preferences and about the true heterogeneity of electoral preferences so that voters can read different things into what parties say. This is the spirit of Otto Kirchheimer's (1966) "catchall" model of party competition where parties refrain from taking clear-cut positions, regardless of whether such positions would be situated close to the median voter.

Extending this revised spatial model of competition to multi-party systems, where the crowd of competitors is large, office-seeking parties have an incentive to target well-defined electorates through distinctive programmatic appeals that clearly diverge from that of their competitors (Enelow and Hinich 1990; Shepsle 1991). Within the context of multi-party competition, then, vote-seeking parties choose not only to diversify their programmatic appeals but also to sharpen the contours of their issue positions. Our first proposition, then, is that *the fragmentation of the party system should be inversely proportional to the programmatic diffuseness of the parties*. Further, holding constant for systemic fragmentation, *the programmatic diffuseness of parties should be directly proportional to their electoral support. Large parties appeal to broad and diverse audiences.*

To complicate matters further, let us consider the interaction between party system format, size of individual parties, and age of democracy. Early in the existence of a democracy, crowds of political entrepreneurs may rush into the electoral marketplace, set up their parties, and begin to advertise their positions. Even where institutional rules discriminate against small parties, the number of competitors may here be very high because it is uncertain which parties will pass the threshold of legislative representation and then later attract strategic voters and politicians who withdraw support from parties unable to win electoral offices. Moreover, given the competitors' lack of experience or time to make investments in party organization and procedures of consensus building, these parties are programmatically diffuse. They tend to run on the personality of their leaders as a ploy to distinguish themselves from their many competitors.[15] In other words, the short-term effects of institutional structure on the party system format and the impact of the party system format on programmatic politics may thus differ dramatically from the long-term equilibrium results in consolidated democracies.[16]

Overall, then, three rival theories advance propositions about the effect of the number of competitors in early post-communist democracies on the programmatic structuring of party systems. First, the theory of equilibrium effects of institu-

---

[15]For this tendency, see Fish's (1995a) study of early Russian party formation.

[16]The first part of this argument, that restrictive institutions that discriminate against small parties do not immediately bring about party systems with little fragmentation, has been empirically confirmed for Eastern Europe by Moser (1995, 1996) and Filippov and Shvetsova (1996).

tions postulates that more systemic fragmentation in electoral systems that discourage charismatic or clientelist competition promotes sharper programmatic crystallization of parties. Second, the theory of transitional institutional effects contends that a large number of parties in the post-communist transition depresses programmatic structuring. Finally, the theory of path-dependent historical legacies argues that the effect of the number of parties on programmatic structuring is spurious and mediated by the pre-existing communist regime and the conditions of the transitions process.

With only four countries, we can hardly claim to set up a decisive test sorting out the explanatory power of each proposition. As a first approximation, we correlate the critical programmatic traits of each country's party systems reported in tables 5.2 through 5.4 – diffuseness, spread/polarization, and systematic asymmetry – averaged for the economic, mixed, and socio-cultural issue areas we have distinguished with two different measures of the "size" of party systems. The first measure of size is the number of parties whose issue stances politicians assess in our survey: five in Bulgaria, nine in the Czech Republic, seven in Hungary, and ten in Poland. Alternatively, we employ the effective number of parties, as measured by the Laakso-Taagepera index reported in chapter 3, in each country's electorate at the most recent national parliamentary election before June 1994.

The results of the simple bivariate correlations in table 5.8 appear to corroborate the theory of equilibrium effects of institutions. Indeed, when we move from systems with a smaller number of parties to larger systems, the diffuseness of their programmatic appeals decreases, their spread/polarization increases, and they produce slightly less systematic asymmetry and valence competition, regardless of which size measure of the party system we employ. There are two problems, however, with this interpretation of the empirical evidence. First, applied to the four countries under comparison, the theory of path-dependent historical legacies would also suggest a correlation between fragmentation and programmatic crystallization, yet interpret it differently. The smallest party system, Bulgaria, offers the worst pre-conditions for programmatic crystallization, followed by Hungary, Poland, and the Czech Republic. The rank order of historical conditions for programmatic capabilities is highly collinear with the number of parties and is expected to affect the structuring of the party systems in exactly the same fashion. Empirically, the effects of system size and historical legacies on programmatic structuring are indistinguishable in our sample of four countries.[17]

Second, it is difficult to determine whether Bulgaria has five or more parties, given that the main anti-communist electoral list, SDS, in 1994 was an alliance of splinter groups with little independent life, but nevertheless no full integration into the umbrella organization. It is possible that the smaller segments of the

---

[17]In fact, if we score patrimonial communism (Bulgaria) = 1, national accommodative communism (Hungary) = 2, bureaucratic-authoritarian communism (Czech Republic) = 3, and Poland as a mixed case (= 2.5), correlations of the legacies variable with the structural parameters of programmatic crystallization are just about the same as with the number of parties.

Table 5.8. *Party system format and programmatic crystallization*

	Number of parties	
	I: Parties included in the politicians' survey in each country	II: Effective number of parties in the electorate at the last parliamentary election preceding the survey
Three issue areas by four countries[a]		
Diffuseness	−.71 (N = 12)	−.61 (N = 12)
Spread/polarization	+.54 (N = 12)	+.49 (N = 12)
Asymmetry	−.30 (N = 12)	−.34 (N = 12)
Three issue areas by three countries[b]		
Diffuseness	−.01 (N = 9)	−.0002 (N = 9)
Spread/polarization	+.18 (N = 9)	−.01 (N = 9)
Asymmetry	−.45 (N = 9)	−.46 (N = 9)

[a]Data points: economic, mixed, and political-cultural issue area averages for Bulgaria, Czech Republic, Hungary, Poland.
[b]Data points: same issue areas as before, but exclusion of Bulgarian data.

Bulgarian party system, were we able to count them separately, would also still display a high level of programmatic diffuseness consistent with the historical legacies theory but not with the argument that institutions shape programmatic strategies. In the second part of table 5.8, we have dropped the Bulgarian case and calculate the correlation between party system format and our structural attributes of programmatic crystallization in the three Central European countries only. Indeed, the correlations the equilibrium argument would expect now disappear, with the partial exception of the case of our probably weakest indicator, systematic asymmetry.

With our systemic measures of party competition, we cannot test the hypothesis of the institutional equilibrium theory that larger parties should have more diffuse programmatic appeals than smaller parties. The historical legacies theory would expect no such link. We will therefore return to these rival accounts of programmatic structuring at the end of the next chapter in which we disaggregate patterns of political competition to the level of individual parties.

CONCLUSION

We have shown in this chapter that our data on programmatic structuring of party competition in four post-communist democracies conform to the historical legacies theory, but we have not yet been able to rule out a rival institutionalist equilibrium argument employing Downsian competitive logic. The difference between these theories is not that one relies on a "cultural" mechanism, while the other presupposes "rational" party competition. The historical legacies explanation also builds on the calculations of rational actors who take into account their resources as well as existing institutional constraints and incentives that shape the path-dependent choice of political strategies in light of ambitions to acquire wealth and power. But, at least implicitly, the historical legacies argument incorporates more cognitive structure in its framework than a Downsian model based on instant institutional equilibrium effects. Consider the strategies of communist successor parties (Ishiyama 1995). Their practices of rule under the old regime shape their own strategic propensities and intra-party coalitions as well as the credibility of their programmatic appeals, as perceived by the electorate.

Our analysis has operated at a very high level of aggregation in this chapter. We have examined general parameters characterizing entire party systems in issue areas, without taking differences of programmatic structuring among individual parties within the same country into account. It is conceivable that one or two highly unstructured small parties in Bulgaria completely muddy the water and conceal that the major Bulgarian parties are programmatically as crystallized as their counterparts in the other post-communist democracies. Conversely, it could turn out that in countries with greater aggregate crystallization the most powerful parties are programmatically diffuse, whereas small parties have clear programmatic profiles. This is a critical problem to be addressed in the next chapter.

6

LINKAGE STRATEGIES WITHIN PARTY SYSTEMS: DIVERSITY AMONG PARTIES

In this chapter we examine the linkage strategies of individual parties with four tasks in mind. First, we explore whether the cross-national differences in programmatic structuring observed at the level of party systems in the previous chapter are merely due to a fallacy of composition. Do our findings reflect cross-nationally varying central tendencies of programmatic linkage building shared by all major parties *within* each polity and setting them apart from those of other polities, or do they derive from the outlier status of maverick parties? Second, we draw on our qualitative open-ended interviews in the pilot phase of our investigation as well as circumstantial evidence to explore whether parties whose programmatic crystallization is weak develop other linkage strategies, such as charismatic leadership appeals or clientelist exchange relations. Third, we examine the extent to which the basic ideological thrust of individual parties and their role in the democratic transition can explain their strategies of linkage building and programmatic competition. Maybe individual party ideology more so than communist legacies or institutional incentives influence politicians' linkage strategies. Finally, we bring the data analysis in this chapter to bear on the rival explanations of alternative linkage strategies discussed in the closing section of the previous chapter – legacies of communism, institutional equilibrium, or transitional party strategies.

PROGRAMMATIC STRUCTURING AT THE LEVEL OF INDIVIDUAL PARTIES

The big disadvantage of our party-level quantitative analysis is that the number of responses on which we base the politicians' assessment of their own party is rather small (see table 4.3). It ranges from an average of twelve respondents per party in

Poland to an average of twenty-one respondents in Hungary.[1] By conventional standards of statistical sampling, these numbers are far too low to generate any confidence in our estimations. We have to take into consideration, however, that our respondents are rather sophisticated, highly involved political participants who enjoy the equivalent of "expert status" on their own parties and their political systems. With such a sample, we would not expect the usual randomness and measurement errors that occur in population surveys on political issues, where many respondents have neither processed much political information nor carefully reflected on the topics of the survey. In political elite studies where experts or politicians are the source of information, scholars generally do not consider small respondent numbers a fatal flaw for descriptive inferences.[2] Moreover, given our reliance on a large number of open-ended interviews, we are able to assess the plausibility of our quantitative estimates against independent evidence.

At the systemic level, we captured national profiles of party competition by four variables: issue salience, programmatic crystallization/diffuseness, spread/ polarization, and systematic asymmetries. In our individual party level analysis, we seek to identify empirical referents for the same theoretical concepts, provided they help us identify meaningful variance across parties. For *issue salience,* we can simply rely on respondents from each party to assess the salience the respective issues have for that party. But as we noted earlier, variance of issue salience across parties is not a terribly interesting phenomenon. We therefore capture the relative salience of different issue areas for individual parties only by separating the already familiar three baskets of highly salient economic, moderately salient mixed, and less salient political-cultural issues in our other measures of parties' competitive strategies.[3] Also *programmatic crystallization* is easy to measure at the level of the individual party. Instead of calculating a party j's position on issue k as the standard deviation of *all parties' respondents,* we base our calculation on only those politicians who also belong to party j. A high standard deviation signals programmatic diffuseness or even serious intra-party conflict *inside* a party. This measure of programmatic crystallization is probably most sensitive to the small-N problem we discussed earlier.

At the individual party level, *spread/polarization* could be measured as the distance between a party j's position on issue k, as assessed by politicians i who belong to that party j, and the mean position of all parties on that issue. For two reasons, we do not pursue the parties' relative positions from the political center in this chapter. First, we already noted that our measure of spread picks up two underlying forces we cannot easily disentangle, the clarity of a party's stance on

[1]This ignores the small regional or splinter parties where we interviewed even fewer respondents: six each in the Czech Free Democrats (SD) and the Moravian-Silesian regionalists (HSD-SMS).

[2]Examples would be Katz and Mair's (1984) expert assessments of western European parties' left-right positions and Laver and Hunt's (1992) political scientist experts.

[3]We keep in mind, of course, that the salience differentials between these three baskets vary somewhat across our four countries.

issue k and its distance from other parties or from the center of the political scale. Second, to the extent that it picks up programmatic clarity, it is correlated with our measure of programmatic crystallization (cf. table 5.7). We therefore confine ourselves to our party-level measure of programmatic crystallization that can be conceptualized in a more unambiguous fashion.

Finally, we need to find an equivalent to our measure of *systematic asymmetry*. What we want to know is the extent to which the public programmatic image a party j's own politicians wish to associate with their party differs from the programmatic image that politicians from other parties try to impose on party j. Where insider and outsider judgments of a party's issue positions diverge, we witness a political battle over "reputation making." In order to capture the forces in that battle, we need to know something about the relative power to communicate party images in the public sphere each of the competitors wields. For example, the Czech prime minister and chair of ODS, Vaclav Klaus, probably had more influence in shaping the public reputation of small competitors, such as that of the Free Democrats or the Moravian-Silesian regionalists, than politicians of these latter parties had influence to shape the public reputation of ODS.

Given the multiplicity of conditions that determine the influence of specific communicators of party images as well as the varying receptivity of different audiences to such messages, it would require a separate study to come up with a theoretically adequate and empirically valid measure specifying each party's capacity to affect another party's reputation on a salient issue k. Lacking the data and the resources to conduct such a study, the measure of systematic asymmetries we have chosen here represents a less than fully satisfying shortcut. We calculate the difference between the mean insider score of party j on issue k – that is, the score the respondents belonging to that party assign to it on issue k – and the mean outsider score given to party j on issue k by all other respondents in our survey. In order to reflect differential powers of persuasion politicians may wield to affect another party's public image, we weight the scores each of the non-j politicians assigns to j on issue k by the electoral size of the party he or she belongs to.[4] Powerful opponents thus leave a deeper mark on a party's asymmetric public image than weak competitors.

If we dichotomize a party's internal programmatic cohesiveness, as evidenced by the standard deviation of issue positions politicians assign to their own party, and systematic asymmetries in its reputation, resulting from different policy positions attributed to it by insiders and outsiders, we generate four ideal-typical patterns of competition (table 6.1). If the insider-outsider differential is small and parties' internal programmatic coherence is great, the party engages in *spatial competition*. This configuration corresponds to configurations 1 and 5 in table 5.6. If the insider-outsider differential is great, while internal party coherence is high,

---

[4]The weights correspond to the percentage of votes parties obtained at the election closest to our survey in 1993 or 1994 (Bulgaria, Hungary, Poland) or to the current opinion polls about halfway through the 1992–96 electoral term (Czech Republic).

Table 6.1. *Patterns of party competition: The perspective of the individual party*

	Internal diffuseness/divisions	
	Low	High
Differences of means between a party's own judges and the evaluation of judges belonging to other parties		
High	Valence competition Diffuseness < 3.57 External differences of a party's issue means > 1.79	Chaos Diffuseness ≥ 3.57 External differences of a party's issue means > 1.79
Low	Spatial competition Diffuseness < 3.57 External differences of a party's issue means ≤ 1.79	Intra-party conflict Diffuseness ≥ 3.57 External differences of a party's issue means ≤ 1.79

parties pursue *valence competition,* a strategy equivalent to configuration 2 and possibly the high asymmetry case of configuration 4 in table 5.6.

Parties may, however, be internally divided on policy, captured by high standard deviations of insiders' issue scores. If at the same time the party's own politicians and the respondents belonging to other parties converge on assigning the same mean value to a party on issue k, parties are primarily engaged in *intra-party conflict,* not a reputational battle with the outside world. If neither a party j's own politicians agree on its stance, nor the central tendency of these conflictual insider judgments agrees with the central tendency of the outsiders' placement of party j, then voters are facing a general *chaos situation* in which the party cannot effectively conduct programmatic party competition at all. A party's politicians do not agree on what it stands for, and the central tendency of their judgments conflicts with the central tendency of what outside politicians try to make the image of the party to be. The level of informational noise is so high that voters receive no cues about a party's policy commitments from the signals emitted by either its inside politicians or its outside competitors. In our systemic analysis, the chaos position would represent the high asymmetry cases captured by configurations 3 and 4, and possibly also 7 in table 5.6.

Instead of presenting complex tables of individual parties' programmatic strategies, we employ geometric displays that map each party's average internal cohesion and external asymmetries on the three issue bundles we have distinguished in the previous chapter. In order to identify alternative patterns of competition, the maps of party positions include demarcation lines between high and low intra-party conflict and high and low insider-outsider differentials. The relevant thresholds are reported in table 6.1. They are the mean values for internal coherence and insider-outsider differentials, as calculated from all the parties and all of their policies across all four countries.[5] The internal diffuseness of parties on an issue basket ranges from a low value of 2.34 to a high value of 5.60, with a grand mean and cutoff point at 3.56. The insider-outsider differential ranges from .1 to 7.40, with a grand mean and cutoff point at 1.79.

If our party-level measures faithfully represent our systemic variables of programmatic crystallization and systematic asymmetry, reaggregating parties to the national system level should yield a similar cross-national configuration as that reported in table 5.6. In other words, in the Czech Republic and in Poland important economic issues should give rise to spatial competition, whereas in Hungary they should involve valence competition. All three countries, however, would have rather clear-cut spatial competition around political-cultural issues. The mixed issues, by contrast, are most likely to yield valence competition. In the case of Bulgaria, finally, we expect high intra-party divisions, if not chaos with comparatively high insider-outsider asymmetries, to be the most common pattern

---

[5]We take the average of the country means, not the average of all thirty parties on each issue, in order to avoid weighting the countries with a larger number of parties, such as Poland and the Czech Republic, more heavily in our analysis than those with fewer parties.

of party competition. Figure 6.1 represents each country as a triangle with each corner indicating the average configurations of competition for one of the three issue areas. Economic issue configurations have the subscript E, mixed economic-cultural issues the subscript E–C, and political-cultural issues the subscript C.

The location of the triangles shows that our expectations are generally borne out. Czech parties are most internally cohesive. Hungarian and Polish parties exhibit somewhat greater intra-party division on economic issues than the grand average across all parties in the four countries. At the same time, systematic asymmetries, signaling valence competition, are quite pronounced on economic or mixed issues in Hungary. All three Central European triangles are visibly set apart from the Bulgarian triangle where competitive configurations prevail, indicating high internal party conflict often combined with substantial insider-outsider disagreements at least over parties' cultural policy positions. Let us now see what we can learn when we examine individual parties in each country and whether the observed aggregate cross-national patterns still represent central tendencies shared by most parties in each country.

BULGARIA

Figure 6.2 disaggregates Bulgaria's pattern of party competition to the level of individual parties. It shows quite clearly that low programmatic crystallization is a widespread phenomenon not confined to a couple of small outlier parties. In fact, the major Bulgarian parties, the post-communist BSP and the anti-communist SDS, at the time of our survey in 1994 appear to be particularly divided internally and vulnerable to external asymmetries, particularly in fights over their reputations with regard to cultural policies. The only approximately coherent party is the small and almost irrelevant "centrist" Bulgarian Social Democratic Party. In all five parties, the salient economic issues generate tremendous internal disagreement among party activists. In light of these results, it is no wonder that Bulgaria failed to produce effective governments with a clear economic policy agenda in the first seven years of democracy. Internal divisions of the governing parties made decisive reform policies impossible under the SDS government of 1991–92, as well as the Berov caretaker government of 1993–94, and finally even the socialist government of 1994–97.

This interpretation is confirmed by our interviews. Unlike their Hungarian and Polish comrades, the Bulgarian communists engaged in a preemptive reform that thwarted a radical break with the past inside the party. As a consequence, they had to cope with deep and continuing divisions in their own ranks between Westernizing quasi-social democrats, middle-of-the-road technocrats, and stalwarts of the old order who maintain their power, particularly in the countryside, through extensive patronage networks. Moreover, extraordinarily high insider-outsider differentials in the BSP's policy assessments indicate that external observers attribute even less capacity for reform to the BSP than BSP politicians

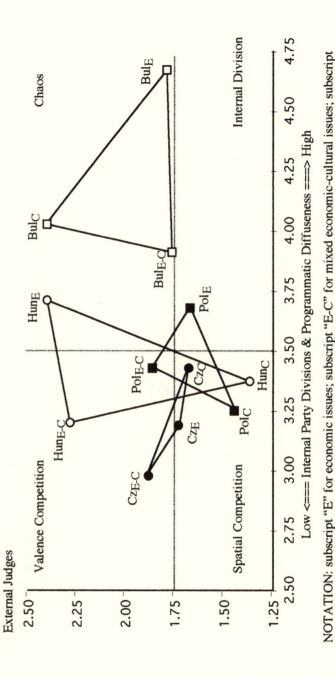

NOTATION: subscript "E" for economic issues; subscript "E-C" for mixed economic-cultural issues; subscript "C" for political and cultural issues

Figure 6.1. Types of party competition: Comparison of countries by issue areas

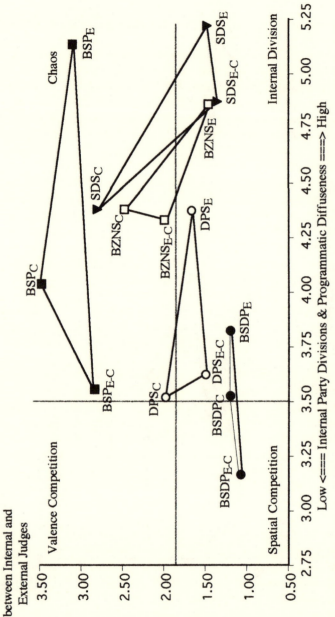

Difference of Means
between Internal and
External Judges

NOTATION: subscript "E" for economic issues; subscript "E-C" for mixed economic-cultural issues; subscript "C" for political and cultural issues

Figure 6.2. Types of competition in Bulgaria: Parties and issue areas

themselves. These external assessments have been borne out by the record of the socialist government of 1994–97.

The BSP's internal division and external asymmetry was its strength and weakness at the same time. The BSP could not engage in decisive reforms and had to produce its organizational coherence through clientelist networks, especially in the sectors of state-run enterprises and collectivized agriculture. Thus, Renata Indzova, prime minister of a short-lived caretaker government before the fall 1994 election, characterized the victorious BSP and its new cabinet as "genetically wedded to corruption and economic criminality."[6] Given corruption and clientelism, Indzova claimed that however closely the new government's program would resemble Czech voucher privatization on the surface, it would only transfer public assets into the coffers of the old cadres. "Red" corporate groups run by former communist officials sometimes descended from Bulgarian state businesses established abroad in the 1980s as fronts for espionage work.[7] The new quasi-private business groups in the BSP's sphere of supporters successfully extracted cheap credits from a compliant government-controlled central bank for non-viable enterprises and export licenses for Bulgarian grain from the socialist cabinet. Involved in trade rather than production, they bought domestic goods poised for international markets cheap, but sold foreign commodities at high world market prices to unviable, debt-accumulating state-owned companies. These practices drove the country into its deep banking, finance, food, and currency crisis in 1996–97.

At the same time, the BSP's clientelism and programmatic "disarticulation" has proved to be an advantage since 1991. Although its disastrous performance in government office from 1994 to 1997 dealt the BSP a severe blow in the April 1997 elections, its organizational resilience and local networks conserved the party as a formidable competitor. Ousted from power, these networks, however, may become difficult to maintain or extend without access to financial state resources. Moreover, the institutional design of Bulgarian democracy may nudge parties toward competitive strategies based on greater programmatic cohesiveness. The fragmentation of the BSP in the 1997 election may be a prelude to such developments.

At the time of our 1994 survey, the main opposition party, the Union of Democratic Forces (SDS), had even deeper internal divisions than the BSP on the critical economic issues. Until 1997, the SDS was a collection of parties and sects with a weak decision center in which extreme anti-communists with only a limited mass following had a lock on the majority vote in the alliance's steering body. As a consequence, the SDS was rather ineffective as a source of policy reform when it furnished the prime minister in 1991–92. From 1992 to 1994, it disintegrated into sectarian politics, spinning off more and more segments as independent parties, most of which, however, proved incapable of surviving elec-

[6]See Indzova's translated interview in *Südosteuropa*, Vol. 44, No. 3 (1995): 218.
[7]Cf. *Transition*, Vol. 6 (1995), No. 3: 5.

torally on their own. Unlike the BSP, a programmatically disarticulated electoral alliance such as the SDS lacked the patronage networks that would entrench it in the Bulgarian polity. The performance of the socialist party government from 1994 to early 1997, however, provided a point of crystallization to rebuild the alliance and overcome internecine struggles. From the vantage point of the mid-1990s, however, the SDS remained far away from offering a coherent programmatic alternative to the BSP that could organize effective citizen-party linkages and a viable party government policy.

High diffuseness and internal division have traditionally also characterized the "historic" peasant party, the Bulgarian Agrarian National Union (BZNS). The peasants' political representatives have been divided since time immemorial. BZNS in 1994 represented the merger of various peasant factions and its internal incoherence shows up in its own judges' placements. Since our survey, the merger with Stefan Savov's Democratic Party has further enhanced the internal diversity of the party.

Among the remaining Bulgarian parties, middle-level elites recognized only the Turkish minority party Movement for Rights and Freedoms (DPS) as a strategic entity of some relevance. As an ethnic lobby, however, it is moderately coherent only on political-cultural issues, yet highly divided on economic issues. Our quantitative measures confirm this perception of the DPS in the press, a picture also corroborated by our open-ended interviews.

According to our data, the only Bulgarian party that has a semblance of programmatic crystallization is the Bulgarian Social Democratic Party. It is telling that this party never commanded more than 2–3 percent of the electorate and failed to win seats in the 1994 election even though it ran in an electoral alliance with a social democratic current that had left the socialist party. In 1996, it became part of the broad anti-BSP alliance, led by the SDS, that won the April 1997 elections. Ironically, judges in 1994 see its policy positions as far removed from the SDS's more liberal-democratic central tendency (cf. chapter 7).

In light of these party-level configurations, our aggregate cross-national comparison does not overstate, but actually understates the lack of programmatic crystallization in the Bulgarian party system. The largest and most powerful Bulgarian parties are also internally most divided and, in the socialists' case, most affected by systematic asymmetries in the assessment of their positions.

HUNGARY

Our analysis of programmatic crystallization in the Hungarian party system indicated greater structuring than in Bulgaria, but more so on political-cultural than economic policy issues. Figure 6.3, with the competitive approaches of the individual Hungarian parties, indeed reveals a rather clear contrast to the Bulgarian situation. In Hungary, parties are much more likely to engage in spatial or valence competition than in Bulgaria. Especially the liberal parties and the Christian Democrats exhibit a spatial competitive approach on the issues we

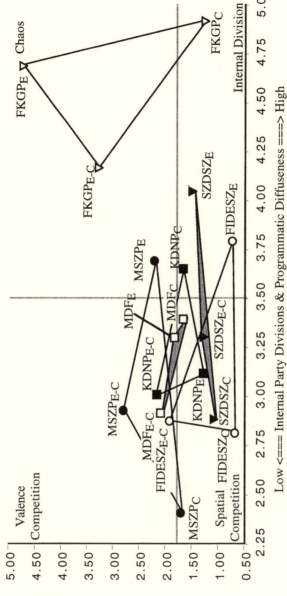

Difference of Means
between Internal and
External Judges

Low <=== Internal Party Divisions & Programmatic Diffuseness ===> High

NOTATION: subscript "E" for economic issues; subscript "E-C" for mixed economic-cultural issues; subscript "C" for political and cultural issues

Figure 6.3. Types of competition in Hungary: Parties and issue areas

already identified in our systemic analysis (culture, politics, "mixed" issues). By contrast, on economics such parties incorporate rather pronounced intra-party conflicts.

A closer look at the individual parties suggests that a single party contributes more to the higher programmatic diffuseness in Hungary than in Poland. This is the Independent Smallholders Party (FKGP), whose politicians express extremely inchoate, conflicting positions in just about every issue area. Moreover, judges in other parties disagree with the FKGP politicians' own representation of the party's general thrust concerning economics and the "mixed" issues. Outsiders suspect the party is much less pro-market and much more for national economic protection and agrarian particularism than FKGP politicians admit themselves, a suspicion that has been confirmed by the changing rhetoric of the party during the socialist-liberal government from 1994 to 1998. It is not by accident that the FKGP's publicity primarily relies on the charismatic appeal of its leader, the populist József Torgyán, while substantive programmatic stances remain in the background. Interviewees maintain that Torgyán runs the party like his personal fief.

In this sense, Torgyán is the equivalent to charismatic party builders such as Ganchev in Bulgaria and Tyminski in Poland, all of whom have relied more on personal than programmatic appeals. What this does not explain is why Tyminski quickly faded and Ganchev's party never grew beyond a modest constituency, while Torgyán's FKGP has proved resilient and able to grow even in the face of internal opposition. Unlike his counter-parts, Torgyán heads not only a "historic" party with some ties to pre-communist era social networks, but also a party with a special interest appeal in the countryside that might be able to build clientelist networks, were it to dominate municipal governments or participate in a national government coalition.

Compared with the FKGP, the other main Hungarian parties demonstrate generally much greater programmatic crystallization. It is noticeable, however, that with the exception of the MDF and the KDNP the three major parties MSzP, SzDSz, and Fidesz all exhibit considerable internal disagreement and in the MSzP's case also external systematic asymmetries with regard to the economic policy realm. The political legacies argument can explain this phenomenon quite easily. Emerging from a negotiated transition, not a single major party in Hungary opposed the introduction of an internationally open capitalist market economy in principle, but all hastened to assure the population of preserving some of the social security experienced under "goulash communism." Parties are torn between the intention to provide social protection while also pursuing economic liberalization. When the socialists and the liberals formed a government in June 1994, however, the internal tensions inside each coalition party over economic policy as well as between them quickly came to the fore. Particularly the MSzP wavered between policies following its social-protectionist working-class and labor-unionist wing and its "liberal" technocratic wing, insisting on tough economic reforms in the first year of the coalition government until its decisive move toward fiscal austerity and economic liberalization in spring 1995.

As in Bulgaria, the post-communist party's position is subject to greater insider-outsider differentials than that of any other party except the agrarians. But these systematic asymmetries unfold within an entirely different competitive context. In Hungary, a reformed and social democratized post-communist MSzP wishes to show credibly that it is economically liberal and culturally modern, whereas politicians belonging to competing parties claim that the MSzP remains much closer to its traditional socialist moorings than MSzP politicians would admit. With a "social market economy" that combines liberalism with social protection perceived as a popular valence position in the eyes of most parties' politicians, the competitive struggle is about the sincerity of each party's commitment to that generally valued position. Examining individual issues, particularly the questions of social security, speed of privatization, international openness, and the general ideological market commitment, involves valence competition, whereas questions of trade-offs between taxation and inflation or unemployment trigger spatial competition.[8]

The former government party MDF and its Christian Democratic ally KDNP show rather similar strategic approaches and thus signal their general political convergence. It is worth noting, however, that the KDNP is internally most divided precisely on those cultural issues where one would expect a Christian party to be most united. Interviews with Christian Democratic politicians indicate a tension between a pragmatic wing that accepts the highly secularized character of Hungarian society and a more fundamentalist wing that insists on the political implementation of Christian values, for example in abortion laws and religious school instruction. Both MDF and KDNP display elements of valence competition with considerable external systematic asymmetries on the mixed economic-cultural issues. Their competitors suspect them to be more protectionist in trade, more opposed to the labor market participation of women, less environmentalist, and more agrarian-particularist than these parties see themselves.

POLAND

The two countries with the highest systemic programmatic crystallization are Poland and the Czech Republic. For Poland, figure 6.4 confirms this picture at the level of individual parties. To make the visual presentation less cluttered, we depict the five Christian-national parties in the upper panel of figure 6.4 (BBWR, KP, PC, Solidarność, and ZCHN) and the five remaining parties in the lower panel (SLD, PSL, UD, KLD, and UP). Just as in Hungary, our systemic measure of crystallization may have understated the programmatic coherence of most parties, because one comparatively small, transitory party that ceased to exist by 1995, Walesa's Non-Party Bloc for Reform (BBWR), was a clear outlier with low internal agreement on the party's policy positions and with significant asymme-

---

[8]In operational terms, the questions generating valence competition among the parties are VAR 30, 32, 34, and 46. For the questions, see Appendix II.

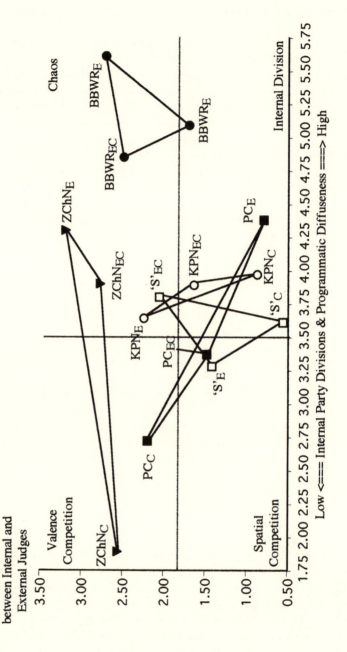

Difference of Means
between Internal and
External Judges

3.50

Chaos

BBWR_E

BBWR_EC

BBWR_E

ZChN_E

Valence
Competition

3.00

ZChN_C

ZChN_EC

2.50

'S'_EC

KPN_EC

PC_E

2.00

KPN_E

'S'_C

KPN_C

PC_EC

1.50

'S'_E

1.00

PC_C

Internal Division

0.50

Spatial
Competition

1.75 2.00 2.25 2.50 2.75 3.00 3.25 3.50 3.75 4.00 4.25 4.50 4.75 5.00 5.25 5.50 5.75

Low <=== Internal Party Divisions & Programmatic Diffuseness ===> High

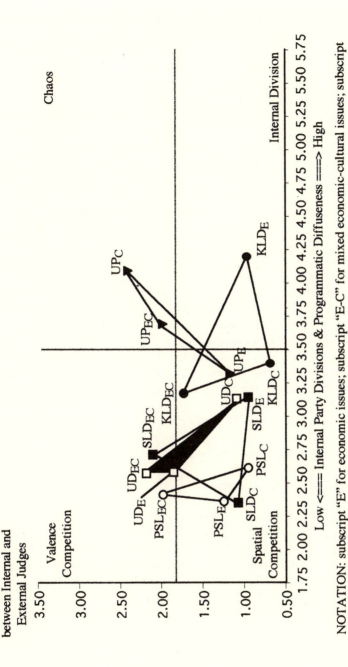

Figure 6.4. *Types of competition in Poland: Parties and issue areas*

tries in its reputation at the time of our investigation in 1994. Its outlier status makes sense in terms of our theoretical model. BBWR was a creation of President Walesa for the purpose of serving as the "presidential party" in the 1993 parliamentary election. It had no direct organizational precursor emerging from the Solidarity movement. As a consequence, even its own representatives could not agree on the Bloc's position at the time of our interviews and politicians in other parties were prepared to dispute what BBWR insiders presented as the central tendency of the party's economic and economic-cultural policy stances. Even more so than Torgyan's Smallholders in Hungary, Walesa's BBWR was the vehicle of personal ambitions expressed by a politician who bet on creating democratic constituency linkages based on charisma more than on program or selective material incentives. During its short duration, however, the BBWR evidences no signs of clientelist constituency linkages.

At the end of the spectrum opposite to the BBWR, the electorally strongest and most durable Polish parties – the PSL, the SLD, and the Freedom Union's (UW) main predecessor, the UD – situate themselves in the realm of spatial competition with rather high programmatic crystallization and limited reputational asymmetries when they address economic or cultural issues. With "mixed" economic-cultural questions, however, valence competition is a more common configuration. Overall, the durable parties display rather sharp programmatic features with quite limited internal disagreements. In our 1994 survey, this applies even to the PSL, a party that as a participant in the 1993–97 government with the SLD sought to build extensive clientelist networks entrenching it in a limited agrarian constituency. The price for relying on such clientelist linkages was a decline of the party's popular appeal to electoral constituencies who cannot easily be reached by agrarian clientelist networks and a resounding defeat in the 1997 parliamentary elections.

Compared with the programmatically focused and electorally successful parties in 1993–94 (SLD, PSL, UW), most parties relying on less programmatic crystallization (less internal cohesiveness and/or more external asymmetries) disappeared by 1995–96 and the single survivor, the Union of Labor (UP), was beaten so badly in the 1997 parliamentary elections that it lost its legislative representation.[9] All the other parties in this sector have regrouped. The liberal KLD merged into the UW. The remaining five parties and electoral lists – ZChN, PC, BBWR, KPN, and NZSS "S" – unraveled, with most of their fission products merging together with further splinter groups into two new party alliances running for the first time in the September 1997 elections under the AWS and the ROP labels.

---

[9]Our data analysis comparing political party elites and electoral constituencies will provide clues as to the reasons for this decline. The Union of Labor attracted an electorate in 1993 that disagreed with the party elite's economic anti-market stance. See chapter 9, especially table 9.A4.

In 1993, these five parties had not only lower programmatic crystallization than their more successful competitors, but also lacked clientelist constituency networks or charismatic politicians that could rally popular support around their labels. These weaknesses of citizen-party linkage building may explain their electoral defeat and subsequent organizational demise. It is notable that the two new party alliances constituted for the September 1997 legislative elections encompass not only Solidarność successor organizations (ZChN, PC, BBWR, and NZSS "S"), but also splinters of the Confederation for an Independent Poland (KPN), a party founded already in 1979 and thus technically the oldest party in the 1993–94 party system. The vagueness of its policy positions and the fading of its would-be charismatic leader, Leszek Moczulski, whom many politicians suspect to have collaborated with the political police in communist Poland, led to an erosion of the party's electorate and prompted its breakup and the assimilation of its politicians into the new opposition alliances.

The question we cannot answer at the time of this writing is whether these new alliances, and particularly the AWS, give rise to programmatically more coherent parties or whether they will prove as transitional as their precursors. Note the high internal divisions on economic and mixed issues in ZChN, KPN, BBWR, and PC. Only the Solidarity electoral list had moderately coherent party positions on economics in 1994. If our data allow any speculation about the future of the Christian-national electoral sector of Polish politics and particularly its dominant component in 1997–98, the AWS, the new umbrella organization may be even more programmatically incoherent on economic issues than its precursor parties. After the electoral success of Solidarity Election Action in 1997, these internal divisions could bring the new alliance quickly to its knees or compel it to build linkages to the electorate primarily based on charismatic or clientelist techniques, particularly if the AWS fails to confront hard choices about the further liberalization of the Polish economy. Given the institutional rules of political competition in Poland, the prospects of successfully engineering clientelist or charismatic voter-party linkage strategies, however, are not good.

CZECH REPUBLIC

At the systemic level, among all four countries we have examined the Czech party system exhibits the highest level of programmatic crystallization. This picture is confirmed by the party-level analysis. A casual glance at figure 6.5 shows that the "chaos" quadrant is empty, indicating that the Czech Republic has no relevant party running on its leader's charisma alone. A potential candidate to be placed in that quadrant is the racist and nationalist Czech Republican party (SPR-RSC), a party that did not cooperate with our research project so that we have no direct information about its internal programmatic cohesion and strategic reputation. Indications are, however, that even this party does not fit into the chaos quadrant,

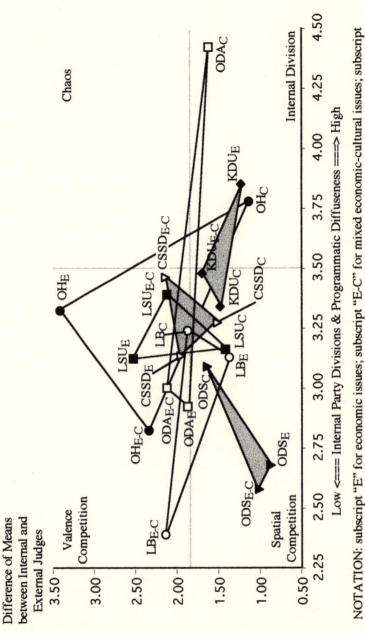

NOTATION: subscript "E" for economic issues; subscript "E-C" for mixed economic-cultural issues; subscript "C" for political and cultural issues

Figure 6.5. Types of competition in the Czech Republic: Parties and issue areas

but combines its exclusionary ethno-cultural politics with social protectionist economics in a programmatically quite crystallized fashion.[10]

Few of the Czech parties reveal high levels of intra-party conflict. Exceptions are the cultural policies of the tiny Free Democrats (OH/SD) and of the more significant Civic Democratic Alliance (ODA). Both parties are torn between libertarian individualism and a more collectivist cultural stance sympathetic to Catholic traditionalism, but these issues are not very salient in Czech politics.[11] The most important division with major consequences in 1997–98 is the internal disagreement within the Christian Democratic KDU-CSL over the extent to which it should buy into economic liberalism. With its internal divisions and intermediate position on economic reform, the KDU has played a pivotal role between the major market-liberal parties of the government camp at the time of our survey, ODS and ODA, and the resurgent, mildly social protectionist opposition represented by the CSSD. The government crisis in the Czech Republic in fall of 1997 and the KDU's willingness to support an alternative to Klaus's ODS government proves this point.

As in the Polish case, it is useful to distinguish between major and minor parties, and between durable and transient parties in assessing the relationship between parties' individual competitive strategies and the more general patterns of competition at the systemic level. Two transient parties that already had lost their electoral significance in 1994 but were included in our study with a small number of interviewees, HSD and KDS, we have chosen not to depict in figure 6.5.[12] All the relevant parties exhibit a strong tendency toward programmatic crystallization and limited valence competition. The most significant government party, ODS, in 1994 competed in spatial terms on the most salient issues of economic strategy and cultural politics. Its coalition partner, ODA, and the two most significant opposition parties, the post-communist KSCM and the most popular opposition party, the CSSD, come close to this configuration, but express more valence competition on economic and mixed issues. In ODA's case, its own politicians project a slightly more radical market-liberal image than other politicians wish to grant them. In the case of the KSCM and the CSSD, the parties' own politicians wish to build a reputation for more centrist economic party strategies that accept a modicum of market liberalism combined with social protection, whereas interviewees belonging to the most market-liberal parties attempt to place KSCM and even CSSD in the corner of hard-line anti-liberal populist-social protectionist policies.

[10]For a further analysis of the SPR's positions, see chapters 7 through 9.

[11]The ODA's internal divisions are particularly pronounced on abortion and church influence in schools (VAR 38 and 39), moral censorship in the mass media (VAR 43), the emphasis on individualism or collectivism (VAR 47), and a more secular or religious political orientation (VAR 49).

[12]In addition to avoiding a too cluttered appearance of figure 6.5, the reason is that we conducted only six interviews in each of these parties and thus have an insufficient base to calculate the standard deviations of internal party positions.

It is revealing that the OH/SD as well as the LSU, both of which lost their electoral significance in the 1996 parliamentary election, faced an even greater valence-type competitive challenge concerning their reputation on economics in 1994. Politicians belonging to these parties try to nurture a more market-liberal image of their own parties' policy stances than their competitors would grant them. Given the resourcefulness of the adversaries LSU and SD were facing, it is no wonder that their own programmatic presentation did not prevail in the public arena of reputation building. The parties were unable to frame their own strategy in a publicly convincing fashion and thus faded or disintegrated (in the case of the LSU) in the 1992–96 legislative term.

After the Czech transition to democracy by implosion, the rapid mobilization of market-liberal political forces, the tenacious persistence of a weak but mostly unreconstructed post-communist alternative gradually displaced by a social democratic contender, and the new institutions of Czech democracy make life difficult for parties unable to engage in vigorous programmatic competition. Each contender within the multi-party system must build a reputation for occupying a distinct programmatic niche in order to attract a modicum of voters. By 1996, only six parties managed to meet these criteria and obtain sufficient votes to send representatives to the legislature – ODS, ODA, KDU-CSL, SPR-RSC, CSSD, and KSCM. Our data on the parties' programmatic cohesiveness in 1993 and 1994 demonstrate why three other contenders – OD/SD, HSD, and LSU – failed to excel in the electoral game.

THE GENERAL PICTURE

Our analysis of individual parties' competitive stances inside each of the four post-communist countries confirms that cross-national differences we identified at the level of party systems in chapter 5 correctly reflect the central tendencies of the major parties in each country. Both systemic and individual party level analysis show that in the early years of the new democracies different legacies of pre-communist and communist rule result in different propensities and capabilities of parties to organize party-voter linkages according to programmatic appeals.

In the Czech Republic and to a lesser extent in Poland, the most durable and electorally popular parties exhibit strong programmatic crystallization around the most salient issues, typically in the realm of economic policy. In Hungary, as the most distinctive case of democratic transition by negotiation, the major parties encounter more difficulties to define cohesive economic policy positions and are exposed to more systematic asymmetries in the assessment of their stances by their competitors. Because all relevant parties endorse a good deal of economic liberalization, economic reform issues have here in part the character of valence issues. Both in Poland and Hungary, however, socio-cultural issues generate very high programmatic crystallization and thus help to structure party competition, although such issues are not as salient as matters of economic distribution.

Compared with the Czech Republic's, Poland's and Hungary's national averages of programmatic crystallization are somewhat reduced by the existence of outlier parties with very low internal cohesiveness and high external asymmetries, the BBWR (Poland) and the FKGP (Hungary). Both of these parties rally around charismatic personalities. Bulgaria is in a different world than the three East Central European countries. Here the continued strong entrenchment of a recalcitrant former ruling party and the weakness of the opposition alliance obfuscated programmatic crystallization and instead promoted clientelist linkage building, at least in the case of the BSP.

Where parties do not crystallize coherent programmatic stances, they may attempt to build clientelist networks or resort to charismatic appeals. For clientelist networking, the Bulgarian BSP provides the most evidence, a strategy that hastened its demise in 1996–97 when party-affiliated rent-seeking groups had brought the economy to its knees. A similar propensity to construct clientelist exchange relations may exist in parties that draw on a narrow sectoral electoral constituency and withdraw from competing in the broader electoral marketplace, such as agrarian parties in Hungary (FKGP) or Poland (PSL). In both cases, the electoral laws are moderately favorable for long-term efforts to construct clientelist networks, particularly in the countryside.

In several instances, parties without sharp programmatic crystallization or without clientelist networks have made respectable electoral inroads primarily based on the charismatic personality of their leaders alone. But such patterns of electoral mobilization are highly volatile. The Polish BBWR, which served as Lech Walesa's instrument, had only a fleeting existence. In a similar vein, after the 1994 Bulgarian legislative election, Georgi Ganchev's Bulgarian Business Bloc, whose programmatic appeal was so diffuse and unintelligible to outside observers, quickly disintegrated in the parliamentary arena, only to be resurrected by Ganchev's charisma to enchant protest voters in the 1997 election. The Hungarian FKGP looks more robust, but as a "historical" party with strong roots in the post–World War II period when it was Hungary's premier party, it has benefited from existing identifications, a special interest group appeal in the countryside, and an opposition status to unpopular governments that have administered economic austerity programs in an environment of slow economic progress.

Our analysis yields no consistent evidence that programmatic coherence varies *within* polities *across* basic ideological tendencies of the various party labels. For example, estimating the internal coherence of liberal, post-communist, and socialist parties on economic issues net of the mean level of programmatic coherence in each country, we find no evidence that one party family tends to be more coherent than others.[13] In a similar vein, we found few indications that some

---

[13]Operationally, we calculated the mean value of all parties' internal programmatic diffuseness and then the average deviance of each party's family values from those figures. The classification of party families proceeds according to the classification provided in table 4.2.

party families are more exposed to valence competition than others. The only partial exception is the cohort of post-communist parties that tends to be internally more coherent, while also more exposed to valence competition, on "mixed" economic-cultural issues and on cultural issues. But even here, the direction of valence competition is contingent upon the polity. In the Czech Republic outside observers see the post-communist party as even more nationalist and anti-Western than it sees itself. Conversely, in Hungary and Poland outside evaluators attribute to the post-communist even more cosmopolitan, secular, and modern sociocultural policies than post-communist politicians wish to admit in an environment where a new cultural conservatism and nationalism enjoys some currency among its competitors.

To sum up our findings and demonstrate the linkage between the disaggregated analysis of individual parties and the systemic level of party competition once again, table 6.2 shows the patterns of competition that characterize all parties in the four countries on each of the individual issues included in our analysis. In contrast to figures 6.1 through 6.5, we do not represent mean values for all issues of a topic, but count how many issues in each party belong in the various quadrants of our two-by-two scheme (table 6.1). Thus, in Bulgaria, we rated five parties on twenty issues, yielding 5×20 competitive configurations, as characterized by internal party cohesion and insider-outsider differentials in the assessment of party positions. According to the first line in table 6.2, 20 percent of all Bulgarian parties reveal issue positions in accordance with a strategy of spatial competition, 14 percent with valence competition, 44 percent with internal division, and 22 percent with a "chaotic" configuration involving high internal disagreements and big discrepancies between averages. In contrast, in the Czech Republic, as the most programmatically structured party system, 67 percent of all issue positions reflect spatial or valence competition, followed by Hungary (64.3 percent) and Poland (59 percent).

In all four countries taken together, just 31 percent of the issues are within the realm of spatial competition and a further 27.6 percent are valence competitive. If we weight each country's contribution to the overall mean equally so that countries with a smaller number of parties (such as Bulgaria or Hungary) do not have a lesser influence on the grand average, then a total of 56.3 percent of cases reflect "structured" spatial or valence competition.

The picture looks somewhat different, however, if we disaggregate the party positions by issue areas and thus, implicitly, also by salience. With regard to the most salient economic issues, only in the Czech Republic does programmatic structuring dominate the parties' competitive approach (spatial + valence competition = 68.5 percent), whereas it is 53.3 percent in Poland, 47.2 percent in Hungary, and only 16.6 percent in Bulgaria. For all economic issues in the four countries, spatial and valence competition prevail only in 51.1 percent of the cases, or 46.3 percent, if countries are weighted equally. These figures underline one more time how difficult it is to organize programmatic competition on economic issues in post-communist democracies.

Table 6.2. *Patterns of party competition by country and issue area*

	Spatial competition	Valence competition	Internal division	Chaos
Countries				
Bulgaria	20 (20%)	14 (14%)	44 (44%)	22 (22%)
Czech Republic	60 (33.3%)	62 (34.4%)	34 (18.9%)	24 (13.3%)
Hungary	43 (34.1%)	38 (30.2%)	33 (26.2%)	12 (9.5%)
Poland	65 (32.5%)	53 (26.5%)	48 (24%)	34 (17%)
All countries	188 (31.0%)	167 (27.6%)	159 (26.2%)	92 (15.2%)
All, weighted	30.0%	26.3%	28.0%	15.8%
Economic issues				
Bulgaria	4 (13.3%)	1 (3.3%)	16 (53.3%)	9 (30%)
Czech Republic	21 (37.0%)	17 (31.5%)	11 (20.4%)	5 (9.3%)
Hungary	9 (25.0%)	8 (22.2%)	12 (33.3%)	7 (19.4%)
Poland	18 (30.0%)	14 (23.3%)	18 (30%)	10 (16.7%)
All economics	52 (28.9%)	40 (22.2%)	57 (31.7%)	31 (17.2%)
All, weighted	26.3%	20.0%	34.4%	18.9%
"Mixed" economic-cultural issues				
Bulgaria	6 (24%)	6 (24%)	13 (52%)	—
Czech Republic	14 (31.1%)	20 (44.4%)	4 (8.9%)	7 (15.6%)
Hungary	9 (30.0%)	14 (46.7%)	4 (13.3%)	3 (10.0%)
Poland	8 (16.0%)	20 (40.0%)	9 (18%)	13 (26%)
All "mixed"	37 (24.7%)	60 (40.0%)	30 (20.0%)	23 (15.3%)
All, weighted	25.3%	38.8%	23.1%	12.9%
Political-cultural issues				
Bulgaria	10 (22.2%)	7 (15.6%)	15 (33.3%)	13 (28.9%)
Czech Republic	25 (30.9%)	25 (30.9%)	19 (23.5%)	12 (14.8%)
Hungary	25 (41.7%)	16 (26.7%)	17 (28.3%)	2 (3.3%)
Poland	39 (43.3%)	19 (21.1%)	21 (22.2%)	11 (12.2%)
All cultural	99 (35.9%)	67 (24.3%)	72 (26.1%)	38 (13.8%)
All, weighted	34.5%	23.6%	26.8%	15.2%

In contrast, our category of "mixed" economic-cultural issues yields more programmatically structured party stances, but here valence competition (40 percent; weighted, 38.8 percent) is most common. Parties tend to be internally quite united on such issues, but they dispute each other's true position on openness of trade and investment, women's role in the economy, the balance between rural and urban interests, environmental protection, and the parties' placement on the left-right axis. The comparatively least salient non-economic political and cultural issues, finally, generate by far the highest degree of spatial and valence structuring.

The lower party structuring around economic issues may reflect the difficult trade-offs and high costs of economic reform parties must face when overcoming the communist planned economy. Moreover, they reveal the systemic obstacles to organizing party competition around alternative economic programs after negotiated transitions where also the previous communist rulers have embraced market-liberal reform essentials (see the economic issues data for Hungary and Poland in table 6.2). In order to create issue linkages to the electorates, politicians therefore single out other, less salient issue dimensions to highlight spatial differences between parties in the competitive space or switch to entirely non-programmatic linkage types such as clientelism (primarily in Bulgaria) or charismatic-personalistic linkages, as demonstrated by the Hungarian FKGP and the Polish BBWR.

ONCE AGAIN: SPATIAL COMPETITION AND PROGRAMMATIC STRUCTURING

In light of our disaggregated, party-level analysis of programmatic structuring of party competition, let us finally return once more to the theoretical challenge we already addressed at the close of chapter 5. Is not the extent of parties' programmatic cohesiveness simply a consequence of the *party system format* rather than of communist regime legacies? With the aid of our individual party level data, we suggest another probe into the validity of these competing arguments. According to the competitive equilibrium argument, large parties can afford to be programmatically more ambiguous – indeed, they have to issue more diverse appeals to cover a broader "catchall" electoral constituency. Conversely, small parties must focus on rather homogeneous bits of the electoral market and express a more coherent message. Further, whereas large parties have the weight and public exposure to engage in valence competition with good prospects of imposing their interpretation of their own and other parties' programmatic stances on the electorate, small parties must find distinctive uncontested niches and usually abstain from efforts to dispute the reputation of competitors. As a consequence, the argument based on an institutionally induced competitive equilibrium would expect *a positive correlation between parties' internal programmatic diffuseness and electoral party size* as well as a positive correlation between systematic asymmetries, as measured by insider-outsider differentials, and the size of the parties. By contrast, *the argument from historical legacy is agnostic about the within-country effects of party size on programmatic structuring.* Its concern is entirely with the overall level or central tendency of programmatic crystallization in a party system that follows from its communist regime background and the associated process of democratic liberalization into which the capacities and orientations of the emerging new political actors are embedded.

As a tentative test of these rival arguments, table 6.3 calculates correlations for each country between the parties' electoral size in the legislative election closest to 1994 and their internal divisions or their insider-outsider differentials for each issue area, as reported in figures 6.2 through 6.5. The resulting correla-

Table 6.3. *Size of party, internal division, and insider-outsider differential*

	Internal division	Insider-outsider asymmetry		
Bulgaria	+.30	+.43	N = 15	(5 parties)
Czech Republic	−.52	+.31	N = 24	(9 parties)
Hungary	−.35	−.05	N = 18	(6 parties)
Poland	−.55	+.21	N = 30	(10 parties)

tions are quite modest, but the signs are consistently in favor of the institutional competitive equilibrium argument only in Bulgaria – and here we have trouble measuring the size of the parties because of the ambiguous status of SDS as an agglomeration of parties but also a single umbrella that fields one electoral list. In the other three countries, the correlations between size and systematic insider-outsider asymmetries are too small and insignificant to be interpretable. The somewhat larger negative correlations between party size and internal programmatic division directly contradict the institutional competitive equilibrium argument.

It appears that larger Central European parties are programmatically *more coherent* than smaller parties, a finding definitely inconsistent with the Kirchheimer-inspired competitive equilibrium model. Small parties tend to be personalistic organizations in the democratic transitions process and crystallize less around programmatic appeals. A survey that asks politicians who belong to such a party to define its political line, therefore, generates a picture of high internal diffuseness.

At first sight, this result also agrees with an argument about the transitional effects of institutions in the early years of democratic competition. A large crowd of political entrepreneurs founds a myriad of parties, none of which has clear programmatic appeals. What is inconsistent with the argument based on the transitional effects of institutions on competitive strategies, however, is that large parties are more cohesive only in the three Central European countries, yet not in Bulgaria. Only the communist legacies argument suggests that the larger parties in the Czech Republic, and to a lesser extent in Poland and Hungary, will craft programmatic party appeals, whereas in Bulgaria, after patrimonial communism, precisely the large post-communist BSP and the anti-communist SDS have extremely diffuse programmatic appeals.

CONCLUSION: POLITICAL ELITES, ELECTORAL CONSTITUENCIES, AND PROGRAMMATIC APPEALS

The communist legacies argument explains why Bulgaria has more diffuse patterns of programmatic competition and voter-politician linkage than Hungary,

Poland, and the Czech Republic, *even though* Bulgaria has closed-list proportional representation electoral institutions and a parliamentary system of executive-legislative power relations. Both institutional components should nurture cohesive programmatic parties. While these institutions may nudge Bulgaria eventually toward more programmatic party competition, for the time being in the first decade of post-communist politics the legacies of the old system and the terms of the democratic transition illuminate why programmatic party competition in that country is less sharply structured than in the post-communist polities we have examined.

In this first empirical part of our study, we have focused on the *form* of political competition more than the *content* of the parties' appeals. Although we now know that the extent to which parties organize their citizen-elite linkages through programmatic appeals varies considerably across post-communist polities, we have said little about the substance of programmatic appeals parties put forward and the lines of competition that result from such practices. This topic is at the center of our concern in the second part of our empirical investigation.

Furthermore, our analysis of programmatic or non-programmatic party competition has focused entirely on the appeals of political elites and the mutual perception of parties in the power struggle. We have thus ignored whether the messages politicians send out to voters about their own party's programmatic concerns and its opponents' appeals successfully structure the parties' electoral support constituencies and actually build linkage relationships. For example, is it the case that parties running on programmatic appeals attract an electorate that rallies around the same programmatic positions and distinguishes itself from that of other parties more sharply than do voters who opt for parties with fuzzier programmatic appeals? Another task of the subsequent parts of our investigation, therefore, is to examine the extent to which elite and constituency patterns of involvement in party competition relate to each other and shape the overall democratic process.

PART IV

POLITICAL ALIGNMENTS AND DIMENSIONS OF COMPETITION

7

POLITICAL DIVIDES AND ALIGNMENTS: THE POLITICIANS' PERCEPTION

The failure of the socialist planned economy is likely to become a crystallizing agenda item in all post-communist countries where parties reach out to voters with more or less programmatic appeals. But beyond this baseline, historically diverse pathways, institutions, and power relations affect the extent to which economics shapes political divisions and the patterns according to which economic appeals relate to an agenda of socio-cultural politics. To recall the result of our theoretical argument in chapter 2 in the roughest approximation, we expect three constellations. After bureaucratic-authoritarian communism, with the Czech Republic as our reference case, we expect economic conflict over the extent of market liberalization to dominate the programmatic diversification of the electorally relevant parties, while other divisions are crosscutting and more or less irrelevant for party competition, although they may bind some constituencies to parties through mechanisms of voter identification on less salient issue dimensions. After national-accommodative communism with negotiated transition, socio-cultural divides play a much greater role for the emerging competitive party system. Such divides may crosscut economic-distributive conflict dimensions and at times be more important for political competition than the latter, particularly where all relevant parties, including the former communists, embrace essentials of a capitalist market economy. Our two empirical reference cases for variants of this configuration are Poland and Hungary. After patrimonial communism, finally, programmatic competition tends to be less crystallized, but the programmatic spectrum that is detectable divides parties over economic policy reform. At the same time, politicians can successfully reinforce this line of conflict by other socio-cultural conflicts that elsewhere tend to yield separate, crosscutting political divides, such as those over religion, traditional social norms, and national identity. Ethno-cultural conflicts, however, tend to relate in diverse ways to this dominant economic-cultural divide in partisan politics, depending on a number of contingencies.

In this chapter, we first explore the extent to which politicians in our four East Central European countries construct the relationship between their own party and its competitors via political divides that bundle issue disagreements among the parties. We then examine the ways politicians relate these substantive conflicts to the purely formal spatial semantics of "left" and "right" placements in their political rhetoric. We expect that the cross-national variance of political divisions and competitive dimensions corresponds to a diversity of meaning politicians attribute to the left-right semantics across our four polities. In the final section, we probe into the extent to which the political divides we identify in our investigation qualify as dimensions of electoral competition or just constitute dimensions of party identification.

POLITICAL DIVIDES IN EAST CENTRAL EUROPE

The main objective in this section is to identify underlying dimensions of political disagreement that signal how and to what extent politicians bundle individual policy issues into relatively coherent "packages" that help voters to simplify their choice among alternatives. The limitation of our analysis, of course, is that we observe such divides at a single time point, around the first half of 1994, and thus cannot capture changes in the spatial arrangement of political issues produced by the dynamic of party competition over time.

Factor analysis provides the most straightforward method to determine the clustering of issues around underlying but not directly observed variables or dimensions. In contrast to other inductive techniques to obtain unobserved variables, its advantage is that it imposes very few further mathematical constraints on the search for such dimensions. Unlike discriminant analysis, for example, it does not impose the objective to maximize differences among the parties' positions on the underlying dimensions. We prefer factor analysis because we want to determine dimensions on which party policies and voter preferences vary, *independent* of finding the technically most efficient tool to discriminate among party positions. Input variables are the fourteen to sixteen concrete policy issues included in each country's partisan middle-level elite survey and already employed in our empirical analysis in chapters 5 and 6. The unobserved factors that underlie parties' positions on these variables can then be related to politicians' judgments of parties' stances on the four abstract ideological scales and each party's left-right placement.

We display the results of varimax rotated factor analyses of the issue positions politicians in our survey attribute to their own parties and their competitors. We provide the usual statistical estimates: factor loadings, explained variance, eigenvalues, and factor scores. In general, *factors* are the unobserved variables that simplify and, in this purely instrumental fashion, "explain" the variance of the units of observation (the ijk policy positions respondents i attribute to parties j on issue k) on a variety of observed variables. *Factor loadings* indicate the extent to which the values on a measured variable relate to the underlying factor, with loadings approximating +/−1.0 indicating (almost) perfect relations between variable and factor. Factor loadings between −.40 and +.40 indicate very weak association of an observed variable with an unobserved factor and contribute little to the substantive interpretation of the underlying factor.

The explained variance and the eigenvalues of a factor indicate how much variance among the observed variable values an underlying factor captures. The maximum eigenvalue corresponds to the number of observed variables. It indicates that an underlying hidden "factor" perfectly maps the variance of values on the observed variables. The actual eigenvalue corresponds to the percentage of variance in the observed variables captured by an underlying factor. Factor scores, finally, provide the value of a unit of observation (the ijk policy positions) on the unobserved factor. We will report the jk mean positions all respondents assign to each party on the factors. We have also run factor analyses for respondents i from each party j separately. Moreover, we have calculated each party j's factor scores based only on the responses by politicians belonging to j. None of these variants that try to capture systematic asymmetries in the perception of the political space by respondents belonging to different parties yields insights sufficiently novel to report here.

In our presentation, we display the results of varimax-rotated factor analyses. Factor analysis, in general, mathematically constrains the search for underlying variables by the objective to explain as much variance in the observed values with as few unobserved variables as possible. But varimax rotation goes one step further and concentrates the *factor loadings* on as few observed variables as possible, once the general form of an underlying factor has been identified. Varimax rotation thus facilitates the interpretation of each factor. Principal components and varimax rotated factor analyses make a further assumption that is important for any interpretation of their results. By virtue of the mathematical estimation technique, the underlying factors are mutually unrelated in statistical terms – that is, they are perfectly orthogonal with a correlation coefficient of 0.0. This does not rule out, of course, that the mean factor scores of groups of observations, such as the mean scores respondents assign to parties on each factor, are correlated with each other.

Our analysis focuses on the 1994 main survey among middle-level politicians in Bulgaria, the Czech Republic, Hungary, and Poland. In most relevant respects, the results of the 1993 pilot study and of the 1994 main survey are identical. This suggests that political divisions in the new East Central European democracies are rather robust and not easily toppled by short-term developments, although a hard test that the emerging political divides solidify into durable cleavages would require a much longer time series. We therefore report findings from the pilot study only occasionally.[1]

---

[1]These results have been analyzed in Kitschelt (1995c).

CZECH REPUBLIC

Table 7.1 shows the results of the factor analysis of issue positions that respondents in our politicians' survey attribute to parties in the Czech Republic. The policy items on which politicians rate the parties have been abbreviated such that the direction in which plus and minus signs of the factor loadings point are semantically clear. We begin with this case of post-bureaucratic authoritarian communism because theoretical considerations lead us to expect rather sharp and polarized divisions on economic issues between a by and large unreconstructed communist party, other social-protectionist parties, and a strong market-liberal camp. Given polarization over economic issues, politicians in the electorally most important parties have comparatively few incentives to highlight other dimensions of competition. This does not rule out, of course, that minor parties located on either side of the economic divide engage in some product differentiation on secondary issue dimensions.

The factor analysis indeed yields an overriding economic protectionism versus market liberalism factor I that captures almost 50 percent of the entire variance of parties' issue positions, translating into an eigenvalue of 7.17.[2] This factor pits social protectionists opposed to market liberalization, indicated by high positive values on this factor, against advocates of market-liberal reform, receiving high negative scores. But it also has some minor socio-cultural and political connotations that link liberal economic policy preferences to anti-communism (VAR 44), religion, and Christian morality (VAR 38 and 39). It is quite telling that decommunization appears on the economic factor in this former bureaucratic-authoritarian country with weak reformism inside the communist successor party, but on the socio-cultural factor in the former national-accommodative communist polities we discuss later.

In the Czech Republic, the greatest share of the remaining socio-cultural issue positions is captured by a second socio-cultural libertarian-secular versus authoritarian-religious dimension. At one end, parties emphasize secular values and civic individualism. At the other end, parties insist on social conduct guided by religious principles and the importance of upholding authority relations in the new societal order. Two further and even weaker factors essentially load on only two issues each. Factor III divides environmentalists who push for a decentralization of the country's polity to the regions against anti-environmentalist centralizers. Factor IV contrasts anti-communists hostile to immigration and ethnic minorities to parties tolerant of both multi-culturalism as well as former communists ("civic tolerance").

The bottom part of table 7.1 reports the mean factor scores of the parties and their standard deviations on each of the four factors. Moreover, it indicates the

---

[2]Mathematically, we obtain the eigenvalue by multiplying the number of observed variables in the factor analysis (in this case 16) by the percentage of variance explained by a factor: $16 \times .448 = 7.17$.

distance, in units of factor scores, between the extreme parties on each dimension as well as the spread between the parties' positions, measured by the standard deviation of the parties' factor scores. The last line in the table shows the average standard deviation of all parties' scores on each factor as an indicator of respondents' uncertainty over the parties' positions on that factor. These concepts quite closely relate to two of our measures of programmatic party competition in chapter 5, spread/polarization and programmatic diffuseness. In the Czech Republic, the first factor yields a divide on which parties' positions show less diffuseness (smaller standard deviations) and more spread (distance between extreme parties) than on the other three factors. The post-communist Left Bloc (LB), the by now defunct Liberal Social Union (LSU), and the Social Democrats (CSSD) all share more or less social-protectionist economic positions and oppose a market liberal sector consisting of the Civic Democratic Party (ODS) and the Civic Democratic Alliance (ODA) at the other extreme of this divide. The Christian parties (the KDU and the tiny KDS) tilt toward the liberal bloc, whereas the Republicans (SPR-RSC) and the Moravian regionalists (HSD-SMS) are more social protectionist.

The other three factors essentially contribute little to programmatic distinctions among the major Czech parties, but define unique "market niches" for minor parties. Factor II identifies the niche of the Christian parties, which distance themselves from the bulk of the more secular and libertarian Czech major parties. The third factor contrasts the Moravian regionalists and the Free Democrats both of whom advocate a decentralization of government and more environmental protection from the anti-environmental centralizers ODS and LB. The fourth factor, finally highlights the unique appeal of the SPR-RSC to civic intolerance, rejecting citizenship rights to asylum seekers and former communists. All parties that articulate outlier positions on the second through fourth factor, taken together, command no more than 20 percent of the 1992 or 1996 electorates,[3] while factor I divides electoral blocs controlling over 60 percent of the vote in these elections. Moreover, factors II through IV give rise to less sharply defined party alternatives, as indicated by the small spread and distance among parties' mean positions on these factors and by the greater fuzziness of parties' perceived stances, signaled by the substantial standard deviations.

It deserves emphasizing that parties with pronounced outlier positions on minor issue dimensions II through IV most of the time do not assume a centrist position on the major economic divide. Thus, the KDU-CSL is not only religious (factor II) but also quite distinctly market-liberal (factor I) in 1994, though less radically so than ODS or ODA. The Republicans are not only xenophobic (factor IV), but also social protectionist (factor I). These parties cannot run on unique, isolated, and relatively low-salience issue positions only, but must achieve some kind of integration of such stances into a broader programmatic offering that

---

[3]KDU and SPR-RSC took 8 percent each, the Free Democrats and the Moravian successor to the HSD-SMS, the CMSS, took only negligible vote shares.

Table 7.1. *Political divides in the Czech party system (varimax-rotated factor analysis)*

	Factors			
	I: Socio-economic protectionism	II: Secular libertarianism	III: Libertarian environmentalism	IV: Civic tolerance
V30 For social protection	+.88	+.10	+.14	−.03
V31 Against market opening	+.90	+.13	−.03	+.07
V32 For fast privatization	−.86	+.01	−.10	+.01
V33 Fighting unemployment	+.92	+.08	+.04	−.03
V34 Limits on foreign investment	+.89	+.14	+.01	−.13
V35 For flat income tax	−.85	−.09	−.04	+.11
V36 Admit asylum seekers	−.26	−.16	+.17	+.81
V37 Child care not a priority	−.75	−.27	+.13	−.12
V38 Pro-choice on abortion	+.35	+.82	−.10	+.12
V39 Against church's public role	+.48	+.72	−.14	+.11
V40 For agricultural subsidies	+.87	+.05	+.16	+.05
V41 For liberal individualism	−.16	+.65	+.44	+.04
V42 For environmental protection	+.18	−.06	+.77	−.07
V43 Moral restraints on mass media	+.02	−.75	+.07	+.36
V44 Against decommunization	+.50	+.30	−.19	+.61
V52 For decentralization	+.04	.00	+.78	+.14
Variance explained (in %)	44.8	12.8	9.7	7.7
Eigenvalue	7.17	2.05	1.55	1.24

Factor scores and standard deviations for Czech parties	Mean	S.D.	Mean	S.D.	Mean	S.D.	Mean	S.D.
LB	+1.50	.47	+.13	.66	-.65	.99	+.63	.84
LSU	+.73	.48	+.22	.51	+.19	.88	+.25	.68
CSSD	+.91	.43	+.30	.54	+.11	.85	+.32	.75
KDU	-.52	.43	-1.59	.69	+.26	.87	-.14	.72
ODA	-1.07	.53	+.61	.78	+.08	.94	+.22	.78
SD	-.04	.49	+.46	.63	+.55	.88	+.39	.80
SPR-RSC	+.48	.55	+.35	.84	-.15	.99	-1.86	.89
HSD-SMS	+.25	.36	+.02	.45	+.57	.58	+.05	.57
ODS	-1.32	.41	+.80	.66	-.93	.95	+.28	.85
KDS	-.91	.41	-1.30	.72	-.03	-.15	.79	
					1.02			
Spread of the parties	1.18		.80		.48		.69	
Distance between extremes	2.82		2.39		1.48		2.49	
Average standard deviation	.46		.65		.89		.75	

Note: Italicized numbers highlight the coefficients that contribute to the interpretation of the factor dimensions.

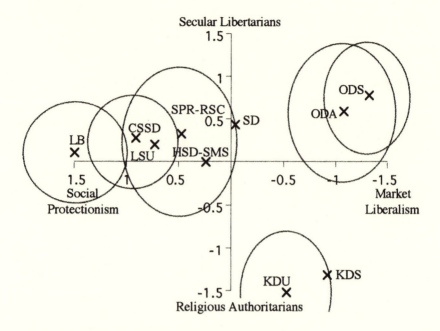

Figure 7.1. Political divides in the Czech Republic

relates to the dominant divide in the Czech party system and thus motivates citizens to invest their vote in a minor party.[4] Overall, the Czech party system approximates a uni-dimensional political divide with minor crosscutting axes. Figure 7.1 visualizes this relationship by depicting parties' mean positions on the first two factors, together with the standard deviations of the factor scores they receive from the respondents.

The politicians' judgment of party positions and the nature of the political divides that result from factor analysis are stable in the time elapsed between the 1993 pilot study and the 1994 main survey. The correlation of the parties' factor scores on the first dimension, the economic divide, at the two time points almost a year apart is perfect ($r = .97$). Because the pilot study there found no separate ethno-national division (factor IV in the main study), some parties' factor scores on the second socio-cultural factor change from the pilot to the main study, most notably that of the Republicans (SPR-RSC). Otherwise, a comparison of the party configuration reveals consistency between the two surveys. Most importantly, all

---

[4] If Christians and Republicans were "single-issue" appeals, directional and issue theories of party competition (Rabinowitz and MacDonald 1989; Budge and Farlie 1983) would have a strong case. But given the actual concatenation of positions on different divides in these parties, a spatial interpretation of parties' strategic "product differentiation" may be, on balance, more adequate.

evidence suggests that in the Czech Republic, a formerly bureaucratic-authoritarian communist polity undergoing an implosion of the old regime, economics dominates the inter-party divisions.

POLAND

Political divisions are quite different in Poland, where a strong mobilization of anti-communist forces around the Catholic Church and the ability of the former communists to embrace fundamental socio-economic and political reform during and after a negotiated democratic transition suggest that economic issues do not capture the bulk of inter-party divisions. In a democracy emerging from national-accommodative communism with a strategically mobile and less tainted former ruling party, democratic politicians may not necessarily focus just on economic policy conflict. Table 7.2 indeed demonstrates that in addition to a first factor that pits socio-economic protectionists against market liberals in ways similar to those found in the Czech Republic, Poland displays a rather strong second factor that rallies secular and libertarian cosmopolitans, on one side, and religious, authoritarian nationalists, on the other. At least in the mind of the political elites, issue positions on questions of religion, moral individualism, and nationalism constrain each other such that a single factor maps the entire cluster of political issues. Because socio-cultural issues congeal around a single factor, Poland does not have further subsidiary political divides comparable with those in the Czech Republic.[5]

Both factors have a strong capacity to divide parties' issue positions, although in different ways. As in the Czech Republic, the economic issue dimension contrasts post-communist parties (assembled in the SLD coalition and the peasant PSL), but also one Solidarność successor organization, the Union of Labor (UP), as well as the electoral arm of Solidarity itself, to liberal parties, primarily the Democratic Union (UD) and the Liberal Democratic Congress (KLD), two parties that joined forces under a single umbrella shortly after our survey. Politicians actually perceive the post-communist SLD as the most *moderate* party in the social-protectionist bloc, considerably outflanked by the peasant party and particularly the UP. The comparatively high standard deviation of the post-communist party's economic stance also signals that the SLD might experience considerable internal strain in its efforts to maintain a common economic policy position.[6]

The second factor in table 7.2 that assembles socio-cultural issue positions reveals a different configuration of polarities between the political parties. The social protectionist UP and SLD, but not the electoral arm of Solidarity or the agrarian PSL, constitute a secular-cosmopolitan pole, whereas Christian parties

[5]Environmentalism loads on a separate factor, but the eigenvalue of that factor falls short of unity.

[6]This message can also be gleaned from figure 6.4, which shows that among all issue positions post-communist politicians have the hardest time finding internal agreement on economics.

Table 7.2. *Political divides in the Polish party system (varimax-rotated factor analysis)*

	Factors			
	I: Socio-economic protectionism		II: Libertarian secular cosmopolitans	
V30 For social protection	+.82		+.06	
V31 Against market opening	+.86		+.11	
V32 For fast privatization	−.85		+.08	
V33 Fighting unemployment	+.87		−.10	
V34 Limits on foreign investment	+.73		−.40	
V35 For flat income tax	−.85		+.02	
V36 Admit asylum seekers	−.26		+.70	
V37 Child care not a priority	−.41		−.59	
V38 Pro-choice on abortion	.00		+.92	
V39 Against church's public role	−.02		+.91	
V40 For agricultural subsidies	+.76		−.17	
V41 For liberal individualism	−.20		+.84	
V42 For environmental protection	−.25		−.22	
V43 Moral restraints on mass media	+.16		−.84	
V44 Against decommunization	+.06		+.79	
Variance explained (in %)	37.0		28.8	
Eigenvalue	5.55		4.33	
Factor scores and standard deviations for Polish parties	Mean	S.D.	Mean	S.D.
SLD	+.53	.62	+1.27	.38
PSL	+.81	.50	−.17	.50
UP	+1.02	.55	+1.13	.50
ZChN	−.10	.50	−1.57	.42
UD	−.81	.47	+.64	.49
KLD	−1.75	.49	+.75	.49
KPN	+.41	.53	−.68	.36
BBWR	−.43	.58	−.35	.50
PC	−.46	.54	−.81	.56
NZSS 'S'	+.81	.47	−.52	.44
Spread of the parties	.88		.93	
Distance between the extremes	2.77		2.84	
Average standard deviation		.53		.47

Note: See table 7.1.

and other fission products of the Solidarity camp are at the other extreme. Also on this second dimension, the parties reveal rather sharp programmatic contrasts, as indicated by the comparatively wide inter-party spread, the distance of extreme parties, and the low average standard deviation of parties' perceived positions, when compared to the Czech Republic's second dimension.

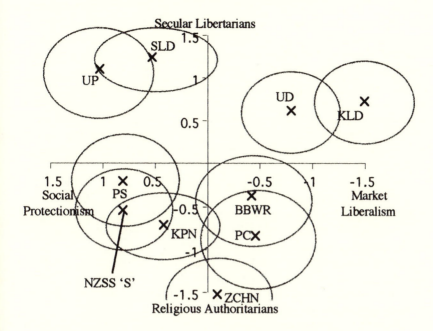

Figure 7.2. Political divides in Poland

Both Polish issue dimensions taken together yield a tri- or quadripolar field of competitors (figure 7.2). One corner of the triangle consists of secular-cosmo-politan-social protectionist parties (UP and SLD) with about 30 percent of the vote in the 1993 and 1997 parliamentary elections, another corner the secular-cosmopolitan-liberal parties (UD and KLD, since 1994 combined as the Freedom Union) supported by about one-sixth of the 1993 and 1997 electorates. The third corner of the triangle, constituted by the Catholic national ZChN, is surrounded by a fairly wide scattering of further parties. Along the side of the triangle leading from ZChN to UP/SLD, we find social-protectionist and national-conservative parties, such as Solidarność, KPN, and even the former communist bloc party PSL. Along the side of the triangle connecting ZChN to UD/KLD, two small national-liberal parties situate themselves, PC and BBWR. In terms of electoral strength, there is little question that in the neighborhood of the ZChN corner parties endorsing social-protectionist policies outweigh the more market-liberal elements.[7] These parties thus tend to combine anti-communism with anti-

[7]PSL, NZSS "S," and KPN, the more social-protectionist parties with a national and/or Christian outlook, received roughly 26 percent of the vote in the 1993 parliamentary election, whereas the more market-liberal ZChN, PC, and BBWR did not exceed 14 percent.

liberalism, a programmatic configuration that plays only a minor role in the Czech Republic.[8]

The intellectual heterogeneity of the third Christian-national sector may suggest an explanation of why it had been so difficult for politicians in the Christian-national camp to build one or two consolidated competitors until 1996. Nevertheless, after the defeat of Lech Walesa's presidential bid in 1995, politicians in this camp have started to rally around the AWS alliance that won the 1997 election, although the AWS has subsequently experienced deep internal divisions over economic policy that relate to the programmatic heterogeneity of its constituents.

The content of the main Polish political divisions revealed by factor analysis with data from the 1993 pilot study differs slightly from the main survey results (cf. Kitschelt 1995c: 91), but the parties' factor scores on the by and large corresponding economic and cultural-religious divisions correlate strongly (r = .81 and .79). Also in Poland, the political actors have a rather stable map of the political divisions and know how the major parties situate themselves relative to each other. Because of the greater weight of the socio-cultural dimension in Poland and the heterogeneity of the Christian national parties, however, that map is more complicated than in the Czech Republic. Given that politicians in the Czech Republic and Poland lack a common anchor point, it is impossible to compare the absolute distances between the parties on the economic divide across the two countries. Nevertheless, our data suggest that this divide is relatively less pronounced in Poland, whereas divisions on the political-cultural dimension are much more polarized.

HUNGARY

Even more so than Poland, Hungary went through a period of protracted bargaining between incumbent reform communists and opposition forces from 1987 to winter 1989–90. What may be even more important, the Hungarian communist regime had advanced market-liberalizing reforms earlier, more forcefully, and at least for some time more successfully in the eyes of the population than its Polish counterpart. For this reason, the communist successor party could claim a commitment to economic reform more credibly than in any other post-communist country and present itself as an agent of socio-political liberalization. This made it less attractive for politicians in the new non-communist parties to focus their appeal primarily on economic reform. Politicians in many upstart parties searched for other policy divisions on which they could advance a distinctive programmatic appeal. As a strategic move in the game of party competition, within Hungary's

---

[8]In fact, a party camp characterized by the joint rejection of socialist redistribution and market liberalism goes back to the inter-war period. The contemporary electoral map of Poland reflects the varying strength of different electoral camps in previous episodes of electoral politics. Cf. Tworzecki (1996), especially chap. 3.

socio-cultural context politicians could seize on Christian, national, and culturally populist, if not authoritarian, positions to make an appeal that would provide a contrast to secular, libertarian, and cosmopolitan positions invoked by rival parties. The Hungarian Democratic Forum (MDF), as winner of the 1990 election, for example, for some time thrived on national-cultural appeals that eventually divided the party and survived in the residues of the radical populist and anti-Semitic Party of Hungarian Life and Justice (MIEP). The MDF's economic policy appeals were always rather bland, calling for incremental economic reforms that did not set the party apart all that much from the economic policies endorsed by the post-communist successor parties.

Table 7.3 demonstrates that in Hungary a religious and political libertarian-authoritarian division structures the parties' issue appeals much more powerfully than any other divide.[9] As signaled by the eigenvalue of factor I, the socio-cultural dimension is not only much stronger than in Poland, but also assimilates a few economic issues. Socio-cultural populists endorse a tradition-bound collectivism (VAR 41), demand tough decommunization (VAR 44), dislike asylum seekers (VAR 36), want to protect Hungarian minorities abroad (VAR 45), and support the positions of the Catholic Church (VAR 38 and 39). They also wish to limit foreign investment (VAR 34) and caution against privatization programs that emphasize speed over distributive concerns (VAR 32). It is a second and much weaker factor that divides party positions purely on questions of economic policy (social protection/market liberalism). A third factor taps environmental policy positions but little else. Although Hungarian politicians attribute greater salience to economic issues than to socio-cultural questions as politicians do invariably throughout post-communist Europe (cf. table 5.1), these economic issues cannot claim the same undisputed prominence in the arena of party competition as in the Czech Republic or even, to a lesser extent, in Poland. The high differentiation among parties and the multiple clustering of issues displayed by the socio-cultural factor dimension in Hungarian party politics suggests that it is critical for the creation of citizen-party bonds. Whether socio-cultural themes contribute more to a *dimension of voter identification* than a *dimension of party competition* we will examine later.

The parties' mean factor scores in table 7.3 show that their spread across the political space is much wider on socio-cultural issues than economics. The parties' socio-cultural positions also display rather small standard deviations, indicating that our respondents attribute highly crystallized programmatic profiles to the individual parties. This applies to a lesser extent to the economic division (factor II). Compared with the situation in Poland, but especially in the Czech Republic, the economic policy differentiation of the parties is less pronounced and their respective positions are more diffuse. High standard deviations around parties' mean scores, indicating great programmatic fuzziness, also characterize parties'

---

[9]For a broadly similar finding, see Evans and Whitefield (1995c: 1183).

Table 7.3. *Political divides in the Hungarian party system (varimax-rotated factor analysis)*

		Factors	
	I: Libertarian secularism	II: Socio-economic protectionism	III: Environmental protection
V30 For social protection	−.01	+.77	+.09
V31 Against market opening	−.12	+.82	−.20
V32 For fast privatization	+.53	−.60	−.01
V33 Fighting unemployment	−.02	+.74	+.03
V34 Limits on foreign investment	−.67	+.25	−.34
V35 For flat income tax	+.37	−.42	−.13
V36 Admit asylum seekers	+.77	−.15	+.03
V37 Child care not a priority	−.80	+.03	+.18
V38 Pro-choice on abortion	+.88	−.14	+.13
V39 Against church's public role	+.91	−.06	−.09
V40 For agricultural subsidies	−.55	+.46	+.28
V41 For liberal individualism	+.87	−.22	+.20
V42 For environmental protection	+.08	+.07	+.92
V43 Moral restraints on mass media	−.82	+.23	−.09
V44 Against decommunization	+.87	−.02	−.15
V52 Protection of Hungarian minorities	−.86	+.10	−.01
Variance explained (in %)	47.6	13.3	7.5
Eigenvalue	7.62	2.13	1.21

Factor scores and standard deviations for Hungarian parties	Mean	S.D.	Mean	S.D.	Mean	S.D.
MSZP	+1.24	.48	+1.21	.84	-.64	.99
FKGP	-1.04	.42	+.16	.82	+.21	.97
KDNP	-.63	.36	+.23	.66	+.05	.81
SZDSZ	+.96	.44	-.69	.82	+.24	1.06
Fidesz	+.81	.38	-.78	.79	+.55	.98
MIEP	-1.07	.39	+.31	.83	-.17	.96
MDF	-.27	.38	-.45	.54	-.24	.77
Spread of the parties	.98		.70		.39	
Distance between the extremes	2.31		1.99		1.19	
Average standard deviation		.41		.76		.94

Note: See table 7.1.

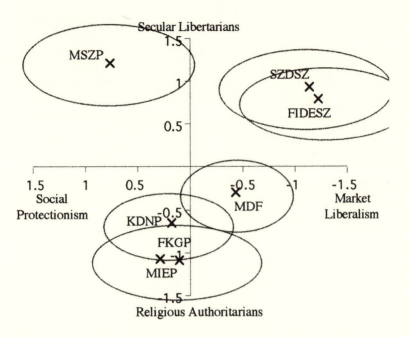

Figure 7.3. Political divides in Hungary

positions on the weak third environmental policy factor that only differentiates quite sharply between the pro-environmental young liberals (Fidesz), on one side, and the anti-environmental post-communists, on the other.

Similar to conditions in Poland, the parties' location in the Hungarian political landscape yields a two-dimensional tripolar arrangement of post-communists, liberals, and Christian-nationalists with each pole in Hungary commanding roughly 25–35 percent of the vote (cf. figure 7.3). In contrast to Poland, however, the Christian-national camp, with intermediate economic, but traditionalist, authoritarian, and populist socio-cultural positions, is a bit more cohesive, even though the Hungarian Democratic Forum (MDF) positions itself between the hardline socio-cultural populists and the liberal parties. The proximity of Fidesz to SzDSz in 1994 might surprise a bit from the vantage point of the further development of the Hungarian party system in the late 1990s, but our survey went into the field just at the time when Fidesz's strategic politicians began to move the party away from a head-on competition with the SzDSz into the territory of the Christian-national camp that Fidesz began to dominate about three years later. Fidesz's movement since 1994 is consistent with the map presented in figure 7.3. It implies only that a different party label supplanted the parties located in the Christian-national sector in 1993–94.

As in the previous cases of the Czech Republic and Poland, the 1994 survey respondents' ratings of the Hungarian parties match those of the 1993 pilot study quite closely (cf. Kitschelt 1995c: 86–90). Both the factors that constitute political divisions as well as the positions of the parties in the space are similar, although the number of policy items rated and the content of the policy issues presented to respondents varies somewhat between the two studies.[10] Similar to Poland, Hungary has a tripolar structure with a significant non-economic dimension on which parties in more centrist economic positions situate themselves near the national-populist-Christian pole.

BULGARIA

Bulgaria reveals rather different issue alignments from those found in the three Central European polities. In this post-patrimonial communist environment, economic conflict plays an important role, but it relates to other conflicts in a mutually reinforcing alignment. Moreover, Bulgaria displays a modicum of ethnic heterogeneity, primarily between the economically and politically dominant ethnic Bulgarians with Christian-Orthodox beliefs and an Islamic Turkish minority.

Consistent with our earlier empirical findings reported in chapter 5, the factor analysis in table 7.4 reveals a programmatically more diffuse landscape of political divides than in East Central Europe. First of all, with four underlying factors evidencing eigenvalues of greater than 1.0, the programmatic description of the Bulgarian party system is less parsimonious than elsewhere. The Czech factor analysis that also yields four factors (table 7.1) produces a single dominant and clearly interpretable economic policy divide. Bulgaria, by contrast, has no factor with an eigenvalue greater than 4.28. The combined explanatory power of all four factors amounts to 61 percent of the total variance compared with 75 percent in the Czech Republic, 66 percent in Poland (with only two factors), and 68 percent in Hungary (with three factors).

The first Bulgarian factor loads most strongly on the issue of decommunization (VAR 44). The centrality of the regime divide is thus greater than in the three Central European countries. Moreover, strong anti-communist positions do not combine with socio-cultural traditionalism and authoritarianism in a single factor, as they do in Hungary and Poland, but with market liberalism (VAR 31), a priority for fighting inflation rather than unemployment (VAR 33), opening the Bulgarian economy to foreign investors (VAR 34), priority for environmental protection (VAR 42), and liberal individualism (VAR 41). This pattern is intelligible against the backdrop of the Bulgarian transition. Environmental protection was the first issue under the umbrella of which members of the opposition dared to organize and to challenge the ruling party in 1989. Given the trajectory of preemptive political reform with continued post-communist party strength, environmentalism then combined with a commitment to free-market politics and

---

[10]The correlation of the parties' mean positions on the socio-cultural factor in the 1993 pilot study and the 1994 main survey is +.93, that between the economic factor scores in both studies is −.84.

Table 7.4. *Political divides in the Bulgarian party system (varimax-rotated factor analysis)*

	Factors			
	I: Post-communist socio-economic protectionism	II: Bulgarian cultural hegemony	III: Economic and cultural reform	IV: Traditional role for women
V30 For social protection	+.43	+.24	-.43	+.42
V31 Against market opening	+.74	+.18	-.21	+.30
V32 For fast privatization	-.28	+.15	+.52	+.04
V33 Fighting unemployment	+.70	+.04	-.29	+.29
V34 Limits on foreign investment	+.58	-.52	-.10	+.06
V35 For flat income tax	+.15	-.06	+.69	-.11
V37 Child care not a priority	.00	-.13	-.01	+.83
V39 Against orthodox church support	+.05	+.77	-.18	+.27
V4O For agricultural subsidies	+.05	+.32	+.55	.00
V41 For liberal individualism	-.55	-.10	+.55	+.15
V42 For environmental protection	-.67	+.15	-.10	+.36
V43 Moral restraints on mass media	+.23	+.23	-.62	+.15
V44 Against decommunization	+.76	+.24	+.05	-.08
V45 Against Turkish instruction	+.02	+.83	+.08	-.23
V52 Turkey a threat	+.41	+.70	+.22	-.16
Variance explained (in %)	28.6	15.4	10.1	7.0
Eigenvalue	4.28	2.31	1.51	1.04

Factor scores and standard deviations for Bulgarian parties	Mean	S.D.	Mean	S.D.	Mean	S.D.	Mean	S.D.
BSP	+1.21	.71	+.83	.69	+.13	1.15	−.13	1.33
BZNS	−.60	.63	+.22	.48	−.53	.79	−.13	.76
BSDP	+.15	.49	+.46	.56	.00	.58	+.35	.71
DPS	+.31	.53	−1.44	.70	−.38	.62	+.32	1.03
SDS	−1.08	.69	−.07	.69	+.77	1.16	−.21	.86
Spread of the parties	.88		.87		.52		.27	
Distance between the extremes	2.29		2.27		1.28		.68	
Average standard deviation		.61		.62		.86		.94

Note: See table 7.1.

libertarian individualism, whereas the communist successor party appealed to social protectionism together with cultural authoritarianism.

Given the comparatively weak programmatic crystallization of the opposition in Bulgarian politics, not all economic variables are tied into the regime-divide, economic reform factor I. Critical micro-economic issues, such as speed or distributive justice in privatization (VAR 32), reform of social security (VAR 30), or taxation (VAR 35) do not load strongly on this factor. Because the opposition to the communist regime is diffuse and relatively unprepared to design policy, the parties have no clear responses to these operational questions of socio-economic reform. Maybe for this reason, a rather fuzzy and weak factor III captures some concrete economic reform issues in a rather idiosyncratic fashion, judged by the clustering of variables in East Central Europe. This factor divides economic and cultural libertarians who are nevertheless willing to provide agricultural subsidies (presumably to reestablish the family farm, a controversial issue in post-communist Bulgaria) from cultural traditionalists and socio-economic protectionists. As in the first economic factor, the anti-communist umbrella organization, the Union of Democratic Forces (SDS), constitutes the libertarian pole supportive of agrarian reorganization, but its most extreme counter-part now is not the communist successor party, but the Bulgarian Agrarian National Union (BZNS), followed by the social-protectionist party of the Turkish minority (DPS).

The second strongest factor in Bulgarian political divisions has to do with ethnicity and religion. It separates supporters of the Turkish minority's claims from advocates of Bulgarian national cultural hegemony (VAR 45, 52). This divide pits the post-communist BSP, as standard bearer of the Bulgarian ethnic majority group, against the Movement for Rights and Freedoms (DPS), while the anti-communist opposition umbrella SDS appears in the middle spectrum on this dimension. The divide has also religious overtones. The anti-Turkish BSP tends to attract secular voters (chapter 8), but as stronghold of Bulgarian nationalism it supports assistance to the Orthodox Church against proselytizers from new Christian sects (VAR 39), a position the DPS obviously cannot endorse. The map of the parties' mean scores on the first two factors in figure 7.4 reveals a rather pronounced linkage between economic social protectionism and ethno-cultural particularism, both on the side of ethnic minority and majority. Among titular Bulgarians, the most populist and authoritarian party, the Bulgarian Socialist Party, is also most opposed to Turkish minority claims, whereas the most liberal and libertarian party, the Union of Democratic Forces, gravitates toward a middle-of-the-road ethnic stance. The Islamic-Turkish Movement of Rights and Freedoms also assumes a muted social protectionist stance that is closer to the BSP than to the SDS.

As we can see from the distance of the extreme parties and the coefficients for the spread of the parties on each factor, the first two factors differentiate party positions rather well. Nevertheless, the average standard deviations for each party's scores on the most powerful factor are much higher than in the three Central European countries, again signaling the comparatively diffuse nature of

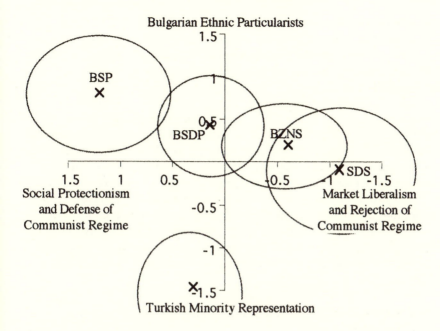

Figure 7.4. Political divides in Bulgaria

Bulgarian party competition. The third and fourth political issue divides do not differentiate between parties very well and yield rather high standard deviations of party positions. They are hence almost useless to characterize Bulgaria's competitive configuration.

Nevertheless, whatever division between nationalist, social protectionist, and authoritarian parties, at one end of the spectrum, and cosmopolitan, market-liberal, and culturally libertarian parties or umbrella organizations, at the other, our factor analysis does reveal that it is quite robust and durable in Bulgaria. We find similar patterns of division both in our February 1993 Bulgarian pilot study as well as in the spring 1994 main survey.[11] The critical difference between Bulgaria, emerging from patrimonial communism by preemptive reform, and democracies originating from a national-accommodative communist regime, represented by Hungary and to a considerable extent by Poland, is the *strategic location of the post-communist party.* In Hungary and Poland, these parties assume a mildly social-protectionist position that is restrained by market-liberal concessions. In

[11] A complication is that in the main study we had to substitute the Bulgarian Social Democrats for the SDS "soft-liners" included in the pilot study (Kitschelt 1995c). The BSDP, however, does draw on many of the same voters and politicians that considered themselves close to the SDS "soft-liners." The correlation of the parties' mean scores on the economic factor in pilot and main study is -.79, that on the ethnic factor is +.89.

Bulgaria, the post-communists are less inclined to liberal market reform, but can also afford to take much less clear-cut positions on the issues because they derive more support from social networks linking them to rent seekers in the old nomenklatura and local communities in the countryside than a policy-oriented urban mass public.

The difference between post-communist parties in Bulgaria and elsewhere in East Central Europe is even starker when we turn to the linkage between economic and socio-cultural issue positions. Whereas in Central European countries most politicians would place post-communist parties closer to a libertarian, individualist, and cosmopolitan position pitted against an authoritarian-traditionalist and semi-social protectionist Christian party camp, in Bulgaria post-communists are identified with authoritarian and nationalist positions.[12] Because of their social-protectionist mass following and continued economic-administrative entrenchment, but also due to the protracted weakness and internal division of the liberal-democratic camp until at least late 1996, BSP politicians emphasize their superiority as the guarantor of social order and stability.

COMPARISON OF PARTY POSITIONS ACROSS COUNTRIES

The factor analyses permit us to situate parties within countries *relative to each other*, but they do not allow us directly to compare the scores of party families on similar issue dimensions across countries or the location of a country's entire political spectrum in a common political space. The variables contributing to an underlying similar factor are never exactly the same in two countries. In order to facilitate cross-national comparison, we now depict the parties' positions in the four countries on some representative issue items that load strongly on the important political dimensions we have identified in each country. Of course, this procedure does not completely get us around all pitfalls of cross-national comparison of survey data. After all, politicians' judgments are relative to national reference parties as "anchor points." Nevertheless, we might focus on the relative differences respondents see between parties *within* each country and compare such configurations *across* our four polities.

In figure 7.5, we present scales with the parties' mean position on representative items that usually load strongly on the socio-economic factors we reported earlier, the social policy issue (VAR 30) and the question of privatization in the face of impending mass unemployment (VAR 31). On social policy, only the Czech liberal-conservative parties (ODA and ODS, which later absorbed KDS)

---

[12]In the pilot study and, to a lesser extent, our main survey, this assessment of the Bulgarian post-communists is subject to challenge through asymmetric judgments. Respondents belonging to the BSP often attribute to their own party a less anti-liberal and less nationalist position than those of the other parties. Compare Kitschelt 1995c: 78.

A. Support for the Welfare State (Public Health Care, V30)

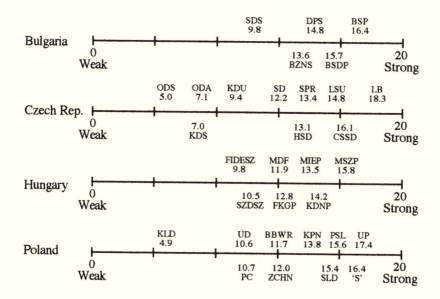

B. Support of Privatization/Market Economics

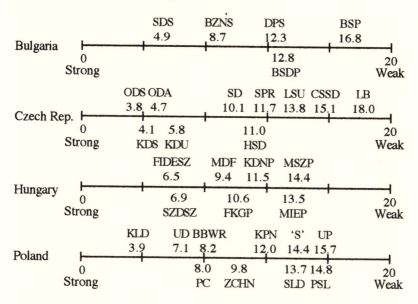

Figure 7.5. The distribution of parties in the four nations on key economic issues

take a pronounced liberal market stance, whereas in the three countries emerging from national-accommodative or patrimonial communism the entire spectrum of parties is situated closer to the strong welfare state pole. The distance between liberal parties and communist successor parties is much smaller in these latter configurations than in the Czech Republic: 13.3 units between ODS and LB in the Czech Republic, 6.6 units between SDS and BSP in Bulgaria, 5.3 between SzDSz and MSzP in Hungary, and only 4.8 between UD and SLD. The Polish KLD is too small to count as an exception to this pattern and, in any case, joined hands with the UD by late 1994.[13]

On liberal market reform (VAR 31), a similar, though less pronounced pattern emerges. The Czech liberals again present themselves as the most ardent standard bearers of market-liberal orthodoxy and economic polarization against an intransigent post-communist party unwilling to embrace reform (distance LB–ODS: 14.2). But also Bulgarian politicians see the SDS as a rather market-liberal party and signal polarization to the BSP (distance BSP–SDS: 11.9). By contrast, after national-accommodative communism in Hungary and Poland, market-liberal parties, excluding the small KLD, restrain their enthusiasm for privatization with huge job losses, while post-communists find market liberalism more palatable than their social-protectionist colleagues elsewhere (distance Fidesz–MSzP: 7.9; distance UD–SLD: 6.6). Former communist regime types thus appear to leave their footprints on post-communist patterns of political competition on economic issues. After national-accommodative communism, successor parties are much less social protectionist on privatization (MSzP: 14.4; SLD: 13.7) than after bureaucratic authoritarianism (LB: 18.0) or patrimonial communism (BSP: 16.8).

Figure 7.6 presents the parties' positions on three prominent socio-cultural issues concerning the influence of the churches in public schools in the East Central European countries: the obligation to defend the Orthodox Church against the encroachment of Christian sects in Bulgaria (VAR 39), the trade-off between the respect for authority and the cultivation of individual autonomy (VAR 41), and the choice between more nationalist or more cosmopolitan orientations (VAR 48), a more abstract ideological conceptualization of national identification not included in our previous factor analyses of parties' issue positions. On the church/school (Bulgaria: defense of the Orthodox Church) question, the formerly national-accommodative communist regimes have parties with highly pronounced pro-religious positions, whereas in the Czech Republic the center of gravity clearly leans toward secularism. Note that liberal parties in all three countries are closer to the socialist parties on this issue than to the proponents of church influence over public affairs. Bulgaria is set apart from the East Central European pattern. The Orthodox Church question we fielded in that country may capture the intensity of rallying to national identity and autonomy more than the

---

[13]The market-liberal pole of the Polish party systems would be somewhat augmented by the Union of Real Politics, which received a touch over 3 percent in the 1993 parliamentary election but failed to make headway in 1997.

A-1. Church and State I: Protection from Proselyting Sects (V39)

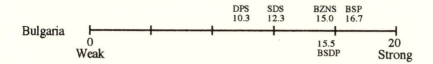

A-2. Church and State II: Church Influence on School Curricula (V39)

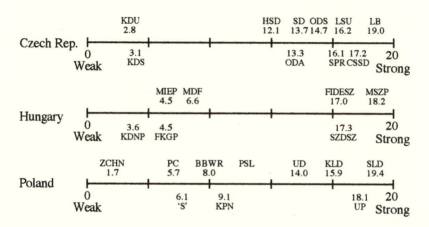

B. Emphasis on Traditional Authority or Individual Autonomy (V41)

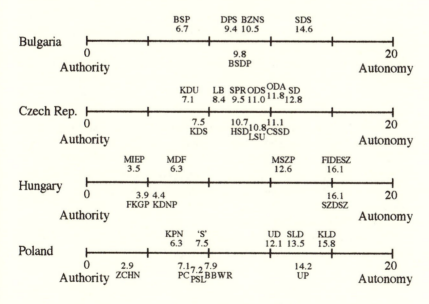

Figure 7.6. The distribution of parties in the four nations on key socio-cultural issues

C. Emphasis on Nationalism (V48)

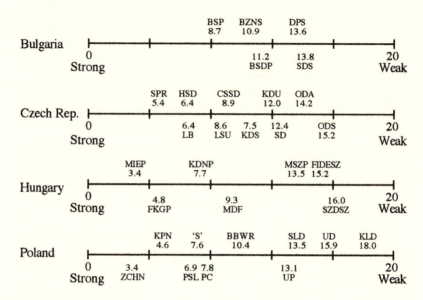

Figure 7.6. (cont.)

protection of personal religious commitments in public life. This may explain why the post-communist party emerges as greatest defender of the Orthodox Church.[14]

A roughly similar cross-national contrast, with one important modification, emerges on the authority/autonomy question (VAR 41). Christian national parties promote collectivist-authoritarian conceptions of social conduct and public life to a much stronger extent in former national-accommodative communism than elsewhere. But in this instance, the position of post-communist parties varies dramatically across our comparison set. In former national-accommodative communism, these parties have acquired a reputation for advocating liberal individualism, whereas in the former bureaucratic-authoritarian and patrimonial polities the intransigence of the old ruling parties is reflected in their placement closer to the authoritarian pole.

A similar pattern emerges with respect to nationalism in display C of figure 7.6. The position of the post-communist parties and the strength of a national-Christian camp correlate with regime type. In Bulgaria and the Czech Republic,

[14]In Bulgaria, the placement of parties on the issue of church influence shows considerable asymmetries (see table 5.4 and figure 6.2), a further difference to Central Europe. BSP advocates think of the party as a much greater defender of the Orthodox Church than the anti-communist politicians would grant.

post-communists are more nationalist, whereas in Hungary and Poland they appear on the cosmopolitan side of the political spectrum. The much greater spread of party positions on the question of national autonomy in the democracies emerging from national accommodative communism may suggest that this issue has much more relevance for parties' support coalitions or even their competitive stances here than in the other two countries.

Our analysis of the political divides that party politicians see in the four East Central European countries has demonstrated cross-nationally varying patterns of political alignments. While everywhere except Hungary an economic divide emerges as the strongest structuring force of political divisions, its relative and absolute capacity to structure ideological alternatives, as reflected by the eigenvalues of the individual factors, varies across post-communist democracies in line with their distinctive regime legacies. Socio-cultural political divides also betray regime legacies. It is not simply socio-cultural background conditions, such as the strength of the Catholic Church, that determine such alignments. Strategic politicians who face differential opportunity structures to craft parties and select their programmatic outreach contingent upon the mode of transition and the emerging party alternatives shape the insertion of socio-cultural appeals into the system of partisan alignments.

IDEOLOGICAL GENERALIZATION OF PARTY COMPETITION THROUGH LEFT-RIGHT DESCRIPTIONS

If parties compete by offering issue bundles to voters, nothing is more convenient than to signal the nature of each package to citizens via summary "right" or "left" positions. Thus, simple ideological "maps" enhance the transparency of the electoral game (Hinich and Munger 1994). Moreover, these simple cues allow parties to gain a *reputation* that transcends the vote of its legislators on individual issues. Parties go through a sequence of complex strategic moves that endow them with reputations in the eyes of their competitors and the voting public. Voters, in turn, base their expectations about the party's future behavior on a condensed and periodically updated view of the party's past record summarized in terms of the left-right spatial metaphor.

If there is a close link between parties' issue stances and left-right placements, the spatial metaphors serve as powerful signals that allow politicians, and to a considerable extent the segment of rationally deliberating voters in the electorate as well, to predict the competitive conduct of parties based on relatively little information. As a consequence, the left-right semantics facilitates relations of democratic accountability and responsiveness. Where left-right placements have a weak predictive power for parties' issue positions, it is much harder for citizens to cast their vote in a deliberate, rational way. The lack of transparency about parties' positions in such circumstances may give rise to profound dissatisfaction with the way democracy operates, unless clientelist or charismatic appeals can offer alternative linkage mechanisms.

The way political actors relate substantive policy issues to the formal left-right semantics, however, varies in time and space.[15] It is therefore plausible to expect some linkage between regime trajectories and the development of post-communist party systems, on the one hand, and the meaning actors attribute to the left-right frame, on the other, in our comparison of post-communist polities. Moreover, the *strength of the association* between parties' substantive policy positions and their left-right stances may vary in accordance with the differential degrees of programmatic structuring we have identified earlier. Compared with voters, of course, politicians are likely to be quite sophisticated in making left-right distinctions, even when party positions are rather close to each other on the issues or politicians deal with a multi-dimensional space. Nevertheless, cross-national differences should still surface in our analysis.

Figure 7.7 depicts for each East Central European country *all* respondents' mean placement of *all* parties on the left-right scale. In other words, each party's score reflects the judgments not just of its own politicians, but also that of politicians belonging to competing parties in the same polity. With few exceptions, the results would have been almost exactly the same had we presented left-right positions by scores politicians assign to their own party only. *Systematic asymmetries,* in the fashion discussed in chapter 5, are negligible in parties' left-right placements.[16]

The range over which respondents distribute the parties is roughly the same in all four countries. The most extreme leftist party is about thirteen to fifteen units removed from the extreme rightist party. Whereas some of the substantive policy issues showed great cross-national variance in party spread, this is not the case with regard to the formal left-right placement of parties. Because politicians employ domestic parties as their reference set, the absolute positions and distances between parties cannot be fully compared across countries.

For cross-national comparison, we therefore focus on the *relative configuration* among competitors within each party system. In line with diverse inter-war and communist legacies, democratic transitions and political experiences, Bulgaria and the Czech Republic reveal a different configuration of parties than Hungary or Poland, as we move from the most leftist to the most rightist positions. Whereas respondents place the post-communist parties in all four countries on the

---

[15] For recent analytical conceptualizations of different left-right semantics, see especially Kitschelt and Hellemans (1990b) and Knutsen (1995).

[16] The correlation between mean self-placement scores of each party's politicians and the general attribution of left-right positions to parties by all politicians are extremely high: r = .99 in Bulgaria, r = .91 in the Czech Republic (without SPR-RSC for which we lack self-placements, because the party refused to cooperate with our project); r = .97 in Hungary and r = .81 in Poland. In Poland, UD politicians locate themselves center-right, whereas politicians in other parties place them center-left. PSL politicians place themselves more to the center than other politicians who place them on the left.

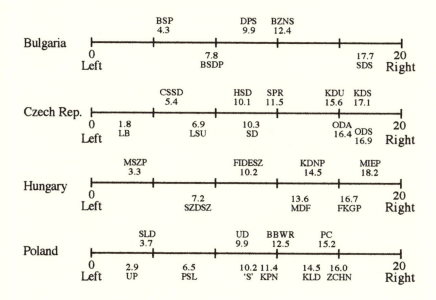

Figure 7.7. The party positions on the left-right scale

extreme left, the placement of different families of non-communist parties varies across these two pairs of countries according to a pattern already familiar from figures 7.5 and 7.6.[17] In Bulgaria and the Czech Republic, the electorally power-ful market-liberal parties SDS and ODS are located near the "rightist" pole of the scale. In Hungary and Poland, by contrast, the market-liberal parties are situated on the center-left (SzDSz and Fidesz in Hungary) or in the center (UD in Poland), while only small liberal parties appear on the right (KLD in Poland). In this second pair of countries, Christian-national parties with middle-of-the-road or even social-protectionist economic policy leanings (cf. figure 7.5) constitute the rightist pole of the space.

The cross-national variation in parties' relative position on the left-right scale may suggest that the issues are not the same according to which politicians attribute left-right positions to parties in different countries. In Bulgaria and the Czech Republic parties' left-right assessments primarily capture economic party stances because non-economic policy issues are politically quite irrelevant after bureaucratic-authoritarian communism or they reinforce regime and economic divides after patrimonial communism. In Hungary and Poland, countries that emerge from national-accommodative communism with a reformist transforma-tion of the old communist parties, parties elaborate a socio-cultural political

---

[17]The only exception to this generalization is that in Poland the Solidarność offspring Union of Labor claims the most leftist position on the scale.

divide that crosscuts economic issues and permits some anti-communist parties to dissociate themselves from their competitors on grounds other than economics. Here non-economic issue stances appear to be more powerful independent contributors to the parties' left-right placements than in the first pair of countries.

A test of this interpretation employs the parties' scores on the factors that capture each country's issue-based system of political divides as predictors of the parties' left-right placements (table 7.5).[18] The results relate to several of our main hypotheses. First, all of the factors have a statistically significant impact on respondents' left-right placements of the parties in the four countries. This finding suggests that politicians consider all the factor dimensions identified in our analysis meaningful and intelligible in these countries. Second, the relative and absolute contribution of different factors to the parties' left-right placement conforms to the expected pattern of cross-national variance. In Bulgaria and the Czech Republic, the economic liberalism–social protectionism factors make by far the greatest contribution to the spatial left-right positions politicians assign to parties. Of course, in Bulgaria, economic issues are confounded with nationalism and authoritarian politics and distributed over two factors. In the Czech Republic, there is a clear-cut dominance of the economic factor in the determination of parties' spatial left-right position.

In the other two countries emerging from national-accommodative communism, by contrast, economics is less dominant (in Poland) or in fact clearly subordinate (in Hungary) in the politicians' assignment of parties' left-right scores. In Hungary, the overwhelming factor for left-right placements is the non-economic divide between Christian, national, and collectivist authoritarians, on one side, and secular, cosmopolitan, and libertarian individualists, on the other. Here the economic dimension, by itself, makes so little difference for left-right party placements that it is outperformed even by the weak third factor, environmentalism, although that factor has relatively little power to structure party alternatives. The negotiated transition to democracy leaves its imprint such that parties cannot credibly differentiate themselves much in economic terms. This, of course, does not automatically imply that economics is irrelevant for party competition, an issue we will address later.[19] In Poland, finally, both economics and

---

[18]The unit of observation here is politician j's placement of party i on the factor dimensions k and the left-right scale. The number of observations ranges from 500 in Bulgaria (100 respondents times 5 evaluated parties) to 1,200 in Poland (120 respondents times 10 parties).

[19]The very proximity of the parties in economic policy terms may in fact facilitate vote switching and retrospective economic voting. Voting for an opposition party is less risky if voters anticipate that a new incoming government makes only small incremental changes in the established policies. Moreover, because the step from one party to another is so small in policy terms, voters are more willing to try out a new alternative. Under conditions of centripetal competition and weak economic performance, retrospective economic voting decisions thus may encourage voters to go "shopping" among parties. For evidence that economics was critical in the 1994 Hungarian election, but socio-cultural issues weighed comparatively heavier in Poland in 1993, see Markowski and Toka (1995).

Table 7.5. *Issue dimensions of party stances as predictors of parties' left-right placements by the politicians' juries (1994 survey)*

	Bulgaria			Czech Republic			Hungary			Poland		
	b	s.e.	beta	b	s.e.	beta	b	s.e.	beta	b	s.e.	beta
Intercept	-.00	.00		-.00	.00		-.00	.00		.00	.00	
Factor I	-3.97*** [post-communist social protectionism (+)]	.18	-.68	-4.84*** [socio-economic protectionism (+)]	.08	-.82	-4.65*** [libertarian, secular cosmopolitans (+)]	.10	-.85	-2.95*** [socio-economic protectionism (+)]	.11	-.53
Factor II	-1.30*** [Bulgarian ethno-national hegemony (+)]	.18	-.22	-1.20*** [secular libertarianism (+)]	.08	-.20	-.48*** [socio-economic protectionism (+)]	.09	-.09	-2.98*** [libertarian, secular cosmopolitans (+)]	.11	-.54
Factor III	+1.17*** [economic and cultural reform (+)]	.18	+.20	+.23* [libertarian environmentalism (+)]	.08	+.04	+.58*** [environmental protection (+)]	.09	+.10	—		
Factor IV	-.38* [traditional roles for women (+)]	.18	-.07	-1.09*** [civic tolerance seekers (+)]	.08	-.18	—			—		
Adjusted R²	.55			.75			.74			.57		

* p < .05; ** p < .01; *** p < .001.

socio-cultural divisions have equally strong effects on the spatial positioning of the parties. Here some economic policy differences between the post-socialist and the other party camps are critical for left-right party placements, but they are complemented by an equally important dimension of cultural political evaluations.

It is interesting to examine how questions of nationalism and multi-culturalism relate to left-right placements. In Bulgaria, the signs of the coeffi-cients of the first two factors show that the divide over national and ethnic identity associates Bulgarian national particularists with the political left. Only in countries emerging from patrimonial communism with extensive clientelist net-works and an absence of vigorous "bourgeois" nationalism before the advent of communism, such as Bulgaria, can post-communist parties successfully associate their appeal with themes of national autonomy and ethno-cultural particularism. In the other East Central European countries, by contrast, politicians place parties supporting nationalism and exclusionary ethno-cultural homogeneity on the right. In the Czech Republic, the acceptance of asylum seekers is an issue that contributes to a more leftist placement of parties. This semantic construct permits respondents to qualify the socio-economically protectionist Republicans (SPR-RSC) as a "rightist" party because it is nationally particularist and rejects immi-grants. In Hungary and Poland, politicians attribute rightist scores to parties with national and authoritarian positions, even though they may support middle-of-the-road or even social protectionist economic views.

The explained variance of each equation in table 7.5 reveals the pattern of cross-national variance we would expect from the differential programmatic struc-turing of party systems we discussed in chapter 5. Where programmatic structur-ing of party competition is high, a smaller number of political divides (factors) explains a greater percentage of parties' left-right placements. In this sense, in Poland two factors explain more variance in left-right placements than four factors do in Bulgaria. In Hungary and the Czech Republic, three or four factors explain a great deal more variance of parties' left-right placements than either two factors in Poland or four factors in Bulgaria. The equations unambiguously show more programmatic structuring, associated with left-right placements, in the three East Central European countries than in Bulgaria. Due to the different number of factors in each equation, however, we cannot establish a clear rank order of programmatic structuring among the three East Central European cases.

The equations in table 7.5 indicate that left-right placements involve cross-nationally varying semantic connotations. With some simplification, we can say that in Bulgaria the "left" implies socio-economic protectionism and anti-liberalism, authoritarian and collectivist politics, nationalism and Bulgarian ma-jority ethnic particularism. In the three Central European countries "left" posi-tions signal a preference for non-market mechanisms of resource allocation as well but, in contrast to Bulgaria, coincide with cosmopolitanism, multi-culturalism, and libertarian individualism. Central European countries thus appear to approach a semantic left-right interpretation that is typical for advanced capitalist countries where both redistributive, social protectionist economics, and political-cultural libertarianism count as leftist (cf. Kitschelt and Hellemans 1990a, 1990b), whereas Bulgaria is closer to a contrasting semantic space where politicians associate leftism with a blend of social protectionism and authoritarian political orientations. In theoretical terms, the semantic differences in the use of the left-right language derive from the discursive capabilities associated with varying types of communist regime, transition politics, and ultimately the resources and symbols that the communist successor parties can mobilize in the new era of democratic competition.

FROM POLITICAL DIVIDES TO COMPETITIVE DIMENSIONS

So far, our analysis has been concerned entirely with "political divides" that help us to locate issue dimensions on which parties' positions may differ. But not all divides are dimensions of party competition. The latter applies only to those divides on which politicians of rival parties find it worth advertising policies in the hope of swaying voters who may otherwise opt for alternative parties. On some issues, voters may be so committed to a policy position and associated party that no modification of its competitors' appeals could convince such voters to change their electoral choice. For that reason politicians who do not "own" a policy position of that type are unlikely to waste their time on such identification issues. In the competitive game to attract new voters, politicians search for issue divides that have either a *spatial* character such that a party's electoral payoff varies with the positions all the competitors advertise or a *valence* character such that rival parties openly compete over demonstrating competence to deliver policies desired by most voters. As we know from chapters 5 and 6, spatial competition appears to be more important on salient issues in post-communist democracies than valence competition.

Political divides involve party competition when the parties' electoral support is elastic to changing strategic party appeals, while the underlying preference distribution of the population remains the same. On dimensions of voter identification, electoral support does not change appreciably, even if parties modify policy positions. Here voters' preference change alone drives variability in party strength. To determine the elasticity of voter responses to changing party appeals, we would need to rely on a time series analysis of citizens' policy preferences and electoral choices, together with politicians' record of electoral appeals and performance in office. Given our lack of data to realize such a research design, as a second best option we rely on politicians' perceptions of the competitive game as a source of clues about political divides that involve party competition or party identification only.

For a political divide to qualify as competitive dimension, first politicians must attribute high salience to the core issues that constitute the divide. Second, politicians must articulate coherent party positions on the bundle of issues contributing to the divide. Third, politicians must spread parties' positions widely over the policy space at least in those instances, where multi-party competition with relatively easy entry of new competitors into the electoral arena prevails, as is the case with multi-member districts and moderate thresholds of legislative representation in all four of our East Central European countries. Vote- or office-maximizing politicians have incentives to diversify their appeals in the competitive pursuit of electoral support.

Our politicians' survey provides some straightforward operational measures of these three attributes of a competitive dimension already discussed as indicators of programmatic crystallization in chapter 5: the salience of issue dimensions, the spread of party positions, and the average diffuseness of parties' political positions. Another baseline for assessing the competitiveness of issue dimensions is the factor analysis of parties' policy positions discussed in this chapter. A factor is more likely to constitute a competitive dimension if many issues load on it. In other words, the greater a factor's eigenvalue, the more likely it is that politicians might seize on it as a competitive dimension. Whether this is actually the case, however, depends on politicians' salience ratings of the issues that load strongly on a given factor.

In table 7.6, the first column reproduces the eigenvalues of each of the factors we identified in our four countries. Eigenvalues serve as an indicator of a factor's capacity to "bundle" issue divides. The second column provides a measure of salience for the issue loadings of the factors. We construct this measure by two operations. First, we identify the variables whose factor loadings exceed .50. Then we express the politicians' average salience rating on that policy issue, as reported in table 5.1, in terms of its standardized z-score relative to the average salience of all issues in that country. Negative signs indicate that an issue is less salient than the average issue in that country, positive signs the reverse. The data in column 2 provide the average standardized salience score for all the issues with factor loadings greater than .5. In order to calculate the interaction effect of salience and strength of a factor divide, we then add 2 to all salience weights so that the salience multiplier contains only positive values.[20] Column 3 presents the result of the interaction between eigenvalues and transformed salience scores of the high-load variables on each factor.

While the factor with the strongest eigenvalue in a country also always constitutes the strongest competitive dimension, note that the relative importance of the second dimension varies across countries and is dependent on the salience multiplier rather than the eigenvalues. In Bulgaria and the Czech Republic, the secondary ethnic (Bulgaria) and socio-cultural (Czech Republic)

[20] In other words, a salience weight of +.36 in column 1 translates into an eigenvalue multiplier of 2.36, a salience weight of −1.72 into a multiplier of .28.

Table 7.6. *Are political divides among issues also dimensions of party competition?*

	1	2	3	4	5	6	7
				Divergence of party appeals			
Factors	Eigenvalues	Salience weights	Competition scores	Spread	Distance of the extremes	Diffuseness of party positions	Determination of left-right party placements
Bulgaria							
I: Economics	4.28	+.36	10.10	.88	2.29	.61	3.97
II: Ethnicity	2.31	-.94	2.45	.87	2.27	.62	1.30
III: Economics	1.51	+.47	3.73	.51	1.28	.86	1.17
IV: Women	1.04	-1.72	.29	.27	.68	.94	.38
Czech Republic							
I: Economics	7.18	+.38	17.07	1.18	2.82	.46	4.84
II: Socio-cultural	2.05	-.97	2.11	.80	2.39	.65	1.20
III: Environment	1.55	[+.68][a]	[4.15][a]	.48	1.48	.89	.23
IV: Ethnicity	1.24	-.64	1.69	.69	2.49	.75	1.09
Hungary							
I: Socio-cultural	7.62	-.10	14.45	.98	2.31	.41	4.65
II: Economics	2.13	+1.17	6.75	.70	1.99	.76	.48
III: Environment	1.21	+.17	2.63	.39	1.19	.94	.58
Poland							
I: Economics	5.55	+.82	15.64	.88	2.77	.53	2.95
II: Socio-cultural	4.33	-.79	5.24	.93	2.84	.47	2.98

Note: Italicized numbers indicate summary index of preceding columns. For its calculation, see text.

[a] No salience ratings available for decentralization (VAR 52), calculation based on VAR 42 (environment) only.

Sources: Column 1: tables 7.1 through 7.4; column 2: calculated from tables 5.1, 7.1 through 7.4; columns 4 and 5: tables 7.1 through 7.4; column 7: table 7.5.

divides yield weak competition scores, amounting to no more than 15 to 25 percent of the value for the dominant (economic) dimension. By contrast, in Hungary, the socio-cultural dimension is strongest, but the (secondary) economic dimension is almost half as strong as the former. In Poland, economic competition comes first, but the competition score on the socio-cultural dimension indicates that it is highly contested as well. Given the imprecision of our competition scores, which result from the unavoidable arbitrariness of the formula we employ to construct them, we wish to draw only a *weak* inference from the pattern of values displayed in the first three columns of table 7.6. It is relatively safe to say that in Hungary and Poland, at times, socio-cultural divides *can be* as intensely contested as economic divides – or even more so. In these two countries, *both* economic and socio-cultural issue divides have the potential of focusing party competition. By contrast, in Bulgaria and the Czech Republic, *only* economic divisions, or economic divisions *reinforced* by socio-cultural issues, structure party competition.

The remaining columns of table 7.6 reproduce parameters of party systems we have already introduced earlier in chapter 5 or in this chapter. If differentiation of party positions on political divides is essential to competitive dimensions in multi-party systems, then the *spread of parties,* as measured by the standard deviation of the parties' average factor scores, and the *distance between the extreme parties,* as measured by such parties' difference in factor scores, are useful indicators (columns 4 and 5). Given that these measures do not take policy salience into account, they are more helpful in eliminating certain issue divides from consideration as competitive dimensions than in positively identifying such dimensions. Based on this benchmark, in Bulgaria factors III (a mixed economic-cultural factor) and IV (women's role in society) and in the Czech Republic and Hungary factor III (environment) fail to produce competitive dimensions.

If competition on issue dimensions requires a rather unambiguous identifiability of a party's appeal, then a *low diffuseness of party positions,* as measured by a small average standard deviation of politicians' assessments that yield a party's average factor score, tells us whether parties can project clear messages on the political divide in the competitive game (column 6).[21] Finally, if party competition requires politicians to simplify issue appeals by invoking parties' left-right positions in order to render alternatives more intelligible to poorly informed voters, then those divides which politicians can easily map on the formal spatial left-right dimension are more competitive. Drawing on table 7.5, political divides indicated by factors with powerful predictive value for politicians' assignment of left-right placements of parties are more likely to be competitive dimensions. Our measure is the *slope coefficient* that signals a policy divide's contribution to a party's left-right placement (table 7.6, column 7).

Our seven quantitative measures characterize overlapping and substantively

---

[21]It does not matter that, at the margin, asymmetric judgments of party positions may affect our measure of diffuseness. Asymmetries indicate that a party's position is contested. They are thus an element of the process that makes parties' appeals more or less ambiguous.

interdependent, but not identical phenomena. They are empirically correlated, but in a less than perfect fashion.[22] A factor divide is likely to constitute a strong competitive dimension, if it (1) bundles many salient issues (high value in column 3), (2) yields a high dispersion of party appeals (high values in columns 4 and 5), (3) makes parties express coherent positions (low value in column 6), and (4) serves as a strong predictor of parties' left-right placements (high value in column 7). By these criteria, Bulgaria and the Czech Republic have only a single competitive dimension each. In both cases, that dimension revolves around economic policy issues, but is slightly "contaminated" by issues of socio-cultural authoritarianism in the Czech Republic and more profoundly shaped by decommunization in Bulgaria. In these two countries, secondary factor divides have a high spread of party positions (columns 4 and 5), but relatively low salience, high diffuseness, and a weak association with parties' left-right positions. Such secondary dimensions identify the position of minor "niche parties" outside the main competitive dimension. The same observation applies with even greater force to Bulgaria's and the Czech Republic's third and fourth political factor divides. The results are in line with our theoretical argument that expects strong political divides on economics, but not on other issues, in countries emerging from bureaucratic-authoritarian and patrimonial communism.

In Hungary and Poland, both countries emerging from national accommodative communism, the competitive alignments are different because there is less room for competition over economic reform. In Hungary, the strongest divide that unambiguously qualifies as competitive has to do with socio-cultural libertarian versus authoritarian issues. Nevertheless, in Hungary the economic divide also has important competitive features, indicated by a comparatively high salience score of the economic dimension (column 2) and considerable spread among parties (columns 4 and 5). At the same time, the Hungarian parties' issue positions on economics are quite diffuse (column 6) and hardly at all affect the politicians' placement of parties on the left-right dimension (column 7). The reformist bandwagon in Hungary makes it difficult to compete with neat alternatives on economic policy issues.

Poland, finally, shows features somewhere between the Czech and the Hungarian pattern. Similar to the Czech Republic, the strongest features indicating competition appear to characterize Poland's economic policy divide. But as in Hungary, socio-cultural divides play a considerable role as well. Poland has a robust secondary socio-political libertarian-authoritarian divide that exhibits most features of a competitive dimension. Hungary's and Poland's political divides are thus most likely to give rise to an electoral and legislative arena with cross-cutting dimensions of competition among the parties, whereas Bulgaria and

---

[22]Interesting are correlations between columns 3, 4, 5, 6, and 7. A high correlation between columns 4 and 5 is partly a matter of mathematical definition. Column 3 (salience * eigenvalues) is related to the subsequent columns with r-squares of .30 to .70. The relations among the remaining columns are even stronger.

the Czech Republic approximate uni-dimensional systems of competition with small niche parties in outlying dimensions of identification.

CONCLUSION

In this chapter we have analyzed the party elites' perception of the political divisions and the competitive space of our four East Central European post-communist democracies. Far from offering a picture of political chaos and lack of structuring, the four party systems display more or less clear programmatic divisions and competitive dimensions on which party rivals advertise alternative appeals. In all countries, with the partial exception of Hungary, the big questions of economic reform have the capacity to structure the political space and to promote party competition. Beyond these similarities, cross-national variance in the alignment and interaction of divisions is associated with pre-communist and communist legacies, combined with the strategic moves of political elites during the transition to democracy in 1989 and 1990.

Central European democracies after national-accommodative communism exhibit an essentially two-dimensional pattern of competitive dimensions yielding a party system with three to four sets or "blocks" of political parties situated in different regions of the competitive space. By contrast, Czech democracy, emerging from bureaucratic-authoritarian communism, and Bulgarian politics, following patrimonial communism, develop party systems with one overwhelming economic political division and competitive dimension and several minor political divisions that identify niches for small parties diversified by ethnic or cultural appeals from the grand alternatives located on the main competitive dimension. Our analysis also shows that the formal left-right semantics is meaningful for politicians in these new democracies, although with a cross-nationally varying policy content. Whether left-right party placements are wedded to the economic dimension of competition or also to a socio-cultural dimension depends primarily on the salience of socio-cultural issues for the competitive struggle.

Let us finally offer some speculations about the implications of our tentative findings for the resilience of the new democratic institutions in East Central Europe. If parties express multiple, mutually reinforcing divisions at least some of which entail non-negotiable cultural conflicts with collective identities at stake, then economic or cultural adversities may threaten the viability of democratic institutions from time to time. Intense conflicts about the merits of the old regime and its political elites also weaken the allegiance of the political actors to the democratic institutions and keep visions of an alternative, non-democratic regime alive. Where regime divides coincide with socio-cultural struggles about collective identities and with conflicts about economic reform and resource distribution, democrats might find it extremely difficult to hold on to their preferred institutions in times of severe economic hardship and open socio-cultural conflict.

None of the Central European countries gives rise to mutually reinforcing regime, economic, and socio-cultural divides in the arena of party competition. Czech democracy is dominated by distributive conflicts, but tends to depoliticize crosscutting conflicts about cultural identity and political regime, as is revealed by the low salience politicians attribute to the decommunization issue. In Hungary and Poland, cultural identity issues do play a role, but they cut across distributive economic conflicts. At the same time, regime questions of decommunization have rapidly lost political currency, even though they may occasionally flare up in highly symbolic episodes, such as the 1995 Polish presidential election campaign. Only in Bulgaria do we see elements of mutually reinforcing political divisions articulated in a party system with rather diffuse programmatic structuring. Here the economic divide between parties coincides to a considerable extent with issues of multi-cultural exclusion and with struggles over the status and treatment of organizations and representatives of the old communist regime. As a consequence, the political discourse often rallies voters more by encouraging them to settle scores of the past than by creating new economic opportunities for the future. Even in Bulgaria, however, the regime divide and ethnic conflicts appear not to be reinforcing conflict dimensions that would have sufficient salience in the 1990s to endanger the constitutional framework of democratic competition.

The procedural quality of democracy in East Central Europe is not just a matter of how politicians think and act on perceived political divisions. If democracy involves the construction of citizen-elite linkages that express relations of representation based on politicians' accountability and responsiveness, then it is important to explore the extent to which the features of democratic party competition we have identified at the elite level correspond to the structure of political attitudes exhibited by each country's electorates. Democracies rest on clay feet, if the cognitive maps, normative orientations, and strategic actions of politicians are not closely related to voters' construction of political life. In the next chapter, we therefore examine the nature of the preference divides among voters that we can detect in our four East Central European countries. This analysis will enable us to engage in a more rigorous analysis of political representation in chapter 9.

8

ELECTORAL CONSTITUENCY ALIGNMENTS: EMERGING POLITICAL CLEAVAGES?

In this chapter, we essentially replicate the analysis of the politicians' view of issue divides, party configurations, left-right placements, and competitive dimensions in each country for mass electorates. The key question is whether political divides and competitive dimensions are simply elite constructs "floating" on an undifferentiated mass audience, or whether they are also entrenched in the population and can be accounted for by the theoretical argument advanced in this book. In addition to this broad theme, there is a second question we pursue in the last but one section of this chapter. We explore the extent to which political divides may in fact give rise to political "cleavages" in the new post-communist democracies. According to our terminological convention introduced in chapter 2, cleavages are divides that exhibit longevity and entrenchment. If we follow Knutsen and Scarbrough (1995), a divide is more likely to constitute a cleavage if it is anchored in social-structural group differences. Political divisions that build on identifiable socio-economic or cultural groups and population sectors may be more durable than parties and divisions confined to the level of political opinion without grounding in distinct social groups.

Our cross-national analysis of programmatic alternatives and socio-structural grounding yields one result that appears inconsistent both with our theoretical framework and our empirical analysis of programmatic structuring in the political elites. In the population surveys, Bulgarian voters articulate sharper programmatic issue alternatives, configured around political parties, than the Hungarian and Polish electorates, *although* Bulgarian political elites engage in rather fuzzy programmatic appeals (chapters 5 through 7). We devote the final section of this chapter to making sense of this discrepancy.

POPULATION SURVEYS AMONG POST-COMMUNIST ELECTORATES

For three of the four countries, we draw on the Central European University semi-annual surveys conducted in the Czech Republic, Hungary, and Poland. We chose the CEU survey wave conducted in fall 1993, only a few months before we fielded our politicians' survey. We have also analyzed the spring–summer 1994 CEU surveys that were typically taken some time after our elite study. We report results from those surveys only in the few instances where they substantively differ from the results obtained with the fall 1993 data.[1] The Bulgarian survey supplied by our colleagues Geoffrey Evans and Stephen Whitefield from Oxford University was conducted in summer 1993. Compared with the CEU surveys, it employs fewer questions with a close semantic match to those included in our elite study, but many items are likely to tap the same underlying political divides.[2]

For our analysis, we have selected public opinion issues according to three criteria. First, a number of the issue opinion scales on which respondents place themselves are sufficiently close to items in the elite survey on party positions to warrant direct comparison. Second, other items are substantively different, but likely to draw on similar divides as those included in the elite survey. Appendix III at the end of this volume lists the precise wording of all items drawn from the population surveys. Third, we selected roughly the same ratio of economic to non-economic opinion issues drawn from the mass surveys as the ratio employed in our elite surveys. While it is quite hazardous to compare results from factor analyses based on a different number and different wordings of issue items, this rule should give us at least a rough bench mark concerning the importance of economic and non-economic issues for structuring voter divides in the various post-communist polities. Roughly half of the population survey items relate to questions of economic distribution and governance. The other half deals with questions of religion and morality, national identity, civic libertarianism, and law and order.

Table 8.1 displays the sub-set of items that exhibit the greatest semantic equivalence between politicians' and voters' surveys. They can be grouped into roughly three classes. First, there are questions of economic distribution and property rights. At the elite level, we chose one item that addresses governments' social-protectionist obligations (health care) and another item that deals with the consequences of liberalizing economic governance structures (market exposure of firms). At the population level, in the CEU survey, a question about governments' responsibility to create jobs approximates the social-protectionist issue, while a question about government policy toward unprofitable enterprises addresses the

---

[1] In the Czech Republic, the survey was conducted in November 1993 by quota selection and has a sample size of 1,117. In Poland and Hungary, the surveys were based on clustered random sampling and include 1,568 respondents (Poland, August 1993) and 1,200 respondents (Hungary, December 1993).

[2] This survey was conducted as a two-step cluster sample with 1,932 respondents.

Table 8.1. *Issue items corresponding in elite and population questionnaires*

Economic issues	
Elite questionnaire	Public provision of health care (VAR 30), for market reform, even if with unemployment (VAR 31)
CEU population questionnaire	Government responsibility to provide jobs (16c), unprofitable factories should be closed immediately (16g)
Bulgarian population questionnaire	Government responsibility to provide jobs (VAR 46), private enterprise as best way to solve Bulgaria's economic problems (VAR 105)
Religious-moral issues	
Elite questionnaire	Choice on abortion (VAR 38), role of church in public school instruction (VAR 39)
CEU population questionnaire	Choice on abortion (16n), church influence in the country (16p)
Bulgarian population questionnaire	Attendance of religious services (VAR 190)
Civic liberty and national collectivity issues	
Elite questionnaire	Liberal individualism (VAR 41), nationalism or cosmopolitanism (VAR 48) For Bulgaria in addition: Turkish language use in school (VAR 45)
CEU population questionnaire	Civil rights or law and order (16m), nationalism or cosmopolitanism (16i)
Bulgarian population questionnaire	Young people do not have enough respect for traditional values (VAR 116) Bulgaria should co-operate with other countries even if it means giving up some independence (VAR 126) Turks in this country should have to be taught in Bulgarian (VAR 134)

liberalization of economic governance structures. In the Bulgarian survey, we found few questions that quite literally address the same opinions as in the CEU surveys.

Our second set focuses on moral-religious issues and here the semantic correspondence between political elite and CEU population survey items on abortion and church involvement in public life is just about as tight as we could have wished for, had we originally designed a population survey to match our elite study. Unfortunately, the Bulgarian survey contains no corresponding items. Our not fully satisfactory fallback option here is a question on the attendance of religious services.

The third set of issues deals with civic libertarianism and national identity. While we analyze these issues separately, taken together they represent the grid/group distinction in conceptions of culture and identity that Thompson, Ellis, and Wildavsky (1989) derive from Mary Douglas's work. Authoritarians seek to erect high external boundaries separating the collective ("group") from strangers and to affirm the internal dominance of binding group norms ("grid") over individual choice. Conversely, libertarian anarchists reject external group boundaries as well as binding internal norms.

The collective whose norms gain particular significance for individual conduct in the modern age is the nation. Items measuring the endorsement of a national or international orientation conveniently capture the emphasis on boundaries both in our elite study as well as in the CEU and Bulgarian population surveys. The elite study frames views on collective norms ("grid") in terms of an item asking politicians to determine how much parties emphasize individual autonomy or compliance with tradition as goals of public education. In the CEU surveys, the closest equivalent is a question on the relative emphasis respondents would place on civil rights (the individualist-libertarian pole) or on law and order (the collectivist-authoritarian pole). In the Bulgarian survey, we employ an item concerning young people's respect for traditional values. Moreover, because of the importance of ethno-cultural divisions in Bulgaria, we include a question about the use of Turkish as a language of school instruction. Equivalent items are both in the elite and population surveys.

POLITICAL DIVIDES IN THE MASS PUBLICS OF EAST CENTRAL EUROPEAN DEMOCRACIES

In the population surveys, respondents do not assess party positions, but express their own personal preferences on policy issues of the day. The underlying dimensions according to which such preferences cluster represent *social divides*. By comparing the mean positions the electoral constituencies of different parties assume on these social divides, we obtain a picture of political divides in the four countries. Because we lack information about the salience respondents attribute to different issues, we cannot directly explore, however, whether *political divides* also translate into *competitive dimensions* or are merely *dimensions of political identification*.

We now proceed to a factor analysis of public opinion in each of our four post-communist countries. Given that the items included in this analysis are roughly similar in content to those in the factor analysis of politicians' assessments of party positions, a similarity between the factors that emerge from the elite and the population surveys would yield a first piece of evidence that post-communist democracies indeed build relations of political representation around programmatic structuring. Of course, the level of cognitive organization and constraint among the issue opinions citizens articulate is likely to be lower than that of the political elites. Political attention, involvement and higher average formal education gives politicians an edge in organizing their ideological maps (cf. Converse 1964; McClosky and Zaller 1984; Converse and Pierce 1986: 236–37). Hence, factor analyses of electorates' preference patterns over policies probably yield a *more complex and less constrained* pattern of factors with *lower factor loadings, lower explained variance,* and *lower eigenvalues* than in the corresponding analysis of political elite surveys.

Tables 8.2 through 8.5 present varimax-rotated factor analyses of the populations' issue preferences in the Czech Republic, Hungary, Poland, and Bulgaria. Compared with the equivalent analyses of the partisan elites' views of parties' issue positions in chapter 7, the opinion factors derived from population surveys indeed reveal more heterogeneity of beliefs – that is, a greater proliferation of independent dimensions along which preferences vary. Nevertheless, the pattern of divides in each country and the contrasts between countries exhibit striking similarities to the politicians' construction of policy alternatives advanced by competing parties.

In the Czech Republic (table 8.2), by far the strongest factor divides issue opinions according to the already familiar polarity between socio-economic protectionism versus market liberalism (eigenvalue 3.3, 25 percent explained variance). This factor addresses questions of privatization, the closure of unprofitable state companies with consequences for a surge in unemployment, and a variety of related issues of economic well-being. This structure of popular beliefs corresponds to an even sharper economic divide among party positions in the Czech elite survey (table 7.1: 44.8 percent explained variance).

In both the Czech elite and population surveys, the second factor constitutes a religion/morality dimension that is much weaker than the economic divide (roughly 12 percent explained variance). Two further even weaker factors tap questions of civil liberties and national autonomy in the Czech population survey. Also these public opinion factors are roughly equivalent to those obtained from the politicians' surveys. The structure of social divisions among Czech citizens is thus fully compatible with the political divides politicians attribute to the parties. The Czech Republic, as a polity succeeding a bureaucratic-authoritarian communist regime and building on considerable citizens' skills, develops a rather sharply articulated landscape of public opinion in which conflict over economic policy clearly dominates.

Just as in our elite surveys, the social divides emerging among Polish and Hungarian citizens are different from those in the Czech Republic. Roughly speaking, both countries have weaker and in Hungary's case more diffuse economic factors (compare tables 8.3 and 8.4), while religious values constitute a second factor with relatively or even absolutely greater explained variance and eigenvalue than in the Czech Republic. In Hungary, a third factor, however, also relates to economic questions (9.4 percent of the variance). Here public opinion separates a divide over issues of economic security and well-being (factor I) from questions concerning economic governance structures (factor III). The diffuseness of the Hungarian electorate's capacity to organize questions of economic governance and distribution around a single comprehensive package demonstrates the absence of sharply contoured elite conflict over economic policy in that country.

Compared with the economic divide, socio-cultural divides are more important in Hungary and Poland than in the Czech Republic, but nowhere do they reach the strength and organization of socio-cultural policy alternatives encountered within the Polish and Hungarian party elites. Whereas the latter assemble all socio-cultural conflicts in one powerful political divide (cf. tables 7.2 and 7.3), Polish and Hungarian mass publics disaggregate these issues into three separate factors quite analogous to the Czech citizens (religion, civic libertarianism, nationalism). Not surprisingly, in Poland the religious factor is somewhat stronger than in the Czech Republic and Hungary, a result in line with the intensity of religious beliefs and the role the Catholic church played in the transition from communism and thereafter.

If voters in all three Central European countries see religion, nationalism, and civic libertarianism as separate issue dimensions, why does this apply only to Czech political elites, but not their counterparts in Hungary and Poland where politicians assemble all socio-cultural issues on a single programmatic dimension? Strategic conditions in Poland and Hungary after national-accommodative communism may be responsible for this mass-elite difference and cross-national contrast to the Czech Republic. Because Polish and Hungarian politicians cannot polarize electoral competition around economic issues in the face of reformist post-communist parties that embrace essentials of market capitalism, they have sufficient incentives to construct a single powerful socio-cultural divide on which to display meaningful programmatic differences and employ those to attract voters.[3]

Current political elites, however, may strive to put more emphasis on socio-cultural divides than the electorates can bear, given their daily concern with economic hardship due to policies of market liberalization. The relative diffuseness of socio-cultural divides in the Polish and Hungarian population surveys may signal that mass publics in these countries are not entirely willing to follow politicians in creating a socio-cultural super-conflict, although mass publics in both countries also appear indisposed toward a powerful polarization over economic issues. Taking all three Central European countries together, the most sharply structured socio-cultural divide is religion in Poland where the church played a critical role in the transition and was perceived to make a bid to dominate the new Polish polity. Not by chance, religious issues appear to have had some capacity to move voters in the 1993 Polish election, whereas in the 1994 Hungarian election economic concerns were most on the mind of the critical swing

---

[3]Of course, these current strategies become more feasible against the backdrop of socio-cultural conflicts in the semi-authoritarian inter-war period and even in patterns of nineteenth- and twentieth-century state formation, particularly in Poland (Tworzecki 1996: chaps. 3, 4).

Table 8.2. *Factor analysis of Czech voters' issue opinions (varimax-rotation): Social divides in the electorate*

	Factors			
	I: Socio-economic protectionism	II: Religious values	III: Cosmopolitans and civil liberties	IV: Nationalism
I. Economic issues				
Government responsible for jobs for everyone (16c)	+.55	—	—	—
Not harmful to reduce income differences (16d)	+.53	—	+.43	—
Economic situation is unfavorable to my family (16e)	+.65	—	—	—
Privatization helps solve country's economic problems (16f)	−.72	—	—	—
Unprofitable factories to be closed immediately, even if this increases unemployment (16g)	−.62	—	—	—
In the present situation, own family has good chance to get ahead (16k)	−.75	—	—	—
II. Religion and morality				
Politicians who are agnostics are unacceptable (16h)	—	+.70	—	—
Allow abortion for women in early months of pregnancy (16n)	—	−.77	—	—
The church has too much influence in our country (16p)	—	−.60	—	—

III. *Nation, law and order*

Politicians should care more about rising crime and deteriorating morality than individual freedom (16m)	+.41	—	—	—
Nationalism always harmful for development of our country (16i)	—	—	-.50	-.91
Prefer politician who is a strong patriot to one who is an expert (16o)	—	—	-.66	—
IV. *Restitution*				
Former property owners should receive no compensation (16r)	+.60	—	—	—
% Explained variance	25.4	12.2	8.1	7.9
Eigenvalue	3.30	1.58	1.05	1.02

Note: Only factor loadings greater than .90 or smaller than -.40 are displayed.

Table 8.3. *Factor analysis of Polish voters' issue opinions (varimax rotation): Social divides in the electorate*

	Factors			
	I: Socio-economic protectionism	II: Religious values	III: Cosmopolitans and civil liberties	IV: Nationalism
I. Economic issues				
Government responsible for jobs for everyone (16c)	+.54	—	—	—
Not harmful to reduce income differences (16d)	—	—	—	+.63
Economic situation is unfavorable to my family (16e)	+.67	—	—	—
Privatization helps solve country's economic problems (16f)	-.67	—	—	—
Close down unprofitable factories, even if this increases unemployment (16g)	-.54	—	—	—
In the present situation, own family has good chance to get ahead (16k)	-.68	—	—	—
II. Religion and morality				
Politicians who are agnostics are unacceptable (16h)	—	+.62	—	—
Abortion for women allowed in early months of pregnancy (16n)	—	-.80	—	—
The church has too much influence in our country (16p)	—	-.77	—	—

III. Nation, law and order				
Politicians should care more about rising crime and deteriorating morality than individual freedoms (16m)	—	—	*−.64*	—
Nationalism always harmful for development of our country (16i)	—	—	—	−.70
Prefer politician who is a patriot to one who is an expert (16o)	—	—	*−.72*	—
IV. Constitutional design				
President should be given exceptional powers (16r)	—	—	*−.61*	—
% Explained variance	17.0	14.6	10.7	8.6
Eigenvalue	2.20	1.89	1.39	1.12

Note: See table 8.2.

Table 8.4. *Factor analysis of Hungarian voters' issue opinions (varimax rotation): Social divides in the electorate*

	Factors				
	I: Optimistic economic outlook	II: Secular cosmopolitans	III: Socioeconomic protectionism	IV: Support of Catholic tradition	V: Nationalism
I. Economic issues					
Government responsible for jobs for everyone (16c)	−.57	—	—	—	—
Not harmful to reduce income differences (16d)	—	—	+.53	—	—
Economic situation is unfavorable to my family (16e)	−.79	—	—	—	—
Privatization helps solve country's economic problems (16f)	—	—	−.68	—	—
Close down unprofitable factories, even if this increases unemployment (16g)	—	—	−.60	—	—
In the present situation, own family has good chance to get ahead (16k)	+.76	—	—	—	—
II. Religion and morality					
Politicians who are agnostics are unacceptable (16h)	—	−.73	—	—	—
Permit abortion for women in early months of pregnancy (16n)	—	−.52	—	—	—
The church has too much influence in our country (16p)	—	—	—	−.72	—

III. Nation, law and order

Politicians should care more about rising crime and deteriorating morality than individual freedom (16m)	—	-.42	—	—	—
Nationalism always harmful for development of our country (16i)	—	—	—	—	-.87
Prefer politician who is a patriot to one who is an expert (16o)	—	-.62	—	—	—
IV. Restitution					
Former property owners should receive no compensation (16r)	—	—	—	+.66	—
% Explained variance	17.3	12.4	9.4	8.2	7.9
Eigenvalue	2.25	1.61	1.22	1.07	1.02

Note: See table 8.2.

Table 8.5. *Factor analysis of Bulgarian voters' issue opinions (varimax rotation): Social divides in the electorate*

	Factors		
	I: Socio-economic protectionism versus market liberalism	II: Authoritarians versus libertarians	III: Turkish minority culture
I. Economic issues			
Aim of creating a market economy (VAR 3)	-.71	—	—
Government responsibility to provide a job for everyone (VAR 46)	+.44	—	—
Capitalism is the best way to solve Bulgaria's economic problems (VAR 105)	-.73	—	—
Large differences in income are necessary for prosperity (VAR 107)	-.61	—	—
II. Religion and morality			
Church attendance (VAR 190)	—	+.43	—
Young people today have not enough respect for traditional values (VAR 116)	—	+.72	—
Censorship of films and magazines is necessary to uphold moral standards (VAR 117)	—	+.64	—
III. Nation and ethnicity			
Turks in this country should be taught in Bulgarian (VAR 134)	—	+.32	-.65
Foreign direct ownership of enterprises acceptable (VAR 136)	+.51	—	—
Emphasis on international cooperation rather than national independence (V 126)	—	—	+.75
% Explained variance	23.2	12.5	11.4
Eigenvalue	2.32	1.25	1.14

Note: See table 8.2.

electorate, even though Hungary has a strong elite politicization of socio-cultural issues (Markowski and Toka 1995).

If we interpret the combined explained variance of the first two opinion factors in the three Central European countries as a rough indicator of issue constraint and programmatic structuring in the electorates, we derive the following rank order: Czech Republic (37.6%), Poland (31.6%), and Hungary (29.7%). This rank order corresponds to our analysis of programmatic structuring at the elite level in chapters 5 and 6 and our proposition that a legacy of bureaucratic-authoritarian communism facilitates programmatic structuring of democratic party competition more so than national-accommodative communist regimes.

In comparison with our findings in Central Europe, we would expect much less popular programmatic crystallization in the Bulgarian electorate, given the rather diffuse programmatic appeal of Bulgarian party politicians in the aftermath of patrimonial communism and the presence of continued strong communist successor parties. But table 8.5 disconfirms this expectation, even if we keep in mind that the number and phrasing of issue items extracted from the Bulgarian survey for our factor analysis are not directly equivalent to the items taken from the Central European surveys. Factor I divides the Bulgarian population over issues of economic reform and is considerably stronger than its Polish, Hungarian, or even Czech counter-parts (explained variance: 26.7 percent). As a secondary factor, Bulgaria displays a clear moral-religious libertarian-authoritarian factor (explained variance: 14.2 percent). There is no evidence for an independent divide along those lines in the elite judgments of party positions. A third factor taps the ethnic division between Bulgarians and the Turkish-speaking Islamic minority population.

Consistent with our theoretical expectations, both in the Czech Republic and Bulgaria economic opinion divides have relatively and absolutely greater power to structure mass opinion than in Hungary or Poland where socio-cultural divides are relatively more important. But combining the first two issue factors in Bulgaria yields 40.9 percent explained variance, an even greater share than in the Czech Republic. The Bulgaria electorate is now at the high end of ideological constraint with voters organizing their political preferences in a relatively more coherent manner than the programmatic diffuseness of the country's political elite would have led us to believe.

In all four East Central European countries, ideological constraint, as measured by the explained variance of the first two factors, is much greater among politicians than electorates. Even the lowest ratio of explained variance at the elite level (Bulgaria: 44 percent) is greater than the highest ratio at the population level (again Bulgaria: 40.9 percent). It would be misleading, however, to argue that the ideological heterogeneity of post-communist mass publics is unique for fledgling democracies and a sure sign of democratic immaturity. West European electorates hardly have more constrained patterns of political belief.[4]

---

[4]McGann and Kitschelt (1995) found in factor analyses of Western mass publics' political

Up to this point, we have analyzed the social opinion divides in East Central European democracies. But do *social divides* translate into *political divides* among parties' electoral constituencies? Each party electorate's mean position on the social divides may provide a "tracer" of the party politicians' actual policy appeals. In the next chapter, we analyze in detail the extent to which politicians' policy appeals in fact coincide with their constituencies' preferences. In this chapter, our aim is more modest. We wish to explore whether social opinion divides capture preference disagreements between the parties' electoral constituencies. Three measures familiar from the preceding chapter are helpful in this regard. First, we can compare the "spread" among parties – that is, the standard deviation of their mean factor scores. Next, we measure the distance between extreme parties on each factor. Finally, the average standard deviation of each party's constituency may serve as a measure of programmatic crystallization in the party system. Low standard deviations signal sharply contoured political alignments with parties enjoying electoral constituencies with rather coherent programmatic opinions.

Table 8.6 provides results for the Czech Republic, where our elite analysis suggests the sharpest political divide around economic issues. Party electorates confirm this alignment. The spread among the various party constituencies' economic policy preferences is greatest on the first, most powerful economic factor and the average standard deviation of each party's constituency opinions is smallest on that factor. Religious values are a close runner-up and actually show the greatest distance between the extreme party opposites, but this result is driven by a single small outlier party, the Christian Democratic KDU-CSL. Were we to calculate the spread of parties weighted by the electoral support of each party, then economic divisions would far surpass the religious divide in the arena of party competition.[5]

The remaining two factors have relatively little power to structure party alignments in the Czech Republic. Just as in our elite analysis, they highlight the distinctiveness of small niche parties, such as the nationalist and xenophobic Republican party which received only about 7 percent of the popular vote (June 1996) and is represented with 4 percent of the respondents in our survey. Overall the most powerful structuring device for political alignments in the Czech Republic is economics.

The Polish results (table 8.7) tell a somewhat different story, consistent with Poland's political alignments at the elite level. Both economics and religious values clearly separate the constituencies of different parties, with religion holding the edge both in terms of revealing the greatest inter-party spread and distance between extremes as well as the highest internal coherence of party

---

beliefs that the strongest factors rarely exceed eigenvalues of 2.8, when we enter about the same number and variety of observed variables into the analysis (respondents' opinion preferences). Only in Germany, the first factor comes close to that in the Czech Republic.

[5] The weighted scores of spread between parties are .65 for economics and .40 for religious values. For the remaining two issue dimensions, they are as low as .13 (nationalism).

Table 8.6. *Czech Republic: The party constituencies' mean positions on the issue dimensions*

	I: Economic populism		II: Religious values		III: Cosmopolitans and civil liberties		IV: Nationalism	
	Average	S.D.	Average	S.D.	Average	S.D.	Average	S.D.
KSCM/LB (85)	+1.17	.76	–.20	1.01	–.10	.90	+.09	.98
CSSD (177)	+.53	.78	–.28	.90	–.09	.94	–.06	1.01
LSU (21)	+.84	.68	+.01	.92	+.21	1.00	–.43	.87
KDU-CSL (52)	+.00	.80	+1.56	1.27	–.22	.99	–.00	.87
ODA (116)	–.36	.78	–.04	.80	+.20	.81	–.06	.89
SPR-RSC (39)	+.62	1.05	–.25	1.03	–.40	1.11	+.40	1.13
HSD-SMS (34)	+.29	.82	+.03	1.10	–.07	.97	+.31	1.11
ODS (382)	–.65	.83	–.01	.79	+.15	1.02	–.01	.99
Non-voters (153)	+.21	.83	+.03	1.09	–.16	1.11	–.07	1.02
Spread of parties	.65		.60		.22		.25	
Distance between extreme parties	1.82		1.84		.60		.83	
Average S.D.	.81		.98		.96		.99	

Table 8.7. *Poland: The party constituencies' mean positions on the issue dimensions*

	I: Socio-economic protectionism		II: Religious values		III: Cosmopolitans and civil liberties		IV: Nationalism and social protection	
	Average	S.D.	Average	S.D.	Average	S.D.	Average	S.D.
SDRP/SLD (112)	+.38	.91	-.66	.75	+.25	1.11	+.18	1.17
PSL (111)	+.27	.81	+.07	1.00	-.24	.92	+.14	1.04
UP (48)	-.10	1.01	-.35	.76	+.30	1.10	-.10	1.10
ZChN (33)	-.35	1.06	+.88	1.15	-.23	1.22	-.02	1.06
UD (103)	-.40	1.09	-.05	.99	+.32	1.15	-.08	1.07
KLD (24)	-.63	1.45	-.27	1.06	+.57	1.35	-.03	1.23
KPN (46)	+.02	.95	-.40	.82	-.29	1.06	+.10	1.11
BBWR (38)	-.42	1.17	+.64	1.16	-.34	.91	-.21	1.08
PC (29)	-.34	1.26	-.14	1.07	+.12	1.21	-.33	1.16
NZSS "S" (39)	+.05	.95	+.12	1.03	-.18	.99	-.06	1.29
Non-voters (310)	-.01	1.07	-.10	1.00	+.02	1.09	+.07	1.13
Spread of parties	.33		.47		.32		.16	
Distance between extremes	1.01		1.54		.91		.51	
Average S.D.	1.07		.98		1.10		1.13	

constituencies. In the elite study, politicians integrate questions of civic libertarianism and national commitment into a broad socio-cultural super-divide. Polish voters not only separate these issues, but also fail to show a clear structuring of party positions on questions of civil liberty or national autonomy. Spread among parties is low, distances among extreme opposites are small, and average standard deviations of each party electorate's opinions tend to be large. Politicians do not attribute much salience to these questions, and with good reason: They can hardly hope to structure party-constituency linkages around such issues.

The Hungarian picture (table 8.8) is even further removed from the neat nearly uni-dimensional structuring of the Czech political space. Moreover, it does not reflect the simplicity of the Hungarian elite's construction of a single powerful socio-cultural political divide. A comparison of the spread among parties and the distance between extreme opposites shows that *only on moral-religious issues are there clear political alignments in Hungarian politics at the time of our survey* (factors II and IV). With regard to the economic factors I and III and the national identity factor V, the spread between the party electorates' mean positions is very small, distances between extreme parties are modest, and intra-party heterogeneity is high. After a "negotiated" transition, preceded by decades of market-liberalizing reform pushed by the ruling communist party, not only political elites but also electorates have a hard time translating economic policy alternatives into political divides that separate party constituencies supporting divergent economic policy options.

In Bulgaria (table 8.9), economics is the main structuring divide of the party system. Measured by inter-party spread and distance between the extreme, the sub-cultural question of Turkish minority autonomy appears to have about equal or greater power to pattern political alignments, but this impression is driven by a single outlier party, the small representative of the Turkish minority, the Movement for Rights and Freedoms (DPS). The libertarian/authoritarian factor II, by itself, has little power to structure party alternatives, but the party constituencies' mean values correlate with the constituencies' scores on the economic divide. The more socio-economically protectionist parties tend to be more authoritarian.[6] Following patrimonial communism, politicians of the former ruling party and the opposition respond to incentives to construct reinforcing economic and non-economic opinion divides. Voter alignments with political parties reflect mutually reinforcing divisions.

Our comparison of political alignments in 1993–94 in the four post-communist countries thus illustrates the differential capacity of economic issues to structure the field of party alternatives both at the politicians' and the voters' levels. This capacity is much greater in the Czech Republic and Bulgaria than in

---

[6]Weighted by party size, the correlation of the parties' mean positions on the two factors is $r = -.68$. Our result conforms to Evans and Whitefield's (1997) discriminant analysis with the same data set which shows a single economic and social libertarian market versus authoritarian socialist factor as the dominant structuring principle of political alignments.

Table 8.8. *Hungary: The party constituencies' mean positions on the issue dimensions*

	I: Optimistic economic outlook		II: Secular cosmopolitans		III: Socio-economic protectionism		IV: Religious values		V: Nationalism	
	Average	S.D.	Average	S.D.	Average	S.D.	Average	S.D.	Average	S.D.
MSZP (169)	-.04	.94	+.33	.85	+.24	1.00	-.40	1.01	-.15	1.09
FKGP (12)	-.02	.88	-.83	1.18	-.44	1.05	+.10	.86	+.48	1.20
KDNP (31)	+.44	1.08	-.48	1.35	-.23	1.36	+.80	1.20	-.25	1.20
SZDSZ (72)	+.24	1.06	+.12	1.00	-.22	.99	-.03	.97	-.05	1.00
Fidesz (88)	+.32	1.16	+.35	.76	-.27	.95	-.14	.96	+.08	1.09
MDF (41)	+.33	1.04	-.60	1.26	-.09	1.23	+.60	1.11	+.04	1.19
Non-voters (257)	-.11	.95	+.10	1.02	+.10	1.07	+.08	1.06	+.02	1.16
Spread of parties	.20		.54		.23		.46		.25	
Distance between extremes	1.05		1.18		.68		1.63		.73	
Average S.D.	1.08		1.06		1.11		1.02		1.13	

Table 8.9. *Bulgaria: The party constituencies' mean positions on the issue dimensions*

	I: Socio-economic protectionism versus market liberalism		II: Authoritarians versus libertarians		III: Turkish minority culture	
	Average	S.D.	Average	S.D.	Average	S.D.
BSP (373)	+.54	.83	-.11	.91	+.23	.85
BZNS (Moser & Petkov) (132)	-.02	.89	-.19	.94	-.09	1.04
BSDP (34)	-.12	.92	-.09	.87	+.29	.69
BBB (62)	-.46	.90	+.22	1.17	-.00	.90
DPS (90)	+.20	.71	+.30	1.00	-.92	1.17
SDS (209)	-.77	.91	+.13	1.06	-.03	1.03
Non-voters (549)	+.06	.97	-.02	.99	+.02	.94
Spread of parties	.47		.18		.51	
Distance between the extremes	1.31		.59		1.21	
Average S.D.	.88		.99		.95	

Poland or Hungary. Socio-cultural divides, in turn, have more capacity to structure the Hungarian and Polish party system.

The cross-national differences in the structuring capacity of different divides are not simply a matter of the Catholic socio-cultural heritage in Hungary and Poland. Were Catholicism the central cause of crosscutting divisions in Hungary and Poland and its weakness or absence the cause of reinforcing divisions in Bulgaria and the Czech Republic, then Poland, not Hungary, should have the strongest socio-cultural and the weakest economic divides. After all, Polish citizens are much more committed to Catholicism and Poland has fewer minority Protestants than Hungary or the Czech Republic. The strength of socio-cultural divides and the weakness of economic divides in Hungary, particularly at the elite level, suggests that political legacies and issue leadership in the new democracies, not just Catholic heritage, frame political alignments.

THE LEFT-RIGHT SEMANTICS IN EAST CENTRAL EUROPEAN MASS ELECTORATES

Left-right spatial metaphors may reduce voters' uncertainty about parties' positions under conditions of high information costs (Downs 1957; Enelow and Hinich 1984; Budge 1984), but a uni-dimensional left-right scale serves information misers best only when programmatic crystallization among voters and politicians is strong and the substantive divisions of the party system involve uni-dimensional or reinforcing alignments rather than multi-dimensional crosscutting alignments. Indeed, previous studies show that the capacity of mass publics to conceptualize left-right scales in terms of substantive policy alternatives varies cross-nationally with systemic conditions of party competition (cf. Granberg and Holmberg 1988; Klingemann 1979). Nevertheless, at least in Western European polities, citizens relate their own and their parties' left-right placements to programmatic issue alternatives, not just to purely symbolic markers (cf. Huber 1989).

In post-communist democracies, however, mass publics may encounter particular difficulties to connect substantive policy positions to the left-right semantics. First of all, the lack of an open discourse on public policy and left-right differences, combined with the trivialized and dogmatic left-right formula under the old communist regimes, deprives East European voters of the familiarity and experience with such concepts in the arena of political competition. Second, in most historical circumstances the meaning of "left" is associated with societal *change* in conjunction with calls for *greater economic equality*. In post-communist countries, however, change typically promotes an increase of social inequality, a traditional "rightist" objective in the Western use of the spatial semantics. Those who endorse change may see themselves as "leftist," because they attack the status quo, or as "rightist," because they welcome more inequality and market allocation of scarce resources.

Third, what makes things even more complicated, those who benefit most from the new capitalist market system are often members of the nomenklatura in the state enterprise system who have sufficient skills and insider information to take advantage of privatization. While their material interests are "rightist" in that they support property, market relations, and liberalization, they may continue to cultivate ties to the post-communist party that now embraces a "leftist" label and a social-protectionist platform. Conversely, many of those who opposed communism are economically worse off in relative or absolute economic terms under the emerging capitalist system than they were under communism. Consider workers and employees in shipyards and manufacturing plants who joined Solidarność in 1980 and possibly again in 1989. Should they place themselves on the "left," if that implies defense of non-commodified work relations, or the "right," because they oppose communist rule? In a similar vein, small entrepreneurs, such as independent farmers in Poland, who resented communist rule, may now worry about international competition resulting from trade liberalization. Do they place themselves now on the "right" because they opposed the communist system or the "left" because they wish to regulate product markets or do they refuse to employ the formal spatial semantics altogether?

In light of these opportunities for semantic confusion about the meaning of left and right in the aftermath of communism, it would demonstrate the formidable power of such formal concepts for the intellectual clarification of party competition if opinion surveys revealed even a modest tendency on the part of respondents to employ left-right placements of self and others (parties) with specific policy positions in mind. This achievement would demonstrate either how much electorates can draw on accumulated cultural capital to make sense of political alternatives or how quickly they can learn the usage of information shortcuts to organize their cognitive maps of the political world in a competitive environment.

Given that average voters do not pay as much attention to politics as partisan politicians and lack their cognitive sophistication, the ability of mass publics to relate policy content to the left-right semantics may systematically vary across contexts of competition that facilitate or impede the organization of knowledge in these formal terms. Where *substantive party alignments* are nearly uni-dimensional, voters have an easier time to affiliate their left-right stances with specific issue preferences and the electoral choice of parties that promote such preferences. Voters have more trouble to employ the left-right conceptualization, when economic and socio-cultural divides vie for politicians' and voters' attention. Voters here have to work through the complex intellectual operation of projecting a two-dimensional space of political divides (and possibly party competition) on a uni-dimensional, formal semantics of left-right attributions.

A further contextual condition affecting voters' use of the left-right language is the *number of competing parties*. A larger number of parties makes it more difficult to project one's own and the parties' positions on a uni-dimensional formal left-right plane. Distinctions between party positions may become too fine for voters to capture by left-right attributions in a consistent way. Finally, the extent to which parties engage in *polarized competition around salient issues* makes left-right attributions more or less difficult. Where parties subscribe to a centripetal competitive dynamic and adopt rather similar issue positions, only the most sophisticated voters are able to conceptualize their own policy preferences or assign party positions within a consistent left-right framework. Polarization, in turn, facilitates the popular intelligibility of left-right notations. Where a deep "regime divide" between communist successor parties and an anti-communist opposition bloc keeps festering in post-communist democracies, the left-right language is more readily intelligible for voters.

Applying these contextually induced mechanisms of information processing to the new East Central European democracies, we would expect voters to be able to link their own policy stances to left-right self-placements and these self-placements to their electoral choice of parties better in the Czech Republic and Bulgaria than in Poland, and in Poland better than in Hungary. The former two countries have a simple dominant divide and comparatively few major parties. Furthermore, shackles of the regime divide still have some salience and provide a simple communist–anti-communist polarity that citizens may project onto the left-right dualism. In Hungary, by contrast, the regime divide began to subside shortly after the negotiated transition. Moreover, the absence of clear-cut party and policy alternatives on economic policy has given politicians incentives to politicize socio-cultural issues which make the arena of party competition inherently more complicated. Poland is situated somewhere between the Czech and the Hungarian configurations by having both a sharply contoured economic divide as well as a strong socio-cultural divide at the elite level, thus making it difficult for citizens to employ the left-right language when confronted with multi-dimensional competition.

The nationally diverging legacies of democratic transition and the emerging settings of party competition in post-communist democracies thus affect both the expected *strength* of the linkage between voters' and politicians' policy positions and their left-right placements as well as the *policy meaning* of "left" and "right" in each country. With regard to the latter, we showed the existence of such differences at the elite level in the previous chapter. We now can explore whether similar cross-national differences surface in the construction of left-right self-placements by mass publics. If competitive dimensions of the party system shape citizens' use of the left-right semantics, then in Bulgaria and the Czech Republic economic policy issues dominate the meaning of left and right, whereas in Hungary and Poland left-right placements are likely to incorporate both economic and socio-cultural issue content. Given the prominence of socio-cultural divides in Hungary both at the elite and the electoral level, socio-cultural meaning may here dominate the left-right semantics.

In line with our previous comparisons of programmatic constraint at the elite and the population level, we expect that in all countries the tightness of linkage between policy content and the left-right semantics is much less pronounced in the

Table 8.10. *The distribution of left and right self-placements in four East Central European countries*

	Left									Right
	1	2	3	4	5	6	7	8	9	10
Czechs 1992	4.4	6.5	8.2	29.5	16.6	20.2	14.7			
Czechs 1993	3.3	7.3	12.3	26.2	19.2	20.8	10.9			
Hungarians 1992	5.7	7.0	17.7	50.5	13.2	3.4	2.6			
Hungarians 1994	6.7	8.2	19.2	43.9	12.1	6.3	3.7			
Poles 1992	3.4	7.1	15.0	44.2	14.8	9.6	5.9			
Poles 1993	6.3	9.3	13.3	39.0	14.5	11.0	6.6			
Bulgarians 1993	4.7	7.5	1.1	13.4	17.3	33.1	8.1	8.4	3.0	3.3

Source: Bulgaria: Evans and Whitefield Bulgarian survey, based on ten categories; all others: Central European University national population surveys, based on seven categories.

mass electorates than among politicians, even when the salient issue space and the party alignments are uni-dimensional. Given that citizens have, on average, less cognitive sophistication and pay less attention to politics than professional politicians, they are likely to express considerably more conceptual slippage, semantic "noise," and randomness in tying their policy preferences to left-right self-placements than politicians. These cognitive limitations weaken the statistical relationship between respondents' issue positions and their left-right self-placements.

Table 8.10 shows the distribution of respondents in the four countries over the left-right dimension. The CEU surveys in the Czech Republic, Hungary, and Poland offer respondents a 7-point scale and we present results of both the 1992 and 1993–94 surveys in order to show the rather high stability of the response patterns. In all three countries, centrist positions command the greatest support, but the distribution of leftist (scores 1 and 2) and rightist (scores 6 and 7) positions varies noticeably between countries. In the Czech Republic, about a third of the respondents place themselves on the right, compared with only one-sixth in Poland and one-tenth or less in Hungary. Relative to the median of the 7-point scale at a value of 4.0, the average Czech left-right self-placement is clearly on the right (4.67 in 1992 and 4.97 in 1993), in Poland in the center (4.12 in 1992 and 4.06 in 1993), and slightly on the left in Hungary (3.79 in 1992 and 3.81 in 1994). In Bulgaria, respondents also place themselves slightly to the left of the midpoint of a 10-point scale (5.46 compared with 5.5). If left-right self-placements have to do with citizens' experience with economic reform (Whitefield and Evans 1994), then rightism in the Czech Republic derives from the country's initial success to engineer market reforms without greatly boosting unemployment.[7] By contrast, the other three countries entered deep crises of economic adjustment accompanied by high unemployment beginning in 1990.

In order to explore the policy content of respondents left-right self-placements, we now could regress each citizen's factor score on the dimensions obtained in our factor analyses (tables 8.2 through 8.5) on their left-right placements. In order to increase the direct comparability between the four countries, we employ original variables from the surveys that load strongly on the relevant opinion factors in each of the countries. These issue items are listed in table 8.1. Where items clearly tap the same dimension, as is the case with the two economic and the two moral-religious issues, we combine them in a single index. Because the range of values is not the same across all variables and all four countries, the size of the slope coefficients showing the impact of respondents' policy preferences on their left-right self-placements sometimes cannot be directly compared across countries. Table 8.11 therefore includes additional information about each variable's range and standardized coefficients in addition to the slope coefficients and the standard errors.[8]

The contrasts between the four countries are quite pronounced. First, cross-national variations in the overall explained variance of left-right self-placements show that respondents' issue positions are more tightly related to their left-right self-placements in the Czech Republic (R^2 = .24) and in Bulgaria (R^2 = .15) than in Poland (R^2 = .11) and Hungary (R^2 = .03). This conforms to our expectation that in countries where a single political divide structures party alternatives respondents are more capable of linking their own issue positions to left-right self-placements. Indeed, the overall explained variance of left-right placements by policy positions closely corresponds to the prominence of economic issues in countries' political divides. Thus, in Bulgaria and the Czech Republic comparatively high standardized beta-scores signal that respondents' economic issue positions explain a considerable share of the variance of their left-right placements. The unstandardized coefficients give a sense of the magnitude of the impact economic issue attitudes exert on left-right placements. A one-point rise of a respondent's score on the economic liberalism scale prompts rather hefty increases on the left-right scale in Bulgaria (+1.19 on a 10-point scale) and especially in the Czech Republic (+1.13 on the 7-point scale), but much smaller movements in Hungary (+.21) and Poland (+.36), both on 7-point scales.

Conversely, socio-cultural issues have an absolutely and relatively greater impact on left-right self-placements in Hungary and Poland. Religion/clericalism

---

[7]With the benefit of hindsight, of course, Czech economic reforms, objectively speaking, look much less impressive (see chapter 3). What counts here is only the perception of economic policy by the population at a time when the Czech economic reform appeared successful to many casual observers.

[8]We report estimations based on the CEU fall 1993 surveys. Calculations based on the spring 1994 surveys essentially yield the same results.

Table 8.11. *Ideological determinants of left-right self-placements*

	Bulgaria			Czech Republic			Hungary			Poland		
	b	s.e.	beta	b	s.e.	beta	b	s.e.	beta	b	s.e.	beta
Constant	.08	.07		4.04***	.16		3.92***	.11		5.04***	.12	
Economic liberalism (index)	1.40***	.13	+.26	1.14***	.08	+.38	+.20**	.06	+.10	+.30**	.08	+.09
Clericalism (index in CEU)	+.19***	.03	+.15	+.53***	.09	+.15	+.22**	.06	+.10	+.71***	.06	+.28
Civic libertarianism	+.47*	.20	+.06	+.78***	.15	+.14	-.13	.10	-.04	-.17	.12	-.04
National autonomy	-.66**	.18	-.09	-.12	.15	-.02	+.30**	.09	+.09	-.12	.12	-.03
Turkish language	+.08	.07	+.03									
Adjusted R-square	.11***			.24***			.03***			.09***		
F	57.82			89.38			9.05			37.42		

Note: All equations replace missing data on the independent variables by mean values. Table 8.1 lists variables employed for the construction of the indices. Economic liberalism: variables 16c and 16g in the CEU survey, variables 46 and 105 in the Bulgarian survey; Clericalism: variables 16n and 16p in the CEU survey, variable 190 in the Bulgarian survey; Civic libertarianism: variable 16m in the CEU survey, variable 116 in the Bulgarian survey; National autonomy: variable 16i in the CEU survey, variable 126 in the Bulgarian survey.
* p < .05; ** p < .01; *** p < .001.

has the greatest effect on people's left-right self-placements in Poland (b = +.87; beta = +.30). In Hungary, a combination of religious opinions and nationalism are significant predictors of rightist self-placements. The predictive power of different issues thus reflects the nature of political divides in each country. In Bulgaria and the Czech Republic, with more or less uni-dimensional economic party competition, economics determines the formal left-right semantics, whereas in Hungary and Poland, with two crosscutting salient divides, socio-cultural concerns are much more influential.

Comparing table 8.11 to the politicians' assignment of left-right scores to political parties in table 7.7, it is clear that political elites and electorates subscribe to a similar interpretation of the left-right semantics within each country. But left-right interpretations of both politicians and voters vary across countries. The statistical strength of association between policy positions and left-right placements of self or parties differs between politicians and voters in predictable ways. Voters' issue opinions are more loosely coupled with their left-right self-placements than are the associations politicians construct between parties' issue positions and their left-right placements. At the elite level, policy positions explain up to three-quarters of the variance in parties' left-right placements (table 7.7), but voters' policy preferences account for no more than 24 percent of the electorates' left-right self-placements.

Both in our population and elite surveys, cross-national differences in the left-right semantics reflect contrasting pathways to democracy, types of communist rule, and socio-cultural background conditions. In Poland and Hungary, where mobilized constituencies struggled for national societal autonomy from the Soviet hegemon since the days of Stalinism and played a critical role in the evolution of an accommodative communist ruler toward a negotiated transition to democracy, non-economic connotations play a relatively greater role for the meaning of the spatial left-right semantics than in the Czech Republic whose democracy emerges against the backdrop of a militant communist and socialist working-class movement in the inter-war democracy, a bureaucratic-authoritarian communism, and a transition to democracy by implosion of the old elites. For different historical reasons, a similar dominance of economics in the left-right semantics occurs in Bulgaria, where the ruling communist party created an industrial society and organized a patrimonial system of rule that undercut the formation of a national or liberal-democratic pole of political opposition against the ruling party.

FROM POLITICAL DIVIDES TO PARTY COMPETITION

The preceding sections on voters' social preference divisions, political partisan divides, and left-right self-placements showed that the perception of political alternatives by the electorate pretty much converges with that of the political elites within each country. Based on politicians' ratings of issue salience, our analysis of politicians' views of the political arena could also explore the divides that are consequential for party competition. Our population surveys unfortunately do not ask respondents to indicate the salience of different issues for their political orientation. Moreover, we have no panel design that would permit us to estimate the elasticity of parties' voter support contingent upon parties' policy positions, performance in government, or voters' changing preferences. We therefore have no independent empirical yardstick to determine the "competitiveness" of different issue divides in the East Central European party systems.

The data at hand permit us only to determine whether the various social and political divides we have identified in the four countries meet necessary, though not sufficient, conditions to contribute to dimensions of party competition. The competitiveness of political divides in multi-party systems, as opposed to two-party systems, requires that parties differentiate their issue stances ("spread") and thus create rather pronounced distances between electorally relevant extreme parties near both ends of a divide.[9] Moreover, in multi-party systems parties emphasize programmatic crystallization on a competitive dimension, as indicated by small standard deviations of respondents' assessments of the parties' policy appeals. Further, a political divide is more likely to be competitive if partisans' own issue positions on that divide predict their left-right self-placements. Given the parsimony of the uni-dimensional, formal left-right scale, voters and politicians may project onto that dimension only what is most salient for their political preferences.

High spread of issue positions among parties, the parties' programmatic crystallization, and strong predictive power of issue positions for left-right (self-)placements, however, also characterize *dimensions of political identification* on which voters' opinions influence their affiliation with a favorite party, but on which they are unresponsive to competing parties' changing policy positions. A party's distinctive position on a policy dimension may signal the existence of a sub-cultural camp. Politicians and voters belonging to that camp express little diffuseness of opinions and strongly relate their position to left-right self-placements. For this reason, our various indicators cannot distinguish whether a political divide actually is a dimension of political identification or a dimension of competition.

The first four columns of table 8.12 collect data from tables 8.2 through 8.8 on the necessary but not sufficient conditions for political divides to constitute dimensions of party competition in multi-party systems. The fifth column gives

---

[9]This presupposes spatial competition as opposed to valence competition where all parties fight to represent one dominant position in the most credible fashion, a type of competition quite implausible for most post-communist politics, as we showed in chapters 5 and 6. In two-party systems, of course, spatial competition also may yield a convergence of the two rivals to similar policy positions, as Downs's theorem demonstrates.

Table 8.12. *From social issue divides via political party divides to dimensions of competition?*

Factors	Explained variance of factors	Spread of parties	Distance between extremes	Diffuseness of the voters' issue positions	Determination of left-right self-placements (beta)	Do configurations match political elite pattern?
Bulgaria						
I: Socio-economic	26.7	.47	1.39	.88	−.43	
II: Civic libertarianism	14.2	.18	.59	.99	−.08	Yes
III: Turkish minority	11.2	.51	1.21	.95	n.s.	
Czech Republic						
I: Socio-economic	25.4	.65	1.82	.81	−.56	
Religious values	12.2	.60	1.84	.98	+.12	
Civic libertarianism	8.1	.22	.60	.96	+.12	Yes
Nationalism	7.9	.25	.83	.99	n.s.	
Hungary						
Economic optimism	17.3	.20	1.05	1.08	n.s.	In elite even
Secular-cosmopolitanism	12.4	.54	1.18	1.06	−.10	stronger weight of
Social protectionism	9.4	.23	.68	1.11	−.11	non-economic
Religious values	8.2	.46	1.63	1.02	+.13	divides
Nationalism	7.9	.25	.73	1.13	+.09	
Poland						
Social protectionism	17.0	.33	1.01	1.07	−.22	Religion plays
Religious values	14.6	.47	1.54	.98	+.30	somewhat less
Civic libertarianism	10.7	.32	.91	1.10	−.13	strong role in the
Nationalism/social protection	8.6	.16	.73	1.13	+.09	elite

Source: Columns 1 through 4 from tables 8.2 through 8.5 and tables 8.6 through 8.9. Column 5 from a regression of respondents' factor scores (factors in tables 8.2 through 8.5) on their left-right self-placements (full regressions not shown).

the beta-coefficients indicating the factor's capacity to determine respondent's left-right self-placements.[10] Table 8.12 clearly demonstrates that in Bulgaria and the Czech Republic the divide between economic social protectionism and market liberalism has the greatest potential to constitute a competitive dimension. Runners-up are the ethnic divide in Bulgaria and religious divisions in the Czech Republic. But they contribute nothing or relatively little to respondents' left-right self-placements.

An assessment of competitive dimensions in Hungary and Poland is more difficult, because the social and political divides are more complex. Just as in the elite survey, in Hungary various socio-cultural issue divides tend to overwhelm economic issues to a greater extent than in Poland. In Poland, parties show more programmatic diversification on economics, and economic issues emerge as a somewhat stronger determinant of people's left-right placements than in Hungary (column 5).[11] The Polish socio-cultural dimension is focused on religious issues. In Hungary, religion is also the lead socio-cultural divide, but it has somewhat less power to organize social and economic divisions and shape left-right self-placements than in Poland and is complemented by other socio-cultural divisions. At the same time, economic issues yield only weak conditions for party competition. These cross-nationally varying patterns again follow from the different political legacies that affect the constitution of multi-party democracies in post-communist polities.

SOCIAL STRUCTURE, POLITICAL PREFERENCES, AND THE VOTE

This chapter has investigated common and diverse patterns of political division in East Central European electorates. Given the recent origins of competitive party democracy in post-communist polities, it is premature to qualify divides as societal or political "cleavages." Nevertheless, if the parties that represent different political preferences on a well-structured divide attract electoral constituencies characterized by distinctive economic resource endowments and locations in the social structure or by unique socio-cultural life-styles, there is some plausibility that the respective divide is here to stay because it is entrenched in the pre-political sphere of social organization.

For a variety of reasons, however, the relationship between voters' socio-economic assets or cultural life-styles, on the one hand, and their party prefer-

[10]These beta-coefficients are quite similar to those obtained in table 8.12, where not factor scores, but original issue questions were employed to predict respondents' left-right self-placements.
[11]In this respect, results reported in table 8.12 differ slightly from those of table 8.11, where the Polish respondents' economic issue opinions do not make a greater difference for their left-right self-placements than in Hungary.

ences, on the other, is likely to be imperfect and tenuous not only in emerging democracies, but also in democracies that have existed for many decades. To begin with, it is hard to measure the complexities of a voter's socio-economic position and trajectory exactly, epecially given social mobility over people's life cycle. Further, voters do not define their interests exclusively in terms of their actual or expected socio-structural location alone, but also let themselves be impressed by current political issues, variable party positions, the economic performance of incumbent governments, the personality of political leaders, or the occurrence of scandals. Through the fog of measurement error and "noise" generated by the dynamic of political competition, it is no wonder that the available crude measures of social structure and citizens' political preferences explain only a small share of the variance in voters' political orientations and partisan choices. This applies to all democracies, but particularly to polities undergoing momentous socio-economic and cultural change, such as post-communist countries.

If conflicts between group interests, however, are somehow "grounded" in the distribution of scarce material and cultural resources in society and show an association with partisan preferences *even* in an era of turmoil due to profound market liberalization and restructuring of the state apparatus, then one might have considerable confidence in the expectation that currently visible group and party alignments have the potential of becoming durable political "cleavages." This applies especially to the entrenchment of economic policy divides in post-communist politics. Even where stable class relations are absent, the unequal distribution of individuals' economic resources may generate a keen understanding of winners and losers that suggests the beginnings of organized electoral coalitions configured around skills, sectors, and occupational affiliations.

Although the transition from planned socialist economies to various modes of private ownership and capitalist market competition creates an exceptional fluidity of winners and losers in post-communist countries that may make it hard for individuals to determine their economic interests, the distribution of human capital embodied in educational and professional experiences, as well as the stock of physical capital invested in different economic sectors is sufficiently rigid to expect some linkage between voters' economic position and their political preferences, at least in the programmatically structured party systems. These "sunk costs" of social organization are likely to leave their mark on the distribution of political preferences over economic reform policies and create rational expectations that guide voters' greater or lesser optimism about the outcomes of the entire process.

In a similar vein, citizens' investments in social and cultural practices, affiliations, and communication networks, such as churches or the communist party before the collapse of the old regime, continue to shape their frameworks of political interpretation and are unlikely to disappear overnight. People's personal biographies consist of sedimented layers of individual and collective experiences that mold their social construction of the political world. People digest dramatic societal ruptures incrementally and with time lags rather than as revolutionary personality breaks.[12]

Three arguments make it likely that the empirical association between voters' position in the social structure and their partisan choices is *indirect*, mediated through political issue preferences and generalized self-interpretations, such as one's left-right self-placement. First, given the absence of party identification in new democracies in most East Central European post-communist democracies, voters are less likely to develop ties to parties based on unreflective affective loyalties rather than on conscious or half-conscious comparisons of party appeals to personal preferences. The relatively high cognitive competence of East European mass publics makes this pattern more plausible compared with other regions of the world where newly installed democracies draw on a much less educated electorate. Second, in an age of mass communication, considerable diversity in the choice of social reference groups, and cheap abundant alternatives to spend one's leisure time, parties are unable to tie voters into sub-cultural "pillars" with strong social and solidary incentives that organize life from cradle to grave. In these respects, post-communist democracies are no different than advanced industrial societies, where similar developments have eroded affective party identification and organizational ties between voters and politicians. On top of these social-structural conditions, of course, the brevity of the democratic experience that has prevented parties from investing in elaborate economically based organizational networks is a third reason why political choices do not directly follow from socio-demographic attributes.

If social structure affects political choice only indirectly, voters' socio-economic or cultural resource endowments may correlate with their policy preferences, policy preferences relate to voters' generalized left-right self-placements, and both of them predict their party preferences. Yet once we control for policy preferences and ideological self-placements, socio-economic position and cultural assets, by themselves, have little direct net effect on voters' party preferences. In Knutsen and Scarbrough's (1995) terminology, there may be "opinion divides" linking political preferences to party choices and "political cleavage voting" associating social structure to voting behavior *mediated by* political preferences, but preciously little unmediated "social structure voting" defined as the direct effect of socio-demographic voter attributes on their partisan choices. We now explore how socio-economic resources and affiliations shape citizens' views on economic policy and how socio-structural traits, together with explicit issue opinions, influence respondents' generalized left-right ideological self-placement and ultimately their party preferences in our four East Central European countries.

---

[12]For Poland, this claim is borne out by Tworzecki's (1996) ecological analysis of voting patterns that show a clear association between regional legacies of political rule before 1918 and current political alignments. A similar message follows from Putnam's (1993) study of Italian politics.

For the three countries covered in the CEU population survey, the Czech Republic, Hungary, and Poland, we tap social structure in terms of the variables age, gender, size of municipality, education, sector of employment, and various crude occupational categories. All of these traits, in one way or another, affect actors' capacities to adapt to and take advantage of market liberalization and therefore may influence their rational expectations over the personal and societal benefits they will derive from alternative economic policy programs political parties advertise in their campaigns. Younger, male, educated individuals with experience in professional employment or as independent businesspeople have probably the brightest prospects in the emerging market capitalism (cf. chapter 2). Because these variables are correlated with each other at least moderately, it is unlikely that all of them simultaneously exercise significant net effects on respondents' attitudes toward market liberalism in a multivariate regression analysis.

Our multivariate regression includes variables for three inter-related concepts, education (5-level scale), occupation, and economic sector. From the original CEU data set, we created five dummy variables that identify occupational groups with high, intermediate, and low chances to gain from capitalist market liberalization. At the top are those who indicate they are professionals or upper management, followed by middle management positions. This group may still incorporate some members of the old nomenklatura, but they have adjusted to the new market order and support economic and social liberalism, regardless of whether they still maintain social ties to the post-communist party networks. Non-management white-collar employees and supervisors of manual workers tend to encounter intermediate opportunities in market-liberalizing economies. White-collar employment in the service sector may grow in size and importance in post-communist economies and thus give employees expectations of some improvement. Conversely, our fourth occupational group, skilled blue-collar workers, face fewer opportunities in the new order and probably suffer significant hardship. This predicament is even worse for the final group, agricultural, semi- and unskilled manual workers as well as retirees, all of whom have very few skills and resources to adapt to a technologically advancing capitalist market economy.[13]

Occupational status correlates, but does not fully coincide, with employment sector. Regardless of occupational skills, employees in some economic sectors may have already benefited from market liberalization, in others they stand to benefit

---

[13]Our division of occupational groups is quite similar to that employed by Evans (1995) based on John Goldthorpe's work on stratification. Groups I (professionals, higher managerial) and II (lower managerial and semi-professional) in that classification are essentially equivalent to our first two occupational categories. Group III (routine non-manual, service workers) and V (foremen, technicians) constitute our third category, and group VI (skilled manual workers) our fourth category. Goldthorpe's groups VIIa (semi- and unskilled workers) and VIIb (agricultural workers) are our fifth category. We do not have separate categories for Goldthorpe's groups IVa (employers), IVb (self-employed), and IVc (farmers) because these distinctions appear in our "sector" category.

from it, and in yet further sectors they have suffered or are likely to suffer under the impact of economic restructuring. On the sector variable, the highest score, indicating the greatest promise of gain from economic reform, goes to respondents who own their business, but are not farmers, followed by individuals employed by private or cooperative firms, as well as farmers. The middle score goes to employees in general public administration, law enforcement, and the military who are likely to stay in the public sector, probably experience the negative effects of budget cuts on their wages in the reform process, but may benefit from capitalist growth in the long run, as state revenue increases. Sectoral losers are the public-service sector (education, health care), which comes under great pressure to rationalize and cut back employment, and particularly the residual sector of state-owned often inefficient and highly subsidized industrial companies.

In addition to these socio-economic attributes and relations, we employ church attendance and membership in the communist party before the demise of the old regime as predictors of salient policy preferences. Both associational memberships yield a wide range of social commitments and frame the cultural interpretation of societal change in a lasting fashion. They should make a difference for citizens' issue positions, net of economic market location.

The Bulgarian survey does not permit us to employ exactly the same specification of independent variables as the CEU survey. It offers identical or very similar measures for age, gender, education, communist party membership, church attendance, and employment sector. But it does not provide suitable urban-rural and occupational dummies. Instead, we include a variable on unemployment. Given the multi-cultural nature of Bulgarian society, we have also added dummy variables for Gypsy and Turkish ethnic minority affiliations.

In all our statistical analyses, we estimate *linear and non-interactive relationships* between voters' socio-economic and cultural traits, on the one hand, and their policy preferences and partisan choices, on the other. We thus ignore potential curvilinear and interactive effects, although ethnographic and some statistical analyses demonstrate the existence of such complex social-structural relations. For example, older entrepreneurs who gained their property before 1990 and benefited from nomenklatura privatization may have close ties to the former communist parties and therefore support them, possibly in the expectation of material gain, such as public-works contracts or subsidies (e.g., grants to farmers), in the event such parties come to government office. In Hungary, support for the socialists in 1994 involved an interaction effect between age and education. Among older voters, the highly educated former apparatchiks overproportionally supported the post-communist party. Among younger age cohorts, highly educated individuals were underrepresented in the MSzP electorate (cf. Toka 1995b). Our presumption of simple, direct, non-interactive, linear relations between social structure, political preferences, and party choices *biases the statistical analysis against identification of a strong socio-economic and socio-cultural "grounding" of voters' party affiliations in a country's pre-political structure.* Given that the analysis of voting behavior serves a limited purpose within the framework of the present study and that we draw on surveys with rather modest sample size, we have refrained from complicating our models to maximize explained variance.

As a first step, we regress social structural traits and organizational affiliations on the two-item economic liberalism versus social protectionism scale based on the indicators of respondents' economic policy preferences reported in table 8.1. Table 8.13 shows the parameter estimates and explained variance resulting from an OLS regression of the independent variables on our index of economic liberalism in the CEU and the Bulgarian surveys. The table reports coefficients only for a reduced form regression in each country after deleting variables insignificant in the full equations.

If economic policy attitudes are grounded in social structure and citizens' resources and if these citizens rationally pursue their economic interests, then young, male, well-educated, urban voters in the private sector and in high-skill jobs should be most inclined to support market-liberal policies. Church attendance should not make much difference and membership in the communist party before 1989 should dispose respondents against market liberalization. In table 8.13, all but one of the signs of the significant predictors of preferences for market liberalism are in the correct direction (the exception is age in Poland). In general, the regressions demonstrate that the impact of social structure on economic policy preferences in post-communist democracies is far from negligible, even taking into account the crudeness of our measures and the conditions of rapid economic change from a command to a market economy. The predictive power of socio-economic variables for political preferences is not much less pronounced in these four post-communist countries than in many advanced capitalist Western democracies.

To illustrate the magnitude of the influence of social structure on citizens' economic policy preferences, compare young, urban, highly educated, and self-employed professionals with older, rural, workers in state industry who live in the countryside. In the three Central European countries our scale of economic liberalism ranges from 2 (least liberal) to 8 (most liberal). Here citizens' differential social background translates into an average difference of political opinions amounting to 1.95 points in the Czech Republic, 2.00 points in Hungary, and 1.67 points in Poland. In Bulgaria, where the scale of the dependent variable ranges from 0 to 2, the difference between these two groups is .36. If the scale is adjusted to the Central European range, this translates into an effect of 1.44 (.36 × 4), only slightly smaller than in Poland.

Associational networks have a mixed influence on respondents' desire to embrace market capitalism. Interestingly, church attendance has no independent effect on market-liberal attitudes except in Bulgaria where few people practice religion, but these individuals stand out in their support of capitalist (or, shall we say, anti-communist?) economic organization. Not surprisingly, communist party membership before 1989 is significantly related to economic policy preferences, but without appropriate controls we cannot yet dissociate the pure effect of

Table 8.13. *Popular preferences for economic liberalism*

	Czech Republic			Hungary			Poland			Bulgaria		
	b	s.e.	beta	b	s.e.	beta	b	s.e.	beta	b	s.e.	beta
Intercept	2.12***			2.84***			2.83***			4.64***		
Age	—	—	—	-.14***	.04	-.10	+.07*	.03	+.06	—	—	—
Gender (female = 2)	—	—	—	—	—	—	-.25***	.06	-.10	-.04*	.02	-.06
Urban residence	—	—	—	+.12***	.02	+.15	—	—	—	—	—	—
Education	+.32***	.06	+.20	+.16***	.04	+.15	+.11**	.04	+.10	+.05***	.01	+.21
Employment sector	+.09***	.03	+.07	+.07*	.03	+.06	+.12***	.02	+.13			
Unskilled labor	—	—		-.22*	.12	-.07	-.26*	.10	-.10			
Skilled manual	—	—		-.28*	.11	-.08	-.33**	.09	-.13			
Lower non-manual	+.20(*)	.12	+.06	—			—					
Middle management	+.36*	.16	+.08	—			+.30*	.15	+.05			
Professionals, higher management	+.31(*)	.17	+.07	—			+.77***	.13	+.06			
Private sector	—			—			—			+.12***	.02	+.13
Unemployed	—			—			—			—	—	—
Turkish	—			—			—			—	—	—
Gypsy	—			—			—			-.08*	.03	-.07
Church attendance	—			—			—			+.02**	.01	+.08
Communist party member (before 1989)	-.61***	.11	-.17	-.24*	.12	-.06	-.25*	.10	-.07	-.06*	.02	-.07
Adjusted R^2	.10***			.09***			.09***			.08***		
N	1114			1200			1468			1585		
F-ratio	21.40			18.80			16.63			25.41		

(*) $p < .10$; * $p < .05$; ** $p < .01$; *** $p < .001$.

membership in the ruling party's social network from more generalized ideological dispositions that come with party affiliation. Nevertheless, the effect of communist party membership varies across the four countries in a meaningful way. Standardized and unstandardized coefficients show the greatest effect of communist membership on the rejection of market liberalization in the Czech Republic. By contrast, in Hungary and Poland former communist party membership has only a minor impact on market-liberal attitudes. This cross-national difference underlines that in a country where the former ruling parties did not engage in a reformist-accommodative policy and did not transform itself into a quasi-social democratic party since 1990, communist party adherence makes a greater difference in terms of stubbornly clinging to social protectionist, anti-liberal economic policies, even once we hold constant for their affiliates' socio-economic resource endowments.

Because of the different model specification, Bulgarian results are not directly comparable with the coefficients obtained for the CEU countries. Nevertheless, the effect of social structure and communist party membership appears to be similar in Bulgaria as in Central Europe. Adjusted for the scale of the dependent variable, the slope coefficient for communist party membership in Bulgaria is exactly the same as in Hungary and Poland (4 × .06 = .24). Because of Bulgaria's more intransigent communist elite and trajectory from patrimonial communism, we might have expected that the effect of communist party membership on views of economic market liberalization is *greater* here than in Hungary or Poland. But party support and inter-party polarization is not necessarily based on programmatic cohesion. We can explore the impact of communist party membership, net of respondents' policy preferences, when we employ their left-right self-placements as the dependent variable. Left-right self-placement is policy-based, if economic liberalism and socio-cultural orientations are its best predictors. But it may be symbolic, organizational, and cultural, if associational affiliations or social-structural group attributes directly determine such placements.

We can sort out these interpretations by means of the equations in table 8.14, where we explore how citizens' socio-economic and cultural attributes, together with various economic and socio-cultural political attitudes, influence respondents' generalized ideological left-right self-placements. Again, we report only reduced equation results from which variables insignificant in the full equations have been dropped. The equations control for respondents' policy opinions by employing the same variables we already presented in table 8.11. Comparing regression coefficients in tables 8.11 and 8.14 shows that policy opinions maintain their effect on left-right self-placements, even once we add socio-economic traits as independent variables. Also the cross-national differences in the intensity of ideological constraint exercised by policy preferences on left-right self-placements stays in place. It is higher in the Czech Republic and Bulgaria, but lower in Hungary and Poland.

Additional variables that have an impact on left-right self-placements, net of issue opinions, are religious practice (church attenders lean to the right) and,

Table 8.14. *Determinants of the population's left-right self-placements*

	Czech Republic			Hungary			Poland			Bulgaria		
	b	s.e.	beta	b	s.e.	beta	b	s.e.	beta	b	s.e.	beta
Intercept	4.33***	.27	—	4.38***	.14	—	5.41***	.17	—	.65***	.05	—
Age	+.01	.00	+.09	—	—	—	—	—	—	—	—	—
Gender (female = 2)	-.15*	.08	-.05	—	—	—	-.19*	.07	-.07	-.23*	.09	-.06
Urban residence	—	—	—	—	—	—	+.06*	.02	+.07	—	—	—
Education	—	—	—	—	—	—	—	—	—	+.16***	.03	+.13
Employment sector	—	—	—	—	—	—	—	—	—			
Unskilled labor	-.42**	.12	-.09	—	—	—	—	—	—			
Skilled manual	—	—	—	—	—	—	—	—	—			
Lower non-manual	—	—	—	—	—	—	—	—	—			
Middle management	—	—	—	—	—	—	+.30*	.15	+.05			
Professionals, higher management	—	—	—	—	—	—	—	—	—			
Private sector	—	—	—	—	—	—	—	—	—	—	—	—
Unemployed	—	—	—	—	—	—	—	—	—	—	—	—
Turkish	—	—	—	—	—	—	—	—	—	—	—	—
Gypsy	—	—	—	—	—	—	—	—	—	—	—	—
Church attendance	+.08*	.03	+.06	+.05*	.02	+.06	+.14	.03	+.13	+.16***	.03	+.13
Communist party member (before 1989)	-1.05***	.10	-.29	-.51***	.08	-.18	-.51***	.10	-.12	-1.42***	.12	-.29
Economic liberalism	+1.00***	.08	+.33	+.20***	.06	+.10	+.24*	.08	+.07	+1.21***	.13	+.22
Secular values	-.40***	.10	-.12	-.16*	.06	-.08	-.62***	.07	-.25	—	—	—
Nationalism	—	—	—	-.18*	.07	-.08	—	—	—	-.14**	.04	-.08
Civic individualism	+.40***	.10	+.10	—	—	—	—	—	—	—	—	—
Adjusted R^2	.34***			.06***			.12***			.19***		
N	1117			1200			1468			1585		
F-ratio	66.11			16.82			30.55			60.99		

(*) $p < .10$; * $p < .05$; ** $p < .01$; *** $p < .001$.

above all, former communist party membership (members lean to the left). Standardized and unstandardized coefficients of the communist party membership dummy variable demonstrate that the effect of political affiliation is much greater in the two countries with unreconstructed or recalcitrant post-communist parties, Bulgaria and the Czech Republic, whereas it is comparatively mild in Hungary and Poland with thoroughly reformist post-communist parties. The communist membership variable now measures the net impact of network association, because we control for social-protectionist, secular, civic libertarian, and nationalist opinions, some of which may be related to party membership. This equation demonstrates that in Bulgaria indeed the social and symbolic importance of communist party membership for self-placement in the leftist camp is greater than anywhere else, if we consider that in Bulgaria the value of communist party membership for left-right placements rivals that of all issue attitudes taken together, whereas in the three Central European countries the impact of issue attitudes on left-right self-placements clearly outweigh that of former communist party membership.[14]

In all four countries, however, voters' political preferences and associational affiliations by and large wash out the independent effect of socio-structural background variables on left-right self-placements.[15] Traits such as citizens' employment sector and occupation have almost no effect on left-right placements, while education maintains modest explanatory efficiency only in Bulgaria. Rather than jumping to the conclusion that social structure does not matter for the political alignments of post-communist polities, however, we should keep in mind the results reported in table 8.13. The effect of social structure on left-right self-placements is *mediated* through issue opinions. Most published research on public opinion and voting rationales in post-communist democracies operates with single-equation models that do not reveal this "causal depth" of phenomena such as citizens' left-right self-placements and party preferences.

The general conclusion that social structure has only an indirect effect on the vote is reinforced by our final statistical model, where the dependent variable is party preference for market-liberal parties (table 8.15). Rather than coding party preference as a set of dummy variables or a nominally scaled variable, our dependent variable replaces each respondent's current party preference by the value elite respondents assign to that party on an index of economic liberalism, as constructed from the issue items dealing with the welfare state and privatization in our elite survey (cf. table 8.1, VAR 30 and 31). In this fashion, we create a

---

[14]Again, a direct comparison of slope coefficients is hampered by the different metric of independent and dependent variables in the three Central European countries from that in Bulgaria. Given that the standardized beta coefficients illustrate our interpretation, we save space and will not demonstrate our argument by numerical examples for each country.

[15]By contrast, when we calculate equations with left-right self-placement as the dependent variable, but only socio-demographic background and associational ties as the independent variables, the former make a significant difference that approximates the results reported in table 8.13.

Table 8.15. *Support for more market-liberal parties*

	Czech Republic			Hungary			Poland			Bulgaria		
	b	s.e.	beta	b	s.e.	beta	b	s.e.	beta	b	s.e.	beta
Intercept	-14.78***	1.21		-9.49***	1.01		-7.12***	1.04		-25.19***	2.64	
Age	—	—	—	-.09***	.01	-.25	—	—	-.07	+.03(*)	.02	+.06
Gender (female = 2)	—	—	—	—	—	—	—	—	—	—	—	—
Urban residence	—	—	—	—	—	—	+.62*	.12	+.18	—	—	—
Education	—	—	—	—	—	—	—	—	—	+.33*	.13	+.07
Employment sector	—	—	—	—	—	—	—	—	—			
Unskilled labor	—	—	—	—	—	—	-.08*	.03	-.08			
Skilled manual	—	—	—	—	—	—	—	—	—			
Lower non-manual	—	—	—	—	—	—	+2.57***	.60	+.14			
Middle management	—	—	—	—	—	—	+2.62**	.73	+.12			
Professionals, higher management	—	—	—	—	—	—	—	—	—			
Private sector	—	—	—	—	—	—	—	—	—	—	—	—
Unemployed	—	—	—	—	—	—	—	—	—	—	—	—
Church attendance	—	—	—	—	—	—	—	—	—	+.32*	.12	+.07
Communist party member (before 1989)	-1.35*	.62	-.06	-2.66***	.58	-.17	—	—	—	-3.39***	.49	-.20
Economic liberalism	+2.58***	.52	+.13	+1.08**	.44	+.09	+1.77*	.49	+.12	+3.46***	.57	+.17
Secular values	-1.85***	.54	-.08	—	—	—	-.89*	.41	-.08			
Nationalism	—	—	—	—	—	—	—	—	—	—	—	—
Civic individualism	+.05*	.02	+.05	—	—	—	—	—	—	+2.21*	.78	+.07
Left-right self-placement	+3.68***	.19	+.57	+1.10***	.19	+.21	+.85***	.15	+.20	+1.55***	.10	+.46
Adjusted R^2	.47***			.19***			.15***			.46***		
N	1117			1200			1468			1585		
F-ratio	217.64			37.51			24.92			52.62		

(*) $p < .10$; * $p < .05$; ** $p < .01$; *** $p < .001$.

continuous, interval-scaled dependent variable of preference for market-liberal parties that is amenable to an ordinary least squared regression analysis.

It is not surprising that respondents' left-right self-placements are the strongest predictor of preference for market-liberal parties. This variable mops up much of the independent effect respondents' issue positions and associational affiliations would exert on party preference, were left-right self-placements deleted from the equation. The strong explanatory power of left-right self-placements shows once again that this formal political semantics is an important simplifier of partisan alignments in post-communist party competition. It serves as a generalized language to characterize the implications of partisan differences in the competitive political space also in new post-communist democracies.

Given that left-right self-placements take this central mediating role in the determination of partisan preferences, it is difficult to interpret the size of the residual coefficients for political preferences and associational affiliations. Partisan preference equations without the left-right variable show essentially the same structure of determination as the equations on left-right self-placements reported in table 8.14. The relative weight of communist party membership and political issue opinions varies across the four post-communist countries in ways consistent with the differential character of their communist regimes and their specific pathways to democracy. With regard to social structure, the message is always that it has no direct impact on party preference, but works indirectly through issue opinions and left-right self-placements.[16] It is worth repeating one final time that it would be entirely misleading to infer from our findings that social structure "does not matter" for current party preferences in post-communist democracies. Voters, on average, support parties that are closer to their ideal positions, particularly on economics, and they choose them for reasons related to their socioeconomic asset endowments and network positions.

Our analysis here has focused on the relation between social structure, political preferences, and partisan choices with regard to the political divide that runs through all four post-communist countries in a roughly similar fashion, issues of economic distribution and governance structures. While the precise salience, intensity, and alignment of this divide with other issue divides varies across post-communist countries, this line of conflict is nevertheless present everywhere. Of course, we could conduct a similar analysis also for other divides, such as sociocultural issues or collective identities. Because the results of our statistical explorations do not add much to the picture we have already drawn, we do not report them here. In general, in all instances social structure has a highly mediated impact on partisan preferences. In single-equation models where political opinions and associational practices serve as controls, social structure shows little statistically significant impact on partisan choices as the dependent variable.

---

[16]In fact, the bivariate correlations between age, education, gender, sector and occupational affiliations, on the one hand, and support of market-liberal parties, on the other, are quite strong.

PROGRAMMATIC STRUCTURING OF PARTY COMPETITION AND THE ELECTORATES' CAPACITY TO PROCESS ELITE SIGNALS

Our analysis generates one unexpected empirical "anomaly" clearly inconsistent with our theoretical framework. Because the elites of the major parties express only weak programmatic crystallization in Bulgaria, voters should also exhibit weakly structured social and political divides. Moreover, Bulgarian voters might be less capable of employing the left-right language as a tool to signal partisan preferences. As a consequence of all this, Bulgarian citizens' socio-economic position may be only a feeble predictor of their ideological and party preferences. None of these expectations has been borne out. Socio-economic position is just as good a predictor of political-economic ideology in Bulgaria as in the Central European countries and Bulgarian voters show considerably more constraint between issue opinions, left-right self-placements, and party preferences than at least voters in Hungary and possibly in Poland, even though a higher proportion of it is mediated through communist party affiliation before 1989 in Bulgaria than anywhere else. What is consistent with our framework, however, is the substance of the policy divisions that characterize the Bulgarian electorate.

To make sense of the Bulgarian anomalies requires a closer look at the contextual conditions of information processing in new competitive democracies that affect citizens' ability to make partisan choices. One cue is the programmatic structuring articulated by the party elites themselves, but there are other cues that organize the cognitive field and the self-understanding of the average voter. After all, citizens have little time and energy to follow political pronouncements between work commitments, family obligations, and the desire to rest and rejuvenate their physical and emotional selves. When politicians express highly organized ideological beliefs and relate them to the left-right semantics, political information misers in the electorate are certainly more likely to devise their own limited political reflections and choices in terms of issue-related, ideology-driven conceptualizations. But other contextual conditions intervene. The more complex the political divides and competitive dimensions and the more numerous the credible party alternatives on offer, the more difficult it is for voters to determine salient programmatic alternatives, relate them to left-right locations, and choose a party in congruence with their own preferences. In established Western party systems, the politicians' reputation and repeated use of programmatic appeals to some extent compensate for the cognitive obstacles voters face in discerning parties' programmatic positions when they are confronted with a cacophony of competitors. But in emerging democracies, politicians and their parties have a brief track record and voters cannot just update an already existing vague image of parties by drawing on a stock of information they acquired, for example, in previous electoral campaigns. In other words, regardless of the programmatic crystallization of party elites, voters have a harder time in choosing between alternatives on programmatic grounds, the larger the number of parties in the competition and the more complex the dimensions of competition on which they relate to each other.

In emerging post-communist democracies, the nature and ongoing relevance of the communist regime division is also likely to affect voters' ability to construct accurate cognitive maps and appropriate political choices. The divide between communists and non-communists provides a simple binary structure of competition that invites voters to project sharply defined policy alternatives on each of the major contenders at the opposite poles of the regime divide, regardless of whether the politicians who impersonate these polar alternatives actually express the policy views attributed to them in a coherent, crystallized fashion. Hence, where the regime divide remains salient, citizens have strong intuitive judgments of who is right and who is wrong, who is good and who is evil, and who is "left" and who is "right." In programmatic terms, voters may thus associate fundamental questions of democracy (for or against) and economic organization (social protectionism or market liberalism) with the regime divide and organize cognitive maps that may have little correspondence to the actual programmatic coherence of parties' appeals. Hence, where the salience of the political regime divide persists over extended periods of time, such as in the aftermath of patrimonial and to a lesser extent that of bureaucratic-authoritarian communism, voters can more easily attribute programmatic structure to the party system, regardless of whether this structure is confirmed or disconfirmed by the politicians' own appeals and actions.

If we score elites' programmatic appeals, the effective number of parties, the number of competitive dimensions in the party system, and the intensity of the regime division as cumulative influences on the average citizens' capacities for political information processing, we arrive at a ranking of our four post-communist countries that renders our Bulgarian results intelligible (table 8.16). The scores are ordinal ranks with higher values indicating contexts more conducive to a greater programmatic structuring and ideological constraint in a country's electorate. For example, Bulgaria has the greatest simplicity of the salient competitive dimension(s) of the four countries and therefore receives a score of 4 in line 3 of table 8.16.

A summary of rank order scores in a single index is always mathematically questionable, particularly when we have no compelling rationale for weighting the different elements that enter the index. Nevertheless, it is a heuristic device to make our comparative logic more transparent. According to this logic, at the time of our elite surveys in 1993–94, the cognitive processing of programmatic differences should have been easiest for electorates in Bulgaria, but hardest in Hungary. This conclusion would not have been predicted based on the programmatic crystallization of the political party elites alone (line 1), the object of our investigation in previous chapters. The rank order of all countries but Bulgaria on that first indicator, however, coincides with their overall ranking on the summary index.

Table 8.16. *The electorate's ability to discriminate programmatic party positions*

	Bulgaria	Czech Republic	Hungary	Poland
The programmatic structuring of party elites in the new post-communist democracies	1	4	2	3
Simplicity of the field of party competitors, as measured by the effective number of electoral parties, 1992–94	4	2	3	1
Simplicity of the salient dimensions of party competition, as measured in table 7.5	4	3	1	2
Intensity of the regime division: repressive or accommodative conduct of the former ruling parties	4	3	1	2
Overall index of voter capacities to construct programmatic distinctions between political parties	13	12	7	8

CONCLUSION

It is obvious that the political professionals whose map of party competition we analyzed in preceding chapters have, on average, much greater capacities to organize programmatic alternatives than their electoral constituencies whose members are, on average, less sophisticated and spend vastly less time processing political information or participating in politics directly. As a consequence, not only in new East Central European democracies but also in well-established Western democracies the capacity of citizens to express opinions, recognize political views, and organize them into coherent frameworks is quite limited (cf. Zaller 1993). At the same time, in Western democracies, at the aggregate level of each party's constituency, we often encounter surprising order and regularity in the organization of political preferences (cf. Feld and Grofman 1988). This chapter presents similar findings for the new democratic polities of East Central Europe. Even though many individual voters may exhibit little organization of their political preferences, at the aggregate level, in each country we encounter social and political divides quite similar to those articulated by party politicians. While it is not possible to compare the extent of the East Central European electorates' cognitive political organization directly with that of electorates in Western democracies, the quantitative parameters that emerge from our analysis resemble the findings produced with comparable methodologies in Western Europe.[17]

Even among four East Central European countries, however, we encounter profound differences in the relative strength of social opinion divides and the translation of social into political partisan divides, let alone competitive dimensions on which teams of politicians appeal to voters in order to boost their electoral fortunes. In all four countries, questions of economic reform pit social protectionist against market-liberal parties. But this political divide combines in diverse fashion with additional socio-cultural divides and yields nationally unique configurations of party competition. In the Czech Republic, secondary socio-cultural divides have much less power to organize political alternatives than in Hungary and Poland. Whereas such secondary political divides crosscut primary economic political divides in these two countries and create multiple "camps" of political parties, in Bulgaria economic and socio-cultural divides tend to reinforce each other, a pattern found also in Russia (Fish 1995b) and Romania (Crowther 1995).

Our analysis established a rough equivalence between the perception of the social and political divides as articulated by both electoral constituencies and party elites in each of our four countries. This suggests that post-communist polities achieve one of the most important regulatives of democratic rules, political representation. In the next chapter, we probe further into the nature of the representative bond that characterizes citizen-elite linkages in these four polities.

[17]Compare, for example, the explained variance and eigenvalues of opinion factors in the four East Central European countries with those obtained for six West European democracies in McGann and Kitschelt (1995).

PART V

POLITICAL REPRESENTATION AND THE QUALITY OF DEMOCRATIC GOVERNANCE

9

POLITICAL REPRESENTATION

If democracies build citizen-elite linkages through programmatic competition, they create feedback loops of accountability and responsiveness that bring about a *systematic relationship* or even a *convergence* of the policy positions supported by party representatives in legislatures and their electoral constituencies. If historical legacies shape patterns of representation in the emerging post-communist democracies, such relations are likely to vary across our four East Central European countries. As we have argued in our theoretical chapter, the nature of representative relations varies with the critical dimensions of party competition in each country.

Because of the moderately to highly fragmented party system format and electoral rules of proportional representation, in all four of our democracies parties face disincentives to converge toward the median voter position on critical competitive dimensions. As a consequence, a political divide that has some significance for party competition is therefore unlikely to give rise to *relations of moderating trusteeship* where party elites take more moderate positions than their constituencies. Instead, on such issue dimensions parties are likely to engage in *relations of polarizing trusteeship* where political representatives often take more pronounced positions than their constituencies. In terms of the more technical characterization of representative relations proposed in chapter 2, parties emphasize *relative representation* at the expense of *absolute representation,* whereas mandate relations of representation combine high relative and absolute representation.

Given communist legacies, trajectories of democratization and competitive dimensions of the party systems, we expect relations of polarizing trusteeship to prevail in the realm of economic policy competition in the Czech Republic, in Bulgaria, to a lesser extent in Poland, and least in Hungary. In the realm of sociocultural policy issues and the politics of collective identity, however, crisp relations of polarizing trusteeship are much more likely in Bulgaria, Hungary, or

Poland than in the Czech Republic. In the former three countries, these non-economic divides have competitive significance, either by reinforcing or crosscutting the economic divides.

Our analysis does not explore the consequences of different patterns of representation. But we are skeptical whether any single pattern of democratic representation promises democratic "stability." As Huntington (1968: 416) quite correctly observed, polarized party systems that are likely to articulate what we call relations of polarizing trusteeship may deeply divide electorates and parties and thus make governing more difficult, but they teach voters that democratic competition matters and thus instill a sense of affiliation with the rules of the political game. Conversely, relations of moderating trusteeship may facilitate governance, but also produce a deep sense of voter cynicism about elite responsiveness to popular demands in a democracy. Effective governance and democratic responsiveness do not necessarily involve trade-offs, and their mutual relationship is sufficiently complicated to avoid rash conclusions about the viability of democracy when analyzing one or the other.

ECONOMIC POLICY REPRESENTATION

In order to assess relations of representation in the economic policy area, we have taken two items from the population and political elite surveys that show considerable semantic similarity (cf. table 8.1). The first item probes into voters' and politicians' preference for the commodification or decommodification of labor and the government's responsibility to protect citizens from the vagaries of the labor market. At the mass level, the question asks respondents to indicate the extent to which governments are responsible for employment. At the elite level, politicians score parties as to their disposition to provide comprehensive state health insurance and workmen's compensation. The second item explores respondents' view of economic governance structures and their willingness to privatize state companies even in the face of rising unemployment. Given that the scales have different ranges on which respondents score their own parties' policy positions (at the elite level) or their own preferences on the policy issues (at the population level), we have converted the mean positions of each party's voters and politicians into a 100-point policy thermometer. For all issues considered in this chapter, tables A9.1 through A9.4 in the appendix report these figures.

For each issue, we analyze relations of representation first by visual inspection of the pattern of mass-elite correspondence, then in terms of some more precise statistical measures. Figure 9.1 depicts relations of representation on the two economic issues in the four countries. In order to gauge the *absolute representativeness* of parties for their electorates, we calculate the average distance D between all the parties' mean voter positions and their mean elite positions on each policy issue in each country. These discrepancies are weighted by the electoral size of each party so that a highly unrepresentative small party cannot overwhelm the overall

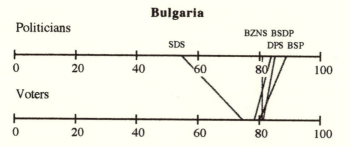

Bulgaria

Politicians

BZNS BSDP
SDS   DPS BSP

0   20   40   60   80   100

Voters

0   20   40   60   80   100

Low Public Protection   **High Public Protection**

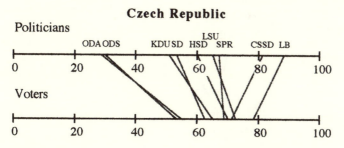

Czech Republic

Politicians

LSU
ODA ODS   KDU SD HSD SPR   CSSD LB

0   20   40   60   80   100

Voters

0   20   40   60   80   100

Low Public Protection   **High Public Protection**

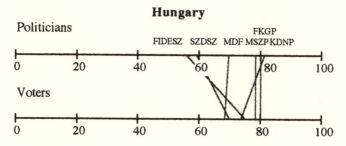

Hungary

Politicians

FKGP
FIDESZ SZDSZ MDF MSZP KDNP

0   20   40   60   80   100

Voters

0   20   40   60   80   100

Low Public Protection   **High Public Protection**

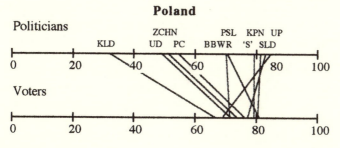

Poland

Politicians

ZCHN   PSL KPN UP
KLD   UD PC   BBWR 'S' SLD

0   20   40   60   80   100

Voters

0   20   40   60   80   100

Low Public Protection   **High Public Protection**

Figure 9.1A. Party representation on the policy of social protection

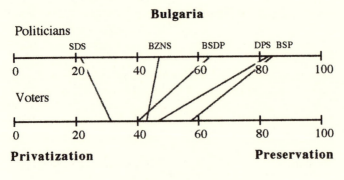

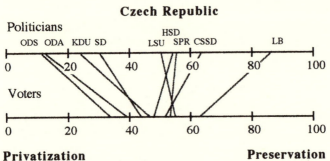

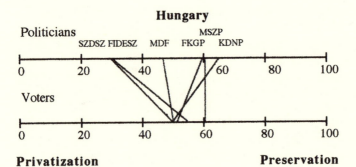

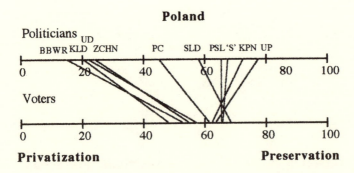

Figure 9.1B. Party representation on the policy of state enterprise

picture for the entire party system.[1] We assess the *relative representativeness* or the responsiveness of parties to their voters by regressing political elites' issue appeals on their partisan constituency's mean issue preferences. Here the regression coefficient and the explained variance are meaningful sources of information to characterize the parties' responsiveness, while the intercept provides another gauge of absolute representation.[2] Table 9.1 provides information related to both absolute and relative representativeness in our four countries on the two economic issues.

Turning first to the issue of social protection, we find that voters in all four countries support defensive, social protectionist policies with only minor differences between the parties' constituencies. In no country does the difference between partisan electorates exceed 15 points on the 100-point scale. Nevertheless, examining the relationship between population and elite level, we discover rather different patterns of elite appeals in the four countries. In Hungary, the positions of all party elites are rather close to those of their electoral constituencies, indicating high absolute representativeness. But relative representativeness is low. Based on knowing the various partisan voters' preferences, it is all but impossible to predict the parties' particular social policy appeal. This observation is borne out by the quantitative parameters reported in table 9.1 for Hungary's social policy issue. The D-value of absolute representativeness is small, the slope coefficient is also rather small, and the explained variance is unimpressive. The issue of economic governance structures yields a similar pattern of high absolute but low relative representation in Hungary. Party elites do not stray very far from their voters' preferences, but they are unresponsive to differences between their respective constituencies.

This configuration signals once more that Hungarian politicians do not treat economics as the prime competitive dimension in the party system. Were economics key for party competition, some politicians would seize the opportunity to differentiate their appeal more starkly from the rest of the parties. The MSzP, for example, would then adopt a more social-protectionist position both on social security as well as the issue of economic governance structures, while the SzDSz would subscribe to a more pronounced market-liberal position. The inability of Hungary's parties to build relations of relative representation and responsiveness on economic matters is consistent with the negotiated character of its democratic transition and the "centrism" of its parties and electorate. In this regard, table 9.2 provides some instructive evidence on the mean economic policy preferences endorsed by the electoral constituencies of the major competing parties between 1992 and 1995. The table reports an index that combines respondents' scores on our two economic variables, social protectionism and state enterprise. The exceptional centrism of the electorate shows up in the very similar average scores of the

---

[1]The weights are the number of respondents who support each party in the population surveys (see tables 9.A1 through 9.A4).

[2]A small intercept is a necessary but not a sufficient condition for high absolute representativeness in a party system.

Table 9.1. *Modes of representation: Economic issues*

	Bulgaria	Czech Republic	Hungary	Poland
Issue I: Social protection				
Absolute representation				
Voter-party discrepancy D	9.7	19.9	4.1	13.0
Intercept of the regression of voter opinions on party elites	−239.1	−110.0	−13.7	−73.3
Relative representation (regression voter-party positions)				
Slope coefficient	4.0	2.52	1.15	1.85
Explained variance	.91	.95	.61	.41
Type of representation	Polarized trusteeship	Polarized trusteeship	Mandate representation	Approaching polarized trusteeship
Issue II: Privatization				
Absolute representation				
Voter-party discrepancy D	20.5	18.7	9.5	16.7
Intercept of the regression of voter opinions on party elites	−46.0	−84.4	+27.2	−167.5
Relative representation (regression voter-party positions)				
Slope coefficient	+2.47	+2.62	+.40	+2.60
Explained variance	.86	.93	.12	.87
Type of representation	Polarized trusteeship	Polarized trusteeship	Mandate relationship but little responsiveness	Polarized trusteeship

Table 9.2. *The position of Hungarian party constituencies on the economic liberalism versus socio-economic protection issues over three years*

	September 1992				December 1993				April 1994				June 1995			
	Mean	SE	SD	(N)	Mean	SE	SD	(N)	Mean	SE	SD	(N)	Mean	SE	SD	(N)
MSZP	2.3	.09	.82	(88)	2.0	.05	.81	(229)	2.1	.05	.79	(216)	2.3	.06	.83	(180)
FKGP	2.4	.13	.82	(38)	2.3	.16	.94	(35)	2.6	.13	.86	(46)	2.6	.08	.83	(96)
KDNP	2.5	.16	.83	(28)	2.6	.14	.90	(44)	2.7	.15	.82	(28)	2.4	.12	.86	(49)
SZDSZ	2.6	.10	.78	(62)	2.3	.09	.83	(84)	2.7	.07	.78	(111)	2.4	.08	.90	(124)
Fidesz	2.4	.05	.83	(276)	2.5	.07	.81	(116)	2.4	.11	.91	(68)	2.4	.08	.86	(118)
MDF	2.8	.10	.93	(93)	2.7	.11	.89	(62)	2.7	.11	.93	(66)	2.6	.12	.90	(59)
Total	2.5	.04	.85	(585)	2.3	.04	.87	(570)	2.4	.04	.86	(535)	2.4	.03	.86	(626)
Standard deviation of parties' mean position	.18				.25				.24				.12			

various parties' voter constituencies. Moreover, except for the MSzP and MDF voters, the constituencies of the other parties change even their relative position vis-à-vis other parties on economic issues over time. By June 1995, after the first year of a socialist-liberal government coalition and shortly after that government imposed a strict market-liberal economic austerity policy, the electorates of all six parties were virtually indistinguishable in their economic policy preferences.[3]

Electoral constituency and party elite centrism on salient economic issues in Hungary have serious consequences for party competition. On economics, voters are not closely tied to parties. When economic issues are salient, as was the case in the 1994 election, the lack of party ties makes large proportions of the electorate available for open competition across the entire menu of credible party alternatives. The comparatively weak determination of left-right preferences and party choices by voters' economic issue opinions in Hungary (tables 8.14 and 8.15) may result from the parties' inability to stake out clear economic policy alternatives in the aftermath of a negotiated transition to democracy. Under conditions of economic strain, weak relations of economic representation, however, may create popular disaffection with democratic politics because voters feel they have no alternatives to choose from. In countries with greater economic policy polarization among voters and parties, cynicism about democratic competition may be less virulent. As a consequence, Hungary more so than Bulgaria, the Czech Republic, or even Poland, does encounter a serious problem of political representation and party responsiveness. But this problem is not due simply to the stubbornness of politicians, but to the lack of preference polarization both among parties' electoral constituencies and politicians.[4]

Going from Hungary, with little capacity to organize relations of representation around economics, to the Czech Republic, where that capacity is high because economics is the by far most salient issue dimension in party competition, reveals sharply different actual patterns of representation. In the Czech Republic, economic issues generate weak absolute, but high relative representation between electoral constituencies and their parties, the reverse pattern of Hungary. In a pattern of *polarizing trusteeship,* political parties in a systematic and predictable way overstate the preference conflict of different partisan electorates at the level of elite political appeals. Not only the visualization of this relationship in figure 9.1, but also high D-values and intercepts, as well as strong slope coefficients (greater

---

[3]The index ranges from 1.0 (social protectionist) to 4.0 (market-liberal). The average values of all party constituencies are within 0.2 points of the scale midpoint of 2.5.

[4]The exceptionally low voter turnout by Hungarian standards in the 1998 legislative election (56 percent in the first round) and the rise of personalist protest parties around Jozsef Torgyan (FKGP) and Istvan Csurka (MIEP) may be a sign of voter disaffection after the socialist government implemented a policy of market liberalization. Also in other countries where socialists pursued market reform rather than social-protectionist objectives close to the heart of their electoral constituencies, electoral turnout fell in subsequent elections and the socialists lost power. Lithuania in 1996 and Poland in 1997 are further examples for this pattern.

than 2) and very high correlations, characterize a polarizing trusteeship mode of voter-elite representation.

Bulgaria and Poland are somewhere between these extremes, although, on balance, both are closer to the Czech pattern of polarizing trusteeship representation on economics. In Poland, we must qualify this assessment because at least the leftist offspring of the Solidarność movement at the elite level represents much more social-protectionist positions than would be warranted by its electorate. More generally, like in Hungary, the social-protectionist spectrum of political parties in Poland is more prepared to represent their voters absolutely than relatively. The competitive shakeout of parties in the Christian-national sector and the rise of the AWS since our survey in 1994 may not have changed this pattern. After elected to government in 1997, the AWS incorporated hetero-geneous electorates and heterogeneous politicians' appeals. Nevertheless, as in the Czech Republic, more market-liberal parties dramatically overstate the economic policy preferences of their voters.

With regard to economic issues, the cross-nationally varying patterns of representation rather closely conform to our expectations about the impact of different legacies and modes of transition on the alignments of party competition and political representation in the new democracies. Where the successors to the communist ruling parties have given up on socialist tenets, as in the former national-accommodative communism, particularly parties of the social-protec-tionist economic left but also sometimes parties of the more market-liberal right encounter great difficulties to organize political competition and representation around economic issues.

SOCIO-CULTURAL POLICY REPRESENTATION

At least in the three Central European countries, our population and elite surveys yield two questions that tap almost identical issue positions on abortion and church-state relations (table 8.1). In Bulgaria, we are lacking the elite question on abortion and we had to resort to different questions on church and religion in the population and elite surveys. For the Bulgarian population, we have only habits of church attendance, whereas the elite question invites respondents to assess the extent to which parties are willing to uphold the Orthodox Church against the influx of new religions. Because of this heterogeneity of response items, our interpretation of the Bulgarian results is highly tentative. Figure 9.2 and table 9.3 provide the same information on absolute and relative representation for the socio-cultural issue in the four countries as previous displays did on the economic issues.

Given the low salience and relative insignificance of socio-cultural issues for party competition in the Czech Republic in the 1990s, we lack strong predictions concerning the form of elite-mass relations on these issues in that country. The empirical results do not fully bear out a relationship of polarizing trusteeship,

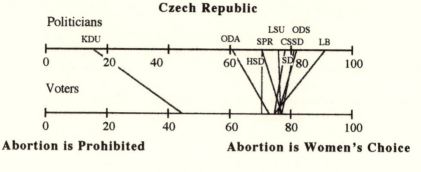

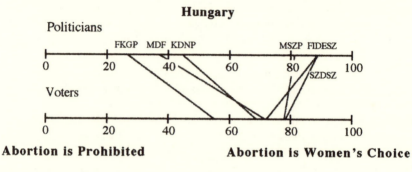

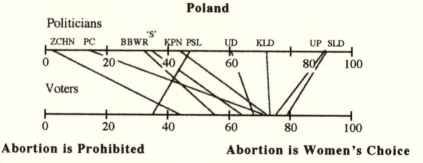

Figure 9.2A. Party representation on the policy of socio-cultural issues: abortion

although the configuration comes closer to that pattern on abortion than on church-state relations where almost all parties have a systematic bias to be less sympathetic to the churches' claims than their voters.

Much more clear-cut patterns of polarized trusteeship emerge in the two countries with national-accommodative communist background, Hungary and Poland. In Hungary, the large average discrepancies between partisan constituencies and their party elites as well as the sizable negative intercepts in the regressions of elite policy appeals on electoral constituency preferences reveal low abso-

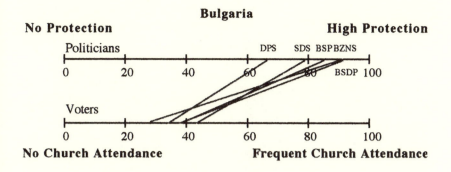

Bulgaria

No Protection   High Protection

No Church Attendance   Frequent Church Attendance

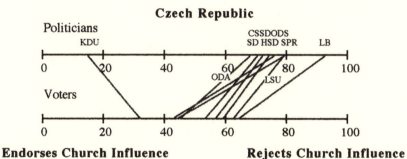

Czech Republic

Endorses Church Influence   Rejects Church Influence

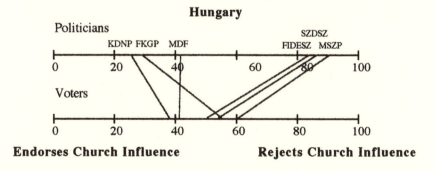

Hungary

Endorses Church Influence   Rejects Church Influence

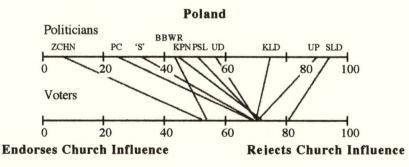

Poland

Endorses Church Influence   Rejects Church Influence

Figure 9.2B. Party representation on the policy of church-state relations

Table 9.3. *Modes of representation: Socio-cultural issues*

	Bulgaria	Czech Republic	Hungary	Poland
Issue III: Socio-cultural issues				
Absolute representation				
Voter-party discrepancy D		8.0	15.9	18.1
Intercept of the regression of voter opinions on party elites		−64.0	−129.3	−27.3
Relative representation (regression voter-party positions)				
Slope coefficient		+1.86	+2.70	+1.20
Explained variance		.95	.80	.57
Type of representation		Ambiguous (between mandate and polarized trusteeship)	Polarized trusteeship	Mostly polarized trusteeship
Issue IV: Church-state relations				
Absolute representation				
Voter-party discrepancy D	46.0	28.6	25.4	19.5
Intercept of the regression of voter opinions on party elites	91.9	−11.3	−78.7	−98.8
Relative representation (regression voter-party positions)				
Slope coefficient	−.27	+1.59	+2.82	+2.23
Explained variance	.15	.74	.77	.69
Type of representation	No representation problem with the question phrasing	Limited mandate relations	Polarized trusteeship	Polarized trusteeship

lute representativeness, but the slope coefficients of greater than 2.0 and the robust correlations in the regressions indicate strong responsiveness and relative representation. On socio-cultural issues, Hungarian parties engage in relations of polarizing trusteeship.

Also in Poland, the absolute representation of voters on abortion and church-state relations is rather weak, but the pattern of relative representation does not yield as high a responsiveness as in Hungary. The quantitative gauges of relative representation, particularly slope coefficients on abortion and correlations on both abortion and church-state relations, are depressed by individual outliers. On abortion, the PSL electorate is much more pro-life than its party elites. On church-state relations, the KPN leadership does not reflect the secular enthusiasm of its voters, while at least BBWR and UD leaders would have had to underwrite more pro-clerical positions to create perfect patterns of polarized trusteeship representation with their constituents.

The Bulgarian figures on socio-cultural issues are hard to interpret not only because of the disparity of questions administered in the population and the elite surveys. Moreover, the general secularization of Bulgarian society and the submission of the Bulgarian Orthodox Church under the state make it difficult to compare our results to those of Central Europe. The post-communist party elite comes out strongest in defense of the Orthodox Church against proselytizing religious sects, although it is the party with the most secular voters. Nationalism and intolerance vis-à-vis non-conformists may drive the communist elite response, not religious commitment. The reverse applies to the SDS whose elite is somewhat more inclined to refrain from restraining civil liberties in the sphere of religious practice, although it attracts more churchgoers. If anything, our data tap civil rights more than religious values, but the questions are inappropriate to draw strong inferences from the observed pattern of responses.

With regard to representation on socio-cultural issues, our theory or our data permit a test of our theoretical propositions only with regard to Hungary and Poland and with regard to these two cases, results confirm our expectations. Both countries display a pattern of polarizing trustee relationships of representation with low absolute but high relative representativeness and responsiveness of the political elites. In both countries, but especially in Hungary where the observed pattern of representation is particularly pronounced, socio-cultural issues constitute dimensions of party competition. This fact is reflected in politicians' modes of representing their constituencies.

REPRESENTATION ON COLLECTIVE IDENTITY ISSUES

Two questions capture collective identity issues in each survey. On the elite level, we ask respondents to score parties on the extent to which they support liberal individualism as opposed to traditional collectivism. There is no directly corresponding question in the Central European survey, but citizens' predispositions toward civil rights as opposed to law and order tap the same trade-off. In the Bulgarian population survey, we employ as a substitute respondents' assessment of whether young people have sufficient respect for traditional values. Things are more straightforward with regard to the second item, national autonomy or international interdependence. Here both elite and mass questionnaires incorporate relatively close equivalents in all four countries (cf. table 8.1). For Bulgaria, we have added an issue on ethnic relations, the use of Turkish as a language of instruction in schools with a high share of minority children, because of the relevance of this item for Bulgarian political divides. Figure 9.3 and table 9.4 provide the by now familiar information on constituency-party relations in the four countries for issues touching on civic norms and collective identity.

In the Czech Republic, none of the items yields clear-cut relations of absolute or relative representation. Because the issues carry low salience, it almost appears as if the elites of all parties go it alone and support issue positions quite different than their voters. With regard to civil rights, elites tend to support liberal individualism, whereas the population tends to opt for law and order. At the same time, party elites are much keener to insist on national autonomy than the electorate. Particularly the party elites of the social-protectionist left (LB, CSSD) are much more wedded to national autonomy than their voters who favor international interdependence. Given the low salience of this issue dimension in the Czech Republic in the 1990s, the lack of political representation on collective identity concerns is unlikely to hurt the parties.

At the other extreme, in Hungary, both civil liberty and national autonomy issues generate rather crisp relations of polarizing trusteeship with high relative but moderate to low absolute representativeness of the parties on both issue positions. As in the Czech Republic, however, there appears to be a slant of the party elites to embrace civil liberties more than their electorates. Inspection of figure 9.3 shows that only one party somewhat disturbs the pattern of polarizing trusteeship by being representative of its voters in absolute terms, but not engaging in issue leadership which in this case would imply positions less favorable to civil liberties and more favorable to national autonomy.[5] But, in general, questions of socio-cultural identity and civic values yield clear relations of representations in Hungary.

The results in Poland are situated somewhere between those of the Czech Republic and Hungary. This time, they are closer to the Hungarian pattern of polarizing trusteeship on civic individualism, whereas they show some resemblance to the Czech pattern on national autonomy. On the former, the presence of two small Polish parties in the Christian national bloc, PC and BBWR,

---

[5] The MDF's values are responsible for the relatively low correlation coefficients reported in table 9.3. Its middle-of-the-road position on identity questions may have prompted the defection of the party's nationalist wing around Csurka and may have hastened its demise in the 1994–98 legislative term.

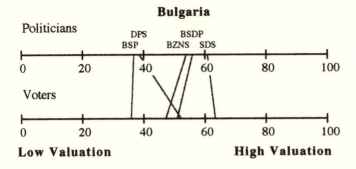

Bulgaria

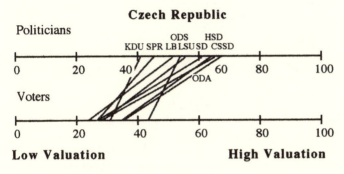

Czech Republic

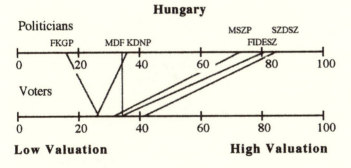

Hungary

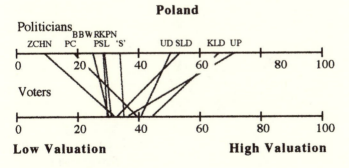

Poland

Figure 9.3A. Party representation on the policy toward civic norms of tolerance and individual autonomy

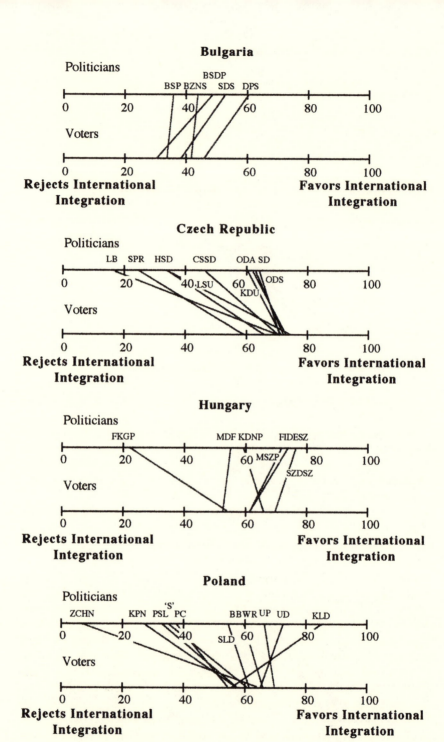

Figure 9.3B. Party representation on policies toward international integration

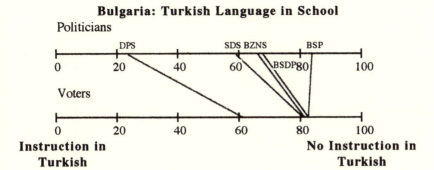

Figure 9.3B. (cont.)

with voter-elite relations inconsistent with the expected pattern disturb the general pattern of representation and substantially weaken the relevant statistical measures. Also SLD and PSL, with more authoritarian electorates but measured or outrightly civil-libertarian elite appeals, dilute the relation of polarizing trusteeship.

On national identity, Polish like Czech voters tend toward a cosmopolitan position, but parties offer wildly different appeals that often lack any consideration of relative or absolute representation. This issue plays a much lesser role in Poland than in Hungary for patterns of responsiveness and representation between voters and political elites.

Finally, the Bulgarian results fully conform to the pattern of reinforcing competitive divisions after patrimonial communism only with regard to the issue of Turkish language use in school. Here political elites take much more radical positions than their voters in a fan-type visual pattern reflecting relations of polarized trusteeship at the elite level. On civil liberties, all parties situate themselves in a middle field with almost perfect mandate representation, disturbed only by the authoritarianism of the DPS leadership that exceeds that of its voters substantially. Otherwise, the ranking of the parties at both elite and mass level follows expectations from the more authoritarian socialist left (BSP) to the more libertarian market-reformist right (SDS). On the question of national autonomy, the overall pattern of mandate representation is quite similar. Here the tiny BSDP undercuts a perfect correspondence between electoral constituencies and political elites, and both SDS and DPS politicians are much more internationalist than their electorates. While not confirming polarizing trusteeship relations, the Bulgarian pattern still comes close to rather organized relations of representation among the parties on issues of collective identity that are certainly more pronounced than in the Czech Republic.

Table 9.4. Modes of representation: Civic norms and collective identities

	Bulgaria		Czech Republic	Hungary	Poland
Issue V: Civic libertarianism					
Absolute representation					
Voter-party discrepancy D	3.5		23.9	32.7	11.7
Intercept of the regression of voter opinions on party elites	+10.8		+40.9	−70.9	−42.6
Relative representation (regression voter-party positions)					
Slope coefficient	+.77		+.49	+3.91	+2.30
Explained variance	.71		.31	.74	.57
Type of representation	Mandate representation		Representation with little responsiveness	Polarized trusteeship	Approximating polarized trusteeship
Issue VI: National identity					
Absolute representation					
Voter-party discrepancy D	21.9[a]	12.4[b]	19.4	10.9	18.0
Intercept of the regression of voter opinions on party elites	+13.8	−121.5	−82.1	−67.3	+.04
Relative representation (regression voter-party positions)					
Slope coefficient	+.90	+2.31	+1.82	+2.04	+.78
Explained variance	.61	.95	.51	.66	.16
Type of representation	Polarized trusteeship on issue b, but not a		Ambiguous, inconsistent relations	Polarized trusteeship	Little representation

[a] In Bulgaria: national autonomy.
[b] In Bulgaria: school instruction in Turkish language.

ASYMMETRIES IN RELATIONS OF POLARIZING TRUSTEESHIP

So far, we have examined only the general pattern of absolute and relative representation across all parties in each country's party system. But where relations of polarizing trusteeship prevail and parties engage in issue leadership that makes their positions much more radical than what their voters endorse, the parties at opposite extremes of the policy scale are not necessarily equally far removed from their electoral constituencies. Consider the patterns of representation on economic issues in the Czech Republic in figure 9.1. On questions of social protection, the liberal party elites are much further removed from their voters in the liberal direction than the post-communists are removed from their voters in the social-protectionist direction. A similar asymmetry applies to the abortion issue in Hungary in figure 9.2 where "pro-life" parties reflect their electorates in terms of absolute representativeness much less than the "pro-choice" parties. By contrast, if we examine the position of Czech parties on the privatization of enterprises in figure 9.1 and the Hungarian parties on church-state relations in figure 9.2, we encounter a more balanced, symmetrical overshooting of electoral constituency differences by the extreme parties on these issue dimensions.

Can we account for which parties have a tendency to "overshoot" their voters' issue preferences most dramatically in relations of polarized trusteeship representation? Table 9.5 examines which parties in the four countries have the greatest propensity to diverge from their own voters' absolute preference positions. The table reveals that on economics particularly the market-liberal party politicians (with scores lower than 40 on the issues of social protection and state enterprise) show the greatest discrepancy to their voters' average policy preferences. The constituency-politician preference gaps are thus not symmetrically distributed over the entire economic divide. *Liberal party elites push the economic reform agenda while their voters are more reticent to abandon the economic status quo, even though such voters still harbor more sympathies toward economic reform than the electoral constituencies of the other parties* (cf. tables 9.A1 through 9.A4). By contrast, parties defending the status quo of a redistributive, planned economy are much closer to their voters' opinions. The lack of representativeness of market-liberal parties in our study is not a unique finding. Already in early 1991, Bialecki and Mach (1992) established in a study of Poland's transitional parliament that Solidarność legislators were the most pro-market group in parliament, but much less representative of their electorate's policy positions than the status-quo-oriented legislators of the post-communist party.

A similar asymmetry in representational gaps between parties advocating change and parties defending the status quo occurs when we examine socio-cultural issues. Compared with the post-socialist status quo, change means (1) restrictions on abortion rights, (2) more power for religious organizations in politics, (3) more civic libertarianism in public life, and (4) more emphasis on national autonomy. With the exception of the church-state question, the gaps

Table 9.5. *Average distance between party politicians' mean position on issues and the mean position of their electoral constituencies*

Average party position on the issue	Social protection (high)	Preservation of state enterprise	Abortion (choice)[a]	Church and public schools (no)[a]	Civic libertarianism	International integration
<40	29.78 ODS, ODA KLD	23.47 SDS KDU, ODA, SD SzDSz, Fidesz ZChN, UD, KLD, BBWR	34.17 KDU FKGP, KDNP ZChN, BBWR, PC, NZSS "S"	15.51 KDU FKGP, KDNP, MDF ZChN, PC, NZSS "S"	17.42 BSP, DPS FKGP, KDNP, MDF ZChN, KPN, BBWR, PC	31.4 BSP LB, LSU, SPR, HSD FKPG PSL, ZChN, KPN, PC, NZSS "S"
40–60	14.90 SDS LSU, KDU, SD, HSD SzDSz, Fidesz ZChN, UD, PC	12.88 BANU LSU, SPR, HSD, ODS FKGP, SzDSz SLD, PC	21.6 MDF PSL, KPN	17.13 PSL, UD, KPN, BBWR	15.33 BANU, BSDP, DPS, SDS LB, LSU, KDU, SPR, ODS SLD, UD	9.04 BANU, BSDP, CSSD MDF, KDNP, SLD, BBWR
>60	6.03 BSP, BSDP, BANU LB, CSSD, SPR MSzP, FKGP, MDF PSL, UP, KPN, BBWR, NZSS "S"	14.11 BSP, BSDP, DPS LB, CSSD MSzP, KDNP PSL, UP, KPN, NZSS "S"	5.65 LB, LSU, CSSD, ODA, SD, SPR, HSD, ODS MSzP, SzDSz, Fidesz SLD, UP, UD, KLD	21.16 LB, LSU, CSSD, ODA, SD, SPR, HSD, ODS MSzP, SzDSz, Fidesz SLD, UP, KLD	34.63 SDS CSSD, ODA, SD, HSD MSzP, SzDSz, Fidesz UP, KLD	11.31 KDU, ODA, SD, ODS MSzP, SzDSz, Fidesz UP, UD, KLD

[a] Bulgaria excluded.

between politicians and their voters are greatest in all those parties that seek to change the status quo in fundamental ways. Religious parties are out of step with their voters on abortion rights, liberal-democrats support civic-libertarian individualism much more than their constituencies, and nationalist parties cannot excite their own voters for the national cause.

REPRESENTATION AND RESPONSIBLE PARTY GOVERNMENT

Even if parties represent voters' issue positions in their public pronouncements, our data do not show whether governments are likely to represent the electoral constituencies of the governing parties, and thus implement responsible party government, or the median voter on a salient issue dimension. Of course, depending on the nature of the governing parties and of coalition government, both responsible party government and median voter representation could coincide.

Our comparative study does not incorporate objective measures of enacted policy that could be related to the governing parties' announced programmatic stances and to their electoral constituencies' preferences. All we can do is to employ several indirect measures that may allow us to gauge the probabilities that governments enact policies diverging from voters' mean and median positions. A first simple measure is to calculate the *difference between the average position of all voters and the average position of parties, reflected in the mean position of their politicians, on issue k,* weighted by the share of voters that support them.

Another way to get at the probability of divergence between governments' enacted policies and mean or median voter positions is to compare the *dispersion of party politicians' and partisan constituencies' mean positions across the policy space.* Where the party politicians are more dispersed, chances are that they form governments enacting highly non-centrist policies. Of course, this proposition assumes that the programmatic diffuseness of the parties is constant while the spread of parties' positions varies. Where governing parties are highly diffuse in programmatic terms, they may be more likely to support median voter policies, regardless of their own mean ideal point. Given that the spread of parties across the political issue space is most of the time negative related to the parties' programmatic diffuseness (table 5.5), we should not worry that our hypothesis about the relationship between spread and non-median voter policies is undercut by the parties' programmatic diffuseness.

A final way to gauge enacted policy representativeness is to compare the central tendency of the government parties' announced policy stances with those of the voters' mean and median positions. We can measure the government's likely policy as the average of each coalition partner's policy position, weighted by the share of legislative seats each coalition partner controls. This measure ignores, however, asymmetries of bargaining power and exit options that may give a smaller party greater weight in a coalition's choice of enacted policy than is revealed by the size of its parliamentary caucus.

Our first measure is the extent to which the central policy tendency of each country's party system, reflected by politicians' perceptions of party policy, corresponds to the national mean voter's policy preference. The first tier of table 9.6 measures the mean issue positions of all voters, regardless of party preference, in the four countries in the six policy domains and compares them with the mean position of all parties' politicians, weighted by the size of each party in the electorate.[6] The results are quite similar to those obtained from calculating the average distances between each party's electoral constituency and political elites in the six issue domains.[7] On economic issues, the center of gravity at the elite level coincides with average electoral constituency preferences most clearly in Hungary. One would therefore expect governments more closely in tune with non-partisan universalist representation in the enactment of policy than elsewhere. Conversely, on church-state affairs and civic libertarianism, the center of gravity in the Hungarian party elite is more out of step with voter preferences than elsewhere. Therefore we would expect here the greatest probability of responsible party government outcomes.

In the Czech Republic, Poland, and Bulgaria, the discrepancies between mean voter and mean party positions are quite large on economic issues, particularly the preservation of state enterprise. But they diverge from the electorate in opposite directions. In the Czech Republic and in Poland, the parties are *much more* committed to economic liberalization than the population; in Bulgaria there is a strong tendency in the opposite direction. In the immediate aftermath of patrimonial communism, economic liberalism remains weak and communist parties entrenched. This also shows up in the orientation of politicians relative to that of voters. To go beyond our data, even where under such circumstances parties with market-liberal ideas come to political power, such as the SDS in Bulgaria in 1991 and 1997 or equivalent forces in Romania in 1996, it is hard for politicians to argue for and to enact practical reform.

The second segment of table 9.6 compares the spread of party positions, as measured by the standard deviation of electoral constituencies' and party elites' mean policy positions, in the four countries. Where the party elites are more polarized on an issue dimension, as indicated by a higher coefficient of parties' spread for politicians than for partisan constituencies, government coalitions may have a greater chance to enact policies with a center of gravity enabling them to enact policies far removed from the mean or median voter and thus to follow a model of responsible party government. If we examine the difference between partisan constituencies' and party politicians' dispersion of the parties' mean positions, we find that these differences are comparatively small (< 12.0) for

---

[6]Weights are each party's share of respondents in the population surveys, as reported in tables 9.1 through 9.A4.

[7]The correlation between the two measures is .74.

Table 9.6. *Opportunities for responsible party government or non-partisan universalist representation*

	Social protection (high)		Preservation of state enterprise		Abortion (choice)[a]		Church and public schools (no)[a]		Civic libertarianism		International integration	
	V	P	V	P	V	P	V	P	V	P	V	P
Average policy position of all voters and politicians (weighted)												
Bulgaria	78.4	78.3	45.9	61.4	78.6	67.8	67.4	85.0	47.2	46.5	37.1	44.3
V/P difference	0.1		15.4		11.8		17.6		0.7		7.2	
Czech Republic	65.3	51.8	45.6	35.8	77.3	78.1	67.4	56.9	35.8	59.7	74.0	54.8
V/P difference	13.5		9.8		0.8		10.5		23.9		19.2	
Hungary	73.6	70.7	54.7	48.7	73.7	73.7	52.9	72.7	33.0	64.0	61.2	65.3
V/P difference	2.9		6.0		0		19.8		31.0		4.1	
Poland	76.4	69.4	61.0	49.6	61.1	56.6	70.0	58.7	34.1	40.2	61.1	48.0
V/P difference	7.0		11.4		4.5		11.3		6.1		11.1	
Average V/P difference	5.9		10.7		4.3		14.8		15.4		12.4	
Dispersion of the parties' mean position												
Bulgaria	3.2	14.0	9.1	26.3	9.0	22.3	3.5	9.9	9.7	10.5	6.2	9.1
Difference	10.8		17.2		13.3		6.4		0.8		2.9	
Czech Republic	7.7	20.6	8.9	25.0	10.8	21.5	10.2	21.9	5.8	9.2	5.0	17.9
Difference	12.9		16.1		10.7		11.7		3.4		12.9	
Hungary	5.8	10.9	4.6	15.6	8.3	28.1	8.4	30.7	5.4	28.8	6.4	20.3
Difference	5.1		11.0		19.8		22.3		23.4		13.9	
Poland	4.9	18.5	5.6	24.0	14.4	30.1	8.6	27.8	5.2	30.7	4.7	23.7
Difference	13.6		18.4		15.7		19.2		25.5		19.0	

Note: V = voters; P = politicians.

[a]Significantly different questions in Bulgaria: Turkish language minority rights in school, and protection of the Orthodox Church from competing proselytizing religions. For question wording, see table 8.1. Bulgaria excluded from average V/P differences.

Hungary on economic issues but large (>12.0) for both Hungary and Poland on socio-cultural issues and issues touching upon collective identities. The reverse is true for the other two countries, except on the Turkish-language question in Bulgaria.

Hungary's negotiated transition offers not much leeway to form government coalitions that adopt widely oscillating economic policies in tune with imperatives of responsible party government. Hungary, as well as Poland, however, displays a much wider spread of party elite positions on socio-cultural issues than corresponds to the parties' constituency preferences, thus permitting cabinets to adopt a responsible party government mode of representation with policies far removed from the mean or median voter. Czech politicians display weaker dispositions to embrace socio-cultural policies diverging from the mean or median voter, while Bulgarian politicians may be so tempted only on the question of Turkish minority rights.[8]

Do the empirical realities of policy making in our four post-communist countries confirm the potential differences between the countries' capacities to enact non-centrist policies inspired by a responsible government model of political representation? To answer that question, we would need a large sample of governments in each of our four post-communist polities and score enacted policies so that we can compare them to the policies desired by the governing parties' electoral constituencies, by the mean voter, and by the politicians in the governing parties themselves. Instead, we are dealing with only a handful of post-communist governments to draw on in each country and lack hard data on each government's policy enactment. Given this predicament, our closest empirical approximation for enacted policy is the center of gravity in the policies *proposed* by the parties at the cabinet table that governed or were about to govern the four post-communist countries at the time of our survey.

In spring 1994, Bulgaria had a caretaker government without clear majority, but primarily supported by the post-communist BSP. This party also won the subsequent election and then formed a new government supported by a majority in the legislature. Our government score therefore reflects the BSP's declared policy position. In the other three countries, we calculate the center of gravity for coalitions consisting of post-communists and peasant party in Poland, post-communists and liberals in Hungary, and market-liberals and Christian Democrats in the Czech Republic. Table 9.7 reports governments' declared center of gravity and the entire electorate's mean and median positions in the six policy domains.

On economic issues, governments' central tendencies are particularly out of line with the mean voter in Bulgaria and the Czech Republic, where the rather

---

[8]Actually, the discrepancy in the spread of the mean positions between party constituencies and politicians on the issue of Turkish school instruction is primarily due to the fact that voters of the DPS are much less sanguine backers of minority language rights than the DPS political elites (see the scores reported in table 9.A1).

deep economic policy divide and potential for political polarization would lead us to believe that governments pursue responsible party government strategies more than non-partisan universalist representation. Consistent with Downsian spatial competition theory, however, these governments are still closer to the median than the mean voter. By contrast to Bulgaria and the Czech Republic, governments in Hungary and Poland are very close to the mean and median voters on the economic issues.[9] One might wonder whether the proximity of the Hungarian and Polish governments' center of gravity to mean or median voters is just a function of governments dominated by reformist post-communist parties that are relatively more status-quo-oriented than might have been a government formed by the contemporary opposition forces. Back-of-the-envelope scenarios of coalition governments among the opposition parties, however, suggest that also liberal-Christian national alliances in Poland or peasant-conservative alliances in Hungary would have probably kept the cabinet's center of gravity on economic policy closer to the respective national mean or median voters than the various actual or potential party governments in Bulgaria and the Czech Republic.[10]

A different picture presents itself when we examine the central policy tendency of governments and voter preferences in the four countries on socio-cultural affairs. Here it is not the case that governments in countries emerging from national-accommodative communism necessarily have more centrist, mean, and median voter-oriented policy dispositions. In fact, the Hungarian socialist-liberal government is further removed from non-partisan universalist representation of the mean voter on religious issues and civic libertarianism than any other government. In Poland, the proximity of the declared government policy to the mean and median voters is primarily due to the cabinet participation of the socially conservative PSL, whereas a socialist-liberal cabinet also here would be likely to drive enacted policy toward a responsible party government model more than non-partisan universalist representation.

Our brief and highly tentative discussion of alternative modes of democratic representation in the enacted policies of governments once again suggests important cross-national differences in the way post-communist democracies operate. At least in the economic policy domain, polities emerging from national-accommodative communism have a greater tendency to serve mean or median voters through enacted government policy, whereas new democracies with greater eco-

---

[9]Moreover, whatever divergence between the government's position and the median voter does exist in Hungary and Poland, particularly on social protection, is in the opposite direction to what a Downsian spatial theory might expect. Opposition parties are not closer to the median voter, than the government coalitions, but even further removed from it on the same side relative to the median voter on which also the government coalition is located.

[10]In Hungary, participation of the KDNP as well as strong currents in the MDF would keep economic government policy close to the mean and median voter. In Poland, social-protectionist demands articulated by Solidarność's AWS constrain the coalition between the Christian-national and liberal-democratic faction in Polish politics since 1987 and keep the coalition's center of gravity near the mean of median voters.

Table 9.7. *Governments' central policy tendency and voters' mean and median positions*

	Social protection (high)		Preservation of state enterprise		Abortion (choice)[a]		Church and public schools (no)[a]		Civic libertarianism		International integration	
	V	G	V	G	V	G	V	G	V	G	V	G
Bulgaria												
Mean voter	78.4	89.0	45.9	84.0	79.6	83.3	67.4	91.0	47.1	37.0	47.2	33.9
Median voter	87.5		70.0		90.0		75.0		30.0		30.0	
Difference/mean	10.6		38.1		3.7		23.6		10.1		11.1	
Difference/median	1.5		14.0		6.7		16.0		7.0		13.3	
Czech Republic												
Mean voter	65.3	30.7	45.6	13.5	77.3	70.7	67.4	69.7	35.8	55.9	74.0	63.0
Median voter	62.5		37.5		87.5		62.5		37.5		62.5	
Difference/mean	34.6		32.1		6.6		1.7		20.1		11.0	
Difference/median	31.8		24.0		16.9		7.2		18.4		0.5	

Hungary

	V	G	V	G	V	G	V	G	V	G	V	G
Mean voter	73.6	71.5	54.7	49.9	73.7	88.8	52.9	88.9	33.0	77.4	61.2	73.3
Median voter	87.5		62.5		87.5		62.5		37.5		62.5	
Difference/mean	2.1		4.9		15.1		36.0		44.4		11.8	
Difference/median	16.0		12.6		1.3		26.4		39.9		10.8	

Poland

	V	G	V	G	V	G	V	G	V	G	V	G
Mean voter	76.4	76.9	61.0	60.6	61.1	67.9	70.0	71.0	34.1	39.8	61.1	43.1
Median voter	87.5		62.5		62.5		87.5		37.5		62.5	
Difference/mean	0.5		0.4		6.8		1.0		5.7		18.0	
Difference/median	10.6		1.9		5.4		16.5		2.3		19.4	

Note: V = voters; G = government.

[a]Significantly different questions in Bulgaria: Turkish language minority rights in school, and protection of the Orthodox Church from competing proselytizing religions. For question wording, see table 8.1.

nomic policy polarization among the parties due to past bureaucratic-authoritarian or patrimonial regimes tend to rely on responsible party government to represent public preferences on salient economic issues.

Our comparison of modes of political representation has emphasized differences among post-communist democracies. At the same time, we should underline that the level of representation between party constituencies and politicians is strikingly high just about everywhere both in absolute as well as relative terms. The average absolute difference between a party and its voters is only about 16 points on the 100-point scales (tables A9.1 through A9.4). Moreover, these discrepancies do not represent random divergence of politicians from their voters, but a tendency on the part of politicians to overstate differences in their electorates and express relations of polarizing trusteeship. For this reason, relative representation of party constituencies by politicians is generally very high (tables 9.1, 9.3, 9.4). With few exceptions, we can predict the policy positions of a party's political elites with great confidence, if we know the central tendencies of its voters, particularly on the most salient economic and socio-cultural issues. The procedural quality of East Central European democracies is such that they have quickly established relations of responsiveness and accountability to their voters.

POLITICAL REPRESENTATION IN THE LEFT-RIGHT "SUPER-DIMENSION"

Many studies of political representation in Western democracies have found that absolute and relative representation in terms of policy advocacy tend to be tighter on the formal "super-issue" of parties' and their constituencies' left-right self-placements than on any substantive policy issue.[11] A simple cognitive explanation drives this result. Many voters may know too little about parties' specific issue positions to choose the party that is closest to their personal positions on salient issues in a reliable way. For them it is easier to compare parties' general left-right location, as a generating principle of policy positions, with their own position on that scale. The relative simplicity of attributing and comparing left-right party and self locations makes it easy for voters to conceive of political competition in spatial terms.

If this argument applies to the new East Central European democracies, then parties' and voters' left-right placements should indicate rather high levels of absolute and relative political representation that generally exceed those found on individual substantive policy issues, including the most salient economic issues. To test this proposition, in table 9.8 we have assembled the same indicators of absolute and relative policy advocacy representation and propensity for enacted

---

[11]This message comes across repeatedly in Converse and Pierce's (1986) comprehensive study of political representation in France.

Table 9.8. *Absolute and relative representation on the left-right scale*

	Bulgaria	Czech Republic	Hungary	Poland
Absolute left-right representation (average distance between the mean position of a party's voters and its politicians, weighted by party size)	9.2	10.0	10.0	10.7
Relative left-right representation (regressing party constituencies' mean left-right positions on those of party politicians)				
Intercept	−33.1	−31.1	−81.5	−46.5
Unstandardized regression coefficient	+1.64	+1.63	+2.83	+1.88
Correlation coefficient	+.95	+.97	+.86	+.85
Dispersion of parties' mean positions (standard deviation of all parties' mean position on the left-right dimension)				
Politicians	21.5	24.0	18.6	25.8
Voters	12.5	14.3	5.7	11.7
Difference	9.0	9.7	12.9	14.1
Governments' central left-right tendency and voters' mean position				
Governments	21.0	69.9	29.0	30.2
Voter means	46.1	62.0	40.1	47.8
Difference	25.1	7.9	11.1	17.6

policies to reflect responsible party government or non-partisan universalist representation we employed in the previous section on individual policy domains.

If we compare line 1 in table 9.8 with the corresponding D-values reported in tables 9.1, 9.3, and 9.4, absolute representation of electoral constituencies by their parties is greater on the left-right dimension than on just about any substantive policy issue. Moreover, there is considerable uniformity in the average distance of electoral constituencies and party politicians on the formal left-right dimension across the four countries. It must be kept in mind, however, that both at the elite and the electoral level left-right placements tap cross-nationally varying substantive policy divides. In Bulgaria and the Czech Republic, economic policies drive the constitution of the left-right space, whereas in Poland and especially Hungary socio-cultural policies are more decisive in voters' and politicians' interpretation of the scale (cf. tables 7.5 and 8.11). In light of this substantive content, the gap between political elites' and electorates' left-right self- and party placements have to do mostly with economics in Bulgaria and the Czech Republic and with socio-cultural affairs in Hungary and Poland.

Measures of relative political representation reveal the extent to which the left-right positions of partisan electorates permit us to predict the relative left-right position and thus the responsiveness of party elites. Regression equations for Bulgaria, the Czech Republic, and Poland show rather small negative intercepts, moderate regression coefficients between 1.5 and 2.0, and very high correlations between their voters' and their politicians' left-right placements in the neighborhood of .85 to .95. *Taken together with the rather high level of absolute representation, this pattern is consistent with a mandate conception of representation. Whereas party elites may exercise issue leadership on economics or socio-cultural questions and thus engage in polarizing trustee relationships vis-à-vis their constituencies, especially if they push societal change rather than defense of the status quo, they are in close touch with their voters' self-image on the formal left-right dimensions.*

The one exception to this pattern is Hungary, where a large negative intercept and a very large regression coefficient indicate that parties engage in issue leadership also on the formal left-right dimension. Elites tend to overstate the differences between the mean positions of partisan constituencies on the left-right dimension. Line 3 in table 9.8, where we compare the spread of parties' mean left-right placements in their electoral constituencies and their elites, provides a lead to account for the Hungarian configuration. Hungarian partisan constituencies are exceptionally reticent to place themselves anywhere but close to the mean on the left-right scale. The spread of parties' mean left-right positions at the electoral level is a paltry 5.7 (on the converted 100-point thermometer), compared with values larger by a factor of two in the other countries, particularly the Czech Republic and Bulgaria. Faced with the imperatives of multi-party competition that calls for the diversification of party positions, the Hungarian party elites, by contrast, attempt to differentiate their left-right locations to a much greater extent than their voters, although they still fall short of the spread among party mean positions observed in the other three countries' political elites. Hungary's negotiated transition and subsequent centripetal political dynamics make it difficult for politicians to articulate divergent positions. These difficulties, in turn, may hamper their efforts to mobilize voters by making them realize that the stakes in democratic competition are high and that their life chances in part depend on who wins or loses.

One might expect that the small dispersion of voters and parties in the left-right space in Hungary compared with the dispersion in Bulgaria, the Czech Republic and Poland also forces the Hungarian government to express a central tendency of policy making closer to the left-right position of the mean voter. As line 4 of table 9.8 reports, the center of gravity in the left-right position of East Central European parties that were in government or about to assume government at the time of our surveys does not bear out this implication. In fact, the Czech Republic displays the smallest discrepancy between the mean voter's and the government's left-right tendency, followed by Hungary, Poland, and Bulgaria.[12] In the interpretation of these findings one must keep in mind that in Hungary and, to a slightly lesser extent, in Poland the left-right semantics is more inspired by socio-cultural than by economic policies, whereas in Bulgaria and the Czech Republic the reverse applies. Hungary's "centrism" exclusively applies to economic affairs. Hence there is no reason to expect the politicians of the governing parties who engage in issue leadership and polarize party competition around socio-cultural divides that define their own and their competitors' interpretation of parties' left-right positions to subscribe to a non-partisan universalist conception of representation.

The high levels of absolute and relative representation evidenced by the left-right placements of parties' electorates and politicians once again confirm that even in new post-communist democracies voters deliberately calculate about which party to support and are not generally disadvantaged by a shortage of information about the parties. Overall, our analysis of political representation on the left-right dimension supports much conventional wisdom derived from studies of Western democracies. The left-right semantics offers an easy scheme enabling voters and politicians to work out relations of representation. Compared with the use of substantive policy issues, it facilitates both absolute and relative representation. The patterns of attributing left-right positions to parties and voters in the four East Central European countries thus contribute further evidence that the new East Central European democracies do not dramatically differ from established Western democracies in a number of important respects.

[12]It is interesting how far to the right the Czech electorate places itself, compared with that of the other three countries. Czech citizens' greater willingness to embrace market liberalism, documented by World Value surveys as far back as 1990, as well as the initial economic success of the ODS/ODA/KDU government articulating an extremely "right-wing" market-liberal rhetoric, contribute to this result.

CONCLUSION

Patterns of representation tend to be quite well structured on competitive political dimensions in the new post-communist polities. The policy dimensions on
which representation takes place vary with the specific legacies and trajectories of
each country. Let us emphasize again that relations of representation do not
necessarily involve a convergence of politicians and their voters on identical policy
preferences (absolute representation). On salient issue dimensions, it appears to be
the more common pattern that party elites in asymmetric fashion overstate the
divergence of issue preferences in their electorates (relative representation). Parties
that advocate policy change tend to be least close to their electoral constituencies.
Although politicians tend to be *responsive* to voter demands on salient issues, they
often engage *in issue leadership* that surpasses their voters' expectations.

Relative representation enables voters to construct a linkage between their
vote choice and potential policy outcomes. Absolute representation without relative representation, by contrast, disempowers voters and discourages them from
participation. No matter how they vote, the policy results will be the same. This
may be a frustrating realization, even if these results pretty much coincide with
the voters' own preferences. Particularly where low responsiveness corresponds to
a non-partisan universalist representation of the median voter through government policy, popular involvement in politics is likely to be low.[13]

Our analysis of representation has revealed familiar patterns of cross-national
variation within East Central Europe, often in interaction with variation across
issue areas.[14] Compared with Bulgaria, the Czech Republic, and even Poland,
Hungary appears to have a problem of relative representation on the salient issues
of economic policy making. Where all relevant parties accept market liberalization after national-accommodative communism, it is difficult for the relevant
political players to offer credible economic policy alternatives. While a "consensual" democracy may yield policy stability despite government alternations, it
may have little capacity to instill a participatory attitude and strong party-voter
ties. As we will see in the next chapter on governance, however, given the variety
of forces that influence the effectiveness of governance, there may be no simple
direct zero-sum linkage between modes of representation and effective
governance.

---

[13]Thus, democracies approximating all-party government, such as Switzerland, produce
low voter turnout and citizens' disengagement from party politics.

[14]For a recent analysis of this theme in Western democracies, see Wessels (forthcoming).

Table 9.A1. *Party elite and electorates' scores on six policy issue domains in Bulgaria*

	Social protection (high)		Preservation of state enterprise		Turkish in school (no)		Defense of the Orthodox Church		Civic libertarianism		International integration	
	V	P	V	P	V	P	V^a	P	V	P	V	P
BSP (N = 366)	80.0	89.0	56.5	84.0	82.6	83.3	28.3	91.0	36.4	37.0	33.4	35.9
BZNS (N = 129)	81.0	80.6	41.4	47.0	81.4	67.3	38.0	90.1	47.2	53.5	41.0	43.2
BSDP (N = 34)	81.0	85.5	40.0	65.8	82.6	68.0	38.2	84.5	51.2	56.3	30.6	48.5
DPS (N = 85)	78.5	84.5	45.4	82.8	61.6	23.5	33.5	67.0	52.4	39.3	46.4	60.0
SDS (N = 209)	73.5	54.4	31.4	21.7	80.2	59.1	43.5	78.8	63.2	60.5	38.4	52.5

Notes: The N in parentheses refers to the number of respondents indicating preference for one of the parties in the population survey. These figures are employed as weights in various calculations. V = voters; P = politicians.

[a] Measures church attendance; no attitudinal indicator relating to religion is available.

Table 9.A2. *Party elite and electorates' scores on six policy issue domains in the Czech Republic*

	Social protection (high)		Preservation of state enterprise		Abortion (choice)		Church and public schools (no)		Civic libertarianism		International integration	
	V	P	V	P	V	P	V	P	V	P	V	P
LB/KSCM (N = 90)	77.5	89.3	63.3	85.7	74.8	90.2	62.3	92.5	23.3	51.5	70.3	17.5
LSU (N = 22)	72.8	63.9	55.8	50.2	77.3	76.6	44.3	78.6	28.5	55.5	75.5	34.2
CSSD (N = 187)	70.8	80.9	50.5	63.0	77.8	80.9	57.3	76.3	27.8	64.9	70.3	47.5
KDU (N = 56)	65.3	51.2	46.5	23.7	43.8	16.5	32.3	14.4	30.8	40.5	71.5	60.2
ODA (N = 123)	55.5	29.2	39.3	13.1	73.5	61.2	45.3	67.9	36.5	67.0	73.5	61.9
OH-SD (N = 25)	62.5	52.5	43.8	30.0	75.0	78.1	54.0	69.8	27.5	60.7	72.5	62.2
SPR-RSC (N = 42)	70.8	(64.5)[a]	54.3	(56.0)[a]	77.5	(70.5)[a]	62.0	(78.0)[a]	26.3	(45.0)[a]	58.8	(24.5)[a]
HSD-SMS (N = 34)	69.0	59.6	50.8	56.3	70.5	70.4	58.8	71.7	35.3	64.0	65.5	34.6
ODS (N = 392)	54.8	28.2	34.3	12.1	76.0	81.4	43.8	78.2	43.3	54.6	71.5	63.8

Notes: The N in parentheses refers to the number of respondents indicating preference for one of the parties in the population survey. These figures are employed as weights in various calculations. V = voters; P = politicians.
[a] Position of the SPR-RSC elites is imputed from issue ratings of the party by politicians belonging to other parties.

Table 9.A3. *Party elite and electorates' scores on six policy issue domains in Hungary*

	Social protection (high)		Preservation of state enterprise		Abortion (choice)		Church and public schools (no)		Civic libertarianism		International integration	
	V	P	V	P	V	P	V	P	V	P	V	P
MSzP (N = 246)	77.8	77.7	60.8	60.2	78.0	88.9	60.0	90.1	31.3	73.8	60.8	71.2
FKGP (N = 56)	80.0	80.5	50.8	59.3	72.0	37.7	50.8	29.0	26.8	17.3	54.0	22.0
KDNP (N = 38)	74.3	80.7	48.8	64.1	55.5	27.1	37.5	24.4	26.5	36.0	66.5	59.1
SzDSz (N = 122)	69.3	59.1	49.5	29.2	72.8	88.6	54.3	86.5	41.3	84.7	69.0	76.7
Fidesz (N = 74)	74.8	56.2	54.8	29.9	77.8	81.8	50.0	83.7	33.3	80.8	61.0	73.6
MDF (N = 81)	67.5	68.7	49.5	45.8	68.0	44.5	40.8	42.1	33.0	33.3	53.3	55.7

Note: The N in parentheses refers to the number of respondents indicating preference for one of the parties in the population survey. These figures are employed as weights in various calculations. V = voters; P = politicians.

Table 9.A4. *Party elite and electorates' scores on six policy issue domains in Poland*

	Social protection (high)		Preservation of state enterprise		Abortion (choice)		Church and public schools (no)		Civic libertarianism		International integration	
	V	P	V	P	V	P	V	P	V	P	V	P
SLD (N = 154)	77.3	84.6	65.5	58.4	79.0	91.7	80.8	93.4	32.8	53.4	61.0	53.8
PSL (N = 177)	80.3	70.2	63.8	62.5	35.0	47.1	70.8	51.5	29.5	28.0	57.5	33.8
UP (N = 62)	68.5	86.7	63.0	76.7	75.8	91.3	71.3	90.0	37.5	70.9	68.8	66.3
ZChN (N = 52)	77.0	50.9	54.0	24.2	44.3	2.5	52.0	7.1	32.0	9.6	63.0	7.1
UD (N = 130)	72.5	48.8	57.8	22.1	67.8	60.4	69.0	57.1	41.3	50.4	64.0	72.5
KLD (N = 27)	67.4	31.7	48.5	20.4	73.5	71.7	70.0	74.6	44.3	66.7	54.8	85.0
KPN (N = 63)	80.3	82.1	62.5	72.5	72.5	43.4	71.8	44.6	31.0	28.8	57.5	27.1
BBWR (N = 55)	75.8	70.0	53.0	15.0	56.5	32.1	53.5	43.4	29.8	25.0	65.5	59.2
PC (N = 14)	73.3	55.0	60.5	45.0	70.3	14.2	68.3	24.6	39.5	18.8	54.3	37.5
NZSS 'S' (N = 52)	81.3	79.2	65.0	67.1	63.5	34.6	69.3	32.5	34.8	33.8	60.3	34.9

Notes: The N in parentheses refers to the number of respondents indicating preference for one of the parties in the population survey. These figures are employed as weights in various calculations. V = voters; P = politicians.

10

THE GOVERNABILITY OF POST-COMMUNIST DEMOCRACIES: COALITION POLITICS BETWEEN PASSIONS AND POLICY INTERESTS

The quality of a democracy hinges not only upon citizens' sense of being represented, but also their perception that the political elites govern effectively. In this chapter, we will not analyze the actual record of governments in post-communist democracies, but employ our elite surveys to explore the *probabilities* that parties in our four East Central European countries form durable legislative and executive majorities. We presuppose that durable majorities are able to deliver more consistent policies and in this vein make governments calculable for market participants. Stability of the political environment, in turn, encourages private investments and thus indirectly economic growth and rising standards of living.

Our analysis is also premised on the assumption that parties' attitudes and dispositions toward mutual collaboration reveal a polity's capacity for governance, particularly in institutional settings that tend to require legislative and executive coalitions among parties to enact binding policies. Toward the end of this chapter, we will briefly confront our survey findings with the actual experience of governing in the four countries and the governments' political-economic record on which we have already supplied some basic figures in the final section of chapter 3.

All four East Central European polities incorporate strong institutional elements of a type of democratic rule Lijphart (1977; 1984) has labeled "consensual" democracy. They involve electoral laws of proportional representation that facilitate multiple-party caucuses in parliament. Moreover, they stipulate cabinet responsibility to parliament, as opposed to a powerful independent executive presidency. Under such institutional circumstances, it is likely that effective governance requires parties to join legislative and/or executive coalition govern-

345

ments. Only inter-party collaboration can overcome legislative stalemate and executive inertia.

Bulgaria and the Czech Republic are parliamentary republics where most of the time whenever there is no single majority party the disposition of multiple parties to cooperate with each other is essential in order to create effective majority governments.[1] Also Polish cabinet government relies on inter-party cooperation to bring together a legislative majority in a parliament elected under the terms of a proportional representation system. But compared with simple parliamentary majority government, in Poland a rather strong executive and legislative presidency with veto powers that require a 60 percent override vote in both houses of parliament under the 1997 constitution and two-thirds majorities before that time may further increase the exigencies for inter-party collaboration to bring about effective governance, if president and prime minister belong to different parties. In the presence of a hostile president, a qualified parliamentary majority must build on rather broad-based party support to pass and implement policy.

Hungarian parliamentary democracy distinguishes itself from the three other post-communist polities among other things through its electoral law. The complicated Hungarian three-tier electoral system tends to produce disproportionality of representation such that large parties benefit. This system sometimes manufactures the majority or near-majority status of a single party, although that party may receive only between a quarter and a third of the popular vote. Compared with the other three polities, the Hungarian democracy thus sometimes tends to reduce the need for collaborative behavior of the parties to ensure effective governance.

Institutional rules of the democratic polity provide a basic bench mark concerning the *demand* for inter-party collaboration that must be met to produce effective governance in the four East Central European democracies. But it is a different question whether political actors, rallied around parties, actually *supply* collaborative pre-dispositions that make possible durable alliances among parliamentary party caucuses in the legislature, beyond the occasional logrolling, and in coalition governments. In our theoretical analysis, we have identified four conditions that affect the ability and willingness of parties to engage in collaborative behavior. In the initial decade after the collapse of communism, the first three conditions directly or indirectly grow out of the diverse legacies on which each polity builds. (1) Crystallized programmatic party cohesion and inter-party competition in the presence of (2) moderate polarization with or without crosscutting cleavages, but definitely with (3) a shallow regime divide, facilitate collaboration among parties. Weak programmatic party cohesion makes legislative coalitions volatile, while a deep regime divide may render parties unable to collaborate with each other, even if their policy positions on the salient issues of a future-oriented legislative agenda are very similar. In a similar vein, deep and mutually reinforc-

---

[1]Such collaboration can express itself in electoral alliances among parties *before* elections and/or in coalition governments negotiated *after* elections.

ing policy divides may produce a centrifugal polarized pluralism that makes inter-party cooperation very cumbersome (Sartori 1966).

The fourth contingency that affects inter-party collaboration has to do with the institutional design of legislative-executive relations. Strong presidencies have incentives and capabilities to undercut stable legislative majorities and thus may hobble democratic governance. Strong presidencies increase the need for legislators to collaborate in order to block presidential initiatives or to over-ride vetoes, but presidential powers also depress the supply of such collaboration.

Comparing the likely supply and demand of inter-party collaboration in the four East Central European democracies, Hungary offers the most promising balance. On the supply side, parties are pre-disposed to collaboration because policy polarization on the most salient economic issues is limited, the regime divide is shallow, and weak presidential power cannot interfere with parties' collaborative strategies in legislature and cabinet. Only the relatively weak pro-grammatic structuring of party competition around economic issues, together with a considerable polarization around socio-cultural policies, may be an impediment to effective governance. On the demand side, Hungary's mixed electoral system tends to manufacture legislative majorities and thus to reduce the need for inter-party collaboration.

Demand and supply conditions are also quite favorable to stable democratic governance in the Czech Republic. Here, economic policy polarization is rather strong, but a weak presidency and the marginalization of an electorally weak and unattractive orthodox post-communist party that creates a deep regime divide tend to remove most non-policy obstacles to collaboration among parties with overlapping policy programs. At the same time, the absence of a highly dispropor-tional electoral system creates greater demand for inter-party cooperation than in Hungary.

In Bulgaria and Poland, by contrast, demand for inter-party cooperation may outstrip the parties' actual supply of collaborative dispositions more frequently. Bulgarian patrimonial communism left behind a deep regime divide that compli-cates efforts to build legislative and government coalitions even among parties with rather similar economic policy positions. Conflicts over how to settle the scores of the past may crowd out efforts to construct a new social order that produces wealth and economic well-being. Veto groups in coalition governments may insist on redistributive zero-sum struggles that trump concerns with creating new assets.[2] In Poland, the regime divide, exacerbated by the bruising confronta-tion between the communist state and Solidarność throughout the first half of the 1980s until the lifting of martial law, has not quite healed by the 1990s and complicates inter-party relations in the new democracy, although the former ruling party has pursued a reformist course and the actual transition to democracy

---

[2]For this reason, from December 1992 until December 1994, the Bulgarian president had to resort to the appointment of a weak "non-partisan" government of "experts" without firm support in the legislature and unable to implement a clear policy program.

proceeded in a more or less negotiated fashion. As an additional obstacle to effective governance, significant presidential veto powers may paralyze legislative majorities and undercut collaborative party relations.

We compare policy and non-policy grounds for cooperative or uncooperative behavior among parties in this chapter. Given each country's historical and institutional setting, Bulgarian and Polish parties may rely in their decision to enter or to abstain from coalitions with competitors on non-policy considerations to a greater extent than parties in the Czech Republic and Hungary. After discussing our basic empirical framework in the first section, we explore this argument with regard to the effects of the regime divide on parties' collaborative dispositions. We then develop a more general model probing into the extent to which the proximity or distance of parties from each other with regard to their policy positions, as opposed to non-policy-related considerations, allows us to predict parties' mutual dispositions to collaborate with each other.

MEASURING CONDITIONS OF GOVERNABILITY

We ascribe dispositions to collaborate with other parties to party leaders, not to electoral constituencies. While leaders may sound out their electorates to select coalition strategies that are electorally beneficial, the ultimate decision about legislative and executive coalition building rests with the party elites. For this reason, our analysis relies on our survey among political elites. Our operational measure of politicians' generalized disposition to work with another party is a 20-point "feeling thermometer" that asks respondents to indicate their sympathy or antipathy toward their own party and toward all its competitors. Technically, we express dispositions to collaborate with another party as the differential between sympathies for one's own party and for that other party (C_D). The greater this sympathy differential, the less sympathetic is the competitor. We wish to explore the extent to which policy distances among parties or purely affective considerations drive C_D. To the extent that policy distances do not explain collaborative dispositions, we examine whether affective relations among parties based on the regime divide or the presence of a strong presidency account for different patterns of legislative and executive coalition politics.

We thus operationalize two of the four forces that affect governability (regime divides and presidential power), having explored the remaining two – programmatic structuring and the alignment of political divisions – in previous chapters. Holding constant for policy distances, the depth of the political regime divide between former communists and their adversaries is likely to reduce mutual political sympathies among parties. Also the presence of a strong presidency is expected to generate issueless dislike among parties. Whereas politicians may resolve policy disagreements among parties through bargaining, they find it much harder to address animosities based on affective orientations. Divisions

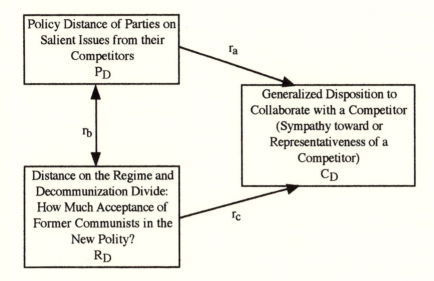

Figure 10.1. Parties' policy distances and dispositions to collaborate

grounded in the actors' passionate personal memories of past injustices and intertwined with narratives and symbols of historical group conflict complicate bargaining among parties over viable democratic governments.

We measure the policy distance P_D of two parties as the differential between
the positions on issue k that each party's politicians assign to their own party on
the 20-point scale in our elite questionnaire. The overall policy distance between
two parties A and B is a vector representing the Euclidean distance or the "city
bloc" distance of these parties in the n-dimensional policy space, with each policy
weighted by the salience the focal party attributes to it.[3] Policy distances between
A and B may be judged differently by politicians belonging to each of the parties.
Depending on party affiliation, politicians may assign different salience weights
to the policy dimensions that enter the overall distance vector between the parties.
We discuss the precise construction of the summary policy distance measure in
the next section and the appendix to this chapter.

If policy concerns shape parties' dispositions toward mutual collaboration,
then a regression of P_D on C_D would yield a high correlation coefficient r_a, a small
intercept, and a large slope coefficient (see figure 10.1). Weak correlations, small
regression coefficients, and high intercepts indicate that sympathies toward other
parties are relatively independent of inter-party policy distances. Do we have any

---

[3]The city bloc method adds up the distances between parties on all policy issues, each
weighted by its salience for the focal party, whereas the Euclidean distance measures the overall
shortest vector connecting two parties in an *n*-dimensional issue space.

positive way to characterize what might drive dispositions to collaboration instead? In our politicians' survey, we ask respondents to rate their own party and their competitors on the question of "decommunization" (VAR 44). It is reasonable to assume that this variable picks up a great deal of the passions associated with the evaluation of the old communist regime and its relevance for current inter-party relations. We can therefore calculate the distance between two parties on the regime divide, as reflected by differences in their attitudes toward decommunization policies R_D, as a measure of political "passions" and "memories" that inspire inter-party relations.

A direct comparison of the simple bivariate linkages r_a (between policy differentials and collaborative disposition) and r_c (between regime divide and collaborative disposition), of course, cannot tell us whether policy or affect have the greater power to shape collaborative dispositions among parties. Consider the case that r_c is much stronger than r_a, but there is a high correlation r_b between policy differentials P_D and differential assessments of the regime divide R_D. Even if a multivariate analysis with dispositions C_D to collaborate as the dependent variable shows that *only* the linkage through r_c is significant and the linkage between P_D and C_D through r_a washes out, one would still have to conclude that policy differentials and regime differentials are so highly intertwined that the dispositions for collaboration are grounded in rational policy calculations to a large extent. The cases we are really interested in are those where the linkage between policy and regime differentials (r_b) is weak and (1) *only* r_c is a strong predictor of dispositions C_D to collaborate with other parties *or* (2) *both* P_D and R_D are strong predictors of C_D (i.e., they have a high r_a and r_c), but multivariate analysis shows R_D to have the greater net effect on dispositions C_D to collaborate.

Disagreement on dealing with the legacies of the past picks up not just passionate relations between the post-communist parties and parties growing out of the communist regime opposition. Also former communist "bloc parties" may be rejected by liberal-democratic parties, regardless of their mutual policy proximity, for historical reasons. Such attitudes dilute the bond between inter-party policy distances P_D and dispositions to collaborate C_D. Even non-policy-based divisions among parties instigated by a strong executive presidency may find their expression in parties' stances on the regime divide. If no clear programmatic issues divide rival political entrepreneurs, they may resort to symbolic and affective concerns such as the political treatment of the agents of the former communist regime.

Regressions of policy distance and of the regime divide on parties' dispositions to collaborate with each other tap general probabilities of cooperative governance in the entire party system, but not specifically the collaborative dispositions of those parties that are indeed close to each other in the competitive policy space. Figure 10.2 describes different relations between dyads of parties, characterized by the policy distances between each party and their mutual dispositions toward collaboration. Stable governance emerges where parties are relatively close to each other in the space of salient policy issues *and* both alliance partners signal a strong

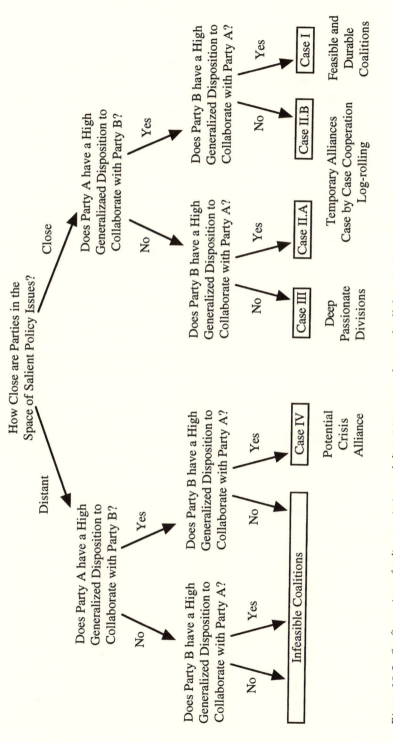

Figure 10.2. Configurations of policy proximity and dispositions toward mutual collaboration in party systems

willingness toward mutual collaboration (case I). All other configurations are likely to yield volatile democratic governance. In cases II.A, II.B, and III, passions interfere with the capacities of one or both parties to cooperate with the other, although they are close in the policy space. These obstacles are greater in configuration III where both elements of a dyad harbor animosities against the other than in configurations II.A and II.B where the problem emanates from only one partner. Short-term legislative alliances may be all that politicians can achieve in these situations.

Conversely, in case IV, good mutual feelings toward rival parties make collaboration possible, but such relations may gloss over fundamental policy divisions. As a consequence, policy disagreements are likely to interfere with ongoing cooperation and eventually disrupt it, provided it is not cemented by clientelist spoils arrangements. Alliances void of overlapping policies or clientelist incentives may be sustainable only in exceptional times of political regime crisis. Even joint crisis management may be impossible in the residual configurations on the left of figure 10.2 where neither policy proximity nor mutual sympathies buttress collaboration. It is extremely unlikely that any sort of alliance will form under such circumstances.

We now examine the extent to which passions fueled by the record of the former communist regime affect parties' willingness to engage in legislative or executive coalitions. Later we turn to a more comprehensive analysis of the political conditions that are likely to affect parties' disposition toward mutual collaboration.

THE REGIME DIVIDE AND POLITICAL GOVERNANCE

Problems of democratic governability may result from a continuing intense regime divide that does not correlate with disagreements among parties over crucial issues of economic and socio-cultural policy. Opponents of the communist regime may be more eager to see their former tormentors ostracized and punished than to engage in joint legislative and executive policy projects with them that may benefit their respective electoral constituencies. The communist successor parties themselves, by contrast, may desperately seek alliances with former opposition parties that would allow them to shed their old reputation and permit them to be recognized as legitimate players in the new democracies. Consequently, postcommunist politicians may express *more* sympathies toward their new competitors than the latter reciprocate in their own evaluations of the former.

As a first empirical exploration of this argument, consider the average sympathy scores all the respondents, regardless of party affiliation, attribute to the various parties (table 10.1). In each country, a minority of evaluators representing between 10 and 20 percent of the respondents, belongs to the party they evaluate.

Table 10.1. *Average sympathy scores for each party*

	Bulgaria	Czech Republic	Hungary	Poland
Post-communists	5.6	4.8	7.2	6.5
Agrarians	13.5	8.2	7.6	7.6
Social democrats	12.5	8.7	—	8.3
Christian democrats	—	10.6	10.2	8.3
Liberals I[a]	—	12.4	10.3	10.5
Liberals II[a]	—	10.6	11.4	10.4
Nationalists	—	3.3[b]	7.1[b]	6.0
Ethno-culturalists	9.2	8.9	—	—
Conservatives I	12.3	10.8	8.9	9.6
Conservatives II	—	—	—	8.6 (PC)
NZSS Solidarność				10.1
Average, all parties	10.6	8.7	8.9	8.6
Average, all parties weighted by electoral size	10.1	9.5	9.0	8.3
Standard deviation of all parties' averages	3.24	2.96	1.72	1.58

[a]Liberals I are ODA (Czech Republic), SzDSz (Hungary), and UD (Poland). Liberals II are SD (Czech Republic), Fidesz (Hungary), and KLD (Poland).
[b]Scores are artificially depressed, because the national samples of politicians did not include members of these parties that would have increased the averages to a certain extent. In the case of SPR-RSC the average is so low, however, that even full scores (sympathy = 20) by twenty politicians belonging to that party would have boosted that party's average sympathy score only into the neighborhood of 5.5 points.

Consequently, they assign it high sympathy scores.[4] The overwhelming majority of respondents who rate that party, however, belongs to a competitor and may therefore assign it a low popularity score. Given that among the respondents in each country, each party has about the same ratio of members to non-members in the pool of survey respondents, each party should receive the same average sympathy score, were there no systematic effects against particular parties. If there is a widespread bias against a party, such as the successor party of the former communists or one of its bloc associates, then that party should receive a lower sympathy score than the overall average for all parties in that country. Moreover, this gap should be larger in countries where the communist regime was more repressive

[4]In Bulgaria, with five parties participating in the politicians' survey, each party's contingent amounts to 20 percent of the respondents. In Poland, with ten parties participating, a party contingent is no more than 10 percent of the respondents. Hungary with six parties (16.6 percent per party) and the Czech Republic with eight parties (and 10 to 18 percent of the total sample belonging to each party) are situated somewhere between Bulgaria and Poland.

and intransigent. Table 10.1 presents parties' average sympathy scores in each of our four countries, on a scale ranging from 1 (least sympathetic) to 20 (most sympathetic); individual party data are followed by the overall average sympathy for all parties in a country, the average weighted by the electoral size of the parties, and the standard deviation of the unweighted party evaluations. These figures bear out our expectations.[5]

In the most repressive former communist regimes, Bulgaria and Czechoslovakia, post-communist parties are by far the least popular parties. The Bulgarian communists receive average sympathy scores no less than 5.0 points below the unweighted country average score. Czech communists end up 3.9 points below the republic's grand sympathy average for all parties. By contrast, in countries where the communists showed greater flexibility during the final phase of their rule, the popularity deficit of their successor parties is only 1.8 points (Hungary) and 2.0 points (Poland). Compared with post-communist parties, liberal and conservative parties typically exceed the country averages. This result suggests that the regime divide is deeper where communist rule was harsher and where post-communist parties are most intransigent.

Also nationalist parties appear extremely unpopular, but at least in the Czech Republic and Hungary, this may in part be the result of sampling bias. Neither the Czech Republicans nor the Party of Hungarian Justice and Life (MIEP) participated in our study. Had we included 20 judges from each of these parties, each of whom had given her own party the maximum sympathy score of 20 and all the other parties the average of 8.7, the Republicans' mean sympathy score would have jumped from 3.3 to 5.5. This is still far below the national average of 8.7, but no further from the mean party popularity than the Bulgarian BSP. In the case of the Hungarian MIEP, a similar counter-factual calculation would bring the MIEP average to the national mean for all parties. Thus, we can say that two of the nationalist parties, the Czech Republicans and the Polish Confederation of Independent Poland (KPN), whose politicians did participate in our study, are extremely unpopular in their countries, but not more so than the Bulgarian or Czech post-communist parties.

Consider now the average levels of sympathy communists and their competitors harbor toward each other (table 10.2). For the CEU population surveys, we can include as an equivalent measure responses to a question where interviewees were asked to assess the "representativeness" of each party in their country for their own interests. While this question invokes policy concerns, it is sufficiently diffuse to mobilize affective judgments as well. Because the figures in table 10.2 always indicate the difference between sympathy for or the representativeness of

---

[5]Because a party's own adherents represent different shares of a country's total sample of evaluators, absolute scores cannot be directly compared cross-nationally. Quite obviously, in a country like Bulgaria where 20 percent of the evaluators belong to the evaluated party, one would expect a higher mean sympathy score for each party than in Poland, where each party supplies only 10 percent of the evaluators.

one's own preferred party and that of a competitor, high scores indicate great antipathy toward and a low attribution of representativeness to the evaluated party.

It is striking that non-communist politicians and voters find the communist parties almost always much less sympathetic or representative than communist respondents reciprocate toward these other parties (lines 1.1.3 and 2.1.3). These asymmetries are particularly pronounced in Bulgaria and the Czech Republic, where the post-communist parties were repressive and have remained intransigent. In Hungary and Poland, however, communists and non-communists evaluate each other in almost symmetrical fashion. Former communists may sometimes inflate their dislike of new competitors, but in general they have reasons to treat their competitors in light of sober policy considerations. By contrast, those who suffered under a repressive communist regime express intense dislike toward communist successor parties, regardless of how close or far they are from the former communists' issue stances. Former communists, in turn, are unlikely to harbor the anger and hatred toward their new opponents that decades of suffering and injustice at the hands of the old regime may have instilled in the latter.

For political governance structures, asymmetric dispositions of parties to engage in collaboration are most relevant among parties close to the post-communists in the policy space. If they reject post-communist parties intensely, no viable "left" coalitions are in the offing. Table 10.2 calculates the average antipathies between post-communist parties and their three competitors closest to them in the left-right space.[6] While post-communist respondents are not all that antipathetic toward these competitors, voters and politicians belonging to these parties want to have nothing to do with the former communists at least in Bulgaria and the Czech Republic and to a lesser extent in Hungary and Poland (lines 1.2.3 and 2.2.3 in table 10.2). Again, cross-national differences reflect the varying levels of repressiveness under the old regimes. In Bulgaria, the non-communist parties closest to the BSP in terms of salient policy positions and left-right placements – BSDP, BANU, and DPS – dislike the BSP much more intensely than the latter reciprocates. The gap is only slightly smaller in the Czech Republic between LSU, CSSD, and HSD-SMS, on one side, and the post-communists on the other. Compared with the Czech Republic and Bulgaria, in the formerly national-accommodationist communist states there is much more symmetry and generally less antipathy among moderate non-communist parties toward the communist successor organizations in Hungary (where SzDSz, Fidesz, and MDF are the most proximate large parties) and Poland (with PSL, UP, and KPN being closest to the post-communists on the left-right scale). This rank order is mirrored by the results from the population surveys (lines 2.2.1 through 2.2.3).

We know from chapter 7 that politicians in the four countries assign parties left-right positions that can be explained in terms of their policy stances to a large

[6]See figure 7.7 to identify these parties in each country.

Table 10.2. *Post-communist parties and collaboration with competitors: The assessment of competitors and the assessment of post-communist politicians and electorates*

	Bulgaria	Czech Republic	Hungary	Poland
Politicians				
1.1.1. Average antipathy (C_D) toward post-communist parties by competitors	17.25	14.90	14.23	14.16
1.1.2. Average antipathy (C_D) of post-communists toward competitors	11.69	11.40	12.76	11.47
1.1.3. Difference	+5.56	+3.50	+1.47	+2.69
1.2.1. Average antipathy (C_D) toward post-communists among three closest parties in the left-right space	16.99	13.12	12.96	10.04
1.2.2. Average antipathy (C_D) of post-communists toward three closest parties in the left-right space	10.18	7.29	11.71	5.87
1.2.3. Difference	+6.81	+5.83	+1.25	+4.17
1.3.1. Left-right distance to the post-communists as predictor of other parties' sympathies toward post-communist parties	+.67	+.95	+.97	+.87
1.3.2. Left-right distance to other parties as predictor of post-communists' sympathies toward other parties	+.91	+.96	+.94	+.79

Electorates

2.1.1. Average antipathy (C_D) toward post-communist parties by competitors	No data	4.04	2.48	2.49
2.1.2. Average antipathy (C_D) of post-communists toward competitors	No data	2.35	2.31	2.47
2.1.3. Difference	No data	+1.69	+0.17	−0.02
2.2.1. Average antipathy (C_D) toward post-communists among three closest parties in the left-right space	No data	3.26	2.14	2.18
2.2.2. Average antipathy (C_D) of post-communists toward three closest parties in the left-right space	No data	1.63	2.39	1.60
.2.2.3. Difference	No data	+1.63	−0.25	+0.58
2.3.1. Left-right distance to the post-communists as predictor of other parties' sympathies toward post-communist parties	No data	+.99	+.86	+.73
2.3.2. Left-right distance to other parties as predictor of post-communists' sympathies toward other parties	No data	+.97	+.55	+.78
			[w/o FKGP: +.91]	

extent (table 7.5). At the voter level, similar but weaker patterns emerge between voters' left-right self-placements and their personal issue positions (table 8.11). If passions play a role in politicians' and voters' evaluations of the desirability of collaboration with another party, then the correlation between parties' left-right placements and political sympathies may be quite weak, because left-right locations tend to express policy positions. In table 10.2, lines 1.3.1 and 1.3.2 (for politicians) and lines 2.3.1 and 2.3.2 (for citizens), we have calculated the correlation between the distances that separate parties on the left-right scales and the levels of sympathy (representativeness) that communist respondents assign to non-communist parties and vice versa.

Line 1.3.1 in table 10.2 shows that non-communist politicians attribute a level of antipathy to communist parties that is closely in line with the left-right distance they see between their own party and all its competitors. The partial outlier is Bulgaria where the regression explains only 45 percent of the variance, not 75 to 93 percent as in the other three countries. This shows that non-communist Bulgarian politicians tend to dislike the BSP regardless of their self-assessed distance from that party in the left-right space. Conversely, communist politicians almost everywhere express sympathies toward other parties based on left-right distances in space (line 1.3.2). A partial outlier is Poland where the regression explains "only" 62 percent of the variance ($r = .79$). In this instance, an examination of the scatterplot is quite revealing (figure 10.3). It shows that SLD politicians tightly link their evaluation of sympathy differentials to competitors and left-right distances between the SLD and its competitors *save* for one exception, the electoral list Solidarity, which is moderately close to the post-communists in its left-right placement, but which post-communist politicians intensely dislike.[7] If we also presented a scatterplot of the approach that non-communist parties take vis-à-vis the post-communists in Poland ($r = +.87$ in line 1.3.1), we would find that a similar antipathy not grounded in left-right distances also motivates the Solidarity politicians' evaluation of the post-communists. The mutual extreme dislike of SLD and Solidarity, unrelated to their "objective" distance in the salient policy space, signals the role of history and memory in inter-party relations and demonstrates that even rather compatible parties in terms of their commitment to social protectionism may be unable to work together.

At the level of electorates, the three countries for which we have displayed relevant data in table 10.2, a similar picture emerges as that encountered among politicians (lines 2.3.1 and 2.3.2). Left-right distances measure the differential between the average left-right scores each party's voters assign to their own preferred party and to its competitors. We regress these values on the differential between the average representativeness each party's voters assign to their own party and to all of its competitors. In all three countries, knowing how far a party's

---

[7]Deleting Solidarność would boost the correlation to $r = .87$. An inspection of table 9A.4 in the appendix to chapter 9 reveals that Solidarność and post-communists are rather close to each other on questions of economic policy, but not on socio-cultural issues.

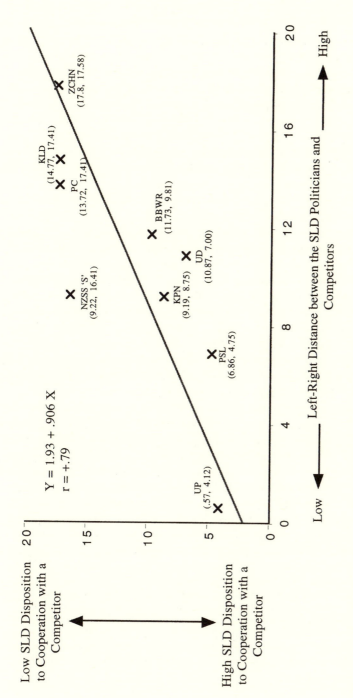

Figure 10.3. Polish inter-party relations: The left-right distance between the SLD politicians and competitors and the SLD politicians' willingness to cooperate with competitors

electorate is removed from the communists on the left-right scale is a very robust predictor of that party's perception of the communists' representativeness for their political concerns (line 2.3.1). Conversely, knowing how representative communist voters find other parties for their own interests provides a good gauge of the differential in left-right self-placements between communists and the electorates of these competitors (line 2.3.2). Only in Hungary do the left-right distances between MSzP supporters and its competitors appear to predict rather poorly how MSzP voters evaluate the representativeness of competing parties (line 2.3.2: r = +.55). Inspection of the scatterplot reveals that the correlation is depressed by the intense dislike MSzP voters display vis-à-vis the smallholders' party, a dislike that is not justified by the left-right self-placement of the FKGP's electorate or its politicians' policy positions.[8]

Our analysis so far shows that the political regime divide indeed does make a difference in parties' mutual dispositions to collaborate. This effect is most pronounced where communist regimes were highly repressive. As a somewhat tougher test of this argument, let us now employ each individual politician's differential between the sympathy score she attributes to her own party and to a competitor as the dependent variable and then determine how much perceived policy distances between the parties or the affective regime divide explain these sympathy differentials.[9] As independent variables, we employ the distances between the scores respondents assign to their own party and to its competitor on each of four representative policy issues: the extent to which privatization should proceed (VAR 31), the relationship between church and state, as measured by church influence on public school curricula in East Central Europe and by state assistance to the Orthodox Church against sectarian proselytizing in Bulgaria (VAR 39), the priority of civic libertarianism or traditional collectivism (VAR 41), and the orientation toward national autonomy or international cooperation in East Central Europe (VAR 48) or the introduction of Turkish as the language of school instruction for minority students in Bulgaria (VAR 45). We capture the continued relevance of the regime divide for the assessment of party sympathy differentials by two independent variables, the difference in the position the respondent ascribes to her own party and to its competitor on the issue of decommunization (VAR 44), and, second, a dummy variable that assumes the

---

[8] The MSzP voters' assessment of the FKGP's unrepresentativeness, however, is much more consistent with the FKGP politicians' issue appeals that are indeed quite far removed from those of the MSzP. In other words, one could regress a party constituency's perception of other parties' representativeness not on the policy or left-right distance of those parties' electorates from the focal party, but on its policy and left-right distances of those parties' politicians. In general, this further complication of the analysis yields no profoundly different insights.

[9] Since each politician scores sympathy differentials to each competing party, the number of units of observation in our regression for each country is the N of respondents multiplied by k − 1 parties. In Bulgaria, for example, 100 respondents express sympathy differentials to four parties each, resulting in an N = 400.

value 1 when a non-communist respondent evaluates a communist party and the value 0 in all other instances (dummy DC).[10]

Table 10.3 reports multivariate regression results for final reduced equations from which variables that turned out to be insignificant in the full model specifications have been omitted. With the exception of civic individualism in Poland, all policy distance variables indeed affect respondents' assessment of sympathy differentials. Overall, coefficients for policy variables are strongest in the Czech Republic, followed by Hungary, Poland, and Bulgaria. Almost the reverse applies to the post-communist variables (VAR 44 and dummy DC) which have the greatest impact on sympathy differentials in Bulgaria, followed at a great distance by Hungary, Poland, and the Czech Republic.

To provide a sense of the magnitude of the regime affect, let us calculate how much a change in respondents' perception of the regime divide would change their sympathy differentials. In table 10.4, scenario I reports how much greater the sympathy differential between a respondent's own party and a competitor would be, if that respondent is a non-communist assessing the sympathy score of a post-communist party and if the distance between the two parties' positions on decommunization increases by 10 points (on a 20-point scale). The effect of the regime divide is strongest in Bulgaria where the fact that a non-communist respondent evaluates the post-communist party reduces the latter's sympathy score by no less than 8.88 points on the 20-point scale compared with another competitor evaluated by the same respondent and subscribing to the same policy position as the post-communist party. In line with our expectation that anti-communist passions are less pronounced after national-accommodative communism, equivalent penalties for communist parties are smaller in Hungary (6.66 points) and Poland (5.12 points) than in Bulgaria.

Surprisingly, the score is even lower in the Czech Republic (4.37 points), but in that country a wide gulf of policy distance that separates the post-communists from their competitors explains why an affective regime divide makes comparatively little difference in predicting party sympathies. If we increase the policy distances between a respondent and her evaluated party by 10 points on each of the four economic, religious, cultural, and national policy variables, indeed the effect on sympathy differentials is nowhere greater than in the Czech Republic (scenario II in table 10.4). In Bulgaria, the fact that a party is on the other side of the regime divide (+8.88) has a greater impact on how politicians perceive the sympathy differentials between their own party and that competitor than a greater distance of that competitor from the respondent's own party position on relevant

---

[10]We also experimented with dummy variables that might affect the sympathy evaluation of former communist bloc parties and of nationalist parties. The expectation was that liberal-democratic parties might find these competitors unsympathetic regardless of policy proximity. Statistical exploration showed that the impact of these dummy variables, however, is too marginal to deserve detailed treatment.

Table 10.3. *Predicting sympathy differentials between parties: Policy distances and affective relations*

	Bulgaria			Czech Republic			Hungary			Poland		
	B	s.e.	beta	B	s.e.	beta	B	s.e.	beta	B	s.e.	beta
Distance on market liberalism (VAR 31)	—	—	—	.39***	.03	.33	.14***	.02	.10	.33***	.03	.27
Distance on church-state relations (VAR 39)	.23***	.05	.17	.06*	.02	.05	.15***	.03	.15	.21***	.03	.19
Distance on civic individualism versus traditionalism (VAR 41)	.26***	.05	.19	.32***	.03	.22	.18***	.04	.17	—	—	—
Distance on national versus international orientation (VAR 48)	—	—	—	.16***	.03	.12	.32***	.04	.26	.14***	.03	.12
Distance on Turkish language in school (only Bulgaria, VAR 45)	.17***	.04	.15	—	—	—	—	—	—	—	—	—
Distance on communists in public life (VAR 44)	.32***	.04	.31	.28***	.03	.24	.30***	.03	.27	.36***	.03	.36
The evaluated party is the post-communist party (dummy variable)	6.08***	.70	.30	1.57**	.47	.07	3.66***	.43	.17	1.52**	.44	.07
Constant	2.37***	.35		2.87***	.24		2.42***	.24		2.91***	.24	
Adjusted R square	.56			.53			.67			.52		
Number of observations	400			1080			756			1080		

Notes: Final equations only, with insignificant variables omitted. * p < .05; ** p < .01; *** p < .001.

Table 10.4. *Elasticity of sympathy differentials to changes in the distance between parties on policies and the regime divide*

	Scenario I plus 10 points in the distance between parties on the regime divide (VAR 44); the evaluated party is post-communist (dummy = 1)	Scenario II plus 10 points in the distance between parties on each of four policy positions (VAR 31, 39, 41, 48)
Change in sympathy differentials		
Bulgaria	+8.88	+7.4
Czech Republic	+4.37	+10.3
Hungary	+6.66	+7.9
Poand	+5.12	+6.8

policy issues (+7.4). Whereas the ratio in the impact of regime and policy variables in our example is 1.2 in Bulgaria, it is only .84 in Hungary, .75 in Poland, and .42 in the Czech Republic.

In Bulgaria, regime divisions thus are a very strong impediment to inter-party collaboration, regardless of parties' convergence or divergence on policies. In the other countries, that impediment is relatively less powerful. Bulgaria may therefore have substantial problems of governance because inter-party relations in general and relations between post-communists and anti-communists in particular are so much driven by considerations relating to the regime divide. In the other three countries, policy considerations have a greater weight in parties' dispositions to collaborate with each other. These results, by themselves, may not provide a full assessment of problems of governability in post-communist democracies, because so far our analysis has focused exclusively on the role of passions vis-à-vis post-communist parties as an impediment to inter-party collaboration and coalition formation.

CONSTITUTIONAL DESIGN, PARTY SYSTEMS, AND GOVERNANCE STRUCTURES

RATIONAL CALCULATION AND PASSION IN COALITION POLITICS

Within a spatial framework of competition, parties act rationally if they seek alliances with rivals close to them in the space of salient policy issues and abstain from liaisons with adversaries distant from their own policy preferences. Parties violate spatial rationality, if they (1) do not wish to ally with parties close to them in the policy space or (2) do seek cooperation with parties distant from them in the policy space. Figure 10.2 has distinguished these configurations. If parties are spatially rational in their strategic conduct, there can be no asymmetric collaborative dispositions in which party A endorses cooperation with B, but B does not reciprocate this disposition. In the previous section, we have shown that the affective communist regime divide may cause just such asymmetric dispositions toward collaboration. Here post-communist parties are favorably disposed toward collaboration with other parties, but the latter do not entertain a political liaison with post-communists, even if they are close to the latter in the policy space.

Deep regime divides are not the only circumstance that might undercut collaboration among parties where spatial coalition politics would mandate it. Intense animosities between parties appealing to similar programmatic objectives, and therefore the failure to collaborate in legislative or executive coalitions, may result from keen personal competition between office-seeking political entrepreneurs in a highly fragmented party system. A powerful legislative and executive presidency may fuel such hostilities. In our sample, Poland's constitutional arrangement and historical legacies are most conducive to conflicts among parties located in the same policy sector. Many of the proto-parties that resulted from the decomposition of Solidarność's Citizens' Committees in 1990 and 1991 exhibited more rivalry among competing politicians than product differentiation in their respective policy programs. From December 1990 on, Walesa as president exploited these rivalries to enhance the president's control over the political process. The president's tactic contributed to the fragmentation of the Polish party system, but also to the momentous defeat of the Christian-national parties in the 1993 election, because the splintering of this political sector into numerous small competitors prevented each from surmounting the newly introduced 5 percent threshold of electoral representation for individual parties or the 8-percent hurdle for party alliances.

The less parties with similar policy preference are able to work together in the legislature or in cabinets, the weaker is the governability of a democracy. In this section, we conduct two simple empirical tests to identify different configurations of governability in the four post-communist countries by means of relating policy distances between parties (P_D) to parties' mutual dispositions to collaborate, measured by the sympathy differentials each party's average respondent sees between her party and each of its competitors (C_D). Where *neither* regime divides *nor* other passions upset the interaction among parties, the perceived distance between parties' policy positions P_D should be a pretty good predictor of their mean sympathy differentials. Because of the feebleness of the regime divide and the existence of a fully parliamentary system of rule, we expect a spatial theory of coalition building to work best in Hungary and the Czech Republic. In Bulgaria, a deep regime divide subverts the rationality of spatial policy calculations in coalition building. How far apart parties' positions on coping with the legacies of communist rule (R_D) are may have a stronger impact on parties' willingness to collaborate with each other (C_D) than their disagreements on policy issues (P_D). In

Poland, the regime divide is not as deep as in Bulgaria, but divisiveness among the various fission products of the Solidarność Citizens' Committees, fueled by presidential power tactics between 1991 and 1993, may have subverted the rationality of spatial coalition building in that era and should be reflected in our politicians' survey from early 1994.

As our first test, we compare simple bivariate correlations between parties' policy distances (P_D), their disagreements on how to cope with the legacies of communist rule (R_D), and their differential dispositions to collaborate with each other (C_D). As a second test, we closely examine the mutual perception of policy distances and the dispositions to collaborate for all dyads of parties in each country.

In the appendix to this chapter, we describe in greater detail how we measure a stylized summary index of parties' distance from their competitors in the policy space. As we know from previous chapters, in each country, policy issues may have somewhat different weights for party competition. Furthermore, the salience of issues may also vary within countries among parties. For each party, we develop a measure that calculates its weighted distance from its competitors on each policy dimension, represented by a single policy variable that loads strongly on it, and then sum these distances in a single score according to the "city bloc" method of spatial representation. For most parties, economic policy differentials receive the strongest weight in calculating their distances to competitors, but in some instances socio-cultural policies or even the question of national autonomy plays a role in a party's perception of the policy space. We compute this index of policy distance for all parties on which we have collected data, except for those few parties that had already lost their significance as electoral and legislative players at the time of our survey.[11] P_D, R_D, and C_D are *aggregate level* measures. For each party, we calculate the average position all of its politicians assign to their own party and then calculate the average distance to the position of their competitors, as identified by the average of their own politicians, on the policy issues and the regime divide. The sympathy differentials between each focal party and its competitors represent the difference between the average level of sympathy respondents attribute to their own party and to each of its competitors. In systems with five parties ($k = 5$), politicians in each party make comparisons to four competing parties ($k - 1 = 4$). In each country, the number of observations that enter the regressions among P_D, R_D, and C_D is thus $k (k - 1)$ – that is, 20 in the Bulgarian and Czech five-party systems, 30 in the Hungarian six-party system, and 90 in the

---

[11]We lack data on two electorally relevant parties, the Czech SPR-RSC and the Bulgarian Business Bloc (BBB). We eliminated four parties from the Czech sample, because these parties had already declined to a support level of less than two percent by the time of our study and later failed to make a comeback in the 1996 Czech parliamentary election: the Free Democrats (SD), the Moravian and Silesian regionalists (then HSD-SDS), and the disintegrating social-ecological agrarians (LSU). In Bulgaria, Hungary, and Poland, all parties included in our survey were relevant at the time of our study or contributed to electorally relevant party alliances in subsequent mergers and divisions.

Bulgaria

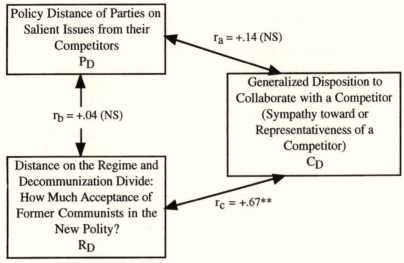

Basis for calculation: five parties (BSP, BZNS, BSDP, DPS, SDS),
N = 20 (5 x 4 observations)

Czech Republic

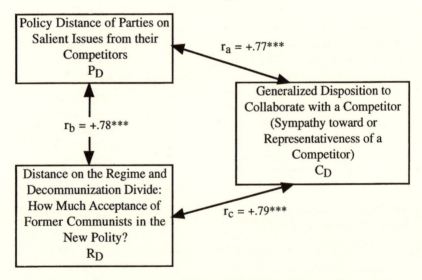

Basis for calculation: five parties (CSSD, KDU, KSCM, ODA, ODS),
N = 20 (5 x 4 observations). No data on the SPR-RSC

* p<.10; ** p<.05; *** p<.01

Figure 10.4. Dispositions to collaborate with rival parties and their determinants

Hungary

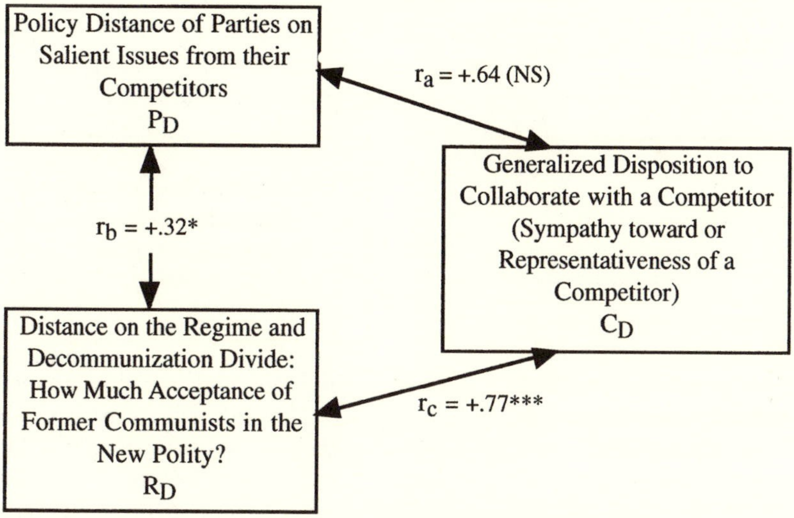

Policy Distance of Parties on Salient Issues from their Competitors P_D	$r_a = +.64$ (NS) →	

Policy Distance of Parties on Salient Issues from their Competitors
P_D

$r_a = +.64$ (NS)

Generalized Disposition to Collaborate with a Competitor (Sympathy toward or Representativeness of a Competitor)
C_D

$r_b = +.32*$

Distance on the Regime and Decommunization Divide: How Much Acceptance of Former Communists in the New Polity?
R_D

$r_c = +.77***$

Basis for calculation: sixe parties (FIDESZ, FKGF, KDNP, MDF, MSzP, SzDSz), N = 30 (6 x 5 observations)

Poland

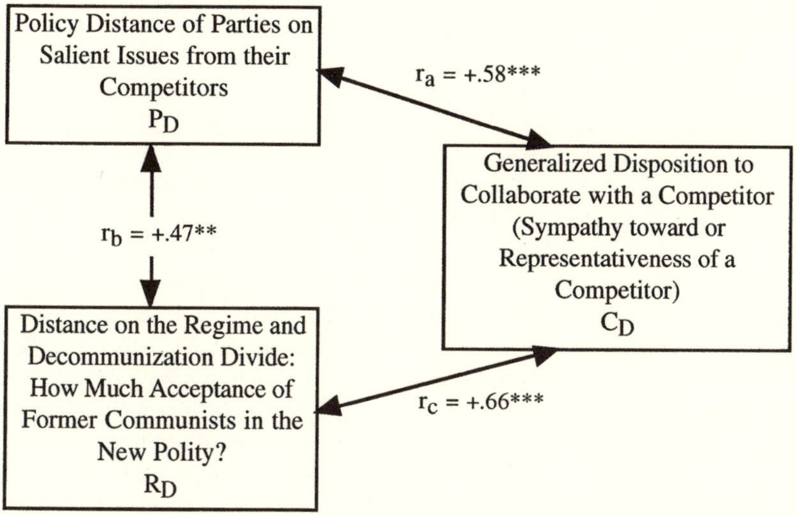

Policy Distance of Parties on Salient Issues from their Competitors
P_D

$r_a = +.58***$

Generalized Disposition to Collaborate with a Competitor (Sympathy toward or Representativeness of a Competitor)
C_D

$r_b = +.47**$

Distance on the Regime and Decommunization Divide: How Much Acceptance of Former Communists in the New Polity?
R_D

$r_c = +.66***$

Basis for calculation: ten parties (BBWR, KLD, KPN, NZSS 'S', PC, PSL, SLD, PD, UP, ZChN)), N = 90 (10 x 9 observations)

* $p<.10$; ** $p<.05$; *** $p<.01$

Figure 10.4. (cont.)

Table 10.5. *Policy distances, regime divides, and sympathy differentials: The regression equations*

	$C_D = P_D$	$R_D = P_D$	$C_D = R_D$
Bulgaria (N = 20)	$C_D = 9.80 + .019\,P_D$	$R_D = 7.58 + .007$	$C_D = 7.16 + .48\,R_D$
Czech Republic (N = 20)	$C_D = 3.53 + .064\,P_D$	$R_D = -1.05 + .070$	$C_D = 5.87 + .73\,R_D$
Hungary (N = 30)	$C_D = 7.59 + .050\,P_D$	$R_D = 5.05 + .033$	$C_D = 7.25 + .59\,R_D$
Poland (N = 90)	$C_D = 6.72 + .050\,P_D$	$R_D = 3.09 + .053$	$C_D = 7.52 + .48\,R_D$

Polish ten-party system. Figure 10.4 presents bivariate correlations among these variables for each country and table 10.5 provides the regression equations. We have also calculated multiple regressions of R_D and P_D on C_D for each country, but they only confirm what can be gleaned from the simple bivariate correlations.

In Hungary and the Czech Republic, we expect to find the highest governability, indicated by a rather tight link between parties' policy distances P_D and their differential dispositions to collaborate C_D. Results for the Czech Republic bear out this expectation. Although parties' disagreements on the regime divide R_D are a slightly better predictor of their dispositions to collaborate with each other than policy distances, positions on the regime divide are highly correlated to parties' perception of policy distances, which are heavily driven by economic policy disagreements. In Hungary, there is a substantial correlation between parties' policy distances and their dispositions to collaboration as well, but parties' relative distances on the regime divide are an even better predictor of their cooperative dispositions. Moreover, differentials between parties' positions in the policy space do not predict their disagreements on the regime divide well (r = .32). In Hungary, the regime divide thus has a somewhat greater independent influence on parties' collaborative dispositions than in the Czech Republic.[12]

In both Hungary and the Czech Republic, however, policy distances among parties appear to make a greater difference for their mutual collaborative dispositions than in Poland and particularly in Bulgaria. In Poland, *both* the regime divide *and* the parties' policy differentials are only moderately strong predictors of their mutual dispositions toward collaboration. Other factors not revealed by our model may affect the parties' collaborative spirits, and we will explore them with our analysis of party dyads. Finally, in Bulgaria, *only* the regime divide can predict parties' dispositions toward mutual collaboration moderately well, but policy distances contribute nothing statistically significant to parties' collaborative dispositions. The relatively modest correlation of .67 between R_D and C_D shows that also in Bulgaria the regime divide is not the only reason why policy differentials among parties fail to predict their collaborative dispositions. Again, an

---

[12]This is borne out by the standardized beta coefficients in the multiple regression of policy and regime distances on dispositions to collaborate.

analysis of party dyads, and here particularly that of relations between the Turkish minority party DPS and the other competitors, is instructive and helps to throw light on this puzzle.

Regression intercepts and slope coefficients reported in table 10.5 essentially confirm the cross-national differences. In the Czech Republic, small intercepts and large slope coefficients indicate that both the differentials between parties' views of the regime divide as well as their disposition to collaborate are most responsive to differences in their policy positions. In Bulgaria, the parties' dispositions to cooperate are least affected by their distances in the policy space, as indicated by the large intercepts and small coefficients in all three equations. Hungary and Poland are situated in intermediate positions.

The regressions covering all parties in each country do not reveal which parties abide by a spatial policy logic of inter-party collaboration and which parties defy this logic and act on non-policy considerations. A closer look at party dyads, however, reveals the precise nature of the obstacles blocking "rational" policy collaboration in each country. For that purpose, table 10.6 distinguishes configurations of policy distance and dispositions toward mutual collaboration for each party dyad in the fashion presented in figure 10.2. We dichotomize each party's distance from its competitors in the policy space and their respective sympathy differentials into high and low values. We rate a party as "close" to a competitor in the policy space if its distance P_D from that competitor is smaller than the average distance of all pairs of parties in that country. In the same vein, a party is favorably disposed toward collaboration with a competitor if its sympathy differential C_D to that competitor is smaller than the mean differential for all conceivable dyads of parties in that country.

Inter-party collaboration is unproblematic where a dyad of parties is close to each other in the policy space *and* is positively disposed toward mutual collaboration (case I: consonant cooperation). Collaboration is out of the question where each party in a dyad is distant from the other in the policy space *and* they mutually reject collaboration (case V: consonant competition). The remaining configurations exhibit a variety of asymmetries and dissonances that should not occur if spatial policy rationality drives parties' strategic actions. Only one party of a dyad is *both* close to its competitor in the policy space *and* willing to cooperate with it, while the other party is hostile to cooperation (dissonant case II). Or both parties are close in the policy space, *but* mutually dislike to cooperate with each other (dissonant case III). Or two parties are clearly distant from each other in the policy space, yet are nevertheless mutually predisposed toward collaboration (dissonant case IV). In our interpretation of the empirical constellations in the four countries, we must keep in mind that our data represent party dispositions and perceptions of policy distances in early 1994. In some instances, these relations are likely to have changed substantially in subsequent years.

At the most superficial level, we can compare the ratio of party dyads that are in cells representing configurations consonant with spatial considerations of policy distance and those that are not. In each country with k parties, there are

Table 10.6. *Coalition potential among parties*

	Bulgaria	Czech Republic	Hungary	Poland	
Case I					
Parties close to each other in the policy space. Both sides willing to cooperate	BNZS - BSDP BNZS - SDS	ODS - ODA ODS - KDU ODA - KDU	MSzP - SzDSz SzDSz - Fidesz KDNP - FKGP KDNP - MDF	SLD-PSL SLD-UP PSL-UP PSL-KPN ZChN-PC	UD-KLD UD-BBWR KLD-BBWR KPN-PC KPN-NZSS "S"
Case II					
Only *one* party close *and* disposed toward cooperation (*in italics*)	*BSP* - BSDP	*LB* - CSSD CSSD - ODA	*MSzP* - Fidesz *MDF* - FKGP *MDF* - Fidesz	*SLD*-KPN *PSL*-UD *PSL*-NZSS "S" *PSL*-BBWR	*ZChN*-BBWR *KPN*-BBWR *UD*-ZChN
Case III					
Both parties close in the policy space, *but both* unwilling to cooperate	BSP - BZNS			PSL - PC UD - PC BBWR - PC	

Case IV
Both parties distant in the policy space, *but both* willing to cooperate

Case V
Both parties distant in the policy space *and* unwilling to cooperate

SD - DPS			UP - UD	
			ZChN - NZSS "S"	
			BBWR - NZSS "S"	
BSP - DSP	LB - KDU	MSzP - FKGP	SLD-ZChN	UP-BBWR
BSP - SDS	LB - ODA	MSzP - KDNP	SLD-UD	UP-PC
BSDP - SDS	LB - ODS	MSzP - MDF	SLD-KLD	UP-NZSS "S"
BSPD - DPS	CSSD - ODS	FKGP - SzDSz	SLD-BBWR	ZChN-KLD
BNZS - DPS	CSSD - KDU	FKGP - Fidesz	SLD-PC	ZChN-KPN
		KDNP - SzDS		SLD-NZSS "S"
		KDNP - Fidesz		UD-KPN
		SzDSz - MDF	PSL-ZChN	UD-NZSS "S"
			PSL-KLD	KLD-KPN
			UP-ZChN	KLD-PC
			UP-KLD	KLD-NZSS "S"
			UP-KPN	PC-NZSS "S"

Number of party dyads

10	10	15	45	

k*(k − 1)/2 pairs of parties. In Hungary and the Czech Republic, the ratio of consonant pairs (cases I and V) to dissonant pairs (cases II through IV) is 4 : 1, whereas it is 2.46 : 1 in Poland and only 1 : 1 in Bulgaria. To show that policy considerations have less weight for parties' collaborative dispositions in Poland and Bulgaria, however, it is more interesting to examine individual party dyads more closely.

In Bulgaria, the regime divide prevents the post-communist BSP from collaborating with social democrats (BSDP) and agrarians (BZNS), although both of these rival parties are close to the BSP in the policy space, particularly on questions of economic liberalization. In the agrarians' case, the antipathies are mutual, a relationship that may go as far back as the conflict between the two parties over Alexandur Stamboliski's agrarian government in 1922–23. Furthermore, the anti-communist SDS and the DPS, as the representative of the Turkish minority, see each other as distant in the policy space, particularly on economic matters, but also on Turkish minority rights. Nevertheless, the two parties signal their willingness to collaborate with each other. However, the quick demise of the 1992 SDS minority government under Dimitrov, which relied on DPS support, illustrates that an alliance between partners that express incompatible policy goals remains precarious and cannot lead to effective governance. The DPS withdrew support from the government when the SDS pushed forward economic liberalization policies that conflicted with the interests of the DPS electoral constituency, consisting primarily of poor peasants. A similar incompatibility of policy goals, but temporary willingness to collaborate, may beset the partners involved in the United Democratic Forces alliance of 1997, a pre-election coalition of the market-liberal SDS (which is still quite heterogeneous internally) with more social-protectionist parties, such as the BZNS, the BSDP, and a number of small splinter groups.

In the Czech Republic, most party dyads represent symmetrical or "consonant" configurations of cooperation (case I) or competition (case V). Feasible and prospectively durable collaboration prevails among the three parties that actually have formed a government in the Czech Republic from 1992 until the time of this writing (ODS, ODA, KDU). In 1993–94, no other coalition configuration appeared feasible in Czech politics.[13] The regime divide articulates itself in one, if not both, of the remaining dissonant pairs. Communists and social democrats perceive each other as relatively close in the issue space, but the social democrats intensely dislike their communist competitor. Social democrats, in turn, find ODA quite sympathetic and see themselves as relatively close to it in policy terms, particularly on socio-cultural issues, but ODA politicians do not reciprocate these overtures.

[13]This general configuration of party dyads is unlikely to change, had we been able to include the nationalist SPR-RSC. All parties, except the post-communists, are quite distant from the SPR on the national issue that is most salient to the latter (see table 9A.2, last column) and no party rates the SPR as a sympathetic prospective coalition partner. In the relations among the other parties since 1993–94, the KDU and the CSSD have gradually converged on moderately social-protectionist economic policy positions and may potentially constitute an alternative to the ODA-ODS-KDU government coalition.

In Hungary, the government coalitions in the first and the second legislative terms (MDF and KDNP; MSzP and SzDSz) are among the feasible consonant dyads with policy distances perceived by both partners as small and mutual sympathies relatively high. Furthermore, alliances between SzDSz and Fidesz as well as between KDNP and FKGP appear feasible, although these parties have received far fewer votes than needed to form a legislative or executive majority. Among the dissonant cases, the MDF extends its sympathies both to the agrarian Smallholders as well as to the Young Democrats, but in 1994 politicians in these two parties did not reciprocate these dispositions, although each dyad comprises parties rather close to each other in the policy space. If we had data for 1996–97, once FKGP, KDNP, MDF, and Fidesz had shared the opposition benches for several years, a coalition between these parties might turn out to be more feasible. Since 1994, Fidesz moved into the Christian-national sector and attracted most of the MDF's and KDNP's supporters and legislators. In addition to this convergence of programmatic appeals, the common experience of opposition changed the dispositions toward collaboration.

As a further dissonant case in 1994, the post-communist MSzP found the Young Democrats quite sympathetic and quite close in the policy space, at least on socio-cultural issues, but Fidesz politicians rejected an alliance with the MSzP. The conflict between SzDSz and Fidesz on the alliance issue with the MSzP was one important catalyst that prompted the Fidesz leadership to rethink its place in the Hungarian competitive political space and move toward the Christian-national camp.

The most complex configuration of inter-party relations appears in Poland with a more fragmented landscape of parties than in any of the other three East Central European countries in 1993–94. Much of this fragmentation is due to the divisions within the Christian national sector of the policy space that was composed of a number of post-Solidarność splinter parties and the KPN. Only a few dyads among these parties actually constituted feasible consonant coalitions (ZChN-PC; KPN-PC; KPN-NZSS "S"). Most of the feasible coalitions (case I) cover parties outside the Christian-national sector. Here we find the actual government coalition of post-communists and agrarians in the 1993–97 legislature as well as the UD-KLD dyad, two liberal-democratic parties that merged under the label of Freedom Union (UW) shortly after we conducted our survey. Further consonant dyads include the most leftist Polish party in economic and socio-cultural terms, the post-Solidarność UP that is favorably disposed to collaboration with both parties of the SLD-PSL government, a pattern that has manifested itself in actual legislative voting in the Polish Sejm. KPN and BBWR, in turn, are able to tie into the agrarian or the liberal political networks with consonant cooperative dyads.

Most of the infeasible coalitions involve dyads in which the PSL or the UP relate to parties of the liberal or the Christian-national sector. Moreover, coalitions between the liberal democrats (UD or KLD) and many elements of the Christian-national sector were out of the question in 1993–94. At that point in time, also a coalition between post-communists and liberals was clearly infeasible for reasons of policy distance and mutual antipathy. Had we been able to repeat our study in 1996–97, after four years of an SLD-PSL government in which the SLD pushed for the continuation of economic reforms against the resistance of the PSL, SLD and UW might have been more compatible in terms of policy distance. Even then, historical sensitivities and an anti-communist affect in the UW might have stood in the way of a government alliance between these two parties. Also in Poland, the regime divide builds up affective orientations that interfere with policy-based coalition making.

When we turn to the "dissonant" dyadic configurations II through IV in Poland, where spatial policy distances and parties' collaborative dispositions do not match, we first encounter evidence of the regime divide in the dissonant dyads of SLD-KPN, PSL-UD, PSL-NZSS "S," and PSL-BBWR. As in the other countries, the former communists or the successors to the agrarian bloc party consider rivals that grow out of opposition movements much more sympathetic than the latter are willing to reciprocate, even when both sides perceive the other as relatively close to their own party in the policy space.

In 1993–94, the most interesting dissonant dyads on the Polish scene, however, concern parties located in the "Christian-national" policy sector populated by post-Solidarność parties and the KPN. First of all, the Christian national parties could not find Solidarność's liberal offshoots, UD and KLD, sympathetic, although some of the former are actually quite close to the liberal democrats in the policy space (UD-ZChN; UD-PC). The only exception to this rule is the presidential party BBWR, which provided a bridge between the market-liberal and Christian-national party sector in 1994. The Christian-national sectors' ability to contribute to effective governance was even further impaired by the prevalence of dissonant dyadic relations among parties *inside* that sector. Thus, ZChN and BBWR (case II) as well as BBWR and PC (case III) had difficulties working with each other, although they were close in the policy space. The divisive tactics that characterized President Walesa's conduct during the 1990–93 period are at least in part responsible for the arduous relations among post-Solidarność parties. At the same time, sentimental recollections about the days of struggle against the communist regime may account for the fact that two Christian-national parties with more market-liberal inclinations, the ZChN and the BBWR, were willing to cooperate with the Solidarność's electoral list, a disposition reciprocated by the latter, *although* the policy positions of these potential partners are very distant from each other, particularly on issues of economic liberalization (case IV: S-ZChN; S-BBWR).

THE REALITIES OF POLITICAL GOVERNANCE AND DISPOSITIONS TOWARD INTER-PARTY COLLABORATION

The realities of coalition politics in the period from 1990 to late 1997 rather closely reflect the politicians' judgments in our four countries in 1994. In the

Czech Republic, a liberal-Christian coalition held firm, until a crisis of its economic reform program led to its demise in late 1997. The left parties cannot offer
an alternative to the ODS-ODA-KDU alliance because the regime divide makes a
coalition between the post-communist KSCM and the social democratic CSSD
impossible. Between 1996 and 1997, from different starting points in the political spectrum, CSSD and KDU began to move toward "center-left" economic
policy positions that expanded the options for coalition making.

In Hungary, consonant and dissonant configurations correspond to the empirical realities of coalition politics as well. Both consonant coalition governments
in 1990 and 1994 survived the entire legislative terms. When the SzDSz joined
the MSzP government in 1994, Fidesz refused to follow and instead began to drift
toward the Christian-national party camp that included the MDF, the KDNP, and
also the FKGP. By 1997, Fidesz's new strategic appeal enabled it to devour pretty
much the entire MDF and KDNP electorates and attracted many of its politicians
as well. The more nationalist-populist forces under the umbrella of the old MDF
and KDNP gravitated toward two parties, the FKGP and in the 1998 election
also Istvan Csurka's MIEP. The FKGP remained outside Fidesz's reach within the
Christian-national sector. Soon after 1990, the FKGP had left the coalition with
MDF over policy disputes involving the restitution of farmland, but also over
personal rivalries between leading politicians of both parties. By 1996–97, however, the FKGP represented a more radical populist-nationalist electoral current
than the Fidesz-Hungarian Civic Party would endorse, but both parties were
nevertheless inclined to work with each other. The 1998 election gave them the
chance to build another consonant coalition government.

As our empirical findings suggest, the realities of coalition politics are much
more complicated in Bulgaria and Poland, though for different reasons. In Bulgaria, the regime divide looms large over the process of coalition building. In
1991, this divide welded together two anti-communist parties with very distant
policy positions, the more market-liberal SDS and the social-protectionist Turkish
minority party DPS. Only their desire to keep the communists out of office
provided the glue of this alliance. Given the policy incoherence of this coalition, it
lasted barely one year. After its failure, politicians were unable to replace it by
another viable government with firm majority legislative support, because neither
the more centrist factions of the SDS nor the DPS dared to enter a coalition with
the BSP. The BSP victory of 1994 heralded an era of majority party government,
but the programmatic diffuseness of the party led to the collapse of its government, precipitated by the catalyst of a national financial crisis and an avalanche of
political corruption scandals. These developments allowed a broad coalition of
programmatically rather heterogeneous elements to reemerge under the new
umbrella of the Democratic United Forces that included not only the old, highly
heterogeneous SDS, but also the more social-protectionist BSDP and BZNS.
While the fear of a communist resurgence holds this coalition together, it is an
open question whether its leading politicians can transform it into a disciplined
party government that produces lasting legislative and executive governance. The

programmatic incoherence of the coalition works against durable governance, but the exigencies of Bulgarian electoral laws and parliamentary government, together with the dynamic of the regime divide, may favor it.

Next to Bulgaria, Poland is the country in our comparison with the most volatile governments. Between 1989 and 1993, the country saw five prime ministers in as many coalition governments. Between 1993 and 1997, the SLD-PSL coalition held steady, but changed prime ministers twice. As of this writing in the first trimester of 1998, the AWS-UW government of Christian-national and liberal political sector formed after the September 1997 parliamentary election remains in place but experiences the strong internal divisions over economic policy as well as non-policy-related personal rivalries one would have predicted based on the programmatic disparities between liberal and Christian-national policy sector and the personal animosities within the latter evidenced by our 1994 survey.[14] In light of the complicated relations among the Solidarność fission products in the period from 1991 through 1996, the refocusing of the Christian-national political sector around two electoral alliances in the run-up to the 1997 legislative election from which the AWS emerged as the core organization may remain quite precarious.

Strong presidential power under Lech Walesa (1990–95) contributed its share to the divisions in the Christian-national sector. In the 1991–93 legislative term, presidential power reinforced extreme party fragmentation, initially precipitated by the dissolution of Solidarność's parliamentary caucus in 1990–91. As a labor union, Solidarność could not generate internal consensus around the construction of capitalism and economic inequalities between workers and owners. But Lech Walesa's presidential rule from December was instrumental in preventing a reconsolidation of those fragments of the Solidarność parliamentary caucus that gravitated toward a common Christian-national programmatic spectrum within democratic Poland's emerging competitive space. In order to satisfy his own ambition to dominate the policy process, Walesa wasted little time to weaken parliamentary parties by a divide-and-rule tactics based on a game of musical chairs that promised and sometimes delivered cabinet positions to those politicians who happened to declare their support for the president's quest to expand his domain of power.[15]

The electoral reform of 1993 and the ensuing defeat of the decomposing post-Solidarność parties in the legislative elections, however, constrained Walesa's ability to affect Poland's democratic governability. Governability further improved when Kwasniewski replaced Walesa as president in 1995. It is not by accident that the Christian-national sector of Polish politics could craft an internal electoral alliance only after Walesa's departure from the presidency. Walesa's

---

[14]The *Economist* therefore entitled one of its feature articles on the Polish government coalition "Solidarity versus Solidarity" (April 25, 1998, pp. 51–52).

[15]For a description of the difficulties to institutionalize the post-Solidarność parties and the role of Walesa's conduct as president in that process, see Wiatr (1996).

defeat in the 1995 presidential election removed a meddlesome and divisive actor from political center stage who employed his considerable institutional leverage to obstruct the unification of the Christian-national party sector. Politicians of the new Solidarność electoral coalition do their utmost to keep Walesa sidelined and prevent his reentry into politics.

The new constitution of 1997 goes some way toward reducing presidential power, particularly in the area of executive appointments and the dismissal of the government. Nevertheless, it preserves considerable presidential veto powers (60 percent veto override in the two houses of parliament) that may tempt a president to undermine legislative and cabinet coalitions hostile to his influence over policy making. Together with the 1993 election law that punishes politicians who engage in a strategy of party fragmentation, however, by 1997 the prospects of stable governance in Poland were considerably better than in the early 1990s.

CONCLUSION

The quality of democratic rule expresses itself in modes of political representation and governability. As a comparison of our findings in chapters 9 and 10 illustrates, patterns of representation do not necessarily coincide with capacities for effective governance. Conversely, there is no simple trade-off between representation, conceived in terms of parties' policy advocacy and efforts to achieve responsible party government, and stable governance. The four East Central European post-communist countries in fact exhibit rather diverse configurations of representation and governance. These configurations are shaped in part by legacies of communist rule but in part also by the new institutions of the democratic polity. Legacies articulate themselves in the salience and alignments of political divides and competitive dimensions, particularly the role that the political regime divide between communists and anti-communists still plays in the new democracy. Institutions concern the electoral laws and the executive-legislative power relations that affect parties' strategies and capabilities to form political coalitions.

Czech democracy produces strong representation in terms of parties' responsiveness to preference divergence among their constituencies and responsible party government, while simultaneously offering conditions conducive to effective governance. The demand for cooperation among parties in a multi-party parliamentary democracy with proportional representation is relatively high, yet at the same time the parties are willing to seek alliances with competitors based on sober policy considerations. Also in Bulgaria we discovered that parties represent diverging partisan constituency preferences quite sharply despite the internal incoherence of their elites. Both bureaucratic-authoritarian as well as patrimonial communist legacies facilitate a polarization of political forces on economic and other reinforcing policy divides that is conducive to parties' responsiveness and responsible party government. Yet in Bulgaria, the patrimonial legacies also keep alive a profound regime division that inflames the passions of both average citizens as well as politicians. As a consequence, conditions of governance are quite poor. Parties have had great difficulties to collaborate with each other, even when their policy positions appear to converge. Conversely, parties with highly disparate policy positions may team up in precarious ineffectual coalitions that follow the imperatives of the political regime divide.

In democracies emerging from national-accommodative communism, conditions for representation through responsiveness and party government are less favorable, because the critical actors can less credibly announce sharply diverging policy positions on the most salient policy issues, especially in the economic arena. As a consequence, particularly Hungary exhibits serious problems of political representation after the comparatively most consensual transition to democracy because the parties can sincerely signal significantly different policy appeals to voters only on secondary socio-cultural dimensions of competition to which citizens may pay less attention than to economics.[16] Disaffection with politics and cynicism may result from this process. Yet at the same time, the relative lack of polarization and the waning relevance of the regime divide create favorable conditions of governance in Hungary. Parties are not very far removed from each other in the policy space and politicians tend to base their attitudes toward collaboration with competitors on policy concerns to a considerable extent.

In all these respects, Poland constitutes an intermediate case. It combines elements of accommodation and confrontation in the old communist regime and experienced a negotiated democratic transition. Moreover, its new democratic institutions incorporate elements of zero-sum competition for the highest office of the state, but also require cooperation of parties in legislature and cabinet. Poland's parties show greater capacity for responsiveness (relative representation) on key economic issues than those of Hungary. But at the same time, Poland's capacity to deliver effective governance has been weakened by historical and institutional factors. A single case study of inter-party relations and obstacles to coalition building in the era of Lech Walesa's presidency certainly does not prove the disadvantages of semi-presidential constitutional arrangements in general. Nevertheless, a close reconstruction of the micro-dynamic of inter-party relations, particularly within the Christian-national sector of competitors, shows how institutional arrangements, combined with a temperamental holder of the chief executive office, can undercut effective political governance.

APPENDIX: A SUMMARY INDEX OF INTER-PARTY DISTANCES IN THE POLICY SPACE

A summary measure of policy "distances" between parties requires several decisions:

---

[16]This does not, of course, prevent socio-cultural traits and opinions from being good predictors of voters' party preferences. Low-salience issues that furnish robust voter alignments constitute identification cleavages, but not competitive dimensions in the party system.

1. Which variables do we select to construct the policy distances?
   1.1. All variables included in the questionnaire?
   1.2. The factors that map the relation of the variables to underlying dimensions (chapter 7)?
   1.3. "Representative" variables that load strongly on factors mapping the underlying policy dimensions?
2. How do we weight inter-party distances on policy variables in light of the varying salience of issues for political competition?
   2.1. No weighting, all distances counted equally?
   2.2. Weighting of variables in the same way for all parties, according to the systemic relevance of dimensions of competition?
   2.3. Weighting of variables in ways that reflect the particular salience of policies for individual parties?
3. How do we construct the multi-dimensional policy space?
   3.1. Euclidean space?
   3.2. "City bloc" method, adding distances on each independent dimension?

For robustness, we calculated interparty distances in different ways, although we did not exhaust the many possible operationalizations that result from the quite different combinations according to which the preceding questions can be answered. Results proved to be robust, regardless of specification. The calculations of P_D, as employed in our calculations for figure 10.5, are based on the following design.

1. We selected "representative" variables that load strongly on factors that map underlying policy dimensions, as revealed by the factor analyses in chapter 7 (tables 7.1 through 7.4). In all countries, we employed the issue of privatization with rising unemployment (VAR 31) to measure inter-party distances on matters of market liberalization. In the Czech Republic, Hungary, and Poland, we employed the church-state school question (VAR 39) to tap the socio-cultural dimension, in Bulgaria the question of Turkish instruction in school (VAR 45). For the Polish KPN, we added the national-cosmopolitan policy issue (VAR 48). The parties' positions on these variables are displayed in tables 9A.1 through 9A.4. Values represent the averages of all respondents belonging to the rated party. Distances P_D between parties are the absolute difference of each party's values reported there.

2. We assign weights for the salience of each policy issue contingent upon the party whose members assess their disposition toward collaboration with its competitors. Our weights are judgmental and draw on the information we have about the parties' major appeals and the nature of competition in the party system as a whole, as discussed in chapters 5, 7, and 8. The sum of weights for the two issue dimensions on which we measure inter-party policy distances is always 3. Some parties focus their attention almost exclusively on economics and the ratio between economic and non-economic policy weights is then either 2.3:0.7 (SDS, KLD) or 2 : 1 (BSP, BZNS, BSDP, LB, CSSD, ODS, SLD, and UD). In a number

of instances, and particularly in Hungary and Poland, we weight the relative importance of economic and socio-cultural issues for the parties' politicians as roughly even, i.e., 1.5 : 1.5 (ODA, MSzP, SzDSz, Fidesz, PSL, BBWR, PC, NZSS "S"). In a few other instances, socio-cultural questions outweigh the salience of economic policies by 2 : 1 (KDU, FKGP, KDNP, MDF, UP, KPN) or even by 2.3 : 0.7 (DPS, ZChN).

There are many alternative ways we could have assigned salience weights to individual parties' policy distances from their competitors. We could have drawn on the raw salience ratings of issues reported in chapter 5. We might have also employed the unstandardized regression coefficients that indicate how well policy positions (distances on VAR 31, 39, 48, or 45) predict politicians' sympathies toward competitors (see table 10.3), because this measure shows how politicians themselves attribute weights to different policy questions, when they assess their dispositions toward competing parties.

3. We calculated the overall index of policy distance P_D according to the "city bloc" method, adding up the weighted distances of each focal party from its competitor on the two policy dimensions.

All measures are at the aggregate level by party, not by individual respondent. Correlations in figure 10.5 reflect aggregate level relations between parties. How well do parties' average policy distances predict their average differences over decommunization (R_D) and their average sympathy differentials C_D, tapping dispositions to collaborate with a competitor?

Interestingly, we experimented with weighted and unweighted measures of inter-party policy distance and different ways to weight policy salience in each country, but such techniques yield equivalent patterns of association between P_D, LR_D, and C_D and cross-national variance of such patterns reported in figure 10.5 for the four countries.

CONCLUSION

11

THE DIVERSITY OF POST-COMMUNIST DEMOCRATIC GOVERNANCE

In the Third Wave of democratization, political scientists first studied the conditions under which polities shifted from authoritarian rule to competitive democracy. Next, they investigated the processes and institutional commitments that turn a volatile, open situation of democratic regime choice into a routinized political process, configured around institutions most citizens and politicians treat as the "only game in town." Most recently, analysts have begun to explore the *quality of the democratic experience* in the new polities, both with regard to the features that characterize the process of democratic competition as well as with regard to the policy outputs that shape people's life chances. Our study of four East Central European post-communist polities is a contribution to the emerging literature on the procedural quality of new democratic polities. It focuses on one central and indispensable aspect of any democracy, the dynamics of party competition, and accounts for cross-national divergence of the democratic experiences in terms of historical legacies and the emerging framework of new electoral, legislative, and executive institutions. Of course, we do not pretend to provide a complete and determinist explanation of the quality of democracy in each of our countries. Political science models do not reflect the full complexity of political life and thus never provide necessary and sufficient explanations. As a consequence, we do not anticipate major political changes, because our models lack sufficient specificity.

If at least one of the following three propositions proves empirically robust in future research, our study will ultimately have been successful. *First,* democratic experience in post-communist democracies varies with regime legacies and institutions. The different resources and strategic orientations of political actors under bureaucratic-authoritarian, national-accommodative, and patrimonial communism affect the transition process to democracy, the choice of new democratic institutions, and the patterns of party competition. The present study of only four democracies does more to illustrate and make plausible this proposition than to test it in a rigorous fashion. Only a future replication of our study with a larger set of countries will tell whether our analysis has broader significance. There will always be cases that defy the logic we have laid out, but our argument is useful if it demonstrates some "carrying capacity" by throwing light on the quality of democratic procedures and party competition in other post-communist countries than our four East Central European reference cases.

Second, citizens and politicians learn to act on well-understood self-interests in new democracies quite rapidly. Even though these democracies are unlikely to have reached lasting equilibrium states in the first five years of democratic competition, politicians' and citizens' political practices reveal a trajectory of practical learning that does point forward toward durable features shaping the new polities for some time to come. Initially, the uncertainties of political action in the new democracies are high, but political actors explore the new setting not simply in a randomized trial-and-error mode but in a directed fashion that makes rational use of information. With each additional round of competition, the actors gain a better understanding of their strategic options within a system of historical and institutional constraints that shape the range of permissible and potentially re-warding moves. If political learning is rational and path-dependent rather than purely random, then empirical observations about the quality of democracy roughly four to five years after the end of communism capture not just a fleeting transitional moment of political flux but potentially lasting and cross-nationally diverging attributes of each country's democratic process. The new political in-stitutions put in place during the transition increasingly structure such patterns. Our analysis, of course, compares the development of these new democratic polities only at a single time point. The dynamic change of post-communist polities, however, can only be satisfactorily captured, if we multiply time points of observation and study the evolution of these democracies in a longitudinal fash-ion. Thus, our analysis does not pretend to identify equilibrium positions of post-communist democracies, but it treats the cross-national diversity we observe among our four countries as a tracer of a widely varying quality of democratic procedures that articulate themselves in different patterns of learning and insti-tutionalization.

Third, democratic processes leave an imprint on political-economic out-comes. Our study has made this claim in an implicit fashion by showing how the potential for economic liberalization, articulated by liberal democrats within the system of party competition, varies across countries with diverging regime legacies. It may currently be too early to test hypotheses about the causal impact of democratic competition on post-communist political economies in a com-prehensive way. Nevertheless, our propositions about the linkage between regime legacies, democratic institutions, and political competition also encourage stu-dents of comparative political economy to relate cross-nationally varying path-ways of market liberalization, privatization, and economic performance to features of the democratic process. The association between democratic procedures and political performance is, of course, not just a matter of political economy but affects socio-cultural areas of policy making as well. For example, we would advance the hypothesis that linguistic and ethnic conflicts will be most difficult to pacify in democracies emerging from a patrimonial communist experience, because here probabilities are highest that voters and politicians crystallize around mutually reinforcing socio-economic and cultural divides in the arena of party competition. In formerly national-accommodative communist countries, it is more likely that such lines of conflict crosscut.

In this concluding chapter, we first restate major findings of our investigation and then debate what we consider to be one key challenge to the thrust of our analysis in the current field of comparative post-communist studies, the tabula rasa theory of post-communist democracy. In the final section, we speculate about the possible linkages between democratic procedures and political outcomes as a way to probe into the future research agenda on the politics of post-communist democracies.

EXPLAINING THE DIVERGING QUALITY OF DEMOCRATIC PROCESSES IN POST-COMMUNIST DEMOCRACY

Political legacies, mediated by the rational strategies of political actors who share an interest in wealth and political office but vary in terms of their resource endowments and cognitive frameworks, do matter for the emerging patterns of accountability and responsiveness and thus ultimately for the procedural quality of post-communist democracies. Our study illustrated these linkages in five respects: the programmatic crystallization of parties and party systems; the political divisions between parties' programmatic appeals; the competitive dimensions on which parties place their appeals; constituency-party configurations of absolute and relative representation; and finally the capacity of parties to solve problems of political governance. Contingent upon the nature of what the former rulers called "real existing socialism" in the past and the associated mode of transition to democracy, the new East Central European party systems in the 1990s have developed different profiles of competition and representation.

The Czech Republic is our example for a democratic polity on the pathway from *bureaucratic-authoritarian communism,* a type of communist rule that grows out of strong working-class and bourgeois mobilization in an industrialized society and inter-war democracy. Here, a resourceful and intransigent communist ruling party tenaciously held on to power until the sudden collapse of its rule in November 1989, while new liberal-democratic and social democratic parties mushroomed quickly and established themselves around highly crystallized rival programmatic agendas that divide the most significant electoral contenders and their voter constituencies primarily over economic issues. These issues become the most salient problems of inter-party competition and policy making. The close association of citizens' and politicians' use of the left-right semantics with economic policy alternatives is testimony to this straightforward alignment of forces in the political landscape. The simplicity and transparency of the political agenda and of ideological party alternatives on offer affect the process of representation. Parties tend to overstate their electorates' proclivities in either direction on the economic social-protectionist versus market-liberal dimension. This undercuts the proximity between party politicians and their voters on salient issues ("absolute" representation) but boosts politicians' electoral responsiveness to differential preferences in the electorate ("relative" representation, relations of polarizing trusteeship). Because the surviving intransigent post-communist party is weak and cornered into a clearly identifiable extreme position on the salient competitive dimension, democratic governance and coalition building among the relevant parties in the legislature are rarely impaired by issueless inter-party conflicts over the assessment of the communist past or the desire to avenge the wrongs of the old regime.

In countries developing democracy after a *national-accommodative communism,* such as Hungary and, to a lesser but still significant extent, Poland, the democratic process develops somewhat different properties. In Hungary, the propensity of the ruling communist party to push toward economic reform created a broad consensus among incumbents and challengers in the late 1980s that a move to some type of market capitalism was desirable. As a consequence, compared with the Czech Republic, Hungary has produced a much less pronounced programmatic crystallization of party alternatives around economic policy packages after the advent of democracy in 1990. Economic issues tend to structure party alternatives weakly, and politicians as well as voters associate the meaning of the left-right semantics less with economic policy than with socio-cultural issues.

At the same time, the socio-cultural foundations and the political dynamic of national-accommodative communism in Hungary gave rise to a pronounced political-cultural division among party elites over questions of national autonomy, traditional moral values, and religion, which crosscut the primary economic issue dimension. Although economic issues are more salient for politicians and particularly for the voters at large, parties develop sharper programmatic contours around socio-cultural issues. This feature has consequences for political representation and governability. On economics, the Hungarian party system tends to represent voters in absolute but not relative terms, whereas on socio-cultural affairs it is the other way round. All parties gravitate toward "centrist" economic positions on social welfare, privatization, and market liberalization and thus are close to the general tendency of the Hungarian public opinion distribution. At the same time, parties do little to reflect the differential economic preferences and policy conflicts among electoral constituencies. Parties' responsiveness to and relative representation of distinct electoral constituencies suffer under the impact of this centripetal tendency. Instead, parties dramatically overstate opinion differences of electoral constituencies on issues of socio-cultural politics (religion, morality, family, nationalism) and here emphasize relations of polarizing trusteeship as their model of representation. While Hungary's party system thus has a problem of economic policy representativeness that results in high inter-bloc volatility of the electorate, there is little evidence of problems of governance. Given the negotiated transition, an issueless, passionate divide over the evaluation of the communist past is sufficiently weak among Hungarian parties that the post-communists managed to enter a government coalition with a leading former opposition party. The policy distance between parties on economic and socio-cultural issues is a fairly good predictor of their propensities to collaborate in legislative or executive coalitions.

In a number of respects, the Polish profile of party alignments and competition is situated somewhere between the Czech and the Hungarian patterns. Like Hungary, Poland experienced a negotiated transition against the backdrop of a moderately conciliatory communist regime ready to tolerate some opposition activity and permitting a modicum of economic and political liberalization at least throughout the second half of the 1980s after the lifting of martial law. Also in line with Hungary, Poland looks back on a semi-authoritarian inter-war polity with a rather strong peasant and urban middle-class political mobilization that forced the ascending communist rulers to make concessions after 1956. At the same time, however, Poland has a history of repeated violent clashes between the regime and a phalanx of opposition forces, the climax of which was reached during the fifteen-month Solidarność mobilization in 1980–81 and the martial law period in its aftermath. This experience structured a more intense antagonism between communists and anti-communists than in Hungary.

In terms of its post-communist party system, Poland shows a rather sharp programmatic crystallization around both economic and political-cultural issues resulting in crosscutting divisions, both of which have some consequence for party competition. Because of the relatively greater programmatic structuring around economic issues than in Hungary, Polish parties provide more relative representation of their constituencies on such issues than their Hungarian counter-parts. In Poland, politicians' and voters' formal left-right conceptions of their own and the competing parties' positions are informed by *both* economic and socio-cultural issues.

In contrast to the Czech Republic and Hungary, however, Poland faces more serious problems of political governance. On the one hand, an issueless regime divide between the principal agents and collaborators of the communist regime and those who rallied to the Solidarność camp is moderately pronounced and may make it difficult to engineer coalitions among parties with similar stances in the two-dimensional issue space but different historical roots in these alternative camps. On the other hand, divisions among the parties that emerged from the Solidarność camp and are now located in the Christian-national sector of the policy space often derive not from policy disagreements but from personal animosities and organizational rivalries. These were initially fueled by the relatively unstructured politics of a labor *movement* and anti-communist umbrella organization against communist rule. Later the strategies of a president with roots in the Solidarność movement who could employ the institutional levers of his office for the purpose of undercutting durable legislative coalitions hobbled the effectiveness of governance in the new Polish democracy. Institutional changes both in the Polish electoral law as well as in executive-legislative relations have reduced these problems since 1993.

Bulgaria, finally, constitutes our example of a country emerging from *patrimonial communism*. Here liberal-democratic forces were weak at the time of the democratic regime transition. Historically, such countries had never experienced a strong urban middle-class or working-class mobilization prior to the advent of communism but had been governed by traditional authoritarian elites who encountered a serious threat only from radical peasant movements. The communist regime created a servile salariat and stratum of intellectuals who were dissuaded from opposition activities by carrot-and-stick practices. At the moment of the democratic regime transition in 1989–90, the more dissatisfied and future-oriented elements of the communist elite themselves instigated a preemptive reform before anti-communist forces could mobilize for a liberal-democratic order. The legacies of patrimonialism and preemptive reform contributed to considerable internal programmatic heterogeneity *both* within the formerly ruling bloc and within the emerging weak, internally divisive, and programmatically embryonic anti-communist camp of proto-parties and factions organized around rival politicians and their personal entourage.

Nevertheless, while the post-communist and the anti-communist blocs produced weak programmatic crystallization, their fuzzy appeals configured around mutually reinforcing political-economic and socio-cultural issue divides that feed into a single overriding dimension of inter-party competition rooted in the antagonism between apologists and opponents of the former communist regime. Parties of the economic social-protectionist "left" also endorse more traditionalist socio-cultural conceptions of moral order and collectivist conformity and appeal to particularist ethno-cultural collective identities. Parties of the economic liberal "right" support more individualist morality and personal autonomy and more universalist ethno-cultural politics.

Because of the organizational polarization between two major rival camps, despite their internal heterogeneity and diffuseness, citizens have little difficulty in recognizing the major alternatives. Hence, politicians tend to pronounce relative representation (responsiveness), often more in symbolic than in substantive terms, as is evidenced by the problems of affective governance encountered by Bulgarian democracy. Because of Bulgaria's deep regime divide that crystallizes intense political emotions around coping with the past and settling open scores resulting from experiences under communist rule, however, Bulgarian politics encounters serious problems of political governance. Parties' dispositions toward mutual collaboration often have more to do with how they see each other relate to the communist past than with the compatibility of their current policy appeals on salient political-economic or ethno-cultural issues. Parties with similar policy positions, but disparate origins inside or outside the communist regime, cannot collaborate with each other, while alliances among parties with disparate policy positions, but similar views of the past, prove fragile and ineffective. This problem surfaced in the short-lived alliance between SDS and DPS in 1991–92 and has also beset the four-party governing coalition that won a legislative majority in the spring 1997 legislative election. Even among SDS politicians, mutual suspicions about each other's role in the communist past and ties to the communist party have fueled internal conflict.

Table 11.1 summarizes our major findings about profiles of party competition and political divisions in the four new East Central European democracies. Future research has to probe into the temporal resilience and the generalizability of such patterns across a broader set of formerly national-accommodative or patrimonial communist countries. With regard to bureaucratic-authoritarian communism, the one other "case," the former German Democratic Republic, is now heavily overdetermined by politics in capitalist Western Germany and thus difficult to compare with the independent post-communist polities.

Of course, with the ongoing learning of democratic practices both by politicians and voters, we expect the quality of democratic procedures to evolve across Eastern Europe. Historical legacies may fade into the past, while the impact of constitutional rules of the game and current political-economic power relations on the arena of party competition takes center stage. These institutions and power relations, however, in part reflect legacies of the communist regimes themselves.

Our analysis emphasizes the *structured diversity* and the *non-randomness* of the post-communist trajectory toward democratic politics and party competition. Rival theories would challenge one or both of these assertions. We take up the challenge of the stronger claim that patterns of post-communist democracy evidence randomness shortly. As with regard to the weaker claim that democratic procedures in post-communist democracies exhibit more similarities than differences, we would be willing to accept the claim that in spite of the many attributes that divide post-communist countries, there are also some elements of the democratic process and the arena of political conflicts most post-communist countries share. In this regard, the *centrality of conflict over economic reform,* the divide between social protectionists and market liberalizers, is common to all post-communist democracies.[1] Everywhere, citizens' policy preferences over the economic alternatives derive from personal self-interests, grounded in their asset endowments and abilities to take advantage of market liberalization. As we have shown in chapter 8, market liberalizers tend to be younger, better-educated, situated in the private sector, and working as professionals or entrepreneurs. Social protectionists, in turn, are older, less educated, more often in public enterprise and working in manual or clerical jobs. Educational, sectoral, and class divisions explain about the same share of variance in respondents' economic policy preferences in all four countries. While it is unlikely that class parties, in the emphatic Marxist sense of proletarian organizations struggling for the abolition or re-

[1] Kitschelt (1992a) emphasized the centrality of economic reform but downplayed the diversity of post-communist democracies.

Table 11.1. *Procedural quality of party competition, representation, and cooperation in East Central Europe*

	Bulgaria	Czech Republic	Hungary	Poland
Programmatic crystallization of party appeals (chapter 5)	Weak	Strong	Moderate	Moderately strong
Political divisions (chapters 7 and 8)	Dominant economic and minor reinforcing cultural	Dominant economic and minor crosscutting cultural	Dominant cultural and minor crosscutting economic	Equally strong economic and crosscutting cultural
Competitive dimensions (chapter 7)	Economics	Economics	Culture and economics	Economics and culture
Modes of political representation (chapter 9)				
Absolute representation	Economics weak, culture medium	Economics weak, culture weak	Economics strong, culture weak	Economics weak, culture medium
Relative representation	Economics strong, culture medium	Economics strong, culture weak	Economics weak, culture strong	Economics medium, culture medium
Capacities for political governance: Balance of supply and demand for inter-party cooperation (chapter 10)	Not favorable	Favorable	Favorable	Intermediate favorable

distribution of private property rights in favor of skilled and unskilled blue-collar workers, could ever regain credibility in post-communist countries, the salience of economic-distributive conflict pervades the dynamic of party formation in all of these polities.

Although post-communist countries thus share essential political-economic challenges that influence their politics, these observations should not lead us to overstate the convergence of post-communist polities across Eastern Europe. As we have shown, economic-distributive conflict is embedded in alignments of democratic competition, relations of representation and governance structures that profoundly differ across our four countries.

THE TABULA RASA VIEW OF POST-COMMUNIST PARTY FORMATION

One interpretive frame that is diametrically opposed to our analysis and has gained wide currency among Western analysts and Eastern intellectuals who reflect on the development of post-communist polities is the so-called tabula rasa view of post-communist democracy. This view denies structured diversity and non-randomness in the articulation of post-communist regimes. It postulates that a host of conditions makes unlikely the creation of parties that engage in programmatic competition, represent and shape conflicts of interest in society, and coalesce with competing parties with the objective of bringing about effective political governance. Tabula rasa theorists put forth a number of arguments to support this expectation. First of all, communist societies are said to have left behind relatively homogeneous, leveled, egalitarian social structures that prevent social actors from formulating individual and collective economic interests. People do not know what their material interests in an evolving capitalist market economy might be, and even if they identify such interests, they do not know how to pursue them. An atomization of society (Schöpflin 1991b: 237) and a lack of social class relations (Ost 1993) undercut the constitution of group interests from the bottom of society up. At the same time, from the top of political elites down, imperatives of fiscal and monetary stabilization policies, imposed and enforced by the International Monetary Fund and a host of foreign country governments, lending institutions, and potential private investors, make it impossible for post-communist political elites to propose economic policy alternatives tailored to the demands of distinct domestic voter groups and to act on such packages when in government. Hence parties cannot credibly compete with alternative economic programs so that voters discount whatever appeals politicians make in electoral campaigns.

Second, tabula rasa theorists are skeptical about the speed at which citizens and politicians are able to learn to articulate interests and act upon them in the fluid environment of post-communist society because interests and interest associations, including parties, have to be constructed from scratch and the new polities face too many challenges at once. Post-communist democracies are often called upon to address the cumulative challenges of state building, nation building, political participation, and economic reform. They would do so with greater chances of success if they had strong vehicles of interest aggregation. But such vehicles are unlikely to emerge, because politicians and voters have feeble cognitive capacities for defining political interests and lack the skills and resources to create effective modes of group representation. Like painters facing an empty white canvas, politicians must build collective organizations in a tabula rasa environment. The only politicians who can rely on pre-existing interest groups and social movements are those affiliated with the successor organizations of the communist regime. The new constitutional system of political rules of the game, moreover, is not a fixed, exogenous, and unalterable framework that could guide the construction of vehicles of interest representation, but is endogenous to the process of political mobilization itself. The very same actors who make the rules are also supposed to compete under them and construct collective actors. This reflexivity of rules and actors yields highly unstable democratic polities, as actors attempt to rewrite the rules of the game whenever power relations change (Mair 1995).

Third, on the cultural level of citizens' beliefs and dispositions, the legacies of the communist system are said to have created orientations amounting to a "civilizational incompetence" that prevents people from participating in the democratic polity: political apathy, schematic friend/foe thinking, disregard for formal rules of conduct, and intense envy rather than the self-regarding pursuit of interests endanger the emergence of a democratic order built on the acceptance of formal constitutional stipulations, majority rule, as well as a respect for minority rights, and a spirit of tolerance for diversity and disagreement (cf. Sztompka 1991). This lack of "cultural capital" conducive to the construction of a civil society that buttresses a competitive polity is likely to endow people with only weak dispositions to participate in democratic party competition.

The political practice of communist rule contributes to a popular revulsion against political parties. In the aftermath of a communist party dictatorship, people turn away from anything that claims to be a political party in disgust and consider such forms of political involvement as remote constructs of intellectuals who cannot put their ears to the ground (Schöpflin 1991b: 239). The political vacuum created by the demise of communist rule may in fact revive fond memories of a happier pre-communist and usually authoritarian past and reinvigorate political practices that were distinctly anti-party and anti-democratic.[2]

---

[2]Rather than treating the pre-communist legacies as a source of diversity in the trajectory of post-communist politics, tabula rasa theorists tend to generalize in vague ways about East European countries' inter-war experiences. Thus Roskin (1993: 60) writes: "The nascent party systems of Central and Eastern Europe bear striking resemblance to those of the interwar years, almost as if the region had awakened in 1990 from a sleep of more than half a century. The earlier period was characterized by extreme fractionalization of the party system, difficulty in forming and maintaining coalitions, immoderate ideological infighting, and general chaos that

Tabula rasa theorists have claimed that since the inception of democratic competition in Eastern Europe in 1989–90, the evidence confirms the extraordinary difficulty to found stable parties and party systems in the post-communist environment.[3] Those organizations that register as parties are often no more than "sofa parties," all of whose members could easily fit into a single living room. Parties command only a tiny membership relative to the size of their electorates and develop few organized linkages to civic associations. Moreover, they have no track record that would permit voters to predict their conduct in the formation of government coalitions or the enactment of public policies. What is most confusing for voters, large crowds of political entrepreneurs found rival parties whose messages are vague and all but impossible to discern and compare. Ironically, the only parties that appear to have the organizational and ideological features enabling them to participate in a competitive democratic polity are the successors of the old communist parties and their allies.

The presence of organizationally and programmatically weak "framework" parties is said to have several consequences for the process of electoral competition and citizens' participation. First, party systems tend to be extremely fragmented and lack programmatic structuring, as political entrepreneurs in competing parties announce the same empty political formula but cannot relate it to operational policy alternatives. On a highly abstract ideological level, party systems may sometimes exhibit strong polarization, as politicians engage in a race to outbid the promises of their competitors with ever more outrageous claims to know the recipe for a restoration of social order, security, and wealth. But because they cannot relate these claims to operational policy programs, they fail to establish their credibility in the eyes of the voters. Second, these patterns of electoral competition contribute to a lack of voter identification with parties and a high level of confusion and disappointment with democratic politics, resulting in low voter turnout and a large proportion of the electorate unable to develop distinct party preferences. Third, fragmentation, polarization, and low voter identification and turnout produce high volatility in the electoral support of parties over time, as measured by the change of parties' voter support from the first "founding" democratic election to subsequent second and third legislative or presidential elections.[4] Electoral volatility demonstrates the absence of a close alignment of voters and parties and delays the consolidation of party alternatives.

Many of these alleged characteristics of East European party systems in the immediate aftermath of the old systems' collapse have also been diagnosed as typical of "founding elections" held after the departure of authoritarian rulers elsewhere in the world as well (O'Donnell and Schmitter 1986: 61–3). Because

ended in authoritarian rule."

[3]Within the sizable literature that emphasizes the problem of building parties in a post-communist societal and political vacuum, see especially Agh (1992, 1993, 1994, 1995a), Cirtautas (1993), Mair (1995), Rose (1995), and Wesołowski (1995).

[4]Mair (1995) and Rose (1995) find much higher volatility in the first East European pair of elections than in comparable elections in Western Europe or Southern Europe.

voters and political entrepreneurs have little democratic experience and face great uncertainties, party identification and party-group linkages usually play only a minor role in creating bonds of accountability and responsiveness between citizens and their representatives. And in post-communist polities that become democratic after many decades without party competition, the obstacles to a consolidation of party-led interest intermediation are likely to be particularly formidable.

In our study, we have empirically refuted many of the arguments that inspire tabula rasa interpretations of post-communist democracy. Social structure, for example, is far less leveled than such arguments presume and citizens' structural positions do help us to predict their policy preferences and – mediated by such preferences – their electoral choices among competing parties. Moreover, our analysis reveals striking patterns of political representation. What is probably most important, we have made sense of some important cross-national patterns of variance in the political divisions, modes of representation, and challenges of governance that come to the fore in a comparison of post-communist democracies. The tabula rasa view may permit the random variation of democratic experiences across the entire cohort of post-communist countries, but not the presence of systematically diverging patterns of democratic competition, as we have observed them in our four East Central European countries and, if we are correct, as they are likely to exist in many of the other post-communist polities as well.

Rather than rehashing points of our empirical evidence that unambiguously refute the tabula rasa interpretation of post-communist politics, let us focus on a number of observations that, at first sight, appear consistent with the tabula rasa view but inconsistent with our own perspective. These controversial pieces of evidence are (1) the high volatility of party support together with (2) an absence of mass membership parties and (3) the parties' lack of responsibility and responsiveness vis-à-vis their voters after elections.

Tabula rasa theories often see a causal linkage between these three phenomena. Voters and parties have little knowledge about each other, because they have failed to build mass organizations that institutionalize a solid citizen-party linkage. The absence of mass organizations, in turn, explains why incumbent politicians can easily abandon their pre-election promises and pursue unexpected policies after coming to office. Weak inter-temporal representation, in turn, accounts for the extreme volatility of party support from one election to the next in post-communist polities and thus ultimately for the unsettled, erratic character of democratic governance, which may give rise to an authoritarian relapse. With regard to each of these three observations and propositions, we will attempt to show that (1) the phenomena said to support tabula rasa theories are not uniformly distributed across post-communist democracies and that (2) tabula rasa theories overestimate the significance of the phenomena on which they focus for assessing the quality of the democratic experience in Eastern Europe. Even some durable Western democracies exhibit many of the features and attributes of party systems that are said to undermine democratic stability in the new Eastern democratic polities.

MASS MEMBERSHIP PARTIES

Parties in post-communist democracies attract few members relative to the size of their electorate. Member-voter ratios tend to be above .02 only for a few Christian democratic parties, such as the Czech KDU and the Hungarian KDNP, some peasant parties, such as the Polish PSL and the Hungarian FKGP, and those post-communist parties that have not thrown their old ideology overboard. Thus, in the mid-1990s the Czech and Bulgarian successor parties still had rather substantial member-voter ratios above .10, while their Hungarian and Polish counterparts had shrunk dramatically to extremely low member-voter ratios in spite of their electoral successes in 1993 and 1994.[5] Liberal-democratic parties everywhere have low voter-member ratios with the partial exception of the Czech ODS. Do such low membership enrollment figures signal a weakness of democratic allegiance that sets the new democracies apart from West European parliamentary democracies?

We would argue that mass party membership is no longer a critical feature that affects the quality of a democracy (cf. Katz 1990). The role party membership has played in the development of democracies must be put in historical perspective. In Western democracies most party members were never active participants in the political discourse of their parties but silent contributors of finance or labor for electoral campaigns. These instrumental activities have not become altogether irrelevant in contemporary democracies, but they are complemented and partially displaced by other resources (public party finance and private donations) and parties now advertise their positions primarily through the mass media. It may not be farfetched to claim that attentive voters today learn more about the parties from easily accessible media than most party members ever learned through membership and instrumental contributions in the first decades of this century. At the same time, the ratio of a party's voters to core activists who participate in the process of interest aggregation, strategic choice, and recruitment of leadership personnel in many parties may not be significantly different from what it was in the past.[6] If citizen-elite linkages involve voter participation in democratic politi-

[5]In Poland, the SdRP organizes about 60,000 to 65,000 members, about 2 percent of the party's voters. In Hungary, the MSzP membership is in the neighborhood of 30,000 to 40,000, also translating into a member-voter ratio of about .02.

[6]This does not rule out, of course, that parties and party families experience a rise and decline in the intensity of internal participation and debates responding to changes in societal cleavage mobilization and in their competitive positions. Thus, without a shadow of a doubt Northern European social democratic parties had more active participants in the aftermath of the social movements of the 1960s and 1970s than either in the first two post–World War II decades or since the middle of the 1980s.

cal deliberation, then the procedural quality of democracy may have hardly *suffered* with the decay of mass party organizations. The decline of mass parties, however, may have intensified the strategic challenges politicians face in their quest for votes and political office. When membership ceases to constitute the glue that binds citizens to parties, then party leaders can no longer take the support of large blocs of voters for granted. A larger share of the electorate becomes available for competing party appeals and forces politicians to remain responsive to new constituency demands.

Thus, substantial cross-national and inter-temporal variance in the party member-voter ratios of West European democracies may indicate differences in the quality of democracy, but not necessarily in terms of the level of public deliberation over policy alternatives. Furthermore, the proven durability of democracies with very different voter-member ratios undercuts the claim that democratic consolidation requires substantial proportions of the electorate to become party members. Today, some of the new East European democracies such as the Czech Republic, Hungary, and Poland, may have overall higher member-voter ratios than such established democracies as the Netherlands, Britain, France, or Denmark in the 1990s (cf. Plasser and Ulram 1992: 33). The absence of mass party membership in Eastern Europe, by itself, is not an indicator that the post-communist democracies lack relations of accountability and responsiveness, but may simply be a result of the fact that these democracies have come into existence in an era of "post-modern" politics. In this period, markets and polities continue to stratify people's access to wealth and power, but citizens' growing physical and cultural mobility, enhanced by decreasing costs of transportation and communication, lead to an individualization of social conduct that undercuts the organization of political discourses through large permanent collectivities.[7] In this environment, the remnants of encompassing mass-membership party organizations easily turn into political deadweight[8] when politicians must show strategic mobility to cope with citizens' dispositions to participate in loose, intermittent political causes and to craft new electoral coalitions in a more complicated political landscape, where parties, interest groups, and social movements pursue not closely connected but highly differentiated goals.[9] The absence of sunk costs in large membership organizations enables East European democracies to enjoy the "advantages of backwardness" and frees its politicians from devoting their energies to

[7] Not by accident, also the most "post-modern" cohorts of Western parties, particularly the left-libertarian parties, have refrained from building mass organizations.

[8] This applies particularly to mass membership organizations based on clientelist linkages. Such practices find little approval in societies whose citizens have comparatively high education and individualist orientation.

[9] In the West European mobilization of religious and class divisions up to the two world wars, for example, social movements, interest groups, and party building were often practically indistinguishable. Since that time, these modes of political interest intermediation have become increasingly independent from each other (cf. Hellemans 1990; Kitschelt 1993a).

fighting armies of party functionaries who attend to empty organizational shells devoid of substantive political relevance. It is thus reasonable to expect that framework or "cadre" parties rather than mass parties will dominate the East European arenas of party competition (cf. Lewis and Gortat 1995: 602).

PROBLEMS OF INTER-TEMPORAL REPRESENTATION

Tabula rasa theorists may claim that politicians in the new post-communist democracies appear to represent electoral constituency interests during political campaigns, but then ignore such commitments after having been elected to government office. This lack of parties' accountability to their voters generates citizens' cynicism about and defection from democracy, phenomena that manifest themselves in low party loyalty and declining voter turnout. In post-communist democracies parties cannot credibly diversify their programmatic stances because the economic imperatives of market liberalization compel whatever parties are voted into executive office to pursue more or less identical economic policies. Thus, while parties may engage in programmatic posturing *before* elections, they must abandon promises that conflict with indispensable reform trajectories *after* elections. As a consequence, the new democracies incur a problem of *inter-temporal representation*. The lack of differentiated class and sectoral interests in the electorate and the weak linkage between socio-economic groups and political parties encourages politicians to engage in opportunistic strategies.

The tabula rasa argument thus involves two interconnected claims. First, government policies in post-communist countries cannot vary on key economic and social policy issues. Second, where politicians promise policies that diverge from the imperatives of economic liberalization they fall victim to problems of inter-temporal representation and have to abandon their campaign commitments.

A comparison of post-communist government policies requires another book, but empirical evidence suggests that economic stabilization policies and privatization strategies vary substantially both across countries and over time between governments characterized by different partisan stripes and coalitional composition (cf. Aslund et al., 1996; Fish 1998; Hellman 1998). Looking closer at our four countries, two of them approximate a model of responsible party government in economic policy making (Bulgaria, Czech Republic), whereas the other two show more continuity across governments of different partisan composition (Hungary and Poland). Communist regime legacies and democratic institutions explain where economics becomes a competitive dimension on which politicians differentiate their electoral appeals. By extension, it is countries where economics is the dominant competitive dimension that show the greatest propensity toward responsible party government.

In the Czech Republic, market liberals have pursued a strategy of responsible party government that overstates underlying variations in the preferences of partisan electoral constituencies (chapter 9), although some enacted policies have made concessions to social-protectionist demands.[10] In Bulgaria, government economic policies have flip-flopped with the partisan stripes of the incumbents from social-protectionist to market-liberal policies in 1992, back to social-protectionism in 1993 and particularly after the BSP victory in 1994, and then again forward to market-liberal reform in 1997. These policies were similar only with regard to their ineffectiveness in turning around the Bulgarian economy. At the other extreme, in Hungary, after national-accommodative communism and a negotiated transition, partisan stripes are less visible in the governments' conduct of economic policy, although the picture is far from unambiguous. The first non-communist government pursued a middle-of-the-road economic policy of gradual liberalization quite consistent with its campaign commitments. The socialist-liberal government in the second electoral term consisted of two parties with rather conflicting economic policy programs. Government policy practically tilted toward the campaign promises of the liberal coalition partner, particularly when the government adopted a decisively market-liberal reform policy about one year into the electoral term. Even in the 1994 campaign, however, the Hungarian socialists expressed social protectionist appeals only in a rather muted fashion and underlined their firm commitment to market liberalization. Moreover, with only a third of the vote, but an absolute majority of the parliamentary seats, socialist politicians found it too risky for their own future electoral prospects to act on the social-protectionist hopes of many voters in their electoral constituency.

Also in Poland, a history of national-accommodative communism and a negotiated transition provide the backdrop against which the gravitation of government parties toward economic reform policies and thus the effective dilution of responsible party government must be interpreted. After 1993, the new government led by post-communist and peasant parties continued basic market-oriented economic policies that had been adopted since 1989 by various Solidarność governments under Finance Minister Balcerowicz. Nevertheless, the socialist-agrarian coalition acted on campaign promises to improve pensions and maintain social services. Furthermore, it embarked only quite slowly on a program of further privatizing state companies and exposing agriculture to market competition. In the 1997 electoral campaign, it was precisely the government parties' reluctance to push economic reform and thus their willingness to abide by their voters' preferences that the market-liberal opposition party, led by economic reformer Leszek Balcerowicz, criticized throughout the campaign.

Even in Hungary where the governing socialists, but not their liberal coali-

---

[10]The lack of financial sector privatization and of an effective enforcement of bankruptcy laws against loss-making industrial enterprises is a case in point. At the same time, the crisis of the Czech financial sector in 1996–97 is a consequence of extreme underregulation of financial institutions, such as investment funds, and thus an example for a highly ideological market-liberal policy.

tion partner, appear to have abandoned pre-election commitments on economic and social policy, the problem of inter-temporal representation involves a further complication. Politicians and voters may consider the *instruments* or the *outcomes* of policy making, when they evaluate inter-temporal representation. If voters are outcome-oriented and assess governments at the time of reelection, responsive politicians may well find it consistent with the imperative of democratic constituency representation to abandon policy instruments they deem to be unsuitable to reach the long-term outcomes desired by their voters, *even if* their campaign promises initially endorsed such instruments. Consistent with a trusteeship conception of representation, politicians may inflict temporary pain on their own electoral constituencies in the hope that bitter economic medicine may benefit their voters eventually and thus their own reelection chances before they face the next election.[11]

In light of these complications, it would be misleading to claim that post-communist governments cannot and will not pursue partisan-oriented economic policies or that a particularly wide gap between promises and actual policies undercuts political representation in the new East European democracies. Government popularity and perception of its voter representativeness depends on a variety of factors. Economic performance affects governments' reelection chances in post-communist democracies just as in the West (Pacek 1994). Voters' cynicism about their own personal effectiveness in influencing politics is high in East Central Europe, but not higher than in many West European democracies such as Austria or Germany.[12] At the same time, mass support for multi-party democracy, and thus a belief in the capacity of democratic regimes to forge a representative linkage, is high in Central European post-communist countries, medium high in Southeastern Europe, and generally more precarious in the successor states of the former Soviet Union (cf. Rose and Haerpfer 1994; Wessels and Klingemann 1994; Wyman et al. 1995). Legacies of communist rule, the nature of the new non-communist political forces, the vigor of economic reform, and the results of such reforms are interdependent factors that shape the mass public's views of democracy. But it is certainly not some uniform problem of inter-temporal representation that impedes the democratic political process and the public perception of the legitimacy of democracy in post-communist countries.

[11]For an initial exploration of the extent to which voters are sufficiently sophisticated to understand problems of inter-temporal representation, compare Stokes (1996) and Przeworski (1996). Even if voters do not understand the logic of trusteeship and abandon governments when they enact unpopular measures, as evidenced by opinion polls, economic improvements at the time of reelection still may help the incumbents. The reelection of several Latin American presidents in the early 1990s (Menem, Fujimori) shows this process at work.

[12]This, at least, is Plasser and Ulram's (1992) result early on in the East Central European countries' experience with democracy. For similar findings, see Tóka (1995: table 11). There is little doubt that satisfaction with democratic institutions is likely to vary more with economic performance in the new democracies than in established Western democracies.

ELECTORAL VOLATILITY

Observers have interpreted Eastern Europe as a democratic tabula rasa because elections in the region exhibit very high electoral volatility, as measured by the net percentage of voters who change their party preference from one election to the next (Mair 1995). High volatility is said to indicate fluid, unstructured relations between parties and electorates that defy linkages of accountability and responsiveness between citizens and politicians. Compared with that in Western Europe (Bartolini and Mair 1990), volatility has been extraordinarily high indeed in post-communist polities. The electorate appears free-floating and "available" to just about any party contender. Before we jump to such conclusions, however, it is important to explore different patterns and causes of volatility.

Following Bartolini and Mair (1990), we should distinguish between volatility *within* blocs of parties that have similar programmatic appeals and volatility *across* party blocs. Furthermore, volatility may occur among *"established" parties* with a track record of legislative presence or *between established and new parties*. Finally, it is important to track trends of electoral volatility from founding elections through subsequent elections. Volatility generates the most chaotic dynamic of party systems where a large proportion of voters moves *across* blocs and *between* established and new parties ("deep volatility"), particularly if this volatility does not subside over time. In this pattern, the electorate is indeed available to a wide range of appeals and does not engage in structured relations to parties. But deep volatility rarely is the prevailing pattern in Eastern Europe and certainly not among the four countries we have examined in this study.

In the Czech Republic, as the most structured party system in our comparison group, electoral volatility from 1992 to 1996 almost exclusively occurred *within* the "leftist" bloc *among* established parties. Also in Poland, much of the electoral volatility in 1991–93 took place within the three major party blocs – the leftist, the liberal, and the Christian-national sector. The same applies to the 1995 presidential and the 1997 legislative elections. The leftist bloc remains by and large stable and experiences relatively little internal volatility. Much of the overall high volatility in these two elections is accounted for by the internal instability of the Christian-national bloc that may have been papered over only temporarily by the success of the AWS in the 1997 legislative election.

Whereas in Poland volatility tends to be intra-bloc but across new parties, in Hungary from 1990 to 1994 volatility primarily occurred between blocs but *among established parties*. In the comparison of the Hungarian elections of 1994 and 1998, the left bloc remains relatively stable, while much of the volatility occurs within the Christian-national camp, now under the leadership of a former liberal party, Fidesz-Hungarian Civic Party.

The only country in which rising electoral volatility suggests a rather highly available electorate across blocs and possibly among new parties is Bulgaria. Here total electoral volatility increased from the 1991–94 elections to the 1994–97 elections. Moreover, a large share of the volatility is across blocs, not just intra-bloc. Whether it also involves new parties is harder to say, given the umbrella character of the anti-communist forces in Bulgarian politics. Whereas the Central European countries show an institutionalization of the party alternatives around five or six durable contenders, Bulgaria exhibits more tenuous and fleeting parties and alliances even in the late 1990s. At least in the three East Central European countries, electoral volatility therefore tends to be "shallow" rather than "deep." Greater depth of volatility and thus less institutionalization of party alternatives appears to be mostly a problem of former patrimonial communist regimes, particularly in those polities that emerge from the former Soviet Union (e.g., Russia or Ukraine).

Finally, any interpretation of the extraordinary levels of electoral volatility in the early years of post-communist democracy must take into account the profound economic crisis with which ordinary citizens in these countries had to cope. Compared with crises in Eastern Europe, in Western Europe the changes in economic performance that create the common swings associated with retrospective economic voting are extremely mild. Moreover, retrospective economic voting varies across time periods, countries, and governments' coalitional configurations (cf. Lewis-Beck 1988; Anderson 1995). Only as a counter-factual can we imagine the level of electoral volatility Western entrenched party systems might face if they suffered through declines of income and surges of unemployment equivalent to those in Eastern Europe after 1989. Alternatively, we can compare East European electoral volatility with that experienced by Western countries during the Great Depression after 1929. Such counter-factual reasoning and historical comparison suggests that in many post-communist democracies electoral volatility is not unexpectedly high and might also occur in democracies that have existed for long periods of time, if they were only exposed to the socioeconomic stress and dislocation encountered by post-communist polities in their first decade of democracy.

EAST CENTRAL EUROPEAN PARTY COMPETITION AND WESTERN EUROPEAN COUNTER-PARTS

There is no question that East European democracies are undergoing a process of learning, both on the part of politicians as well as that of voters. This process takes place within a rather tumultuous environment of far-reaching macro-economic stabilization and micro-economic institutional reform policies, including a fundamental transfer of property rights. In some cases, the exigencies of state and nation building further increase the complexity of policy making. It is not surprising that the uncertainties generated by these processes give rise to some false starts and trial-and-error politics. Amazingly, these conditions in many instances do not lead to a picture of party competition that is consistent with the tabula rasa interpretation. Particularly the East Central European countries we have analyzed in this book appear to develop post-communist party systems with a limited set of permanent players who have rather well-understood appeals and reputations. The actual electoral strength of parties then depends on the interaction between government status and economic performance, together with the politicians' ability to fine-tune their parties' appeals within the one- or two-dimensional competitive issue spaces monitored by a segment of rather sophisticated and attentive electoral constituencies.

From this perspective, many features of the East European party systems resemble attributes of established Western democracies. First, democratic competition takes place within a low-dimensionality space. Second, the basic policy alternatives expressed on the most salient competitive dimensions are rather similar to those in Western democracies. They involve issues of income distribution and economic governance structures or socio-cultural issues dealing with the authority of the collective or individual autonomy to choose life-styles and social affiliates. Two attributes of the party systems, however, set East Central and Western European democracies apart: first, the concrete issues voters and politicians map on these dimensions and, second, the way politicians combine positions on the two dimensions in their political appeals. Whereas in Western Europe in the 1980s and 1990s economic social protectionism typically goes with libertarian political-cultural positions, the relationship between the two dimensions is less determinate in Eastern Europe where it varies cross-nationally. In democracies succeeding bureaucratic-authoritarian or patrimonial communism, the overriding competitive dimension tends to combine economic market liberalism with socio-cultural libertarian individualism at one pole, and social protectionism with traditional collectivism, if not authoritarianism, at the other pole. In these countries, we encounter a single dominant division or mutually reinforcing divisions feeding into the same competitive dimension. In the two democracies emerging from national-accommodative communism, the economic and the political-cultural issue divides generate crosscutting competitive dimensions that constitute three of four competing camps of political parties.

As in Western Europe, voters' socio-demographic position in society influences their ideological outlook in ways systematically related to their material economic self-interests. At the same time, socio-demographic positions influence voters' electoral choice only indirectly, because they are mediated by their issue positions. A similar trend can be observed in advanced industrial democracies, where social structure has a declining independent influence on electoral choice. But whereas in Western Europe the increasing importance of voters' issue positions for their electoral choice results from an erosion of affective party identifications and cultural milieu-based subconscious commitments to a party, in Eastern Europe issue positions count because voter identifications and party-affiliated socio-cultural milieus had rather little chance to emerge.

Also with regard to modes of representation and patterns of governance, the post-communist experience discussed in this book does not strike us as completely foreign to what participants in Western democracies may have encountered. Also in Western democracies, politicians may engage in relations of *polarizing trustee-*

ship, going beyond the preferences of their electorates for policy reform, as exemplified by politicians from Margaret Thatcher to Helmut Kohl. Government formation and stability in both Western and Eastern democracies build to a large exent on the programmatic compatibility of the coalition partners. Of course, the particular complications that result from the recent regime transition in Eastern Europe constitute unique features of post-communist coalition politics, but equivalents probably could be studied in the conduct of parties after democratic transitions in Southern Europe.

Overall, we find a great deal of structure and only limited randomness in the patterns of representation and governance of East Central European countries. The democratic process evolves not primarily according to chance or pure trial-and-error variation, but according to intelligible patterns of action chosen by rationally deliberating politicians and by voters, many of whom have a rather firm understanding of their preferences and how to map them onto the menu of party alternatives. We interpret our findings as powerful evidence suggesting that political reasoning and conscious deliberation play a significant role both for the strategic conduct of political elites as well as for the preferences and choices of significant segments of East European mass publics.

DEMOCRATIC PROCESS AND POLITICAL ECONOMIC PERFORMANCE: A CRITICAL RESEARCH FRONTIER

Our study has analyzed process features of the emerging East Central European democracies at a rather early stage in their development, less than five years after the collapse of communist rule. By the mid-1990s, in all four countries, the relevant political forces consider political democracy as the "only game in town." No party, movement, or state institution, such as the military, has seriously proposed a non-democratic governance structure to replace democracy. While these East Central European democracies have thus consolidated their support base in a very short period of time, citizens experience qualitatively different policy processes in each of the four democracies. Whereas Hungary, and to some extent Poland, develop a *consensual democracy with centripetal competition* around key issues of economic policy making but highly polarizing inter-party competition around socio-cultural issues, the Czech Republic produces a more *competitive democracy* with significant party divisions over economics but also incentives for parties to collaborate and form coalitions that moderate the government output of enacted policies. Bulgaria, finally, is caught up in a process of creating a more polarized, centrifugal polity with sharply antagonistic but internally diffuse party camps that clash over mutually reinforcing issues of socio-economic reform, the regime divide, and socio-cultural arrangements.

The main task of our study has been to describe and explain these democratic process features. While the procedural quality of democracy is an intrinsically important topic of comparative analysis, political science may be ultimately interested in the *consequences* such features have for the subjective sense of well-being and the material life chances of their citizens. On the one hand, democratic procedures themselves may instill a greater or lesser sense of satisfaction with the political order in the population. Endorsement of the political order, in turn, may affect people's life satisfaction more broadly conceived at least in a modest way. On the other hand, citizens' satisfaction with democracy depends on the *outputs* and *outcomes* of the political process – the production of individual and collective goods and the (re)distribution of power and wealth in society. This linkage directs political scientists to explore how democratic process features shape the ways in which polities allocate scarce resources, produce new wealth, confer power, and thus affect popular perceptions of the legitimacy of the core institutions of social order.

It is beyond the scope of our current study and maybe even too soon after the collapse of communist regimes to address these big questions of empirical democratic theory with respect to the performance of East European democracies. Nevertheless, our study provides conceptual tools and systematic descriptions that should enable future research, preferably based on a more comprehensive set of post-communist countries, to probe into the linkages between the organization and perception of democratic processes and the political-economic effectiveness as well as the normative justification of the political order. Let us therefore devote the final paragraphs of our study to a few speculations about the interaction between processes and performance in post-communist polities. Even if our hypotheses turn out to be wrong, they illustrate the kinds of research questions we deem fruitful to pursue in the future.

At this time, it is empirically controversial whether basic political freedoms and democratic governance boost economic growth when compared with the economic capacity of authoritarian regimes.[13] Not all democratic polities incorporate institutions and power alignments conducive to the enactment of public policies that secure property rights, produce collective goods, and thus encourage private citizens to make long-term investments likely to result in economic growth and a broad-based improvement of the quality of life. Nevertheless, the experience of the four East Central European democracies gives us some confidence in the proposition that the regime form of the communist past, mediated through current institutions, procedures, and alignments in the new democratic polities, do affect the performance of post-communist regimes in instrumental economic as well as symbolic cultural respects. Among the three legacies and communist regime types we have distinguished, formerly patrimonial communist rule offers the least promise to deliver strong democratic performance. It tends to

---

[13]For a review of the burgeoning literature on this topic and an empirical analysis that finds no independent effect of democratic regimes on economic growth, see Davis and Wu (1996).

produce feeble, internally divided liberal-democratic forces, a landscape of pro-grammatically diffuse political parties, and a deep regime divide between former agents and antagonists of the old communist system. These features tend to undercut the performance of the emerging democratic polities both in terms of popular legitimacy as well as political-economic effectiveness. In our four-country comparison, these attributes characterize the Bulgarian case, but we expect simi-lar conditions to hold in other post-patrimonial communist polities. Weak liberal-democratic forces make it difficult to enact a consistent and comprehensive package of political-economic reforms. Where liberals control government power, they may lack the skills, competence, and organizational networks to bring about reform effectively and displace the old rent-seeking elites. Indecisive incremental-ism, in turn, may give reform a bad name altogether and may drive many citizens back to a defense of the status quo rather than a radicalization of the reform process. When communist successor parties come back to power, they may abide by democratic rules, but exploit their control of the policy process to (re)build clientelist networks and to funnel public assets into the hands of rent-seeking groups affiliated with the party. As Hellman (1998) has argued persuasively, partial economic reform creates anti-reform constituencies not only among the losers of the reform process, but also among the winners who try to lock in their gains through institutions that perpetuate their rent-seeking activities and block further liberalization. This halfway house of reform is most likely where pa-trimonial communist parties remain powerful political actors that can channel reform such as to benefit the old elite stratum of communist regimes.

A deep regime divide complicates conditions of effective political gover-nance, thus further reducing the chances of decisive reform because even those politicians who share economic policy objectives may fall out over ways to right the wrongs of the past (chapter 10). Moreover, where the regime divide orients politicians toward revenge and retribution, they tend to regard economic policy making as a zero-sum game over the allocation of existing wealth, rather than as an effort to design novel institutions that maximize the production of new wealth, regardless of how those who held most of the assets under communist rule may be faring under the terms of the new practices. Concerns with redistribution tend to serve rent-seeking groups that invoke the past to appropriate current resources.

Threats to democratic legitimacy and effectiveness intensify in formerly pa-trimonial communist countries, if politicians find it advantageous to construct competitive dimensions that combine multiple reinforcing political-economic and socio-cultural divides. This is particularly likely where politicians invoke questions of collective national autonomy or ethno-cultural relations within the arena of party competition. Ethno-cultural politics increases the chances that policy making evolves into zero-sum games among rent-seeking groups (cf. Horowitz 1985).

Democratic polities emerging from patrimonial communism may attempt to sidestep some of these problems by building voter-elite linkages based not on programmatic appeals but on clientelist electoral relations. In principle, clientelist democracies may constitute an equilibrium, but we are skeptical that any of the post-communist countries meet the pre-conditions it takes to entrench a clientelist system of elite-voter relations for very long periods of time. Clientelist politics works best where poverty and low education depress the level of political mobilization and where the domestic economy is protected from external competitive forces that make rent-seeking politics costly. Clientelist polities tend not to produce the collective goods (education, health care, infrastructure) that improve the productivity and competitiveness of domestic industries. As a consequence, those post-communist countries that lock in clientelist politics will find themselves at a progressively greater disadvantage vis-à-vis competitors that embrace different institutional arrangements.

Compared with former patrimonial communist countries, democracies emerging from bureaucratic-authoritarian or national-accommodative communism grow out of settings that promote stronger liberal-democratic forces, greater programmatic structuring of parties, and a weaker crystallization of political passions around the regime divide. Furthermore, salient socio-cultural divides have greater chances to cross-cut rather than reinforce economic group conflict or to be sidelined altogether. In such settings, politicians and their constituencies express not only greater propensities to pursue political economic reform, but they are also more likely to develop cooperative dispositions that facilitate effective governance.

Advocates of liberal democratic reform in formerly patrimonial communist regimes have sometimes argued that their only chance to overcome the weakness of public support for liberalism and the disorganization of liberal-democratic parties is to ensure that a reformer is elected to the presidential office and manages to endow it with far-reaching executive and legislative powers that can undercut societal and political veto groups. But an extremely powerful presidency that can block, if not overrule, legislative action is a two-edged sword. No one can guarantee that the officeholder will back liberal-democratic reforms for a time period sufficiently long to make them irreversible. The semi-dictatorial powers of the presidency may too soon revert to a protagonist of the political economic status quo. Moreover, the very institutional arrangement of a strong presidency may give incentives to the incumbent to weaken the cohesiveness of political parties, including those of the liberal-democratic camp, and to govern with the aid of personal clientelist networks. Such arrangements may fuel popular cynicism and disaffection with the legitimacy of democratic governance structures and may undercut the operational efficiency of economic reform.

It goes without saying that the empirical evidence about the dynamic of East Central European party systems we have assembled in this book cannot bear out the speculations we have offered in the preceding paragraphs. Comparisons of democratic performance require information on long periods of time in which features of the policy process and its outputs can be tracked. Moreover, such studies must include a wider variation in the institutional arrangements of democratic politics than we have incorporated in our current study. In the not too distant future, however, a longer performance record of post-communist democracies and more information about their democratic procedures will make it an attractive research project to explore the linkage between the procedural quality of party systems and democratic institutions, on the one hand, and the economic and political-cultural performance of the new post-communist polities, on the other.

APPENDIX I

LIST OF POLITICAL PARTIES
AND ELECTORAL ALLIANCES

BULGARIA

BBB	Balgarski Buzines Blok	Bulgarian Business Bloc
BSDP	Balgarska Socialdemokraticeska Partija	Bulgarian Social Democratic Party
BSP	Balgarska Socialisticeska Partija	Bulgarian Socialist Party
BZNS	Balgaski Zemedelski Naroden Sajuz	Bulgarian Agrarian National Union
DPS	Dvizenije sa Pravata i Svobodite na Turzite	Movement of Rights and Freedom of the Turkish Minority
SDS	Sajuz na Demokraticeski Sili	Union of Democratic Forces

CZECH REPUBLIC

ČMSS	Českomoravska strana středu	Czech-Moravian Center Party
ČSSD	Česka strana socialně demokraticka	Czech Social Democratic Party
HSD-SMS	Hnuti za samospravnou demokracii – Sdružení pro Moravu a Slezsko	Movement for Democratic Self-Governance/Moravian and Silesian Association (later CMSS)
KDS	Křest'anská-demokratická strana	Christian-Democratic Party
KDU-ČSL	Křest'anská-demokratická strana – Československá strana lidová	Christian Democratic Union – Czech People's Party

KSČM	Kommunstická strana Čech a Moravy	Communist Party of Bohemia and Moravia
LB	Levý Blok	Left Bloc
LSU	Liberálné sociální unie	Liberal Social Union
ODA	Občanská demokratická aliance	Civic Democratic Alliance
ODS	Občanská demokratická strana	Civic Democratic Party
OF	Občanské forum	Civic Forum
OH	Občanské hnuti	Civic Movement
SD	Svobodní demokraté	Free Democrats
SPR-RSČ	Sdruženi pro republiku – Republikánská strany Čzeske republiky	Colition for the Republic – Republican Party of the Czech Republic

HUNGARY

Fidesz	Fiatál Demokraták Szövetsége	Alliance of Young Democrats
FKGP	Független Kisgazda-, Földmunkás-és Polgári Párt	Independent Smallholders Party
KDNP	Kereszténydemokrata Néppárt	Christian Democratic People's Party
MDF	Magyar Demokrata Fórum	Hungarian Democratic Forum
MIEP	Magyar Igazság es Élet Pártja	Party of Hungarian Justice and Life
MSZMP	Magyar Szocialista Munkáspárt	Hungarian Socialist Workers' Party
MSZP	Magyar Szocialisa Párt	Hungarian Socialist Party
SZDSZ	Szabad Demokraták Szövetségé	Alliance of Free Democrats

POLAND

AW	Akcja Wyborcza "Solidarność"	Electoral Action "Solidarity"
BBWR	Bezpartyjny Blok Wspierania Reform	Non-Party Bloc to Support Reforms
KLD	Kongres Liberalno-Demokratyczny	Liberal Democratic Congress
KPN	Konfederacja Polski Niepodleglej	Confederation of Independent Poland
OKP	Obywatelski Klub Parlamen-tarny	Parliamentary Citizens' Club (Solidarity Parliamentary Caucus 1989)
OPZZ	Ogólnopolskie Porozumienie Związków Zawodowych	National Trade Union Alliance

PC	Porozumienie Centrum	Center Alliance
PSL	Polskie Stronnictwo Ludowe	Polish Peasant Party
ROP	Ruch dla Rzeczypospolitej	Movement for the Republic of Poland
'S'	Solidarność	Solidarity
SdRP	Socjaldemokracja Rzeczypospolitej Polskiej	Social Democracy of the Republic of Poland
SLD	Sojusz Lewicy Demokratycznej	Alliance of the Democratic Left
UD	Unia Demokratyczna	Democratic Union
UP	Unia Pracy	Union of Labor
UW	Unia Wolności	Freedom Union
ZCHN	Zjednoczenie Chrześcijańsko-Narodowe	Christian National Union

APPENDIX II

QUESTIONNAIRE FOR THE ELITE STUDY

We provide here the Polish version of the questionnaire on the basic questions covered in all four national surveys. The Czech and Hungarian versions differ in slight nuances on the core questions and have additional questions listed below. The Bulgarian questionnaire does not have questions 6 and 8, but substitutes questions on the use of Turkish language in Bulgarian school instruction, the defense of the Orthodox Church against proselytizing religions, and foreign relations with Turkey.

The format of the questions and the response options given to the interviewees is identical in all four surveys.

QUESTIONNAIRE: POLISH POLITICIANS

Rer resentatives of all relevant Polish parties have been asked to respond to this questionnaire. In a similar vein, a panel of Polish political scientists has been assembled to provide their expert judgments on the parties' voter appeals and organizational development. The identity of the respondents to this questionnaire will be held confidential and the information will be used for scientific purposes only.

I. YOUR POLITICAL OFFICE

1. What is your current party membership?
2. What political offices in party and elected assemblies do you presently hold?
3. Where is your local party organization? (city, county)

II. YOUR OWN PARTY'S VOTER APPEAL AND YOUR COMPETITORS

On the following pages, you will find twenty-one issues on which parties in the new East Central European democracies may take different positions. For each objective, please complete the following three tasks: (1) indicate whether the issue is important for your own party; (2) indicate where your party's position is on this issue; and (3) indicate your political competitors' position on the issue, compared with your own party's.

To indicate how important an issue is, use the following scale throughout:

Not important   1 – 2 – 3 – 4 – 5   Very important

To indicate your party's position and your political competitors' position, use the following scale throughout:

Democratic Union	1 2 3 4 5 6 7 8 9 10 11 12 13 14 15 16 17 18 19 20
Democratic Left Alliance	1 2 3 4 5 6 7 8 9 10 11 12 13 14 15 16 17 18 19 20
Polish Peasants' Party	1 2 3 4 5 6 7 8 9 10 11 12 13 14 15 16 17 18 19 20
Non-Party Bloc to Support Reform	1 2 3 4 5 6 7 8 9 10 11 12 13 14 15 16 17 18 19 20
Confederation for an Independent Poland	1 2 3 4 5 6 7 8 9 10 11 12 13 14 15 16 17 18 19 20
Fatherland Catholic Coalition	1 2 3 4 5 6 7 8 9 10 11 12 13 14 15 16 17 18 19 20
Union of Labor	1 2 3 4 5 6 7 8 9 10 11 12 13 14 15 16 17 18 19 20
Liberal Democratic Congress	1 2 3 4 5 6 7 8 9 10 11 12 13 14 15 16 17 18 19 20
Center Alliance	1 2 3 4 5 6 7 8 9 10 11 12 13 14 15 16 17 18 19 20
Solidarity	1 2 3 4 5 6 7 8 9 10 11 12 13 14 15 16 17 18 19 20

1. Social Policy and Health Insurance
Some politicians believe that social policy should not protect citizens from all risks, but that citizens must be self-reliant to a certain extent and take responsibility for some risks. For example, citizens should participate in the costs of health care by covering a substantial share of medical expenses out of their own pockets or through voluntary private insurance. *Other politicians* declare that it is the obligation of social policy to protect citizens from social risks in a comprehensive way and not force them to look out for themselves. For example, most health expenses should be covered by a public insurance system.

How important is social policy legislation for your party?

Please characterize the position of all of the following parties on the issue of social policy legislation:

No comprehensive risk protection through social policy:
citizens should pay a signifi-   Comprehensive risk protection
cant share of health care ex-   through social policy: public
penses   insurance should cover most
                                                                of citizens' health care expen-
                                                                diture

2. Management of the Economy

Some politicians argue that most businesses and factories should be run by private entrepreneurs to improve the efficiency of the Polish economy. No efforts should be made to save state firms that are economically not viable and they should be allowed to go bankrupt. *Other politicians* advocate that many state companies that are presently not economically viable should stay in public hands, receive state subsidies, and be modernized through industrial policy.

How important is the question of comprehensive privatization of state companies for your party?

Please characterize the position of all of the following parties on the question of privatizing the remaining state-owned businesses and factories.

                                                                A substantial number of busi-
Most businesses should be pri-   nesses should stay in the
vate; non-viable state com-   hands of the state; modernize
panies should go bankrupt   them before decision on sell-
                                                                off

3. Strategy of Privatization

Some politicians argue that, consistent with liberal market economics, the over-riding goal of privatizing state companies should be the economic efficiency and speed of transferring property into the private sector. The privatization process should not be needlessly burdened and slowed down with political considerations. *Other politicians* retort that also social and political principles of justice must be considered in the privatization process. Property cannot just be handed over to the strongest and most efficient claimants, but the fair distribution of property to all employees and citizens or the political loyalty of the new owners to the new democratic regime must be taken into account.

How important is the debate about liberal market and political criteria of privatizing state enterprises for your party?

Please characterize the position of all of the following parties on the choice of criteria for the privatization of state enterprises.

Priority for social and political principles of justice in the creation of private ownership rights Priority for economic criteria of speed and efficiency in the choice of new private owners

4. Fighting Inflation versus Fighting Unemployment

Some politicians believe that Polish economic policy should put priority on the fight against inflation. It should therefore pursue high real interest rates and deep budget cuts, even if such measures increase unemployment and poverty temporarily. For these politicians, monetary stability is a pre-condition of economic growth in the long run. *Other politicians* believe that Poland now has to fight high unemployment and poverty as its highest economic policy priority. Investments in industry must be increased, even if this accelerates inflation temporarily. Once industrial production is rising, it will be less painful to fight inflation.

How important is the question of economic policy priorities for your party?

Please characterize the position of the following parties on the issue of economic policy priorities.

Priority for fighting inflation now and reducing unemployment later Priority for fighting unemployment now and reducing inflation later

5. Foreign Capital in the Polish Economy

Some politicians sense that there is too much foreign capital, and especially German capital, coming into the Polish economy. This is said to create a dependency of the Polish economy on foreign owners and their economies. *Other politicians* suggest that it does not matter where capital is coming from as long as it provides productive investments in the Polish economy.

How important is the question of international capital inflows and ownership in the Polish Republic for your party?

Please characterize the position of the following parties on the question of international capital inflows and ownership in the Polish Republic.

It is irrelevant where capital is coming from, as long as it stimulates investments, production, and job growth There is too much foreign capital inflow that may make the Polish economy dependent and thus vulnerable to foreign interests

6. Income Taxation

Some politicians advocate the introduction and enforcement of progressive income taxes so that people with higher incomes pay higher tax rates. By having the affluent pay more for government services through taxation than the less well-off, government would contribute to an equalization of living conditions. *Other politicians* argue that progressive income taxes would dampen the incentive to create wealth and are counter-productive to economic growth. The less well-off should seek a greater equalization of living conditions through hard work, not through government redistribution based on progressive taxation.

How important is the question of income taxation for your party?

Please characterize the position of the following parties on the question of progressive income taxation.

For progressive income taxation: needed for income redistribution toward the less
well-off

Against progressive income
taxation: undermines incentives to create wealth and the
work ethic of the poor

7. *Controlling the Flow of Asylum Seekers (Czech Republic, Hungary, and Poland only)*

Some politicians charge that Poland is in danger of being flooded by political asylum seekers who are really economic refugees, particularly from regions of the former Soviet Union and from Romania, and that tight immigration and asylum laws are justified. Others argue that the problem has been vastly blown out of proportion and that Poland should opt for less restrictive laws regulating immigration and the right to political asylum.

How important is the question of political asylum and immigration laws for your party?

Please characterize the position of the following parties on the question of asylum and immigration laws.

Asylum and immigration laws
should be restrictive because
immigrants are a social problem now

Asylum and immigration laws
should be less restrictive because immigrants are not a social problem now

8. *Women in the Labor Market and Public Child Care Facilities*

Some politicians argue that it is a priority of social policy to provide public child care facilities so that young mothers are able to go back to work and earn money. *Other politicians* retort that mothers should attend to their young children at home rather than be employed outside the house and that other social policies should have priority than child care facilities.

How important is the question of women with children in the labor market for your party?

Please characterize the position of the following parties on the question of women with children in the labor market.

Public child care deserves high priority; young mothers should be able to go to work		Other social policies deserve more priority than public child care; young mothers should stay home

9. Women's Rights to Abortion (Czech Republic, Hungary, and Poland only)

Some politicians maintain that abortion is immoral and criminal, because it amounts to murder of a human being. Hence the state should ban all forms of abortion. *Other politicians* argue that it is the sole moral responsibility and right of pregnant women to decide whether to bear a child or not.

How important is the question of abortion policy for your party?

Please characterize the position of the following parties on the question of abortion.

State should outlaw abortion as a crime		Pregnant women should decide themselves on the morality of abortion

10. Role of the Church in Public Education (Czech Republic, Hungary, and Poland only)

Some politicians think that religion has to provide the new moral guidelines for post-communist Poland. It is therefore the state's responsibility to promote religious faith and to grant the church significant influence over the content of public school education. *Other politicians* argue that religion is a private affair and that it is not the state's obligation to promote religion. Therefore the church should not enjoy significant influence over the content of public school education.

How important is the question of the church's role in schools for your party?

Please characterize the position of the following parties on the question of the church's role in school.

The church provides the post-communist ethic and should play a critical role in public education		The church is a private organizations and should not play a significant role in public school education

10a. Protection of the Orthodox Church (Bulgaria only)
Some politicians think that the state should exercise its influence and forbid the entrance of foreign sects into the Bulgarian religious space. *Other politicians* think that religious beliefs are a personal matter and state institutions should not deal with limiting the influence of particular sects.

How important is the question of protection of Bulgarian religion for your party?

Please characterize the position of the following parties on the question of the protection of Bulgarian religion.

| Foreign sects should be per- | | The entrance of foreign sects |
| mitted access | ←——→ | should be prohibited. |

11. Assistance to Agriculture
Some politicians call for subsidies to family farms or for agricultural tariffs protecting their survival from cheap subsidized competition by the members of the European Community and other states. *Other politicians* believe that tariffs and subsidies are counter-productive for the economic health of Polish agriculture and should not be introduced.

How important is the question of agricultural subsidies/tariffs for your party?

Please characterize the position of the following parties on the question of tariffs and subsidies for agriculture.

Subsidies/tariffs are counter-		Subsidies/tariffs are essential
productive for agricultural	←——→	to guaranteeing the viability
efficiency		of Polish agriculture

12. Order, Authority, and Public Democratic Education
Some politicians believe that public democratic education should teach respect for the traditional values of authority and social order because a democracy works well only if citizens show respect for the government as well as authority relations in the family and at the workplace. Others counter that respect for traditional authority and order should have less priority in democratic education than developing a spirit of individual autonomy and an ability to question authority in government, the workplace, and the family.

How important is the question of traditional authority and order in democratic education for your party?

Please characterize the position of the following parties on the question of priorities in democratic education.

Priority for respecting tradi-
tional authority and social or-   Priority for developing indi-
der   vidual autonomy and the
    capacity to question authority

13. Environmental Protection

Economic modernization and environmental protection often go together, but sometimes they lead to goal conflicts. In these instances, *some politicians* argue that Poland cannot afford to enforce strict environmental laws at this time because it has to produce more goods and to create more jobs that would not become available if costs of investment and production were driven up by environmental regulation. *Other politicians* retort that environmental degradation is so significant that environmental laws should be enforced, even if jobs must be sacrificed in order to meet environmental standards.

How important is the question of enforcing environmental laws for your party?

Please characterize the position of the following parties on the question of enforcing environmental laws if jobs are endangered by environmental regulatory requirements.

Industrial investment should
have priority if environmental
law enforcement endangers   Environmental laws should
    have priority if law enforce-
jobs   ment leads to the loss of jobs

14. Freedom of the Mass Media and Morality

Some politicians maintain that in a democracy films and magazines have the right to publish materials that contradict prevailing standards of morality and proper conduct. *Other politicians* argue that even in a democracy moral restraint in films and magazines should be enforced by the laws to maintain popular standards of decency.

How important is the question of moral standards in the mass media for your party?

Please characterize the position of the following parties on the question of enforcing moral standards in the mass media.

The mass media should be
free to publish materials not
conforming with prevailing
morality   ←—→   Some enforcement of moral
    standards in the mass media is
    justified in order to maintain
    prevailing norms of morality

15. Participation of Former Communists in Public Life

Some politicians argue that former middle- and high-ranking communist officials should be kept out of political life and business by existing or new legal, administrative, and political rules because they fought democracy and market capitalism in the past. *Other politicians* reason that former communists should get the same chance to enjoy political and economic liberties as anyone else and that existing or new legal, political, and administrative measures to keep them out of economic or political life are unjustified.

How important is the question of former communists in public life in your party?

Please characterize the position of the following parties on the treatment of former communists in political and economic life.

Former communists should be
kept out of public life by
legal, administrative, and political means

Former communists should
have the same rights and opportunities as other citizens to
participate in public life.

15.a. Relations with Turkey (only in Bulgaria)
Some politicians think that Turkey is a potential partner of Bulgaria. *Other politicians* are of the opinion that Turkey is a potential threat to our national security.

How important is the question of relations with Turkey for your party?

Please characterize the position of the following parties on the question of relations with Turkey.

Turkey is a potential partner
of Bulgaria

Turkey is a potential threat to
Bulgaria

15b. Signing a Basic Treaty with Neighboring Countries (only in Hungary)
All politicians say we need to develop good relations with neighboring nations and improve the conditions of Hungarians who live in these countries. But they propose different policies to reach these goals. For instance, some politicians think that Hungary must be prepared to sign such basic treaties with each of the neighboring countries that would confirm the inviolability of the current borders. Other politicians think that such treaties would only deprive us of the possibility of protecting the interests of the Hungarians who live there. According to them the Hungarian government must not give such guarantees to any of the neighboring countries.

How important is this topic for your party?

Please characterize the position of the following parties.

Hungary must be prepared to recognize the inviolability of the current borders in the case of every neighboring country None of the neighboring countries should be given such guarantees

15c. Turkish Language in School (only in Bulgaria)

Some politicians think that the Bulgarian Turks ought to be instructed in all courses at school in Turkish. *Other politicians* think that Turkish language instruction should be confined to the family setting.

How important is the question of Turkish language in schools for your party?

Please characterize the position of the following parties on the question of Turkish language in schools.

Turkish should be the language of school Turkish should be taught only in the family

16. Economy

Please place each party on a scale ranging from preference for state intervention in the economy to a liberal market economy.

State intervention Liberal market economy

17. Tradition

Please place each party on a scale ranging from preferences for values of liberal individualism to preferences for values of traditional Polish cultural community and solidarity.

Cultural individualism Traditional cultural community and solidarity

18. History

Please place each party on a scale ranging from an emphasis on creating a strong national popular consciousness of Poland's unique history and cultural destiny to an emphasis on creating a strong cosmopolitan consciousness for Poland's interdependence with Western Europe and the global development of humankind.

Emphasis on national consciousness, history, and cultural destiny Emphasis on cosmopolitan consciousness of regional links to Western Europe and global problems of humankind

19. Religion

Please place each party on a scale ranging from preferences for religious principles in politics to secular conceptions of politics.

Christian principles in politics   ←——→   Secular principles in politics

20. Politics
Please place each party on a scale ranging from the political "left" to the political "right."

Left   ←——→   Right

21. Sympathy
Please indicate for each party whether you find it sympathetic or not sympathetic.

Not sympathetic   ←——→   Sympathetic

APPENDIX III

POPULATION SURVEY QUESTIONS (POLICY OPINIONS)

A. THE CENTRAL EUROPEAN SURVEY (CZECH REPUBLIC, HUNGARY, POLAND)

16. Please tell me how much you agree or disagree with the following statements, using the following scale: (1) definitely agree, (2) rather agree, (3) rather disagree, (4) definitely disagree.

    c. It should be the government's responsibility to provide a job for everyone who wants one.

    d. It is harmful for the economy if the government tries to reduce income differences between rich and poor.

    e. The present economic situation is very unfavorable to me and my family.

    f. Transferring the former state-owned companies to private property is going to help very much in solving the economic problems of our country.

    g. Unprofitable factories and mines should be closed down immediately, even if this leads to unemployment.

    h. Politicians who do not believe in God should not perform public functions.

    i. Nationalism is (always) harmful for the development of our country.

    k. With the way things are in [name country], people like me and my family have a good chance of getting ahead in life.

    m. Politicians should care more about rising crime and deteriorating morality than about individual freedom and human rights.

    n. A woman should be allowed to have an abortion in the early weeks of pregnancy, if she decides to.

    o. In case of a politician, I prefer a strong patriot to an expert.

    p. The church has [the churches have] too much influence in our country.

24. Please tell me after each of the following goals which party or parties in [name country] you think really wish to reach that objective. You can name a maximum of three parties in each case.

   c. Strengthen national feelings.
   d. Preserve freedom of speech and democracy in our country.
   e. Increase pensions and benefits.
   h. Increase the influence of religion and the church(es).
   i. Speed up privatization of state-owned companies.
   k. Guarantee that women can have an abortion if they decide to.

B. THE BULGARIAN SURVEY

The following attitudinal items from the Evans and Whitefield 1993 Bulgarian survey were employed in the calculations for Bulgarian voters presented in chapters 8 and 9. Each item was measured using a Likert-style 5-point response format (strongly agree, agree, neither agree nor disagree, disagree, strongly disagree).

   Thinking next about the economic system, how do you feel about the aim of creating a market economy with private ownership and economic freedom for entrepreneurs. Are you a strong supporter, supporter, opponent, strong opponent, or neither supporter nor opponent? (VAR 3)
   Private enterprise is the best way to solve the country's economic problems. (VAR 105)
   Large differences in income are necessary for prosperity. (VAR 107)
   The government should see to it that every person has a job and a good standard of living. OR: The government should just let each person get ahead on his own. (VAR 46)
   Young people today do not have enough respect for traditional values. (VAR 116)
   Censorship of films and magazines is necessary to uphold moral standards. (VAR 117)
   Turks in this country should have to be taught in Bulgarian. (VAR 134)
   Foreign ownership of enterprises might be accepted if it improves our state of the economy. OR: It is better that we should continue to own our enterprises even if it means more hardship in the future. (VAR 136)
   Bulgarians should cooperate with other countries even if it means giving up some independence. (VAR 126)

In addition we employed a 10-point left-right scale and a 7-point attendance in religious service scale.

BIBLIOGRAPHY

Achen, Christopher H. 1977. "Measuring Representation: Perils of the Correlation Coefficient." *American Journal of Political Science,* Vol. 21, No. 4: 805–15.
1978. "Measuring Representation." *American Journal of Political Science,* Vol. 22, No. 3: 475–510.
Agh, Attila. 1992. "The Emerging Party Systems in East Central Europe." *Budapest Papers on Democratic Transition.* Department of Political Science, Budapest Economics University.
1993. From Nomenklatura to Clientura. The Emergence of New Political Elites in East Central Europe. Paper presented at the conference of the Center for Mediterranean Studies, University of Bristol, September 17–19.
1994. "The Hungarian Party System and Party Theory in the Transition of Central Europe." *Journal of Theoretical Politics,* Vol. 6, No. 2: 217–38.
1995a. "Partial Consolidation of the East-Central European Parties. The Case of the Hungarian Socialist Party," *Party Politics,* Vol. 1, No. 4: 491–514.
1995b. The East Central European Party Systems: From "Movements" to "Cartels." Paper presented at conference of the Central European University, Budapest, June 15–17.
Aldrich, John. 1983. "A Downsian Spatial Model with Party Activism." *American Political Science Review,* Vol. 77, No. 4: 974–90.
1995. *Why Parties?* Chicago: University of Chicago Press.
Alesina, Alberto, and Howard Rosenthal. 1995. *Partisan Politics, Divided Government, and the Economy.* Cambridge: Cambridge University Press.
Almond, Gabriel A. 1956. "Comparative Political Systems." Reprinted in Gabriel A. Almond, *Political Development: Essays in Heuristic Theory.* Boston: Little, Brown, 1970.
Almond, Gabriel A., and James S. Coleman, eds. 1960. *The Politics of the Developing Areas.* Princeton, N.J.: Princeton University Press.
Almond, Gabriel A., and G. Bingham Powell. 1978. *Comparative Politics: A Developmental Approach.* Rev. ed. Boston: Little, Brown.

Almond, Gabriel A. and Sidney Verba. 1963. *The Civic Culture*. Princeton, N.J.: Princeton University Press.

Alt, James E., Jeffry Frieden, Michael J. Gilligan, Dani Rodrik, and Ronald Rogowski. 1996. "The Political Economy of International Trade. Enduring Puzzles and an Agenda for Inquiry." *Comparative Political Studies*, Vol. 29, No. 6: 689–717.

Ames, Barry. 1994. "The Reverse Coattails Effect: Local Party Organization in the 1989 Brazilian Presidential Election." *American Political Science Review*, Vol. 88, No. 2: 95–111.

—— 1995a "Electoral Strategy under Open-List Proportional Representation." *American Journal of Political Science*, Vol. 39, No. 2: 406–33.

—— 1995b. "Electoral Rules, Constituency Pressures, and Pork Barrel: Bases of Voting in the Brazilian Congress." *Journal of Politics*, Vol. 57, No. 2: 324–43.

Anderson, Chris. 1995. *Blaming the Government: Citizens and the Economy in Five European Democracies*. Armonk, N.Y.: M. E. Sharpe.

Ashley, Stephen. 1990. "Bulgaria." *Electoral Studies*, Vol. 9, No. 4: 312–18.

Aslund, Anders, Peter Boone, and Simon Johnson. 1996. How To Stabilize. Lessons from Post-Communist Countries. Paper prepared for the Brookings Panel on Economic Activity, Washington, D.C., March 28–29.

Balcerowicz, Leszek. 1995. *Socialism, Capitalism, Transformation*. Budapest: Central European University Press.

Bankowicz, Marek. 1994a. "Czechoslovakia: From Masaryk to Havel." Pp. 142–68, in Sten Berglund and Jan Ake Dellenbrant, eds., *The New Democracies in Eastern Europe: Party System and Political Cleavages*. 2nd ed. Aldershot: Edvard Elgar.

—— 1994b. "Bulgaria: The Continuing Revolution." Pp. 219–37 in Sten Berglund and Jan Ake Dellenbrant, eds., *The New Democracies in Eastern Europe: Party System and Political Cleavages*. 2nd ed. Aldershot: Edvard Elgar.

Bankowicz, Marek, and Jan Ake Dellenbrant. 1988. "The Party System of Czechoslovakia." Pp. 89–108 in Sten Berglund, Marian Grzybowski, Jan Ake Dellenbrant, and Marek Bankowicz, eds., *East European Multi-Party Systems*. Helsinki: Finnish Society of Sciences and Letters.

Barany, Zoltan D., and Louisa Vinton. 1990. "Breakthrough to Democracy: Elections in Poland and Hungary." *Studies in Comparative Communism*, Vol. 39, No. 2: 191–212.

Bartolini, Stefano, and Peter Mair. 1990. *Identity, Competition, and Electoral Availability*. Cambridge: Cambridge University Press.

Baylis, Thomas. 1996. "Presidents versus Prime Ministers. Shaping Executive Authority in Eastern Europe." *World Politics*, Vol. 48, No. 3: 297–323.

Bell, John D. 1977. *Peasants in Power: Alexander Stamboliski and the Bulgarian National Union, 1899–1923*. Princeton, N.J.: Princeton University Press.

—— 1986. *The Bulgarian Communist Party from Blagoev to Zhivkov*. Stanford, Calif.: Hoover Institution Press.

—— 1997. "Democratization and Political Participation in 'Postcommunist' Bulgaria." Pp. 353–402 in Karen Dawisha and Bruce Parrott, eds., *Politics, Power, and the Struggle for Democracy in South-East Europe*. Cambridge: Cambridge University Press.

Berelson, Bernard R., Paul F. Lazarsfeld, and William N. McPhee. 1954. *Voting: A*

Study of Public Opinion Formation in a Presidential Campaign. Chicago: University of Chicago Press.

Berend, Ivan T. 1986. "The Historical Evolution of Eastern Europe as a Region." *International Organization,* Vol. 40, No. 2: 329–46.

Berglund, Sten, and Frank Aarebrot. 1997. *The Political History of Eastern Europe in the 20th Century: The Struggle between Democracy and Dictatorship.* Cheltenham: Edvard Elgar.

Bermeo, Nancy. 1990. "Rethinking Regime Change." *Comparative Politics,* Vol. 22, No. 3: 359–77.

Bialecki, Ireneusz, and Bodgan W. Mach. 1992. "The Social and Economic Orientations of Polish Legislators against a Background of the Views of Polish Society." *Polish Sociological Bulletin,* No. 2: 167–86.

Binder, Leonard et al.,. 1971. *Crises and Sequences of Political Development.* Princeton, N.J.: Princeton University Press.

Boix, Carles. 1997. Choosing Electoral Rules. Structural Factors of Political Calculations? Department of Political Science, Ohio State University. Unpublished manuscript.

Bozoki, Andras. 1988. "Critical Movements and Ideologies in Hungary? A Socio-Political Analysis of Alternative Ways to a Civil Society." *Südosteuropa,* Vol. 37, Nos. 7–8: 377–87.

——— 1990. "Political Transition and Constitutional Change in Hungary." *Südosteuropa,* Vol. 39, No. 3: 538–49.

——— 1993. "Hungary's Road to Systemic Change: The Opposition Roundtable." *East European Politics and Society,* Vol. 7, No. 2: 276–308.

Bratton, Michael, and Nicolas Van de Walle. 1994. "Neopatrimonial Regimes and Political Transitions in Africa." *World Politics,* Vol. 45, No. 4: 453–89.

Brokl, Lubomir, and Zdenka Mansfeldova. 1992. "Von der 'unpolitischen' zur 'professionellen' Politik. Aspekte der politischen Kultur der CFSR in der Periode des Systemwechsels." Pp. 163–202 in Fritz Gerlich, Fritz Plasser, and Peter A. Ulram, ed., *Regimewechsel. Demokratisierung und politische Kultur in Ost-Mitteleuropa.* Vienna: Böhlau.

Brown, J. F. 1988. *Eastern Europe and Communist Rule.* Durham, N.C.: Duke University Press.

Bruszt, Laszlo. 1990. "1989: The Negotiated Revolution in Hungary." *Social Research,* Vol. 57, No. 2: 365–87.

Bruszt, Laszlo, and David Stark. 1991. "Remaking the Political Field in Hungary: From the Politics of Confrontation to the Politics of Competition." Pp. 13–55 in Ivo Banac, ed., *Eastern Europe in Revolution.* Ithaca, N.Y.: Cornell University Press.

Budge, Ian. 1984. "Parties and Democratic Government. A Framework for Comparative Explanation." *West European Politics,* Vol. 7, No. 1: 95–118.

Budge, Ian and Dennis Farlie. 1983. *Explaining and Predicting Elections: Issue Effects and Party Strategies in Twenty-Three Democracies.* London: Allen and Unwin.

Budge, Ian, and Michael Laver, eds. 1992. *Party Policy and Government Coalitions.* New York: St. Martin's Press.

Budge, Ian, David Robertson, and Derek Hearl. 1987. *Ideology, Strategy, and Party*

Change: Spatial Analysis of Post-War Elections: Programmes in 19 Democracies.
Cambridge: Cambridge University Press.

Carey, John M., and Matthew Soberg Shugart. 1995. "Incentives to Cultivate a Personal Vote: A Rank Ordering of Electoral Formulas." *Electoral Studies,* Vol. 14 No. 4: 417–39.

Castles, Francis, and Peter Mair. 1984. "Left-Right Political Scales: Some Expert Judgments." *European Journal of Political Research,* Vol. 12, No. 1: 73–88.

Cavarozzi, Marcelo. 1992. "Beyond Transitions to Democracy in Latin America." *Journal of Latin American Studies,* Vol. 24, No. 4: 665–84.

Chazan, Naomi, Robert Mortimer, John Ravenhill, and Donald Rothchild. 1992. *Politics and Society in Contemporary Africa.* Boulder, Colo.: Lynne Rienner.

Chirot, Daniel, ed. 1986. *The Origins of Backwardness in Eastern Europe.* Berkeley: University of California Press.

Cirtautas, Arisa Maria. 1993. "In Pursuit of the Democratic Interest. The Institutionalization of Parties and Interests in Eastern Europe." Pp. 36–57 in Christopher G. A. Bryant and Eduard Mokryzcki, eds., *The New Great Transformation? Change and Continuity in East Central Europe.* London: Routledge.

Collier, David, ed. 1979. *The New Authoritarianism in Latin America.* Princeton, N.J.: Princeton University Press.

Collier, David, and Steven Levitsky. 1997. "Democracy 'With Adjectives.' Conceptual Innovation in Comparative Research." *World Politics,* Vol. 49, No. 3: 130–51.

Collier, Ruth Berins, and David Collier. 1991. *Shaping the Political Arena.* Princeton, N.J.: Princeton University Press.

Colomer, Josep M. 1991. "Transitions by Agreement: Modelling the Spanish Way." *American Political Science Review,* Vol. 85, No. 4: 1283–1302.

Comisso, Ellen, Steven Dubb, and Judy McTigue. 1992. "The Illusion of Populism in Latin America and East-Central Europe." Pp. 27–57 in György Szoboszlai, ed., *Flying Blind: Emerging Democracies in East-Central Europe.* Budapest: Hungarian Political Science Association.

Comisso, Ellen, and Paul Marer. 1986. "The Economics and Politics of Reform in Hungary." *International Organization,* Vol. 40, No. 2: 421–54.

Converse, Philip. 1964. "The Nature of Belief Systems in Mass Publics." Pp. 206–61 in David E. Apter, ed., *Ideology and Discontent.* New York: Free Press.

Converse, Philip, and Roy Pierce. 1986. *Political Representation in France.* Cambridge, Mass.: Harvard University Press.

Cox, Gary W. 1990. "Multicandidate Spatial Competition." Pp. 179–98 in James Enelow and Melvin J. Hinich, eds., *Advances in the Spatial Theory of Voting.* Cambridge: Cambridge University Press.

⎯⎯⎯ 1997. *Making Votes Count: Strategic Coordination in the World's Electoral Systems.* Cambridge: Cambridge University Press.

Cox, Gary W., and Frances Rosenbluth. 1995. "Anatomy of a Split. The Liberal Democrats of Japan." *Electoral Studies,* Vol. 14, No. 4: 355–76.

Cox, Gary W., and Matthew Soberg Shugart. 1995. Strategic Voting under Proportional Representation. University of California, San Diego. Unpublished manuscript.

Crampton, Richard J. 1987. *A Short History of Modern Bulgaria.* Cambridge: Cambridge University Press.

    1994. *Eastern Europe in the Twentieth Century.* London: Routledge.

    1995. "The Bulgarian Election of December 1994." *Electoral Studies,* Vol. 14, No. 2: 236–40.

Crawford, Beverly, and Arend Lijphart. 1995. "Explaining Political and Economic Change in Post-Communist Eastern Europe. Old Legacies, New Institutions, Hegemonic Norms, and International Pressures." *Comparative Political Studies,* Vol. 28, No. 2: 171–99.

Crowther, William. 1995. Party Formation and Elite Strategies in Romania and Moldova. Paper presented at the Workshop on Parties and Party Systems, Duke University, Durham, N.C., March 24–25.

Cusak, Thomas, and Rolf-Dieter Eberwein. 1993. "The Endless Election: 1990 in the German Democratic Republic." Pp. 188–212 in Dirk Berg-Schlosser and Ralf Rytlewski, eds., *Political Culture in Germany.* London: Macmillan.

Cutler, Lloyd, and Herman Schwartz. 1991. "Constitutional Reform in Czechoslovakia: U Duobus Unum?" *Chicago Law Review,* Vol. 58, No. 2: 511–53.

Dahl, Robert R. 1971. *Polyarchy.* New Haven: Yale University Press.

    1989. *Democracy and Its Critics.* New Haven: Yale University Press.

Dalton, Russell. 1985. "Political Parties and Political Representation. Party Supporters and Party Elites in Nine Nations." *Comparative Political Studies,* Vol. 18, No. 3: 267–99.

Davies, Norman. 1984. *Heart of Europe: A Short History of Poland.* Oxford: Clarendon Press.

Davis, Otto A., and Wenbo Wu. 1996. Two Freedoms and Economic Development and Growth: An Empirical Study. Carnegie Mellon University. Unpublished manuscript.

Dawisha, Karen, and Bruce Parrott. 1997. *Authoritarianism and Democratization in Postcommunist Societies.* 4 vols. Cambridge: Cambridge University Press.

de Weyenthal, Jan B. 1978. *The Communists of Poland: An Historical Outline.* Stanford, Calif.: Hoover Institution Press.

De Winter, Luc, Donatella della Porta, Kris Deschouwer. 1996. The Italo-Belgian Partitocratic Type Compared to Fourteen West European Countries. Paper prepared for the annual meeting of the American Political Science Association, San Francisco, August 28–September 1.

Deschouwer, Kris, and Bruno Coppieters. 1994. "A West European Model for Social Democracy in East Central Europe?" Pp. 1–18 in Michael Waller, Kris Deschouwer, and Bruno Coppieters, eds., *Social Democracy in a Post-Communist Europe.* Newbury Park, Calif.: Cass.

Deutsch, Karl W. 1953. *Nationalism and Social Communication.* Cambridge, Mass.: MIT Press.

Dimitrov, Roumen. 1993. "Bewegungsende zum Demokratiebeginn? Institutionalisierungsprobleme des politischen Vermittlungssystems in Bulgarien." *Forschungsjournal Neue Soziale Bewegungen,* Vol. 6, No. 2.

DiPalma, Giuseppe. 1990. *To Craft Democracies.* Berkeley: University of California Press.

Dix, Robert. 1989. "The Cleavage Structures and Party Systems in Latin America." *Comparative Politics,* Vol. 22, No. 1: 23–37.

Dodd, Larry C. 1976. *Coalitions in Parliamentary Government.* Princeton, N.J.: Princeton University Press.

Downs, Anthony. 1957. *An Economic Theory of Democracy.* New York: Harper and Row.

Duch, Raymond. 1993. "Tolerating Economic Reform: Popular Support for Transition to a Free Market in the Former Soviet Union." *American Political Science Review,* Vol. 87, No. 3: 590–608.

———. 1995. "Economic Chaos and the Fragility of Democratic Transition in Former Communist Regimes." *Journal of Politics,* Vol. 57, No. 1: 121–58.

Duverger, Maurice. 1954. *Political Parties.* London: Methuen.

Eisenstadt, Shmuel N., and Luis Roniger. 1981. "The Study of Patron-Client Relations and Recent Developments in Sociological Theory." Pp. 271–95 in Shmuel N. Eisenstadt and René Lemarchand, eds., *Political Clientelism, Patronage, and Development.* Beverly Hills, Calif.: Sage.

———. 1984. *Patrons, Clients and Friends. Interpersonal Relations and the Structures of Trust in Society.* Cambridge: Cambridge University Press.

Ekiert, Grzegorsz. 1996. *The State against Society: Political Crises and Their Aftermath in East Central Europe.* Princeton, N.J.: Princeton University Press.

Elster, Jon. 1993–94."Bargaining over the Presidency. Myopic Bargains among the Framers in Poland, Hungary and Bulgaria." *East European Constitutional Review,* Vol. 2, No. 4 and Vol. 3, No. 1: 95–98.

Enelow, James, and Melvin J. Hinich. 1984. *The Spatial Theory of Voting: An Introduction.* Cambridge: Cambridge University Press.

———. eds. 1990. *Advances in the Spatial Theory of Voting.* Cambridge: Cambridge University Press.

Engelbrekt, Kjell. 1992. "The Fall of Bulgaria's First Noncommunist Government." *Radio Free Europe/Radio Liberty Research Report,* Vol. 1, No. 45: 1–5.

Enyedi, Zsolt. 1996. "Organizing a Subcultural Party in Eastern Europe. The Case of the Hungarian Christian Democrats." *Party Politics,* Vol. 2, No. 3: 377–96.

Etzioni-Halevy, Eva. 1993. "The Anatomy of Elites and Transitions from Non-Democratic Regimes. The Cases of the Former Soviet Union and Poland." *Research in Political Sociology,* Vol. 6: 257–76.

European Bank for Reconstruction and Development. 1997. *Transition Report 1997: Enterprise Performance and Growth.* London: EBRD.

Evans, Geoffrey. 1994. Mass Political Attitudes and the Development of Market Democracy in Eastern Europe. Paper presented at the conference of the Social Science Research Council, Madralin, Poland, September 23–25.

———. 1995. "Social Class and Interest Formation in Post-Communist Societies." Pp. 225–46 in David Lee and Bryan Turner, eds., *Conflicts about Class.* London: Longman.

Evans, Geoffrey, and Stephen Whitefield. 1993. "Identifying the Bases of Party Competition in Eastern Europe." *British Journal of Political Science,* Vol. 23, No. 4: 521–48.

———. 1995a. "The Politics and Economics of Democratic Commitment: A Preliminary Study of Support for Democracy in Transition Societies." *British Journal of Political Science,* Vol. 25, No. 4: 485–514.

———. 1995b. "Economic Ideology and Political Success. Communist Successor Parties in the Czech Republic, Slovakia and Hungary Compared." *Party Politics,* Vol. 1, No. 4: 565–78.

1995c. "Social and Ideological Cleavage Formation in Hungary." *Europe-Asia Studies,* Vol. 47, No. 7: 1177–1204.

1997. The Social Bases of Political Preferences in Eastern Europe. Nuffield and Pembroke College. Unpublished manuscript.

Fearon, James D., 1991. "Counterfactuals and Hypothesis Testing in Political Science." *World Politics,* Vol. 43, No. 2: 169–95.

Fearon, James D., and David D. Laitin. 1997. "Explaining Interethnic Cooperation." *American Political Science Review,* Vol. 90, No. 4: 715–35.

Feld, Scott, and Bernard Grofman. 1988. "Ideological Consistency as a Collective Phenomenon." *American Political Science Review,* Vol. 82, No. 3: 773–88.

Feng, Yi. 1997. "Democracy, Political Stability and Economic Growth." *British Journal of Political Science,* Vol. 27, No. 3: 391–418.

Filippov, Mikhail, and Olga V. Shvetsova. 1995. Political Institutions and Party Systems in New Democracies of Eastern Europe. Paper delivered at the annual meeting of the American Political Science Association, Chicago, August 30–September 2.

1996. Direct Presidential Elections and Party Systems in Eastern Europe. Paper delivered at the annual meeting of the American Political Science Association, San Francisco, August 29–September 1.

Finifter, Ada. 1996. "Attitudes toward Individual Responsibility and Political Reform in the Former Soviet Union." *American Political Science Review,* Vol. 90, No. 1: 138–52.

Finifter, Ada, and Ellen Mickiewicz. 1994. "Redefining the Political System of the USSR: Mass Support for Political Change." *American Political Science Review,* Vol. 86, No. 4: 857–74.

Fish, M. Steven. 1998. "The Determinants of Economic Reform in the Post-Communist World." *East European Politics and Societies,* Vol. 12, No. 1: 31–78.

Fish, Stephen. 1995a. *Democracy from Scratch: Opposition and Regime in the New Russian Revolution.* Princeton, N.J.: Princeton University Press.

1995b. "The Advent of Multipartism in Russia, 1993–95." *Post-Soviet Affairs,* Vol. 11: 340–83.

Fishkin, James. 1991. *Democracy and Deliberation.* New Haven: Yale University Press.

Frankland, Erich G. 1995. "Green Revolutions? The Role of Green Parties in Eastern Europe's Transition, 1989–1994." *East European Quarterly,* Vol. 29, No. 3: 315–45.

Frieden, Jeffrey. 1991. *Debt, Development and Democracy.* Princeton, N.J.: Princeton University Press.

Frieden, Jeffrey, and Ronald Rogowski. 1996. "The Impact of the International Economy on National Policies: An Analytical Overview." Pp. 25–47 in Robert O. Keohane and Helen V. Milner, eds., *Internationalization and Domestic Politics.* Cambridge: Cambridge University Press.

Friedheim, Daniel V. 1992. "Bringing Society Back into Democratic Transition Theory after 1989: Pact Making and Regime Collapse." *East European Politics and Society,* Vol. 7, No. 3: 482–512.

Friszke, Andrzej. 1990. "The Polish Political Scene (1989)." *East European Politics and Society,* Vol. 4, No. 2: 305–41.

Frye, Timothy. 1997. "A Politics of Institutional Choice: Post-Communist Presidencies." *Comparative Political Studies,* Vol. 30, No. 5: 523–52.
Ganev, Venelin T. 1992. "The Mysterious Politics of Bulgaria's Movement for Rights
and Freedoms." *East European Constitutional Review,* Vol. 4, No. 1: 49–53.
      1995. "Prisoners' Rights, Public Services, and Institutional Collapse in Bul-
garia." *East European Constitutional Review,* Vol. 4, No. 4: 76–83.
Garrett, Geoffrey, and Peter Lange. 1996. "Internationalization, Institutions, and
Political Change." Pp. 48–75 in Robert O. Keohane and Helen V. Milner,
eds., *Internationalization and Domestic Politics.* Cambridge: Cambridge Uni-
versity Press.
Gebethner, Stanislaw. 1991. "New Party System in the Making in Poland of the
1990s." Pp. 239–58 in Gerd Meyer and Franciszek Ryszka, eds., *Political
Participation and Democracy in Poland and West Germany.* Warsaw: Osrodek
Badan Spolecznych.
      1993. "Political Parties in Poland (1989–1993)." Pp. 310–38 in Gerd Meyer,
ed., *Die politischen Kulturen Ostmitteleuropas im Umbruch.* Tübingen: Franke
Verlag.
Geddes, Barbara. 1994. *Politician's Dilemma: Building State Capacity in Latin America.*
Berkeley: University of California Press.
Gellner, Ernest. 1983. *Nations and Nationalism.* Oxford: Blackwell.
Gibson, James L. 1994. Political and Economic Markets: Connecting Attitudes to-
ward Political Democracy and a Market Economy within the Mass Culture
of Russia and Ukraine. University of Houston. Version 2.2.
      1996. "Political and Economic Markets. Changes in the Connection between
Attitudes toward Political Democracy and a Market Economy within the
Mass Culture of Russia and Ukraine." *Journal of Politics,* Vol. 58, No. 4:
954–84.
Gibson, James L., and Raymond Duch. 1993. "Political Intolerance in the USSR, the
Distribution and Etiology of Mass Opinion." *Comparative Political Studies,*
Vol. 26, No. 3: 286–29.
Goetz, Klaus. 1995. "Ein neuer Verwaltungstyp in Mittel- und Osteuropa? Zur
Entwicklung der post-kommunistischen Verwaltung." Pp. 538–53 in
Hellmut Wollmann, Helmut Wiesenthal, and Frank Bönker, eds., *Transfor-
mation sozialistischer Gesellschaften. Am Ende des Anfangs.* Opladen: West-
deutscher Verlag.
Goldstein, Judith, and Robert Keohane. 1993. "Ideas and Foreign Policy. An Analyt-
ical Framework." Pp. 3–30 in Judith Goldstein and Robert Keohane, eds.,
Ideas and Foreign Policy. Beliefs, Institutions, and Political Change. Ithaca, N.Y.:
Cornell University Press.
Goldthorpe, John. 1987. *Social Mobility and Class Structure in Modern Britain.* 2nd ed.
Oxford: Oxford University Press.
Goodwin, Larry. 1991. *Breaking the Barrier.* Oxford: Oxford University Press.
Gordon, Stacy, and Gary M. Segura. 1997. "Cross-National Variation in the Political
Sophistication of Individuals: Capability or Choice?" *Journal of Politics,* Vol.
59, No. 1: 126–48.
Gortat, Radzislawa. 1994. "The Development of Social Democracy in Poland." Pp.
136–53 in Michael Waller, Bruno Coppieters, and Kris Deschouwer, eds.,
Social Democracy in a Post-Communist Europe. Newbury Park, Calif.: Cass.

Granberg, Donald, and Sören Holmberg. 1988. "Attitude Constraint and Stability among Elite and Mass in Sweden." *European Journal of Political Research,* Vol. 29, No. 1: 59–72.

Grew, Raymond, ed. 1978. *Crises of Political Development in Europe and the United States.* Princeton, N.J.: Princeton University Press.

Grofman, Bernard, and Arend Lijphart, eds. 1986. *Electoral Laws and Their Political Consequences.* New York: Agathon Press.

Grzybowski, Marian. 1988. "The Polish Party System in Transition." Pp. 30–55 in Sten Berglund, Marian Grzybowski, Jan Ake Dellenbrant, and Marek Bankowicz, eds., *East European Multi-Party Systems.* Helsinki: Finnish Society of Sciences and Letters.

———. 1994. "Poland: Towards Overdeveloped Pluralism." Pp. 36–73 in Sten Berglund and Jan Ake Dellenbrant, eds., *The New Democracies in Eastern Europe: Party System and Political Cleavages.* 2nd ed. Aldershot: Edvard Elgar.

Haggard, Stephan. 1990. *Pathways from the Periphery.* Ithaca, N.Y.: Cornell University Press.

Haggard, Stephen, and Robert Kaufman. 1995. *The Political Economy of Democratic Transitions.* Princeton, N.J.: Princeton University Press.

Hajdu, Tibor, and Zsusza L. Nagy. 1990. "Revolution, Counterrevolution, Consolidation." Pp. 295–318 in Peter F. Sugar, ed., *A History of Hungary.* Bloomington: Indiana University Press.

Hanson, Stephen. 1995. "The Leninist Legacy and Institutional Change." *Comparative Political Studies,* Vol. 28, No. 2: 306–19.

Hardin, Russell. 1995. *One for All.* Princeton, N.J.: Princeton University Press.

Harmel, Robert, and Kenneth Janda. 1982. *Parties and Their Environment.* London: Longman.

Harmel, Robert, and Lars Svasand. 1993. "Party Leadership and Party Institutionalization: Three Phases of Development." *West European Politics,* Vol. 16, No. 1: 67–88.

Heinrich, Hans-Georg. 1986. *Hungary: Politics, Economics and Society.* London: Pinter.

Held, David. 1987. *Models of Democracy.* Cambridge: Polity Press.

Held, Joseph, ed. 1992. *The Columbia History of Eastern Europe in the Twentieth Century.* New York: Columbia University Press.

Hellemans, Staf. 1990. *Strijd om de moderniteit. Sociale bewegingen en verzuiling in Europa sinds 1800.* Leuven: Kritak.

Hellman, Joel. 1996. "Constitutional and Economic Reform in Postcommunist Transition." *East European Constitutional Review,* Vol. 5, No. 1: 46–57.

———. 1998. "Winners Take All. The Politics of Partial Reform in Postcommunist Transitions." *World Politics,* Vol. 50, No. 2: 203–34.

Hibbing, John R., and Samuel C. Patterson. 1992. "A Democratic Legislature in the Making. The Historic Hungarian Elections of 1990." *Comparative Political Studies,* Vol. 24, No. 4: 430–54.

———. 1994. "Public Trust in the New Parliaments of Central and Eastern Europe." *Political Studies,* Vol. 42, No. 4: 570–92.

Hinich, Melvin J., and Michael C. Munger. 1990. A Spatial Theory of Ideology. University of Texas at Austin. Unpublished manuscript.

———. 1992. "The Spatial Theory of Ideology." *Journal of Theoretical Politics,* Vol. 4, No. 1: 5–27.

1994. *Ideology and the Theory of Political Choice.* Ann Arbor: University of Michigan Press.

1996. Changing Mind: New Issues and Political Choice. University of Texas, Austin, and University of North Carolina, Chapel Hill. Unpublished manuscript.

Holmberg, Sören. 1989. "Political Representation in Sweden." *Scandinavian Political Studies,* Vol. 12, No. 1: 1–16.

Holzer, Jerzy. 1992. "Polen nach dem Kommunismus – Quo Vadis?" *Aus Politik und Zeitgeschichte,* Vol. 42, No. 6: 11–23.

Höpken, Wolfgang. 1990. "Die Wahlen in Bulgarien. Ein Pyrrhus-Sieg für die Kommunisten?" *Südosteuropa,* Vol. 39, No. 6: 11–23.

Hoppe, Hans-Joachim. 1991. "Bulgariens dorniger Weg zur Demokratie." *Osteuropa,* Vol. 41, No. 9: 887–904.

Horowitz, Donald. 1985. *Ethnic Groups in Conflict.* Berkeley: University of California Press.

Hough, Jerry. 1977. *The Soviet Union and Social Science Theory.* Cambridge, Mass.: Harvard University Press.

1994. "The Russian Election of 1993: Public Attitudes toward Economic Reform and Democratization." *Post-Soviet Affairs,* Vol. 10, No. 1: 1–37.

Huber, John. 1989."Values and Partisanship in Left-Right Orientations: Measuring Ideology." *European Journal of Political Research,* Vol. 17, No. 5: 599–621.

Huntington, Samuel P. 1968. *Political Order in Changing Societies.* New Haven: Yale University Press.

1991. *The Third Wave: Democratization in the Late Twentieth Century.* Norman: University of Oklahoma Press.

Inglehart, Ronald. 1990. *Culture Shift.* Princeton, N.J.: Princeton University Press.

Ishiyama, John T. 1995. "Communist Parties in Transition. Structures, Leaders, and Processes of Democratization in Eastern Europe." *Comparative Politics,* Vol. 27, No. 2: 147–66.

1996. "Red Phoenix? The Communist Party in Post-Soviet Russian Politics." *Party Politics,* Vol. 2, No. 2: 147–75.

1997. "The Sickle or the Rose? Previous Regime Types and the Evolution of the Ex-Communist Parties in Post-Communist Politics." *Comparative Political Studies,* Vol. 30, No. 3: 299–330.

Iversen, Torben. 1994. "Political Leadership and Representation in West European Democracies. A Test of Three Models of Voting." *American Journal of Political Science,* Vol. 38, No. 1: 45–74.

Jackman, Robert. 1987. "Political Institutions and Voter Turnout in the Industrial Democracies." *American Political Science Review,* Vol. 81, No. 2: 405–24.

Jackson, John, Jacek Klich, and Krystyna Poznanska. 1996. Democratic Institutions and Economic Reform: The Polish Case. Paper prepared for the annual meeting of the American Political Science Association, San Francisco, August 29–September 2.

Janos, Andrew. 1982. *The Politics of Backwardness in Hungary, 1825–1945.* Princeton, N.J.: Princeton University Press.

1989. "The Politics of Backwardness in Continental Europe, 1780–1995." *World Politics,* Vol. 41, No. 3: 325–58.

1994. "Continuity and Change in Eastern Europe. Strategies of Post-Communist Politics." *East European Politics and Societies,* Vol. 8, No. 1: 1–3.

Jasciewicz, Krzysztof. 1992. "From Solidarity to Fragmentation." *Journal of Democracy,* Vol. 3, No. 2: 55–69.

Jelavich, Barbara, and Charles Jelavich. 1977. *The Establishment of the Balkan Nation States, 1804–1920.* Seattle: University of Washington Press.

Jenkins, Robert M. 1992. Movements into Parties: The Historic Transformation of the Hungarian Opposition. Paper presented at the Eighth International Conference of Europeanists, Chicago, March 22–29.

Jowitt, Kenneth. 1992. *New World Disorder: The Leninist Extinction.* Berkeley: University of California Press.

Juberias, Carlos Flores. 1992. "The Breakdown of the Czecho-Slovak Party System." Pp. 147–76 in György Szoboszlai, ed., *Flying Blind: Emerging Democracies in East-Central Europe.* Budapest: Yearbook of the Hungarian Political Science Association.

Karasimeonov, Georgi. 1992. "Vom Kommunismus zur Demokratie in Bulgarien." *Aus Politik und Zeitgeschichte,* Vol. 42, No. 14: 13–21.

1993. Political Parties and the Challenges of Transition to Democracy. Bulgaria and Portugal Compared. Paper presented at the Conference of the Center for Mediterranean Studies, University of Bristol, September 17–19, 1993.

1994. "Parliamentary Elections of 1994 and the Development of the Bulgarian Party System." *Party Politics,* Vol. 1, No. 4: 579–87.

1995. Between Democracy and Authoritarianism. Department of Political Science, University of Sofia. Unpublished manuscript.

Karl, Terry. 1990. "Dilemmas of Democratization in Latin America." *Comparative Politics,* Vol. 23, No. 1: 1–21.

Karl, Terry, and Philippe Schmitter. 1991. "Modes of Transition in Latin America, Southern and Eastern Europe." *International Social Science Journal,* No. 128: 269–84.

Katz, Richard. 1980. *A Theory of Parties and Electoral Systems.* Baltimore: Johns Hopkins University Press.

Katz, Richard 1990. "Party as Linkage: A Vestigial Function?" *European Journal of Political Research,* Vol. 18, No. 2: 143–61.

Katz, Richard, and Peter Mair. 1984. "Left-Right Political Scales: Some 'Expert' Judgments." *European Journal of Political Research,* Vol. 12, No. 1: 73–88.

Katzenstein, Peter. 1985. *Small States in World Markets.* Ithaca, N.Y.: Cornell University Press.

Kaufman, Robert R. 1979. "Industrial Change and Authoritarian Rule." Pp. 165–253 in David Collier, ed., *The New Authoritarianism in Latin America.* Princeton, N.J.: Princeton University Press.

Kircheimer, Otto. 1966. "The Transformation of the Western European Party Systems." Pp. 177–200 in Joseph LaPalombara and Myron Weiner, eds., *Political Parties and Political Development.* Princeton, N.J.: Princeton University Press.

Kitschelt, Herbert. 1986. "Political Opportunity Structures and Political Protest: Anti-Nuclear Movements in Four Democracies." *British Journal of Political Science,* Vol. 16, No. 1: 57–86.

1989. *The Logics of Party Formation.* Ithaca, N.Y.: Cornell University Press.

1992a. "The Formation of Party Systems in East Central Europe." *Politics and Society,* Vol. 20, No. 1: 7–50.

1992b. "Structure or Process Driven Explanations of Political Regime Change? A Review Essay." *American Political Science Review,* Vol. 86, No. 4: 1028–34.

1992c. Explaining the Choice of Electoral Laws in New Democracies: The Experience of Southern and Eastern Europe. Paper submitted to the Eighth International Conference of Europeanists, Chicago, March 27–29.

1993a. "Social Movements, Political Parties, and Democratic Theory." *Annals of the American Academy of Political and Social Science,* Vol. 528: 13–29.

1993b. "Comparative Historical Research and Rational Choice Theory. The Case of Transitions to Democracy. A Review Essay on Adam Przeworski's *Democracy and the Market.*" *Theory and Society,* Vol. 22, No. 4: 413–27.

1994a. *The Transformation of European Social Democracy.* Cambridge: Cambridge University Press.

1994b. Designing Government Institutions in East European Constitution Making: Parliamentarism and (Semi-)Presidentialism. Paper presented at the Ninth International Conference of Europeanists, Chicago, March 31–April 2, 1994.

1995a. "The Formation of Party Cleavages in Post-Communist Democracies." *Party Politics,* Vol. 1, No. 4: 447–72.

1995b. In collaboration with Anthony J. McGann. *The Radical Right in Western Europe: A Comparative Analysis.* Ann Arbor: University of Michigan Press.

1995c. *Party Systems in East Central Europe: Consolidation or Fluidity?* Studies in Public Policy, No. 241. Center for the Study of Public Policy. University of Strathclyde.

Kitschelt, Herbert, Dimitar Dimitrov, and Asen Kanev. 1995. "The Structuring of the Vote in Post-Communist Party Systems. The Bulgarian Example." *European Journal of Political Research,* Vol. 27, No. 2.

Kitschelt, Herbert, and Staf Hellemans. 1990a. *Beyond the European Left.* Durham, N.C.: Duke University Press.

1990b. "The Left-Right Semantics and the New Politics Cleavage." *Comparative Political Studies,* Vol. 22, No. 2: 210–38.

Kitschelt, Herbert, and Regina Smyth. 1997. Issues, Identities, and Programmatic Parties: The Emerging Russian Party System in Comparative Perspective. Paper prepared for the annual meeting of the American Political Science Association, Washington, D.C.

Klingemann, Hans-Dieter. 1979. "Ideological Conceptualization and Political Action." Pp. 279–305 in Samuel Barnes and Max Kaase, eds., *Political Action.* Beverly Hills, Calif.: Sage.

Klingemann, Hans-Dieter, Jürgen Lass, and Katrin Mattusch. 1994. "Nationalitätenkonflikt und Mechanismen politischer Integration im Baltikum." In Dieter Segert, ed., *Konfliktregulierung durch Parteien und politische Stabilität in Ostmitteleuropa.* Franfurt am Main: Peter Lang.

Knight, Jack. 1992. *Institutions and Social Conflict.* Cambridge: Cambridge University Press.

Knutsen, Oddbjorn. 1995. "Value Orientations, Political Conflicts and Left-Right Identification. A Comparative Study." *European Journal of Political Research,* Vol. 28, No. 1: 63–93.

Knutsen, Oddbjorn, and Elinor Scarbrough. 1995. "Cleavage Politics and Value Conflict." Pp. 492–523 in Jan van Deth and Elinor Scarbrough, eds., *The Impact of Values.* Oxford: Oxford University Press.

Kopecky, Petr. 1993. Developing Party Organizations in the Czech Republic: What Type of Party Is Likely to Emerge? Paper prepared for the Conference on the Emergence of New Party Systems and Transition to Democracy, Center for Mediterranean Studies, University of Bristol, September 17–19.

———. 1994. "Developing Party Organizations in East-Central Europe. What Type of Party Is Likely to Emerge?" *Party Politics,* Vol. 1, No. 4: 515–34.

Körösenyi, Andras. 1991. "Revival of the Past or New Beginning? The Nature of Post-Communist Politics." *Political Quarterly,* Vol. 62, No. 1: 52–74.

Kovrig, Bennett. 1979. *Communism in Hungary: From Kun to Kadar.* Stanford, Calif.: Hoover Institution Press.

Krejci, Jaroslav. 1990. *Czechoslovakia at the Crossroads of European History.* London: Tauris.

Kubicek, Paul. 1994. "Delegative Democracy in Russia and Ukraine." *Communist and Post-Communist Studies,* Vol. 27, No. 4: 423–41.

Kukorelli, Istvan. 1991. "The Birth, Testing and Results of the 1989 Hungarian Electoral Law." *Soviet Studies,* Vol. 43, No. 1: 137–56.

Kuran, Timur. 1991. "Now out of Never: The Element of Surprise in the East European Revolution of 1989." *World Politics,* Vol. 44, No. 1: 7–48.

Laitin, David D. 1991. "The National Uprisings in the Soviet Union." *World Politics,* Vol. 44, No. 1: 139–77.

Laver, Michael, and Ben Hunt. 1992. *Policy and Party Competition.* London: Routledge and Kegan Paul.

Laver, Michael, and Norman Schofield. 1990. *Multi-Party Government.* Oxford: Oxford University Press.

Laver, Michael, and Ken Shepsle. 1996. *Making and Breaking Governments: Cabinets and Legislatures in Parliamentary Democracies.* Cambridge: Cambridge University Press.

Leblang, David A. 1997. "Political Democracy and Economic Growth: Pooled Cross-Sectional and Time-Series Evidence." *British Journal of Political Science,* Vol. 27, No. 3: 453–72.

Leff, Carol Skalnik. 1987. *National Conflict in Czechoslovakia: The Making and Remaking of a State, 1918–87.* Princeton, N.J.: Princeton University Press.

Lehmann, Susan Goodrich. 1996. The Mystery of the Urban Vote in the 1995 Russian Election. Paper prepared for the annual meeting of the American Political Science Association, San Francisco, August 28–September 1.

Lehmbruch, Günther. 1977. "Liberal Corporatism and Party Government." *Comparative Political Studies,* Vol. 10, No. 1: 91–116.

Lemarchand, René. 1981. "Comparative Political Clientelism: Structure, Process, and Optic." Pp. 7–32 in Shmuel N. Eisenstadt and René Lemarchand, eds., *Political Clientelism, Patronage, and Development.* Beverly Hills, Calif.: Sage.

———. 1988. "The State, the Parallel Economy, and the Changing Structure of Patronage Systems." Pp. 149–70 in Donald Rothchild and Naomi Chazan, eds., *The Precarious Balance: State and Society in Africa*. Boulder, Colo.: Westview.

Levine, Daniel H. 1988. "Paradigm Lost: Dependence to Democracy." *World Politics,* Vol. 40, No. 3: 377–94.

Lewis, Paul G. 1994. "Political Institutionalization and Party Development in Post-Communist Poland." *Europe-Asia Studies,* Vol. 46, No. 5: 779–99.

———. 1997. "Theories of Democratization and Patterns of Regime Change in Eastern Europe." *Journal of Communist Studies and Transition Politics,* Vol. 13, No. 1: 4–26.

Lewis, Paul G., and Radislawa Gortat. 1995. "Models of Party Development and Questions of State Dependence in Poland." *Party Politics,* Vol. 1, No. 4: 599–608.

Lewis-Beck, Michael. 1988. *Economics and Elections: The Major Western Democracies.* Ann Arbor: University of Michigan Press.

Lijphart, Arend. 1977. *Democracy in Plural Societies.* New Haven: Yale University Press.

———. 1984. *Democracies.* New Haven: Yale University Press.

———. 1992. "Democratization and Constitutional Choices in Czecho-Slovakia, Hungary and Poland, 1989–91." *Journal of Theoretical Politics,* Vol. 4, No. 2: 207–23.

———. 1994a. *Electoral Systems and Party Systems: A Study of Twenty-Seven Democracies, 1945–1990.* New York: Oxford University Press.

———. 1994b. "Presidentialism and Majoritarian Democracy: Theoretical Observations." Pp. 3–87 in Juan Linz and Arturo Valenzuela, eds., *The Failure of Presidential Democracy: Comparative Perspectives.* Baltimore: Johns Hopkins University Press.

Lijphart, Arend, and Markus L. M. Crepaz. 1991. "Corporatism and Consensus Democracy in Eigtheen Countries. Conceptual and Empirical Linkages." *British Journal of Political Studies,* Vol. 21, No. 2: 235–46.

Lindstrom, Ulf. 1991. "East European Social Democracy: Reborn to Be Rejected." Pp. 269–301 in Lauri Karvanen and Jan Sundberg, eds., *Social Democracy in Transition: Northern, Southern and Eastern Europe.* Aldershot: Dartmouth.

Linz, Juan. 1994. "Presidential or Parliamentary Democracy: Does It Make a Difference?" Pp. 3–87 in Juan Linz and Arturo Valenzuela, eds., *The Failure of Presidential Democracy. Comparative Perspectives.* Baltimore: Johns Hopkins University Press.

Linz, Juan, and Alfred Stepan. 1996. *Problems of Democratic Transition and Consolidation: Southern Europe, South America, and Post-Communist Europe.* Baltimore: Johns Hopkins University Press.

Linz, Juan, and Arturo Valenzuela, eds. 1994. *The Failure of Presidential Democracy: Comparative Perspectives.* Baltimore: Johns Hopkins Unversity Press.

Lipset, Seymour Martin. *Political Man.* Rev. ed. 1981. Baltimore: Johns Hopkins University Press.

———. 1994. "The Social Requisites of Democracy Revisited. 1993. Presidential Address." *American Sociological Review,* Vol. 59, No. 1: 1–22.

Lipset, Seymour Martin, and Stein Rokkan. 1967. "Cleavage Structures, Party Systems, and Voter Alignments. An Introduction." Pp. 1–64 in Lipset and

Rokkan, eds., *Party Systems and Voter Alignments: Cross-National Perspectives.* New York: Free Press.

Lipski, Jan Jozef. 1985. *KOR: A History of the Workers' Defense Committee in Poland, 1976–1981.* Berkeley: University of California Press.

Lohmann, Susanne. 1994. "The Dynamics of Information Cascades. The Monday Demonstrations in Leipzig, East Germany, 1989–91." *World Politics,* Vol. 47, No. 1: 42–101.

Luebbert, Gregory. 1991. *Liberalism, Fascism or Social Democracy.* New York: Oxford University Press.

MacDermott, Mercia. 1962. *A Short History of Bulgaria, 1393–1885.* London: George Allen and Unwin.

MacKuen, Michael B., Robert S. Erikson, and James A. Stimson. 1992. "Peasants or Bankers? The American Electorate and the U. S. Economy." *American Political Science Review,* Vol. 86, No. 3: 597–611.

Madsen, Douglas, and Peter G. Snow. 1991. *The Charismatic Bond: Political Behavior in Time of Crisis.* Cambridge, Mass.: Harvard University Press.

Magaloni, Beatriz. 1997. The Dynamics of Dominant Party Decline. The Mexican Transition to Multipartism. Ph.D. Dissertation, Department of Political Science, Duke University.

Mainwaring, Scott. 1991. "Politicians, Parties, and Electoral Systems. Brazil in Comparative Perspective." *Comparative Politics,* Vol. 24, No. 1: 21–43.

——— 1993. "Presidentialism, Multipartism, and Democracy. The Difficult Combination." *Comparative Political Studies,* Vol. 26, No. 2: 198–228.

Mainwaring, Scott, and Timothy R. Scully. 1995. "Introduction. Party Systems in Latin America." Pp. 1–34 in Mainwaring and Scully eds., *Building Democratic Institutions: Party Systems in Latin America.* Stanford, Calif.: Stanford University Press.

Mainwaring, Scott, and Matthew Soberg Shugart, eds. 1997. *Presidentialism and Democracy in Latin America.* Cambridge: Cambridge University Press.

Mair, Peter. 1995. What Is Different about Post-Communist Party Systems? Stein Rokkan Memorial Lecture, University of Bergen, November 10.

Mamatay, Victor S. 1973. "The Development of Czechoslovak Democracy, 1920–1938." Pp. 99–166 in Victor S. Mamatay and Radomir Luza, eds., *A History of the Czechoslovak Republic, 1918–1948.* Princeton, N.J.: Princeton University Press.

Mangott, Gerhard. 1992. "Parteienbildung und Parteiensysteme in Ost-Mitteleuropa im Vergleich." Pp. 99–127 in Fritz Gerlich, Fritz Plasser, and Peter A. Ulram, eds., *Regimewechsel. Demokratisierung und politische Kultur in Ost-Mitteleuropa.* Vienna: Böhlau.

March, James Gardner. 1978. "Bounded Rationality, Ambiguity, and the Engineering of Choice." *Bell Journal of Economics,* Vol. 9, No. 2: 587–608.

March, James Gardner, and Herbert A. Simon. 1958. *Organizations.* New York: Wiley.

Markowski, Radek, and Gábor Tóka. 1995. "Left Turn in Poland and Hungary Five Years after the Collapse of Communism." *Sisyphus,* Vol. 9, No. 1: 75–99.

Markus, György. 1994. "Parties, Camps and Cleavages in Hungary." Pp. 154–70 in Michael Waller, Bruno Coppieters, and Kris Deschouwer, eds., *Social Democracy in a Post-Communist Europe.* Newbury Park, Calif.: Cass.

Martz, John D. 1997. *The Politics of Clientelism: Democracy and the State in Colombia.* New Brunswick, N.J.: Transaction Books.

McAdam, Doug. 1982. *Political Protest and the Development of Black Insurgency.* Chicago: University of Chicago Press.

McAdam, Doug, John D. McCarthy, and Mayer N. Zald, eds. 1996. *Comparative Perspectives on Social Movements: Political Opportunities, Mobilizing Structures, and Cultural Framings.* Cambridge: Cambridge University Press.

McAllister, Ian, and Stephen White. 1995. "Democracy, Political Parties and Party Formation in Postcommunist Russia." *Party Politics,* Vol. 1, No. 1: 49–72.

McClosky, Herbert, and John Zaller. 1984. *The American Ethos: Public Attitudes toward Capitalism and Democracy.* Cambridge, Mass.: Harvard University Press.

McCubbins, Tim, and Arthur Lupia. 1998. *The Democratic Dilemma.* Cambridge: Cambridge University Press.

McDonough, Peter. 1995. "Identities, Ideologies, and Interests: Democratization and the Culture of Mass Politics in Spain and Eastern Europe." *Journal of Politics,* Vol. 57, No. 3: 649–76.

McGann, Anthony J., and Herbert Kitschelt. 1995. Electoral Trade-Offs and Strategic Choices of Social Democratic Parties in the 1990s. Paper prepared for the annual meeting of the American Political Science Association, Chicago, August 31–September 3, 1995.

Meisel, John. 1974. *Cleavages, Parties and Values in Canada.* Beverly Hills, Calif.: Sage.

Michels, Robert. [1911] 1962. *Political Parties.* New York: Free Press.

Mildner, Kirk. 1995. "Korruption in Rußland: Wurzeln, Effekte und Strategie." Pp. 346–64 in Hellmut Wollmann, Helmut Wiesenthal, and Frank Bonker, eds., *Transformation sozialistischer Gesellschaften. Am Ende des Anfangs.* Opladen: Westdeutscher Verlag.

Millard, Frances. 1994a."The Shaping of the Polish Party System, 1989–93." *East European Politics and Societies,* Vol. 8, No. 3: 467–94.

1994b. "The Polish Parliamentary Election of September 1993." *Communist and Post-Communist Studies,* Vol. 27, No. 3: 295–313.

Miller, Arthur, Vicki L. Hesli, and William M. Reisinger. 1994. "Reassessing Mass Support for Political and Economic Change in the Former USSR." *American Political Science Review,* Vol. 88, No. 2: 399–411.

1996. "Understanding Political Change in Post-Soviet Societies. A Further Commentary on Finifter and Mickiewicz." *American Political Science Review,* Vol. 90, No. 1: 153–66.

Misiunas, Romuald J., and Rein Taagepera. 1993. *The Baltic States: Years of Dependence, 1940–90.* Expanded ed. Berkeley: University of California Press.

Mizgala, Joanna. 1994. "The Ecology of Transformation: The Impact of the Corporatist State on the Formation and Development of the Party System in Poland, 1989–93." *East European Politics and Societies,* Vol. 8, No. 2: 358–69.

Moser, Robert G. 1995. "The Impact of the Electoral System on Post-Communist Party Development. The Case of the 1993 Russian Parliamentary Elections." *Electoral Studies,* Vol. 14, No. 4: 377–98.

1996. The Impact of the Electoral System on Post-Communist Party Development: A Comparison of the 1993 and 1995 Russian Parliaments. Paper prepared for the annual meeting of the American Political Science Association, San Francisco, August 29–September 2.

Müller, Wolfgang C. 1993. "The Relevance of the State for Party System Change." *Journal of Theoretical Politics,* Vol. 5, No. 4: 419–54.

Nagel, Joanne. 1995. "Resource Competition Theories." *American Behavioral Scientist,* Vol. 38, No. 1: 442–58.

Nathan, Andrew J., and Tianjin Shi. 1995. China's Ideological Landscape. Paper presented at the Workshop on Parties and Party Systems, Duke University, March 24–25.

Nelson, Joan. 1993. "The Politics of Economic Transformation. Is Third World Experience Relevant for Eastern Europe?" *World Politics,* Vol. 45, No. 3: 433–63.

O'Donnell, Guillermo. 1973. *Modernization and Bureaucratic Authoritarianism.* Berkeley, Calif.: Institute of International Studies.

———. 1979. "Tensions in the Bureaucratic-Authoritarian State and the Question of Democracy." Pp. 285–318 in David Collier, ed., *The New Authoritarianism in Latin America.* Princeton, N.J.: Princeton University Press.

———. 1992. "Transitions, Continuities, and Paradoxes." Pp. 17–56 in Scott Mainwaring, Guillermo O'Donnell, and J. Samuel Valenzuela, eds., *Issues in Democratic Consolidation.* South Bend, Ind.: University of Notre Dame Press.

———. 1993. "On the State, Democratization and Some Conceptual Problems: A Latin American View with Glances at Some Post-Communist Countries." *World Development,* Vol. 21, No. 8: 1355–70.

———. 1996. "Illusions about Consolidation." *Journal of Democracy,* Vol. 7, No. 2: 34–51.

O'Donnell, Guillermo, and Philippe C. Schmitter. 1986. *Transitions from Authoritarian Rule: Tentative Conclusions about Uncertain Democracies.* Baltimore: Johns Hopkins University Press.

Offe, Claus. 1991. "Capitalism by Democratic Design? Democratic Theory Facing the Triple Transition in East Central Europe." *Social Research,* Vol. 59, No. 4: 865–92.

———. 1994. *Der Tunnel am Ende des Lichts.* Frankfurt am Main: Campus Verlag.

Olson, David M. 1993. "Compartmentalized Competition: The Managed Transitional Election System of Poland." *Journal of Politics,* Vol. 55, No. 2: 415–41.

Olson, Mancur. 1992. *The Rise and Decline of Nations.* New Haven: Yale University Press.

Olszak, Susan. 1992. *The Dynamics of Ethnic Competition and Conflict.* Stanford, Calif.: Stanford University Press.

Ordeshook, Peter C. 1995. "Institutions and Incentives." *Journal of Democracy,* Vol. 6: 46–60.

Oren, Nissan. 1973. *Revolution Administered: Agrarianism and Communism in Bulgaria.* Baltimore: Johns Hopkins University Press.

Ormos, Maria. 1990. "The Early Interwar Years, 1921–1938." Pp. 319–38 in Peter F. Sugar, ed., *A History of Hungary.* Bloomington: Indiana University Press.

Osiatynski, Victor. 1994. "Poland's Constitutional Ordeal. Avoidable and Unavoidable Detours on the Path to Reform." *East European Constitutional Review,* Vol. 3, No. 2: 29–38.

Ost, David. 1990. *Solidarity and the Politics of Anti-Politics: Opposition and Reform in Poland since 1968.* Philadelphia: Temple University Press.

1993. "The Politics of Interest in Post-Communist East Europe." *Theory and Society*, Vol. 22, no. 4: 433–86.

Pacek, Alexander C. 1994. "Macroeconomic Conditions and Electoral Politics in East Central Europe." *American Journal of Political Science*, Vol. 38, No. 3: 733–44.

Pempel, T. J., ed. 1990. "Exclusionary Democracies: The Postauthoritarian Experience." Pp. 97–118 in Peter J. Katzenstein, Theodore Lowi, Sidney Tarrow, eds., *Comparative Theory and Political Experience: Mario Einaudi and the Liberal Tradition*. Ithaca, N.Y.: Cornell University Press.

Pierson, Paul. 1994. *Dismantling the Welfare State? Reagan, Thatcher, and the Politics of Retrenchment*. Cambridge: Cambridge University Press.

Piven, Frances Fox, and Richard Cloward. 1977. *Poor People's Movements*. New York: Random House.

Plasser, Fritz, and Peter A. Ulram. 1992. "Zwischen Desillusionierung und Konsolidierung. Demokratie- und Politikverständnis in Ungarn, der CSFR und Polen." In Fritz Gerlich, Fritz Plasser, and Peter A. Ulram, eds., *Regimewechsel. Demokratisierung und politische Kultur in Ost-Mitteleuropa*. Vienna: Böhlau.

Popkin, Samuel. 1979. *The Rational Peasant*. Berkeley: University of California Press.

Powell, G. Bingham. 1986. "American Voter Turnout in Comparative Perspective." *American Political Science Review*, Vol. 80, No. 1: 18–43.

Poznanski, Kazimierz. 1986. "Economic Adjustment and Political Forces: Poland since 1970." *International Organization*, Vol. 40, No. 2: 455–88.

Przeworski, Adam. 1986. "Some Problems in the Study of Transitions to Democracy." Pp. 47–63 in Guillermo O'Donnell, Philippe C. Schmitter, and Laurence Whitehead, eds., *Transitions from Authoritarian Rule: Comparative Perspectives*. Baltimore: Johns Hopkins University Press.

1991. *Democracy and the Market*. Cambridge: Cambridge University Press.

1996. "Public Support for Economic Reforms in Poland." *Comparative Political Studies*, Vol. 29, No. 5: 520–43.

Przeworski, Adam, Michael Alvarez, Jose A. Cheibub, and Fernando Limongi. 1996. "What Makes Democracies Endure?" *Journal of Democracy*, Vol. 7, No. 1: 39–55.

Przeworski, Adam, and Fernando Limongi. 1993. "Political Regimes and Economic Growth." *Journal of Economic Perspectives*, Vol. 7, No. 1: 51–69.

Putnam, Robert, with Robert Leonardi and Raffaella Y. Nanetti. 1993. *Making Democracy Work: Civic Traditions in Modern Italy*. Princeton, N.J.: Princeton University Press.

Rabinowitz George, and Stuart Elaine McDonald. 1989. "A Directional Theory of Issue Voting." *American Political Science Review*, Vol. 83, No. 1: 93–121.

Racz, Barnabas. 1991. "Political Pluralization in Hungary: The 1990 Elections." *Soviet Studies*, Vol. 43, No. 1: 107–36.

Rae, Douglas. 1967. *The Political Consequences of Electoral Laws*. New Haven: Yale University Press.

Rae, Douglas, and Michael Taylor. 1970. *The Analysis of Political Cleavages*. New Haven: Yale University Press.

Ragin, Charles. 1987. *The Comparative Method*. Berkeley: University of California Press.

Rapaczynski, Andrzej. 1991. "Constitutional Politics in Poland: A Report on the Constitutional Committee of the Polish Parliament." *University of Chicago Law Review*, Vol. 58, No. 2: 595–631.
Remington, Thomas F., and Steven S. Smith. 1995. "The Development of Parliamentary Parties in Russia." *Legislative Studies Quarterly*, Vol. 20, No. 4: 457–89.
——— 1996. "Political Goals, Institutional Context, and the Choice of an Electoral System. The Russian Parliamentary Election Law." *American Journal of Political Science*, Vol. 40, No. 4: 1253–79.
Remmer, Karen L. 1991. "New Wine in Old Bottlenecks? The Study of Latin American Democracy." *Comparative Politics*, Vol. 23, No. 4: 479–93.
——— 1997. "Theoretical Decay and Theoretical Development. The Resurgence of Institutional Analysis." *World Politics*, Vol. 50, No. 1: 34–61.
Riker, William. 1982. *Liberalism versus Populism*. San Francisco: Freeman.
——— 1986. *The Art of Political Manipulation*. New Haven: Yale University Press.
Robertson, John. 1976. *A Theory of Party Competition*. London: Wiley.
Rodrik, Dani. 1995. The Dynamics of Political Support for Reform in Economies in Transition. Discussion Paper No. 1115. Center for Economic Policy Research. London.
Rogowski, Ronald. 1987. "Trade and the Variety of Democratic Institutions." *International Organization*, Vol. 41, No. 2: 203–23.
——— 1989. *Commerce and Coalitions*. Princeton, N.J.: Princeton University Press.
Rokkan, Stein. 1977. "Towards a Generalized Concept of *Verzuiling*." *Political Studies*, Vol. 25, No. 4.
Ronas-Tas, Akos. 1991. The Selected and the Elected: The Making of the New Parliamentary Elite in Hungary. University of California, San Diego. Unpublished manuscript.
Roniger, Luis. 1981. "Clientelism and Patron-Client Relations. A Bibliography." Pp. 297–329 in Shmuel N. Eisenstadt and René Lemarchand, eds., *Political Clientelism, Patronage and Development*. Beverly Hills, Calif.: Sage.
Roos, Hans. 1986. *Geschichte der Polnischen Nation 1918–1985*. 4th ed. Stuttgart: Kohlhammer.
Rose, Richard. 1995. "Mobilizing Demobilized Voters in Post-Communist Societies." *Party Politics*, Vol. 1, No. 4: 535–48.
Rose, Richard, and Ellen Carnaghan. 1994. Generational Effects on Attitudes to Communist Regimes: A Comparative Analysis. Studies in Public Policy, No. 234. Center for the Study of Public Policy, University of Strathclyde.
Rose, Richard, and Christian Haerpfer. 1994. *New Democracies Barometer III: Learning from What Is Happening*. Studies in Public Policy, No. 230. Centre for the Study of Public Policy, University of Strathclyde.
Rose, Richard, and William Mishler. 1996. Political Patience in Regime Transformation: A Comparative Analysis of Post-Communist Citizens. Paper prepared for the annual meeting of the American Political Science Association, San Francisco, August 29–September 2.
Roskin, Michael G. 1993. "The Emerging Party Systems of Central and Eastern Europe." *East European Quarterly*, Vol. 27, No. 1: 47–63.
Rothschild, Joseph. 1974. *East Central Europe between the Two World Wars*. Seattle: University of Washington Press.

1989. *Return to Diversity: A Political History of East Central Europe since World War II.* Oxford: Oxford University Press.

Sani, Giacomo, and Giovanni Sartori. 1983. "Polarization, Fragmentation and Competition in Western Democracies." Pp. 307–40 in Hans Daalder and Peter Mair, eds., *Western European Party Systems. Continuity and Change.* Beverly Hills, Calif.: Sage.

Sartori, Giovanni. 1966. "European Political Parties. The Case of Polarized Pluralism." Pp. 137–76 in Joseph Lapalombara and Myron Weiner, eds., *Political Parties and Political Development.* Princeton, N.J.: Princeton University Press.

1986. "The Influence of Electoral Systems: Faulty Laws or Faulty Method?" Pp. 43–68 in Bernard Grofman and Arend Lijphart, eds., *Electoral Laws and Their Political Consequences.* New York: Agathon Press.

Schmitter, Philippe C. 1974. "Still the Century of Corporatism?" *Review of Politics,* Vol. 36, No. 1: 85–131.

Schofield, Norman. 1993. "Political Competition and Multi-Party Coalition Governments." *European Journal of Political Research,* Vol. 23, No. 1: 1–33.

Schumpeter, Alois, 1946. *Capitalism, Socialism, and Democracy.* New York: Harper.

Schöpflin, George. 1991a."Obstacles to Liberalism in Post-Communist Polities." *East European Politics and Societies,* Vol. 5, No. 1: 189–94.

1991b. "Post-Communism: Constructing New Democracies in Central Europe." *International Affairs,* Vol. 67, No. 2: 235–50.

1993. *Politics in Eastern Europe.* Oxford: Blackwell.

Scott, James. 1969. "Corruption, Machine Politics, and Social Change." *American Political Science Review,* Vol. 63, No. 4: 1142–59.

1976. *The Moral Economy of the Peasant.* New Haven: Yale University Press.

Shain, Jossi, and Juan Linz. 1995. *Between States: Interim Governments and Democratic Transitions.* Cambridge: Cambridge University Press.

Share, Donald, and Scott Mainwaring. 1986. "Transitions through Transaction. Democratization in Brazil and Spain." Pp. 175–215 in Wayne Selcher, ed., *Political Liberalization in Brazil.* Boulder, Colo.: Westview.

Shefter, Martin. 1994. *Political Parties and the State: The American Historical Experience.* Princeton, N.J.: Princeton University Press.

Shepsle, Kenneth. 1991. *Models of Multiparty Electoral Competition.* Chur: Harwood Academic Publishers.

Shugart, Matthew Soberg. 1993. "Of Presidents and Parliaments." *East European Constitutional Review,* Vol. 2, No. 1: 30–3.

1995. "The Electoral Cycle and Institutional Sources of Divided Presidential Government." *American Political Science Review,* Vol. 89, No. 2: 327–43.

1996. *Politicians, Parties, and Presidents: An Exploration of Post-Authoritarian Institutional Design.* University of California, San Diego. Unpublished manuscript.

Shugart, Matthew Soberg, and John Carey. 1992. *Presidents and Assemblies: Constitutional Design and Electoral Dynamics.* Cambridge: Cambridge University Press.

Shugart, Matthew Soberg, and Scott Mainwaring. 1997. "Conclusion. Presidentialism and the Party System." Pp. 394–439 in Scott Mainwaring and Matthew Soberg Shugart, eds., *Presidentialism and Democracy in Latin America.* Cambridge: Cambridge University Press.

Skilling, H. Gordon. 1983. "Interest Groups and Communist Politics Revisited." *World Politics,* Vol. 36, No. 1: 1–27.

Staniszkis, Jadwiga. 1984. *Poland's Self-Limiting Revolution.* Princeton, N.J.: Princeton University Press.

Stark, David. 1992. "Path Dependency and Privatization Strategies in East-Central Europe." *East European Politics and Societies,* Vol. 6, No. 1, 17–53.

Stark, David, and Laszlo Bruszt. 1997. *Postsocialist Pathways: Transforming Politics and Property in East Central Europe.* Cambridge: Cambridge University Press.

Steinbruner, John. 1974. *The Cybernetic Theory of Decisions.* Princeton, N.J.: Princeton University Press.

Stepan, Alfred, and Susan Skach. 1994. "Constitutional Frameworks and Democratic Consolidation. Parliamentarism versus Presidentialism." *World Politics,* Vol. 46, No. 1: 1–22.

Stokes, Susan. 1996. "Introduction: Public Opinion and Market Reforms. The Limits of Economic Voting." *Comparative Political Studies,* Vol. 29, No. 5: 499–519.

Stone, John. 1995. "Race, Ethnicity, and the Weberian Legacy." *American Behavioral Scientist,* Vol. 38, No. 1: 391–406.

Strom, Kaare. 1990. *Minority Government and Majority Rule.* Cambridge: Cambridge University Press.

Suda, Zdenek. 1980. *Zealots and Rebels: A History of the Communist Party of Czechoslovakia.* Stanford, Calif.: Hoover Institution Press.

Sztompka, Piotr. 1991. "The Intangibles and Imponderables of the Transition to Democracy." *Studies in Comparative Communism,* Vol. 24, No. 3: 295–311.

1992. "Dilemmas of the Great Transition." *Sisyphus, Social Studies,* Vol. 2: 9–27.

1993. "Civilizational Incompetence: The Trap of Post-Communist Societies." *Zeitschrift für Soziologie,* Vol. 22, No. 2: 85–95.

Taagepera, Rein, and Matthew Shugart. 1989. *Seats and Votes: The Effects and Determinants of Electoral Systems.* New Haven: Yale University Press.

Tarrow, Sidney. 1990. *Struggle, Politics, and Reform.* Ithaca, N.Y.: Cornell University Press.

1994. *Power in Movement: Social Movements, Collective Action and Politics.* Cambridge: Cambridge University Press.

1996. "Making Social Science Work across Space and Time: A Critical Reflection on Robert Putnam's *Making Democracy Work." American Political Science Review,* Vol. 90, No. 2: 389–97.

Thompson, Michael, Richard Ellis, and Aaron Wildavsky. 1990. *Cultural Theory.* Boulder, Colo.: Westview Press.

Tilkovsky, Lorand. 1990. "The Late Interwar Years and World War II." Pp. 339–55 in Peter F. Sugar, ed., *A History of Hungary.* Bloomington: Indiana University Press.

Tóka, Gábor. 1993. Parties and Electoral Choices in East Central Europe. Paper prepared for the conference of the Centre for Mediterranean Studies, University of Bristol, September 17–19.

1995a. Political Parties and the Bases of Party Support in East Central Europe. Paper prepared for the Conference on Consolidating the Third Wave Democracies: Trends and Challenges, Taipei, August 27–30.

1995b. "Parties and their Voters in 1990 and 1994." Pp. 131–58 in Bela K.

Kiraly and Andras Bozoki, eds., *Lawful Revolution in Hungary, 1989–94*. New York: Columbia University Press.

Tökés, Rudolph L. 1996. *Hungary's Negotiated Revolution: Economic Reform, Social Change, and Political Succession, 1957–1990*. Cambridge: Cambridge University Press.

Touraine, Alain, François Dubet, Jan Strzelecki, and Michel Wieviorka. 1982. *Solidarité*. Pairs: Fayard.

Tworzecki, Hubert. 1996. *Parties and Politics in Post-1989 Poland*. Boulder, Colo.: Westview.

Tyson, Laura d'Andrea. 1986. "The Debt Crisis and Adjusted Responses in Eastern Europe. A Comparative Perspective." *International Organization*, Vol. 40, No. 2: 239–85.

Verba, Sidney. 1967. "Some Dilemmas of Political Research." *World Politics*, Vol. 20, No. 1: 111–28.

Vermeersch, Jan. 1994. "Social Democracy in the Czech Republic and Slovakia." Pp. 119–35 in Michael Waller, Bruno Coppieters, and Kris Deschouwer, eds., *Social Democracy in a Post-Communist Europe*. Newbury Park, Calif.: Cass.

Walicki, Andrzej. 1991. "From Stalinism to Post-Communist Pluralism: The Case of Poland." *New Left Review*, No. 185: 93–121.

Waller, Michael. 1995. "The Adaptation of the Former Communist Parties of East-Central Europe. A Case of Social-Democratization?" *Party Politics*, Vol. 1, No. 4: 473–90.

Walters, E. Garrison. 1988. *The Other Europe: Eastern Europe to 1945*. Syracuse, N.Y.: Syracuse University Press.

Wasilewski, Jacek. 1992. "Dilemmas and Controversies concerning Leadership Recruitment in Eastern Europe." Pp. 113–27 in Paul G. Lewis, ed., *Democracy and Civil Society in Eastern Europe*. New York: St. Martin's Press.

Watt, Richard M. 1979. *Bitter Glory: Poland and Its Fate, 1818–1939*. New York: Simon and Schuster.

Weber, Max. 1978. *Economy and Society*. Berkeley: University of California Press.

Wesolowski, Wlodzimierz. 1990. "Transition from Authoritarianism to Democracy." *Social Research*, Vol. 57, No. 2: 435–61.

_____ 1992. "The Role of Political Elites in Transition from Communism to Democracy: The Case of Poland." *Sisyphos, Social Studies*. Vol. 2: 77–100.

_____ 1994. The Formation of Political Parties in Post-Communist Poland. Conference of the Social Science Research Council, Madralin, Poland, September 23–25.

_____. 1995. "The Nature of Social Ties and the Future of Postcommunist Society: Poland after Solidarity." Pp. 110–35 in John A. Hall, ed., *Civil Society: Theory, History, Comparison*. Cambridge: Polity Press.

Wessels, Bernhard. Forthcoming. "System Characteristics Matter: Empirical Evidence from 10 Representation Studies." In Warren Miller et al., *Political Representation in Western Democracies*.

Wessels, Bernhard, and Hans-Dieter Klingemann. 1994. Democratic Transformation and the Prerequisites of Democratic Opposition in East and Central Europe. Science Center, Berlin. Unpublished manuscript.

White, Stephen, Matthew Wyman, and Olga Kryshtanovskaya. 1995. "Parties and

Politics in Post-Communist Russia." *Communist and Post-Communist Studies,* Vol. 28, No. 2: 183–202.

Whitefield, Stephen, and Geoffrey Evans. 1994. The Ideological Bases of Political Competition in Eastern Europe. Paper prepared for the 1994 annual meeting of the American Political Science Association, New York, September 1– 4.

———. 1997. From the Bottom Up? Explaining the Structure of Ideological Cleavages in Post-Communist Societies. Pembroke College and Nuffield College. Unpublished manuscript.

Wiarda, Howard, and Harvey F. Kline. 1990. "The Latin American Tradition and Process of Development." Pp. 3–125 in Wiarda and Kline, eds., *Latin American Politics and Development.* 3rd ed. Boulder, Colo.: Westview Press.

Wiatr, Jerzy J. 1996. "Executive-Legislative Relations in Crisis: Poland's Experience, 1989–1993." Pp. 103–15 in Arend Lijphart and Carlos H. Waisman, eds., *Institutional Design in New Democracies.* Boulder, Colo.: Westview.

Willerton, John P. 1992. *Patronage and Politics in the USSR.* Cambridge: Cambridge University Press.

World Bank. 1996. *From Plan to Market: World Development Report, 1996.* Oxford: Oxford University Press.

———. 1997. *The State in a Changing World: World Development Report, 1997.* New York: Oxford University Press.

Wyman, Matthew, Stephen White, Bill Miller, and Paul Heywood. 1995. "The Place of 'Party' in Post-Communist Europe." *Party Politics,* Vol. 1, No. 4: 535–48.

Zaller, John. 1993. *The Nature and Origins of Mass Opinions.* Cambridge: Cambridge University Press.

Zubek, Voytek. 1991. "Walesa's Leadership and Poland's Transition." *Problems of Communism,* Vol. 40, No. 1: 69–83.

———. 1994. "The Reassertion of the Left in Post-Communist Poland." *Europe-Asia Studies,* Vol. 46, No. 5: 801–37.

———. 1995. "The Phoenix out of the Ashes. The Rise to Power of Poland's Post-Communist SdrP." *Communist and Post-Communist Studies,* Vol. 28, No. 3: 275–306.

INDEX